WALLPAPERS

WALLPAPERS

AN INTERNATIONAL HISTORY
AND ILLUSTRATED SURVEY FROM
THE VICTORIA AND ALBERT MUSEUM

CHARLES C. OMAN AND
JEAN HAMILTON

Bibliography by E. A. Entwisle

HARRY N. ABRAMS, INC.,
PUBLISHERS, NEW YORK

IN ASSOCIATION WITH THE
VICTORIA AND ALBERT MUSEUM, LONDON

Library of Congress Catalog Card Number: 81–69549
International Standard Book Number: 0–8109–1778–5

Published by permission of the Controller of
Her Majesty's Stationery Office, London

Published in 1982 by Harry N. Abrams, Incorporated,
New York.

Designed and produced for Harry N. Abrams, Incorporated, New York, and Sotheby Publications, London, by Philip Wilson Publishers Limited, Russell Chambers, Covent Garden, London WC2E 8AA, England

Printed in Great Britain by
BAS Printers Limited, Over Wallop, Hampshire,
and bound by Webb Son & Co Ltd, Glamorgan, Wales

Contents

Foreword

Among its many functions, the Victoria and Albert Museum houses the national collection of historic wallpapers and consequently, when the catalogue of the Museum's collection was published in 1929, it at once took its place as a standard work of reference on the subject.

The introduction to the 1929 catalogue was written by Charles Oman, later internationally known as Keeper of the Department of Metalwork, but at that time on the Print Room staff. It discusses the history of wallpaper in England from the late fifteenth century to the time of William Morris and in France to the Second Empire, with a section on the Chinese export wallpapers, which form an important part of the collection. This detailed and authoritative account has been reprinted, with some minor amendments, in the present edition. In addition Jean Hamilton has contributed a brief historical outline of English and French wallpaper over the last hundred years and added short sections on American, German and Scandinavian wallpaper.

Since the 1929 edition of the catalogue was published, the Museum's collection of wallpaper has increased over sixfold: the present catalogue contains 1,313 entries, as against the 220 of its predecessor, and we have attempted to provide as full a corpus of illustrations as possible.

The Museum's thanks are due in the first instance to Mr E. A. Entwisle, for providing a revised version of his monumental bibliography. Thanks are also due to the editorial assistance of Anne Jackson and Rosemary Amos of Sotheby Publications, and to Michael Graham-Dixon, who prepared the text for press and compiled the indices.

C. M. KAUFFMANN
Keeper of Prints and Drawings

102

INTRODUCTION

Part One
by Charles C. Oman

English Wallpapers

The Fifteenth to the Mid-Eighteenth Century

It is not necessary to go very far to find a natural explanation of the invention of wallpaper in Europe. By the end of the fifteenth century paper was being manufactured all over Europe, with the result that its price was no longer as great as formerly. Paper that had been used on one side could be obtained for considerably less. Everything, indeed, was propitious at the end of the Middle Ages for the introduction of paper to decorate walls for those who could not afford the more costly tapestries, painted cloths, mural paintings, leather and panelling that were used by the rich. The main incentive for the introduction of wallpaper was its relative cheapness, combined with the possibility of decorating it in such a way as to make it a very passable imitation of its more expensive rivals. Its most formidable rival in this respect was the practice of stencilling patterns on plaster, a method used considerably during the sixteenth century. Though the effect produced might not be so good, paper had the advantage of offering a drier and less cold surface, as well as of being portable.

At no time has the inspiration for wallpaper been entirely original. From the beginning, textiles and mural painting were the most popular things to imitate; at later dates sculpture (including stucco work) and panelling were copied. Some attempt was made in the early eighteenth century to imitate Cordovan leather hangings, but the inspiration from leatherwork cannot be said to have started until Japanese hangings were copied at the end of the last century.

Though it has been possible to trace the origin of so many of the decorative arts of Europe to the East, there does not seem to be any reason for seeking such an inspiration in the case of wallpapers. During the Middle Ages there had been an almost constant stream of traders and missionaries between Europe and China, but the goods that reached Europe by such channels were, naturally, only the most valuable and the most portable. It is doubtful whether wallpaper was in general use in China earlier than it was in Europe. The use of Chinese designs in European wallpapers appears only in the latter part of the seventeenth century, when Europe had been importing Chinese goods on a considerable scale for nearly a century. There does not seem to be any evidence for the use of wallpaper in the Middle East which would form the link between the earliest wallpapers of China and those of Europe.

In the year 1481 occurs what still appears to be the earliest mention of the use of wallpaper in Europe.[1] A payment, on behalf of Louis XI, was made to Jean Bourdichon for having painted fifty great rolls of paper blue, for inscribing them with the legend *Misericordias Domini in aeternum cantabo* and for colouring three angels, three feet high, to hold this paper at the word *Misericordias*. These hangings were subsequently hung in several places at the royal Château of Plessis-les-Tours. This seems, on the whole, clearly to indicate wallpaper, though it must be allowed that doubt remains as to whether these papers were intended to be permanent. It is interesting to note that the paper is described as being 'grands rouleaux', showing that sheets had been pasted together before painting—a practice of which we find no other indication until the latter part of the seventeenth century.

A passage in a statute passed in Richard III's reign (1483),[2] which has hitherto been overlooked, must now be quoted. This Act was intended to prevent unemployment in England through the importation of cheap foreign manufactured goods. At the request of the various guilds it was ordained 'That no merchant stranger, after the feast of Easter next coming, shall bring into the realm of England to be sold any manner of . . . painted glass, painted papers, painted images, painted cloths, etc.' The term 'painted papers' is curious, for it seems difficult to construe it as meaning illuminated manuscripts, and the mention of painted cloths so near to it may not be without significance, as this is the regular term, to be found in all inventories, for the cheaper imitations of tapestries. If the King of France had already started to use wallpaper in his castle, it might be argued that its use was already more extensive than has been suspected, and that paper-staining might already have begun in England. During the eighteenth century this Act was clearly taken to refer to wallpaper, and as such was repealed in George III's reign (1723);[3] but if we remember how far the constitution has been moulded by the misinterpretation of ancient statutes, a certain scepticism must be allowed.

Leaving aside for the moment the question of flock wallhangings, we can now reach less disputable ground. In the course of the restoration of the Master's Lodgings at Christ's College, Cambridge, in 1911,[4] the remains of paper bearing a printed design were found adhering to the beams of the entrance hall and the current Master's study. The paper had decayed, except where preserved by some quality in the ink, but sufficient remained to show the original design. This was clearly an imitation of an oriental velvet or brocade, taken from some of these goods which the Venetians had made so popular all over Europe. The central motif is a highly conventionalized pine-cone surrounded by strapwork and foliage. Half-way up the design on the left-hand side is a Lombardic H, which was matched on the other side by a bird. It would seem that the paper was printed from a wood block measuring sixteen by eleven inches. This is an inch longer than the standard proportions which persisted till the eighteenth century. The back of this paper was found to provide useful material for supplying a date.[5] The design had been printed on the reverse side of a chance collection of documents that had been discarded as waste paper. Among them was a proclamation of the first year of Henry VIII, a poem on the death of Henry VII, an indulgence bearing the Della Rovere arms, probably issued by Julius II, and a few lines of a poem printed in the style of Caxton and Wynkyn de Worde. This all seems to agree with the accepted theory that the Master's Lodgings were approaching completion in 1509.

It is clear that the H and the bird were the trade-marks of the printer. The most probable candidate seems to be a certain Hugh Goes of Beverley, who was working at York at about this time. Beverley was also the birthplace of Bishop Fisher, confessor to Margaret, Countess of Richmond and Derby, and founder of Christ's College, and it has been suggested that he may have acted as the patron of his fellow-citizen. The character of the fragment shows it to have been the work of one who had studied carefully the possibilities of this type of mural decoration, and makes it improbable that this was a first attempt. It is also obvious that the design was not intended for a ceiling paper to be pasted on beams, but for a flat surface. To be seen at its best, it would have to be used to cover the upper portion of the wall of a room above panelling.

In the spring of 1925 an important discovery was made by Canon A. W. Goodman. Some restoration in the chantry of Bishop Thomas Langton (d. 1501) in Winchester Cathedral involved the removal of part of the panelling, between which and the wall were discovered a few fragments of paper, with plaster adhering to the back. The painting is in grey and sepia, but the small amount remaining does not permit us to establish the character of the design. The panelling of the chapel cannot have been erected till some time after the bishop's death,[6] and it seems possible that a temporary covering of paper may have been given to the walls pending its arrival. This is the earliest example of a hand-painted wallpaper that has been discovered, and is the only indication that we have of the use of paperhangings in churches.

There is at least one piece of documentary evidence to show that wallpaper was already a recognized means of mural decoration in the reign of Henry VIII. In an inventory of the goods of the nunnery of St Mary and St Sexburga at Minster in Sheppey,[7] made in 1536, there is a list of the hangings of the eight nuns' chambers. These are all of painted cloth or 'saye', except that belonging to one 'Dame Margaret . . . ock' (here the sheet is torn), which had a hanging of painted paper. So far, this seems to be the only reference to wallpaper that has come to light in the monastic inventories of this time, though other types of hangings are specified. This must not be taken, however, to mean that the use of wallpaper was still very exceptional, but rather that as the papers of this period were probably always pasted on to the walls, they would not be considered as goods separately marketable at the sales of monastic effects at the Dissolution. It is possible that many of the apartments for which no hangings are mentioned in the inventories of the monasteries may really have been decorated in this manner.

The number of wallpapers datable to the second half of the sixteenth century was considerably increased by discoveries made during the 1920s, mainly by Hilary Jenkinson, of the Public Record Office; it thus became possible to trace a connected tradition in the designing of paperhangings from this point down to the beginning of the eighteenth century.

It is necessary, however, to say something of the uses of papers for wall decoration at this period before proceeding further. Only a minority of what have been identified as wallpapers have been found hanging on walls. For the greater part of the period we are at present concerned with the principal source of the examples to be cited are wallpapers that have been used to line deed-boxes or chests, or to bind books. While, however, wallpaper was continuously used for these purposes, other papers were also produced especially for lining boxes and for bookbinding. It is necessary, therefore, to differentiate between these two classes. The essential difference is that the sheets of true wallpaper are printed with designs which are not complete in themselves, so that several sheets have to be juxtaposed in order to obtain the complete repeat of the pattern. The lining- and binding-papers, on the other hand, are printed with designs which are complete on every sheet and which sometimes could not be placed together to form complete designs without the cutting off of a margin.

The three sheets of specimens of binding-paper in the Victoria and Albert Museum (2733. 21–24) appear to have been used for churchwardens' account books, and, from their design, are obviously unsuitable for use as wallpapers. Though we have classified the designs complete in one sheet as probably intended for lining boxes, it is probable that certain of these may also have been used on walls. The design of some of these papers, such as that of no 3 (E. 4012–1915), with its pattern of roses in stripes, is obviously unsuitable for mural decoration. It is less easy to speculate about other lining papers—especially some of those which fall into what we may call the pictorial class, such as no 26, which has a design of figures emblematic of the Four Seasons surrounding a roundel filled with the arms of the Haberdashers' Company. It is known that wallpapers composed of small pictures of religious and fabulous subjects were in use in France during the sixteenth and seventeenth centuries, and so it may be supposed that the same was the case in England. The only criterion that can validly be applied to these papers must be the suitability of their designs for mural decoration. The rude and irregular eighteenth-century paper[8] formerly in the Leverhulme Collection may definitely be rejected as a possible wallpaper, just as the Haberdashers' paper, and the paper at Sulgrave Manor depicting Charles II and Catherine of Braganza,[9] may be regarded as possible, if improbable, wall hangings. It must, therefore, be kept in mind that the present classification of wall- and lining papers may subsequently have to be changed in order to enlarge the former category.

Our first example of a sixteenth-century wallpaper in the Victoria and Albert Museum collection is an excellent instance of the use of the same paper both for mural decoration and for other purposes. The paper from an old house at Besford Court, Worcester (no 4), was discovered adhering to the lath and plaster. Another example, however, of this design had previously been found lining an old box at Longwitton Hall, Morpeth,[10] and a tracing presented to the Museum (D. 1074–1904) served to prove, for the first time, the connection between wallpaper and paper used to line boxes. The design of this paper is typical of a large class of the papers of this period. The principal motif is heraldic: the arms of Queen Elizabeth I, surrounded by the Garter, form the centre of the sheet, while in each corner is the quarter of a Tudor rose, the complete flower being formed by the junction of adjacent sheets. The rest of the design belongs to another class—that of conventional decoration—and is composed of vases of fruit, grotesque masks and strapwork. The frequent appearance of coats-of-arms on these papers naturally reflected the growth of the use of heraldry, which was one of the most marked signs of the close of the Middle Ages. The conventional decoration here may very probably be attributed to the fact that the printers of wallpapers at this time were also the designers of the title-pages of books, though it must be admitted that very similar work also appears stencilled and painted directly on to the plaster in houses of this period.

A variant of this design was found at the Public Record Office, and must clearly date from the same time.[11] Instead of the mask above the central coat-of-arms is a medallion of St George on horseback, wearing a morion, and spearing the dragon in a somewhat casual manner.[12] In the corresponding space at the bottom of the design is the Tudor rose crowned, and supported by two wild men. A similar paper[13] from the same source includes the same arms, but the Garter is here used to surround the initials, 'ER', of the Queen. A box formerly in the possession of A. T. Bartholomew, of Cambridge, is lined with another example of the combination of conventional and heraldic styles. The principal motif here is a pair of demi-figures supporting a pole from which depends an orb. The Tudor rose and portcullis are worked into the bottom and sides of the paper, but the completed design is only shown when nine sheets are placed together. The paper discovered at Howbridge Hall, Essex,[14] belongs artistically to the same class as this one, but it has been suggested that it may antedate it.

The early years of the seventeenth century saw no important innovations in the design of wallpapers. The conventional style is represented by a paper (no 9) now in the Ashmolean Museum, Oxford,[15] which was found lining a box containing a licence to alienate in mortmain, dated 1615. The centre of the design is a vase of very classical appearance containing flowers. This is surrounded by strapwork and conventional foliation. The continued use of heraldic motifs is attested in the Public Record Office by papers bearing the Stuart royal arms, and attributable to the time of both James I and Charles I,[16] but the earlier of these is of greater interest, as it introduces as the decoration surrounding the armorial achievement a third motif: the imitation of the 'Spanish stitch' textiles, so popular at this period.

A few specimens of the 'Spanish stitch' papers exist in the Museum collection. The best of these (no 8) lines a deed box.[17] Its date can be given with some exactness, as it is printed on the reverse of sheets of paper which had been used for a partial printing of William Camden's *Remaines concerning Britaine*, of 1615. It belongs to a class of papers whose pattern is so small as to raise a doubt as to whether it was really intended for mural decoration—a question which could only be satisfactorily settled by its discovery pasted on walls. It is, however, an excellent example of the use of this type of textile design, and is composed of Tudor roses and squares, which leave no doubt of its being an imitation of stitchery. Another paper (no 16) in this style, but with a larger pattern, also lines a deed box. It has a pomegranate design, but is not a good specimen of the best work of this period.

Two very fine examples of papers of this description, discovered by Mrs R. L. Poole in the Oxford University Archives, are now in the Ashmolean Museum, Oxford.[18] They date from about the same time as the last mentioned design, but are composed of large flowing designs of fruit and flowers. The floral design is represented with extreme naturalism, and it is possible to name all the flowers depicted, despite a certain inevitable conventionalism. In one of them caterpillars and butterflies are added to the pattern, and a pomegranate obtrudes on a design of objects which could all otherwise be met with in the English countryside. A design showing all the characteristics of the Oxford papers was found in the Public Record Office, and also at Archbishop Abbot's Hospital, Guildford.[19] In 1974 a paper with the same design as another paper from Archbishop Abbot's Hospital was found on the walls of a closet room at Gable Cottage, Dinton, near Aylesbury with a pattern of floral motifs, including the 'clove gilly-flower', formerly found only on lining papers.[20]

A later example[21] of the 'Spanish stitch' papers—but, like the specimens in the Museum, probably not intended for use on walls—is in the Public Record Office, and another is in the Guildhall Library.[22] The design of the former is more conventional than the earlier ones; it is a pattern of crosses and foliations, instead of the more usual floral motifs. It is printed on the back of an Act of 1650, while the box at the Public Record Office which it lined bears a date formed by nails on the lid: 1655.

This habit of printing designs on the back of paper which had been previously printed and used for books, and so forth, leads to a curious sidelight on the history of paper hangings and box linings of the later seventeenth century. It would seem that this was the usual way of disposing of the books that offended against the political and religious opinions of the times. From the records of the Stationers' Company we learn that the latter end of censored copies of Hobbes' *Leviathan* was to serve this new purpose. The following is a letter from the Bishop of London to the Master and Wardens of the Stationers' Company: 'These are to require you to Damask or obliterate whatsoever Sheets you have seized of a book called Leviathan, and for your doing so this shall be your warrant. Given under our hand this 11th Day of December 1673. Hump. London.'[23] Similar orders lay down that any profits arising from the sale of the damasked paper should be applied to the poor of the Company, and that books unfit for damasking should be burnt in the garden adjoining the Company's Hall. (Another example of this usage is no 23, overprinted on an edition of the Prayer Book of the first half of the eighteenth century.)

That the word 'damask' was used to denote the printing of rough designs in imitation of textile and other patterns is shown by a passage in Kersey's revised edition of Edward Phillips' *New World of Words, or, Universal English Dictionary* (1706), where we find this definition: 'Damask or Damasquine, to imprint the Figures of Flowers on Silk, or Stuff, to Stamp rude Draughts on waste Paper, etc.' Damasking was not necessarily used in reference to the over-printing of waste paper, for clearly a much more ambitious article is inferred in the advertisement of the Blue Paper Works, to which allusion will be made later. The word 'damasking' also appears, along with 'veining' and 'marbling', in the patent of Richard Redrich and Thomas Jones, of 1724.

A paper (no 28) of the late seventeenth century in the Museum collection seems to hold at present an almost isolated position as an indubitable specimen of wallpaper of pictorial design.[24] In the centre of the sheet is the episode of Diana and Actæon, which is surrounded by other mythological scenes, all more or less held together by garlands of flowers into which spirited representations of birds are introduced. It will be noticed that the design is not complete on the one sheet, nor would it fit together if only sheets from the same block were used. It would seem, therefore, that the complete design must have been made up by several similar sheets, but arranged so as to join together at the sides. It appears that this is an early attempt to overcome the limitation of the constant repeat in wallpapers. It should be noted that this paper was printed from an engraved metal plate, instead of from the usual wood block.

Between the early sixteenth century and the late seventeenth century there is very little that can be positively asserted about the use of coloured wallpapers. A paper which was discovered in 1896 at Borden Hall, Kent,[25] with a coloured floral design in black and blue on a red ground, was dated by its discoverer, Philip Johnston, as being between 1550 and 1600. It was unfortunately lost and survives only in copies. A second paper, discovered in the same place, of which a small fragment remains, was printed in black on a white ground, with flowers roughly coloured in vermilion, and has been dated to *circa* 1650. A fragment (no 13), dating from about the same time as the first of these papers, was discovered at the Monastery House, Ipswich, prior to its demolition in 1913. Scarcely enough of it remains to enable one to determine the design, but it seems to have been rudely coloured in green and yellow. It seems fairly certain that coloured papers were being used throughout the seventeenth century, as Hilary Jenkinson discovered two lining papers that can be positively dated to the first half of the century,[26] while a paper which lines a box in the Stationers' Hall is, judging from its design, clearly of the last years of the century.[27] It is an all-over floral pattern printed in black, while the colours have been added by means of a stencil. The untidiness in the colouring (which is in watercolour), inevitable when a stencil is used, is well illustrated in this specimen, and goes far to explain the preference for uncoloured papers which would seem to have existed at this time. It cannot be said, however, that these early English papers are inferior in this respect to their French contemporaries.

Though there is nothing at present that can be taken as positive evidence for the existence of freehand-painted wallpapers in the seventeenth century, it is not difficult to believe that these were also manufactured when we take into consideration the existence of hand-painted designs and the subsequent well established use of hand-painted papers of the early years of the eighteenth century.

The most important development in the history of wallpaper in the seventeenth century was the popularizing of the use of flock. Flock is the minute shearings of wool which are left over as waste in the manufacture of cloth. The earliest use for this waste by-product seems to have been that which is forbidden in a statute passed in Richard III's reign.[28] Dishonest merchants had been in the habit of lightly painting their coarser cloths with an adhesive, and then scattering flock over it, with the result that an appearance of a material with a high pile was created and a higher price was charged accordingly. The legitimate use of flock is only a variant of this, but it is extremely difficult to fix its age, as the idea might have occurred to any ingenious craftsman after the date when Venetian and Genoese brocades and velvets became popular for hangings. Small religious pictures decorated with flock are even said to date from as early as the fifteenth century.

The process of manufacturing flock hangings is quite simple. The paper or canvas to be flocked is first painted over with the colour which is wanted for the background. When this is dry, the flock design is painted in an adhesive over this background, and the flock scattered over it. As the flock sticks only to the parts which have been painted in adhesive, an effect very like the pile of velvet can be obtained. Though the painting in adhesive can be done freehand, it has almost always been done with the aid of a stencil or has been printed from a wood block. It would be natural to suppose that the first attempts at flocking for hangings were probably done on cloth or canvas, rather than on the weaker paper.

The earliest reputed maker of flock paper hangings is a certain Le François of Rouen, but it is very doubtful whether much faith should be put in a story whose authorities are so late, and which is not without obvious discrepancies. In 1756, at the height of the fashion for English flock papers, a patriotic Rouennais was able to produce two of Le François' original blocks, bearing the dates 1620 and 1630.[29] The invention, he asserted, had received only a moderate amount of attention in France, but had been much more popular abroad. The reputed inventor's son abandoned the manufacture of flock paper half a century later, as foreigners had learnt to make the paper for themselves, and there was no home market for it.

Even if there were any truth in this story, there does not seem to be much reason to suppose that the art of making flock hangings was brought to England from beyond the channel, though our present data on this subject are inconclusive. In 1626, however, the Painter Stainers' Company claimed that flock work was among their monopolies,[30] from which we may presume that some members of the Company had already started this line of business. Unfortunately, we have no information as to the date of the first attempt to flock on paper,[31] but it seems probable that this had become the usual medium by the end of the seventeenth century. To about this date may be assigned a flock paper once in the Manor House at Saltfleet, Lincolnshire (see no 18, note). A central motif is an arched recess enclosing a conventionalized bunch of flowers.[32] The colouring of the flock is pink, and the background white. The design is printed on sheets about two feet square, and appears to be of a seventeenth-century character, and so this may be claimed as the earliest flock paper extant.

One of the most important innovations of this period was the practice of pasting the sheets of paper together and issuing them in rolls before painting. By this means the horizontal joins of the paper might be disguised to some extent by the paint. It became easier to make large spreading designs, and less scope was left for the unskilful paper-hanger. The change seems to have started in the last decade of the seventeenth century, as the new method is described in John Houghton's *A Collection of Letters for the Improvement of Husbandry and Trade,* June 1699, and also in the advertisement of the Blue Paper Warehouse, Aldermanbury, quoted below. The new system must have become the normal one quite early in the eighteenth century, for even the earliest legislation for taxing of wallpapers anticipates the difficulty of measuring the sheets of paper that have been joined together.

It is therefore probable that the fragment of wallpaper from Lumley Castle (no 32), which formerly hung in one of the rooms decorated by Vanbrugh in 1721, must date from *circa* 1700, as it preserves the old type of joint. It could not be later than the first year of George I's reign, 1714, as it shows no excise stamp. The fragment was painted with a flowing floral pattern on a thick white distemper ground, but little can be seen of the general design.

A painted paper which formerly existed at Bradbourne Hall, Derbyshire, must clearly date from the same period.[33] The sheets were about twenty inches square, and were fixed to the walls with nails with washers on them. This device was probably also intended to obviate the running of the colours when paper was being pasted—a fault which was very common in the early papers.

It is clear that by the end of the seventeenth century wallpaper was passing out of its infancy and was becoming an article of common use, though probably chiefly among people of the middle and lower classes. There is little more that can be said of the papers of this period, but we may conclude by mentioning that a certain William Bayley obtained a patent in 1691 for an invention in connection with wallpaper.[34] As he did not take the Patent Office sufficiently into his confidence to leave any record of the details of his discovery, it can only be instanced as evidence that a healthy interest was now being taken in the industry.

It was not long before the growing importance of the paper-hanging industry received statutory recognition. In the year 1712 a tax of 1d per square yard of paper to be painted, printed or stained for hangings was imposed, in addition to the tax on the various types of plain paper scheduled in the same Act.[35] Though alleged to be of only a temporary character, this tax ended by becoming a regular item in the national budget for over a hundred years. In 1714 the tax was raised to 1½d, and in the first year of George I's reign each sheet of paper which was intended to be painted, printed or stained in the kingdom was ordered to be marked by the excise officers with stamps similar to those in use for cotton goods. The importance of this last regulation is considerable, as it affords us a positive dating point by which we can place all papers with the stamp after the passing of the Act. The statutes dealing with the subject of the stamps order that these should be changed periodically, in order to prevent counterfeiting. If it were possible to discover the sequence of these stamps, their value as a means of identifying dates would naturally be increased, but so far only tentative solutions of this problem have been put forward.[36] It is unfortunate that for the whole period during which this regulation was in force, until the reign of William IV, all the kings of England used the monogram of the double 'GR' surmounted by a crown.

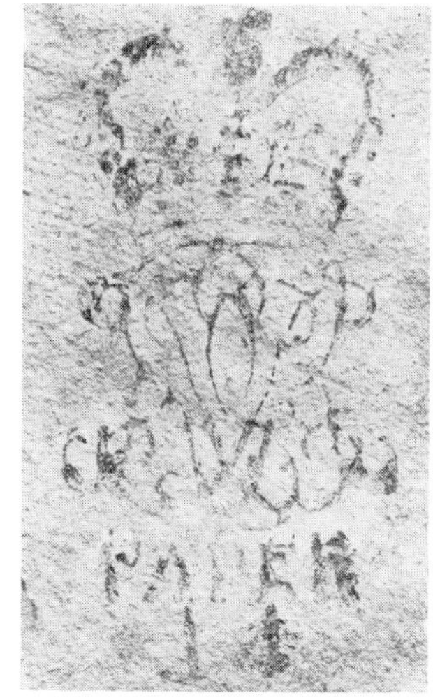

Excise stamp on the back of wallpaper (no 83, mid-eighteenth century) from The Chantry, Dursley, Gloucestershire.

The recognition by the Treasury that wallpaper was now a commodity sufficiently popular to be worth taxing is not the only evidence for the prosperity of the industry. Advertisements, as early as the reign of Charles II, by firms which sold wallpaper have been found, and the following extract from an advertisement, bearing the monogram of William and Mary, in the Bagford Collection in the British Museum, presents several interesting points.[37]

> At the Blue Paper Warehouse in Aldermanbury London are sold the true sorts of Figured Paper Hangings in pieces of twelve yards long and others of the manner of real Tapistry, and in imitation of Irish stitch, and flowered Damask and also of marble &

> other Coloured Wainscot, fitt for the hanging of rooms, and staircases, with great variety of Skreens, Chimney pieces, sashes for windows and other things of curious figures and colours.
>
> The Patentees for the sole making thereof doe hereby signify that their s^{d} pieces are not only more substantial and ornamental as well as Cheaper than the Counterfeits sold in other places but are also distinguished by these words on the back of each piece as their true mark viz
>
> 'Blew Paper Society's Manufacture'.

At the foot of the advertisement are instructions and illustrations showing how to hang the papers. A curious *chinoiserie* paper, to be hung in panels with ornamental borders, is depicted.

A newspaper advertisement of the same firm, which appeared in the *Postman* on 10 December 1702, gives us a few more indications of the wallpapers in fashion at this time. After beginning with phrases almost identical with those of the advertisement just quoted, it continues,

> . . . others in imitation of Irish stitch, flowered Damasks, Sprigs and Branches, others yard wide in imitation of marble and other coloured wainscoats, and other yard wide Embossed work, and others curious sort of flock work in imitation of Caffaws and other hangings.
>
> The Patentees for making the said Figured Hangings (observing the same to be counterfeited upon a thin and common Brown Paper, daubed over with a slight and superficial Paint) do hereby give Notice, that the said True Sorts may be distinguished from Counterfeits by their Weight, Strength, Thickness and Colour. Dyed through, and are every way more lasting and serviceable.

Besides the evidence that coloured grounds were beginning to become usual in paperhangings, this advertisement offers several other points for comment. The meaning of the 'Embossed work' is shown in another newpaper advertisement of a year later, where it is shown to be an imitation of gilded leather. No specimens have yet been found of it, nor of the marble papers, but it is possible to recognize examples of almost all the other types that are mentioned. The black-and-white designs with floral motifs, which have been described, are clearly alluded to, though they are here said to be in imitation of Irish stitch. The mention of coloured flock papers should also be noted. 'Caffaws' or 'Caffoys' were other names for damasks.

The first half of the eighteenth century was a period during which fashions in wallpaper experienced many changes, the sequence of which is not at all easy to trace. The first point that is to be remarked is the disappearance of the old black-and-white papers. Though specimens belonging to this century do exist (no 68), they do not seem to have survived for long after the date of the advertisement of 1702, quoted above, and no specimen bearing a tax stamp appears to be known. The lining papers in the same style seem also to have gone out of fashion similarly : a rude pictorial paper formerly in the collection of Lord Leverhulme[38] (see no 29, note) is probably as late as any. The workmanship of these black-and-white wall- and lining papers shows a very marked decline in design.

There seems to have been a greater demand for coloured papers. Though, as has been said, it is probable that the production of painted papers had been continuous from the early days of the industry, they seem to have won new popularity towards the end of the seventeenth century. Though neither the second Borden Hall paper nor the fragment from Lumley Castle (no 32) shows a particularly oriental feeling in its design, it seems very probable that the new demand for coloured papers was largely due to the importation of the brilliantly coloured Chinese hangings. As will be shown later, the earliest of these seem to have reached this country just at the end of the seventeenth century, and it is significant that quite a number of the surviving wallpapers of this time have *chinoiserie* designs.

There seem to have been two principal methods of producing these coloured papers up to the middle of the century. The first of these was simply to draw the design and to colour it by hand. To this class belong the Lumley Castle fragment (no 32) and the most interesting *chinoiserie* paper from Wotton-under-Edge, Gloucestershire (no 67), now removed and rehung in the Department of Furniture and Woodwork in the Museum. The closeness of the resemblance of these imitation Chinese wallpapers to the originals varies from paper to paper. As a rule, the English character is evident, but in a few cases the resemblance is good enough to baffle critics. As an imitation, the Wotton-under-Edge paper ranks high. It copies the bird-and-flower type of Chinese paper. The drawing of the birds and plants might pass as the work of a Chinese artist, especially when seen in a photograph, although the arrangement of the bushes would be exceptional if genuine. Around the paper is a narrow border of a sort of lattice pattern, rather more than an inch broad, which was subsequently covered by a heavier festooned border when the paper was restored later in the eighteenth century. Two points, however, give away its English origin: firstly, the paper is undoubtedly English and bears the relevant watermark of long parallel lines across it; secondly, paper-tax stamps are discernible in several places on the back.

Besides having the advantage of cheapness, these papers were especially convenient in that they could be made to order for decorating rooms with dadoes and low ceilings, as the designs could easily be modified to suit the taste of the purchaser.

It is possible to date the Wotton-under-Edge paper (no 67) with considerable precision, owing to the fortunate survival of a letter from Thomas Hancock, of Boston, to John Rowe, stationer, of London, dated 1738,[39] in which the former tells how much he admires a new wallpaper that has just arrived in America, and orders papers for two rooms to be painted like the enclosed pattern. He continues,

> The pattern is all that is left of a Room Lately Come over here, and it takes much in the Town and will be the only paper-hanging for Sale wh. am of opinion may answer well. Therefore desire you by all means to get mine well Done and as Cheap as Possible, and if they can make it more beautiful by adding more Birds flying here and there, with some Landskips at the Bottom, Should like it well. Let the ground be of the same Colour of the Pattern. At the Top and Bottom was a narrow Border of about 2 inches wide wh. would have to mine. About three or four years ago, my friend Francis Wilks, Esq. had a

> hanging Done in the Same manner but much handsomer, Sent over here by Mr. Sam Waldon of this place, made by one Dunbar in Aldermanbury, where no doubt he, or some of his successors may be found. In the other parts of these Hangings are Great Variety of Different Sorts of Birds, Peacocks, Macoys, Squirril, Monkys, Fruit and Flowers, &c.

Another very interesting example of English *chinoiserie* work (no 69) came from Longnor Hall, near Shrewsbury. This imitates one of the most popular of the figure-subject papers: scenes from the daily life of the Chinese. Though it is not of such good workmanship as the Wotton-under-Edge paper, there is undoubtedly a certain Chinese flavour about it.

The second process for producing coloured paper hangings was that already in use in the seventeenth century, of printing the outlines, and adding the colours either by hand or by stencil. Few specimens of this period have remained, but among these is a paper in a shop in the Market Place, Uppingham. This has a fantastic *chinoiserie* design, and is filled with figures dancing, flying kites and engaged in other pastimes to which the inhabitants of the Far East were popularly supposed to be addicted. The colouring is as untidy as in most of the work done in this manner.

The use of coloured inks in printing had been known from the early seventeenth century, but the transition from printing a mere outline in colour to printing a paper in several colours by means of a succession of wood blocks did not occur till very much later. Red and blue inks seem to have been the main obstacle to progress, as a wide range of greys and browns had been in use in chiaroscuro printing since the middle of the Italian Renaissance. Hilary Jenkinson's discovery[40] of some small pattern papers used for book-covers, with indications that they were printed from wood blocks, shows that attempts in this direction were being made. In one of these the outlines are printed in green, to which red has been added by another block. The designs are small—a fact which makes it unlikely that these were used for wall decoration—and the success of the process was not sufficient to make it of any great importance immediately. Although these book-covers, dated by their discoverer to *circa* 1720, clearly show that the date of colour-printing must be advanced into the early years of the eighteenth century, the task of tracing the sequence of these early attempts is far from easy.

There is in the Museum collection, however, a fragment of a paper which seems to belong stylistically to the years 1740 to 1750 and which comes from an old house at Dursley, Gloucestershire (no 82). The design is composed chiefly of parrots and exotic birds and plants, but into the midst of it a sleeping grey cat is obtruded. While there can be no doubt that the remainder of the design is printed from a wood block, the cat appears to be printed from a copper plate, though, by some means, all trace of the plate mark has been removed. The cat is an enlarged copy, printed in reverse, of 'A Cat Sleeping', an engraving by Cornelius Visscher. The edges of the paper were bound by a trellis-work border, similar to that used at Wotton-under-Edge. Although it is difficult to eliminate the possibility of this paper having been coloured by stencils, the appearance seems to suggest that it may be an early example of the use of a succession of wood blocks. The colours used are of light distemper, which would make this possible, while it is also noticeable that, though the registration is bad, there are no bad smudges such as are inevitable when stencils are used. The whole had been carefully finished with a paintbrush after the main part of the colouring had been applied from blocks. The use of distemper colours for printing was not destined to become popular immediately, as prolonged attempts to use oil colours were made *circa* 1750. If we recognize in this paper the use of printing from wood blocks, it may be necessary to deprive John Baptist Jackson (to whom we shall return later) of the credit for having produced the first marketable papers coloured by this process.

In the interval between the disappearance of the old black-and-white papers in the early eighteenth century and the appearance of numerous coloured printed papers *circa* 1760, by far the most important type of paperhangings were made with flock. Though the Wotton-under-Edge paper is a very fine piece of imitation, it must be admitted that the coloured papers which have survived must, as a whole, be considered to be more interesting or amusing than artistic. The flock papers of this period, on the other hand, are, almost without exception, the work of very capable designers. Their decorative qualities were such that their supersession by other types of wallpaper later in the century was clearly due to a change in taste, rather than to the growth of greater artistic appreciation. The Museum possesses a fine series of these papers, though the static conventionalism of the designs makes it difficult to arrange them more than tentatively according to date. The majority of them appear to have been made from *circa* 1730 onwards.

A paper of very original design is that from Hurlcote Manor, Easton Neston, near Towcester (no 48). The design is a large one, occupying two rolls of paper and taking about five feet before the repeat. The central motif is a large hexagonal pagoda surrounded by pillars; beneath are Chinese wooden houses, and palm trees. A water carrier is seen approaching a well. Stags are seen in the groves around the pagoda, and behind is a bird-catcher in pursuit of his quarry. The background is of a cream colour, and the flocking is done in a dark brown. The largeness of the design has necessitated a join down the middle, which, in the case of this paper in the Museum, has been badly executed. This may merely be the handiwork of a careless paper-hanger, and not an indication that the flock technique had not reached its later perfection, when no joins remained visible. It is known that this paper was already hanging in 1740, while a paper-tax stamp shows that it cannot be of earlier date than 1715, though it was probably made not long afterwards.

Two very fine examples come from the Offices of H.M. Privy Council (nos 59, 60). They are both mounted on wooden panels with glue and nails, and have duty stamps on the reverse. One of them has a pink background on which the pattern is printed in dark red. The pattern is so large that it does not repeat in the six feet of the panel in the Museum. It depicts broad conventional foliage, and flowers with large petals and seed-vessels. The pattern is said to be the same as that of the flock paper which formerly hung in the Queen's Drawing Room at Hampton Court, and which was removed when the paintings by Antonio Verrio were found underneath in 1899. The other paper has a yellow background with a pattern of small clustered flowers in an olive-green flock. Here, the design repeats itself in each sheet of paper, though the flocking was clearly done after they were joined.

Another fine design (no 65), with the usual pomegranate subject in dark green on a light ground, is represented by a fragment from All Souls College, Oxford. The key-pattern border used with it has also survived, and this paper is also exceptional in that it was hung on the walls entirely by a series of nails, without paste. Perhaps this may have been done in order that it might be removed without being damaged.

Two other fragments of papers (no 61), from Christ Church Mansion, Ipswich, are also of interest.

Reference will be made to the later flock papers in due course, but it is now necessary to return to the colour-printed papers which were destined to oust the flock examples from the place of honour in the latter part of the century.

The Second Half of the Eighteenth Century

THE WORK OF JOHN BAPTIST JACKSON

Before proceeding to trace the development of the art of printing in distemper colours, it is necessary to refer to a rival process which for a few years in the middle of the eighteenth century seemed likely to eclipse it.

Experiments in printing with oil colours seem to have been made in the first quarter of the eighteenth century, but the results were invariably poor. The designs of the end-papers at the Public Record Office, however, make it certain that these cannot have been intended for mural decoration. In this connection certain examples of end-papers in this Museum should be mentioned (E. 4512–6326–1897). Among them are a number of examples of equally poor execution, but of rather uncertain nationality and date, which, on the other hand, might possibly have been intended for use as wallpapers. Thus, though the possibility of printing in oil colours had already been discovered, no appreciable progress seems to have been made in it before the second quarter of the eighteenth century, when we come to the name of John Baptist Jackson, to whom can be given the credit for raising this technique from a condition of primitive barbarity to the status of an art.

Since he was the only English paper-stainer in the eighteenth century whose career can be reconstructed at all, and was also a craftsman and designer who attracted much attention from his contemporaries, it is necessary to deal here with his career and his works at some length.

Jackson seems to have been born *circa* 1701 and to have become a pupil of the engraver Kirkhall; but, finding little scope for himself in England, he went, *circa* 1726, to Paris, where he came into contact with the famous French paper-stainer and author, the younger Papillon. The characters of these two, which were so evenly matched, soon gave rise to a deadly enmity between them, and Papillon in his treatise[42] is always ready to depreciate his rival's abilities. During his stay in Paris, Jackson had already begun to interest himself in the subject of printing in chiaroscuro, and he claims to have invented a process by which his wood blocks might be passed through a rolling-press, and to have convinced the masters of the art in Paris, like Nicolas Le Sueur, that he had discovered something superior to their own methods.[43] He claims also to have invented a way of printing ten positive shade tints which could be achieved with only four blocks. Jackson, however, failed to find a livelihood in Paris, and went to live in Rome, then to Venice, where he is said to have married.

In Venice he became interested in the work of the Italian Renaissance chiaroscuro engravers, and produced a series of reproductions after Titian, Tintoretto and Veronese in this style, bearing dedications to several of his English patrons. Though unequal in merit, they are not at all the work of a man without ability. Thomas Bewick, who was so largely responsible for the revival of wood-engraving in England, gives the following criticism of these works of Jackson: 'They were well drawn, and perhaps correctly copied from the originals, yet in my opinion none of them looked well.'[44]

In 1746 Jackson returned to England, and, after having done some ordinary copper-engraving, seems suddenly to have determined to apply the experience which he had gained abroad to the production of wallpapers.

Our next piece of information about Jackson comes from Horace Walpole, and shows that, even before the publication of the *Essay* (which contains his famous advertisement), his work was becoming well known. In a letter from Walpole to Sir Horace Mann, dated 12 June 1753, when the process of decorating Strawberry Hill was in full swing, we find the following passage: 'Now you shall walk into the house. The bow window leads into a little parlour hung with a stone-colour Gothic paper and Jackson's Venetian prints, which I could never endure while they pretended, infamous as they are, to be after Titian, &c., but when I gave them the air of barbarous bas-reliefs, they succeeded to a miracle; it is impossible at first sight not to conclude that they contain the history of Attila or Totila done about the very era.'

In the following year Jackson produced a book entitled *An Essay on the Invention of Engraving and Printing in Chiaro Oscuro as practised by Albert Dürer, Hugo di Carpia, and the Application of it to the making of Paper Hangings of Taste, Duration and Elegance. By Mr. Jackson of Battersea. Illustrated with Prints in proper Colours.* Beneath appears a quotation from Pascal: 'Ceux qui sont capables d'inventer sont rares, ceux qui n'inventent point sont en plus grand nombre et par conséquent plus forts.' The price was two shillings and sixpence.

The essay is written entirely in the third person, and, as far as it pretends to be a history of wood-engraving, is inaccurate, if not intentionally deceptive, with a constant tendency to magnify the inventive powers of the author in the most effusive manner. The following passage shows the character of the book, and also shows how Jackson was to revolutionize the wall decoration of his time:

> Having thus brought this Manner of Engraving on Wood to the Perfection abovementioned, Mr. Jackson has imagined a more extensive Way of applying this Invention than has hitherto been thought of by any of his Predecessors; which is the printing Paper for the Hanging of Rooms. By this Thought he has certainly obtained the most agreeable and most useful Ends for the Generality of Mankind, in fitting up Houses and

Apartments, which are Elegance, Taste, and Cheapness. By this way of printing Paper, the Inventor has contrived that the Lights and Shades shall be broad and bold, and give great relief to the Figures; the finest Prints of all the antique Statues which imitate Drawings are introduced into Niches of Chiaro Oscuro in the Pannels of their Paper; these are surrounded with a Mosaic Work, in Imitation of Frames, or with Festoons and Garlands of Flowers, with great Elegance and Taste.

Thus the Person who cannot purchase the Statues themselves, may have these Prints in their Place; and may effectually shew his Taste and Admiration of the ancient Artists in this manner of fitting up and finishing his Apartments, as in the most expensive. 'Tis the Choice, and not the Price which discovers the true Taste of the Possessor; and thus the Apollo of the Belvedere Palace, the Medicean Venus, the dying Mermillo, the fighting Gladiator, or the famous Group of the Laocoon, may be disposed of in so many Pannels, and all the other Parts of the Paper correspond to this original Intent.

Or if Landscapes are more agreeable, for Variety Sake Prints done in this Manner, taken from the Works of Salvator Rosa, Claude Lorrain, Gaspar Poussin, Burgher, Waverman, or any other great Master in the Way of Painting, may be introduced into Pannels of the Paper, and show the Taste of the Owner.

The different Views of Venice by Canaletti, the Compositions of Paolo Panini after the Ruins of Rome, the Copies of the Pictures of all the best Painters of the Italian, French, and Flemish Schools, the fine sculptur'd Vases of the Antients which are now remaining; in short every Bird that flies, every Figure that moves upon the Surface of the Earth from the Insect to the Human; and every Vegetable that springs from the Ground, whatever is of Art or Nature, may be introduced into this Design of fitting up and furnishing Rooms, with all the Truth of Drawing, Light and Shaddow, and great Perfection of Colouring.

Saloons in Imitation of Stucco may be done in this Manner, and Stair-Cases in every Taste as shall be most agreeable, fitted up with the utmost Elegance. No Figure is too large for this Invention, Statues and other Objects may be taken off in full length, or any size whatever.

It need not be mentioned to any Person of the least Taste, how much this Way of Finishing Paper exceeds every other hitherto known; 'tis true, however, that the gay glaring Colours in broad Patches of red, green, yellow, blue etc. which are to pass for flowers and other Objects that delight the Eye that has no true Judgement belonging to it, are not to be found in this as in Common Paper; but Colours softening into one another, with Harmony and Repose, and true Imitations of Nature in Drawing and Design. Nor are there Lions leaping from Bough to Bough like Cats, Houses in the Air, Clouds and Sky upon the Ground, a thorough Confusion of all the Elements, nor Men and Women, with every other Animal, turn'd Monster, like the Figures in the Chinese Paper, ever to be seen in this Work.

A little later Jackson continues:

Besides the Superiority of Taste, which Paper done in this Way has to all others, there is yet a very essential Advantage belonging to it, which is, that being done in Oil, the Colours will never fly off; no Water or Damp can have the least Effect upon it, the whole Body of the Paper being impregnated with the Oil which is used in fixing the

> Colours. By this means the same Beauty continues as long as the Paper can hold together: Whereas in that done with Water-colours, in the common way, six Months makes a very visible Alteration in all that preposterous Glare, which makes its whole Merit; and one Year or two, carries off all that which at first was so greatly admired, and it becomes a Disgrace to the very Wall it covers, and to which it was designed as an Ornament.

Eight illustrations are appended to the book to give the reader some idea of the possibilities of the invention, but, unfortunately, the choice does not by any means represent Jackson's work at its best. Four of the illustrations are chiaroscuro representations of statuary, including the Apollo Belvedere. These are more successful than the remainder, which depict classical ruins, a pheasant and a lion, and are printed in colour. Though the register of the blocks is fairly good, the oil colours have followed the tendency of that medium to spread and to give a smudged effect. The red used in the illustrations is particularly unpleasant, although the browns and greens are not much better.

Much more favourable examples of Jackson's art are two small panels of wallpaper in the Museum (nos 1018, 1019), each measuring $16\frac{3}{4} \times 23\frac{1}{2}$ inches. They both depict Italian landscapes with a background of classical ruins and picturesque peasants, and a town with tumble-down houses and tall mediaeval towers. At east eight different shades of colour were used in each of these, but only one of Jackson's blocks has not registered correctly in the print held by the Museum.

A most important accession to the known works of Jackson was obtained by the Museum in 1920, in the form of a book of original sketches and proofs of wallpapers belonging to the artist (no 1020).[45] Some of these drawings have been printed in colour from wood blocks, but have been finished in watercolours, so that they must be regarded as trial proofs. Others are mere pencil designs, partially finished in watercolours. Among these are two cornices in chiaroscuro, mostly classical in inspiration, though a sort of Gothic tracery is obtruded into one. Others have remained only as pencil drawings, including a series of what we may describe as the 'Trophies of Art, Science, and War', probably intended to be framed as monochrome plaster-work panels. The 'Trophy of Art', which represents an easel bearing a painting, with a palette, a mallet and chisel beneath, and two pieces of statuary on either side, is of particular interest. After having made his first drawing, the artist stretched a tracing-paper over it and drew in as much as he intended to be printed by each block. The white indent of the pencil is visible in this and in about four other designs. There are two drawings of classical vases, and one drawing of the capital of a Corinthian pilaster decorated with the royal monogram. Whether we may infer from this last that Jackson was ordered to decorate some public building, or whether this is no more than an architectural drawing made by way of a pastime, must remain an open question.

It has not hitherto been suggested that Jackson produced wallpapers with fruit and flower motifs, but in this volume there are about twenty such designs, besides a number bearing such inscriptions as 'Drawn from Nature, August 8th, 1753, by J. B. J. at Batersea' and clearly suited for mural decoration. From all these designs it appears that Jackson must have been a most accomplished draughtsman, and, unless his colour schemes suffered greatly by being transferred to the wood blocks, the results must have been most decorative.

It might be inferred from his strictures on Chinese wallpapers that Jackson would adhere rigidly to nature in his floral papers. This, however, was far from being the case. Most of the flowers and fruit that he depicts are well drawn and easily recognizable as belonging to well known species, but he does not scruple to make them all spring from the same stem, or to add creations of his own, such as blue strawberries and camellias rendered in equally impossible colouring.

If we admit that Jackson did not adhere to the rules which he set for others, we can find little else to complain of in these designs. One or two are gaudy, and show the artist as perhaps aiming at a victory for his technique rather than at a sound and satisfactory effect. Most of the patterns are made up of at least seven different shades of colouring, although in a few a sort of monochrome effect has been sought. All except one of these floral designs consist entirely of flowing patterns without any adjuncts, but in one there occurs very weak and meaningless classical ornament and a sort of fragmentary trellis-work.

Our historical data for the latter part of Jackson's career are extremely scanty. We do not really know how far his factory at Battersea was a financial success, or at what age he retired from business. It is probable that he was still at work *circa* 1760, and that he died some time in the following decade. This would fit in well with Bewick's brief note that 'Jackson left Newcastle quite enfeebled with age, and, it is said, ended his days in an asylum under the protecting care of Sir Gilbert Elliot, Bart., at some place on the border near the Teviot or on Tweedside.'[46]

It is necessary to say something of certain papers that have been attributed to Jackson. Some fragments of wallpapers from Doddington Hall, Lincolnshire (nos 130, 132–136), represent small chiaroscuro miniature pictures, some depicting men and women, others ruins and insects on blue and yellow backgrounds. The small pictures of classical ruins may suggest Jackson, but, on the other hand, the medium is tempera and not oil, and we have no information that Jackson ever departed from the use of oil colours. Some other examples of work in the same style, from the Manor House, Bourton-on-the-Water, Gloucestershire (nos 99–101), are also in the Museum. Some time later a group of three wallpapers made up of designs in common, two of which are in the United States and one in England, were assigned to Jackson.[47] The designs consist partly of military trophies in chiaroscuro and partly of large pictures of Italian scenes framed in imitation stucco frames. The historical data appended to the descriptions of the papers seem, however, to conflict with the attribution, and in any case appear to be inaccurate. For one of the American papers no date is suggested, but the other is stated to have been bought at 11 Regent Street, London, in 1768. As this street was only planned thirty-five years later, it is clear that the documentation is not entirely reliable. The English paper at Harrington House, Bourton-on-the-Water, Gloucestershire, is stated to have been bought in 1786. It may have been made at that time, but not by Jackson, who, if alive, might well have been described as 'enfeebled by age' at the age of eighty-five! It is clear that in this group of wallpapers we have the work of one of the important paper-stainers of the late eighteenth century who has not yet been identified.

If Jackson was not as great a man as he claimed to be, or as some later writers have believed him to have been, his career must not be belittled. His influence as a designer can be rightly traced in the distemper-printed papers which have just been described, though he certainly had no share in their production. More important, however, was his insistence on careful workmanship, so that, despite the greater elaboration of his work, there are few signs of the clumsy registration of blocks which spoils the work of his contemporaries. Though he failed fully to realize his conceptions artistically, his pre-eminence as a craftsman cannot be disputed. His failures must be attributed to his attempt to perfect the obsolescent oil-colour technique, instead of developing the newer medium of distemper.

TECHNICAL PROGRESS

If Jackson's work stands out conspicuously among that of the English paper-stainers of this period, he must be considered only as one of a number of enterprising paper-stainers who were experimenting in new techniques at this time. It was not even destined that the technique which he favoured should overcome its competitors. The use of oil colours never became general, for, despite the superiority which he claimed for them, there could be no doubt about the unsatisfactory nature of the effects which were produced with them. Distemper colours, such as had been used in the Dursley paper (no 82), were better in this respect, though bad workmanship in their application might often detract from their real merits. If we suppose this paper to have been one of the earliest examples of the use of wood blocks, we may suppose that during the period 1750–60, when Jackson was producing his best work, printing in distemper was still at a fairly rudimentary stage, though a fragment from Ramsbury Manor, Wiltshire (no 22), said to be dated *circa* 1685, appears to have been printed in a distemper colour. Hilary Jenkinson discovered at the Public Record Office some undoubted specimens of distemper papers of fairly successful execution, which may be dated *circa* 1762. In the years 1760–65 a certain Boulard began to flood France with papers printed in distemper colours, but there seems to be no doubt that this method had been known in England for some years previously. Papillon, in his book published in 1766,[48] mentions the process as a new English invention; and though he is known to have spent many years in writing his work, this passage seems to be of late date. Robert Dossie, in his *Handmaid to the Arts*, published in 1758, treats printing in colour from wood blocks as already one of the principal methods of producing wallpapers, and, by his descriptions, shows that the process was practically the same as has prevailed during the present century. It would seem, however, that it was not till *circa* 1770 that enough experience had been gained in the use of the medium for workmen to do justice to the designs with which they were confronted.

While the new process was still being perfected, the use of stencils was not very much affected. It was not till comparatively late in the century that competition from printing in colour from wood blocks became really serious, and the use of stencils became restricted to the making of flock papers with large designs and to the unimportant classes of paper-hangings for which they have still been used in modern times. It is rather surprising to find, however, that the slow and laborious method of colouring papers by hand was not abandoned till well into the reign of George III. By decorating rooms with white paper and afterwards having it painted, it was possible to elude the vigilance of the excise officers, who stamped all wallpapers produced at the authorized factories. As late as 1778, special instructions had to be issued to the excise officers to search for this sort of fraud against the revenue.[49]

Horace Walpole, in a letter to Richard Bentley dated 20 November 1754, makes mention of having had his Gothic wallpaper hung with the intention of having it coloured afterwards, thus demonstrating that he was still living at a time before the colour-printing processes had been perfected. The paper in question was, moreover, of such a sort that the subsequent colouring might be considered superfluous, as is shown by his remark on seeing it also at Latimers,[50] at Chalfont in Buckinghamshire, so that, in this case, the tax must clearly have been paid for the paper. How general was the desire to evade the tax is shown by a revival of the art of painting directly on to the plaster of walls, as may be seen in large scenic designs which are often to be found in the country houses of this period. A petition was addressed to Lord North by the principal paper-stainers of London in the summer of 1778, begging him to extend the wallpaper tax to wall paintings, in order to crush this temporary revival of a venerable art. The hand-painted wallpaper did apparently disappear by the end of the century, and there does not seem to have been any revival in England to correspond with that which was to flourish in France and America from the time of Napoleon till the 1840s. Such papers were created in imitation of the great printed scenic wallpapers of the time, which only reached England in quite limited quantities and had no influence on native art.

Though the great revolution in the history of paper hangings caused by the introduction of cylinder printing machines did not take place till early in the nineteenth century, the records of the Patent Office, from the middle of the eighteenth century onwards, are full of descriptions of inventions embodying the principle that was ultimately to succeed.

Among the earliest of the attempts in this direction is the machine invented by Thomas Fryer, Thomas Greenough and John Newberry, who obtained a patent on 28 February 1764. The colours were printed by engraved cylinders which were fed 'by small cylinders which are put in motion by other plain cylinders'. The whole work of 'filling in, cleansing off, and stamping the impressions' was performed by the 'assistance of sundry springs and the intermediums of cogs and rings turned by a wheel'. Nothing is known of the paper produced by these inventors, but the principle of their machine was not forgotten. Eight years later, Joseph Adkin, father and son, Charles Taylor, and Thomas Walker patented another machine which seems to have been a simplification of the one just described. Both these machines were intended for printing silks and calicoes, as well as paper hangings, a practice which was probably not uncommon at this time and which does much to explain the similarity of the designs of the several materials. The tradition is maintained by the patent of

J. Burnett of March 1786, following on the same lines. Though not all these attempts were destined to bear immediate fruit, it is important not to forget that the generation which designed some of the artistic and expensive wallpapers for which it is renowned was also feeling its way along the deadly path leading to mass production.

In 1753 a patent was granted to Edward Dighton, who aimed at producing papers from engraved and etched plates of copper and brass passed through a rolling press. The colouring was to be done by hand. No paper that can be attributed to Dighton has yet been found, but the technique which he invented appears to have been used to a limited extent till towards the close of the century. The examples surviving seem all to date from considerably later than Dighton's patent, and no clue to their authorship has been discovered. A series of panels in the Museum (no 98), which formed part of a series of *chinoiserie* designs, show the occidental influences hardly disguised by the oriental setting. A Chinaman on a camel of distinctly equine appearance is seen regarding benevolently, in the manner of the conventional English farmer, a child with an inordinately large head, holding a greyhound on a leash. Gigantic flowers roughly frame the scene. Another panel (no 97), composed of several sheets of paper pasted together, clearly dates from the same period and was probably produced by the same firm. The motif here is half Chinese and half classical, the latter style being represented by a large vase filled with carnations and other flowers. Perching among the stalks, and flying around, are birds drawn to imitate those familiar to us from Chinese papers. A companion design, from the same source, bore an inscription engraved on a piece of foliage: 'Accordg to Act of Parlt Decr 1st 1769'. This enables us to date the small group to which this example belongs.[51]

Mention has already been made of the combination of copper-plate and wood-block printing in connection with the Dursley paper (no 82). Another, but much less crude, example of this technique is the magnificent paper at Temple Newsam, near Leeds. The design consists of bands of classical decoration dividing scenes of various types of exotic birds. The birds here have been etched, though the rest of the design was produced by blocks. The date of the paper is clearly the close of the century, and the authorship of A. G. Eckhardt, one of the best known of the paper-stainers of the end of this century, does not seem impossible.

In the year 1792 Eckhardt took out a patent for a device for laying on coats of composition or paint for receiving impressions from copper plates. It is not known for how long he made use of this technique, or how far he was successful, but it would seem that his attempt was the last of these to be made in this direction, except for William Morris's unsuccessful ventures in 1862.[52]

Though, as will be shown later, flock wallpapers had not the same popularity in the later eighteenth century as they had enjoyed in the earlier part, changes were made in the art of flocking parallel to those in the other branches of the industry. Papillon mentions[53] the introduction of flock papers produced by a series of wood blocks arranged so that each printed part of the design, as in ordinary colour-printing. Flocking could thus be done in different coloured wools, instead of in one only. The new method would be much less difficult to manipulate than the old method of flocking in different colours, by which the designs had to be painted in adhesive by hand and the various coloured flocks scattered on successively. An example of this use of wood blocks for flocking is no 75. Blocks have been used not only for printing the design for the flock in adhesive, but also for the design in distemper on the 'ground' of the paper. Another good instance of this new method is the paper from Glamorgan Street House, Brecon (no 117).[54] In this instance, however, wood blocks were used not only in the actual flocking, but also to add fresh colours to the paper after the first process had been completed.

This new process never ousted the old method of flocking with stencils of leather and oil-cloth which was described by Robert Dossie in 1758 and which has not been materially changed up to the present century. The chief beauty of the old flock papers lay in the breadth of design which could be obtained, and this was almost inevitably lost by the smaller and multi-coloured wood-block papers. It should have been recognized that it was better to continue to design in one colour, rather than to aim at producing complete imitations of tapestries.

DESIGN AND DEVELOPMENT

It is impossible to regard the wallpapers of the beginning of the eighteenth century as anything more than the attempt by those of more modest means to ape the hangings of the rich, even though the artistic merit of these imitations might be very considerable. The advent of flock papers raised the status of the whole industry, so that paper-stainers might receive not only the unwelcome attentions of the Chancellors of the Exchequer, but also the favours of all those who claimed to direct public taste. By the time of Horace Walpole the question of the choice and method of hanging a wallpaper was a matter of very careful consideration. The increased demand for paper hangings gave occasion for the production of papers in varied styles to meet every taste, while sometimes innovation was the result of the ingenuity of some wealthy patron.

During the period when Horace Walpole was furnishing Strawberry Hill, his letters contain frequent mentions of his wallpapers, and further information is to be obtained from his *Description of the Villa at Strawberry Hill*, published in 1784. A number of his papers were plain blue or crimson; others bear witness in a most striking manner to the eccentricities of his taste. The gothic wallpaper he had chosen for his hall, and which he afterwards saw repeated at Latimers, Chalfont, was no less than a copy of the chantry of Prince Arthur in Worcester Cathedral, executed by a paper-hanger named Tudor.[55] It caused the author of the letters no little surprise when he discovered the original to be of stone, and not of brass, as he had thought when he had had it painted.[56] Another room at Strawberry Hill was papered in imitation of Dutch tiles,[57] while it seems highly probable that the 'strawberry papers', which are sometimes mentioned in contemporary records, may really have been called after some designed by Walpole himself. He seems, at any rate, to have had a hand in the designing of a *chinoiserie* paper for his friend Rigby's house in Essex.[58]

By a casual mention in one of the descriptions of Strawberry Hill he enables us to discover the originator of one of the most popular styles of wallpaper at this period: 'The room on the ground floor . . . hung with yellow paper and prints, framed in a new manner invented by Lord Cardigan,[59] that is with black and white borders printed.'[60] The chief interest of this manner of decorating rooms with prints pasted on to the wallpaper and framed in paper lies in the fact that it was in this style that Thomas Chippendale, the author of *The Director*, published in 1754, is known to have decorated several houses. Matthew Darly and François Vivares also published sets of engraved and etched 'frames' for use in print rooms (Department of Prints and Drawings, No 25084.5 etc). The following is the bill for the decoration carried out by Chippendale at The Hatch, Ashford, Kent, in 1762:

		£	s	d
To size Paste & Hanging the dressing room with 2 papers		£ 1	5	0
To Lumberhand and Cartridge Paper			10	6
To Verditure & Colouring the Room		4	6	0
180 Feet of Papie Mashie Border Painted Blue & White @ 6		4	10	0
Pins and Fixing up the Border			12	6
To Cutting out the Prints, Borders & Ornaments & Hanging them in the Room Complete		14	10	0
To 506 Printed Borders	2 @ 2	4	4	4
106 ditto Festoons	,, 3	1	5	9
91 ditto Corners	,, /2½		18	11½
11 Bustos 18 Satyrs & Lions Masks	,, /4		9	8
39 Rings and 12 Masks	,, /1½		6	4½
74 Knots	,, /1½		9	3
28 Baskets & 8 sheets of Chains			12	0
18 Patterns & 3 Pedestals	,, /2		3	6

It will be seen that Chippendale has elaborated Lord Cardigan's simple black-and-white framing into a much more fanciful and complete scheme, where busts are seen in alcoves over doors and swags of fruit hang between masks to form a frieze, while the engravings hang in their paper frames suspended by paper chains from paper nails. Two plates in the third edition of *The Director* serve to illustrate what he considered to be suitable designs for these friezes.

At Rokeby, Yorkshire, there still exists a room papered in this style,[62] and, in all probability, by Chippendale also. The house was at this time owned by Sir Thomas Robinson, who was a well known friend and patron of Chippendale. It was he who proposed Chippendale for membership of the Society of Arts in 1760, and he had previously subscribed to *The Director*.

At about this time 'print rooms' of this sort were very common in big country houses, and were excellently adapted for showing the individual tastes of the owners. At Rokeby, the prints are largely copies of portraits of the seventeenth and eighteenth centuries; at Woodhall, Piranesi's etchings of the churches of Rome are well represented;[63] at the Thrales' house at Streatham, Hogarth's engravings were on the walls.[64] Other examples of this style of decoration, in less fantastic framing, may be seen at Stratfield Saye; at The Vyne, near Basingstoke (the home of Walpole's friends, the Chutes); and at Heveningham Hall, Suffolk.[65]

The verditure paper mentioned in the above account appears also in the bill for the decoration of Nostell Priory, Yorkshire,[66] by Chippendale in 1767, in which we find a mention of 'blue verditer' for covering chimney boards. Its exact nature is not clear.

Time has on the whole been unkind to the products of the English paper-stainers of the late eighteenth century, for comparatively little of their work has survived. The great number of Chinese wallpapers which have come down to us are not paralleled by corresponding English examples. It is probable that this is largely due to the fact that canvas backing for wallpapers was falling into disuse, giving place to paper mounting, or to direct pasting on to the wall. The designs of this period, often inspired by contemporary light-coloured textile designs, were also more liable to fade than the flock hangings which had preceded them. The papers from Doddington Hall, Lincolnshire (nos 130, 132–136), long attributed to J. B. Jackson, and the fragments from Bourton-on-the-Water, Gloucestershire (nos 99–101), are good examples. One of the Doddington Hall papers (no 135), consisting of some curious little scenes of Gothic ruins twice repeated, and evidently intended for cutting up and pasting on the wall, is insufficient to supply us with an idea of the appearance of the paper as a whole, far less of the period which it represents. More interesting is a fragment (no 90) depicting a fine classical archway on a blue ground, and with the usual trellis-work border, which dates from shortly after the middle of the century. Too little of this example remains, however, to allow us to form an adequate judgment of the whole.

To obtain a clearer idea of the styles of paper in vogue at this time it is scarcely more profitable to scrutinize contemporary representations than to turn to the chance fragments that have survived. The greater English artists of this time unfortunately painted few pictures of interiors, and a large proportion of the examples that do exist show panelled rooms or walls decorated in a manner which is difficult or impossible to determine. It is rare to find good representations of wallpapers, as in George Morland's *Industry* and *Dressing for the Masquerade*, in the 'Laetitia' series, engraved in 1789. Both of these show wallpapers decorated in stripes, with conventional decoration in between.

More interesting are the trade cards of the period, which are sometimes decorated with representations of the various styles stocked by the advertiser. The card of Matthew Darly, who is known also as an engraver of some of the plates of *The Director*, is an excellent example.[67] Panels of *chinoiserie* paper, very like the etched examples in the Museum (nos 97, 98), are clearly depicted. Several examples of conventional trellis- and strap-work also appear, but it would seem that during this period, as always, floral patterns were the most popular. Some of these are composed of bouquets of flowers diapered all over the paper; others show continuous flowering bushes. A design of a more architectural character, in imitation of panelling, is just visible in one of the corners. Except that we are unable to recognize any flock decoration, we may accept the samples shown on Darly's card as representative of what was in demand at the time.

The flock papers of the late eighteenth century bore small resemblance to those of the great period of 1715–45. Allusion has previously been made to the deleterious effect on the designs caused by the introduction of printing in colour from wood blocks. Although this process was not always used for flock papers, the other uses of flock were scarcely more successful. The attempt made at Eltham Lodge, Kent, to combine a key-pattern border and arabesques of red flock with large brown imitation-painted panels is deplorable. The designer had entirely forgotten that the only legitimate use of flock can be the imitation of textile designs; when flock is combined with pseudo panelling the result is inevitably distasteful. Between the middle of the eighteenth and the middle of the nineteenth centuries, nearly all the flock hangings produced violated this canon, while a tendency to reduce the size of the pattern in otherwise correctly designed papers made these lose the charm of the broad effects which this material should give.

The use of wallpaper to imitate large architectural designs dates, as we have seen, from the days of J. B. Jackson. During the remainder of the century this style received considerable attention, and was used almost exclusively for the decoration of the halls and staircases of great houses. The example at Harrington House, Bourton-on-the-Water, to which allusion has already been made, is extremely fine and is said to date from 1786. It is inspired by the elaborate rococo stucco work of the time, and represents large framed pictures of classical ruins. Small panels of trophies and cherubs are interspersed with the larger designs where space necessitates it.[68] Another staircase, with upper and lower hall, decorated in a similar style, may be seen at Eltham Lodge, Kent. The design imitates oak panelling decorated with figures in alcoves from classical mythology, and includes an arcade of Corinthian columns. All the sculptural and architectural portions of this paper have been cut out and pasted on to the background, while the shadows and the perspective have been so cleverly arranged that, from some points of view, the effects are most deceptive.

Though the arabesques of J. B. Réveillon were imported into England, the use of Pompeian designs does not seem to have been as popular here as in France. England did not really turn for inspiration to classical paintings till the heavier style of the Empire was the vogue. Though the great paper-stainer, John Sherringham, gained a great reputation for his arabesques, no examples of his work in this style have yet been identified.

A number of foreign designers were, however, employed in England at this time. At the Eckhardts' factory at Whitelands, in Chelsea, established in 1786, the Frenchmen Boileau, Feuglet, and Joinot were employed. At this time, Sherringham had Rosetti and Louis as his designers. As far as we can judge from extant specimens of paper, the types of English paper-hanging maintained their national character, and more interest was taken in mechanical inventions than in novelty of design. In 1774, for instance, A. G. Eckhardt patented a device by which the drawings of wallpaper designers made on squared paper could be transferred faithfully on to wallpaper by the use of small squares of wood, as with printing type. In 1793 F. Eckhardt took out a patent for making gold and silver paper hangings by a process resembling that used for flocking, but it does not seem to be known whether this was any more successful than the method adopted by Joachim and Andreas Bahre, which had been patented in 1755. In 1796 J. Hancock patented a device for making embossed wallpapers—which had been attempted, as we have seen, more than a hundred years earlier.

Before tracing the history of wallpaper into the next century, it will be useful to examine some of the valuable material provided by public records relating to the industry in the second half of the eighteenth century.

In the year 1773 the ban placed on the importation of foreign painted papers in the time of Richard III[69] was expressly repealed,[70] but a customs duty of 1½d was imposed instead, in order to balance the excise duty on English papers. The papers of the East India Company, however, could still be imported free. The passing of this Act raises a very interesting problem. Are we to believe that hitherto foreign papers had really been excluded from England, or was the discovery of the old Act the work of an antiquary, and its repeal merely the removal of an anomaly that had lingered unnoticed on the Statute Book? On the one hand, it must be admitted that the importation of wallpapers from the Continent does not seem to have been extensive at any time in the eighteenth century. Undoubted examples seem scarcely to exist,[71] while it would seem rash to lay too much stress on the vague assertions about the trade which Le François of Rouen (see p. 16) is said to have had with foreign countries, because of the difficulties which surround the whole story. Chinese wallpapers, however, had been imported in very considerable quantities, although, owing to the privileged position held by the East India Company, it does not seem safe to infer that free trade had previously existed. English paper-stainers, up to this time, had little to fear from foreign competition, as they could produce goods that compared favourably with anything that was being made on the Continent. If foreign papers had been allowed to be imported previously, it is unlikely that many people would have availed themselves of the opportunity.

Whatever interpretation we put on this new duty, it was ultimately destined to prove the first step towards a type of protection, achieved by the virtual exclusion of foreign papers as a result of duties which became increasingly heavy.[72] In 1792 the basis of the customs duty was changed to 6d per pound weight, in addition to any duties on paper, and papers imported from China were now no longer exempt from taxation. In the meantime, the excise duty on English paper hangings had been increased from 1½d to 1¾d in 1777,[73] while, under the stress of the French Revolutionary War, licences at the rate of £4 were imposed on all paper-stainers.

The following figures, obtained from G. H. Morton's pamphlet,[74] give the amounts received from wallpaper tax in successive periods of ten years in the later eighteenth century:

	£	s	d
1770	13,242	8	11
1780	11,955	4	3
1790	19,204	18	8
1800	24,811	8	7

The following figures, obtained from the records of the Customs House, dated Christmas 1774, will help to give some idea of the extent of the English export trade in stained paper at about this time. The exported paper received a complete drawback of the excise duty:

Channel Islands	7,060 sq. yds	Russia	21,453
Ireland	2,471	Scandinavia and Eastern Baltic	9,184
Flanders	96,230	Spain	171,859
France	2,800	Africa	350
Germany	27,521	British West Indies	23,994
Holland	101,295	Canada	26,964
Italy	32,946	Florida	2,842
Portugal	110,612	Nova Scotia	294

From these figures it may be seen that the industry was in a very flourishing condition, and that British stained papers[75] were appreciated all over the known world. Undoubtedly the figures would vary considerably from year to year, and the American colonies, unrepresented in this list, would take their share. The importance of the West Indies at this time is fully borne out by their large imports. The smallness of the exports to France bears witness to the efficiency of the French protective legislation.

It must not be supposed that all the stained paper exported to the Continent would be used as paper hangings. All over Europe, especially in Italy, wallpaper was used for the end-papers and covers of books, as well as for such uses as the lining of drawers and cupboards. A considerable number of the end-papers in the collections of the Victoria and Albert Museum and in the British Museum are suitable for wall decoration, and even flock paper was used for end-papers (E. 5968–1897). The general standard of the artistic and technical skill displayed in this type of work was low, so that designs suitable for wallpapers were usually preferred for bookbinding to the cheap local products intended solely for this purpose.

Although wallpapers were not taxed nearly as severely in the last decade of the century as was to be the case later, there seems to be little doubt that the decline in the industry's standards of artistry and workmanship, which was to be so marked in the first half of the nineteenth century, started at about this time. A considerable proportion of English wallpapers had always been of the cheaper sort, and this proportion was no doubt reflected in the papers which had been exported for use for book-binding abroad. The general overthrow of stable conditions in Europe, moreover, gradually throttled the British Continental market. Since the American rebellion, the demand for wallpapers in the New World had been increasingly met by French paper-stainers and by the two factories which had long been established in America. It became increasingly clear to English manufacturers that it must be the home market alone for which they must cater. The insular character of the industry was becoming ever more perceptible, while the tendency to look for quick returns and to save on outlay was accentuated by the mounting weight of taxation. Chinese papers were still high in favour among those who could afford them, but there appeared to be an element of risk in spending large sums on the production of a really high-class paper which might not sell after all. The lines on which British wallpaper was to be manufactured in the nineteenth century were being laid down. When it became possible to sell large quantities of relatively cheap and inferior wallpapers, makers began to neglect the less remunerative part of their business.

The Nineteenth Century, up to the Time of William Morris

The history of English wallpapers during that part of the nineteenth century with which we are here concerned falls roughly into two periods. The first period is that of taxation at home and the practical exclusion of foreign wallpaper by customs duties; the second may be described as the period of free trade and mass production.

The influence of taxation and Government control on the formation of styles of wallpaper in the early nineteenth century was so great that it is necessary to deal with this aspect of the history of the industry before we pass on to others. Although the excise duty at the rate of $1\frac{3}{4}$d per square yard, which had been in force since 1787, was not increased, the licences for paper-staining businesses were raised in 1809 to £20 per year.[76] Along with the heavy taxation, the industry had to bear all the inconveniences of close Government supervision. In 1806 the falsification of wallpaper stamps was even added to the list of offences punishable by death.[77] Doubtless the offenders, against whom repeated legislation had been enacted since the beginning of the duties, were the smaller house-decorators and occasional paper-stainers, rather than the larger, well supervised businesses. In 1801 John Gamble tried to reap the benefit of his rights in Louis Robert's invention for making continuous lengths of paper for hangings. The officers of the excise had always been accustomed to encounter paper for staining in the forms of sheets, and as the new method would involve economies in the quantity of paper used (since none would have to be wasted on joins), and consequently might reduce the revenue to be collected, the invention was vetoed for about thirty years. Ireland was even more unfortunate than England in the manner of its treatment by the revenue officers, as, besides its wallpaper taxes, similar to the British after the Union, it had to bear the extra burden of licences for retailers of wallpapers from 1805 to 1822.

The customs duties on foreign wallpapers rose steadily during the period of the Napoleonic wars. In 1803[78] the tax was raised to 9d per pound weight. An extra 3d was voted for the period of the war and six months after it in 1809,[79] but when this period had elapsed the duties remained in force. It was not till the theories of free trade began to be propounded, when the reign of Queen Victoria was well advanced, that the duties were suddenly lowered from 1s to 2d in 1847,[80] to be further reduced to 1d six years later,[81] and finally to disappear, practically unnoticed, in 1861.[82]

There can be no doubt about the damaging effects of the heavy excise and customs duties. In 1835 it is declared in the Official Report of the Excise Commissioners, under Sir Henry Parnell, Bt., that on every 'piece' of wallpaper produced in this country costing 2s 6d the duty was 1s 3d. While the quantity of paper hangings was increasing annually, the price at which they could be put on the market was so high that there was no demand for expensive papers. It was for this reason that, whereas French manufacturers were producing scenic papers by means of large numbers of colour blocks, English paper-stainers preferred less costly designs. The demand for scenic papers in England was not sufficiently large to encourage any English firm to embark on the huge initial outlay, so that, though a certain number of these papers are to be found in England, they are all of French origin. The days when the fastidious few, like Horace Walpole, could settle the correct style for decorating their houses, and then force it on the manufacturers, were passing in the early years of the nineteenth century. The aim of the greater number of manufacturers was to produce wallpapers within the financial reach of all.[83] The report of Sir Henry Parnell's Commission on the wallpaper tax, after it had fully examined the facts of the case, was so outspoken that there was no course left for the Government but to remove the duties. After being in force for nearly a century and a quarter, the duty disappeared, and with it disappeared the use of the tax stamp and the licences for paper-stainers.

It is now time to turn to examples of some of the styles of wallpaper made at this time. Many of those in the Museum collection came from the stock of a builder, Thomas Avery, who represented a firm which had been in existence for nearly 150 years in Tenterden, Kent. A few of these papers might date from the end of the eighteenth century, but most of them form a series which represents fairly adequately some of the styles in vogue in the first half of the nineteenth century. Unfortunately, none of the names of the makers of any of these papers is known.

The most pleasing examples of the early years of the century represented in this series are a number of patterns of papers imitating painted panelling.[84] There is no sign of the Pompeian designs of the preceding century in these papers,[85] which are characterized by extreme simplicity. The moulding of the edge of the panel is of a different colour or shade from the panel itself, and the colours mostly used are light browns and blues, mauve, and olive green. As far as one can judge from these specimens, it would seem that the centres of the panels were left undecorated. It is probable that these papers were used largely in conjunction with pictures. In the corners of the panels, however, there are simple classical motifs, sometimes imitating painting, and sometimes stucco work. Similar decoration appears in the spaces between the panels. The angle decoration is sometimes in gold, which has not tarnished, and in other cases in flock. Possibly many of these papers were intended for use in rooms with wooden dados. A number of narrow borders for use with these are in the Museum collection, as well as examples of friezes. The borders are mostly simple key-pattern designs or floral motifs; some are flocked. The upper border is usually in imitation of a stucco cornice, but in some cases it develops the dimensions of a frieze. Some of the later and less successful examples of these represent in flock the bunched linen decoration which was also popular in France at about this time, and one example, probably not earlier than 1830, represents heavy cords and tassels. Taken as a whole, this type of decoration was fairly successful, at any rate in the earlier years. These designs involved no extravagant outlay, as most of them required few wood blocks. The use of flock in these papers is in very questionable taste, for few of the designs are inspired by textiles, but in practice this error is not as noticeable as might be expected.

Textile designs copying flowered silk were as popular during the early years of the century as they have always been since. They present few remarkable features, however. In the design of one example (no 206), made by Messrs Duppa and Slodden, of Oxford Street, London, dated 1833 and bearing the tax stamp of William IV, we see indications of the decline which culminated in the work of the middle of the century. The use of satin papers towards the end of the first half of the nineteenth century was considered a great triumph by contemporaries, and added to the popularity of these designs.[86] The polish of these papers was obtained by rubbing them with French chalk. Tom Cobb's device for embossing and twilling paper, patented on 15 September 1829, also added to the textile appearance of these papers.

We have already made mention of the early attempts in the eighteenth century to print wallpapers by means of cylinders with raised patterns on them. Attempts to perfect this technique did not end with the century, but it was a considerable time before anything could be produced by these machines which could be regarded as a marketable commodity. William Troutbeck, of Liverpool, who was working as early as 1837, claimed to be the first to use the calico-printing machine to print both calicoes and paper hangings, although the idea is much older. Although his machine was equipped with a cylinder, he is said not to have availed himself of it. At about the same time, C. H. and E. Potter, of Darwen, also calico-printers, began some experiments in power-driven machine-printing. After many years, this firm succeeded in adapting this machinery to the engraved roller-printing of wallpaper.[87] The main problem (how to obtain a constant supply of colour) was largely solved by the invention of Harold Potter's employee, Walmsley Preston, patented in 1846.[88] The limitation of the cylinder-printing process is the frequency of the repeat of the pattern, but the cheapness of the article produced compensated for its artistic demerits. Already in 1851 machines were working which could produce two hundred pieces of paper, each twelve yards long, in one hour.[89] The immense output of these machines, together with the cheapness of the work which they produced, was largely responsible for the bad workmanship characteristic of the wallpapers manufactured in the latter half of the last century.

Attempts to produce machine-made papers by techniques other than cylinder-printing had made a certain amount of headway at an earlier date. Nothing is known of the fate of Edward Cowper's machine for printing papers, patented in 1816, but it is clear that it cannot have met with success. The machine invented by William Palmer, and patented in 1837, on the other hand, is known to have been still in use five years later. It printed by means of a block, which was raised, lowered, and fed with colour by the mechanism. Hand-machines, working with roller and block, continued to be used till 1850. Messrs Evans and Fisher, of Tamworth, seem to have been the first English firm to produce machine-made papers which could be sold. They continued to work for about twenty years, but finally ceased production, owing to the hostility of the excise officials, who objected to their combining paper-making and staining in the same works. They do not seem to have succeeded in printing anything more elaborate than plain-line papers.

Although block-printed papers were beginning to be regarded as being among the more expensive type of paper hangings, great technical improvements were made before the middle of the century, so that this better process could, to some extent, compete with the cylinder. While Jackson, a hundred years before, could produce only 'ten positive tints' by means of four wood blocks, in 1850 papers could be produced, using the same number of blocks, with twenty or thirty colours. In this way it was possible to sell papers in twenty-three colours at 3½d per yard, instead of 10d, which they would have cost if produced by the old method.[90]

Unfortunately, technical progress far outstripped artistic quality in this as in so many other branches of Victorian art. The restraint enforced by taxation, which had trammelled the industry in the early years of the century, had now passed away with the repeal of the 1714 Act in 1836, but the designers, turning from the enforced simplicity of earlier years, now indulged in an orgy of complicated designs. The Gothic revival must bear the blame for the production of some of the most offensive designs. Now that there was practically no restriction on imports of foreign wallpapers, British manufacturers had to bear the burden of French competition. Although the papers of Réveillon had passed away, and French decoration was assuming the style known as the Second Empire, there could be no doubt of the superiority of the French over the English papers. Efforts to undersell foreign wallpapers might be successful in the lower reaches of the market, but this could not affect the demand for decorations in better styles. Throughout the second quarter of the last century there was a conscious effort on the part of the English paper-stainers to compete with France in meeting this demand. If reference be made to the Museum's collections of papers of this period, and particularly to the later part of the stock of Thomas Avery of Tenterden, two main trends reveal themselves: the servile imitation of French designs by craftsmen incompetent to judge quality; and the desire to be original, resulting in the production of wallpapers such as no reputable designer had hitherto dared to produce. As instances of the former class, we cannot do better than cite no 266, which can only be described as constituting crude parodies of flowered-silk designs.

Among innovations in design we may note the new idea of the nursery paper, which was to bring into existence such a quantity of charming designs in the latter years of the century. The early nursery papers, however, are remarkable only for their gaudiness and for the badness of their execution. If the artistic taste of children can be ruined in the nursery, a paper such as no 349 (E.1114) may have been responsible for many intellectual murders. Though less reprehensible for its design, no 349 (E. 1113) is noteworthy in that none of the colour blocks have registered accurately—a quite inexcusable fault. No 409, which consists of a number of views of the Great Exhibition of 1862, is another example of this type of paper.

Though flock was still frequently misused in the decoration of flowered borders, as we have remarked with regard to papers earlier in the century, there seems to have been a quite perceptible tendency to use flock once more in the old colour designs imitating velvets, such as had been made in the eighteenth century. Among the cuttings of wallpapers in the *Journal of Design and Manufactures* of 1849 and the succeeding years, a number of designs of considerable merit may be found side by side with others, from the same manufacturers, which show no improvement. Though a certain improvement is visible in no 223, which has a grained background, no 266 is more typical, as an example of the worst class of flock paper of this period.

The year of the Great Exhibition of 1862 may be taken as the date of the beginning of a new era for English paper hangings. The firm of Morris, Marshall, Faulkner and Co. had come into existence in April 1861, but it was not till the following year that the designing of wallpapers was included in the business. Although hitherto it had been the practice of the firm to execute all their orders themselves, the large space required for paper-staining forced Morris to hand over the execution of his designs to Metford Warner, of Jeffrey's works in Islington. This gave Morris's firm the great advantage of dealing with workmen who had experience of their craft, so that the business of supervision could be carried on without the attendant fatigues of the organization of a factory. The importance of William Morris in the history of English paper hangings lies in his insistence on the necessity of providing good designs. The rules which had been recognized in the making of their designs by Papillon, Réveillon and the more shadowy English makers of flock paper of the eighteenth century, were rediscovered and restored to the industry. In the case of paper hangings, an attempt to restore craftsmanship did not involve a hopeless war against economic facts, as was the case with other industries. Morris's papers, after his first attempt to work with etched plates, were produced by exactly the same methods as were in use among his contemporaries, and differed from them only in minor details of technique. His insistence on obtaining the best and purest colours, and his use of hatching to show shadows, merely show him to have possessed that constant desire to improve his work in every way, which was lacking in the other British makers of wallpapers in the middle of the last century.

It was, however, as a designer that Morris did most for English paper hangings. Here, the artistic training which he had undergone, especially in the study of the Middle Ages, was of especial use. He knew the art of combining bright colours without producing merely gaudy results, and evolved for himself general rules which had to be observed in the making of every pattern. The beauty, imagination and order which he described as being the necessary components of every good design were the abstractions of what he saw most lacking in the work of his contemporaries. There is no room here for fuller treatment of the work of William Morris, of which, thanks to the generosity of two donors, the Museum possesses a rich and comprehensive collection.[91] The revival brought about by Morris begins the period in the history of wallpapers in which we still live, and an adequately close scrutiny of the artistic development of the last sixty years lies outside the scope of this survey.

French Wallpapers

To the Mid-Eighteenth Century

Although, as has been seen already, there is evidence that wallpaper was being used abroad at as early a date as in England, our information about this is still elementary. Nearly two hundred years elapse between our record of the activities of Jean Bourdichon and the discovery of the earliest examples of a foreign wallpaper. From this it must not be thought that the increase in the use of wallpaper was less marked on the Continent than in England in the second half of the sixteenth century. In the course of the trial in 1568 of Hermann Schinkel, of Delft, for publishing an heretical book, it appeared that he was in the practice of printing sheets of ballad paper with stripes and roses for use as wallpaper.

In the year 1586 the paper-hanging industry had progressed sufficiently in France to justify the formation of a guild of *Dominotiers, Tapissiers, et Imagiers.*[92] The two last terms denote makers of wallpapers of all types, including those with pictures.

The *domino* was in quite a different line of business. The word was the French term for the Italian papers, imitating marble, which had become fashionable for the bindings of books. These binding papers were produced in an entirely different way from the ordinary printed or painted wallpapers, and it seems very doubtful if the real *domino* was ever used to decorate walls, as the earliest record of marbleized wallpapers dates from the last decade of the seventeenth century in England. Because *Dominotiers* was the first of the titles of the guild, by lax usage the word *domino* began to be used for wallpaper, the sphere in which the guildsmen chiefly encountered the public. Already, at the beginning of the seventeenth century, this change had almost ousted the former use of the word.

There seems no reason to suppose that the work of the early *dominotiers* was in advance of that of their English contemporaries. Their higher-class work was probably composed chiefly of the printed papers which were common in England, sometimes coloured by hand or stencil, whilst their cheaper work seems to have been mainly small religious pictures, or comic scenes with printed explanations. Although no actual specimens of the wallpapers produced by the *dominotiers* in the first half of the seventeenth century have so far been discovered, it will be easily realized how nearly their work approached that of the book-illustrators. It is not, therefore, surprising to find that the *dominotiers* often succumbed to the temptation of adding explanatory captions to their pictures to make them intelligible, thereby infringing the privileges of the printers. The litigation between the trades of the printers and the *dominotiers* is, indeed, virtually the only documentary evidence that we have for the activities of these obscure artists at this time. As a result, a series of rulings on the use of printed pictures and explanations was made in 1586, 1618, 1649 and 1723, with a view to putting an end to this cause of friction. Explanations, when necessary, were to be engraved on the block, no movable type was allowed when a printer was employed, and then the inscription might not exceed six lines. Precise regulations were made as to the supervision of the *dominotiers* when at work, and they were not permitted the use of the ordinary kind of printing press. Paris and Rouen seem to have been the main centres of the industry in its early days.

Allusion has already been made to the invention by Le François, of Rouen, of flock papers, and, in the absence of any further evidence, the story must be taken for what it is worth. It may be remarked that there is nothing inherently improbable in the invention of flock papers at such an early date, but the ignorance of this invention shown by so many of the French authorities on the eighteenth century makes it all the more probable that the flock papers of Le François made little headway in the market.

As we approach the eighteenth century, our information about French wallpapers becomes less vague. This is due mainly to three authorities: *Dictionnaire Universel de Commerce*, by Jacques Savary des Bruslons, published in 1723; the *Encyclopédie ou Dictionnaire Raisonné des Sciences*, by Denis Diderot and Jean Le Rond D'Alembert, published from 1751 to 1757, and *Traité Historique et Pratique de la gravure en Bois*, by Jean Michel Papillon, published in 1766.

The *Dictionnaire Universel* is valuable in that it is an independent work, and is a necessary corrective to Papillon, though it must not be assumed that Savary des Bruslons was always correct, as he did not possess the same intimate knowledge of *dominotiers* as his rival.

The *Encyclopédie* incorporates verbatim much of what had appeared in the book of Savary des Bruslons, but, in addition, it has some independent articles of considerable interest by Papillon.

Papillon is therefore the primary authority for the history of paper hangings up to the middle of the eighteenth century in France. This is not to deny that his book has shortcomings. For example, as a history of the art of wood-engraving, it is extremely inaccurate. Also, even when dealing with the discoveries in the making of wallpaper during his own lifetime, Papillon can be shown to be misinformed.[93] Moreover, it should also be remembered that he was a far from impartial witness. He was the son of the greatest *dominotier* of his time, and he loses no opportunity of glorifying all the members of his family. Apparently, down to nearly the end of the century the *dominotiers'* activities were confined to the traditional manufacture of the picture papers and to the *papiers marbrés*. Under this last heading Papillon seems to include papers with flower patterns stencilled on them.[94] A well known maker of these papers was a certain Le Breton, who was able to produce very decorative sheets polished like playing cards, until the work of Papillon's father finally drove them from the market. The work of Le Breton must have included the making of paper hangings, for improved paper hangings of Papillon could only have had a very limited effect on the production of end- and lining-papers.[95] The abuse of the term *papiers marbrés* thus adds one more difficulty to an already obscure work.

Jean Papillon, father of the author of the *Traité*, was born at St Quentin in 1661. Besides acquiring the art of making small woodcuts after an apprenticeship spent in designing and cutting blocks for printed petticoats, he was led by a natural transition to the manufacture of wallpapers. His greatest invention, alleges his son, was the introduction of *papiers de tapisserie*, which he began to bring into fashion in 1688. The difference between these papers and the earlier ones was that the designs were printed so as to join together when the sheets were pasted on to a wall.[96] If J. M. Papillon is correct in his claim, it will be seen that by the end of the seventeenth century the *dominotiers* had discovered a device which had in fact been known in England about 170 years before.

The colouring of all Papillon's papers, and of those of his imitators, was done with brush and stencil. When producing works on a large scale by hand, such as wallpapers, it is impossible to avoid a certain amount of untidiness, which these papers unfortunately illustrate. It is very difficult to hold a stencil by hand so that it will not smudge, or so that the colours will not overflow. The colours used by Papillon and his followers were either watercolours or ink. The colouring is, unfortunately, the weak point of these papers, as it is almost always too washy.

In *circa* 1730 a certain Boulard began to work, who used to colour his papers with one distemper colour applied by stencil. As none of his work has survived, we do not known how far he was successful.[97]

The elder Papillon was a man who spared no pains to understand his craft, and insisted on superintending all the processes of manufacture, from the cutting of the wood blocks to the pasting of the completed articles on the wall. From this practice he learned the difficulties to be encountered, and used his ingenuity to overcome them. It was probably with the intention of increasing the size of his designs that he began to use larger wood blocks than had been commonly in use among the *dominotiers*. The fewer the joins in the paper made after printing, the better would the paper appear as a whole. This advantage, however, was bought very dearly. The blocks, three feet in length and made of pear or service wood, were, as used by him, extremely unwieldy. It was impossible to print with them in the ordinary way, so that Papillon was forced to lay his wood blocks on their backs, with the paper on top, and to take the impression by means of a roller or mallet. Many of his imitators continued to use this method down to 1766, but it never became universal, in spite of his prestige.

Papillon's ingenuity is further shown by his attempt to produce a type of lustre paper.[98] He painted a pattern with glue on the paper, and then scattered powdered paint over it, in the same way as makers of flock papers. The adhesives must have been bad, however, for no example produced by this technique seems to have survived.

The interest of Papillon's book was greatly enhanced in our own day by Henri Clouzot's discovery of the sketches prepared by him for accompanying his articles in the *Encyclopédie des Sciences*.[99] These had been rejected wholesale by the editor, as the artist had not contented himself with illustrating extremely fully all the processes of making and hanging wallpapers, but evidently considered essential such details as a view of the street in which his father's shop stood. But, however trivial some of Papillon's sketches may have appeared to his editor, to us they are invaluable, as they help us to visualize so many of the details which his texts had left obscure, such as the printing of wallpapers with the paper above the wood blocks—a technique about which some writers had expressed scepticism. The possiblity of removing for use elsewhere a wallpaper which had been already hung, by extending a damp cloth over it, is also illustrated. No less interesting is the variety of designs of wallpapers which are shown. A great number of these are stripe and diaper patterns, and also flowing designs of foliage, sometimes with larger designs produced by several different wood blocks which were joined together. Others have small framed pictures printed on them, and there are also large pictorial designs which filled the whole side of a room. Though Jean Michel Papillon never asserted that his father had ever attempted colour-printing from wood blocks, certain papers in which traces of this process have been seen have been attributed to him. It should be added, however, that, although none of these sketches shows colour-printing in progress, one of them does show a group of hand-colourers at work.

Papillon seems to have raised paper-hanging in France from an expedient of the poor to an art which even the rich might patronize. In the seventeenth century, the *Dictionnaire Universel* informs us, the use of paper hangings was confined to the houses of the poor and the lesser *bourgeoisie*, but by about the turn of the century there was scarcely a house in Paris which had not wallpaper somewhere in it. Although this seems to point to a very large output of wallpaper, the number of papers that can, with any probability, be attributed to Papillon remains quite small. It must also be added that, even supposing that these were produced in Papillon's workshop, it is quite possible that his part in their manufacture may have been confined to mere criticism, as we know that he had a staff of very capable assistants.

Some interesting fragments of a Papillon paper are in the Musée des Arts Décoratifs, Paris. There is a small classical panel containing inside it a smaller one, coloured blue, and depicting a torch with a small bearded figure on either side. Another fragment of the same paper shows diaper work and the lower part of a classical panel. A good design, clearly based on the printed textiles which were then becoming fashionable, is shown in a paper now in New York.[100] The background is yellow, and a branch of a flowering shrub climbs diagonally across the sheet, affording a perch to a bird of the golden pheasant species. Another paper[101] is interesting as being an early example of the European imitation of Chinese papers. The upper part of the sheet is filled by a bouquet of flowers, while in the lower part a grotesque little figure with a skipping rope is seen among more floral decoration. In this, as in most of the French *chinoiserie* papers, the influence of the Far East has been reduced almost to the minimum. It was generally considered sufficient that a design of this sort should be fantastic in order to pass as Chinese. Designs that made more serious attempts to imitate Chinese papers were also produced during this time, but the correctness of the imitation was seldom more than superficial. In depicting the Chinese themselves, little attempt is made to show the true Chinese type, though it would easily have been possible for the artists to see this in specimens of Oriental art, nor were Chinese entirely strangers to France, as a small number of converts came to Paris under the tutelage of the Jesuits. According to J. M. Papillon, in the middle of the eighteenth century *chinoiserie* papers were produced that might easily be mistaken for genuine Chinese papers.[102] Some of these were actually painted on Chinese paper, but they were imported into France from the Low Countries and Germany.

It was natural that Papillon should have had many imitators, and, as he never took any steps to obtain patents for his designs, others were at liberty to copy him as closely as they could. One of the most successful of his rivals must have been a certain Dufourcroy, whose name and address in the Rue Jacob, Saint-Germain, Paris, appear on the margin of a fragment of a paper in the Musée des Arts Décoratifs.[103] The design is one of intertwining chrysanthemums, with small birds perching on the stems. The block, measuring $16\frac{1}{2} \times 12\frac{5}{8}$ inches, is not as large as those used by Papillon, and the whole design is shown on one sheet, but is made so as to form a continuous hanging. It is certainly a masterpiece of its kind. After having admired this design in a photograph, it is impossible not to be disappointed, on seeing the original, by the untidiness in the application of the colouring and in the washiness of its pinks, blues and olive-green.

Another paper of this period, in the same museum, comes from the Château de Marcour, near Dijon.[104] It is of a much more conventional character, and consists of a frame of strap work containing *fleurs-de-lis*, mostly surmounted by crowns. The colours of the strap work and *fleurs-de-lis* are yellow and red.

Jean Papillon died in February 1723, but his son, Jean Michel, the author of the *Traité*, continued to carry on the business. Despite his book, he remains, as a paper-stainer, a much more shadowy character than his father. The latter had determined that his son should succeed him as the leading *dominotier* of Paris, and had begun his education in the art of cutting wood blocks when he had reached the age of only nine.[105] A print of his first paper—a design of poppies—is preserved in the Cabinet des Estampes at the Bibliothèque Nationale, Paris, in the 'Recueil des Papillons', which the artist presented to the Royal Library in order to preserve specimens of the work of his family. His father praised his first essay, but he did not succeed in passing on to his son his own enthusiasm. For the ambitions of the younger Papillon lay more in the field of illustrative woodcuts than in the making of wallpapers. The *Traité* is full of mentions of his more successful cuts, but the allusions to his real business are few and incidental. It is probable that its *morale* was such that it was able to carry on fairly well without the supervision of its owner. That it still continued to command good labour is shown by the fact that Jacques Chauvau, who popularized wallpapers printed in oil colours, was once among its employees. It is not known exactly how long the younger Papillon continued his father's business, but he appears among a number of other well-known *dominotiers* in a prosecution of 1739.[106]

It would seem that he sold his blocks for printing wallpapers very shortly after this to 'Veuve l'Anglois,'[107] for he tells us that *circa* 1740 she was prosecuted by another well known *dominotier*, Didier Aubert, for using the Papillon sign of the butterfly, and that she lost her case. Didier Aubert, also an employee of the younger Papillon, had married the daughter of an engraver who had also used the sign of a butterfly, and, as he had set up in business earlier, could prove that he had a better right to it than the widow. The son of the 'Veuve l'Anglois' was still carrying on the business at the time of the writing of the *Traité*.

After retiring from his paper-hanging business, Jean Michel Papillon devoted himself to making woodcuts. The *Traité* was started as early as 1734, but proceeded no further than its first volume, and was entirely recast for the edition of 1766. In 1759, he succumbed to some mental trouble, from which he recovered after a short time. As was natural, his interest in the development of paper hangings waned somewhat when they were no longer his personal concern, and we find in his writings only too few references to contemporary work. Many of the *dominotiers* of his time whom he mentions are mere names to us.

The introduction of the refined *papiers de tapisserie* did not drive out all the older types of paper hangings. The old-fashioned *dominoterie* still continued to be made for the lower classes, especially at Rouen and other places in the provinces. There was still the demand for inexpensive paper bindings and lining-papers, and the peasant would still need his pictures of sacred or comic subjects with which to decorate his cottage. Many of these *domino* papers, even at the end of the eighteenth century, show no development, either in design or in execution, from work of the seventeenth century, and fully bear out the disparaging remarks of the *Dictionnaire Universel*. The changes in fashion which are so evident in the superior types of wall hangings in the middle of the eighteenth century seem to have left no sign in the production of these humbler wares.

Allusions have already been made to the continuance of the manufacture of flock papers during this period. Our main authority on this subject is the *Dictionnaire Universel* of Savary des Bruslons,[108] published in 1723. Savary gives us a careful account of the manufacture of these papers, showing them to have been of a very different character from those which came into fashion *circa* 1750. They were intended to imitate tapestries, and not velvets and damasks, like the English flock papers. The process of manufacture was as follows: flocks of all shades and colours required for the tapestry were first collected in little trays beside the workmen. The outlines of the design were sketched on the paper, and the painter then began to paint in each successive colour, using the ordinary *dominotier's* paints mixed with adhesive. As he worked, another workman scattered the appropriate flocks on the design, till the whole was finished. The results of this process were so good that they were scarcely distinguishable from real tapestries. They had a fatal defect, however: the adhesive used would not resist damp. So grave was this fault that not a single example has survived.

Savary des Bruslons was aware, unlike Papillon, that the earliest flock hangings had been made at Rouen, where the backing of the flock had been usually of cloth, and not of paper.[109] The industry spread to the Faubourg Saint-Antoine, where it reached that state of perfection which he describes. It was at this time that Claude Audran was connected with the business, but there seems to be no support for the theory that he was the first to imitate tapestries, nor does he appear to have used a backing of paper for the flock.[110]

Although these flock hangings, which imitated tapestry, were so manifestly unsatisfactory, there seems to have been a continuous effort to maintain their manufacture. In 1735 a certain Simon secured a patent for an invention for the production of flock papers imitating tapestries.[111] It would seem that his invention also failed to overcome the real shortcoming of all these flock hangings, the failure to resist damp, for no more is known of his work. The French manufacturers appear definitely to have failed in their attempts to perfect the manufacture of flock, and an entirely new beginning, arising from imports from England, was required to restart the industry on sound lines.

The Second Half of the Eighteenth Century

In the second half of the eighteenth century the wallpaper industry in France began to lay its foundations anew. Hitherto, there can be no doubt that France had been relatively backward in this industry, as compared with England, and, in all probability, Holland. Papillon, in popularizing *papiers de tapisserie*, had undoubtedly taken a great step forward, but, even at its best, his technique was faulty, and for at least a generation after his death no appreciable progress was made.

A sudden deluge of superior foreign wallpapers, together with a revival of interest in new technical experiments among native manufacturers, served to put fresh life into the industry. By the end of the century French wallpapers were as good as any that could be produced in Europe, and by the first half of the nineteenth century they were to be immeasurably ahead of their competitors.

The English flock papers, which gained such popularity in France *circa* 1750, did not reach such heights of artistic quality as contemporary French work, but as hangings they were infinitely preferable. Instead of imitating tapestries,[112] they continued to copy velvet and brocade hangings, and were limited, as a rule, to one shade or colour for the ground and another for the flocking. They were produced with stencil and wood block, instead of by the elaborate process described earlier (see p. 46). It was not so much the design, as the superior manufacture, which gave the English flock papers the preference. Papillon, indeed, tells us that in his time the English flock was made with a series of wood blocks in the manner of colour-printing, so that flock papers using several colours were made.[113] If he is correct in describing the technique, no such papers have, so far, been discovered.[114] The method of colouring with wood blocks paper that had already been flocked was, however, well known, and may be presumed to have been introduced before 1760, when colour-printing for wallpapers was becoming popular. The number of English flock papers of this date that have survived are the best witnesses of the soundness of the technique. It would appear that the French manufacturers, when flocking, used their ordinary colours mixed with turpentine and an oil with adhesive powers.[115] The *Encyclopédie des Sciences*[116] gives walnut oil, white lead, and litharge as the mixture then in use.

One of the earliest to patronise English flock papers was Madame de Pompadour, who is mentioned in the *Livre Journal* of Lazare Duvaux[117] as having had her wardrobe and the passage to the chapel at Versailles decorated in this manner. Four years later she had 'English paper' hung in the bathroom at the Château de Champs.

The trade must have developed very considerable proportions. For some years the *Affiches de Paris* and the *Annonces, affiches et avis divers* record a number of sales of these goods, although caution must be used in accepting all that is termed *papiers d'Angleterre* as being of English manufacture. Among the most interesting of these is one in the former series, dated 1759, in which J. B. Réveillon, who was to become the greatest of French paper-stainers of the eighteenth century, drew the attention of the public to his goods by an announcement that he had for sale at his establishment in the Rue de l'Arbre Sec a large quantity of real English flock hangings imitating Persian hangings, Utrecht velvets and damasks, to serve for hangings and screens.

It was not to be expected, however, that French manufacturers would tolerate the continued importation of English goods without attempting to copy them. The outbreak of the Seven Years' War must have done much to help them, for though, perhaps, a Madame de Pompadour might get her flock hangings, as the Empress Josephine was to get her muslins, it would not have been possible to meet all the French demand by smuggling from England and from the prizes taken at sea.

As early as 1754, a certain Roguie,[118] living in the Rue du Cloître Saint Germain l'Auxerrois, announced that he had discovered the secret of the English flock papers. Didier Aubert, who had been one of the most prominent of the second generation of the makers of *papiers de tapisserie*, was forced to follow the trend of public opinion and, in 1755, is found advertising his papers as being equal to the English.[119] In this notice he also asserts that his papers are infinitely superior to the Chinese and other painted wallpapers. They cost less than damask and wore well, while they had the advantage that the adhesive used preserved them from being eaten by moths, like woollen tapestries. His method of hanging his papers was unusually elaborate, for, besides the usual cloth at the back, he inserted a layer of grey paper over which he pasted the flocked paper. In this way he avoided any swelling of the paper while it was being hung. An interesting point which is illustrated by the advertisements and the accounts of sales of this time is that, owing to this elaborate method of hanging, it was possible to move the paper from house to house. When a landlord refused to take over the paper of an outgoing tenant, the latter was able to try to find a purchaser elsewhere. We may instance sale advertisements mentioning 'Tentures de papier velouté, à baguettes[120] dorées';[121] 'À vendre, Rue Saint Honoré, vis-à-vis l'Oratoire: tenture de salon, de papier cramoisi velouté, collé sur toile.'[122]

At the close of the Seven Years' War it may be supposed that English papers began to appear once more in considerable quantities on the French market. This time the French government imposed a customs duty, at the rate of a hundred *sous* per quintal, on all paper hangings entering the kingdom, while exporters of French papers had to pay ten *sous* per quintal.[123] In the following year a further ordinance rated imported flock papers at twenty *livres* per quintal.[124] These must have been very severe blows to the English exporters, as may be judged from the fact that the British Customs Records from Christmas 1774 to Christmas 1775 show that the stained paper exported to Jersey was exactly double the amount exported to France, and that exports to France were exceeded even by those to Florida.

The number of manufacturers of flock papers grew immensely from the date of the protective measures, if we may judge from the quantities of names that appear in the advertisements. Among the most enterprising of these paper-hangers was a certain Lecomte of Lyons, who invented a type of flock hanging made from silk shearings *circa* 1769. *L'Année Littéraire* for 1769[125] gives him very high praise both for his designs and for their execution. They did not at all resemble the English flocks in appearance: some were designed to imitate Chinese hangings, while others were composed of flowers bound with ribbons. The papers were sold at prices ranging from twenty-five to forty-five *sous* per *aune*.[126] They took the place, however, of genuine silk hangings, which would cost the purchaser from sixty to eighty sous per *aune*.

The inventor unfortunately died soon after, and although his widow set up a shop in Paris in the Rue des Deux Écus, the business did not last long. The invention was one that would appeal only to the most expensive tastes, and did not overcome the main drawback of silk hangings, which was their tendency to fade. It might appeal to some that the silk flock hangings were much cheaper than the real silk examples, but there would be a very limited market for hangings that would require to be replaced about every eighteen months.

Although for about thirty years flock hangings maintained their supremacy in French fashion, their use was never so exclusive as to hinder the development of other types of wallpaper. In the middle of the century, they had been superior to any other type of wallpaper that could be made in France, and their only rivals in popularity were the Chinese wallpapers. Though these were imported in very considerable quantities, their cost, coupled with the customs duties and the difficulties of obtaining a continuous supply, prevented them from being very extensively used. The rich, and those with commercial interests in the East, might be able to obtain them, but they could not seriously affect the home market.

It was the improvements in the technique in colour-printing from wood blocks that finally put an end to the reign of flock papers in France. It is necessary to go back to *circa* 1740 to see this process beginning. We cannot pretend to decide who introduced colour-printing for wallpapers, while even the credit for bringing it to a reasonable state of efficiency is disputed. The first persons to be mentioned in this connection are Jacques Chereau and Jacques Chauvau, for some time the pupil of the author of the *Traité Historique et Pratique de la Gravure en Bois*. Jacques Chereau is said to have produced his wallpapers printed in colours *circa* 1740, and a specimen of work attributed to him was shown by Follot at the Paris Exhibition of 1900.[127] Nothing else concerning his invention seems to be known, but if it is authentic it would have been developed at about the same time as Jackson was producing his prints in Italy.[128] No mention is made of the medium with which Chereau printed.

The date usually given for Chauvau's essays in colour-printed wallpapers is 1750, several years after the production of Jackson's Venetian prints, but three years before the first mention of him as a paper-hanger. For the rest, it must be admitted that Chauvau remains a very shadowy figure. No work of his has yet been identified, and our only other information about him is from a few scattered references in Papillon's book.[129] Like Jackson's, his work was done in oil, and it is claimed that his papers did not suffer from damp, like the English papers printed in distemper colours. Judging from the fact that his business must have been carried on for at least sixteen years, it may be inferred that his work attained a certain amount of popularity.

If it was the flock papers that struck the first blow at the *papiers de tapisserie*, it was the papers printed in colours that finally drove them off the market. There is a small class of papers which date from the middle of the century, before the painting of papers by hand became economically impossible. Someone in France appears to have copied the experiment, made by Dighton in England, of printing wallpapers from etched plates and colouring them by hand. A couple of rolls of paper executed in this manner are in the Museum collection (no 540). They show an extraordinary mixture of East and West in their inspiration. In one example, a young man and woman are fishing; in the other, another pair are seen fleeing from a burning cottage; but in the backgrounds of both are the familiar trees and butterflies of the Chinese papers. Some other examples exist in the Musée des Arts Décoratifs. These are, however, in pure *chinoiserie* style. One of them depicts two Chinese with guns and a dead rabbit;

nearby is a diminutive stag, and a tree from which birds are flying. Another depicts a Chinese house, on the balcony of which a woman is standing and admiring a child held up to her by another woman on the ground below. These are panels from the same room.

We gather from Papillon that the definite overthrow of the *papiers de tapisserie* by the wood-block papers occurred *circa* 1760–65. He tells us in his book[130] that a certain Boulard, who had for thirty years been producing stencilled papers, had lately started to produce papers printed in distemper, which he was selling at so low a price at his shop in the Rue de la Pelleterie that the old type of paper hanging was disappearing. He had evidently made such a success of the business that he had started to make such papers at Chartres and Orléans as well. The use of distemper-colours instead of Chauvau's oil-colours is an innovation[131] of great importance, especially after the discovery in 1783 by the Duc de Chambres of colours which were insoluble in cold water.[132]

In 1778 a regulation was introduced which laid down that the minimum length of a roll of wallpaper was fixed at nine *aunes*, an arrangement which survived the introduction of the metric system till 1840.[133] In 1771 another regulation enforced the printing of the maker's name and address at both ends of every roll. This gave a legal sanction to a practice that had been observed for a long time by some of the best manufacturers.[134]

Just as Jean Papillon overshadows the other *dominotiers* of the beginning of the eighteenth century, so Jean Baptiste Réveillon overshadows his contemporaries towards its close. It is definitely from the date of his rise that the superiority in paper-staining can be said to have passed from England to France. English manufacturers still continued to make all the technical discoveries of the industry, but, despite this, they never obtained their full share of success. While English manufacturers tried in every way to cut down the initial cost of producing wallpapers, Réveillon taught his countrymen the advantage that could be gained by a large but judicious outlay. The charge of short-sighted economy which was made by Crace in 1839[135] was true of English makers fifty years earlier.

Réveillon, initially a stationer, started as a retailer of wallpapers in the Rue de l'Arbre Sec *circa* 1752. He passed from this to the manufacture of wallpapers, and gave to two of his assistants his stationery business, which had been worth about twenty-five or thirty thousand livres a year to him. In 1765 he was able to buy La Folie Titon, a large mansion built by the *Commissaire de Guerre*, Titon du Tillet, in the Faubourg Saint-Antoine, which now became his factory. In 1770 he bought a paper factory at Courtalin-en-Brie, as he found that he could not buy paper of the quality he needed.

In his early days, while still a stationer, Réveillon had sold papers in every style, but soon after he set up he started to specialize in the style for which he became renowned. These were the days when Pompeii and Herculaneum were beginning to give up their treasures, with the consequence that light classical arabesques, adhering closely to the Roman originals, had become highly fashionable for wall decorations. While some patrons of this style were able to afford to have their rooms painted in the classical manner, the introduction of wallpaper of this sort made it possible for a greater number to indulge their taste, although the prices might still remain relatively high.

There can be no doubt that Réveillon's wallpapers are the most artistic that have ever been produced, nor is it difficult to see the reason. He paid his artists well, and, having good taste as well as business ability, saw that he got good value for his money. While the designers of most wallpapers have remained anonymous, the artists of a number of Réveillon's papers are known. Among these were the Italian Cietti, and J. B. Fay, Huet, Lavallée-Poussin, Méry père, Prieur and others. Cietti was particularly skilled in his imitations of stucco,[136] and among his known work is a series of 'The Senses' in this manner[137]. Other designs of his, imitating Pompeian marble, also exist. The effects that he gives are always delightful, even though his nymphs are in somewhat strained attitudes.[138]

Jean Baptiste Fay specialized in the imitation of Pompeian wall paintings, and if, when he attempted a Pompeian design, he erred by lacking cohesion, this is a fault that was due to his faithfulness in copying his originals, and his best work is undoubtedly that in which he allowed himself to turn his arabesque into a more purely floral decoration, interspersed with birds. Perhaps the most attractive of all Réveillon's papers is one of Fay's design, showing a floral arabesque on a light-blue ground, and having peacocks, parrots, cocks and other birds at the foot of each panel.[139] Perhaps rather less attractive is a similar paper, showing classical arabesques on a pale-green ground. Both of these papers are supposed to have been issued *circa* 1785–88. It is interesting to be able to record that these two papers are the only examples of Réveillon's work that have so far been found in England.[140] The customs duties to be paid, both on export from France and on import into England, coupled with Réveillon's high charges, would make a large export trade improbable. The fragments of these papers are now in the Museum (no 962), and it is recorded that they were supplied in 1793 to a house at Longford, Newport, Salop, by a firm called Elliott. In the bill for £39 3s, reference seems only to be made to the green paper, so it must be supposed that the light blue was either supplied on a separate account, or else pieces of it were used to fill up odd spaces, such as door-heads.

Lavallée-Poussin, like Fay, imitated Pompeian paintings,[141] while examples of the work of Prieur, Méry and Huet are hardly less successful.

Réveillon did not neglect floral patterns for use in rooms where decoration in panels was not wanted. These are equally well executed, but they are not as distinctive as his classical and panel designs. A roll of a very fine paper (no 546), almost certainly produced by Réveillon, has a background which represents a silk hanging decorated by designs inspired by Etruscan vases in panels.

In 1784, in recognition of the success of his work, Réveillon received permission to call his factory a *Manufacture Royale*, and to stamp the ends of every roll of his paper with this title.[142] In the following year he received the gold medal instituted by Necker for the encouragement of the useful arts. And yet it was destined that his carefully built up business, employing three hundred workmen, should collapse in one day.

Réveillon had as a private enemy a certain Abbé Roy, who had tried to pass a forged bill in settlement of his account for goods which he had bought. At the end of April 1789 the prosecution of the Abbé was proceeding, and his conviction was expected daily. He spread a rumour that Réveillon had declared that a workman could live on fifteen *sous* a day, and that he had expressed his intention of making a great cut in his employees' wages. Réveillon afterwards denied all this, and pointed to the fact that even the children in his factory received from eight to fifteen *sous*, while his most skilled workmen earned from fifty to one hundred *sous* a day. Any sort of rumour was sufficient to cause an upheaval in Paris at that time, and on 27 April a mob collected to burn the factory. They were dispersed, but the next day they returned, and effected their purpose. Réveillon and his wife were fortunate enough to escape, and a few days later he was able to write to Necker, giving an estimate of the immense losses he had incurred. In reply he received a letter from Necker promising to replace the gold medal which was among the objects lost, the maintenance of the title of *Manufacture Royale* and its extension to the factory at Courtalin, the remittance of ten thousand francs for which he was surety, and an indemnity of thirty thousand francs. In spite of all this, Réveillon did not feel that the times were secure enough, so he retired to England, from whence he disposed of what was left of his business to Jacquemart and Bénard.

The time when the wallpaper industry in France could be said to be in the hands of a dozen firms in Paris and Rouen had by now passed away. Paris, by the second half of the century, seems to have had several dozen flourishing businesses, but in the provinces wallpaper was being made at Besançon, Bordeaux, and Marseilles, as well as at Rouen. Though Réveillon's business may be taken as the most successful of this time, it is necessary to say something about a few of the most important of his contemporaries and successors, in order to bridge the gap between the destruction of his works and the close of the century.

The most prominent of these was the firm of Arthur and Robert. Besides producing papers in the ordinary style of the time, they also undertook work of a most ambitious type, including the imitation of pictures in grisaille. These were produced from copper plates, and were intended to fill large panels, a lunette filled with a lunette, filled with a smaller picture, being placed above. Examples in this style are 'The Sacrifice of Iphigenia', after Charles Delafosse (1636–1716); 'Apollo pursuing Daphne,'[143] after Louis Michel Vanloo (1707–71); 'Pygmalion and his Statue', 'An Offering to Pan', 'Orpheus and the Beasts' and other papers representing such subjects. It is interesting to compare these carefully finished works with the clever, but never satisfactory, wood-block prints of Jackson. The Revolution, which had deprived Réveillon of his fortune, cost Arthur his head, so that Robert had to continue the business alone.

The Revolution, curiously enough, did not cause any diminution in the demand for expensive wallpapers, and for the first few years Jacquemart and Bénard were engaged in producing papers often indistinguishable from the costly productions of Réveillon.[144] There was still a demand for Pompeian designs, but, at the same time, papers of a more topical interest were being manufactured.

The 'Altar of Liberty,' as designed by Huet[145] for Jacquemart and Bénard, is still thoroughly Pompeian, but designs more extravagantly Republican were now required by popular taste. Panels surrounded by tricolour ribbons and framing a trophy of fasces, caps and Liberty and scales of Justice could not be made to look as decorative as the work of Réveillon, however orthodox the sentiments might be inspiring them, while negroes fêting Liberty is a subject still more difficult to treat artistically.[146] Citizens Demosthène Dugour and Anisson-Duperson opened a factory in the Place du Carrousel especially for Republican wallpapers, but some error of taste, perhaps, brought the junior partner to the guillotine, and Citizen Dugour thought it safer to seek employment elsewhere.

Although, for the time being, public taste might have gone astray, there was no need for despondency for the future of the wallpaper industry at the end of the eighteenth century. Old firms might be disappearing, but new ones filled their places. There was no depression in the industry, and the skill of Réveillon's employees was such that they need have no fear of unemployment.

The imitations of classical decorations were now changing in character. The heavier and more finished style, which is typified in sculpture by Canova, was in the ascendant, but it was left for the nineteenth century to render classical forms so oppressive that any alternative might seem attractive. By the closing years of the eighteenth century we can see the Pompeian decoration of Réveillon, which had survived his overthrow, being supplanted by the later style,[147] even in work produced by firms like Jacquemart and Bénard, which could claim direct descent from the great paper-hanger. Although by the year 1799 the change had already taken place, it will be more convenient to deal with the work of these last years of the century in conjunction with the papers of the early years of the nineteenth century.

The Nineteenth Century to the Period of the Second Empire

Although the Revolution did not cause any break in the production of wallpapers in France, or any sudden change, the last few years of the eighteenth century foreshadowed many of the developments of the succeeding one. Most of the firms which were destined to come to the forefront during the Empire were being set up at this time.

Mention has already been made of Jacquemart and Bénard, Réveillon's successors, who had started in 1791. Though Jacquemart died in 1804, the firm continued under his son with great success till 1840. In 1836 it opened a shop in the Rue de la Paix, and that it was highly esteemed is shown by the award to it of five medals during this period.[148]

Hardly less important than this Paris firm was that connected with the name of Jean Zuber in Alsace. Zuber started as a salesman for the firm of Nicolas Dolfus, of Mulhouse, which was engaged in textile and wallpaper printing. In 1793 they took into their employment Jean Laurent Malaine, a designer from the tapestry works of Les Gobelins, who co-operated with Zuber when he was put in charge of the wallpaper business of Hartman Rissler, which succeeded Dolfus in 1797. New premises for the business were found in the former Hospice of the Teutonic Order near Rixheim. In 1802 Zuber obtained complete control of the business, which continued to prosper throughout this century.

The third great manufacturer of this period who must be mentioned is Joseph Dufour, who, after having worked at Mâcon for some time, moved to 10, Rue Beauveau, Paris. In 1820 the firm became Dufour and Leroy, which it remained till 1860.

It is now necessary to turn to the alterations of fashion during this period. The influence of Réveillon did not disappear suddenly, and changes in the designing of wallpapers occurred almost insensibly. One of the new motifs which were discovered was that of representing silk and other draperies in loose folds, instead of stretched tight, as previously. This was doubtless intended to give a richer effect, by the representation of a greater amount of material, but there was no gain artistically. It remained a very popular device till nearly the middle of the nineteenth century. In some cases the whole paper was designed to represent these folds; in others, the frieze only was so treated. Good examples of this fashion are nos 552, 554 and 563 which came from Vaison, near Avignon. Even when the style is used in moderation, as in the first of these papers, the weakness of the design is apparent, though this is not nearly so blatant here as in no 552, where the design is composed of a series of knotted draperies in folds held together by cords and tassels all the way down the paper; the result rivals in heaviness the paper decorated with the insignia of the Order of the Holy Ghost, produced in 1825 by Jacquemart, now in the Musée des Arts Décoratifs.[149]

The production of wallpapers representing stretched textiles went on concurrently with this somewhat tasteless fashion. A revival of the use of flock also took place, but, as in England, the proper use of the material was not adhered to, and we find flock used to pick out details of designs, where colour-printing from a wood block would have been sufficient. In the best designs, as in nos 574 and 575, the use of flock is not at first apparent, and it is only on closer inspection that the incongruity of its use becomes visible. In other papers, including some in the Musée des Arts Décoratifs, the flocking is much more obvious and the results are proportionately less successful. Of the many wallpapers inspired by flowered textiles which were produced throughout this period, nos 555 and 565 may be taken as typical. Another, no 548, shows cherubs among garlanded flowers, and is slightly reminiscent of Réveillon, although of considerably later date.

The firm of Jacquemart and Bénard may be said to have led in the production of wallpapers with designs imitating textiles in the early part of the century, and, it must be admitted, were responsible for some of the more dubious experiments which have been mentioned, as well as for much of the better work. Although they habitually used flock in the manner described above, their designs were too good to make flock appear as unsightly as it did in the work of some of their contemporaries.

The decline in the quality of designs imitating textiles, which was so marked in England towards the middle of the century, was also notable, only to a much lesser degree, in France. A greater continuity of sound workmanship is apparent, and although Zuber introduced mechanical printing into France in 1850, no general deterioration resulted immediately from this. Good specimens of designs imitating textiles which date from this time may be seen among the papers designed by Victor Poterlet for the firm of Balin, now in the Musée des Arts Décoratifs. Starting *circa* 1840, this artist worked through the middle of the century, and if he gave way to the weaknesses of the times in some of his early papers, he was also able to produce others which were eminently successful. Some of his flock designs on embossed paper deserve special mention. Good specimens of the work of the firm of Balin will be found among the thirty-five examples (no 755) presented to the Museum by this manufacturer.

The use of friezes imitating stucco work and sculpture was very popular at this time in France. Nos 564 and 570 are excellent examples of this style, which was to reach its fullest development in Dufour's paper 'Cupid and Psyche' (no 1040).

The most typical and interesting development of this period was, however, the scenic paper. The earliest scenic wallpapers, derived from the art of decorating walls in tempera, were produced by hand-painting in the late eighteenth century. Some of the inspiration for this form of decoration may have been derived from Chinese scenic papers, and also from the large imitation oil paintings in stucco frames produced by Arthur and Robert, which are not unlike the English examples at Harrington House (see p. 26). The earliest of these hand-painted European scenic papers which have so far been identified seem to date from the last decade of the eighteenth century. A fine example of this date, formerly at Givry, near Verdun, depicts a harbour scene, and shows tricolour flags on some of the buildings and caps of Liberty on the heads of some of the inhabitants.

The essence of these papers was that they should show no repeat, but form a continuous picture all round the room, like the Chinese papers. They could be seen to advantage only where there was no type of mural decoration other than a dado, and where as few pieces of furniture as possible were placed against the walls. Some time seems to have elapsed before any of the wallpaper printers attempted to imitate this type of decoration, as the initial outlay on wood blocks to print such large designs was so high. The earliest printed scenic papers did not achieve the completely continuous design, but repeated at intervals round the room. An example of this compromise may be seen in a paper at the Metropolitan Museum, New York, and two other examples also exist in the United States.[150]

The first of the great series of scenic wallpapers without a repeat seems to have been Zuber's 'Vues de Suisse,' which appeared in 1804 and was designed by a certain Mongin. After this pioneer example, which suffers from a certain crudeness in colouring, Zuber did not make another attempt till 1825. Almost at the same time, Dufour produced at Mâcon his 'Les Sauvages de la Mer du Sud' ('Les Sauvages de la Mer Pacifique'), to popularize which he published a descriptive pamphlet. This paper was composed of twenty rolls of paper, and represented Captain Cook's principal adventures and his death in the South Pacific. A number of other papers succeeded this after Dufour's move to Paris in 1807. Among these were the 'Les Français en Egypte' (1814), 'Les Campagnes Français en Italie' and 'Galerie Mythologique' (1814), a selection of classical deities in chiaroscuro. As soon as Napoleon was overthrown, a great number of these papers were exported. A considerable number found their way to the United States, and some examples still exist in Britain.

One paper of this type, 'Monuments de Paris,' published by Dufour in 1814 at the price of fifty francs, is in the Museum (no 776). The south bank of the Seine is represented as grassy meadows, while all the more remarkable buildings of Paris are arranged arbitrarily along the other bank in such a way as to show them to greatest advantage. This paper has a certain historical interest. The obnoxious statue of the Emperor has been removed from the chariot on the top of the Arc de Carrousel, but the horses of St Mark's have not yet been sent back to Venice. This shows the paper to have been designed between the fall of Napoleon in March 1814 and the removal of the horses in 1815. It will be noticed also that the grenadiers on guard beside the arch are wearing the white cockade of the Bourbons, instead of the Imperial red and green. The succeeding years saw the production of a number of other topographical papers. 'Vues d'Italie' shows a view of the Bay of Naples and other Italian scenes (no 577), while another exists which shows a fanciful panorama of Venice. 'Les Rives du Bosphore' is a similarly imaginative design. In 'Vues de Londres', which appeared *circa* 1840, great care was taken in depicting the principal buildings, although they are arranged fancifully, as in the case of Paris, noted above. The view of London is taken from somewhere in Southwark. The Shot Tower and Southwark Bridge and Cathedral are prominently in the foreground, and London, Waterloo and old Westminster Bridges can all be seen, indicating that the paper dates from after the opening of the new London Bridge in 1831 and before the building of the new Westminster Bridge, which was completed in 1846.

Literature, as well as topography, was illustrated by Dufour's scenic papers, for besides the classical mythological series he produced a complete 'Lady of the Lake' and a 'Cid' wallpaper. The former is a very spirited production, and is especially good in the lake scenery. The latter has an additional interest, as the background used in the representations of the deeds of the Spanish hero had previously been used for a French paper called 'Le Petit Décor,' with contemporary costume. The latter paper, which showed costumes of the early years of the century, had been reworked *circa* 1830 and the figures re-dressed in the later fashion; and finally, the background was used for the entirely new theme of the Cid shortly afterwards. This practice seems to have been quite exceptional, for no other papers produced thus economically are known.

Enough has been said to show the extent of Dufour's activities, and it is necessary to turn now to some of his rivals. The firm of Jacquemart and Bénard, which had started so much under the influence of Réveillon, never really threw off its preference for designs imitating painted panels and textiles. Only one scenic paper has, as yet, been attributed to it: 'La Chasse de Compiègne' ('La Chasse aux Courses'), 1814. As the name implies, it represents a hunting scene and probably dates from the later years of the First Empire. The hunt is seen starting from in front of a large house (which may be the Château de Compiègne), where the ladies in their carriages have come to see the meet. All the details of the hunt are shown in the succeeding panels, down to the death of the stag. There is a copy in the Museum (no 567). At least two other examples of this paper exist in England: one is at Eslington Park, Northumberland; the other belonged to Lady Horner.

The first of the scenic papers to be issued by Zuber, after a twenty years' interval, was called 'Paysage des Lointains,' and after this he continued to issue others down to the end of the period with which we are concerned. One of the more interesting is the chiaroscuro 'Courses des Chevaux,' which appeared in 1838 and of which examples can be seen in the Museum (no 585) and in the Musée des Arts Décoratifs. This shows hurdle-racing in France, flat-racing in England and the Palio in Italy. This last is clearly represented not at Siena, but in Rome, where the horses are seen starting from the Piazza del Popolo in one view, and ending in the Piazza Venezia in another. High stands are shown, holding an excited crowd eager to witness this scene. In the same year Zuber produced a paper showing events from the War of Independence, especially intended for the American market. Several events—like the surrender of Yorktown—are recognizable, and considerable care has clearly been expended on making the paper more or less historically correct. Shortly before, Zuber had produced another paper for sale abroad, depicting the Niagara Falls, Boston and other views of America.

Though scenic wallpapers were being produced well into the second half of the nineteenth century in France, the later ones have much less to recommend them artistically, though they show no decline in technical achievement. Desfossé's paper (in the Musée des Arts Décoratifs) of classical ruins covered by trailing creepers and flowers, published in 1855, is uninspired, and the same may be said of Delicourt's paper, 'La Jeunesse,' of the same year, designed by Charles Muller.

Besides the full-size scenic wallpapers, mention must be made of another type which belongs to this species of decoration. These are the scenic friezes, of which quite a quantity were produced in the first half of the century. A typical example (no 576) shows an Italian cloister filled with figures in seventeenth-century costume, perhaps forming part of some continuous story.

The idea of depicting religious scenes on wallpapers, which had died in the early eighteenth century with the old school of *dominotiers*, had also a revival in the nineteenth. Dufour, indeed, produced in 1825 a grisaille picture of Saint Teresa, and a number of similar papers with religious subjects, such as the 'Acts of St Vincent de Paul' and the episode of 'Christ and the Woman of Samaria', were also designed.

Space does not permit of a more general examination of the many other types of wallpaper produced in France in the nineteenth century. While in England a reformation in the designing of wallpaper was required in the middle of the last century, in France no such revolution took place, so that our conclusion, at this point, must not be regarded as denoting the end of a great epoch. French mural decoration has changed since this period, but, although it may be claimed that the work of Morris was in part reflected in them, French wallpapers have maintained their national characteristics. Just as in the eighteenth century the French wallpaper industry seemed likely to be crushed by superior English work, but replied with the magnificent productions of Réveillon, so in the last century the English paper hangings produced by Morris replied to the deluge of French imports, not by imitation, but by the expression of the individuality of their designer.

Chinese Export Wallpapers

By the beginning of the seventeenth century, Europe was beginning to trade with China on a considerable scale. None of the earliest accounts of the goods imported mentions wallpaper, and it would seem that it cannot have been brought to Europe in any large quantity until the middle of the century. Evelyn in his *Diary*, on 13 July 1693, mentions 'China and Indian cabinets, screen and hangings' in the possession of Queen Mary, and although these last are not specified as being of paper, they may well have been.

The inspiration of Chinese wallpapers was the painted silk hangings in use among the rich in China, but it is questionable whether papers of this sort were used there to any great extent before their manufacture was popularized by the demands of the European market. The earliest use of wallpaper by the Chinese had been for tomb decorations, and although it had spread to the houses of the living, such examples do not usually appear to have been of the highly artistic quality with which we are familiar.

Father Louis Le Compte, one of the early Jesuit missionaries to China, gives some account of the interior decorations of the Chinese houses of his day.[151] He describes the painted silk hangings which appear to have been in general use, but adds, 'Others only whiten the Chamber, or glew Paper upon it.' This would seem to show that when wallpaper was used, it was not necessarily the highly elaborated species that held sway in Europe for 150 years. Whether the Chinese painted paper screens preceded, or were copied from, the wall-paintings is another question difficult to answer, for in European records they both appear about the same time.

Sir William Chambers, in his *Designs of Chinese Buildings* (1757), describes rooms in which the lower part of the walls are covered with a matted dado, above which are white, crimson or gilt papers, apparently quite plain. This same austere type of decoration is also mentioned in an account of Lord Macartney's embassy to China in 1793;[152] the members of the Embassy were lodged in Pekin in the palace of the Governor of Canton, where they found that 'the apartments were very spacious, and hung with the most elegant paper enriched with gilding.' It is probable, indeed, that the papers which we now admire were made originally by the Chinese for the European market, and are, in reality, cheap copies of the painted silk hangings which European visitors to the Far East describe as decorating the houses of the rich merchants and officials whom they visited.

It is probable that the Dutch, who were the leading power in the Chinese trade in the seventeenth century, were also the first to import Chinese wallpapers, and that the English and French followed them. As these Chinese papers were imported in the ships of the British and French East India Companies both into France and into England, they were referred to as 'Indian' in contemporary documents. Although they are also sometimes described as 'Japan papers,' there does not seem to be any doubt that this name was entirely erroneous.

Although the art of printing had been known in China for centuries, practically no attempt was made in that country to use it for wallpapers. In the very few examples where printing has been used, as in no 655, the colours have all been added by hand. In the hand-painted papers the colours are of various kinds of gouache and tempera.

If the use of hand-painting avoided the monotony of the repeated wood block, the range of subjects recognised by the Chinese was so small that there must remain in Europe several hundreds of these papers differing from each other only in slight variations of colour and arrangement. In many cases, the dating of these papers can accordingly be estimated only from slight alterations in the technique.

Chinese wallpapers are easily divided, according to their designs, into three classes. The first class, in which are found designs consisting of bird- and plant-forms, comprises the majority, as well as the most artistic, of the surviving examples. Though no two are identical, the general design for these papers offers few varieties. The usual design is shown in a magnificent paper in the Museum (no 657). The lower part shows ground covered with coarse grass, amid which are the roots of flowering shrubs, roses, peonies, and bamboos, the intermingling stems of which form the central part of the design. The boughs reach almost to the top of the paper, but in many cases this is wanting, owing to the necessity of fitting the hangings to the height of the walls. Among the roots of the shrubs and in the branches are seen numerous birds, while other birds and butterflies are depicted in flight at the top of the paper. The backgrounds of these papers are always of a single colour—in the present example, a rich blue.

Having noted the convention of the silhouetted trees and shrubs with their accompanying birds, one must remark on the strict adherence to nature in the drawing and colouring. The fidelity with which both birds and plants were depicted is worthy of the illustrations to scientific works. Despite the complicated nature of the designs, extending over many rolls of paper, it is rare to find that the artist has attributed two types of flower and fruit to the same plant, and such errors are almost invariably confined to papers of late date. The birds and butterflies are equally representative of well known species.[153]

The earliest papers of this class are usually the simplest in design. In answer to a European demand for variety, caged birds are sometimes depicted hanging from the upper boughs in some papers, as in no 660. In others the bottom is filled with reedy pools with water-fowl and trellis-work enclosures, while porcelain vases filled with small shrubs stand among the roots of the larger bushes, as in nos 671 and 673.

Of the examples in the Museum, the paper from Eltham Lodge (no 654) shows signs of an early date (the second quarter of the eighteenth century). The design is free from the rather tiresome minor adjuncts which have just been mentioned, and is of an exceptionally graceful form. Unfortunately, the paper has suffered in the course of time from the extremely pasty character of the colours employed, which were very liable to crack and flake. As the trade in these papers increased, this fault was remedied by the use of thinner colours which would not suffer when the rolls were packed for transit. The surfaces of most eighteenth-century papers were painted comparatively lightly and have lasted well. In one example (no 674), of nineteenth-century date, the background has only been slightly silvered, so that the danger of damage in transit was almost negligible. This last example shows, however, some of the most noticeable defects of the later papers—a tendency to adhere less closely to nature, and to produce harsh colour schemes.

Papers of the 'bird and flower' type which differ from those described above are rare, but an interesting example at Oakley House, near Bedford, may be mentioned. It is clearly an imitation of the European 'all-over' floral design, which could be fitted into rooms of small proportions more easily than the ordinary spreading Chinese designs. The background is green, and the design consists entirely of the twining stems of flowering plants with small flying birds. The soil is not seen at the base, nor do the plants thin out at the top. A feature which should be noted in this paper, as well as in several examples in the Museum, is the addition, after hanging, of extra boughs and birds. These were evidently sent from China so that they could be cut out and pasted on, to cover joints in the paper, dirty patches, or even weak portions of the design.[154]

The second class of Chinese paper consists of those in which human figures are the dominant features. The most common subject depicted the varied activities of a Chinese city. The Museum possesses a rare printed example (no 655), with colours added by hand, but examples hand-painted throughout may be found at Messrs. Coutts' Bank in the Strand, London,[155] Ramsbury Manor, Wiltshire,[156] and elsewhere. The city is depicted in a conventionalized form, and consists of a number of islands on which stand the dwellings of the citizens, who are seen following their various callings. The islands are linked by architectural bridges, while boats are seen in the intervening waters, and in the distance, at the top of the paper, appears a range of mountains. The historical interest of these papers is considerable, as they give us a good impression of the appearance of a large Chinese city on which Western influences have not yet had any perceptible effect. Silk-weaving and china-making can be seen in the workshops, while all the processes of the growing and preparation of tea are shown, beginning with the fields at the top of the paper and ending with the shops at the bottom.[157]

In some papers the life of the Chinese city is depicted with figures on a much larger scale. A fragment in the Museum (no 666) is of a more unusual sort. It depicts an open-air theatre. A wild dance is in progress on the stage, while at one side is a box for the ladies, and in front a very large audience of men and children. In the foreground are two gamblers, and a man with a refreshment stall selling food to a father with two children. Unfortunately, there is no record of what scenes were shown on the rest of the paper.

As an alternative to representations of Chinese city life, a number of papers representing hunting scenes were produced. A magnificent example exists at Lockleys, Hertfordshire,[158] showing huntsmen on horseback and foot surrounding the retreat of some unsuspecting deer. Portions of a similar paper (no 667) combine a hunting scene on a rocky island with representations of a religious festival. A number of mythological figures in an open boat are seen approaching the hunters, who seem to be chiefly engaged in catching monkeys.

The third class of Chinese papers consists of a combination of the 'bird and flower' type with the hunting and industrial scenes which appear in the second class. The top three-quarters of the paper consists of birds and flowering shrubs, around the roots of which, in the lowest quarter, are seen the minute figures of the hunters, as in no 672, or figures drinking tea, as in no 668. None of the papers of this class seem to be older than the last quarter of the eighteenth century.

The great period for Chinese papers was between 1740 and 1790, when all over England they are found replacing the decorations of earlier ages. In the inventory of Charlton House, Kent,[159] when occupied by Lord Ancram fron 1763 to 1769, the Jacobean panelling is recorded as giving way to the new wallpapers, while in the last quarter of the century the great architects of the day, like Sir William Chambers and Robert Adam, seem to have followed the prevailing fashion in the renovation of old houses.[160]

The documents dealing with the importation of Chinese papers are, unfortunately, much rarer than might be expected, considering the extent of the trade. The papers seem mostly to have been exported from Canton, but the British East India Company dealt only in the major products of China; the minor products, such as wallpapers, were carried as the captain's 'private trade'. The records of 'private trade' have, unfortunately, only survived between the years 1825 and 1833, when Chinese papers were going out of fashion, so that in these years they must have been included under the heading of 'sundries'. In earlier days, the trade had special privileges. In 1773, when a duty was first laid on imported wallpapers, those imported through the East India Company were specially exempted. It was not until 1794, when England was faced with the cost of the Revolutionary War, that the duty was extended to Chinese wallpapers.[161]

There can be no doubt that, at the end of the eighteenth century, the fashion for Chinese wallpapers was dying out rapidly. Besides the change of fashion, there were several other contributory causes. At the beginning of the century, there was no article on the market, with the possible exception of the very best flock papers, which could compare in technical quality with the Chinese papers. This was no longer the case at the close of the century, when the art of colour-printing with wood blocks had been brought to such perfection by such artists as Réveillon. Against this, one must balance a perceptible decline in the workmanship of the later Chinese papers. Though Chinese papers continued to be imported into Britain well into the second decade of the nineteenth century, they were no longer in much demand. The paper hung by Sir Walter Scott at Abbotsford must be considered as one of the latest of the long series of these hangings.[162] Fashion demanded less exotic, if not less fantastic, designs, and the Chinese papers, at no time cheap, and now heavily taxed, disappeared from the market. It was not until the present century that public opinion once more began to recognize their attraction, and created a fresh demand for copies.[163]

115

INTRODUCTION

Part Two by Jean Hamilton

British Wallpapers from the later Nineteenth Century to the Present Day

Most large collections include work by the outstanding designers of the periods during which they have been assembled, and the Victoria and Albert Museum collection of wallpapers is no exception in this respect. More unusual is its considerable content of workmanlike but 'run-of-the-mill' specimens, which serve to build up a picture of the place which wallpaper has taken in the decoration of thousands of ordinary homes in the past. During the second half of the nineteenth century it would have been difficult to find a house with unpapered walls, for mass production, begun in the 1840s, had resulted in the marketing of goods so inexpensive that practically everyone could afford them. An entry in *Novelties, Inventions and Curiosities in Arts & Manufacture*, published by George Routledge and Company in 1853, which describes the new cylinder-printing methods, records that it was then possible to make wallpapers at a cost of a farthing per yard.

Examples of 'run-of-the-mill' wallpapers are shown in John Line and Sons' first pattern book for the year 1880 (no 701), which contains over two hundred specimens of cheap, machine-printed patterns, but even these show that the principles of design set forth by Owen Jones and William Morris had by then become widely influential. A new generation, educated in design and reacting against the 'indiscriminate' taste of the mid-nineteenth-century majority, provided a market for the products not only of Morris and Company, but of the big, more overtly commercial firms of Jeffrey and Company, Essex and Company and Shand Kydd Limited. Metford Warner, director of Jeffrey and Company, had taken over the production of Morris's designs, and had also adopted a general policy of commissioning artists and architects, among them Walter Crane, William Burges, E. W. Godwin and C. L. Eastlake, to design wallpapers for his firm. In 1873 Warner won admission for wallpaper designs to the London Annual Exhibition of All Fine Arts, held at the Albert Hall, and the work of Bruce J. Talbert, E. W. Godwin, Owen Jones and others was shown there for the first time. These artists all created a new form of wallpaper design, produced by Jeffrey and Company in the 1870s, in which the frieze, filling and dado were combined in one overall design (no 700), with angled versions for staircase walls. At this time too Talbert and Godwin in particular developed the influential new 'Japanese style'. The products of Essex and Company, founded in 1887, were distinguished by the art nouveau patterns of C. F. A. Voysey and Lindsay P. Butterfield (qq.v.). Shand Kydd Limited, founded by William Shand Kydd in 1885, introduced into the industry the block-printed outline enclosing a stencilled pattern, and with it a range of large, beautiful friezes, of which the 'Ravenna' (no 1033), designed by their founder, is perhaps the most memorable.

The Silver Studio, brought into being by Arthur Silver (no 1143) in 1880 and continued by his son Rex (nos 1145–1147), supplied Lightbown, Aspinall and Company with a fine series of conventionalized flower and plant designs. The series entitled 'The Silvern Stencils' were produced in Alexander Rottmann's factory in Yokohama, Japan. Rottmann was himself an advocate and supporter of the English art nouveau movement, and many of his best wallpapers in this genre were designed by Harry Napper (no 1080 etc).

A society known as the Century Guild, founded in 1882 by A. H. Mackmurdo and Selwyn Image, numbered among its members Herbert Horne, who designed many patterns, including the distinctive frieze and filling entitled 'The Bay Leaf' (no 1011), produced in 1885 by Jeffrey and Company.

One of the more important aspects of the history of nineteenth-century wallpaper printing was the development of washable papers, which became known as 'sanatories'. Varnished grounds intended to strengthen wallpaper had been described in Robert Dossie's *Handmaid to the Arts* (1758), and these may have had the effect of making wallpaper cleanable to some degree; also, a process of varnishing after printing, invented by Crease, of Bath, in 1802, was apparently effective in rendering such papers washable with soap and water. Another method, tried by W. B. Simpson, which consisted of hardening the distemper colours after the printing, was advertised by this firm in the Great Exhibition as 'washable', but no method had been widely adopted, either because of the expense involved in the production, or because of the inadequacy of the process itself, until in 1853 John Stather, of Hull, printed paper from a metal roller engraved with an oak-grain pattern, in oil-based colours, and produced the first washable paper on a commercial basis. In 1884 Lightbown, Aspinall and Company succeeded in manufacturing multi-coloured 'sanatories', while in the 1890s David Walker of Middleton was specializing in shaded floral patterns in this medium (no 403) and Wyllie and Lochhead's washable papers were distinguished by the excellent designs of Arthur Gwatkin (no 980) for staircases and halls. The 'sanatories', as a type, enjoyed a popularity which lasted well into the twentieth century.

A survey of the important collection of Order Books of the interior decorators Cowtan and Sons (no 692) demonstrates the very wide range of quality and design in wallpaper during the latter part of the nineteenth century, and reflects the increased demand, not only for the best contemporary papers, but for the traditional block and flock patterns of the late eighteenth and early nineteenth centuries, which many owners of older houses continued to prefer when repapering. For example, orders for a diaper *chinoiserie* design, known as 'Chinese Trellis' (no 265), appear in these volumes over the period from 1833 until 1861. The Cowtan Gift also includes a pattern book of papers supplied for the decoration of the Houses of Parliament between 1851 and 1859 (no 696).

By 1896 Metford Warner felt able to say, in an essay, 'The History of Paper-hangings', which he read before the Artworkers' Guild, that there had been a marked improvement in the design and production of machine-printed papers, while the artistic quality of those printed by hand or blocks had been fully maintained.

In March 1905 the monthly journal *The World* expressed the view that 'It is difficult in these days, when ideas are so quickly copied and appropriated, to find anything original in the way of decoration. . . .' The writer goes on to praise Jeffrey and Company for maintaining their high standards into the early twentieth century with the designs of Lewis F. Day, Heywood Sumner, W. J. Neatby and Sidney Haward. Also, the firm's annual pattern books received enthusiastic reviews in the artisan journals, not merely on grounds of design, but for the variety of materials, including embossed copper and reinforced 'canvas' paper, which they offered among their wall coverings. Wallpapers made to simulate other materials (such as marble, granite, wood and plasterwork) had been manufactured from the eighteenth century onwards, but the last quarter of the nineteenth century and the beginning of the twentieth saw a great increase in the number of firms producing raised or embossed patterns, and the specialist firms which marketed them, such as Lincrusta Walton, Anaglypta and Scott Morton Tynecastle, became household words. A handsome example of Tynecastle 'canvas' is the gilded embossed paper designed by William Scott Morton (no 1077), and among others in the collection are the 'Spanish Leatherwork' pattern from Arnsbrae, Alloa (no 392), and a design of 'Grasses and Fans' (no 686) from 180, Queens Gate, London (a Norman Shaw house, now demolished). Many papers of this sort were made in Japan from British designs, as in the case of Alexander Rottmann's Yokohama Factory. Shand Kydd Limited, in particular, specialized in delicately shaded stencilled hangings, printed on a textile known as 'Japanese grass paper' (nos 487–489).

Over forty major firms were producing wallpapers in Britain by the end of the nineteenth century, when the Wallpaper Manufacturers Limited was formed as a joint stock company to give financial support to smaller firms still using hand printing methods, enabling them to survive against foreign competition in the home market, which had increased as a result of the removal of customs duty on imported papers in 1861. Nevertheless, prior to the First World War it was estimated that between seventy and eighty million pieces (rolls) of wallpaper were sold on the home market and millions more were exported.[164]

At the outbreak of the war the manufacturers, in agreement with the Wallpaper Merchants Association, decided not to issue pattern books of machine-printed paper for 1915, but to draw on existing stocks. It was discovered that the presses used for embossed papers could be applied to shell-body forging and the varnishing processes could also be applied to shell cases.[165] In the third year of the war a limited amount of new wallpaper was produced in the prevalent style, with black backgrounds; the cessation of imports of aniline dyes from Germany had reduced the range of colours available. Supplies of paper became increasingly curtailed (though substitutes, mainly in the form of old newspapers, were used), and eventually flour pastes, and other pastes containing edible substances, were prohibited. The export of wallpaper had virtually ceased and supplies to merchants at home were rationed, though borders could still be sold outside the rationing quotas, a fact which may have been influential in the revival of a mid-Victorian fashion for plain panels with decorative surrounds, which emerged with its own period flavour in the 1920s and 1930s.

The vast variety of patterns formerly available was largely replaced either by the 'Jazz Age' designs, or by bland plain or textured fillings with appliqué borders, though for a brief period in the mid-twenties the 'leaf' pattern filling was popular; a prominent designer in this style was A. J. Baker, of C. and J. G. Potter (no 754). Other papers were either traditional, with emphasis on the Tudor revival (such as Henry Butler's hunting scene, based on a textile: no 785), or in the art deco style, a typically geometric example of which is a sample of the wallpaper used in the Council Chamber at Chester Town Hall in 1935 (no 519).

The influence of the art schools of the 1930s is seen in Edward Bawden's designs (no 756), which were printed directly from his lino cuts by Cole and Son and lithographically reproduced by the Curwen Press Limited. The perennial vogue for *chinoiserie* and designs in the Japanese style, which reappeared in the twenties in the guise of the 'Japanese lantern' patterns (no 510), was also evident in some designs of the 1930s, and the demand for wallpaper remained constant during the inter-war period, until 1939, when production was again interrupted by the outbreak of the Second World War.

In 1945 the Central Institute of Arts and Design organized on behalf of the British Wallpaper industry the first post-war industrial exhibition in London, and this, together with the renewed availability of raw materials, gave fresh impetus to the wallpaper trade. With government encouragement to promote exports, the Wallpaper Manufacturers launched their 'Lancastria' collection, principally aimed at the American market and containing papers which were semi-washable; this led to the production of washable wallpapers as a standard market requirement in the following years.

In 1950 the Council of Industrial Design issued a series of folios, one of which contained a selection of approved contemporary designs in wallpaper for small rooms (no 709); among the manufacturers represented in the folio were Cole and Son, A. Sanderson and Sons, John Line and Shand Kydd. The molecular structure of natural objects seen under micro-photography had considerable influence on the design style of the 1950s, after a set of patterns based on the crystalline structure of insulin, afwillite, myglobin and other substances was shown at the Festival of Britain in 1951 (no 707). In the same year John Line brought out the first British screen-printed wallpaper in a pattern book entitled *'1951' Wallpapers Limited Editions* (no 710), which included designs by John Minton, Sylvia Priestley and Lucienne Day. In the early 1950s A. Sanderson and Sons had begun to reprint papers from the William Morris wood blocks, which they had acquired *circa* 1941 at the dissolution of the Morris Company. Among their reprints are designs by J. H. Dearle, Kate Faulkner and May Morris (William Morris's daughter). In 1956 the Sanderson branch of the Wallpaper Manufacturers brought out the first of their 'Palladio' series, presenting the public with a new set of fresh and lively designs by young artists. A typical example of the new designs in *Palladio 8* (Wallpaper Manufacturers' first book of screen printed vinyl papers) is Margaret Cannon's 'Crescendo' (no 719).

Advances in photographic printing led to the production of photomurals, and photogravure wallpaper with the naturalistic 'brick wall' type of pattern pre-

dominated in the decor of coffee houses, bars and restaurants in the 1960s. Shand Kydd, which merged with John Line in 1958, began to produce their own original style in design with the first of the *Focus* pattern books in 1964–65 (no 715). The emphasis throughout this volume was on making the papers resemble fabric, linen, silk, hessian or textured cotton. A review in the *Decorator* of November 1963 commented on *Focus* that 'for the first time a costly photogravure machine, similar to that used in magazine work, has been used to create facsimiles of artists' works. Designs now look like screen-printed papers but cost less than half the price.' The design by Donald Melbourne entitled 'Festival' (no 715) is probably the first example in this country of printing by the Heidemann ink-embossing process.

A genre which came into being at about the middle of the nineteenth century was the nursery wallpaper, but the first artist of note who designed papers for the nursery was Walter Crane, whose 'Nursery Rhymes' (no 810) was produced by Jeffrey and Company in 1876. By the beginning of the twentieth century the works of many illustrators, among them Kate Greenaway, Randolph Caldecott, Mabel L. Attwell, Cecil Aldin, John Hassall and Beatrix Potter, had been translated into wallpaper, which was popular and widely used. A pair of borders with the Mickey Mouse theme was produced by Sandersons *circa* 1930 (no 515), and Jacqueline Groag's 'Kiddies Town' (no 977) and Christina Risley's 'Joanna' (no 1132) are typical of the 1950s. Crown Wallpaper encompassed the current juvenile demands for aeroplanes, vintage cars and the 'spacemen' and 'Flintstones' mythologies. Shand Kydd's *Focus* series, mentioned above, devoted sections of their volumes to designs for the nursery or playroom; two of the most attractive papers are Donald Melbourne's 'Dolls' (no 715) and a paper, produced in the late 1970s, based on Peggy Fortnum's illustrations to Michael Bond's *Paddington Bear* stories (no 536). A recent form of decoration for the playroom is the 'Photodoor', depicting such cartoon characters as 'Snoopy' or 'The Muppets', for pasting to the modern flush door.

The 1970s saw a revival of the small 'textile' patterns of the early nineteenth century, and a trend for matching paper and fabrics, begun in the mid-1960s, was catered for by firms like Osborne and Little (no 529), Designers Guild Ltd (no 726) and Laura Ashley, a textile designer who extended her business to include paints and wallpapers in 1975.

The period after the Second World War has seen the virtual disappearance of hand block-printing from the commercial scene; it has been replaced by rotary screen-printing, rotagravure, flexographic and ink-embossing techniques, but an aspect of wallpaper manufacture which has been stimulated in recent years by the increasing interest in the restoration of historic interiors has resulted in hand block-reprinting and the reproduction by silkscreen printing of wallpapers which date from the seventeenth to the early twentieth centuries. In this the needs of organizations like the National Trust have been influential, and have been fulfilled by such firms as Cole and Son, Sanderson and Watts and Company.

French Wallpapers from the Mid-Nineteenth Century until the Present Day[166]

Two of the most important manufacturers of wallpaper in France during the nineteenth century were Jean Zuber and Isidore Leroy. By the 1820s Zuber had adapted the engraved cylinders of Thomas Bell's calico-printing machinery to wallpaper production, and was using new dyes and colours, including chrome yellow and Schweinfurt green. The Zuber firm had put into production the *iris* ground, invented by the German Michael Sporlin (see p. 70) *circa* 1821, and was also manufacturing satin and jaspé grounds. During the years 1830–40 Zuber employed the lithographer Engelmann and was developing a new printing process by 'lithographic cylinder'.

The firm of Isidore Leroy, founded *circa* 1842, began by printing from relief cylinders, and in 1858 patented a process embodying felting between the raised metal outlines of the designs to hold the colour. French manufacturers of the first half of the nineteenth century inherited and benefited from the variety of hand-printed designs of high quality produced by the great eighteenth-century firm of Réveillon, but although they added more technical skills and inventions, they were unable to improve on Réveillon's standards of design.

By *circa* 1860 there were three hundred wallpaper factories in Paris alone. A reporter at the International Exhibition in Paris, 1861, noted that machine products were outnumbering and gradually replacing hand-printed papers and expressed the view that they should receive assessment as a separate class of product. A *tour-de-force* of machine-printing on a large scale, typical of this period, was acquired by the Museum in 1947, in the form of a panel entitled 'Le Souper à la Maison D'Or' (no 954), produced by Desfossé et Karth, 1862. Another huge panel imitating a tapestry, composed of five non-repeating lengths, over one-and-a-half metres in height, was shown in the 1878 Exhibition, and these show-pieces continued to be fashionable for the next decade at least.

In France, as in England, the proliferation of technically skilled but over-elaborate design finally aroused adverse criticism. Charles Blanc published his *Grammaire des Arts Décoratifs* (1882), in which he discussed the rules of good design, including its application to wallpaper, and Emile Cardon, in *L'Art au foyer domestique* (1884), set similar limitations on the use of wallpaper in the decor of the home, but with little effect on public demand, which continued to encourage the production of highly imitative designs, including wallpapers which simulated Eastern silks, Genoese velvets and tapestries of all kinds. Charles Blanc had found a new source of design in the old wallpapers of a country house at Charolais, and was also inspired by the work of William Morris and Walter Crane, which had been imported from England. Artists like Hector Guimard and Eugène Grasset began to design for wallpapers and textiles in fresh, light colours based on patterns of the past, but general commercial standards of design had not improved by the early years of the twentieth century. In the Exposition des Arts Décoratifs, held at the Salon d'Automne in 1912, Ferdinand Roche commented on the prevalence of room decors spoilt by the choice of wallpapers; even the new designs of André Mare and André Groult for Raymond Duchamp-Villon's 'maison cubiste' were not received with enthusiasm by informed critics.

After the First World War the emergence of the art deco style marked a new era in textile and wallpaper design, with the work of such artists as René Georges Hermann-Paul, Jean-Emile Laboureur, René Gabriel and Henri Stéphany. An abstract pattern of leaves and blossom in silver and blue (no 1161) by Stéphany, produced by the Société Francais des Papiers Peints *circa* 1925, an example of the best work of the period, was acquired by the Museum in 1967. In the 1930s silkscreen printing began to be used in wallpaper production in France, while the firm of Nobilis was printing wallpaper from a combined method of collotype and *pochoir*.

The firm of Paul Dumas returned to the methods of printing wallpapers from wood-block cylinders in relief used by Leroy in the 1840s, with the result that many of the designs of the art deco artists gained in textural quality. A pattern book produced by Dumas for the London market in 1927 (no 727) is in the Museum's collection. As in England and Germany, the French wallpaper industry expanded rapidly after the Second World War with the modernization of machinery and the production of durable, washable papers, a period represented in the collection by the pattern books *Collection Leroy de Paris 1974–75* (no 728), *Collection Zuber* (1977 and 1979; nos 730, 732), and *Europa IV* and *VI* (1974–75, 1978–79; nos 729, 731).[167]

German Wallpapers

Less is known about the early history of the manufacture of wallpapers in Germany than in England or France. A modern silkscreen reproduction of the oldest datable German wallpaper (*circa* 1530) is in the Museum collection (no 803). This paper is a reconstruction based on the original block-printed fragments, but there are several examples of large original sixteenth-century woodcuts used as wallpapers in German buildings, notably in the Kloster Wienhausen.[168] There was a considerable output of *Buntpapier*, or decorative papers, in South Germany, particularly in Augsburg; a fine example is one with a *chinoiserie* theme which has been dated to *circa* 1729 and is in the Albgaumuseum, Ettlingen. Some flocked wallpapers, such as those found at Arnsdorff, dated *circa* 1700, are probably of German manufacture, and there is reference to the production of flocked papers in Berlin by the second quarter of the eighteenth century. The *Wachstuchtapeten*, a genre of wall-coverings which consisted of linens saturated in heated wax and linseed oil, with oil-painted designs, was especially favoured in Germany, although also known in England and France, and was first produced in the early eighteenth century. It is known that a few factories in Berlin and Potsdam, making flocked or printed linens and *Wachstuchtapeten*, also experimented with block-printed wallpapers.

There is, however, relatively little documentation of the German wallpaper industry until the second half of the eighteenth century, although a description of J. B. Nothnagel's *Wachstuchtapeten* factory in Frankfurt appears in Goethe's autobiographical work, *Dichtung und Wahrheit*, which must be dated prior to 1775.

This firm, which formerly imported French and English wallpapers, began production of its own paper-hangings towards the end of the century.

During the years 1775–80 a Leipzig factory founded by Gottfried P. Wilhelm was advertising rolls of wallpaper in the latest fashions, together with *Buntpapier*, and some other manufacturers were specializing in imitation 'marble' wallpapers. Similarly, by *circa* 1790, Joel of Potsdam, which amalgamated with Wessely and Neumeister of Berlin, was producing designs in the Etruscan style based on those of the Réveillon factory in Paris. Many other centres of wallpaper production and distribution existed throughout Germany, though wallpaper had still not attained the predominance among wall-coverings that it enjoyed in France and England at this period. By 1813 there were five wallpaper factories in Berlin alone, and a pioneer of German wallpaper, J. C. Arnold of Cassel, founded a branch of his firm in Berlin in 1830. The earliest original example in the Museum collection (no 1135) is a *dessus-de-porte* panel of *circa* 1840–48, with a rare political theme caricaturing King Ludwig I of Bavaria and his mistress, the dancer Lola Montez, after drawings by Katharina Sattler, which was produced by Sattler of Schweinfurt, a firm founded by Wilhelm Sattler in 1821.

Michael Spörlin of Elsässer, who founded the firm of Spörlin and Rahn in Vienna in 1809, is credited with the invention of the *irisé* effect: a form of grounding in which the colours, delicately blended, merge together. In 1821 the first *Iristapeten* were produced by Zuber of Rixheim, and later by Arnold of Cassel. Johann Becker, a watchmaker born in Mainz in 1778, founded a factory at Nordhausen am Harz, which flourished from 1827 to 1910, and is said to have been the first German manufacturer to construct a wooden cylinder-printing machine, *circa* 1835. This machine proved unsatisfactory, however, and in 1838 Becker took out a patent for a lithographic technique of wallpaper printing. He died in 1841 and the business was carried on by his son, who introduced a four-colour printing machine *circa* 1860.

Karl F. L. Herting of Einbeck, born at Holzmunden in 1803, was the inventor (*circa* 1860) of the 'Perlmutt' ('mother of pearl') wallpapers, famous for the purity and delicacy of their colour.

In the late nineteenth century a branch of the English firm Lincrusta Walton, which produced a special form of relief wallpaper, was founded in Hamburg and employed a German designer working in the 'Moorish' style, Georg Böttlicher. G. L. Peine of Hildesheim, founded in 1868, was one of the largest German wallpaper firms towards the end of the nineteenth century, producing three million rolls of wallpaper per year, both hand- and machine-printed, and with an important export trade by 1880. In 1939 this firm began to produce the flock papers for which it became famous.

In 1889 sixteen German firms formed an association of manufacturers, soon to number fifty-two members, similar to that established by the Wallpaper Manufacturers Limited in England some years later.

The aftermath of the First World War, with the shortage of materials and the period of inflation, naturally affected the wallpaper industry, but by 1928 Germany had recovered its pre-war position as a major producer and exporter of wallpaper. Among the artists of the Wiener Werkstätte was Dagobert Peche (1887–1923), who

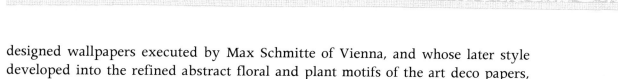

designed wallpapers executed by Max Schmitte of Vienna, and whose later style developed into the refined abstract floral and plant motifs of the art deco papers, which were produced by Flammerstein and Steinmann of Cologne. In 1929 three pattern books of Bauhaus wallpapers were produced by the firm of Gebrüder Rasch, which sold over three million rolls of the paper.

German wallpaper produced since the Second World War is represented in the Museum by a collection of papers of the 1950s, which includes the work of designers of international repute, such as Maria May, Josef Hillerbrand, Margit Hildebrand and the British Lucienne Day. Other designs of the 1950s are from Erismann and Cie of Breisach (founded in 1838), Tapetenfabrik H. Strauven KG of Bonn, and the Werkkunstschule, Krefeld (produced by the Rheinische Tapetenfabrik Schleu and Hoffmann of Breul). The first German wallpapers imported into Britain after the war were contained in John Line's 1960 *Folio* edition. They included examples of 'the *tiefdruck* plaster effects which were printed and gave the feel and quality of deep embossing on flat paper. Also designs printed from etched steel rollers, which had never before been seen in this country, and complex abstract patterns printed after two or three separate processes.'[169] The *tiefdruck* process, a form of rotagravure, in which colours, graded in intensity, could give the effect of depth by shading, was first used in wallpaper production in Germany, and is now widely used elsewhere in the industry. The pattern book *Europa VI* (1978–79; no 731), produced by Cole and Son (Wallpapers) Ltd, contains a few imported German papers.

Scandinavian Wallpapers

Apart from a native tradition of stencilled mural decoration and painted textiles in Sweden, the early history of wall-coverings in that country consists mainly of imports from France, England and Germany; the first paper-hangings of quality were examples imported from the Réveillon factory in Paris, flocks from England and, after 1800, wallpapers from Germany. The earliest printed paper in Sweden known to have been used as a wallpaper is a wood-engraving with a floral and strap-work design at Rosingenvinge, a house at Malmö. The same pattern occurs as a ceiling paper in a room at the Kloster Wienhausen, Germany, with the date, 1564, incorporated within the pattern. The style of the pattern, with its Tudor roses and marigolds, suggests that it is probably of English origin, and, according to Ingemar Tunander,[170] English papers were imported into Sweden as early as the sixteenth century.

A decorative paper in the style of the French printer, J. M. Papillon, with a bird and flower design, is stamped 'Skenninge Fabrique', a firm active in Skanninge *circa* 1720, and there appears to have been a *wachstuchtapeten* industry in Stockholm in the eighteenth century. Towards the end of the century the Swedish firm of C. F. Torsselius was operating in Stockholm, producing small decorative papers and wallpapers; during the first quarter of the nineteenth century it also produced classical panels and borders.

An apparently unique form of wall-covering is the *Spantapet*, which consists of thick strips of wood, basket-woven, and, in the case of a sample, datable to *circa* 1800, printed with a small diaper pattern. A wallpaper imitation of this form of covering decorates the walls and ceiling at the Lusthus vid Vallinge, Soderland. The Swedish national collection of historic wallpapers is housed in the Nordiska Museet, in Stockholm.

Denmark had an embryo wallpaper industry by the eighteenth century, and small hand-printed pattern papers were available from *circa* 1800.

The collection of post-war Scandinavian wallpapers in the Museum illustrates the freshness and simplicity of Scandinavian design in the work of the Danish artists, Preben Dahlström and Bent Karlby, the Norwegian Folke Sundberg and the Finn Viola Gråsten. The Swedish firm Duro presented the Museum with a set of its pattern books for 1976–77, some of which contain designs by Jonas Wallström, Gunel Ginsburg and Inez Svensson; a few of the machine-printed papers, produced by a special process, have a quality comparable to that achieved by hand-block printing.

American Wallpapers

Prior to the Revolution, English wallpapers were widely imported into America; in fact, the most detailed description extant of an early eighteenth-century English wallpaper, a *chinoiserie* design, is contained in a letter written in 1737 by Thomas Hancock of Boston to John Rowe, a London stationer. During the first half or more of the nineteenth century, however, French wallpapers, in particular the panoramas, replaced the English work in popularity. Hundreds of American houses contain sets of these spectacular scenic papers, which were available 'at least as early as 1808, when Dufour's *Savages of the Pacific Ocean* was offered for sale in New Orleans'.[171] The history of American wallpaper production can, however, be dated back to the middle of the eighteenth century by an advertisement, issued in 1756 by John Hickey for his wallpaper printed 'in the English manner'. A factory was established by John Rugar in New York in 1765, and by the end of the eighteenth century several more were in operation in East Coast cities. By the 1830s Philadelphia had become one of the chief centres of manufacture, and a Philadelphia firm, Howell and Brothers, which imported the first wallpaper-printing machine in 1844 and exhibited at the 1851 Exhibition in London, developed into the largest manufactory in America in the 1860s and 1870s. In 1860 New York was producing more wallpaper than Philadelphia and Boston, and the industry was expanding rapidly during this period of mass production. A twelve-colour printing machine was shown in operation at the Central Exposition held in Philadelphia in 1876, and by the end of the century there were fifty wallpaper factories in America.[172]

The firm of M. H. Birge and Company, established in Buffalo, New York, in 1834, specialized 'in a variety of papers, including complex panel decorations. In 1889 it advertised such exotic wares as "Ecclesiastical Decorations, studied from the Mural paintings of Notre Dame"'.[173] A large proportion of the Museum collection consists of floral and pictorial papers, friezes, panels and imitation leather work produced by Birge in the late nineteenth century. The American painter Charles Burchfield worked for the firm 1921–29.

The practice, encouraged by Jeffrey and Company in England, of employing artists to improve the standard of wallpaper design found its counterpart in America during the 1880s in the efforts of Warren Fuller and Company of New York, who engaged such distinguished American designers as Louis Comfort Tiffany, Candace Wheeler and Lockwood de Forest.[174] Although the best English standards were to influence the design from this period until the early twentieth century, and American trade journals carried many advertisements for 'art' wallpapers in the English style, production to meet the general public's demand for very ornate, technically elaborate wall-coverings continued to dominate the market. The use of ingrain papers, or papers dyed in the pulp for wallpaper production, if not initiated in America appears to have been widespread there from about the 1880s, whereas such 'ingrains' only began to be fashionable in Britain in the early years of the twentieth century. As in Britain, the demand for wallpaper showed a continuous growth until the beginning of the First World War. During the war pictorial papers were produced, showing such patriotic themes as the flags and banners of the United States and the Allies, including the papers designed by Charles Jeltrup, one of which depicts soldiers drilling in City Hall Park, New York. Many papers at this time were copied from those in historic American buildings, including the Paul Revere House in Boston and Longfellow's birthplace at Portland, Maine.

During the late 1920s wallpaper was experiencing some decline in America: 'The average domestic paper was still strongly influenced by the over embellished Victorian patterns . . . the best papers, both domestic and imported, were copies of good 18th century design'.[175] The influence of the European *avant garde*, however, among them the German Tommi Parzinger, who emigrated to the United States in the 1930s, began to stimulate American designers during the ensuing decades. In 1934 washable papers were introduced, and by the mid-1940s the wood block was being replaced by hand-printing by silkscreen. The Museum collection includes some lively silkscreen designs based on the drawings of the American cartoonist Saul Steinberg, notably 'Views in Paris', produced by Piazza Prints Inc. in 1946 (no 1158). The 1950s are represented by some of the productions of C. M. Stockwell and Company of California, Harben Papers of New York and F. Schumacher and Company of New York. The architect Frank Lloyd Wright also designed carpets, textiles and wallpaper; the Museum has acquired some of his designs for wallpapers in the 'Taliesin Line' (nos 1310–1313) range, produced by Schumacher in 1956, of which 'Design 103', Design 705' and 'Design 706' were also manufactured as furnishing fabrics. The work of Jack Denst, President of Denst Designs Inc., Chicago, is represented by four screen-printed papers (*circa* 1968), including 'A Dialogue of Color', in white on silver 'mirror' paper (no 951).

Since the large-scale restoration of Colonial Williamsburg inaugurated by John D. Rockefeller in the late 1920s, there has been continuous and growing interest in American historic buildings and their interiors. The Cooper-Hewitt Museum in New York, opened in 1897, with its well preserved and well documented collection, is an important centre in the United States for the study of historic wallpaper and of methods of preserving it.

NOTES TO THE INTRODUCTION

[1] H. Havard, *Dictionnaire de l'Ameublement et de la Décoration depuis le 13me siècle jusqu'à nos jours* (Paris, 1887–90), IV, col. 70.
[2] I, Richard III, cap. 12.
[3] 13, George III, cap. 67.
[4] A. E. Shipley, 'The Master's Lodgings, Christ's College, Cambridge', *Country Life* (1916), vol 40, 406–12.
[5] C. Sale, 'Cambridge Fragments', *Library* (1911, 1912), 3rd series, 11, 340.
[6] It bears the Bishop's arms impaling those of the See of Canterbury, to which he was elected a few months before his death, but where he was never enthroned.
[7] *Archaeologia Cantiana*, VII, 296.
[8] Illustrated in *Connoisseur* (1922), LXII, 156.
[9] Illustrated in H. Jenkinson, 'English Wallpapers of the Sixteenth and Seventeenth Centuries', *Antiquaries' Journal* (1925), V, 246–47.
[10] A fragment was found lining a small deed box at the Public Record Office.
[11] Illustrated in H. Jenkinson, *op. cit.*, V, pl XIX.
[12] Wallpaper fragments with this pattern have recently been uncovered at Hampton Court Palace.
[13] Illustrated in H. Jenkinson, *op. cit.*, V, pl 20.
[14] B. Ionides, 'Wallpaper in a Sixteenth-century House', *Architectural Review* (1924), LVI, 195.
[15] Illustrated in H. Jenkinson, *loc. cit.* H. Jenkinson, *op. cit.*, V, pl XIX and p 244.
[16] Illustrated in *The Antiquaries Journal* (1925), V, 224.
[17] Illustrated in *Old Furniture* (1927), 1, 276.
[18] Both reproduced in *Connoisseur* (1922), LXII, pls 1, 11, and in H. Jenkinson, *op. cit.*, 245, pl XIX, fig 1. A facsimile of nine sheets of one of these is in the Museum collection (no 9). Some slight restoration was required in making this reproduction as, when the original was being pieced together at the Ashmolean Museum, the original form was slightly altered owing to stretching of the paper.
[19] Another specimen of this paper lines a deed box in the Department of Woodwork (no 15).
[20] Illustrated in H. Jenkinson, *op. cit.*, V, 246, fig 2.
[21] *Ibid.*, V, 246 (fig 2), 253.
[22] *Ibid.*, V, 250.
[23] C. R. Rivington, *The Stationers' Company* (London, 1883).
[24] A fragment of another wallpaper of pictorial design is in the Castle Museum, Norwich. It also seems to date from the close of the century. It depicts a hunting scene. A. V. Sugden and J. L. Edmondson, *A History of English Wallpaper* (London, 1926), 40–41.
[25] Lindsay P. Butterfield, 'Discovery and Restoration of Two Wallpaper Designs', *Artist* (1898), 102.
[26] One of these lines a box belonging to the Court of Wards, which came to an end in 1645, and is in the Public Record Office. It consists of a diaper pattern in green, pink and orange. The other, a pictorial design, shows the letters 'CP', with the Prince of Wales' feathers for Charles I or Charles II, and was in the possession of Colonel Croft Lyons (see H. Jenkinson, *op. cit.*, V, 252, pl XXV.)
[27] *Ibid.*, V, 251.
[28] I, Richard III, cap. 8.
[29] H. Clouzot, 'La tradition du papier peint en France', *Gazette des Beaux-Arts* (1912), 4 période, vii.
[30] W. A. Englefield, *History of the Painter Stainers' Company* (London, 1923), 97.
[31] The claim that Jerome Lanyer, an Englishman, was an inventor of flock paper cannot be maintained. The patent granted him by Charles I shows that his flock hangings were made of materials other than paper (T. Rymer, *Foedera*, 21 May 1634).
[32] Illustrated in *Journal of Decorative Art* (1906), 323, and in A. V. Sugden and J. L. Edmondson, *op. cit.*, 15.
[33] *Notes and Queries* (1910), 11th series, i, 350.
[34] A. V. Sugden and J. L. Edmondson, *op. cit.*, 43.
[35] 10 Anne, cap. 18.
[36] The earlier 'GR' stamps do not appear to change at all in the shape of the monogram or crown, and the only visible change is in the numeral under the word 'PAPER'. Those stamps that I have seen have borne numbers from 1 to 16. In some cases more than one stamp was used (for example, the Wotton-under-Edge paper, no 67, which bears the numbers 1, 4, 5). If anything can be deduced from the stamps, the key must be sought in these numerals. I have been unable to obtain any help in this direction either from the statutes or from the instructions to excise officers. The suggestion that each of the various excise offices in the kingdom had a number seems to be contradicted by the presence of more than one stamp on the same wallpaper. Another hypothesis, that the numbers may refer to the years of the sovereign's reign, is much more plausible. 'Paper 8', which appears on a flock from Clandon Park, Surrey, was hung *circa* 1735—that is, in the eighth year of George II's reign—and 'Paper 14' in the illustration (p. 17) thus becomes 1741, which also bears out this suggestion. It is necessary to admit the possibility that paper might lie unused for as long as five years

after it had been stamped for use as paper hangings. This, although unlikely, is not impossible, as a paper-stainer might quite well keep a stock of odd bits for several years with which to make up the 'piece' when necessary. The practice is indicated in *Instructions for Collectors, Supervisors, and Officers in the Country* (1778), where it is ordered that a certain proportion of the sheets of paper should bear two stamps, so that, should they have to be cut into two, the paper-stainer would have no excuse for not being able to show a stamp on the fragment. This seems also to be the subject of some regulations in 26 George III, cap. 78. Another stamp, with 'First Account Taken', is also found on some later papers.

[37] Illustrated in A. V. Sugden and J. L. Edmondson, *op. cit.*, pl 33.

[38] Illustrated in *Connoisseur* (1922), LXII, 156, pl III.

[39] *Journal of Decorative Art and British Decorator* (1909), XXIX, 447.

[40] *Op. cit.*, V, 252.

[41] This collection of end-papers includes a number of fragments with designs, produced by several techniques, which would be equally suitable for wallpapers. There is even a fragment of a flock paper among them. When acquired by the Museum, the end-papers had already been separated from the books which they had bound, and of which no record has been kept. It is possible to decide the age and nationality of only a few examples, and it has not been possible to separate categorically the wallpapers used as end-papers from those originally intended for the binding of books. End-paper design is extremely traditional, and techniques otherwise obsolete appear to have survived in this industry for a surprisingly long time. Although the collection covers practically the whole of the eighteenth and nineteenth centuries, the possible wallpapers appear mostly to date from before the end of the eighteenth century.

[42] J. M. Papillon, *Traité Historique et Pratique de la Gravure en Bois* (1766), I, 327.

[43] J. B. Jackson, *Essay on the Invention of Engraving and Printing in Chiaro Oscuro* (1754), 8.

[44] *Memoirs of Thomas Bewick* (1862 edition), 248.

[45] J. Kainen, in *John Baptist Jackson: 18th-century Master of the Color Woodcut* (Washington, 1962), states that this volume is the work of Jackson's studio, rather than his own.

[46] *Memoirs of Thomas Bewick, loc. cit.*

[47] N. V. McClelland, *Historic Wallpapers . . .* (Philadelphia and London, 1924), 324.

[48] *Op. cit.*, I, 535.

[49] *Instructions for Collectors, Supervisors, and Officers in the Country* (London, 1778).

[50] Letter to Richard Bentley, July 1755.

[51] A photograph of this paper is in the Museum. An example of this panel is in the London Museum, where there are also others from the same series.

[52] J. W. Mackail, *The Life of William Morris* (1889), 156.

[53] *loc. cit.*

[54] An English copy of 'Les Deux Pigeons' (*circa* 1785), by Jean Baptiste Réveillon.

[55] *Description of Strawberry Hill* (1784), 401.

[56] Letter to Richard Bentley, September 1753.

[57] Letter to Sir H. Mann, 1753.

[58] Letter to Sir H. Mann, August 1750.

[59] George Brudenell, 4th Earl of Cardigan (1712–90).

[60] Letter to Sir H. Mann, June 1753.

[61] *Country Life* (1925), LVII, 202–3.

[62] Illustrated in *ibid.* (1897), II, 405.

[63] Illustrated in *ibid.* (1925), LVII, 202.

[64] J. Boswell, *Life of Samuel Johnson* (Everyman ed., 1906), II, 249.

[65] Illustrated in *Country Life* (1925), LVIII, 476–78.

[66] O. Brackett, *Thomas Chippendale* (London, 1925), Appendix.

[67] Illustrated in *Connoisseur* (1922), LXII, 25.

[68] A fragment (no 99) from the Manor House, Bourton-on-the-Water, Gloucestershire, is in the same style.

[69] See note 2.

[70] See note 3.

[71] An interesting example of a French paper, depicting a naval engagement in the East Indies in 1784 between a French and an English ship, is at The Grange, Rottingdean, Sussex. Illustrated in *Country Life* (1928), LXIII, 625.

[72] 32 George III, cap. 54.

[73] 27 George III, cap. 68. The duty on certain other grades of paper was removed, while that on wallpaper was increased.

[74] *History of Paper-hangings* (London, 1875), 26.

[75] This term includes coloured papers used not only for wall decoration, but also for other purposes.

[76] 49 George III, cap. 81.

[77] 46 George III, cap. 112.

[78] 43 George III, cap. 68.

[79] 49 George III, cap. 98.

[80] 9 and 10 Victoria, cap. 23.

[81] 16 Victoria, cap. 106.

[82] 24 Victoria, cap. 20.

[83] The following figures, extracted from G. H. Morton's pamphlet (see note 74), illustrate the growth of the industry in the early nineteenth century: in 1810, the proceeds of the wallpaper tax were £32,228 18s 2d; in 1820, £34,246 6s 4d; in 1830, £44, 835 4s 9d; in 1834, £63,794 16s 9d. The report of the Excise Commissioners, 1835, gives the following details of the productivity of the tax in the three divisions of the United Kingdom: England, £58,851 14s 6d; Scotland, £435 18s 6d; Ireland, £4,508 4s 1d. The amount of wallpaper produced in Ireland in early days, as compared with Scotland, was remarkable. The Irish paper-hanging industry, however, was declining in the first half of the nineteenth century, and by the present century had ceased to be of importance. According to Morton, formerly a number of paper-stainers in the Liverpool and Manchester districts were Irish. An example of the

wallpaper tax stamp in use in Ireland is illustrated in McClelland, *op. cit.*, 44.

[84]Good examples of this style are nos 212, 253, 266.

[85]The paper from Shelsley Bank, Stanford Bridge, Worcester (no 164), is an exception, as it shows traces of the lingering influence of classical wall paintings.

[86]*Journal of Design and Manufacture* (1849), I, 170.

[87]See S. V. Sugden and E. A. Entwistle, *Potters of Darwen* (Manchester, 1939).

[88]G. H. Morton, *op. cit.*, 34.

[89]*Journal of Design and Manufacture* (1851), IV, 174.

[90]*Ibid.* (1852), V, 173.

[91]In 1915 Allan F. Vigers presented two volumes of cuttings of Morris's wallpapers, and these were followed by two more pattern books, presented by Messrs Morris and Company. These illustrate almost every pattern designed by Morris in almost every combination of colours.

[92]N. McClelland, 'The Inventors of Wall-papers', *Arts and Decoration* (1923), XX, 59.

[93]One of the most remarkable of his statements (111, 121) is that the invention of flock papers was due to Audran, painter and *concierge* of the Palais du Luxembourg, between 1712 and 1716. He goes on to say that he had seen one of the earliest of these at the Château de Bruyères, which depicted a comic repast of apes. It was as good, he says, as the modern (1766) English flock papers. Even if we were to take this as a reference to the type of flock papers imitating tapestries in every colour of flock, it does not explain why he never mentions that the activities of the seventeenth-century *dominotiers* included the making of even the simpler types of flock papers, which he entirely leaves out of account. Considering the interest that had been shown in England in this technique during the seventeenth century, it is hard to believe that flocking, at any rate on cloth, was well known in France.

[94]J. M. Papillon, *op. cit.*, 1,536.

[95]That some of the papers which were made by Papillon were used for such purposes is shown in an anecdote in *ibid.*, I, 83.

[96]'Sur quoi je ferai remarquer que leurs papiers n'etoient pas à rapport à pouvoir former avec une tenture pour une chambre ou un cabinet, comme les papiers de tapisserie d'aprésent dont mon Père a fait à Paris les premiers en ce genre qu'on y ait fabriqués' (*ibid.*, I, 21).

[97]*Ibid.*, I, 535.

[98]See *Encyclopédie des Sciences*, II, 860, where the author is merely called Sieur Papillon. This has always been taken to mean the father, but it might equally refer to J. M. Papillon.

[99]See H. Clouzot, 'Le papier peint au début du xviii siècle', *La Renaissance de l'Art Francais* (1925), VIII, 149.

[100]Illustrated as in the possession of Miss Marbury, Sutton Place, New York, by N. V. McClelland, *Historic Wallpapers* (Philadelphia and London, 1924), 71.

[101]*Ibid.*, 72.

[102]J. M. Papillon, *op. cit.*, I, 380.

[103]Illustrated in F. Follot, *Museé Rétrospectif de la Classe 68, Paris Exposition* (1900), 54.

[104]Illustrated in *ibid.*, 31.

[105]J. M. Papillon, *op. cit.*, III, 4.

[106]*Ibid.*, III, 85.

[107]*Ibid.*, I, 327.

[108]Savary des Bruslons, *Dictionnaire Universel de Commerce* (1723), III, col. 1060.

[109]*Loc. cit.*

[110]Germain Brice, *Description de Paris* (1725), III, 347.

[111]*Gazette des Beaux-Arts* (1912), 4 période, VII, 138.

[112] The Blue Paper Warehouse advertisement (see pp. 17–18) mentions papers in imitation of 'real tapestry', but if these were flock papers there is no other indication that the French style of flocking was ever attempted in England.

[113]J. M. Papillon, *op. cit.*, I, 535.

[114]Eighteenth-century flocks in two colours have since been acquired (nos 50, 117). A piece from Blyth Hall, Warwickshire, of the early eighteenth century, is printed in red and green.

[115]Savary des Bruslons, *loc. cit.*

[116]IX, 197.

[117]Quoted by H. Havard, *Dictionnaire d' Ameublement* (see note 1), IV, 60.

[118]*Annonces, affiches et avis divers*, 10 July 1754 (quoted by H. Havard, *ibid.*, IV, col. 61).

[119]*Ibid.*, 9 July 1755 (quoted by H. Havard, *op. cit.*, IV, col. 76).

[120]*Baguettes* were the battens on which the paper was stretched.

[121]Sale of the goods of Mme de Bastard, Rue Sainte-Anne, 2 July 1782 (quoted by H. Havard, *op. cit.*, IV, col. 61).

[122]*Annonces, affiches et avis divers*, 1 April 1783 (quoted by H. Havard, *loc. cit.*).

[123]F. Follot, *op. cit.*, 15.

[124]*Arrêt du Conseil d'Etat*, 1 December 1766 (quoted by J. M. Papillon, *op. cit.*, III, 95.

[125]H. Havard, *op. cit.*, IV, col. 76.

[126]The *aune* was equivalent to the old English 'ell'.

[127]F. Follot, *op. cit.*, 12.

[128]I have failed to find the original authority for Chereau's invention, but, although it might be tempting to merge Chereau and Chauvrau into one man, this course does not seem possible. Papillon, indeed, never mentions Chereau's invention, but, on the other hand, Jacques appears among the plaintiffs in the case of the Dominotiers v. Gilde de Saint Luc in 1739, mentioned in Papillon, *op. cit.*, III, 83. At a later date he appears selling flock papers.

[129]J. M. Papillon, *op. cit.*, I, 535.

[130]*Loc. cit.*

[131]Chereau may have used them, for all we know.

[132]H. Havard, *op. cit.*, IV, 81.

[133]P. Gusman, *Panneaux Décoratifs et Tentures Murales du XVIIIième Siècle* (1913).
[134]F. Follot, *op. cit.*, 19.
[135]J. G. Crace, 'History of Paper-hanging', reprinted in *Decorator* (22 January 1925).
[136]Illustrated in P. Gusman, *op. cit.*
[137]F. Follot, *op. cit.*, 21.
[138]Illustrated in P. Gusman, *op. cit.*, 23.
[139]Illustrated in *ibid.*, pls IX–XI.
[140]The Palladio Room at Clandon Park, Surrey, is hung with an English copy of Réveillon's 'Les Deux Pigeons', a sample of which is no 117.
[141]Illustrated in *ibid.*, pls V–VII.
[142]Illustrated in F. Follot, *op. cit.*, 59.
[143]Illustrated in *ibid.*, 67.
[144]Illustrated in *ibid.*, 27, 37.
[145]Illustrated in *ibid.*, 25.
[146]Illustrated in *ibid.*, 64.
[147]Illustrated in *ibid.*, 26, 27.
[148]For a closer study of the period under review, see McClelland, *op. cit.*, 192; F. Follot, *op. cit.*; H. Havard, *op. cit.*
[149]Illustrated in F. Follot, *op. cit.*, 100.
[150]N. V. McClelland, *op. cit.*, 208.
[151]*Memoirs and Observations made in a late Journey through the Empire of China* (London, 1697), 160.
[152]A. Anderson, *An Accurate Account of Lord Macartney's Embassy to China* (London, 1795).
[153]Among the very few exceptions are some fragments of a paper in the Museo Petriano, Rome, where the birds are clearly of a fantastic nature.
[154]One of the great advantages of the Chinese papers was the fact that there was little beginning or end to their designs. Odd pieces could, therefore, be made into fire screens, or to cover the space over a door. As a result of this use of small pieces, a type of miniature paper panels of Chinese papers came into existence to serve these purposes, and also to be formed into larger designs by being pieced together.
[155]Illustrated in *Old Furniture* (1928), III, 17.
[156]Illustrated in *Country Life* (1920), XLVIII, 475.
[157]Good examples are at Beaudesert, Staffordshire (illustrated in *Country Life*, 1919, XLVI, 692), and at Brasted Place, Kent.
[158]Illustrated in *Country Life* (1920), XLVIII, 54.
[159]*Ibid.* (1920), XLVIII, 475.
[160]As at Brasted Place, Kent, and Nostell Priory, Yorkshire, restored by Adam, and at Coker Court, Somerset, built by Chambers.
[161]Tax stamps are said to have been found on the back of the Chinese paper at Wrest Park, Silsoe, Bedfordshire.
[162]The Chinese paper at Moor Park (no 656), supplied by Cowtan's in 1829, is another example of a late importation of this kind of wallpaper.
[163]There were several methods of hanging Chinese wallpapers. The best and most expensive was to mount them on canvas stretched on battens, as was done in the downstairs room at Oakley House. The next best was to mount them on a lining paper, but often the paper was pasted straight on to the wall. It was not usual to varnish the front of the paper.
[164]A. V. Sugden and J. L. Edmondson, *op. cit.*, 190.
[165]A. V. Sugden and E. A. Entwisle, *Potters of Darwen . . .* (Manchester, 1939), 75.
[166]As the collection of foreign wallpapers does not encompass a historical representation, and the absence of sufficient material precludes a proper assessment from the Museum's resources, only very brief historical outlines are given in the following accounts.
[167]For French wallpapers of the period covered in the above text, see Jean-Pierre Séguin, 'Trois Siècles des Papier-peints', catalogue of the exhibition held at the Musée des Arts Décoratifs, Paris, 1967.
[168]H. Appuhn and C. von Heusinger, *Reisenholzschnitte und Papiertapeten der Renaissance* (Unterschneidheim, 1976).
[169]Edward Pond, 'The Wallpaper Manufacturers Ltd 1945–1971', catalogue of *Historic Wallpapers in the Whitworth Art Gallery*, an exhibition held at the Whitworth Art Gallery, Manchester, 4 March to 8 April 1972.
[170]I. Tunander, *Tapeter* (Nordiska Museet, Stockholm, 1955).
[171]Polk Douglas, ed., 'French Panoramic Wallpaper . . .', *Arts and Antiques* (November–December 1980), 62.
[172]Catherine L. Frangiemore, 'Wallpapers used in nineteenth century America', *Antiques* (December 1972), and *Wallpapers in Historic Preservation* (Washington, 1977).
[173]Samuel J. Dornsife, 'Wallpaper', *The Encyclopaedia of Victoriana* (New York, 1975).
[174]C. L. Frangiemore, *op. cit.* (see note 172).
[175]L. and W. Katzenbach, *The Practical Book of American Wallpaper* (Philadelphia and New York, 1951), 2.

1007

List of Colour Plates

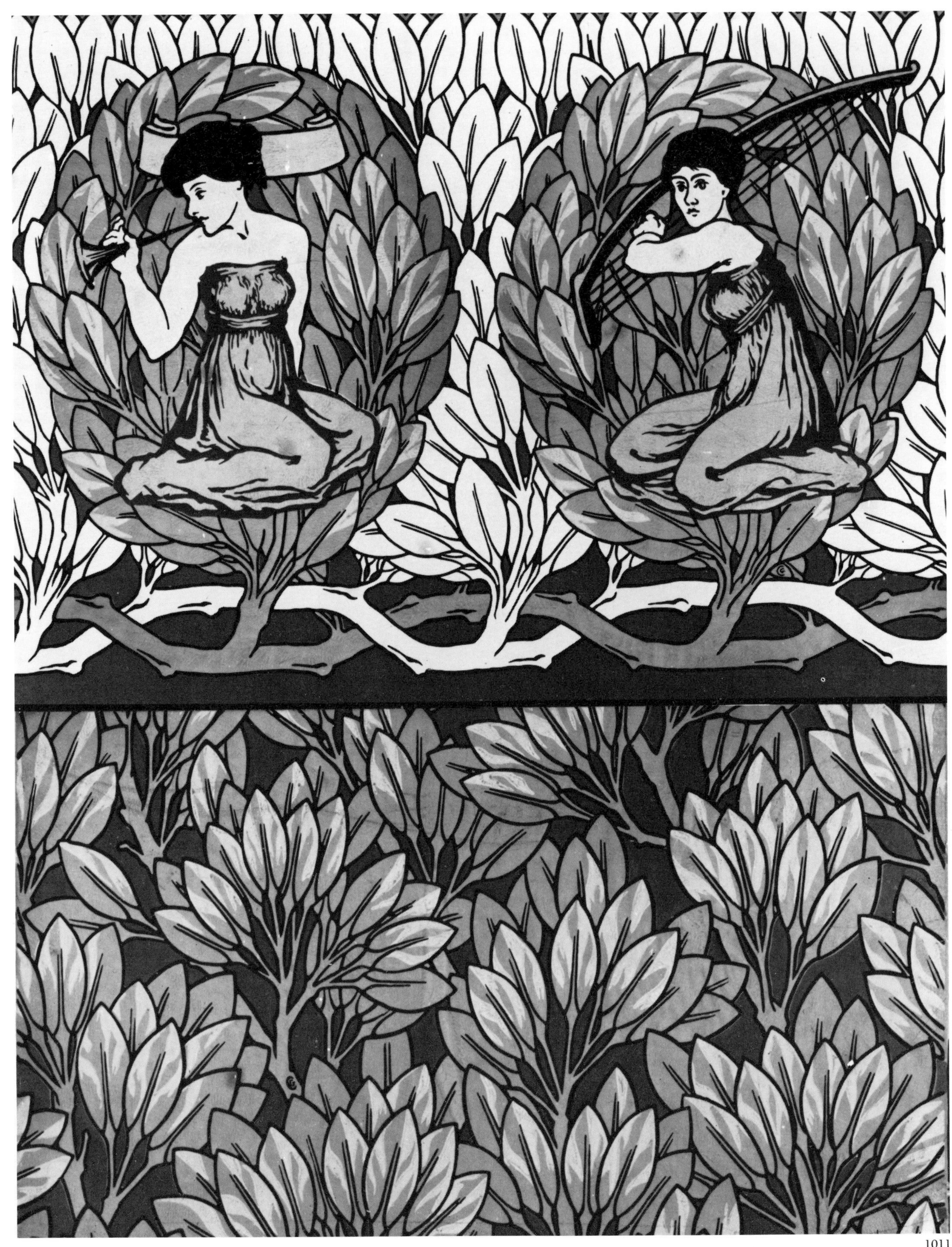

1011

How to use this Book

The wallpapers listed in the catalogue have been grouped in three sections: 'Anonymous Wallpapers and Wallpaper Designs', 'Pattern Books' and 'Designers'.

The first section includes papers or designs which cannot be ascribed to a known designer. Conjectural attributions, or former attributions which are now regarded as obsolete, are mentioned in the notes below the few entries concerned. The papers are arranged in chronological order within the sub-sections devoted to each country of manufacture. In some instances the years of production have been obtained from documentary sources; in others it has been possible to relate the patterns of the papers to their counterparts in the dated order books or pattern books of the manufacturers. For the most part, however, the suggested order (often necessarily approximate) has been based on stylistic grounds.

The second section, 'Pattern Books', includes books or collections of designs which are the work of more than one designer, as well as a few other items (such as manufacturers' order books) which could conveniently be grouped with them. The books are listed in chronological order of production, within sub-sections on the relevant countries. Designers who are named within a catalogue entry (as having contributed a design to the pattern book in question) are listed in the third section of the catalogue ('Designers'), with a cross-reference to the relevant entry or entries in the 'Pattern Books' section. In cases where a designer has contributed more than one design to a particular pattern book the number of designs is given between brackets after the catalogue number in the cross-reference.

Pattern books which consist of the work of a single designer are listed under the designer's name in the 'Designers' section. It should be added, however, that in the single case of William Morris, and the firm which bore his name, it was considered impracticable to separate the pattern books to which other designers, apart from Morris himself, had contributed, from those which consist solely of his own designs, and they have accordingly been included under Morris' name in the 'Designers' section.

The third section, 'Designers', includes works which can be ascribed to known designers, who are listed in alphabetical sequence. Each designer's works are given in chronological order, undated (or undatable) works being placed last. Except in cases where a date is given in an inscription (normally the date of completion of the design, if the inscription is the designer's), the dates given are those of production by the manufacturer.

For designers who have contributed to works listed in the 'Pattern Books' section, see above.

Technical Terms

Portion A sizeable piece of wallpaper, either unused or, if used, in good condition

Length A portion of wallpaper of average wall-height

Panel A piece of wallpaper showing the design complete on one sheet

Fragment A damaged, irregularly shaped, much used piece of wallpaper

These terms are only included in the catalogue descriptions in cases where the item is not illustrated.

List of Abbreviations

AJ	*Art Journal*
ASJ (1)	A. S. Jennings, *Wallpapers and Wall Coverings* (London, 1903)
ASJ (2)	A. S. Jennings, *Wallpaper Decoration* (London and New York, 1907)
BGM	Bethnal Green Museum
Clouzot	Henri Clouzot and Charles Follot, *Histoire du Papier Peint en France* (Paris, 1935)
Clouzot, *TT*	Henri Clouzot, *Les chefs d'oeuvres du Papiers Peints. Tableaux-tentures de Dufour et Leroy* (Paris, 1931)
Entwisle	E. A. Entwisle, *The Book of Wallpaper* (2nd ed, Bath, 1970)
Entwisle, *FS*	E. A. Entwisle, *French Scenic Wallpaper 1800–1860* (Leigh-on-Sea, 1972)
Entwisle, *LH*	E. A. Entwisle, *A Literary History of Wallpaper* (London, 1960)
Entwisle, *V*	E. A. Entwisle, *Wallpapers of the Victorian Era* (Leigh-on-Sea, 1964)
Greysmith	Brenda Greysmith, *Wallpaper* (London, 1976)
HJ	Hilary Jenkinson, 'English Wallpapers of the Sixteenth and Seventeenth Centuries', *Antiquaries Journal* (1925), vol v, no 3
JDA	*Journal of Decorative Art*
McClelland	Nancy V. McClelland, *Historic Wallpapers from their Inception to the Introduction of Machinery* (Philadelphia and London, 1924)
Paulson Townsend	W. G. Paulson Townsend, *Modern Decorative Art in England*, pt I (London, 1922)
RA	Royal Academy
RCA	Royal College of Art
RI	Royal Institution
RIBA	Royal Institute of British Architects
SE	A. V. Sugden and J. L. Edmondson, *A History of English Wallpaper. 1509–1914* (London, 1926)
VAM	Victoria and Albert Museum
WM	Wallpaper Manufacturers Ltd

THE CATALOGUE

Anonymous Wallpapers and Wallpaper Designs

ENGLAND

16th Century

1 Reconstruction of a piece of a conventional pomegranate design; incorporated within the design, the letter *H* and a goose (a rebus of Hugo Goes)
Circa 1509
Machine print
76.4 × 53.3 cm
PROVENANCE The Master's Lodge, Christ's College, Cambridge
Given by Sir Charles Allom
E.1783–1914 neg 49088

See SE pls 1–3; Greysmith, pl 10. A lithographed facsimile was given by Professor W. R. Lethaby (E.539–1912). The pattern relates to Italian textile designs imported into this country in the 15th century; it also bears comparison with a leather hanging, possibly Spanish, on the walls of a house, which is now part of the Plantin–Moretus Museum, Antwerp (J. W. Waterer, *Spanish Leather* (1971), pl 8).

Hugo Goes was a maker of woodcuts and a printer who, after leaving Beverley, settled at York, where he was in 1509. He may subsequently have come to London.

The pattern was printed on the back of sheets of paper with letterpress and contains certain references to the first year of Henry VIII's reign (1509). This was the year in which the Lodge is known to have been built. The reconstruction was the work of Horace Warner (q.v.) of Jeffrey & Co. See C. Sayle, 'Cambridge Fragments', *The Library* (1911–12), 3rd series, vol II, p 340; A. E. Shipley, 'The Master's Lodgings, Christ's College, Cambridge', *Country Life* (1916), vol 40, 406–12.

1 E.539–1912

2

3

2 Royal crown surmounted by a crowned lion, within a decorative border, and below, a shield charged with a portcullis with the royal motto
First half of 16th century
Print from wood block
25.4 × 10.2 cm (fragment)
Given by an anonymous donor
E.276–1961 neg GE.432

The royal device is that used by Henry VII and Henry VIII. The donor stated that the paper was removed from a wall of 'Nacton Hall, Suffolk', but such a building cannot be traced. There is, though, a Broke Hall at Nacton, Suffolk, which was built in the first half of the 16th century. There is also a Necton Hall, Norfolk, which has been in the possession of the Mason family since the reign of Henry VIII. A similar armorial design is no 4. See J. Hamilton, 'Early English Wallpapers', *Connoisseur*, July 1977, 201, pl 1; Greysmith, pl 11.

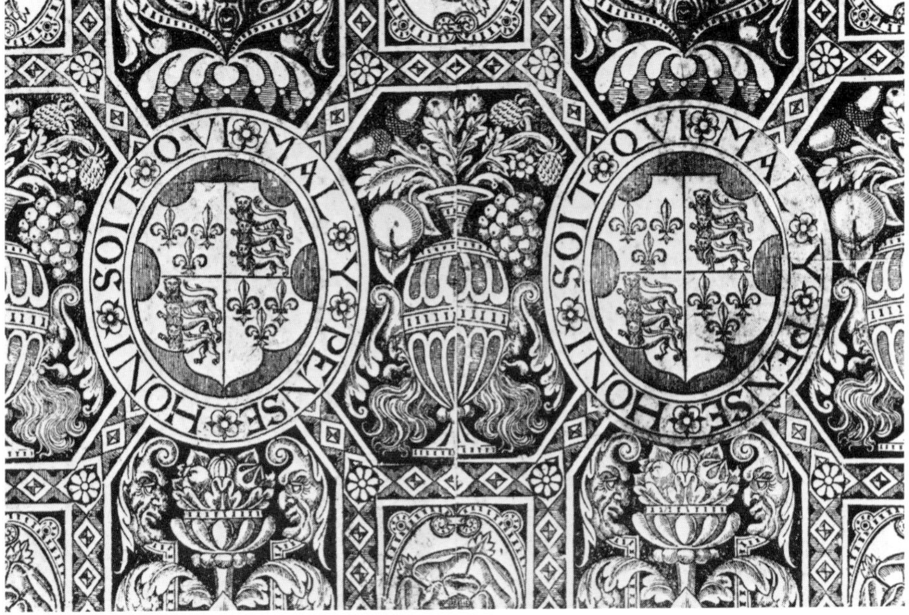

4

6

7

3 Lining paper with a pattern of Tudor roses
Circa 1550
Print from wood block
20 × 17.8 cm (first fragment);
19.5 × 36.5 cm (second fragment)
Given by the Reverend J. Harvey Bloom
E.73–1910; E.4012–1915; E.73 neg 77388

See Greysmith, pl 12.

4 Pattern of panels containing the arms of England, Tudor roses, vases of flowers and masks
Circa 1550–75
Print from wood block
42 × 57.2 cm (portion)
PROVENANCE Besford Court, Worcestershire
Given by Mrs Randell Wells
E.3593–1913 neg 51380

Another portion of the paper, still adhering to the original wattle and daub is E.2431–1918. The same pattern was used on the lining of an oak chest of the latter half of the 16th century, in the possession of Mr C. H. Spencer Percival (see tracing, D.1074–1904). A note about the chest and the lining paper is in the *Connoisseur*, September 1906, 52. The wallpaper is discussed in HJ, pl 19; SE, p 15; Greysmith, pl 15. A silk-screen reproduction in 3 colourways, produced by Cole & Son (Wallpapers) Ltd, is no 526. Recently, a variation of this pattern has been found in a room in the Base Court at Hampton Court (HJ, pl XIXa; J. Hamilton, *op. cit.* (see no 4), pl 1); the mask motifs are replaced by George and the Dragon, and figures supporting a crowned rose. Yet another sample is to be found at the Public Record Office.

5 Two wall hangings with panels painted to simulate walnut and tortoiseshell (?), and small roundels painted blue
Circa 1600
Tempera on canvas
195.7 × 99 cm; 132 × 66 cm
PROVENANCE Lockley's, Hemel Hempstead, Hertfordshire
Given by Mr D. Hart
Department of Furniture and Woodwork, W.42–1952

17th Century

6 Small 'black stitch' pattern of Tudor roses and other flowers within a trellis
Early 17th century
Print from wood block
32.4 × 28 cm (fragment)
Given by Mr Alfred Newett
E.1974–1927 neg 71286

7 Lining paper with a design of horizontal lines of flowers and various devices, a cock, a mermaid, a camel, etc, alternating with moralities from the scriptures, made into rough couplets
Early 17th century
Print from wood blocks
PROVENANCE Lining an early 17th-century box given by the late Colonel G. B. Croft Lyons per Mill Stephenson Esq, FSA, in the Department of Furniture and Woodwork (V & A)

8

Department of Furniture and Woodwork, W.51–1926 neg 68589

The box also contains part of a calender dated 1680.

8 Wall- or lining paper used for lining a deed box, with a small 'black stitch' pattern of Tudor roses, etc; printed on the reverse of paper begun to be printed with William Camden's *Remaines concerning Britaine* (1615)
Circa 1615
Print from wood block
Department of Furniture and Woodwork, W.17–1910 neg 64500

See Introduction, p 13; also C. C. Oman, 'Old Wall-papers in England', *Old Furniture* (1927), vol I, plate on p 276.

9 Design reconstructed from a portion of Jacobean paper, printed from a wood block with floral pattern in black and white
Circa 1615
Photo-lithograph
122 × 111.2 cm
PROVENANCE Lining a deed box dated 1615 in the Ashmolean Museum, Oxford
Given by Hillary Jenkinson, MA, FSA
E.1149–1925

See Introduction, p 13; also Margaret Jourdain, 'Some Early Printed Papers', *Connoisseur*, March 1922, 159, fig 11; SE, pl 9

10 Design on 4 sheets, reconstructed by Wyndham Payne from fragments of a lining paper found in a box dated 1635, showing a plume of 3 ostrich feathers enfiled by a royal coronet, with the motto *Ich Dien* and the initials *HP*, the badge of Henry Frederick, Prince of Wales (1594–1612), within a sunburst enclosed by an oval of strap work surrounded by 4 quadrants containing formalized flowers in a vase
Circa 1635
Lino cut
28 × 26.8 cm
Given by Wyndham Payne
E.456, 456 A–C–1951 neg GE.429

See Greysmith, pl 18. Henry Frederick was created Prince of Wales in 1610.

11 Arms and supporters of the House of Stuart and the letters *CR* (Carolus Rex?)
Circa 1645
Print from wood block
36.9 × 33 cm (lining paper)
Given by the Reverend J. Harvey Bloom
E.362–1940 neg B.61

10

11

12

13

14

12 Design representing the sun (?), surrounded by Tudor roses, with winged cherubs and conventional flowers
Mid-17th century
Print from wood block
14.6 × 47.6 cm (fragment of lining paper)
PROVENANCE Taken from a chest of drawers
Given by Olive Baker
E.155–1933 neg 69183

A variant of this pattern, showing a version of the coat-of-arms of the Haberdashers' Company in place of the motif possibly representing the sun, lines the drawer of a late 17th-century mulberry-veneered chest of drawers, in private possession.

13 Trellis pattern in green and yellow
Mid-17th century
Print from wood block and watercolour
10.2 × 50.9 cm (fragment)
PROVENANCE The Old Monastery House, Turret Lane, Ipswich, Suffolk
Given by Mr Thomas Parkington (junior)
E.1735–1913 neg 51381

14 In an oval, surrounded by cherubs, the half-length figures of Charles II and Catherine of Braganza; the pattern repeated in a second oval in which the figures appear inverted
Circa 1662
Print from wood block
49.5 × 42 cm (fragment of lining paper)
PROVENANCE A contemporary oak box
Given by Mr H. Lambert Williams
E.1258–1933 neg 69994

Another version of this paper, in the Public Record Office, was found in a chest at Sulgrave Manor.

15 Wall- or lining paper with a small 'black stitch' design
Circa 1670 (?)
Print from wood block
PROVENANCE A deed box from Lacock Abbey in Wiltshire, given by C. H. Talbot to the Department of Furniture and Woodwork, VAM
Department of Furniture and Woodwork, 501–1898 neg J.726

Another specimen of this paper is to be seen in the Public Record Office, HJ, pl XXVa.

16 Wall- or lining paper with a conventional gilly flower and pomegranate design in the 'black stitch work' style
Circa 1670 (?)
Print from wood block

PROVENANCE A deed box from Lacock Abbey in Wiltshire, given by C. H. Talbot to the Department of Furniture and Woodwork, VAM
Department of Furniture and Woodwork, no 500–1898 neg J.726

This paper differs slightly in minor details from another example found in a charter box in Corpus Christi College, Oxford, possibly to be dated *circa* 1670. See A. J. B. Wace, 'Lining Papers from Corpus Christi College', *Oxoniensia* (1935), vol 2, 166 ff, fig 27; see also no 17. Two other versions of the pattern are recorded.

17 Panel of wall- or lining paper with a conventional gilly flower and pomegranate design, in the 'black stitch work' style
Circa 1670 (?)
Print from wood block
72.4 × 60.3 cm (overall size, which is composed of four printings)
PROVENANCE Removed from a leather-covered, studded coffer, with the initials *TG* and dated 1671 on the lid
Given by Mrs Helen Wace
E.693–1959 neg GJ.9208

This is a slightly cruder version of the paper found in a charter box at Corpus Christi College, Oxford. See A. J. B. Wace, *op. cit.*, fig 27; also no 16.

18 Architectural and floral motifs, alternating with a panel of leather embossed with a design of cherubs, garlands and fruits, and painted gold-bronze and white
Circa 1680
Crimson flock on a white micared background
137.3 × 106.7 cm (panel)
PROVENANCE Ivy House, Worcester Cathedral precincts
Given by the Very Reverend W. Moore Ede, Dean of Worcester
E.337–1932 neg 67816

The whole room from which these panels were taken was decorated in this way with the 2 alternating patterns. The house was built in 1679 on the site of the old Charnel House (see Valentine Green, *History and Antiquities of the City of Worcester* (1796), vol I, p 56), and these wall decorations may be ascribed to about the same date, since they were found applied directly to the unplastered bricks and are discoloured with brick dust at the back. They had been subsequently buried under a canvas lining and many layers of later papers. After these had been stripped, the flock and leather were found intact, as originally arranged, in alternate patterns, with the flock paper always

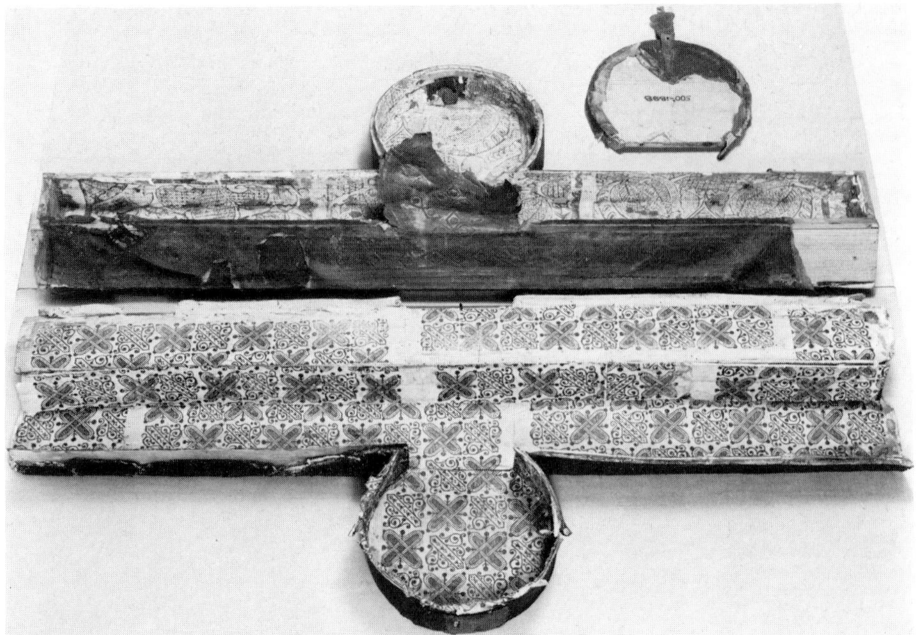

15

17

18

overlapping the leather. The flock paper is the earliest known in this country, the only other example of the same paper being at the Manor House, Saltfleet, Lincolnshire (E.2203–1925 neg 57211; see SE, pl 25, where it is wrongly dated to 1560–1600). Fragments of a very similar pattern are at Gwernhaylod (see Entwisle, 'Early Wallpapers', *Country Life* (1953), vol 114, 213, fig 3). The whole of the leather, embossed pattern as well as ground, was at one time laid with extremely thin silver foil. Over this are traces of a gold-bronze varnish, and over this in turn there is a coat of white paint, confined to the ground only. A portion of the leather was cleaned under the direction of Dr Scott of the British Museum laboratory with a solution of methylated spirit and pyradine, in order to expose some of the original silver ground.

J. W. Waterer in *Spanish Leather* (1971), p 62, pl 41, states that there is an affinity with Dutch leather patterns, but thinks that the pattern is probably a simplified English version; he dates it *circa* 1690 (?). J. Sturt's engraved trade-card for Abraham Price's warehouse (*circa* 1710–20) shows his interpretation of the flock pattern, or one very similar. See Entwisle, 'The Blew Paper Warehouse in Aldermanbury, London', *Connoisseur*, May 1950, 94; *Country Life* (1932), vol 72, 80; *Connoisseur*, October 1932, 274; Greysmith, pl 25.

19 Formalized floral design
Circa 1680 (?)

20

Print from wood block
54 × 48 cm (portion)
PROVENANCE Boots the Chemist, 14, Market Place, Kingston-upon-Thames, Surrey
Given by Boots the Chemist, Kingston-upon-Thames, Surrey
E.1003–1976 neg GF.5635

The paper bears a fleur-de-lis watermark of *circa* 1680, and the design is closely related to that of the border of a printed cotton, bearing a characteristic lace pattern of the second half of the 17th century (Department of Textiles, no 1605–1872). The building used by Boots is dated *circa* 1599. The paper was on a wooden partition wall, uncovered by subsequent decoration, and presents an unusual example of the preservation of original décor. A lining paper with the same pattern, slightly cruder in execution and with the background omitted (E.313A–1940 neg B.63), is lettered *Roger Hudson Trunk Maker, Coney Street, York*. It was found in a small wooden box and given to the Museum by the Reverend J. Harvey Bloom. It measures 36.8 × 34.3 cm (E.373–1940; E.373A–1940 neg B.63). See Jean Hamilton, 'Early English Wallpapers', *Connoisseur*, July 1977, 201, pl 1. Another example of the same pattern, with additional stencilled colouring, was found at the Shrubbery, Epsom, Surrey.

20 Design representing the Five Senses
Circa 1680
Print from wood block
33 × 42.9 cm (lining paper)
PROVENANCE A travelling trunk dated 1688 (property of Mr O. Baker)
E.1135–1931 neg 66603

This pattern was also used to line a box in the antechamber to the Jerusalem Chamber, Westminster Abbey.

19

21

22

21 Same design as no 20, re-engraved on another block with slight variations
Circa 1680
Print from wood block
32.2 × 41 cm (another portion)
PROVENANCE A travelling trunk dated 1688 (property of Mr O. Baker)
E.1136–1931 neg 66604

22 Foliate design
Circa 1685 (?)
Colour print from wood block
13.6 × 31 cm (fragment)
PROVENANCE Ramsbury Manor, Wiltshire
Given by Mr John B. Fowler
E.2230–1966 neg GJ.9209

23

28

The paper was nailed to the plaster wall beneath the Chinese wallpaper in the Chinese Room next to the saloon.

23 Stylized flowers and leaves, overprinted on a proof sheet of an edition of *The Prayer Book*
Circa 1690–1710
Print from wood block
39.5 × 51 cm (lining paper)
Given by Mr John B. Fowler
E.2232–1966 neg GJ.9220

In the Science Museum there is a box (no 1927–1150) containing a weighing balance, with the same pattern printed on a proof sheet used to cover the bottom of the box.

24

24 Conventional floral design, surmounted by a crown
Second half of 17th century
Print from wood block
38 × 29.6 cm (portion of lining paper)
Given by Mrs G. C. Arnot
E.678–1947 neg GJ.9210

25 Stylized floral pattern
Second half of 17th century
Wood block and reddish-brown flock
68.6 × 63.6 cm (portion)
PROVENANCE The King's Drawing Room, Kensington Palace
Given by Mr H. Clifford Smith, FSA
E.859–1954 neg GJ.9211 CT 8640

A modern reproduction: see no 476, note.

26 Two fragments of a pattern of a lining paper, showing the arms of the Haberdashers' Company with the initials *GM* (Guillelmus Maria), and in the

25

corners 4 figures emblematic of the Seasons
Circa 1689–1702
Print from wood block
45 × 43 cm (overall size)
Given by Colonel H. H. Mulliner
E.203, 204–1913 neg GJ.9212

Another version of this paper, with the Haberdashers' arms replaced by 3 crowns and a lion and unicorn, is at Colonial Williamsburg, USA. See also no 528. Peter Sturt lists 'The Four Seasons' among his stock, *circa* 1660.

27 Two fragments: one with a 'flame stitch' pattern on a background of trailing foliage; the other a repeat pattern of snowdrops and 2 borders with leaf and bead motifs
Last quarter of 17th century; early 19th century (fragment with borders)
Print from wood blocks and colour stencil
14 × 26.6 cm (first fragment);
4.2 × 22.9 cm (second fragment: overall size); 4 × 22 cm; 4 × 29.5 cm (borders)
PROVENANCE A 14th-century house in Faversham, Kent
Given by Mrs Joan Bygrave
E.1347, 1348–1963; E.1347 neg GJ.9213

The fragment of the late 17th-century wallpaper is similar to some found at Brympton D'Evercy, Somerset (Entwisle, pl 6). A 'flame stitch' pattern appears on an illustrated trade-card of the Blew Paper Warehouse, *circa* 1710–20.

28 Pattern of flowers, birds and groups of figures, including Diana and Actaeon, Venus and a satyr, and a figure possibly emblematic of Charity

26

27

Late 17th century
Engraving
54.3 × 38.1 cm (portion)
E.901–1924 neg 56517

See Greysmith, pl 21.

29 Repeat pattern of a woman fishing in a pond and a house in the background
Late 17th century
Print from a wood block
77.7 × 47 cm (portion of lining, or wallpaper)
PROVENANCE Found on an early 17th-century box from the Croft Lyons Bequest in the Department of Furniture and Woodwork, W.51–1926, VAM
E.405–1968 neg GE.430

This appears to be a contemporary reworking of a lining paper found in a drawer of a chest belonging to Lord Leverhulme (SE, pl 17; Greysmith, pl 13). In the background, the palings and trees are practically identical to those shown in another scene, from Colonial Williamsburg, USA, which was a companion piece to the hunting scene from Clandon Park (no 30). This companion piece shows a chinoiserie figure walking over a hill. There is obviously a common source, perhaps a painted cloth hanging, for all 3 scenes, which may have been intended to be shown in conjunction with one another, forming an early example of a panoramic paper.

29

30 Scene of a stag hunt; in the foreground a gate, an oak tree, a house and a peacock
Late 17th century
Print from a wood block
29.4 × 29.4 cm (first fragment);
30.5 × 22.2 cm (second fragment)
PROVENANCE A deed box found at Clandon Park, Surrey
Given by Mr John B. Fowler
E.2232, 2232A–1974 neg GG.5870

The same scene with variant details is shown on a wallpaper, said to have come from Aldford House (now demolished), Park Lane, London (Entwisle (1970) pl 26), and now in the Whitworth Art Gallery, Manchester. This has additional hand-colouring, as has another piece at Colonial Williamsburg, Virginia, USA, (see no 29), and also a third piece, discovered recently at The Shrubbery, Epsom, Surrey. See Greysmith, pl 31.

30

31

31 Six portions forming a repeat pattern of squirrels, peacocks, parakeets and chinoiserie figures among flowers and foliage
Circa 1700
Print from wood block and colour stencil (varnished)
250.7 × 60.4 cm (overall size)
PROVENANCE Ord House, Berwick-on-Tweed, Northumberland
E.5311–1958 neg S.489 CT 7785 (see col pl)

See Greysmith, pl 30.

32 Fragment with a floral design which is mounted on original handwoven backing
Circa 1700 (?)
Tempera
61 × 45.8 cm
PROVENANCE Lumley Castle, County Durham
Given by the Rt Hon Lord Scarborough
E.2111–1924

This paper is anterior to the restoration of the Castle by Vanbrugh in 1721. The design is nearly obliterated.

33

33 Conventional flower design in black, green and orange, apparently stencilled, on a cream ground
English or Dutch
17th century
Flock on canvas
256.6 × 81.3 cm
Given by Mr A. V. Sugden
E.3635–1932 neg 71288

See SE, pl 24 (colour), where it was tentatively attributed to Herman Schinkel of Delft (*d.* 1568?); H. Olligs, *Tapeten* (1970), vol I, fig 84, where it is designated as a Dutch production, dated second half of 17th century. (See Greysmith, pl 16, and no 623.)

34

18th Century

34 Formal pattern of flowers and acanthus leaves, in black on a white ground
Early 18th century
Print from wood block
54.1 × 40.3 cm (fragment)
PROVENANCE No 5, The Grove, Highgate, London
Given by Messrs James & Bywaters and S. Rowland Pierce
E.554–1935 neg 74095

Another slightly cruder version of this pattern, reconstructed from separate fragments, is from Whitmores, the Dorking Road, Epsom, Surrey (E.966–1963). (See Cloudesley S. Willis FSA, 'Old Houses in Epsom, Ewell and Cuddington', *Surrey Archaeological Collections* (1950), vol 51; also Greysmith, pl 20.)

35 Design of birds, fruit and flowers, on a pale blue ground
Early 18th century
Print from wood block and colour stencil
47.8 × 48.2 cm (portion)
PROVENANCE The Bell Inn, Sawbridgeworth, Hertfordshire
Given by Benskin's Watford Brewery
E.340–1914 neg 51383

A later copy of this paper, made by Swedish block-cutters, is said to be in existence (SE dates this paper *circa* 1700).

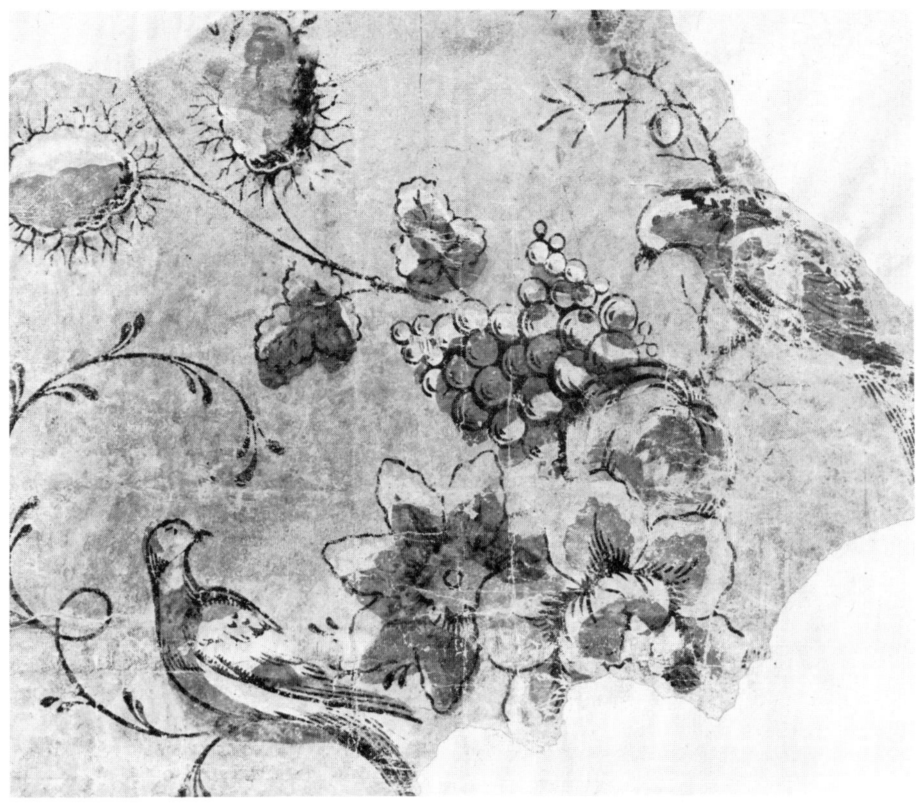

35

36

36 Three portions with a simplified pattern of oak stems and lattice work, each stamped on the back with the Excise duty stamp and numbered *127*
Early 18th century
Dark green flock
94 × 58.4 cm; 96 × 59.1 cm;
91.5 × 58.4 cm
PROVENANCE Welwick House, South Lynn, King's Lynn, Norfolk
Given by King's Lynn Museum and Art Gallery, Norfolk
E.851, 851A,B–1970; E.851B neg GE.463

The duty stamp includes the royal coat-of-arms, but the printing is too indistinct for the heraldry to be positively identified. As the stamp is of a type hitherto unrecorded and differs from the Georgian stamps, it is likely to be that used during the reign of Anne. If this is so, the paper may be dated *circa* 1714; the stamping of papers commenced on 2 August and the Queen died on 7 August in that year. See Greysmith, pl 24.

37 Two fragments with a design of birds and blossom in the Chinese style, each stamped on the back with the Georgian Excise duty stamp and *Paper J7*
Early 18th century
Print from wood block and stencil
51 × 40.5 cm; 45.1 × 31.8 cm
PROVENANCE Welwick House, South Lynn, King's Lynn, Norfolk
Given by King's Lynn Museum and Art Gallery, Norfolk
E.865–1970

The genuine Chinese papers brought over by the East India Company were exempt from import duty until 1792. The style and execution of this paper is close to that of no 49.

38 A section consisting of 13 layers of wallpaper and 1 border
Dating from the early 18th century to the second quarter of the 20th century
Flock, prints from wood block, engraved rollers etc
11.5 × 17.5 cm (overall size);
3.3 × 17.5 cm (border)
PROVENANCE Welwick House, South Lynn, King's Lynn, Norfolk
Given by the King's Lynn Museum and Art Gallery, Norfolk
E.852–864–1970

The earliest layer, a dark green flock, is a fragment of no 36.

39 Fragment with a small floral and rope design
Early 18th century
Print from wood block and stencil
12.1 × 8.9 cm
Given by Capt. R. Lane
E.1154–1930

40 Two fragments of a baroque floral pattern on a diaper background: one of the fragments used as a book cover
Early 18th century
Red flock on a red ground
27.7 × 39.3 cm; 17 × 22.9 cm
E.5967, 5968–1897

The background diaper is the same as that in no 75, but the floral pattern differs.

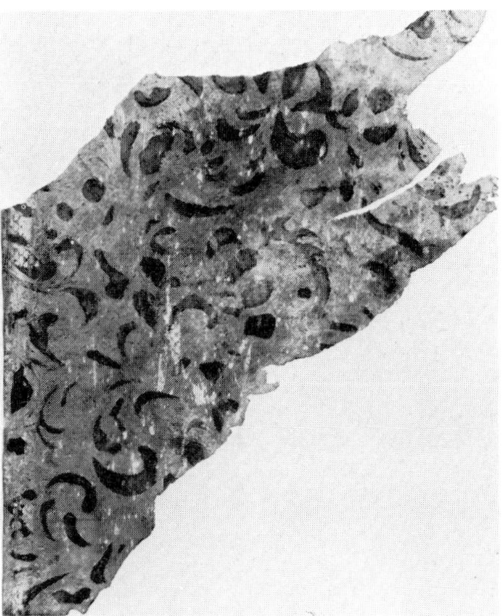

41

41 Red leaves or petals on a white ground
Early 18th century
Wood block and stencil
47.3 × 36.9 cm (fragment)
PROVENANCE No 5, The Grove, Highgate, London
Given by Messrs James & Bywaters and S. Rowland Pierce
E.555–1935 neg 74413

42

45 Pattern of flowering shrubs
Early 18th century
Print from wood block and stencil
63 × 55 cm (fragment)
PROVENANCE Hampden House, Great Missenden, Buckinghamshire
Given by the Earl of Buckinghamshire
E.886–1979 CT 7786 (see col pl, p 105)

Other fragments of this paper bear the duty stamp with *Paper J8*.

46 Portion with a pattern of a baldacchino (fruit, drapery and figures of gods and goddesses), perhaps based on a leather hanging or a tapestry border
Circa 1712 (?)
Print from wood block
PROVENANCE Lining one door of a child's wardrobe in the Department of Furniture and Woodwork, VAM
Given by Mrs Guy Trafford
Department of Furniture and Woodwork, W.36–1930 neg 65021

The wardrobe bears the name Edmund Joy and the date 1712. A piece of the same pattern was found as a wallpaper at the Royal County Hotel, Durham. (See also no 47.)

42 Red and blue flowers and foliage, on a white ground with red dot trellis
Early 18th century
Colour print from wood blocks
38.7 × 47.7 cm (fragment)
PROVENANCE No 5, The Grove, Highgate, London
Given by Messrs James & Bywaters and S. Rowland Pierce
E.556–1935 neg 74096

43 Formal pattern of flowers and leaves enclosed in ellipses and quatrefoils in white on a black ground
Early 18th century
Print from wood blocks
51.6 × 41.4 cm (fragment)
PROVENANCE No 5, The Grove, Highgate, London
Given by Messrs James & Bywaters and S. Rowland Pierce
E.553–1935 neg 74094

44 Fragment with a floral design in red and green on a white ground
Early 18th century
Print from wood blocks and colour stencil
20.6 × 17.8 cm
Given by the WM
E.1558–1934

43

46

47 Portion with a pattern in the chinoiserie style, of flowering trees, birds, animals and a hunter
Circa 1712 (?)
Print from wood block and stencil
PROVENANCE Lining one door of a child's wardrobe in the Department of Furniture and Woodwork, VAM
Given by Mrs Guy Trafford
Department of Furniture and Woodwork, W.36–1930 neg 65021

On the other door of this wardrobe is another piece (see no 46).

48 Chinoiserie design
Circa 1720
Red-brown flock
196.8 × 106.7 cm (panel)
PROVENANCE Hurlcote Manor, Easton Neston, Towcester, Northamptonshire
E.677–1921 neg 71289 CT 975 (see col pl, p 106)

Another fragment of this flock from Hurlcote Manor is stamped on the back with the Georgian Excise duty stamp. The condition of the Manor is known back as far as 1740, at which date this paper was already on the walls. See SE, pl 26; Entwisle, pl 13; Greysmith, pl 26.

49 Bird and flower design in the Chinese style; stamped on the back of each sheet with the Georgian Excise duty stamp in brown and *Paper 5*
Circa 1720
Print from wood block and colour stencil
62.3 × 122 cm (portion)
PROVENANCE Haigh Hall, Bretton, Yorkshire
Given by the WM
E.1554–1934 neg B.65

See *JDA* (1929), vol XLIX, 26. A similar paper is no 37, from Welwick House.

50 Portion imitating damask with a conventional floral pattern in yellow on a dark red and buff ground; stamped on the back with the Georgian Excise duty stamp
First quarter of 18th century

49

Colour print from wood block and flock
94 × 61 cm
PROVENANCE Culham House, near Abingdon, Berkshire, built 1710
Given by Mr G. Houghton-Brown
E.616–1939 neg GJ.9214

51 Fragment of a ceiling paper with a design of square and oblong panels, each containing formalized flower and foliate motifs, connected by bands of laurel and a border with a formal flower pattern; stamped with the Georgian Excise duty stamp and *Paper 8*
First quarter of 18th century
Print from wood block and colour stencils
56 × 46 cm (overall size); 5.3 × 42 cm (border)
Given by Mrs Joan Bygrave
E.1345, 1346–1963; E.1345 CT 7787 (see col pl, p 107)

As the duty stamp bears the initials *GR*, the paper cannot be earlier than 1714. It is stated by the donor to have come from a 14th-century house in Faversham, Kent.

52 Ten fragments with a design of conventional flowers
First quarter of 18th century
Colour print from wood blocks
Various sizes
PROVENANCE A house at Guildford, Surrey
Given by Dr G. C. Williamson
E.2150–1929

53 Leaves and flowers between vertical bands of small motifs, printed in white,

50

grey and black, and green ground
Circa 1730
Colour print from wood blocks
24.8 × 26 cm (fragment)
PROVENANCE Used to line a chest in the Bishop of London's Registry, St Paul's Cathedral, London
Given by the Reverend J. Harvey Bloom
E.4590–1920

A similar paper is no 55, from St Nicholas' Rectory, Shepperton, Middlesex.

54 Thirteen portions forming a continuous pattern with a floral and foliate design on a background of diaper pattern, with a chinoiserie strapwork border; each stamped on the back with the Georgian Excise duty stamp
Circa 1730
Red and gold flock
153.7 × 103.6 cm (overall size); 5.3 × 25 cm (border)
PROVENANCE St John's College, Cambridge
Given by the Master and Fellows of St John's College, Cambridge
E.3868–1953

The paper was found beneath a later paper (no 113). It was taken from a panelled wall, beside and above a doorway in a room in the College. The design closely resembles a red flock paper installed at Webb House, Wethersfield, Connecticut, USA in 1781. See C. L. Frangiamore, *Wallpapers in Historic Preservation* (1977, Washington), p. 18.

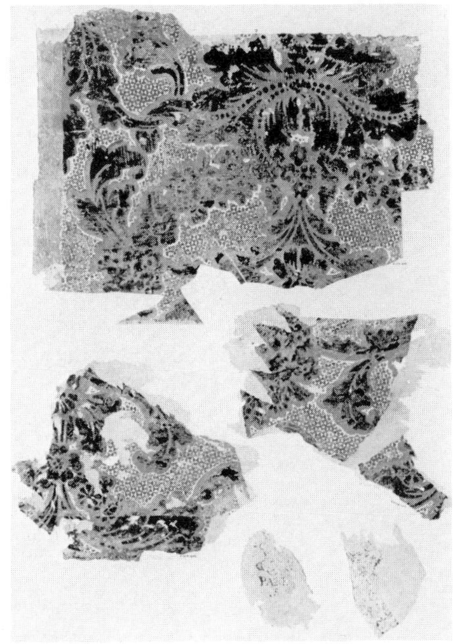

55

55 Three fragments with an Italian damask design, with a superimposed diaper pattern; each stamped on the back with the Georgian Excise duty stamp and *Paper [J ?] 5*
Circa 1730
Colour print from wood blocks
34.6 × 45.7 cm; 24.2 × 27.3 cm; 22.2 × 28 cm
PROVENANCE St Nicholas' Rectory, Shepperton, Middlesex
Given by the Reverend H. Scholfield
E.523, 523A, B–1956 neg GH. 6140

This paper was taken from a bay in a front room on the first floor of the Rectory. Above it was found the paper and border (no 93). The papers and borders (nos 55, 93, 111, 155, 181, 215, 282, 332, 434, 440) were superimposed upon each other in this room. See also no 53.

56 Portion with a damask pattern: formalized flowers and foliage, and pine-cones, within a trellis; stamped on the back with the Georgian Excise duty stamp and *Paper 4*
Circa 1730–40
Print from wood block and stencil
46 × 55 cm
PROVENANCE A cupboard at Wichenford Court, Worcestershire
Given by Colonel Patrick G. Britten
E.1082–1978 CT 7789 (see col pl, p 108)

Wichenford Court, originally the property of the Washbourne family, was sold in 1712 to Edmund Skinner, who later became Sheriff of Worcestershire. The house came into the possession of the donor's family in 1856.

57 Two fragments with an alternating half-drop pattern of single formalized flowers, within a trellis made up of small diamond shapes, printed in blue, black and white on a grey ground; E.970 with matching border affixed; E.969 with the Georgian Excise duty stamp and *Paper 8*
Circa 1730–40
Prints from wood blocks
26.5 × 38 cm (first fragment); 20 × 16.5 cm (overall size of second fragment); 4.6 × 15 cm (border)
PROVENANCE Whitehall, Malden Road, Cheam, Surrey
Given by the Greater London Council
E.969, 970–1977 neg 5859

See also no 220.

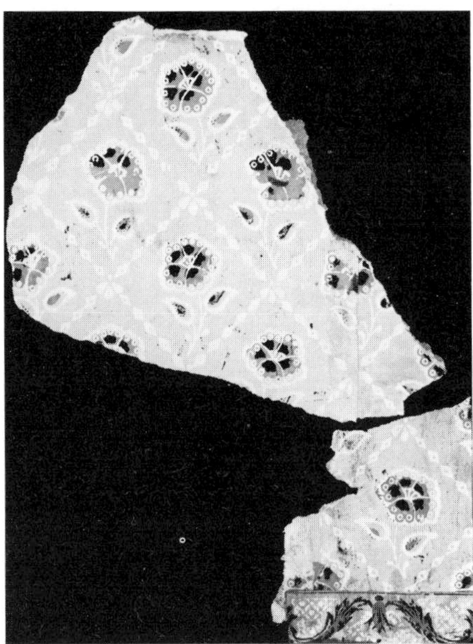

57

58 Portion (3 sheets joined) with a baroque floral pattern
Circa 1734
Flock and stencil (?) on stained paper
127 × 42 cm
PROVENANCE The south-east side bedroom, Clandon Park, Surrey
Given by Mr John B. Fowler
E.31–1971 (see col pl, p 117)

Lengths of the same pattern are at Withepole House (Christchurch Mansion), Ipswich (SE, pl 27). Clandon Park, which was built *circa* 1735, belongs to the National Trust.

59 Design of conventional foliage
Circa 1735
Green and yellow flock
171.5 × 59.8 cm (panel)
PROVENANCE The offices of HM Privy Council
Given by HM Office of Works
E.3595–1922 neg M.1202

59

60 Panel with two and a half lengths of a large design of conventional flowers and foliage
Circa 1735
Red flock in two shades
185.5 × 153.8 cm
PROVENANCE The offices of HM Privy Council
Given by HM Office of Works
E.3594–1922 neg 56578

This paper appears to be identical in pattern with the flock paper which was formerly hung in the Queen's Drawing Room at Hampton Court Palace. This was removed when the mural paintings by Antonio Verrio were found underneath in 1899. An Italian brocade of this design is in the Department of Textiles, VAM, no 715–1864. A derivative pattern is no 78. A reproduction based on this design, entitled 'The Earl of Onslow', was produced by Arthur Sanderson & Sons Ltd in 1907. See *Decorators' and Painters' Magazine* (1907).

Flowering shrubs. English, early 18th century (no 45)

A ceiling paper. English, first quarter of 18th century (no 51)

(*opposite*) Chinoiserie design. English, *circa* 1720 (no 48)

A damask pattern. English, *circa* 1730–40 (no 56)

60

61

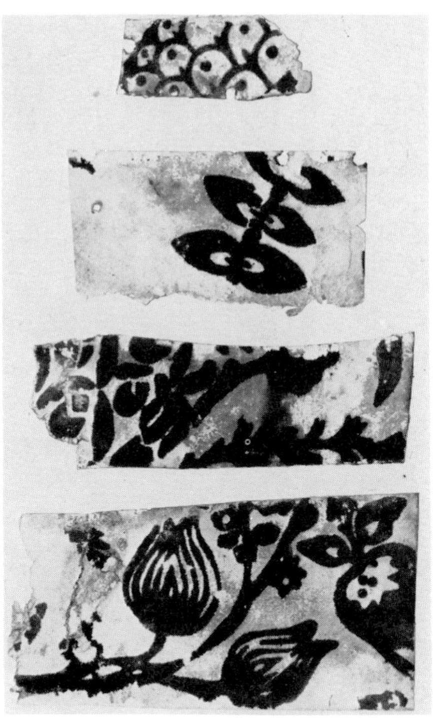

62

61 Two fragments of the same pattern, stamped on the back with the Georgian Excise duty stamp; E.685 stamped with *Paper J9*
Circa 1735
Crimson flock
42.5 × 56 cm; 74.3 × 45.7 cm
PROVENANCE Christchurch Mansion, Ipswich, Suffolk
Given by the Ipswich Corporation through Mr J. S. Corder
E.239–1918 neg 51385; E.685–1918 neg 51386

See Oliver Brackett, 'English Wallpapers of the 18th century', *Connoisseur*, October 1918, 83–88.

62 Four fragments from the same pattern as no 65
Circa 1740
Green flock mounted on half imperial size sheet
Various sizes
PROVENANCE St Edmund Hall, Oxford
Given by Mr A. B. Emden
E.2523–1929 neg 71284

63 Several fragments of the same pattern and a border of key and flower pattern
Circa 1735
Green flock
Various sizes; 5 cm (depth of border)
PROVENANCE The former State Dining Room, Clandon Park, West Clandon, Surrey
Given by Mr John B. Fowler
E.2210, 2210A–1974

This paper was found behind the door heads during the restoration of Clandon Park between 1969 and 1971. The door heads were probably added on the accession of Arthur George, 3rd Earl of Onslow. A border of the same pattern in red flock, from the State Bedroom at Clandon Park, is E.2234–1974.

64

64 Design of carnations, daisies and other flowers, in blue and pink, on a white ground
1740
Colour print from wood blocks
22 × 25.2 cm (fragment)
PROVENANCE A room at Horsenden Manor, Buckinghamshire
Given by Miss A. F. Oakes
E.13–1934 neg GJ.2915

65

65 Baroque floral and leaf pattern and a border of Greek key pattern; the paper, originally attached to the walls by nails alone, stamped on the back with the Georgian Excise duty stamp and *Paper J4*
Circa 1740
Green flock
124.5 × 111.2 cm (overall size of portion)
PROVENANCE The lumber room between the Hall and the Chapel at All Souls' College, Oxford
Given by the Warden and Fellows of All Souls College, Oxford
E.288–1925 neg H.932

See Greysmith, pl 22. This pattern was reproduced by Watts & Co. as a block print entitled 'Pear'.

66

66 Pattern of red, green and black flowers on white grounds
Circa 1740
Colour prints from wood block and stencil
14.3 × 72.3 cm (first fragment);
11.5 × 55.2 cm (second fragment)
PROVENANCE Thomas Hearne's Room, St Edmund Hall, Oxford
Given by Mr A. B. Emden
E.284–1933 neg 68994

See Entwisle, *LH*, pls 27, 28.

67 54341

67 Complete paper hangings of the room of a house, with a design of bird and plant forms in the Chinese style
Circa 1740
Tempera
171.5 cm (height)
PROVENANCE The Berkeley family, Berkeley House, Long Street, Wotton-under-Edge, Gloucestershire
Given by F. C. Harper
Department of Furniture and Woodwork, W.93–1924

negs 54339–54342

The original trelliswork border was replaced at the end of the 18th century by another of festoons of flowers. The usual Georgian Excise duty stamp was discovered on the backs of the lengths whilst they were being remounted. The stamps were lettered and numbered *Paper 1,4,5*. See Entwisle, p 22, who also illustrates a similar example from Dalemain, Cumberland (pl 23).

67 54339

67 54340

68

68 Two fragments with a floral design in stripes
Circa 1740
Print from wood blocks
21 × 33 cm (overall size)
PROVENANCE Formerly lining a cupboard in the donor's possession
Given by Mrs Curgenven
E.2904, 2905–1908 neg 32204

69 Daily life of the Chinese
Circa 1740
Tempera and block-printed foliage
218.5 × 104.9 cm (panel)
PROVENANCE Longnor Hall, Shrewsbury, Salop
Given by Major E. R. Trevor Corbett
E.990–1921 neg B.120

The design has been painted on English paper, which has been laid down on wood. The painting is restored direct on the wood in several places where the paper has been destroyed. See John Cornforth, 'Longnor Hall, Shropshire: Part II', *Country Life* (1964), 395, pl 8.

70 Pattern of formalized foliage, flowers and pomegranate on a grey ground scattered with mica; stamped on the back with the Georgian Excise duty stamp
Circa 1740
Print from wood block and yellow flock
94.6 × 98.4 cm (portion)
PROVENANCE Fairford Park, Gloucestershire
Given by Mr Derek Sherborn
E.350–1955 neg GJ.9216

69

70

71

73

71 Floral design stamped on the back with the Georgian Excise duty stamp and *Paper* [*?J 8*]
Circa 1740–50
Green and red flock and block on a mica ground
41.4 × 46.1 cm (portion)
Given by Arthur Sanderson & Sons' Branch of the WM
E.1963–1934 neg GJ.9217

72 Floral design in red on a white background
1749
Colour print from wood block
27.3 × 20.3 cm (fragment)
Given by the WM
E.1556–1934 neg GJ.9218

73 Lining paper with a trellis pattern in pin-print, each segment containing a small flower; overprinted on a proof sheet of an edition of Ovid's *Metamorphoses*
Circa 1750
Print from wood block
14.1 × 38.1 cm
Given by the Reverend J. Harvey Bloom
E.371–1940 neg B.62

74 Three fragments with a pomegranate and pineapple pattern; E.237 stamped on the back with the Georgian Excise duty stamp
Circa 1750–80
Yellow flock
55 × 57 cm; 76.8 × 54 cm; 13.7 × 55.6 cm
PROVENANCE Eagle House, Bathford, Somerset
Given by Miss Margaret Lester-Garland
E.237, 237A, B–1968; E.237 neg GJ.9225

Eagle House was built *circa* 1750 in the style of John Wood the Elder. It should not be confused with Eagle House at Batheaston, which John Wood built for himself in 1727.

74

75 Large floral pattern on a background of diaper
First half of 18th century
Green flock and wood block
155 × 73.7 cm (portion)
PROVENANCE Longnor Hall, Shrewsbury, Salop
Given by Major Trevor Corbett
E.1112–1924 neg 57212

This paper was taken from the back of a screen, the front of which was covered with Chinese paper (no 655). Another portion is Circ. 956–1924.
See also no 40.

72

75

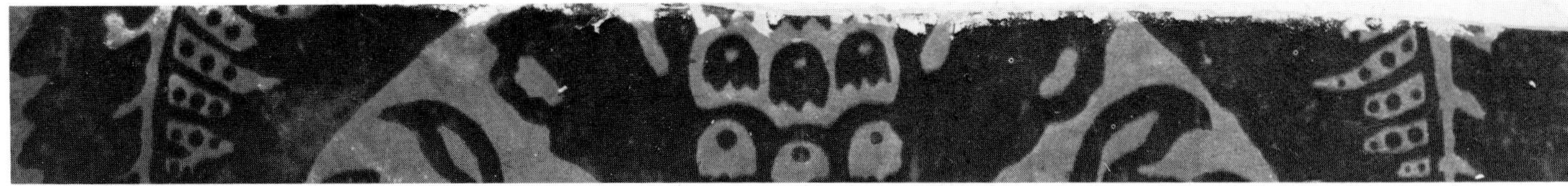

78

76 Four fragments with a foliate pattern, mounted on canvas
First half of 18th century
Prints from a wood block in green
29.5 × 29 cm (overall size)
PROVENANCE The Green Drawing Room, Clandon Park, Surrey
Given by Mr John B. Fowler
E.185–1972

Greysmith, pl 2 (colour), reproduces the panels of this paper from Clandon Park, and erroneously describes them as flock. The Georgian Excise duty stamp, with *Paper J9*, is on the back of samples of the same paper.

77 Portions (4 sheets joined) with a foliate design and a border of Greek key pattern; stamped 3 times on the back with the Georgian Excise duty stamp
First half of 18th century
Green flock
139.8 × 63.5 cm (overall size); 4.5 cm (depth of border)
PROVENANCE The attic storey of Clandon Park, Surrey
Given by Mr John B. Fowler
E.704, 704A–1970

Another sample of this paper is E.184–1972

78 Pomegranate design
First half of 18th century
Crimson flock
7 × 56.5 cm (fragment)
Given by Mr John B. Fowler
E.2234–1966 neg GJ.9219

The derivation of this pattern would seem to be that of the flock from HM Privy Council Offices (see nos 59, 60), so it may be of a later date.

79 Fragment and a border with a design of stylized leaves and branches; stamped twice on the back with the Georgian Excise duty stamp
First half of 18th century
58.4 × 102.9 cm (overall size); 5.1 × 43.2 cm (border)
PROVENANCE The Holly Trees, Colchester, Essex
Given by the Colchester and Essex Museum
E.517, 517A–1964

79 E.1452–1929

80

The Holly Trees, which was built *circa* 1716, was altered in 1748. The main panel appears to be a crude imitation of the Chinese wallpapers fashionable in the early 18th century. A larger sample of this paper is E.1452–1929 neg 72929; it measures 193 × 113 cm with a border of 4.5 × 113 cm. See H. Jenkinson, 'A Recently Discovered Wallpaper in Colchester', *Essex Archaeological Society. Transactions* (1930), vol 19; see also Greysmith, pl 4 (colour).

80 Pineapple design, in black and white on grey
Mid-18th century
Colour print from wood blocks
45.7 × 101.5 cm (fragment)
PROVENANCE A room in Sir Joshua Reynolds' house, Leicester Square, London, demolished early in 1937
Given by Mr Percy W. Lovell
E.468–1937 neg B.60

H. Olligs, *Tapeten*, vol I, shows a French silk hanging of *circa* 1725 with a not dissimilar design.

81 Pattern of scrolling leaves and formalized floral motifs, within a cartouche, on a background of diaper and fragments of stamped gilt paper superimposed
Mid-18th century
Yellow flock
35.3 × 35.9 cm (portion)
Given by Mr James Ivory
E.2207–1929 neg 62276

82 Pattern of flowers and foliage interspersed with parrots and cats; a border pasted on
Mid-18th century
Colour print from wood blocks and (for the cat only) engraving
182.8 × 110.6 cm (overall size); 4.5 × 111 cm (border)
PROVENANCE The Chantry, Dursley, Gloucestershire, a house once belonging to the Vizard family
Given by Mr H. Hickling
E.1440–1925 neg 56519

The cat is an enlarged copy, printed in reverse, of 'A Cat Sleeping', an engraving by Cornelius Visscher (W. Smith, *A Catalogue of Works of Cornelius Visscher* (1864), Bungay, no 46).

83 Fragments from the above paper, one stamped on the back with the Georgian Excise duty stamp and *Paper J 4*
Mid-18th century
Various sizes
Given by Mr H. Hickling
E.628–1925

See Introduction, p 17

84 Portion with a floral pattern, a fox and a bird on a blue ground; stamped on the back with the Georgian Excise duty stamp and *Paper* [*8* ?]
Mid-18th century
Colour print from wood blocks
48.2 × 33 cm
Given by Walpole Brothers
E.546–1928

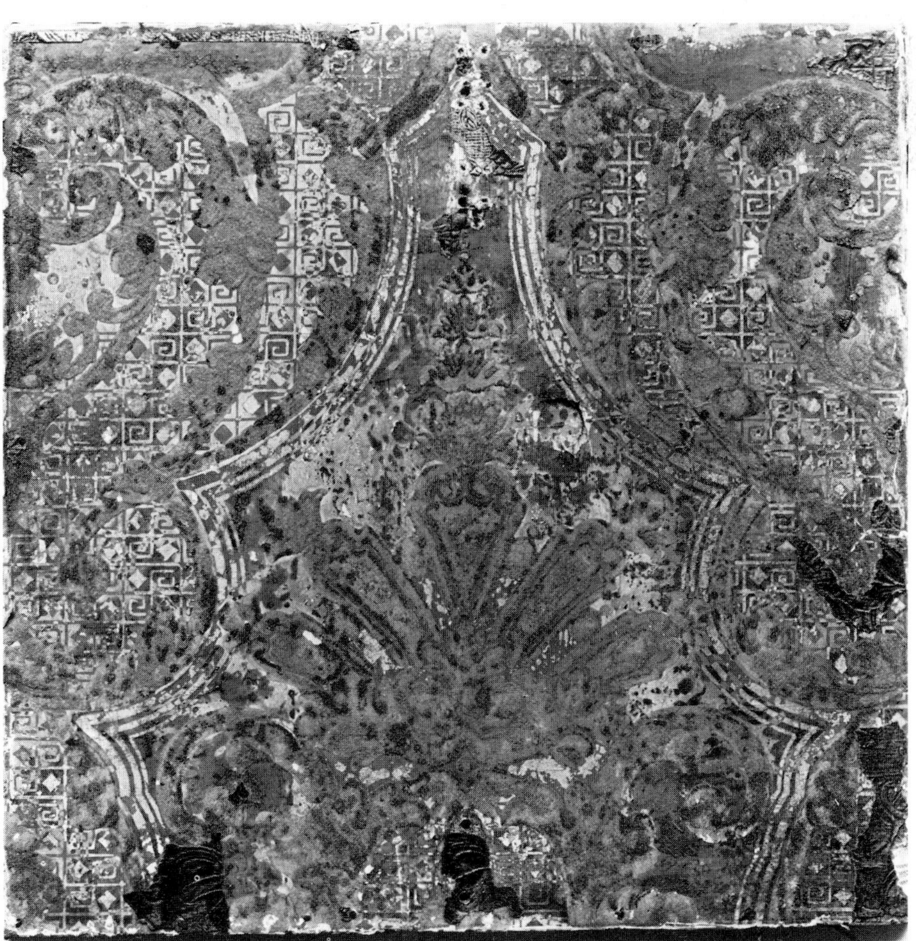

81

82

85 Portion with a repeated chinoiserie pattern of blue vases from which issue branches of flowering trees; on one branch, a bird
Mid-18th century
Body colour
90.5 × 184.8 cm
PROVENANCE A house in Twickenham
Given by Mr Noel P. W. Viner Brady
E.2789–1929

86 Stylized floral design on a green background
Mid-18th century
Gold flock
22 × 32.8 cm (fragment)
Given by Mr John B. Fowler
E.2233–1966 neg GJ.9221

87 Portion (3 pieces joined) with a pattern of roses, carnations, dahlias and other flowers, some in vases, linked by a foliate rococo motif; stamped on the back with the Georgian Excise duty stamp
Mid-18th century
Colour print from wood blocks

86

68.5 × 120 cm (overall size); 5.3 × 120 cm (border)
PROVENANCE A recently demolished house in the High Street, Brentford, Middlesex
Given by Mr John B. Fowler
E.2296, 2296A–1966 CT 6586 (see col pl, p 118)

88 Two fragments joined, forming part of a design with formalized floral motifs within rectilinear and curvilinear borders, on a background of 2 different diaper patterns
Mid-18th century
Colour print from wood blocks
28 × 8.9 cm (overall size)
PROVENANCE Skipton Castle, Yorkshire
Given by Mr Wilfred Fattorini
E.2662–1962 neg GJ.9226

89 Three fragments: 2 with a design of trees within circular medallions, the

88

(*opposite*) A flock wallpaper. English, *circa* 1734 (no 58)

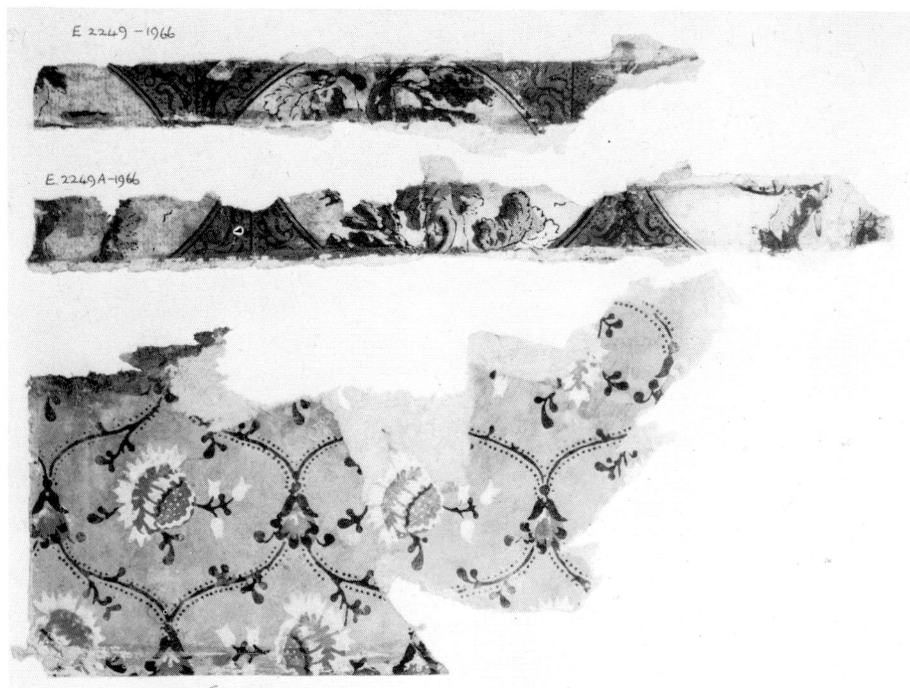

89

third with a design of stylized sprigs of flowers within ovals formed by the stems
First two fragments, mid-18th century; third fragment, 19th century
Colour prints from wood blocks
4 × 23.5 cm; 3.5 × 30.8 cm; 14 × 25 cm
PROVENANCE The back basement of No 44, Berkeley Square, London
Given by Mr John B. Fowler
E.2249, 2249A, 2250–1966 neg GJ.9222

90

90 Portion with a design of an elaborate gateway and floral decoration, together with a border pasted below
Mid to late 18th century
Colour print from wood blocks
87.6 × 55.9 cm (overall size); 4.5 × 54.5 cm (border)
Given by Mr Francis Harper
E.4474–1923

This paper was formerly thought to be in the style of J. B. Jackson.

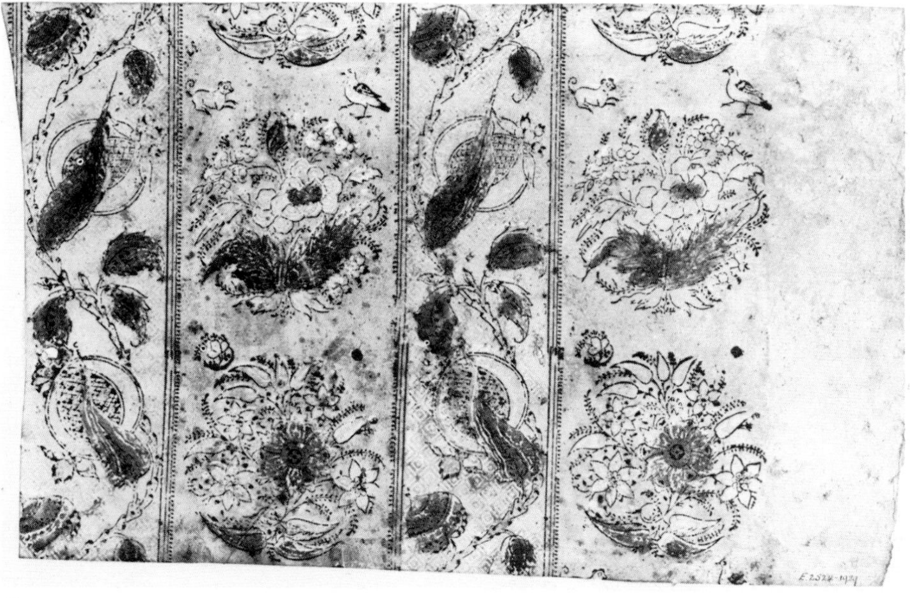

91

91 Pattern of pomegranates, leaves, a dog and a bird, within vertical bands
Circa 1760
Print from a wood block and stencil
26.4 × 43 cm (portion)
PROVENANCE St Edmund's Hall, Oxford
Given by Mr. A. B. Emden
E.2524–1929 neg 71290

92

92 Formal floral design on a diapered ground; stamped on the back with the Georgian Excise duty stamp and *Paper 4*
Circa 1760
Yellow flock and wood block
57 × 54 cm (portion)
Given by Arthur Sanderson & Sons' Branch of the WM
E.1961–1934 neg GJ.9223

93 Portion showing a design of classical ruins, birds and flowers, with chinoiserie borders (2); stamped 3 times on the back with the Georgian Excise duty stamp and *lo bs 52* (?)

(*opposite*) Floral pattern with vases and rococo motifs. English, mid-18th century (no 87)

Circa 1760
Print from wood block and stencil
155 × 118.2 cm; 3.8 × 82.6 cm; 3.8 × 127 cm (borders)
PROVENANCE St Nicholas' Rectory, Shepperton, Middlesex
Given by the Reverend H. Scholfield
E.524, 525–1956

The paper was taken from a bay in a front room on the first floor of the Rectory. The wallpapers and borders (nos 55, 93, 111, 155, 181, 215, 332, 434, 440) were superimposed upon each other in this room. This unusual stamp numbering is also to be found on no 104, dated *circa* 1770.

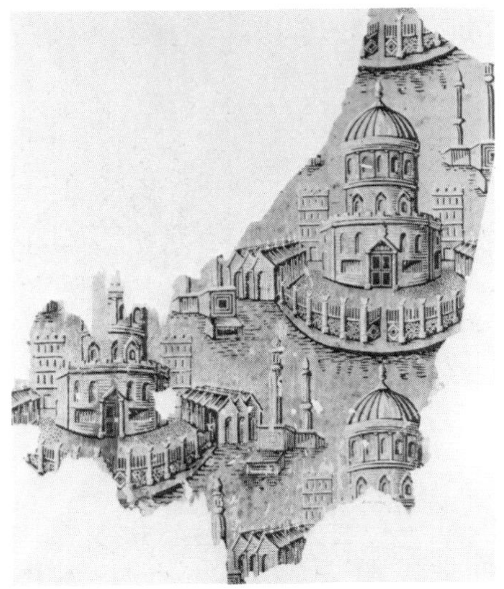

94

94 Architectural design reminiscent of the Radcliffe Camera, Oxford, in brown and white on a buff ground
Circa 1760
Colour print from wood blocks
54.6 × 49.5 cm (portion)
PROVENANCE Norwood House, Milton Regis, Kent
Given by Mr C. O. Masters
E.12–1934 neg GJ.9224

See *JDA* (1933), vol LIII, 86.

95 Portion and 2 smaller pieces showing repeat sections of the same design: building on rising ground with a fence before it, a hound killing a hare, a bird, flowers and foliage; E.2975B stamped on the back with the Georgian Excise duty stamp and *Paper J*
Circa 1760
Print from wood block and colour stencil
74.5 × 54.3 cm (portion); 69.3 × 49.8 cm; 48.3 × 45.8 cm
PROVENANCE No 44, Lincoln's Inn Fields, London
Given by the President of the Royal College of Surgeons
E.2795, 2795A, B–1948 neg G.59

95

96 Three portions, in different colourways, with spot patterns (wall- or lining papers)
Circa 1760
Colour prints from wood blocks
57.5 × 47 cm (approximately for each)
Given by Mr Francis Harper
E.4475–4477–1923

97 Vase with flowers, bird and insect ornaments, in the Chinese style
Circa 1769
Etching, coloured by hand
83·2 × 90·2 cm (panel)
Given by Messrs Green and Abbott
E.2001–1919 neg 49550

97

100

This paper is from a set, one of which is lettered *Accordg to Act of Parlt Decr 1st 1769*. Other examples of paper in this style, and in the style of no 98, are at the London Museum. At the Whitworth Art Gallery, Manchester, is a copy of the design, probably made by the donors.

98 Man on a camel talking to a boy with a greyhound on a leash, in the Chinese style
Circa 1769
Etching, coloured by hand
83·2 × 90·2 cm
Given by Miss Violet M. Morley
E.1852–1919 neg 51387 CT 6585 (see col pl, p 135)

See SE, pl 60 (colour).

99 Archway with garlands of flowers over a semicircular colonnade of Greek pillars, with a vase of flowers in the foreground, on a yellow ground; stamped on the back with the Georgian Excise duty stamp and *Paper 4*
Circa 1769
Chiaroscuro print from wood blocks
105 × 53.4 cm
PROVENANCE Left over from the decoration in 1769 of the Old Manor, Bourton-on-the-Water, Gloucestershire
E.964–1926 CT 7790 (see col pl, p 136)

See SE (colour frontispiece) where it is attributed to the firms of Bromwich of Ludgate Hill, or Spinnage of Cockspur Street.

100 Design of landscape vignettes, in foliated scroll borders imitating stucco work, on a yellow ground; stamped on the back with the Georgian Excise duty stamp and *Paper 4*
Circa 1769
Chiaroscuro print from wood blocks
74.3 × 54 cm
PROVENANCE Left over from the decoration in 1769 of the Old Manor, Bourton-on-the-Water, Gloucestershire
E.965–1926 neg 57511

See SE, pl 39A.

101

101 Flying angel trumpeter, in a circular border imitating stucco work, on a grey ground
Circa 1769
Chiaroscuro print from wood blocks
53.3 × 53.3 cm (portion of ceiling paper)
PROVENANCE Left over from the decoration in 1769 of the Old Manor, Bourton-on-the-Water, Gloucestershire
E.966–1926 neg 59578

See SE, p. 39B.

102 Panel, made up of 4 pieces joined together, of unused paper with pastoral scenes between flowering branches; stamped 5 times on the back with the Georgian Excise duty stamp and *Paper 5*
Circa 1770
Colour print from wood blocks and stencils
235.6 × 59.1 cm
PROVENANCE Left over from the decoration, in 1776, of a house at Williton, Somerset
Given by Miss E. E. G. Welch
E.1852–1938 neg B.66

103 Flower and ribbon pattern in red, grey and white, on a yellow ground; stamped twice on the back with the Georgian Excise duty stamp
Circa 1770
Colour print from wood blocks
80 × 57.2 cm (portion)
Given by the WM
E.1559–1934 neg J.1152

102

Another piece of this paper is E.2138–1913, which dates from the first half of the 19th century, and was probably printed from the old blocks. See SE, pl 68.

104 Two fragments with a design of panels, framed in foliated scroll work, containing architectural pastiches; each stamped on the back with the Georgian Excise duty stamp *lo bs 30*(?)
Circa 1770
Chiaroscuro prints from wood blocks on a red ground
64.1 × 44.3 cm; 40.9 × 46 cm
PROVENANCE A house at Wallbridge, Stroud, Gloucestershire
Given by Mr David Verey
E.49–1971; E.50–1971 neg GG.5871 CT 8461

Another paper which bears this unusual duty stamp is no 93, dated *circa* 1760.

105 Two portions of a ceiling paper with an architectural pattern in the gothic style; E.91 stamped with the Georgian Excise duty stamp and *Paper J*
Circa 1775
Print from wood block and stencil
55.9 × 52.7 cm; 50 × 56.4 cm
PROVENANCE Stubbers, North Ockendon, Essex
Given by Miss Marjorie Russell
E.91–1937 neg B.64; E.92–1937

104

105

106 Diaper design of formalized flower and leaf motifs; stamped on the back with the Georgian Excise duty stamp
Circa 1780
Green flock on a green ground
44.5 × 24.6 cm (portion)
Given by Arthur Sanderson & Sons' Branch of the WM
E.1962–1934 neg GJ.9228

Another piece of this flock, with the duty stamp on the back and *J8*, from a room on the top floor of Uppark, West Sussex, is E.2235–1974.

107 Flowers, cable pattern and quatrefoil motifs
Circa 1786
Colour print from wood blocks
5.4 × 26 cm (border)

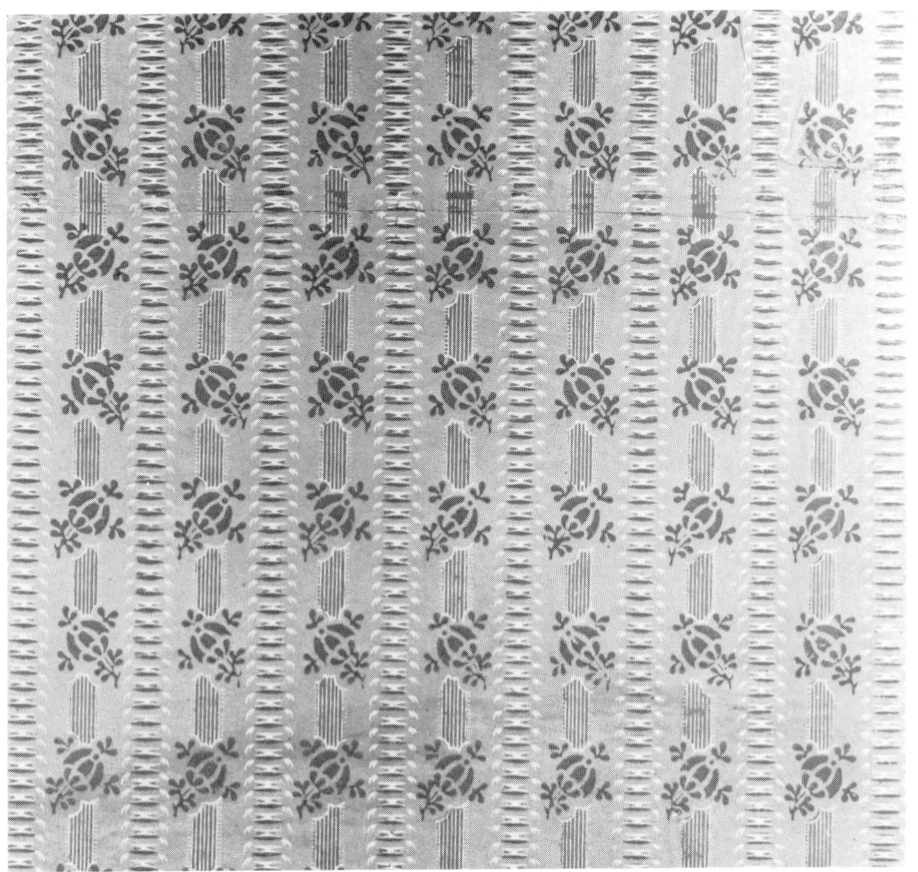

103

106

PROVENANCE Admiralty House, Whitehall, London
Given by Sir Vincent Baddeley, KCB
E.2304–1924 neg GJ.9229

108 Black and red floral design on a green ground, used as border to a gothic scenic paper
Circa 1786
Colour print from wood blocks
5.8 × 64.8 cm (portion)
Given by the WM
E.1560–1934 neg GJ.9230

109 Exotic flowers and leaves; stamped on the back with the Georgian Excise duty stamp and *Paper L*

110

Circa 1790–1800
Pen and ink and watercolour
152.4 × 53.4 cm (portion)
E.3885–1920 neg 51387

J. G. Crace noted that this paper was not printed, and suggested that an accurate repeat may have been worked out with tracing paper. It has been attributed to John Sherringham or the Eckhardt brothers. SE, pl 56 (colour); Entwisle, *LH*, pl 33 (colour); Greysmith, pl 9 (colour). A printed paper with the same serial letter *L* after the duty stamp is no 166. Another example of the same design is in the Cooper Union Museum, New York.

110 Fragment with a pattern of vertical and horizontal stripes on a pink ground, containing oblong panels showing deer, alternating with square panels showing symbols of the chase; also 3 fragments from margins; with a frame-type Excise duty stamp *2L 1562 72 62 1794; 2L*

109

107

108

112

15617 (rest cut off); Georgian Excise duty stamp *Charged on Paper 34 Stained* and *First Account Taken*
Circa 1794
Colour prints from wood blocks
24.8 × 72.4 cm (fragment); various sizes (margin fragments)
PROVENANCE Cranford House, Middlesex
Given by the Borough of Heston and Isleworth
E.1244–1937 neg GJ.9231

111 Four fragments with a foliate design; each with a frame-type Excise duty stamp truncated *66 57* (?) . . . *1250* and date *98*
1798
Print from wood block
Various sizes
PROVENANCE St Nicholas' Rectory, Shepperton, Middlesex
Given by the Reverend H. Scholfield
E.526, 526A–C–1956

This paper was taken from above the fireplace in a front room on the first floor of the Rectory. The wallpapers and borders (nos 55, 93, 111, 155, 181, 215, 282, 332, 434, 440) were superimposed upon each other in this room.

112 Lining paper with a floral pattern in colours and gold; lettered *B. Moore Newgate Street London 1763*
1763
Print from wood blocks
32 × 38 cm
Given by Miss Helen Freeman
E.1972–1927 neg 77387

Presumably this is Benjamin Moore, who received a premium from the Society of Arts for the introduction of the manufacture of embossed paper to this country (SE, p 134).

113 Portion with a trailing floral design on a background of diaper pattern; stamped on the back with the Georgian Excise duty stamp
Late 18th century
Print from wood blocks
55.9 × 53.7 cm
PROVENANCE St John's College, Cambridge
Given by the Master and Fellows of St

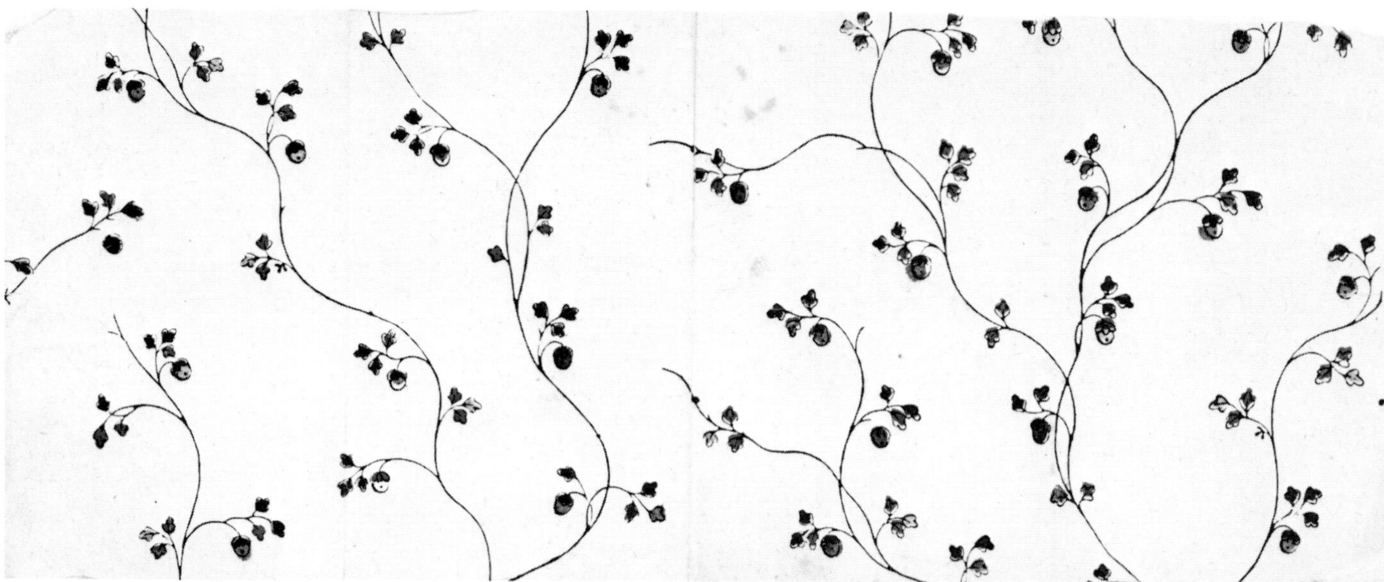

114

John's College, Cambridge
E.3869–1953

This paper was superimposed upon an earlier paper (*circa* 1730, no 54). It was taken from a panelled wall, on one side and above a doorway, in a room in the College.

114 Trailing fruit and leaves; inscribed in ink on the back *Brook Great Queen Street N 61* (the rest illegible) and stamped with the Georgian Excise duty stamp and *Paper J3*
Last quarter of 18th century
Print from wood block and stencil
22 × 53.7 cm (portion)
Given by Mr E. Cursley
E. 192–1955 neg GJ.9232

This portion was produced by John Boover Brook, a paper stainer of 61, Great Queen Street, Lincoln's Inn Fields. The manufacturer's name appears in a London directory for the year 1783. Presumably he is connected in some way with John Brook of 39, Great Queen Street, who appears in the 1769 directory.

115 Trailing blue flowers and a border with a simplified cable pattern; stamped twice on the back with the Georgian Excise duty stamp and *Paper J*
Last quarter of 18th century
Print from wood block and stencil
46.1 × 38 cm (overall size of fragment)
PROVENANCE Uppark, West Sussex
Given by Mrs Jean Meade-Fetherstonhaugh
E.797–1969 neg GG. 5872

115

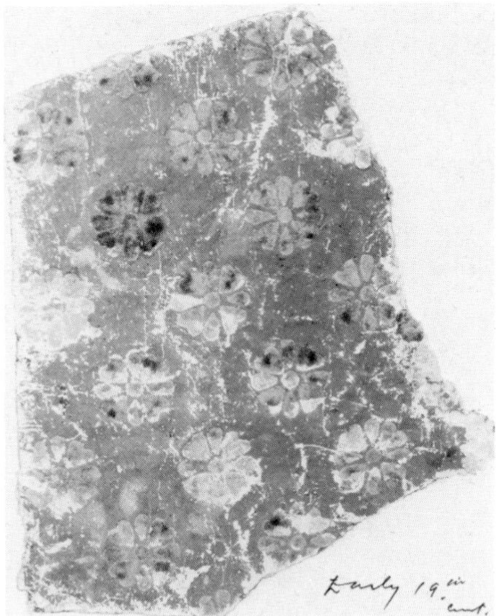

116

116 Stylised roses
Last quarter of 18th century
Flock on a distemper ground
25.5 × 20.8 cm (fragment)
PROVENANCE Strawberry House, formerly the Rectory, Barnes, Surrey
Given by Mr John B. Fowler
E.2248–1966 neg GJ.9233

The paper was superimposed upon no 145. Another piece of this paper was found at Somerset House, together with the accounts of Robert Stark, paper hanger, for 1779. This pattern seems likely to be the 'Green on green pretty rose' listed in the accounts.

117 Flowers, birds, festoons of drapery and foliage
Late 18th century
Colour print from wood blocks and flock
134 × 54.3 cm (panel)
PROVENANCE Glamorgan Street House, Monmouth
Given by Colonel H. P. Jones-Williams
E.453–1924 neg 55589

117

40.6 × 21 cm
Given by Mrs Nesfield Cookson
E.2722–1914 neg GJ.9234

This paper is a copy in reverse of 'Les Deux Pigeons', a wallpaper by Jean-Baptiste Réveillon (1765–89), *circa* 1785. The same pattern is also to be found at Clandon Park, Surrey (a property of the National Trust), a portion of which is E.2239–1974.

118 Sheet of wallpaper borders with a formalized flower and leaf motif against a background of horizontal stripes, in brown and 2 shades of grey; originally used as a lining paper covering the bottom of an 18th-century drawer
Late 18th century
Colour print from wood blocks

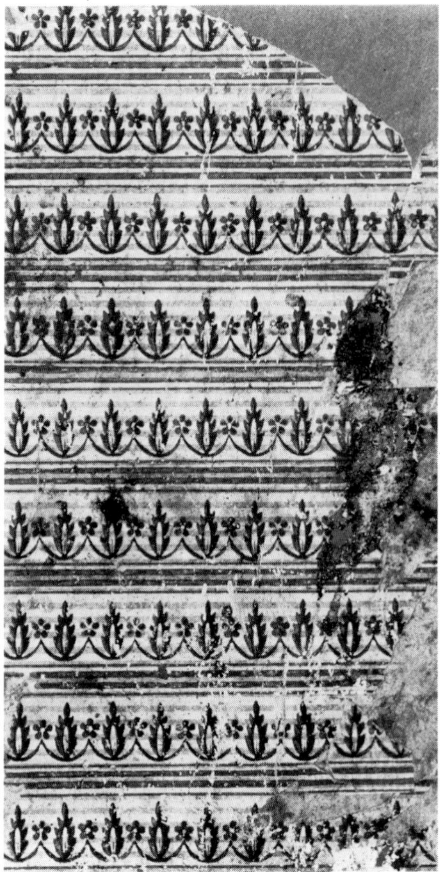

118

4.5 × 15 cm; 11 × 5 cm
Given by Mr John B. Fowler
E.2238, 2239–1966 neg GJ.9235

119 Two fragments: one with a design of fleur-de-lis on a dotted background, the other with a gold lattice pattern printed on silk
Late 18th century
Colour prints from wood blocks

119

120 Portion with a design of garlands of bell-shaped flowers joined by ribbons, and a matching border
Late 18th century
Flock, originally yellow (?)
47.7 × 27.7 cm (overall size); 3.5 × 11.4 cm (border)
PROVENANCE The Book Room, Blithfield Hall, Staffordshire
Given by Mr John B. Fowler
E.2235, 2235A–1966

121 Two fragments with a multicoloured floral design on a plain background, and a matching border
Late 18th century
Colour print from wood blocks and stencil
25 × 51 cm (first fragment); 17 × 9 cm (overall size of second fragment); 4.5 × 50 cm (border)
Given by Mr John B. Fowler
E.2240, 2241–1966

122 Fragment (2 pieces joined), with a rococo design; stamped on the back with the Georgian Excise duty stamp
Late 18th century
Colour print from wood block and distemper
17.9 × 62.5 cm
PROVENANCE Earls Hall Farmhouse, Prittlewell, Essex
Given by the Corporation of Southend-on-Sea
E.1210–1965

Earls Hall Farmhouse, the main building of which dates from the early 17th century, was demolished in 1964.

123 Fragment with a design of sprays of flowers and trailing fruits and leaves
Late 18th century
Print from wood block and stencil
33 × 18.4 cm
PROVENANCE The bathroom in the Angel Bedroom, Quenby Hall, Hungarton, Leicestershire
Given by the Squire de Lisle
E.2219–1974

124 Portion (on 2 sheets joined) of a frieze, with a pattern of classical scenes within panels
Late 18th century
Colour chiaroscuro print from wood blocks
13.4 × 79.7 cm
PROVENANCE Daylesford House, Gloucestershire
Given by Mr Roger Warner
E.34–1971 CT 6584 (see col pl, p 137)

Daylesford House, Gloucestershire (Worcestershire until 1931), built by Samuel Pepys Cockerell for Warren Hastings, begun in 1787, has decoration throughout the ground floors in the classical style.

125 Diaper flower design, in red and 2 greens, on white paper
Late 18th century
Print from wood blocks
35.2 × 22.9 cm (portion)
Given by the WM
E.1561–1934 neg 79256

The marks of 'pitch pins' can be seen in the border.

125

126 Portion (5 sheets joined) with a pattern of single flowers, on a dotted lattice background
Late 18th century
Colour print from wood blocks
109 × 74 cm
PROVENANCE No. 44, Berkeley Square, London
Given by Mr John B. Fowler
E.2231–1966 neg GJ.9236

The house was built by William Kent, 1742–44. The paper was also found at Sudbury Hall, Derbyshire, and a silk-screen reproduction of the pattern was produced by Cole & Son (Wallpapers) Ltd.

126

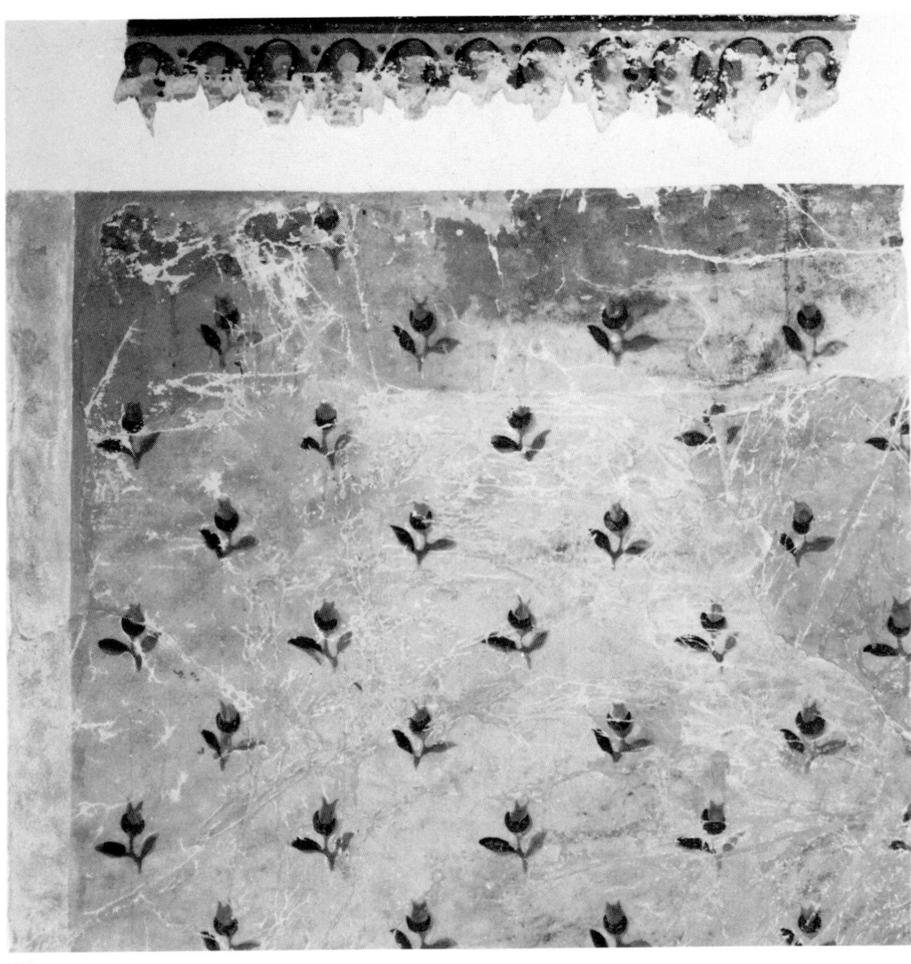

127

129 Panel with sprays of foliage, and pink, white, blue and orange flowers, on a pale green ground, in the Chinese style
Second half of 18th century
Tempera
238.9 × 49.5 cm
Given by Mr A. V. Sugden
E.3636–1932

130 Foliate pattern; stamped on the back with the Excise duty stamp and *First Account Taken J60*
Second half of 18th century
Green flock on a cream-coloured ground
28.6 × 24.5 cm (portion)
PROVENANCE Doddington Hall, Lincolnshire
Given by Mr G. E. Jarvis
E.477–1914 neg 71283

See also 'France', no 581.

131 Fragment with a design, partly in the gothic style, partly following a Chinese design
Second half of 18th century
Colour print from wood blocks
86.5 × 16 cm
PROVENANCE Found behind the cornice of the Warden's dining room, Winchester College, Hampshire
Given by the Warden and Fellows of Winchester College, Hampshire
E.4067–1923

127 Rosebuds, in black and green, on a green ground with a border of stylised leaves; stamped on the back with the Georgian Excise duty stamp and *Paper J6*
Late 18th century
Print from wood blocks
37 × 32 cm (overall size of fragment); 4 × 25 cm (border)
PROVENANCE Sudbury Hall, Derbyshire
Given by Mr John B. Fowler
E.2238, 2238A–1974 neg GJ.9237

128 Fragment with a drop pattern of single formalised flowers between bands of leaves and a border of Greek key pattern, together with a sample of the reproduction of the design made by the donor
Late 18th century
Prints from wood blocks and red flock, on a red background
37.4 × 12.8 cm; 39.4 × 18.5 cm
PROVENANCE The State Bedroom, Clandon Park, Surrey
Given by Mr John B. Fowler
E.2234, 2247, 2247A–1974 neg GJ.9238

128

130

133

134

132 Portion with a design of trophies, circular medallions with profile heads, panels with landscape, floral festoons, etc, printed in white, blue, brown and grey on a yellow ground; stamped on the back with the Georgian Excise duty stamp
Second half of 18th century
Colour print from wood blocks
47 × 54 cm
PROVENANCE Doddington Hall, Lincolnshire
Given by Mr G. E. Jarvis
E.472–1914

133 Another portion of the above
Second half of 18th century
Colour print from wood blocks
22.5 × 40.6 cm
PROVENANCE Doddington Hall, Lincolnshire
Given by Mr G. E. Jarvis
E.473–1914 neg 66457

See SE, p 37. Doddington Hall was 'Georgianized' by Sir John Hussey Delaval, *circa* 1760. These and nos 134, 135 were formerly attributed to John Baptist Jackson.

134 Medallions containing insects, and panels with landscapes and figures, interspersed with flowers, printed in white, black, brown, pale blue and grey, on a bright blue ground; stamped on the back with the Georgian Excise duty stamp
Second half of 18th century
Colour print from wood blocks
81.6 × 54.3 cm (portion)
PROVENANCE Doddington Hall, Lincolnshire
Given by Mr G. E. Jarvis
E.474–1914 neg 46880 CT 8638

One of the medallions shows a pair of lovers seated on a garden bench, a design which relates to one by C. N. Cochin the Younger, of *circa* 1745, and to designs engraved by Robert Hancock for use on Battersea enamels, Worcester and Bow porcelain (see Cyril Cook, *The Life and Work of Robert Hancock*, London, 1948, item 2, fig 3 and pp 29 and 59). Examples of an enamel and of porcelain showing variants of this design are in the Department of Ceramics (VAM): a Bow plate, printed in red (no 2908–1901), Worcester cups and saucers (*Schreiber Collection*, vol I, p 651) and a Staffordshire enamel snuff-box (*Schreiber Collection*, vol III, p 344). See SE, pl 3; Greysmith, pl 36.

135 Design of 2 landscapes, printed in various shades of brown, green, grey etc
Second half of 18th century
Colour print from wood blocks
51.1 × 57.1 cm (portion)
PROVENANCE Doddington Hall, Lincolnshire
Given by Mr G. E. Jarvis
E.475–1914 neg 66458

See SE, pl 39.

136 Floral and lattice pattern on a blue ground
Second half of 18th century

136

Brown flock
89.3 × 48.1 cm (portion)
PROVENANCE Doddington Hall, Lincolnshire
Given by Mr G. E. Jarvis
E.476–1914 neg GJ. 9227

This is probably the flock described as covering the walls of the Great Parlour over the hall. See A. H. Tipping, *English Homes: Elizabethan and Jacobean* (1912), p 392. It was formerly attributed to John Baptist Jackson.

137 Seven fragments of plain blue paper (2) and green paper (5)
18th to 20th centuries
Distemper
Various sizes
PROVENANCE The Long Gallery, Osterley Park, Middlesex
E.1767–1773–1973

These fragments were found when the Long Gallery was being redecorated in 1972. The 2 blue papers are presumed to be part of the colour scheme introduced by Sir William Chambers for the Long Gallery, which was completed in 1759, and it is thought that the pea-green paper was introduced by Robert Adam to match his damask upholstery, *circa* 1765–70. E.1773 is a sample of the paper that was used in 1972.

135

Late 18th to Early 19th Century

138 Fragment with a pattern in grisaille of panels enclosing stylised floral motifs
Late 18th or early 19th century
Print from wood blocks on grey-toned paper
22.8 × 38.1 cm
Given by Mr John B. Fowler
E.2233–1974

139 Small stylised flowers within diamond shapes, joined by broad bands to form a lattice pattern; numbered in ink on the back *210*
Late 18th or early 19th century
Colour print from wood blocks
22.5 × 50 cm (fragment)
Given by Mr John B. Fowler
E.2245–1966 neg GJ.9239

140 Fragment with a design of sprigs of leaves and stylised floral shapes
Late 18th or early 19th century
Colour print from wood blocks
32 × 36.3 cm
PROVENANCE Weston Park, Staffordshire
Given by Mr John B. Fowler
E.2255–1966

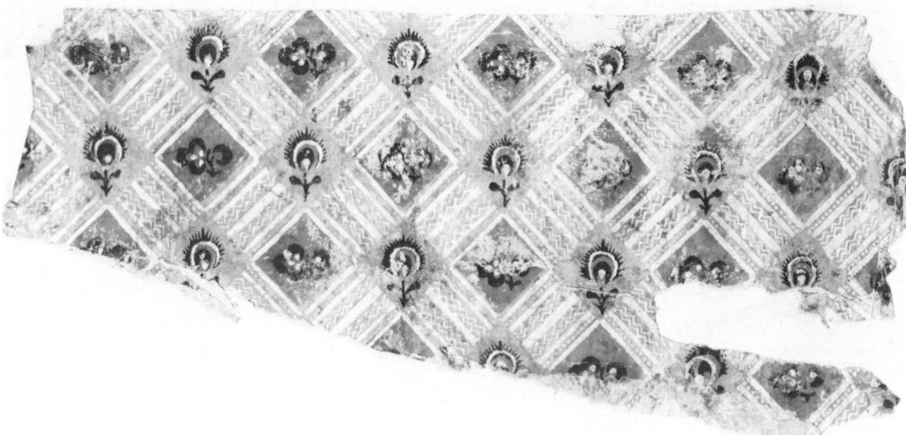

139

142

143

141 Portion of a facsimile of the above
Produced by Mauny of Paris
Circa 1939
Colour print from wood blocks
38.7 × 47.5 cm
Given by Mr John B. Fowler
E.2256–1966

142 Sprigs of bell-like flowers, tied with ribbons, joined by an undulating line of dots
Late 18th or early 19th century
Colour print from wood blocks
18 × 30.5 cm (fragment)
Given by Mr John B. Fowler
E. 2236–1966 neg GJ.9240

Another fragment of this paper had been stamped with the Excise duty stamp *First Account Taken*.

143 Two fragments with a design of stylized 4-petalled flowers with a trellis of flowers and leaves; E.2251 stamped on the back with the Excise duty stamp (partly truncated) and *Paper JJ*
Late 18th or early 19th century
Colour prints from wood blocks
16 × 21.5 cm; 14 × 16 cm
PROVENANCE A small room on the first floor of Haseley Court, Oxfordshire
Given by Mr John B. Fowler
E.2251–1966; E.2251A–1966 neg GJ.9241

144 Two fragments joined, with a design of quatrefoils and circles containing stylized single flowers, and a matching border
Late 18th or early 19th century
Colour print from wood blocks
32 × 26.5 cm (first fragment); 48 × 26 cm (second fragment); 3.5 × 23 cm (border)
Given by Mr John B. Fowler
E.2246, 2246A, B–1966; E.2246 neg GJ.9242

145 Fragment (2 sheets joined) with a design of small sprigs of flowers, printed in dark blue on a light-blue background; stamped on the back with the Georgian Excise duty stamp
Late 18th or early 19th century
Print from wood block
35 × 37 cm (overall size)
PROVENANCE Strawberry House, formerly The Rectory, Barnes, Surrey
Given by Mr John B. Fowler
E.2247–1966 neg GJ.9243

This paper was underneath no 116.

146 Scrolling flowers, leaves and ribbons, between vertical bands of beading
Late 18th or early 19th century

144

146

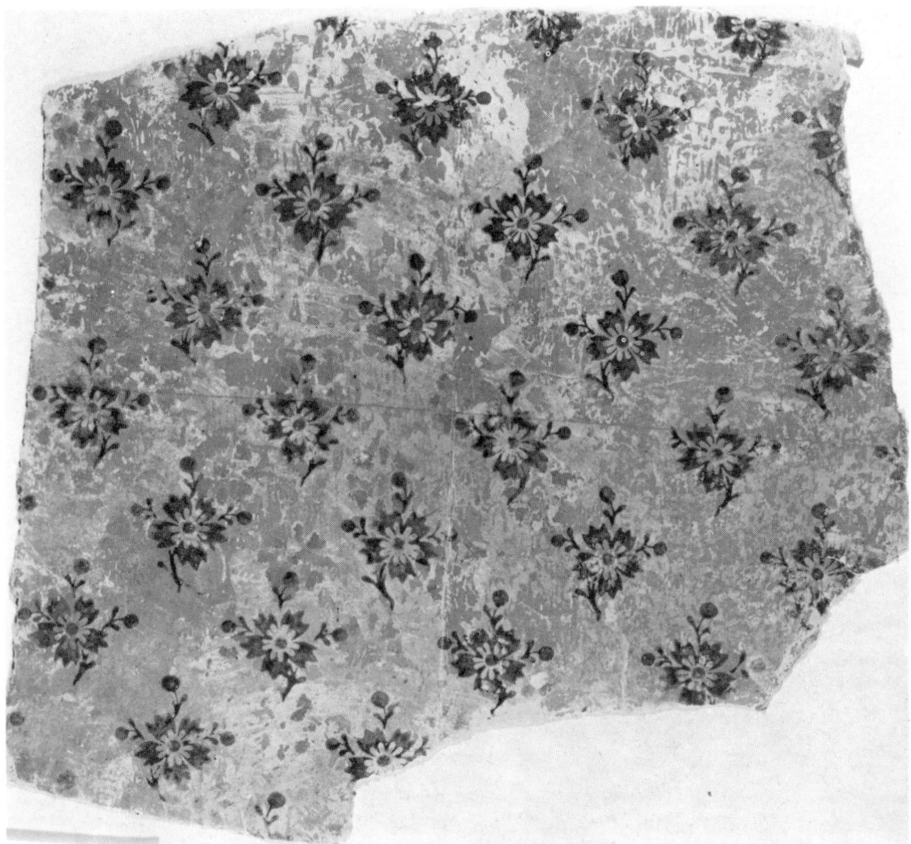

145

Colour print from wood blocks
35 × 37 cm (fragment)
Given by Mr John B. Fowler
E.2244–1966 neg GJ.9244

147 Small trailing flowers and leaves, printed in green and black, on a pink background
Late 18th or early 19th century
Print from wood blocks
23.8 × 20 cm (fragment)
Given by Mr John B. Fowler
E.2242–1966 neg GJ.9245

148 Fragment with a design of vertical gold lines, and sprigs and lines of green foliage
Late 18th or early 19th century
Colour print from wood blocks
10 × 28 cm
Given by Mr John B. Fowler
E.2266B–1966

This paper was found beneath nos 355, 171A.

149 Two fragments with a design of small single flowers on a background of regular dots, and a fragment of a border with a pattern of daisy flowers
Late 18th or early 19th century
Colour prints from wood blocks

147

13 × 32.5 cm; 14 × 36 cm; 3.5 × 7.6 cm (border)
Given by Mr John B. Fowler
E.2253, 2253A, 2254–1966; E.2253A neg GJ.9246

150 Nine fragments of floral and formal designs, with chain border (E.788) and a chinoiserie fretwork border with blue broad and narrow striped paper
Late 18th to mid-19th century
Colour prints from wood blocks (E.794 machine-printed)
Various sizes
PROVENANCE Mrs Offley Shore's apartment, The Clock Tower, Hampton Court Palace
Given by H M Office of Works
E.786–793–1936; neg J.1153

It is possible that E.788 is a sample of the 'stone link-chain' pattern which appears in Robert Stark's bill for paper hanging at Somerset House in 1779. For a later (*circa* 1870) machine-printed paper of the same provenance, see no 335.

150

149

152 GJ.9247

19th Century

152 Four fragments (3 on one sheet) from the upper apartments of Kew Palace; one piece lettered *Sanitary (Wall-paper)*
Circa 1800–1880
Colour prints from wood blocks, prints from engraved rollers, etc
Various sizes
Given by the Department of the Environment
E.621–1972 neg GJ.9247; E.621A–1972 neg GJ.9248

153 Border with a design of Egyptian motifs and a strip of edging, made for the drawing room at Crawley House, Bedfordshire
1806
Colour print from wood blocks and flock
11.4 × 40.9 cm (border); 1.2 × 10.7 cm (edging)
Given by Mr John B. Fowler
E.2498, 2498A–1966 CT 7792 (see col pl, p 138)

See M. Jourdain, 'Old English Wall-papers and Wall Hangings', *Country Life*, 29 March 1924 (vol 55), p 501, fig. 7. The pattern of this paper is identical to that of E.2259–1966, except that the design is vertical. These papers are similar in style of production to a French paper, *circa* 1800, no 550.

154 Five fragments with a repeating pattern of gothic windows interspersed with canopies
Circa 1810
Colour print from wood blocks and stencil
Various sizes
PROVENANCE Redwood, Low Road, Auchtermuchty, Fife
Given by Mrs Bell
E.775–1963

155 Fragment of plain lemon yellow wallpaper, and border with a design of roundels and flowers; the fragment stamped with the Excise duty stamp and *Paper 35 Stained; First Account Taken J 63*; frame mark *81/K.10303. 12/58*
Circa 1810
Print from wood block and stained paper; colour print from wood block
9.4 × 26.4 cm (overall size of fragment)
PROVENANCE St Nicholas' Rectory, Shepperton, Middlesex
Given by the Reverend H. Scholfield
E.527, 528–1956 neg GJ.9257

(*opposite*) Chinoiserie design. English, *circa* 1769 (no 98)

Archway with garlands of flowers.
English, *circa* 1769 (no 99)

A frieze with classical scenes. English, late 18th century (no 124)

Border in the neo-classical style. English, first quarter of 19th century (no 182)

Border with Egyptian motifs. English, 1806 (no 153)

This paper was taken from above the fireplace in a front room on the first floor of the Rectory. The wallpapers and borders (nos 55, 93, 111, 155, 181, 215, 282, 332, 434, 440) were superimposed upon each other in this room.

156 Two corner-pieces of wall- or lining paper: classical panels, printed in gold on blue
Early 19th century
Colour prints from wood blocks
63.5 × 63.5 cm; 66.1 × 52.8 cm
Given by Mr W. D. Dawkins
E.523, 524–1914

157 Portion with classical panels, in yellow on grey; stamped on the back with the Georgian Excise duty stamp and *Duty Ch. on Paper Stained*
Early 19th century
Colour print from wood blocks
63.5 × 57.1 cm
Given by Mr W. D. Dawkins
E.525–1914

158

158 Pattern of beading and palmettes, in the neo-classical style; traces of the Georgian Excise duty stamp on the back
Early 19th century
Colour print from wood blocks
4.5 × 10.2 cm (fragment of border)
PROVENANCE Stourhead, Wiltshire
Given by Mr John B. Fowler
E.164–1972 neg GJ.9249

The wings and 2-storey pavilions of Stourhead House were added by Sir Richard Colt Hoare (1758–1838). The paper was found in a drawer of Colt Hoare's desk by the National Trust at Stourhead. A border of the same design appears in *Wedgwood's First Pattern Book, 1769–1814*, a record of painted borders for Queen's Ware, in the collection of the Wedgwood Museum, Burslem, Staffordshire. It is pattern no 341, described as 'running honeysuckle'.

159 Half-drop design of small sprigs of flowers in grey, black and white
Early 19th century

152 GJ.9248

155

159

Print from wood blocks
14 × 19 cm (fragment)
Given by Mr John B. Fowler
E.2240–1974 neg GJ.9250

Another sample of this pattern, in green and white with matching border, is no 163.

160 Fragment with formal flower, dot and line design
Early 19th century
Colour print from wood blocks
21.6 × 8.3 cm
PROVENANCE Stubbers, North Ockendon, Essex
Given by Miss Marjorie Russell
E.93–1937

161 Sheet of borders with a quasi-Egyptian design in grey, white and blue on a red ground; stamped on the back with the Georgian Excise duty stamp and *First Account Taken 296*
Early 19th century
Colour print from seven wood blocks
57.8 × 73 cm
Given by the WM
E.1562–1934 neg J.1151

162 Portion with a design of rocks, bridge and foliage in green and brown; border stuck on, with a leaf and flower pattern
Early 19th century
Print from wood blocks, border block and flock
97.8 × 67.3 cm
Given by the WM
E.1563–1934

163 Small sprigs of flowers in green and white, and a matching border
Early 19th century
Print from wood blocks
23.5 × 55.5 cm (overall size); 18.3 × 3.7 cm (border)
Given by Mr John B. Fowler
E.2252–1966 neg GJ.9251

164 Floral arabesque design incorporating the Garter Star; stamped on the back with the Georgian Excise duty stamp and *First Account Taken*
Early 19th century
Colour print from wood blocks
149.9 × 53.1 cm (panel)
PROVENANCE Shelsley Bank, Stanford Bridge, Worcestershire
Given by Mrs E. G. Hill
E.710–1921 neg 56523

165 Fragment with a grisaille leaf pattern, and a border of cable pattern
Early 19th century
Colour print from wood blocks

161

163

35 × 29.8 cm (overall size); 5.5 × 61 cm (border)
PROVENANCE A boudoir on the second floor (the master bedroom), Quenby Hall, Hungarton, Leicestershire
Given by the Squire de Lisle
E.2222–1974

164

166 Five sheets with floral and 'moulding' patterns; each stamped on the back with the Georgian Excise duty stamp and *Paper L*
Early 19th century
Colour prints from wood blocks and flock
Various sizes
Given by the WM
E.2141–2145–1929

See also no 109 (note).

167 Portion with a scrolling foliage pattern in red on a gold background imitating silk
Early 19th century
Colour print from wood block
36.6 × 26.2 cm
29301.17

168 Fragment with a grey basket-weave pattern
Early 19th century
Print from wood block
21.6 × 44.4 cm
PROVENANCE The Old Manse, Bean Street, Nayland, Suffolk
Given by Mrs Joan Kennedy
E.475–1968

A page in J. S. Hayward's sketch book (E.1628–1939), inscribed *Scraps from Recollections of Papers 20 decr. 1801*, illustrates 2 basket-weave patterns.

169 Trailing pattern of small white flowers with black leaves and twigs, and a piece of border with yellow and pink flowers; stamped on the back with the Georgian Excise duty stamp *First Account Taken* and numbered *347*
Early 19th century
Colour prints from wood blocks
54 × 54.7 cm (overall size); 21.6 × 2.9 cm (border)
Given by Mr John B. Fowler
E.355–1972 neg GJ.9252

170 Portions (2 on one mount) of borders, with a pattern of winged putti riding hippocampi, within ovals
Early 19th century
Colour print from wood blocks and flock
8.9 × 8.9 cm; 8.9 × 17.2 cm
PROVENANCE Lulliement House, Perthshire

169

Given by Mr John B. Fowler
E.166–1972

These borders (one horizontal, one vertical strip) were, together with no 180, removed from behind a scenic paper.

171 Two borders: one, acanthus moulding; the other, leaves and flowers
Early 19th century
Multicoloured flock, and wood block
50.8 × 6.4 cm (each border)
Given by Mr Sydney Vacher
E.2243, 2244–1913

171A Design of roses, divided by an undulating dotted band
Early 19th century
Colour print from wood blocks (fragment)
10 × 28 cm
Given by Mr John B. Fowler
E. 2266A–1966

This paper was found beneath no 355 and above no 148.

172 Design imitating plaster moulding
Early 19th century
Gouache (monochrome)
46.7 × 9.1 cm
Given by Mr W. D. Dawkins
E.527–1914 neg GJ.9253

173 Fragment with a pattern of stylized sprigs of flowers within ogival lattice formed by the stems
Early 19th century
Colour print from wood blocks
14 × 25 cm
PROVENANCE The back basement of No 44, Berkeley Square, London
Given by Mr John B. Fowler
E.2250–1966

174 Fragment with a stylized snowdrop pattern and 2 borders, one with palmettes in red on black, the other with oak leaf and beading
Early 19th century
Colour prints from wood blocks
22.8 × 51.1 cm (overall size); 4.1 × 22.9 cm (border); 3.7 × 21.9 cm (border)
Given by Mrs Joan Bygrave
E.1348–1350–1963

175 Two fragments: one, a design simulating marble panels; the other, a design of panels of stylized daisies and imitation marble
Early 19th century
Colour print from wood blocks
28.5 × 23 cm (each)
PROVENANCE An old house near Exeter
Given by Mr John B. Fowler
E.2258, 2258A–1966 neg GJ.9254

E.2258 was superimposed upon E.2258A.

172

175

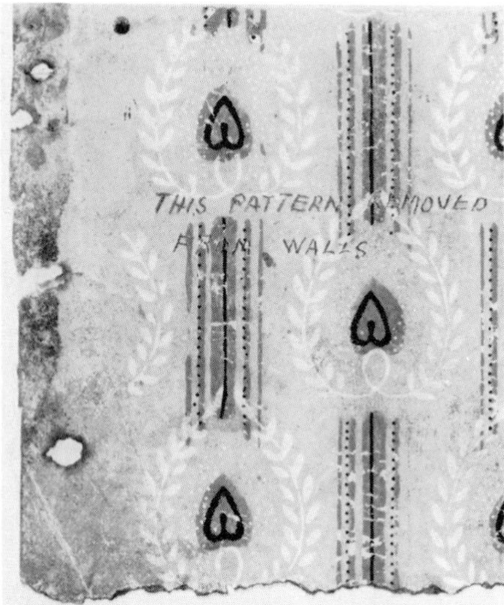

176

176 Small heart shapes contained within larger ones formed of leaves, connected by vertical bands, printed in white, green and black on a pink background
Early 19th century
Print from wood blocks
13.3 × 16.5 cm (fragment)
Given by Mr John B. Fowler
E.2257–1966 neg GJ.9255

177 Two fragments with a pattern of windows and columns in the neo-gothic style
Circa 1820
Colour print from wood blocks
33.7 × 29.9 cm
PROVENANCE Great Jenkins Farm, Hallingbury, Essex
Given by Mr Edwin Light
E.26–1936 neg Z.2437

See Entwisle, *V*, pl 13, fig 25.

177

179

178 Two fragments with a foliate design incorporating formalized pineapples and tendrils
Circa 1820
Print from wood blocks
48 × 43.7 cm; 8 × 45.5 cm
PROVENANCE Said by the donor to have come from a 14th-century house in Faversham, Kent
Given by Mrs Joan Bygrave
E.1353–1963

This paper was found beneath nos 209, 211.

179 Saints and trophies in the neo-gothic style
Circa 1820
Colour print from wood blocks
66.1 × 54.7 cm (portion)
PROVENANCE The Ostrich Hotel, Castleacre, Swaffham, Norfolk
Given by Mr T. Taylor
E.2538–1913 neg Z.2445

See Entwisle, *V*, pl 13, fig 24.

180 Portion with a pattern of trailing flowers, and birds
Circa 1820–30
Colour print from wood blocks
41.3 × 32.1 cm
PROVENANCE Lulliement House, Perthshire
Given by Mr John B. Fowler
E.156–1972

This paper and the border (no 170) were removed from behind scenic paper. A similar type of paper from St Nicholas' Rectory, Shepperton, is no 55.

181 A portion and a fragment with a trailing flower and leaf design, also 2 borders with a formal leaf pattern; each stamped with the Georgian Excise duty stamp *First Account Taken J 74*
Circa 1820–30
Colour print from wood blocks and stencil
70.5 × 52.1 cm (portion); 2.9 × 54.6 cm

(fragment); 17.2 × 24.5 cm (border); 2.9 × 24.8 cm (border)
PROVENANCE St Nicholas' Rectory, Shepperton, Middlesex
Given by the Reverend H. Scholfield
E.529, 529A, 530, 530A–1956

This paper was taken from above the fireplace in a front room on the first floor of the Rectory. The papers and borders (nos 55, 93, 111, 155, 181, 215, 282, 332, 434, 440) were superimposed upon each other in this room.

182 Mouldings, stylized lotus leaves and palmettes in the neo-classical style
First quarter of 19th century
Black flock on a dark pink ground
8.5 × 60.3 cm (border)
PROVENANCE A cupboard in Montacute House, Somerset
Given by Mr John B. Fowler
E.2242–1974 CT 7791 (see col pl, p 137)

183

183 Fragment of a border in 3 shades of blue; stamped with the Georgian Excise duty stamp and *Duty Ch. on Paper 228 Stained*
First quarter of 19th century
Colour print from wood blocks
15.5 × 17.7 cm
Given by Mr Martin Battersby
E.63–1947 neg GJ.9295

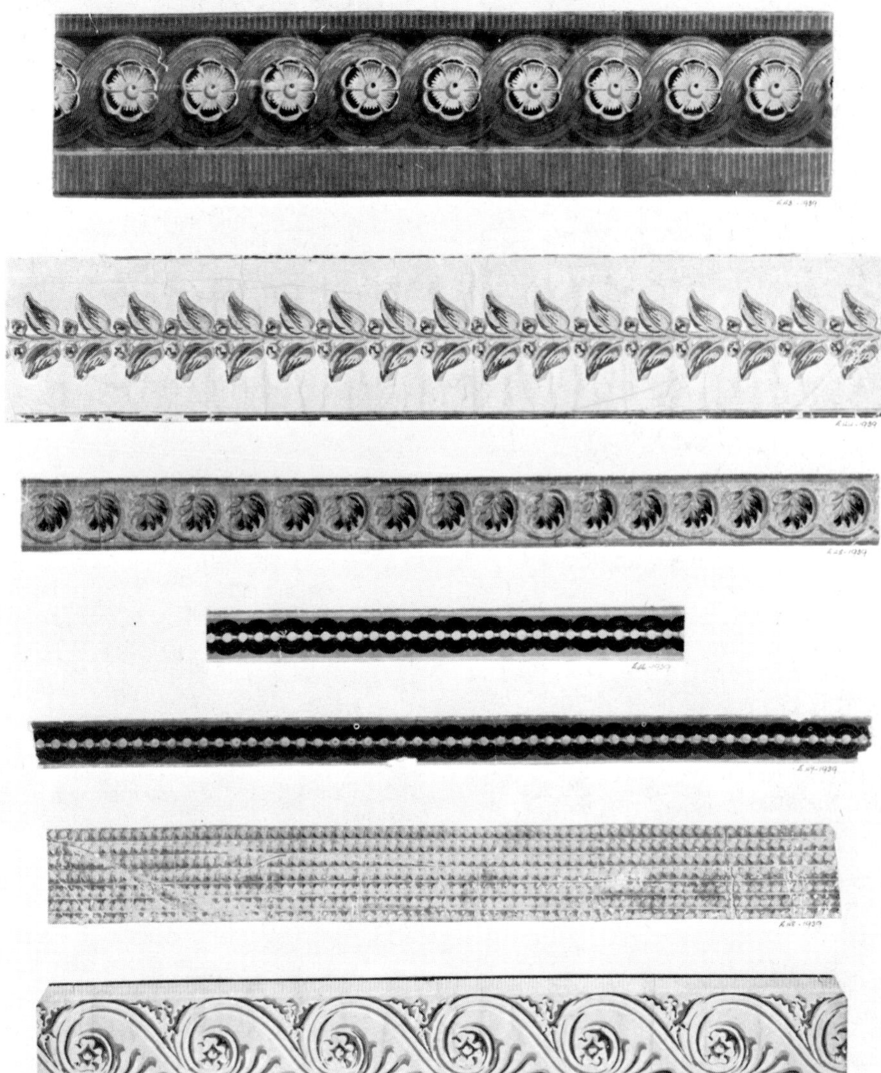

184

184 Thirteen borders of mouldings etc
First quarter of 19th century
Colour prints from wood blocks, flock, etc
Various sizes
PROVENANCE The stock of Cowtan & Sons, successors of J. Duppa, J. G. Crace, etc
Given by Mr A. L. Cowtan in memory of his father, Arthur Barnard Cowtan, OBE
E.43–65–1939; E. 43–49 neg GJ.9256

185 Portion (consisting of 2 sheets joined) of a border with a striped design; stamped on the back with the Georgian Excise duty stamp and *First Account Taken 307*
Possibly produced by Crace & Sons
Possibly *circa* 1829
Colour print from wood blocks
39.4 × 58.5 cm
PROVENANCE The Royal Pavilion, Brighton, Sussex
Given by Brighton Corporation
E.9845–1958

This paper (and nos 1024–1027, which were probably designed by Robert Jones and produced by Crace & Sons) was intended for rooms on the upper floor of the Pavilion, which included the Duke of York's and the Duke of Clarence's bedrooms and the lobbies to them, all on the east side, the King's old bedroom on the south east and the west bedrooms. Since Robert Jones is known to have worked for Crace & Sons only from 1817 until 1823, it is less likely that no 185 is by him.

186 Portion with a pattern (much worn) of scrolling foliage, flowers and a pedestal (?)
Circa 1830
Colour print from wood blocks
93.4 × 81.3 cm
PROVENANCE The Commercial Hotel, Knaresborough, Yorkshire
Given by the WM
E.2938–1934

See *JDA* (1934), vol LIV, 258.

187

188

187 Stylized floral design
Circa 1830
Red flock
46 × 20.2 cm (fragment)
PROVENANCE Tyninghame, East Lothian
Given by Mr John B. Fowler
E.2260–1966 neg GJ.9258

The order for this paper for the Earl of Haddington, Tyninghame, East Lothian, dated 8 September 1832, appears on p 274 of Cowtan & Sons Ltd's Wallpaper Order Books, E.1863–1946 (see PATTERN BOOKS, no 692).

188 Pseudo-Spanish design, showing a troubadour and a man and woman dancing on a terrace, within white cartouches, alternating with bowls of flowers; each fragment with an appliqué border of roses and leaves above a partition
Circa 1830
Colour prints from wood blocks
29.5 × 49.5 cm (first fragment);
37.4 × 50.2 cm (second fragment)
PROVENANCE The drawing room of Pardons, Ditchling, Hassocks, Sussex
Given by Miss Sylvia Thursfield
E.1006, 1007–1970 neg GJ.9259

Off-printed on the back of each fragment is the pattern of an earlier wallpaper, with a pin-print design.

189 Floral design on a striped background
Circa 1830
Colour print from wood blocks
16.3 × 26.3 cm (fragment)
PROVENANCE Stubbers, North Ockendon, Essex
Given by Miss Marjorie Russell
E.95–1937 neg GJ.9260

190 Fragment with a conventional foliage design printed in mauve
Circa 1830
Colour print from a wood block
48.3 × 28 cm
Given by Messrs Green & Abbott
E.360–1917

191 Portion of a ceiling paper (2 fragments joined) with a pattern of octagonal and diamond-shaped panels, containing floral and foliate motifs; stamped on the back with the Georgian Excise duty stamp
Circa 1830
Chiaroscuro print from wood blocks

189

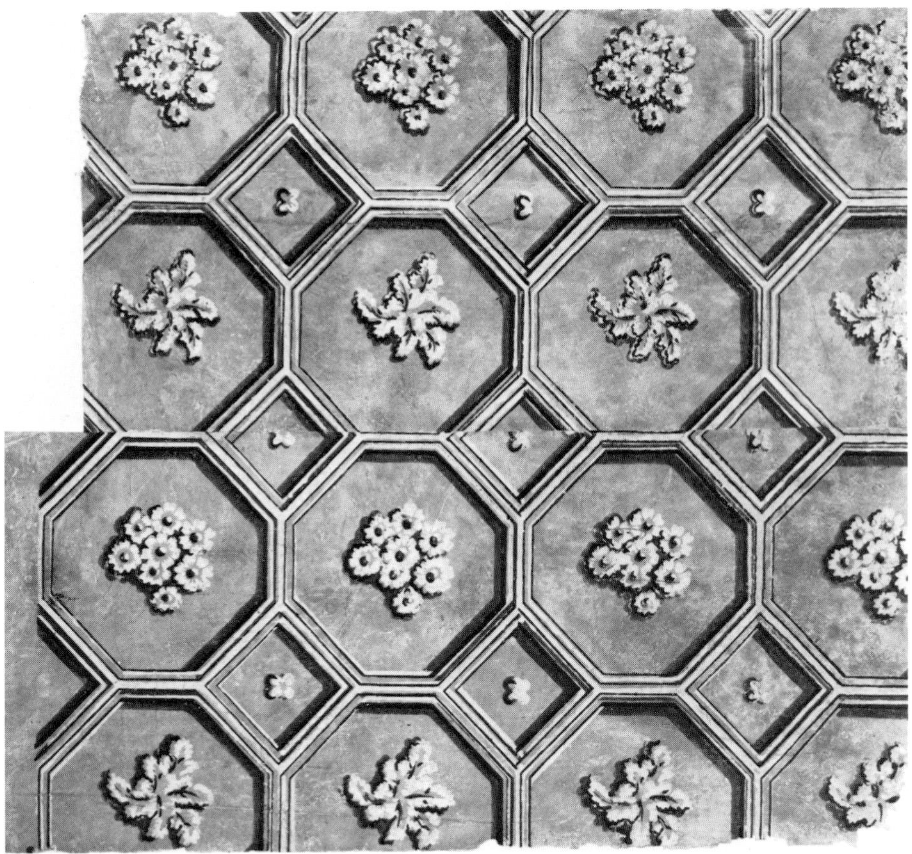

191

51 × 45 cm
PROVENANCE Clandon Park, West Clandon, Surrey
Given by Mr John B. Fowler
E.32–1971 neg GJ.9261

192 Green and red 'Moorish' design on a white ground
Circa 1830
Colour print from wood blocks
62.3 × 29.3 cm (fragment)
PROVENANCE Luddesdown Court, Kent
Given by Mr W. Cobbett-Barker
E.1191–1935 neg GJ.9262

193 Stylized design of leaves and flowers, and other decorative motifs
Circa 1830
Red flock
35.5 × 14 cm (fragment)
PROVENANCE The Ballroom, Lydiard Tregoze, Wiltshire
Given by Mr John B. Fowler
E.2261–1966 neg GJ.9263

See Christopher Hussey, 'Lydiard Tregoze', *Country Life* (1948), vol 103, plate on page 629. SE, pl 30, show a flock of the same pattern at Temple Newsam House, Leeds, which they date *circa* 1720. There has been support for a date *circa* 1745, when the Long Gallery was remodelled, but a reference from the memoirs of Lady Mary Meynell (1933), who lived there in the 19th century, states that it was hung in 1826. Possibly there was an 18th-century pattern, copied by a firm such as Cowtan & Sons, in the 1820s and 1830s.

194 Two fragments: one with a floral design with a striped background; the other (pasted over it) with a *ferronerie irisé* pattern
Circa 1830 and *circa* 1840–50 respectively
Colour prints from wood blocks
16.3 × 26.3 cm (overall size)
PROVENANCE Stubbers, North Ockendon, Essex
Given by Miss Marjorie Russell
E.94, 95–1937

195 Portion with a lattice and window design in brown and white
Circa 1830–40
Print from wood blocks
145.5 × 54.2 cm
Given by Mr John B. Fowler
E.2264–1966

196 Arcading in the gothic style
Circa 1830–40
Colour print from wood blocks
13.5 × 24 cm (fragment)
PROVENANCE The basement of Upton House, Alresford, Hampshire
Given by Mr John B. Fowler
E.2265–1966 neg GJ.9264

192

193

196

197

197 Twenty-four borders with classical mouldings, ribbons, fruit, flowers etc; E.71–74 stamped on the backs *First Account Taken*
Circa 1830–40
Colour prints from wood blocks, flock etc
Various sizes
PROVENANCE The stock of Cowtan & Sons Ltd, successors of J. Duppa, J. G. Crace etc
Given by Mr A. L. Cowtan in memory of his father, Arthur Barnard Cowtan, OBE
E.54–61–1939 neg GJ.9266;
E.66–90–1939; E.66, 67 neg GJ.9267

198 Fragment (2 sheets joined) with a pattern of imitation marble panels
Circa 1830–40
Colour print from wood blocks
43.2 × 43.2 cm
Given by Mr John B. Fowler
E.705–1970 neg GJ.9268

199 Two portions with a design of a gothic ruin with stags and trees; each stamped on the back with the Excise duty stamps, and E.1568 with *First Account Taken*
Circa 1830–40
Colour prints from wood blocks
127.7 × 55.2 cm (overall size)
Given by the WM
E.1567, 1568–1934

200 Portion with a baroque floral pattern, possibly a copy of an 18th-century paper
Probably *circa* 1830–40
Pink, green and mauve flock, on a white glazed paper
62 × 27 cm
Given by Mr John B. Fowler
E.2237–1966

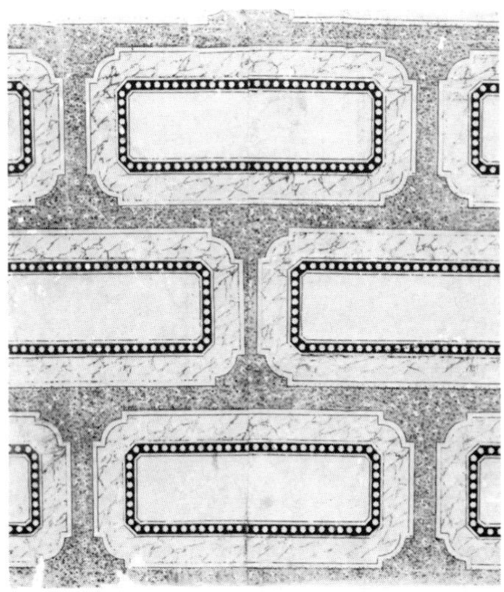

198

201 Fragment with a design of a gothic gateway
Probably *circa* 1830–40
Colour print from wood blocks
54.6 × 28.7 cm
Given by the WM
E.1565–1934

202 Fragment of the same design as the above, but reversed and printed in different colours
Probably *circa* 1830–40
Print from wood blocks
38.2 × 29.3 cm
Given by the WM
E.1566–1954

203

203 Rose pattern
Probably *circa* 1830–40
Red flock
10.4 × 10.6 cm (fragment)
PROVENANCE Shardeloes, Amersham, Buckinghamshire
Given by Mr Archibald G. B. Russell
E.335–1915 neg GJ.9265

Catalogued originally as 'late 18th century', this seems more likely to have been produced in the second quarter of the 19th century, because of the texture of the paper and flock.

204 Four portions; one with a red damask pattern, another with a floral design, a third with a pattern of pendants and fringed hangings
The illustrated portion has a border of cabled ribbon and a pattern of Michaelmas daisies
Circa 1830–50
Multicoloured flock
Various sizes
Given by Arthur Sanderson & Sons Ltd
E.473–476–1921; E.476–1921 neg GJ.9269

204

205

205 Repeat pattern of geometrical floral shapes
Circa 1832
Colour machine print
79.7 × 52.6 cm
PROVENANCE Coleshill House, Berkshire
Given by Mrs K. H. D. Pleydell-Bouverie
E.1062–1965 neg GJ.9270

This paper with colour variations appears from 1832 to 1852 in Cowtan & Sons' Wallpaper Order Books (see PATTERN BOOKS, no 692). Coleshill House was burnt down in 1952.

206

206 Two fragments with a floral design in 2 shades of yellow; one of the pieces stamped on the back with the manufacturer's name and address, the Excise duty stamp of William IV, and frame mark *B 2426 1258* [?] *1832*, and inscribed in ink *Silvanus Sharp April Thirtieth 1833*
Produced by Slodden & Co, 314, Oxford Street, London
1832–33
Colour print from wood block
74.2 × 31.8 cm (overall size)
Given by Messrs Green & Abbott
E.358, 359–1917 neg GJ.9271

207 Fragment with a formalized floral design in cartouches, interspersed with a foliate motif, on a background of diaper pattern
Circa 1835
Colour print from wood blocks

208

45.8 × 39.5 cm
PROVENANCE No 1, The Cloisters, Hereford Cathedral
Given by Mr F. C. Morgan
E.2658–1962

This paper was found beneath no 293.

208 Double lattice bamboo pattern
Circa 1835
Colour print from wood blocks
7.5 × 37 cm (fragment)
Given by Mr John B. Fowler
E.2263–1966 neg GJ.9272

209 Fragment with a pin-print pattern: diamonds with zig-zag borders
Circa 1835–40
Machine print
44.5 × 45.8 cm
PROVENANCE A 14th-century house in Faversham, Kent, according to the donor
Given by Mrs Joan Bygrave
E.1352–1963

This paper was found beneath no 211 and superimposed on no 178. A similarly produced paper with the pattern adapted from a calico-print design is illustrated in SE, pl 88, reprinted from the *Journal of Design and Manufacture*, March 1849.

210 Formal leaf pattern
1837
Crimson flock
22 × 21.4 cm (fragment)
PROVENANCE The old coffee room of the former Angel Inn, 83, High Street, Oxford
Given by Mr H. Clifford Smith
E.392–1943

The paper was backed by a copy of *The Times*, 2 March 1837.

211 'Thorn Damask'
Probably produced by the firm later known as Jeffrey & Co.
Circa 1837
Machine print and colour print from wood block
47.6 × 49.6 cm (fragment)
PROVENANCE A 14th-century house in Faversham, Kent, according to the donor
Given by Mrs Joan Bygrave
E.1351–1963 CT 7793 (see col pl, p 155)

This paper was superimposed upon nos 178, 209. A specimen of the same design, printed on a different background and entitled 'Thorn-Damask', is pasted in a pattern book preceding a page dated January 1839. This pattern book was probably issued by the firm later known as Jeffrey & Co. (see PATTERN BOOKS, no 692A).

212

212 'Bamboo Decoration'
Circa 1837–44
Colour print from wood blocks
55 × 39.7 cm (portion)
PROVENANCE 'Found among the stock of Thomas Avery, builder, etc, of Ivy House, Tenterden, Kent, which business had been in existence nearly a century and a half' (extract from a letter from the donor)
Given by Mr Alexander Reynell
E.2161–1913 neg GJ.9273

A colour variant of this paper appears in the record books of a firm which is probably that later known as Jeffrey & Co. (see PATTERN BOOKS, no 692A).

213 'Lyre'
Circa 1837–55
Colour print from wood blocks
18.4 × 26.8 cm (portion of border)
PROVENANCE As for above item
Given by Mr Alexander Reynell
E.2160–1913 neg GJ.9273

213

214 Portion with a repeat pattern of trailing flowers
Circa 1838
Colour machine print
108 × 53.2 cm
PROVENANCE The Honeymoon Room, Coleshill House, Berkshire
Given by Mrs K. H. D. Pleydell-Bouverie
E.1064–1965

An order for this paper printed on a background simulating watered silk, dated June 1838, appears on p 258 of Cowtan & Sons Ltd's Wallpaper Order Books (see PATTERN BOOKS, no 692). Coleshill House was burnt down in 1952.

215 Fragment with a striped design
Circa 1840
Colour print from wood block and stencil
7 × 37.7 cm
PROVENANCE St Nicholas' Rectory, Shepperton, Middlesex
Given by the Reverend H. Scholfield
E.531–1956

This paper was taken from above the fireplace in a front room on the first floor of the Rectory. The papers and borders (nos 55, 93, 111, 155, 181, 215, 282, 332, 434, 440) were superimposed upon each other in this room.

216 Panel of 'satin' paper with pink and yellow convolvulus, within a flock border of tasselled green cords
Circa 1840
Colour print from wood blocks
268 × 127 cm (overall size)
PROVENANCE The Queen's Hospital, Sidcup, Kent
Given by the London County Council
E.2145–1930

217 Fragment with coloured roses and rose leaves and white foliage on a blue ground
Circa 1840
Colour print from wood blocks
72.8 × 53.4 cm
PROVENANCE Cranford House, Middlesex
Given by the Borough of Heston & Isleworth
E.1246–1937

218 Sheet of borders with a pattern of pink roses on mouldings
Circa 1840
Colour prints from wood blocks and flock
48 × 68.9 cm (overall size)
PROVENANCE 'Found among the stock of Thomas Avery, builder, etc, of Ivy House, Tenterden, Kent, which business had been in existence nearly a century and a half' (extract from a letter from the donor)
Given by Mr Alexander Reynell
E.2183–1913

219 Panel of 'satin' paper with roses and other flowers interspersed with pink ornaments on a cream ground, within a flock border of cable pattern
Circa 1840
Colour print from wood blocks
243.9 × 108.1 cm (overall size)
PROVENANCE The Queen's Hospital, Sidcup, Kent
Given by the London County Council
E.2146–1930

220 Seaweed pattern
Circa 1840
Colour print from wood blocks
43 × 9 cm (fragment)
PROVENANCE Whitehall, Malden Road, Cheam, Surrey
Given by the Greater London Council
E.1033–1977 neg GJ.9274

A copy of *The Times* for February 1839 was used as a backing for this paper. See also no 57.

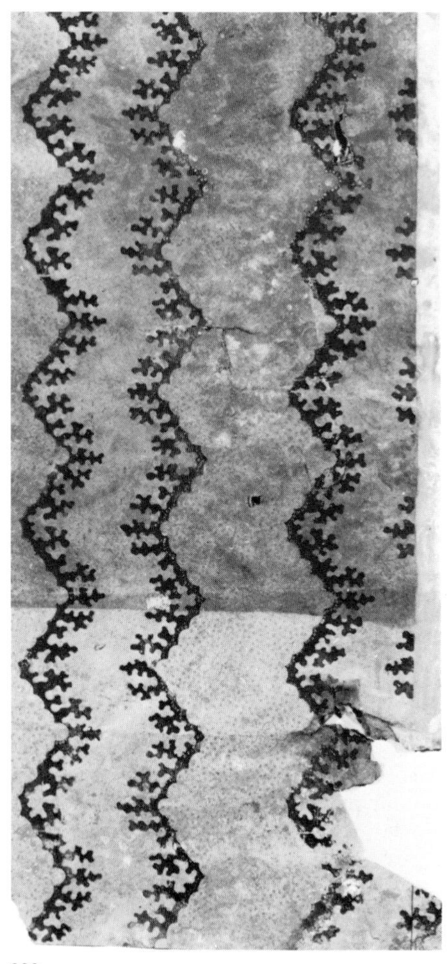

220

221 GJ.9275

PROVENANCE The stock of Cowtan & Sons Ltd, successors of J. Duppa, J. G. Crace etc
Given by Mr A. L. Cowtan in memory of his father, Arthur Barnard Cowtan, OBE
E.80–89–1939; E.80–86–1939 neg Z.2439; E.87–1939 neg GJ.9275

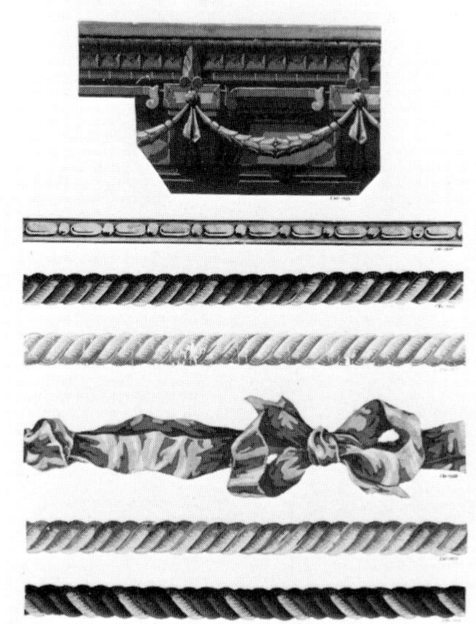

221 Z.2439

221 Borders of mouldings etc; E.88 stamped on the back with *First Account Taken*
Circa 1840
Colour prints from wood blocks, flock etc
Various sizes

222 Pattern of roses and leaves
Circa 1840
Colour print from wood blocks and blue-green flock
93.7 × 53.6 cm (portion)
Given by the WM
E.2146–1929 neg Z.2441

222

223

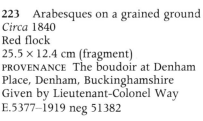

223 Arabesques on a grained ground
Circa 1840
Red flock
25.5 × 12.4 cm (fragment)
PROVENANCE The boudoir at Denham Place, Denham, Buckinghamshire
Given by Lieutenant-Colonel Way
E.5377–1919 neg 51382

229

224 Two fragments joined: the top piece with a pattern of blue flowers on a background of vermicelli dots; the lower piece with a flower and leaf motif, within a framework of dots
Circa 1840–50
Colour prints from wood blocks
31.2 × 15.3 cm (overall size)
Given by Mr John B. Fowler
E.2237, 2237A–1974

225 Portion with a pseudo-Renaissance strapwork pattern, printed in brown
Circa 1840–50
Colour print from wood block
24.5 × 53 cm
Given by Mr John B. Fowler
E.2277–1966

226 Two fragments with an arabesque design on an *irisé* background
Circa 1840–50
Colour prints from wood blocks
22 × 25.8 cm; 53.6 × 27.7 cm
PROVENANCE Stubbers, North Ockendon, Essex
Given by Miss Marjorie Russell
E.94, 95–1937

227 Fragment consisting of part of 2 lengths joined to form a pattern of strap work and formalized leaves and flowers
Circa 1840–50
Print from a wood block, on red paper, with a slight emboss
55 × 45 cm (overall size)
PROVENANCE The King's Gallery, Kensington Palace, London
Given by the Directorate of Ancient Monuments & Historic Buildings, Department of the Environment
E.381–1975

The King's Gallery was divided into separate compartments during the 19th century, until the restoration of *circa* 1895.

228 Fragment with a pattern of leaves, and stems of roses, and other flowers
Circa 1840–50
Colour print from wood blocks
25.4 × 17.8 cm
PROVENANCE Quenby Hall, Leicestershire
Given by the Squire de Lisle
E.2223–1974

229 Pattern of gothic canopies
Circa 1840–50
Colour print from wood blocks
75 × 54.5 cm (fragment of wall- or lining paper)
Given by Mr R. P. Bedford
E.4728–1922 neg F.34

See Greysmith, pl 85; Entwisle, *V*, pl 11, fig 21.

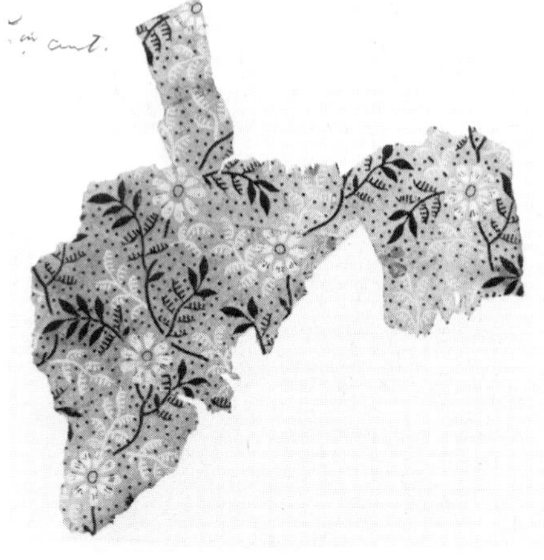

230

230 Leaves and flowers, in black and white, on a background of dots
Circa 1840–50
Colour print from wood blocks
20.1 × 19.2 cm (fragment)
Given by Mr John B. Fowler
E.2245–1974 neg GJ.9276

231 Floral 'Paisley' pattern
Circa 1840–50
Colour machine print
19.3 × 49 cm (fragment)
Given by Mr John B. Fowler
E.2262–1966 neg GJ.9278

This appears to be an early roller print.

231

236 Stylized floral pattern
Circa 1840–50
Red flock
12 × 11 cm (fragment)
Given by Mr John B. Fowler
E.2244–1974 neg GJ.9279

237

232 Fragment of wall- or lining paper with a pattern of escutcheons in blue and brown
Circa 1840–50
Colour print from wood blocks
36.9 × 30.5 cm
Given by Mr R. P. Bedford
E.4729–1922

233 Fragment of frieze or dado: sculptured vase with acanthus, flanked by panels, with moulded surrounds
Circa 1840–50
Machine print in several shades of brown
59.5 × 72.5 cm
Given by Mr Martin Battersby
E.71–1947

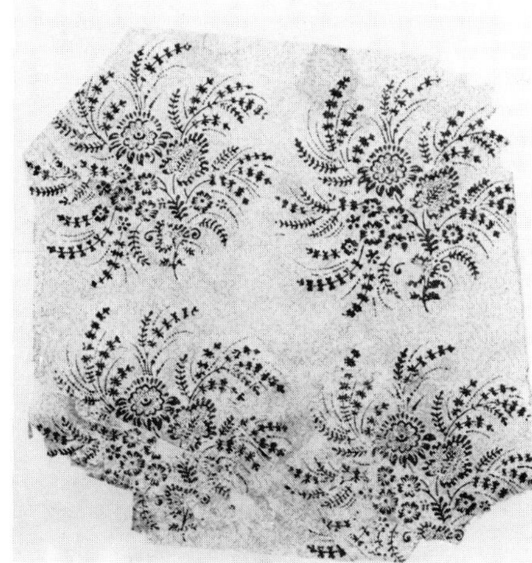

234

234 Sprays of stylized flowers and leaves, on a background of vermicelli dots
Circa 1840–50
Colour print from wood blocks
63.5 × 42 cm (portion)
PROVENANCE Montacute House, Somerset
Given by Mr John B. Fowler
E.2236–1974 neg GJ.9277

235

235 Design of geometrical shapes within vertical stripes, printed in white on pink
Circa 1840–50
Machine print (?)
23.5 × 13 cm (fragment)
Given by the WM
E.2267–1966 neg GJ.9281

237 Sixty-one specimens of borders and corners, with patterns of ribbons, palmettes, mouldings, flowers, Greek keys etc; most inscribed in ink with serial numbers in the margins etc; some inscribed *Destroyed 1874* [*1876* and *1880*]; one dated *June 1885*
Circa 1840–50
Colour print from wood blocks and flock (E.1811 machine-printed)
Various sizes
PROVENANCE A log book of Arthur Sanderson & Sons
Given by the WM
E.1764–1779, 1801, 1803–1816–1934; E.1801–1934 neg GJ.9280

'Archer's Cornice' (E.1764), 'Bourbon Rose' (E. 1765), 'Inlaid' (E.1766), 'Raglan' (E.1767), 'Oxford' (E.1768), 'Japan Damask' (E.1769), 'Fern and Poppy' (E.1772), 'Huntington Rosette' (E.1773, see no 1016), 'Nemophilia Sprig' (E.1774), 'Pinks and Iris' (E.1775), 'Valentia Damask' (E.1776)

238 Portion (2 fragments joined) with a pseudo-Renaissance strapwork design
Produced by Cowtan & Sons Ltd
Circa 1841

236

Print from wood block and flock
35 × 37.5 cm
PROVENANCE Said, by the donor, to have come from a room added to Grenofen House, Tavistock, Devon
Given by Captain H. P. Chichester-Clark
E.28–1956

239 Two portions with beggar boys, after paintings by Murillo in Dulwich Art Gallery
Produced by Jeffrey, Allen & Co.
Circa 1843
Chiaroscuro prints from wood blocks
80.6 × 53.4 cm (each)
E.390, 391–1923; E.391–1923 neg FD.50

These papers are mentioned in the *Art Union Monthly Journal* (1847), p 110, as being submitted by Robert Horne. They were exhibited by Jeffrey, Allen & Co. at the Great Exhibition in 1851. E.391 is illustrated in SE, pl 107; see also Greysmith, pl 83.

240 Fragment with panels of 'Paisley' shawl patterns in green, red, pink and black, on a grey and white ground
Circa 1845
Colour machine print
45.8 × 34.3 cm
PROVENANCE Ivy House, Worcester Cathedral precincts
Given by the Very Reverend Dr W. Moore Ede, Dean of Worcester
E.339–1932

This is an early roller print.

239

241

241 Formal 'Paisley' shawl pattern in crimson and white
Circa 1845
Colour print from wood blocks
62.3 × 47 cm (fragment)
PROVENANCE Ivy House, Worcester Cathedral precincts
Given by the Very Reverend Dr W. Moore Ede, Dean of Worcester
E.338–1932 neg Z.2444

See Entwisle, *V*, pl 4, fig 7.

242 Portion of a border entitled 'Swiss Crymp'
Circa 1845–52
Colour print from wood blocks
4.3 × 43.1 cm
PROVENANCE A log book of Arthur Sanderson & Sons
Given by the WM
E.1788–1934

A different colourway of this border appears in the record books of a firm which is probably that later known as Jeffrey & Co. (see PATTERN BOOKS, no 692A).

243

'Thorn Damask'. Probably produced by the firm later known as Jeffrey & Co, *circa* 1837 (no 211)

View of a railway station. Produced by Potters of Darwen, *circa* 1853 (no 270A)

249

243 Flowering branches between bands of interlaced ovals
Probably produced by the firm later known as Jeffrey & Co.
1847
Colour machine print
90 × 51 cm (portion)
PROVENANCE The drawing room of Auchmacoy House, near Ellon, Aberdeenshire
Given by Dr Alastair Rowan
E.144–1972 neg GJ.9282

A sample of this pattern, entitled 'Oval and Pink Stripes', in another colourway, is in the pattern book for 1847 probably produced by the firm later known as Jeffrey & Co. (see PATTERN BOOKS, no 692A). The house, which is in the Tudor style, was designed by William Burn (1789–1870) in the early 1830s, and the paper was apparently an original one.

244 Sheet of wallpaper borders with a pattern of imitation cord
Possibly produced by Hinchliff & Co.
Circa 1849
Colour prints from wood blocks and flock
44 × 20.1 cm
Given by Mr John B. Fowler
E.2342–1974

The same pattern, but from another block, a sample of which is affixed to p 169 of *The Journal of Design and Manufactures* (1849), vol I, was produced by Hinchliff & Co.

245 Fragment with a stylized floral design
Second quarter of 19th century
Red flock
30.5 × 27.8 cm
Given by Mr John B. Fowler
E.2243–1974

246 Fragment with a pattern of spiralled vertical bands
Second quarter of 19th century
Red flock
12.3 × 14 cm
PROVENANCE Uppark, West Sussex
Given by Mrs Jean Meade-Fetherstonhaugh
E.803–1969

247 Border with a pattern of garlands of leaves and medallions, on a background of zig-zag dots
Second quarter of 19th century
Colour print from wood blocks
13 × 31.1 cm
PROVENANCE Uppark, West Sussex
Given by Mrs Jean Meade-Fetherstonhaugh
E.804–1969

248 Portion and fragment (mounted on 1 sheet), with a scrolling damask pattern
Second quarter of 19th century
Colour print from wood blocks
55.5 × 39.1 cm (portion); 42 × 19.7 cm (fragment)
PROVENANCE The Cloisters, Hereford Cathedral
Given by Miss P. E. Morgan
E.115–1972

This paper was pasted on to a newspaper dated 13 September 1843. It was found beneath no 321.

249 Three portions of a frieze with a design reproducing part of the Parthenon marbles
Second quarter of 19th century
Colour chiaroscuro print from wood blocks with machine printed background
29.8 × 50.8 cm (average size)
Given by Mr Roger H. M. Warner
E.33A–1971; E.33B–1971 neg GG.5861 CT 8593

This paper is probably part of the reproduction of the Elgin marbles, which was exhibited as a frieze (7.32 m long) by Jeffrey, Allen & Co. at the Great Exhibition in 1851.

250 Eight borders of flowers, mouldings, cornices etc, and a Greek key pattern
Second quarter of 19th century
Colour prints from wood blocks
Various sizes
PROVENANCE 'Found among the stock of Thomas Avery, builder, etc, of Ivy

House, Tenterden, Kent, which business had been in existence nearly a century and a half' (extract from a letter from the donor)
Given by Mr Alexander Reynell
E.2170–2177–1913

251 Two borders of flowers and leaves, and of acanthus
Second quarter of 19th century
Colour prints from wood blocks and flock
Various sizes
PROVENANCE See above item
Given by Mr Alexander Reynell
E.2142, 2143–1913

252 Two borders of tasselled ropes, and of vines and acanthus pattern
Second quarter of 19th century
Colour prints from wood blocks, and flock
32.4 × 53.4 cm; 18.5 × 49.6 cm
PROVENANCE See no 250
Given by Mr Alexander Reynell
E.2154–1913 neg Z.2433; E.2155–1913

Entwisle, pl 9, fig 17.

253 Panel with a bunch of flowers, and a dado of simulated masonry
Second quarter of 19th century
Colour prints from wood blocks
42.5 × 45 cm (panel); 21.6 × 45.1 cm (dado)
PROVENANCE See no 250
Given by Mr Alexander Reynell
E.2162, 2163–1913

254 Two sheets of borders: one, with small conventional flower pattern; the other, cornices with classical mouldings
Second quarter of 19th century
Colour prints from wood blocks
53.4 × 34.4 cm; 53.4 × 47 cm
Given by Mr Basil Ionides
E.1115–1921; E.1116–1921 neg Z.2438

255 Three corner-pieces and 2 borders, also a fragment with a plumed helmet
Second quarter of 19th century
Colour prints from wood blocks and flock
Various sizes
PROVENANCE See no 250
Given by Mr Alexander Reynell
E.2148–2153–1913 neg GJ.9292

256 Border of draped curtains, surmounted with a cornice of acanthus pattern
Second quarter of 19th century
Colour print from wood block and flock
35.5 × 64.8 cm

252

254

255

PROVENANCE See no 250
Given by Mr Alexander Reynell
E.2156–1913 neg GJ.9290

257 Corner-pieces with scrolling, palmettes and cornucopiae
Second quarter of 19th century
Colour prints from wood blocks
Various sizes

Given by Mr Alexander Reynell
E.2165–2169–1913; E.2167–1913 neg GJ.9293

258 Scrolling branches of exotic flowers
Second quarter of 19th century
Colour print from wood blocks
70.5 × 53 cm (portion)
PROVENANCE See no 250
Given by Mr Alexander Reynell
E.2186–1913 neg GJ.9286

259 Portion with strap work surrounding medallions containing, respectively, an Imperial eagle and a circular spray of formalized leaves
Second quarter of 19th century
Print from wood block and colour stencil
87.7 × 71.2 cm
PROVENANCE Alton Towers, Cheadle, Staffordshire
Given by the Ministry of Local Government and Planning
E.852–1951

Alton Towers was partially demolished in 1951.

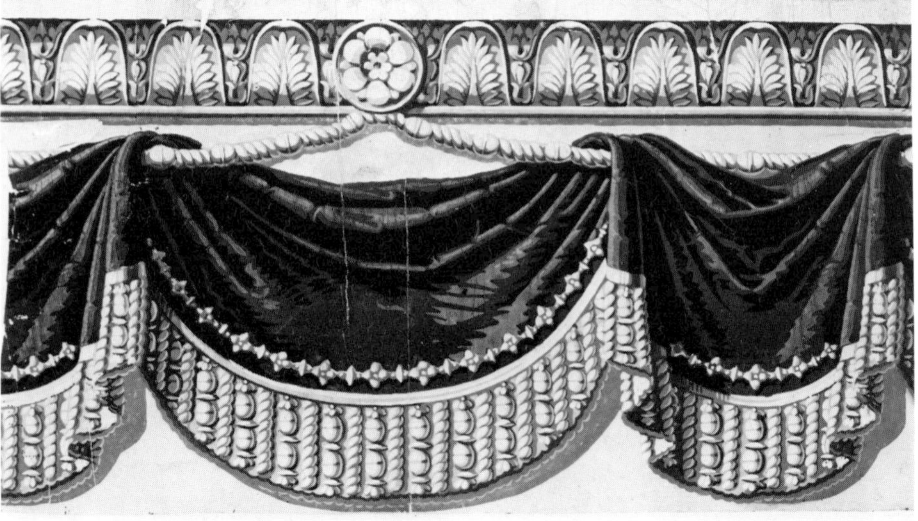
256

263 **263** Design of roses on a background simulating watered silk
Second quarter of 19th century
colour print from wood blocks
15.6 × 27.8 cm (fragment)
Given by Mr John B. Fowler
E.2268–1966 neg GJ.9287

264

257

258

260 Border of architectural motifs and curtains
Second quarter of 19th century
Colour print from wood blocks and flock
48 × 43.3 cm
Given by Arthur Sanderson & Sons Ltd
E.475–1921

261 Two fragments with a design of small flowers and leaves within a rococo framework
Second quarter of 19th century
Colour prints from wood blocks
17 × 30.5 cm; 33.5 × 15.7 cm
Given by Mr John B. Fowler
E.2269–1966

262 Fragment with a design of stylized floral quatrefoils
Second quarter of 19th century
Colour print from wood blocks
63 × 19 cm
Given by Mr John B. Fowler
E.2271–1966

263

264 Floral and scrollwork pattern in white and chocolate
Second quarter of 19th century
Colour print from wood blocks, on brown paper
40 × 58.4 cm (fragment)
PROVENANCE Uppark, West Sussex
Given by Mrs Jean Meade-Fetherstonhaugh
E.821–1969 neg GJ.9288

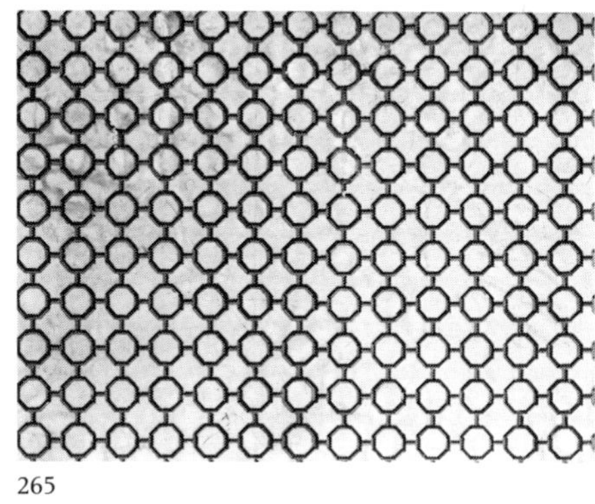
265

265 Pattern of linked bamboo octagons
Second or 3rd quarter of 19th century
Colour print from wood blocks
41.1 × 51.7 cm
PROVENANCE Uppark, West Sussex
Given by Mrs Jean Meade-Fetherstonhaugh
E.798–1969 neg GJ.9285

A similar pattern occurs in the Wallpaper Order Books of Cowtan & Sons Ltd, for 1833–61, and in pattern books, probably from the firm later known as Jeffrey & Co, for 1837–52; in the latter the design is entitled 'Chinese Trellis'. (See PATTERN BOOKS, nos 692, 692A.)

266 GJ.9291

266 GJ.9284

266 Ninety specimens, including borders, friezes, mouldings, decorative panels, motifs and corner pieces
The greater part of the first half of the 19th century
Various media and sizes
PROVENANCE 'Found among the stock of the late Thomas Avery, builder, etc, of Ivy House, Tenterden, Kent, which business had been in existence nearly a century and a half' (extract from a letter of the donor)
Given by Mr Alexander Reynell
E.2126–2138, 2142–2143, 2145–2147, 2156–2159, 2162–2164, 2166, 2168–2185, 2187–2194–1913; E.2162, 2163 neg GJ.9291; E.2170–2177 neg GJ.9284; E.2178 neg GJ.9289; E.2181 neg GJ.9283

266 GJ.9289

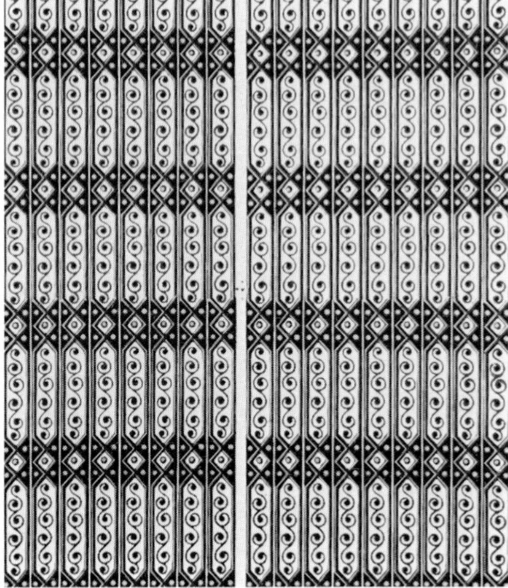

266 GJ.9283

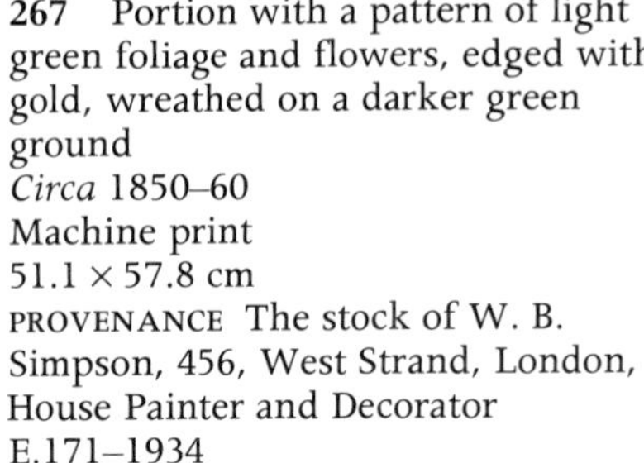

267 Portion with a pattern of light green foliage and flowers, edged with gold, wreathed on a darker green ground
Circa 1850–60
Machine print
51.1 × 57.8 cm
PROVENANCE The stock of W. B. Simpson, 456, West Strand, London, House Painter and Decorator
E.171–1934

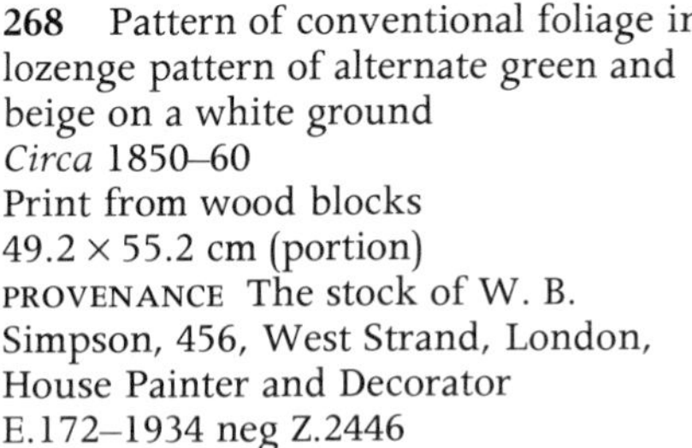

268 Pattern of conventional foliage in a lozenge pattern of alternate green and beige on a white ground
Circa 1850–60
Print from wood blocks
49.2 × 55.2 cm (portion)
PROVENANCE The stock of W. B. Simpson, 456, West Strand, London, House Painter and Decorator
E.172–1934 neg Z.2446

269 Twelve panels with various patterns, including single quatrefoil gold flowers, fleur-de-lis, etc
Circa 1850–60
Flock
Various sizes
PROVENANCE The stock of W. B. Simpson, 456, West Strand, London, House Painter and Decorator
E.159–170–1934

268

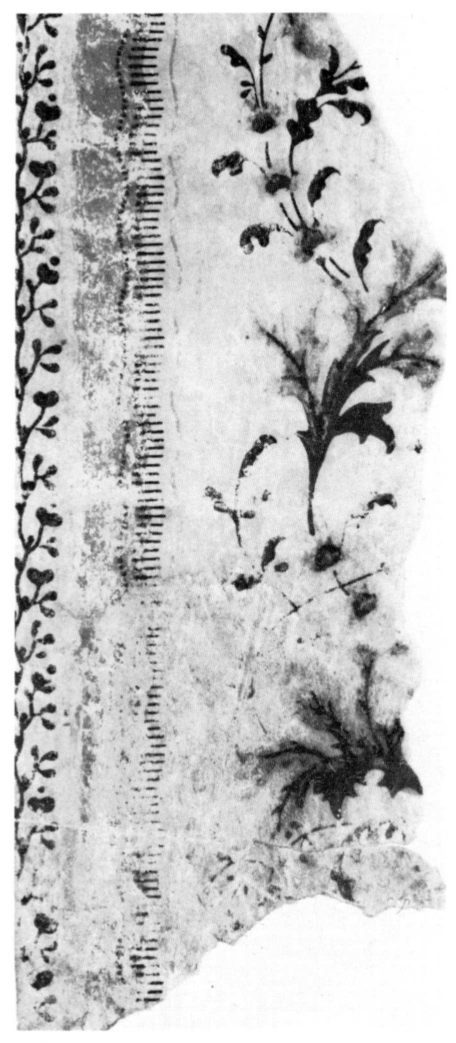

270

272

270 Trailing foliage and seaweed, within vertical bands
Produced by John Woollams & Co.
1851
Colour machine print
28.4 × 11 cm (fragment)
PROVENANCE A demolished house in Ringwood, Hampshire
Given by an anonymous donor
E.474–1968 neg GJ.9294

A specimen of this paper is in the *Journal of Design* (1851), between pp 174 and 175.

270A Six samples of pictorial wallpapers, used to demonstrate 'False Principles of Decoration' at the Museum of Ornamental Art, Marlborough House, Pall Mall, London; four of the samples bearing labels with the numbers etc
Listed in the catalogue of the Marlborough House collection, issued by the Department of Science and Art, 1853
Colour prints from wood blocks, and some machine printing
53.5 × 53 cm (average size)
E.558–563–1980 E.558 neg CT 8749 (see col pl, p 156)

no 27 Perspective representations of a railway station, frequently repeated and falsifying the perspective (produced by Potters of Darwen)
E.558
no 31 Perspective representations of architecture
E.559
[no 32]? Imitations of a picture repeated all over a wall, although it could be correctly seen from only one point
E.560
no35 Horses, water, and ground floating in the air; landscape in perspective
E.561
no 36 Objects in high relief; perspective representations of architecture employed as decoration for a flat surface
E.562
[no 36a] Perspective representations of battles frequently repeated
E.563

Another piece of the pattern no 28, described in the catalogue as 'Perspective representation of the Crystal Palace and Serpentine; with flights of steps and architectural framework, causing the same error as in No. 27', is in the Department of Prints and Drawings
(E.158–1934).

271 Crystal Palace seen through a garden archway
Probably produced by Heywood, Higginbottom & Smith, Manchester
Circa 1853–55
Colour machine print
99.4 × 53.4 cm (panel)
E.158–1934 CT 4209 (see col pl, p 181)

See also no 270A

272 Design commemorating the Duke of Wellington and his victories
Probably produced by Heywood, Higginbottom & Smith, Manchester
Circa 1853–55
Colour machine print
65.5 × 43.8 cm (portion)
Given by Mr Reginald Guy Francis Hussey
E.21145–1957

Another piece of this paper is E.157–1934 neg 82622 (Greysmith, pl 78).

273

273 Stylized design of roses, ribbons and bamboo
Circa 1854
Colour print from wood blocks
32.5 × 23.5 cm (fragment)
Given by Mr John B. Fowler
E.2272–1966 neg GJ.9310

An order for this paper in another colourway, dated 17 May 1854, appears on p 53 of Cowtan & Sons Ltd's Order Books (see PATTERN BOOKS, no 692)

274 Eight portions with various floral patterns
Produced by Hinchliff & Co., 15, Piccadilly, London
Circa 1855
Colour prints from wood blocks; flock, some on embossed, some on glazed paper
Various sizes

These samples are in T. H. Saunders, *Illustrations of the British Paper Manufacture* (1855), in the VAM Library. Hinchliff was forerunner to Scott Cuthbertson.

275 Fragment with a pattern of ivy leaves on a dotted background
Mid 19th century
Colour print from engraved rollers
22.8 × 14 cm
PROVENANCE The third floor gallery of Quenby Hall, Hungarton, Leicestershire
Given by the Squire de Lisle
E.2224–1974

276 Roses and foliage with gilt beading
Mid-19th century
Colour print from wood blocks
16.1 × 25.5 cm (fragment of border)
Given by Mr Martin Battersby
E.80–1947 neg GJ.9295

277 Four specimens with floral patterns
From the stock of Cowtan & Sons, successors of J. Duppa, J. G. Crace etc
Mid-19th century
Colour prints from wood blocks and flock
Various sizes
Given by Mr A. L. Cowtan in memory of his father, Arthur Barnard Cowtan, OBE
E.90–93–1939

E.92, in the neo-grecian style, is possibly French, *circa* 1860 (see no 550).

278 Two fragments of scenic paper showing repeat motifs of 2 men duck shooting and fishing in a mountain stream
Mid-19th century
Colour prints from wood blocks
42.3 × 52.4 cm (overall size)
PROVENANCE The Rectory, Southfleet, near Gravesend, Kent
Given by the Reverend W. M. Falloon
E.1251, 1251A–1937 neg 82658

279 Fragment of a design of stylized roses and a ribbon motif
Mid-19th century
Colour print from wood blocks
33.5 × 15.7 cm
Given by Mr John B. Fowler
E.2270–1966

278

280 Two fragments with strap work and arabesque
Mid-19th century
Colour prints from wood blocks
6.1 × 13.8 cm; 59.2 × 37.5 cm
PROVENANCE Stubbers, North Ockendon, Essex
Given by Miss Marjorie Russell
E.96, 196–1937

281 Portion with an arabesque pattern in green and brown
Mid-19th century
Colour print from wood blocks and brown flock
72.4 × 53.3 cm
PROVENANCE Cranford House, Middlesex
Given by the Borough of Heston & Isleworth
E.1243–1937

This paper was analysed and was found to have been printed with Scheele's green, a copper–arsenic green of a poisonous type, the use of which was abandoned later in the century.

282 Fragment with a design of moss roses and fern
Mid-19th century
Colour print from wood block and stencil
7 × 38.2 cm
PROVENANCE St Nicholas' Rectory, Shepperton, Middlesex
Given by the Reverend H. Scholfield
E.532–1956

The paper was taken from above the fireplace in a front room on the first floor of the Rectory. The papers and borders (nos 55, 93, 111, 155, 181, 215, 282, 332, 434, 440) were superimposed upon each other in this room.

283 Three fragments with small floral and formalized leaf patterns
Mid-19th century
Machine printed, one from an engraved roller
Various sizes
PROVENANCE Bedrooms at Berrymead Priory, Acton, Middlesex (formerly a convent of the Sacred Heart)
E.930–932–1933

The design of E.932 seems to be a slightly sophisticated version of the paper in the Strawberry Room of Lee Priory, Kent, *circa* 1785 (Department of Furniture and Woodwork, W.48–1953).

284 Three fragments with a green floral pattern on black and white striped ground
Mid-19th century
Colour prints from wood blocks
35.5 × 38.1 cm (largest fragment)
PROVENANCE Whiteways, Sissinghurst, Kent
Given by Mr Matthew J. Dawson, FRIBA
E.1136–1926 neg Z.2449

284

285 Three fragments with blue arabesques on a white ground with blue and grey stripes
Mid-19th century
Colour prints from wood blocks
15.3 × 15.9 cm (largest fragment)
PROVENANCE Whiteways, Sissinghurst, Kent
Given by Mr Matthew J. Dawson, FRIBA
E.1137–1926

286

286 Large formalized flowers and scrolling foliage
Mid-19th century
Print from wood block and flock
88.9 × 53.4 cm (portion)

PROVENANCE Alton Towers, Cheadle, Staffordshire
Given by the Ministry of Local Government and Planning
E.851–1951 neg GJ.9296

Alton Towers was partially demolished in 1951.

287 Portion (2 pieces joined) with a design of a stone bridge over a rocky gorge, and a border with a floral design; 2 rectangular sections cut out of the portion
Mid-19th century
Print from wood blocks
85.7 × 68.7 cm (portion); 113.7 × 5.1 cm (border)
Given by the Geffrye Museum
E.783, 783A–1959

The border does not seem to have been designed for use with the main portion.

288 Portion (2 pieces joined) with a design of convolvulus and tasselled cords tied in bow-knots
Mid-19th century
Print from wood block
114.4 × 71.1 cm
Given by the Geffrye Museum
E.784–1959

289 Portion (2 pieces joined) with a floral design interspersed with arabesques
Mid-19th century
Print from wood block and colour stencil
114.3 × 102.9 cm
Given by the Geffrye Museum
E.785–1959

291

290 Fragment with a Moorish-style tile pattern
Possibly produced by Messrs Lightbown, Aspinall & Co.
Mid-19th century
Colour machine print
30.5 × 15.2 cm
PROVENANCE The third floor gallery of Quenby Hall, Hungarton, Leicestershire
Given by the Squire de Lisle
E.2220–1974

291 Trailing flowers and leaves, with a tile-pattern background
Mid-19th century
Print from wood block and colour stencil
200.7 × 78.8 cm (portion)
PROVENANCE Fulbeck Hall, Grantham, Lincolnshire
Given by Mr Henry William Newman Fane
E.708–1961 neg GJ.9297

This paper was found in a lift shaft built *circa* 1890 in one of the landings which had previously been part of a bedroom. The bedroom may have been redecorated *circa* 1840 on the return of General Sir Henry Fane from India.

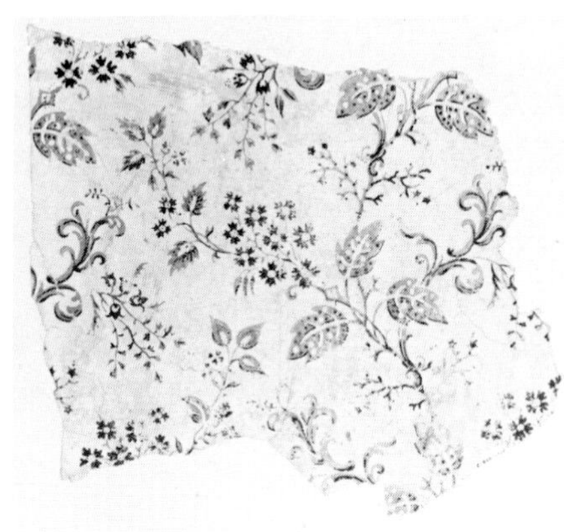

292

292 Pattern of sprays of foliage and small flowers, printed in red and grey on a cream distemper ground
Mid-19th century
Colour print from wood blocks
31.8 × 36.5 cm (portion)
PROVENANCE The Manor of Dean, Petworth, Sussex
Given by Captain W. Slade Mitford
E.1802–1946 neg GJ.9298

293 Portion with a stylized fleur-de-lis pattern
Mid-19th century
Print from wood block and flock
57.5 × 27.6 cm

PROVENANCE 1, The Cloisters, Hereford Cathedral
Given by Mr F. C. Morgan
E.2659–1962

This paper was superimposed upon no 207. Another sample is Circ. 535–1962.

294 Fragment with a design of vertical gold lines, and sprigs and lines of green foliage
Mid-19th century
Colour print from wood blocks
10 × 28 cm
Given by Mr John B. Fowler
E.2266B–1966

This paper was found beneath nos 361, 519, 355, 511.

295 Portion with a repeat pattern of lilac and convolvulus and stocks
Mid-19th century
Colour machine print
113 × 58 cm
Given by Mrs K. H. D. Pleydell-Bouverie
E.1060–1965

296

296 Trellis pattern of formalized foliage and small flowers
Mid-19th century
Colour machine print
51.4 × 56.2 cm (portion)
PROVENANCE Coleshill House, Berkshire
Given by Mrs K. H. D. Pleydell-Bouverie
E.1061–1965 neg GJ.9299

Coleshill House was burnt down in 1952. A sample of paper with very similar motifs, dated May 1861, appears on p 340 of Cowtan & Sons Ltd's Wallpaper Order Books (see PATTERN BOOKS, no 692).

297 Portion with a repeat pattern of floral sprays on a background simulating watered silk
Mid-19th century
Colour print from wood blocks
154.5 × 43.6 cm

PROVENANCE Coleshill House, Berkshire
Given by Mrs K. H. D. Pleydell-Bouverie
E.1063–1965

This paper was used to decorate the downstairs boudoir of Coleshill House. A photograph showing the paper *in situ*, surrounding an overmantel by William Kent, is in H. Avray Tipping, 'Coleshill House', pt 2, *Country Life*, August 1919, vol 46, 144.

298 Portion with a design of small oval shapes within a trellis pattern of coral stems
Mid-19th century
Colour print from wood blocks and green flock
37.3 × 54.5 cm
Given by Mr John B. Fowler
E.2279–1966

299 Portion with a design of stylized foliage within strap work, printed in gold and red
Mid-19th century
Colour print from wood blocks
55 × 42 cm
Given by Mr John B. Fowler
E.2278–1966

300 Portion with a design of vertical stripes with trailing brambles, and clubs and diamonds
Mid-19th century
Colour machine print
50.8 × 56.5 cm
Given by Mr John B. Fowler
E.2276–1966

301 Fragment with a design of stylized floral shapes within variously shaped medallions
Mid-19th century
Colour print from wood blocks
48 × 37 cm
Given by Mr John B. Fowler
E. 2275–1966

302 Portion with a scrolling floral and foliate design, printed in green on a lighter green background
Mid-19th century
Colour print from wood blocks
89.5 × 4 cm
Given by Mr John B. Fowler
E.2273–1966

303 Fragment with a design of gold-edged flowers and leaves on a royal blue background
Mid-19th century
Colour print from wood blocks
61 × 57 cm
PROVENANCE The Cloisters, Hereford Cathedral
Given by Mr F. C. Morgan
E.2525–1966

This paper, which was found beneath no 361, was pasted over a copy of *The Times*, dated Monday, 6 February 1854.

304 Portion of a plain blue-green paper
Mid-19th century
Distemper
33.9 × 36.4 cm
PROVENANCE Uppark, West Sussex
E.799–1969

A plain blue and grey-green paper from Osterley Park, dating from the period of William Chambers, is no 137. Similar pieces, however, dating from the mid-19th century, are also to be found in the Cowtan Order Books. (See PATTERN BOOKS, no 692).

305 Portion (2 sheets joined) with a design of semi-naturalistic flowers, on a background of small honeycomb pattern
Mid-19th century
Colour print from wood blocks
78 × 65.5 cm
PROVENANCE Uppark, West Sussex
E.801–1969

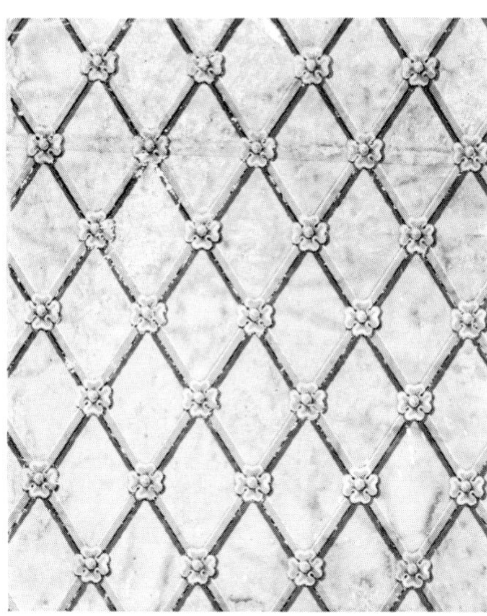

306

306 Portion (2 sheets joined) with a trellis and rosette pattern in blue and green
Mid-19th century
Colour print from wood blocks
49 × 41.1 cm
PROVENANCE Uppark, West Sussex
E.802–1969 neg GJ.5876

This paper was beneath no 362 (third quarter of 19th century).

307 Fragment with a pattern of stylized trailing plants, on a background imitating watered silk; another fragment of the same design, but the end of a length of paper, without the background printing
Mid-19th century
Colour machine print
22.4 × 46 cm 37.6 × 57.5 cm
PROVENANCE Uppark, West Sussex
E.805, 806–1969; E.805–1969 neg GJ.9300

307

308

308 Fragment with a damask pattern in 2 shades of green; another fragment of the same design in blue and pink, including the end of the length, showing the pattern printed from the blue block only
Mid-19th century
Colour print from wood blocks
36.3 × 46.5 cm; 36 × 58.5 cm
PROVENANCE Uppark, West Sussex
E.807, 808–1969; E.807–1969 neg GJ.9301

309

312 Large scrolling pattern in blue, grey and olive, stamped on the back with the trademark (a lion couchant) of an unidentified manufacturer
Mid-19th century
Colour print from wood blocks, on a white ground
43.2 × 58.6 cm (fragment)
PROVENANCE Uppark, West Sussex
E.812–1969 neg GJ.9305

309 Egg and dart pattern
Mid-19th century
Colour print from wood blocks
10 × 50.5 cm (border)
PROVENANCE Uppark, West Sussex
E.809–1969 neg GJ.9302

310 Damask pattern in ochre, brown and blue
Mid-19th century
Colour print from wood blocks
22.6 × 51 cm (fragment)
PROVENANCE Uppark, West Sussex
E.810–1969 neg GJ.9303

310

311

311 Pattern of exotic birds among semi-naturalistic flowers and foliage
Mid-19th century
Colour machine print on embossed, glazed paper
56.6 × 57.8 cm (fragment)
PROVENANCE Uppark, West Sussex
E.811–1969 neg GJ.9304

313 Design of broad stripes, with alternating trellis and scrolling patterns, stamped on the back with Jeffrey & Co.'s trademark
Produced by Jeffrey & Co.
Mid-19th century
Colour machine print
47.2 × 45.3 cm (fragment)
PROVENANCE Uppark, West Sussex
E.813–1969 neg GJ.9306

314 Trellis and rosette pattern in blue and brown
Mid-19th century
Colour print from wood blocks
34 × 58 cm (fragment)
PROVENANCE Uppark, West Sussex
E.814–1969 neg GJ.9307

315 Fragment with a diamond-shaped pattern imitating sections of granite
Mid-19th century
Colour machine print
36.2 × 48 cm
PROVENANCE Uppark, West Sussex
E.815–1969

316 Damask pattern in pink and grey (English or French)
Mid-19th century
Colour machine print, on embossed, glazed paper
49.4 × 41.2 cm (fragment)

312

PROVENANCE Uppark, West Sussex
E.816–1969

317 Portion of a semi-circular border of wall- or decorative paper, with a gold and blue vine pattern between oval medallions, on a dappled background, with scenes of cupids engaged in various activities
Mid-19th century
Colour print from wood blocks, embossed, on glazed paper
45 × 21.5 cm (semicircular)
PROVENANCE Uppark, West Sussex
E.817–1969

313

314

318 Trailing plants on a background of vermicelli dots
Mid-19th century
Colour machine print
67.7 × 38.2 cm (fragment)
PROVENANCE Uppark, West Sussex
E.818–1969 neg GJ.9308

The above 15 items, nos 304–318, were given by Mrs Jean Meade-Fetherstonhaugh

319 Fragment with a pattern of quatrefoils
Mid-19th century
Machine print
PROVENANCE 12, Hillside, London, SW19
E.572–1971

318

320 Two identical borders on 1 sheet with an interlaced cable pattern
Mid-19th century
Colour print from wood blocks and flock
140.4 × 15.3 cm
Given by Mr John B. Fowler
E.167–1972 neg GJ.9309

This design, showing variant details and printed from different blocks, appears in a pattern book of samples of wallpaper supplied for the decoration of the

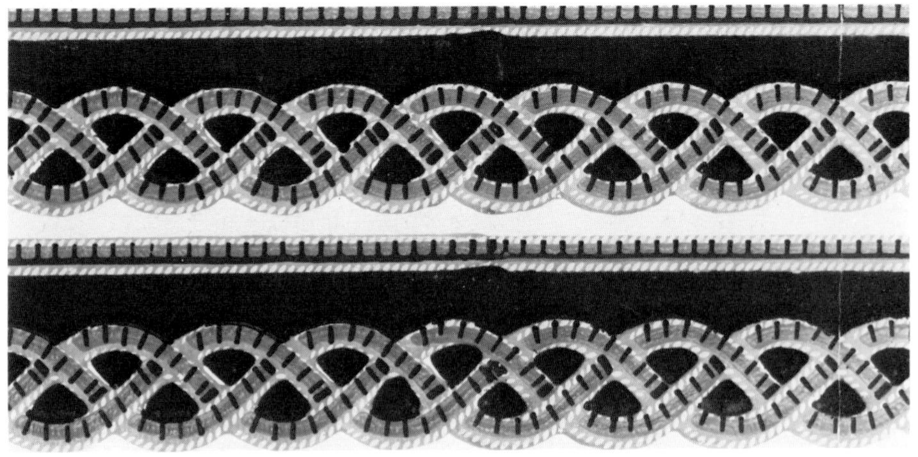

320

Houses of Parliament between 1851 and 1859. The sample on which E.167 is based, entitled 'Delicourt 1910', is on p 83 of the pattern book and was ordered on 26 September 1853 (see PATTERN BOOKS, no 696).

321 Fragment with a pattern of scrolls and flowers
Mid-19th century
Colour machine print (?)
PROVENANCE The Cloisters, Hereford Cathedral
Given by Miss P. E. Morgan
E.116–1972

This paper was pasted over no 248 (*circa* 1843)

322 Fragment with a pattern of single star shapes, half-dropped
Mid-19th century
Colour machine print
PROVENANCE The Cloisters, Hereford Cathedral
E.117–1972

This paper was found over the above item

323 Three fragments with alternate vertical bands of flowers between borders
Circa 1860
Colour prints from wood blocks
Various sizes
PROVENANCE Stubbers, North Ockendon, Essex
Given by Miss Majorie Russell
E.197–199–1937

324 Vertical design of trailing coral stems and a border of flowers on a black background
Circa 1860
Colour prints from wood blocks
27 × 32.2 cm (fragment)
PROVENANCE Radburn Hall, Derbyshire
Given by Mr John B. Fowler
E.2280, 2280A–1966 neg GJ.9311

325 Portion with a floral chintz pattern, inscribed in red ink *8–18″ rollers*, with colour key and numbered *65*
Circa 1860–70
Colour machine print
52.5 × 50.8 cm
Given by the WM
E.1817–1934

326 Portion with a trellis pattern of ribbons against a background simulating watered silk
Circa 1860–70
Colour machine print
52.5 × 49.5 cm
PROVENANCE See no 250
Given by Mr Alexander Reynell
E.2131–1913

327 Five portions with designs in various colours imitating marbling
Produced by John Stather & Sons Ltd
Post 1860
Colour machine prints, with additional colour by hand
Various sizes
PROVENANCE The stock of F. Scott & Son, 26, High Street, Hawick, Roxburghshire
Given by the Royal Scottish Museum, Edinburgh
E.794–798–1970

SE record that J. Stather & Sons Ltd added 'marbles' to their repertoire after 1860, when the firm moved their factory to Beverley Road, Hull.

328 Design adapted from William Collins's painting *'I'm as happy as a King'* (1836)
Circa 1862
Colour machine print
96.5 × 55.6 cm (portion)
No 21249 neg Z.2442

329 Portion with a pattern imitating Spanish leatherwork; flowers and foliage, within scrolling strap work borders
Circa 1867
Colour print from wood blocks, embossed
42 × 47 cm
PROVENANCE Lockwood-Matthews House, Norwalk, Connecticut, USA
Given by Mr Samuel J. Dornsife, AID
E.12–1975

The Lockwood-Matthews House was built 1864–67. The paper is almost certainly English.

324

328

330 Portion with a pattern of conventionalized poppy flowers and foliage in slate blue on a light blue ground
Circa 1870
Colour machine print
104.8 × 53.3 cm
PROVENANCE Cranford House, Middlesex
Given by the Borough of Heston and Isleworth
E.1249–1937

331 Fragment with a formal floral pattern in gold on a white ground
Circa 1870
Machine print
76.2 × 50.5 cm
Given by Mr W. L. Wood
E.2899–1938

332 Fragment with a design of flowers and foliage
Circa 1870
Print from wood block
5.8 × 48.9 cm
PROVENANCE St Nicholas' Rectory, Shepperton, Middlesex
Given by the Reverend H. Scholfield
E.533–1956

This paper was taken from above a fireplace in a front room on the first floor of the Rectory. The papers and borders (nos 55, 93, 111, 155, 181, 215, 282, 332, 434, 440 were superimposed upon each other in this room.

333 Portion with a pattern of birds and pine branches
Circa 1870
Colour machine print
48.3 × 55.9 cm
Given by Lieutenant-Colonel E. F. Strange, CBE
E.563–1899

334 Grotesque and comic scenes of men and animals
Formerly attributed to Ernest Henry Griset (1844–1907)
Circa 1870
Lithograph
61 × 50.5 cm (portion)
E.626–1945 neg GJ.9312

335 Fragment with a floral design in green
Circa 1870
Print from engraved roller
37.5 × 17.5 cm
PROVENANCE Mrs Offley Shore's apartment, The Clock Tower, Hampton Court Palace
Given by HM Office of Works
E.794–1936

336 Portion with a pseudo-Chinese pattern
Formerly attributed to Heywood, Higginbottom & Smith, Manchester
Circa 1870
Colour machine print
157.6 × 55.3 cm
Given by the WM
E.2147–1929

337 Design of salmon fishing in the Highlands
Circa 1870

334

337

Colour print from wood blocks
105.8 × 53.3 cm (panel)
PROVENANCE The gun room of Blatherwycke Hall, Peterborough
Given by Mrs O'Brien
E.347–1932 neg 82621

338 Three fragments with a pink floral pattern
Circa 1870–80
Colour machine prints
Various sizes
PROVENANCE The Old Monastery House, Turret Lane, Ipswich, Suffolk
Given by Mr Thomas Parkington
E.1736–1738–1913

339 Z.2440

339 Z.2436

340

339 Five sheets with floral and pin-print patterns
Circa 1870–80
Colour prints from engraved rollers, etc
Various sizes
Given by Mr H. C. Andrews
E.155–159–1925; E.156 neg Z.2440; E.159 neg Z.2436

E.159 is reproduced in Entwistle, V, pl 6, fig 11; E.156 in pl 7, fig 12.

340 Scenic paper, 'Skating'
Probably produced by Heywood, Higginbottom & Smith, Manchester
Circa 1870–80
Colour machine print
76.2 × 51.5 cm (panel)
E.1818–1934 neg GJ.9313

This paper is reproduced in *Country Life* (1974), vol 155, 94; E. A. Entwisle dates the paper *circa* 1890.

341 Medallion design of horse-racing scenes
Probably produced by Heywood, Higginbottom & Smith, Manchester
Circa 1870–80
Colour machine print
42.6 × 56.2 cm (portion)
E.1819–1934 neg 82623

The above 2 items, nos 340, 341, were given by the WM

341

346 Portion with a vertical pattern of roses and wreaths
Third quarter of 19th century
Colour print from wood blocks, on a micared ground embossed to simulate watered silk
70.5 × 54 cm
Given by Mr Sydney Vacher
E.2240–1913

347 Pattern of broad stripes with trailing flowers and leaves, alternating with bands of interlaced ovals
Third quarter of 19th century
Colour machine print
68 × 53 cm
PROVENANCE See no 250
Given by Mr Alexander Reynell
E.2180–1913 neg Z.2447

Entwisle, V, pl 5, fig 9.

348 Four samples of felted paper curtain material, with floral designs; each with pattern number stamped on the back

342 Sheet of uncut floral borders
Circa 1870–80 (?)
Colour machine prints
46.5 × 71 cm
PROVENANCE See no 250
Given by Mr Alexander Reynell
E.2144–1913

343 Portion with a design of red currants and light green and brown foliage on a darker green ground
Produced by Jeffrey & Co.
1872
Colour print from wood blocks
47.6 × 51.4 cm
E.1820–1934

344 Frieze with a design of stems and blossom, with a chequered edge, on a gold background
Circa 1875
Print from wood block and flock
34.7 × 52 cm
E.1893–1934

345 Chrysanthemums on a gold background
Circa 1875
Colour print from wood blocks
58.6 × 47.7 cm (frieze)
E.1856–1934 neg Z.2435

See Entwisle, V, pl 22, fig 38.

The above 3 items, nos 343–345, were given by the WM

345

347

348

Probably produced by Pavy, Pretto & Co.
Third quarter of 19th century
Colour prints from wood blocks
69.2 × 52.1 cm
Given by Miss Olive M. Flower
E.336–339–1971; E.21161–21167–1957; E.21164–1957 neg GJ.9314

Eugène Pavy, with Auguste and Jean Le Roy, took out a patent in 1853 for improvements in the production of fabrics whereby clothing, curtains, carpets, etc could be produced at low cost. 'Wallpaper curtains' are referred to in *The International Exhibition Review and Trade Directory* (1872–73). These were printed in England and France, and were produced by Pavy, Pretto & Co. Examples of curtains made up from this material are E.34, 35–1910. Other samples, with the manufacturer's label attached to the back of some of them, are E.21161–21167–1957.

349 Two portions of nursery paper: one depicting children in late 18th-century costume; the other with pictorial representations of the Four Seasons, within a trellis pattern
Third quarter of 19th century
Colour prints from wood blocks; engraved rollers
53.4 × 53.4 cm; 76.3 × 53.3 cm
Given by Mr Basil Ionides
E.1113–1921 neg GJ.9315; E.1114–1921 neg 60366 CT 8584

E.1114 reproduced in SE, pl 178 (colour).

350 Portion with a diaper pattern
Third quarter of 19th century
Red flock
74.3 × 54.5 cm

349 GJ.9315

349 60366

PROVENANCE The Great Room of the Society of Arts, Adelphi, London
Given by Mr Arthur T. Bolton
E.455–1924

351 Fragment with red flowers, green foliage and chocolate background, on a pink ground
Third quarter of 19th century
Colour print from engraved rollers
68.2 × 55 cm
PROVENANCE Cranford House, Middlesex
Given by the Borough of Heston and Isleworth
E.1245–1937

352 Fragment with a design of sparrows amid branches, in the Japanese style
Third quarter of 19th century
Colour machine print
16 × 29 cm
Given by Mr L. S. Wood
E.481–1946

353 Eight ceiling papers with floral and imitation plasterwork patterns
Possibly produced by B. J. Allan & Son
Third quarter of 19th century
Colour machine prints
52.1 cm (average size of diameter)
Given by Mr Martin Battersby
E.72–79–1947; E.77 neg Z.2434

See Greysmith, pl 82a (E.77–1947); Entwisle, V, pl 37, fig 65. B. J. Allan & Son exhibited similar pieces at the Paris International Exhibition of 1878.

353

PROVENANCE Uppark, West Sussex
Given by Mrs Jean Meade-Fetherstonhaugh
E.798–1969

357 Portion with a pattern of small leaves and flowers
Third quarter of 19th century
Colour machine print
PROVENANCE The Cloisters, Hereford Cathedral
Given by Miss P. E. Morgan
E.118–1972

The paper was pasted over no 322.

358 Pattern of vertical bands with Moorish motifs
Third quarter of 19th century
Colour print from wood blocks and red flock
81.4 × 53.1 cm (portion)
PROVENANCE See no 250
Given by Mr Alexander Reynell
E.2147–1913 neg Z.2448

Entwisle, V, pl 6, fig 10.

359 Two portions of a pictorial paper showing sections of a scene with figures in a pseudo-Chinese setting
Third quarter of 19th century
Colour machine print
59.5 × 45 cm; 45.8 × 33 cm
Given by Mr John B. Fowler
E.2274, 2274A–1966

354 Fragment of a frieze or dado, with a design of a sculptured vase with acanthus, flanked by panels with moulded surrounds
Third quarter of 19th century
Machine-printed in several shades of brown
50 × 74 cm
Given by Mr Martin Battersby
E.71–1947

355 Fragment with a design of trailing roses
Third quarter of 19th century
Colour print from engraved rollers
10 × 28 cm
Given by Mr John B. Fowler
E.2266–1966

This paper was superimposed upon no 148.

356 Portion with a pattern of linked bamboo octagons
Third quarter of 19th century
Colour print from wood blocks
41.1 × 51.7 cm

358

360 Fragment with a pattern of large pink-and-brown flowers on a background of small scrolling foliate shapes and crowns in red
Third quarter of 19th century
Colour machine print on terracotta coloured paper
Irregular shape
PROVENANCE Uppark, West Sussex
Given by Mrs Jean Meade-Fetherstonhaugh
E.819–1969

361 Fragment (3 sheets joined), with a pattern of gold-edged fleur-de-lis on a dark-blue background
Third quarter of 19th century
Colour print from wood blocks
61 × 47 cm
PROVENANCE The Cloisters, Hereford Cathedral
Given by Mr F. C. Morgan
E.2526–1966

This paper was superimposed upon no 303.

362 Pattern of sprays of blue roses
Third quarter of 19th century
Colour print from engraved rollers
45.4 × 49.4 cm (portion)
PROVENANCE Uppark, West Sussex
Given by Mrs Jean Meade-Fetherstonhaugh
E.800–1969 neg GJ.9316

This paper was superimposed over no 305 (mid-19th century).

363 Fragment with star shapes composed of formalized leaves and flowers within interlocking arabesques
Third quarter of 19th century
Colour prints from wood blocks
26.8 × 34.9 cm
PROVENANCE Lanhydrock House, Bodmin, Cornwall
Given by the National Trust
E.1765–1973

The paper apparently dates from a period after alterations to Lanhydrock House in 1857.

364 Two fragments: one, a border of moulding; the other, a rose and curvilinear trellis
Third quarter of 19th century
Colour print from wood block and flock, and machine print
14 × 6 cm; 12 × 17 cm
Given by Mr L. S. Wood
E.481A, B–1946

365 Fragment with a floral and scrollwork pattern in white and chocolate
Third quarter of 19th century
Colour machine print on brown paper
55.4 × 57.4 cm
PROVENANCE Uppark, West Sussex
Given by Mrs Jean Meade-Fetherstonhaugh
E.821–1969

366 Fragment with pseudo-Indian scenes
Reputed to have been made for an Indian Rajah
Circa 1876
Colour print from engraved rollers
53.4 × 54 cm
Given by the Reverend J. Harvey Bloom
E.681–1921

367 Fragment with a pattern of birds and insects amid willow-leaves, with a border of flowers affixed
Circa 1879
Colour machine print

362

60.5 × 55.9 cm
Given by Mr Roger Warner
E.42B–1971

The paper was taken from a screen. On the back is pasted a page from *The Graphic* for 1879. See also nos 809, 810

368 Fragment with a stylized leaf design
Circa 1880 (?)
Colour print from wood blocks
14 × 10.1 cm
PROVENANCE The Morning Room, Quenby Hall, Hungarton, Leicestershire
Given by the Squire de Lisle
E.2221–1974

369 Fragment with a floral brocade pattern in 2 shades of brown
Circa 1880–90
Colour machine print on embossed beige paper
56 × 53.7 cm
PROVENANCE Uppark, West Sussex
Given by Mrs Jean Meade-Fetherstonhaugh
E.820–1969

370 Paper from the series entitled 'Hindoo Gods'
Produced by Allan, Cockshut & Co. for the Indian market
Circa 1880–90
Colour machine print
67.3 × 51.5 cm (portion)
Given by the WM
E.1821–1934 neg GE.427

See SE, pl 169; Greysmith, pl 77.

371 Nursery paper with illustrations of nursery rhymes, the subjects separated by decorative rectangular borders; lettered with titles of rhymes
Circa 1880–90
Colour machine print
112.4 × 80 cm (portion)
Given by Mr A. G. Coates
E.769–1955 neg GJ.9317

372 Two portions, in different colourways, with a scrolling pattern of flowers and foliage
Produced by Jeffrey & Co. (?)
Circa 1880–90
Colour machine prints
63 × 48.3 cm
PROVENANCE Cranford House, Middlesex
Given by the Borough of Heston and Isleworth
E.1247, 1248–1937

C. O. Masters of Sanderson & Sons stated (7 December 1942), 'The motif of the design was found in wrought iron gates

370

at one of the historic country houses, but which house, I have so far failed to discover. I should put the date at the earliest about 1880—it was probably later. The blocks are still, I believe, at our Perivale works and had been frequently used for printing up to the period of the present War. The drawing was made by one of the Turner brothers.'

373 Fragment with a pattern of convolvulus-like flowering plants
Circa 1880–90
Colour print from wood blocks
33.4 × 16 cm
PROVENANCE The gallery of the Theatre Royal, Bath
Given by Mr Charles Clarke
E.9–1975

The gallery was closed in 1904. This fragment was found beneath no 395.

374 Medallion of a still-life subject in an ornamental gilt frame
Produced by Heywood, Higginbottom & Smith, Manchester
Circa 1880–90
Colour print from wood blocks
101.1 × 65.5 cm
Given by Mr A. V. Sugden
E. 605–1936

375 Portion with a foliated design based on a Louis XVI gilt-bronze wall clamp
Circa 1880–90
Colour print from wood blocks
112.1 × 57.2 cm
E.82–1937

This and the following three items were formerly catalogued as French, *circa* 1840. See Entwisle, V, pl 32, fig 56.

376 Portion with a still life of fruit, framed in an imitation of a Louis XVI gilt cartouche
Circa 1880–90
Colour print from wood blocks
116.9 × 78.8 cm (size of sheet)
E.83–1937

377 Portion with a scene with a chalet at the side of a lake and peasants in a mountain landscape, framed in an imitation of a Louis XVI gilt cartouche
Circa 1880–90
Colour print from wood blocks
148.3 × 69.9 cm (size of sheet)
E.84–1937

The above 3 items, 375–377, were given by Mr William McEwan, through the WM

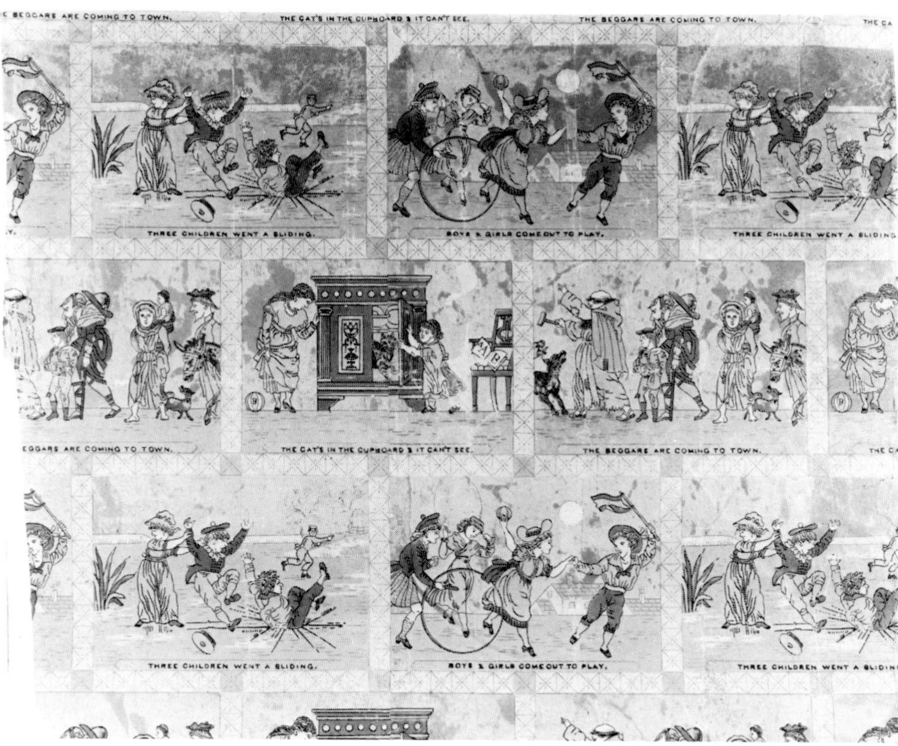

371

378 Panel, with dead game-birds hanging in an ornamental gilt frame
Circa 1880–90
Colour print from wood blocks
160 × 67.3 cm (size of sheet)
Given by Mr Martin Battersby
E.58–1947

See Entwisle, V, pl 32, fig 57.

379 Panel with a design of roses on a black ground
Circa 1880–90
Colour machine print
203.2 × 56.5 cm
Given by Mr A. V. Sugden
E.535–1936

380 Nursery paper, with a design of foliage medallions and cycling scenes
Probably produced by Heywood, Higginbottom & Smith, Manchester
Circa 1880–90
Colour machine print
58.5 × 53 cm (portion)
Given by the WM
E.1822–1934 neg B.57

381 Portion with a trailing pattern of roses and lace, within vertical bands on a black ground
Circa 1880–90
Colour machine print
47 × 53.4 cm
Given by Mr Henry Butler
E.2770–1914

380

382 Roll of 'Tile'
Produced by Shuffrey & Co.
Circa 1880–90
Colour machine print
702 × 56.5 cm
E.84–1972

383 Roll of 'Wigmore'
Produced by Shuffrey & Co.
Circa 1880–90
Colour machine print
294.7 × 55.8 cm
E.85–1972 neg GJ.9319

384 Roll of 'Welbeck'
Produced by Shuffrey & Co.
Circa 1880–90
Colour machine print
850.9 × 55.8 cm
E.86–1972

383

387

385 Roll with a pattern of entwined cornucopiae, tulips, lily-of-the-valley and other flowers
Produced by Shuffrey & Co.
Circa 1880–90
Colour machine print
850.9 × 56.5 cm
E.87–1972

386 Roll of frieze with a pattern of large scrolling leaves and dandelion plants
Produced by Shuffrey & Co.
Circa 1880–90
Colour machine print
1028.8 × 56.5 cm
E.88–1972

387 Roll with a pattern of trailing flowers and stems against a dark background
Produced by Shuffrey & Co.
Circa 1880–90
Colour machine print
1021.1 × 56.5 cm
E.89–1972 neg GJ.9320

Jeffrey & Co. printed a private range of papers of L. A. Shuffrey (*d.* 1927) in 1879 (see SE, p 211).

388 Portion with a pattern of vertical ribbons with garlands of roses, in imitation of watered silk
Circa 1880–90
Print from wood block on mica ground (embossed)
72 × 50.5 cm
E.2240–1913

389 Portion with a design of a vase of flowers and rococo scrolls, in imitation of watered silk
Circa 1880–90
Print from wood block on embossed ground
72 × 50.5 cm
E.2242–1913

The above 2 items, nos 388, 389, were given by Mr Sydney Vacher.

390 Panel entitled 'Japanese Decoration', showing flowers in a vase with borders of flowers and geometrical patterns; lettered with the title
Circa 1880–95
Colour machine print
90.2 × 55 cm
Given by Mr J. Robertshaw
E.1944–1952

391 Portion of a dado and border showing a design of foliage and tulips
Circa 1885
Colour machine print (varnished)
12.8 × 54 cm (overall size)
Given by Miss Joan Hassall, RE
E.768–1955

This paper was used for the decoration of the hall and staircase of 88, Kensington Park Road, London, *circa* 1905.

392 Roll of unused paper, with fruit and floral pattern within ogival borders, simulating a 17th-century Spanish leather hanging
Circa 1885
Embossed paper, coloured by hand and varnished
280.7 × 50 cm; 70.3 × 49.9 cm
PROVENANCE Arnsbrae, Cambus, Alloa, Scotland
Given by Sir James Younger
E.144, 144A–1974; E.144A neg GJ.9321

There is a piece from the end of the printing of this paper which shows the stages of production. The paper is probably of the type known as 'Cordelova', first produced by Brown, of

392

Pitt Street, Edinburgh. Arnsbrae was built by Alfred Waterhouse, RA, FRIBA (1830–1905). The paper, which was hung in 1886, was embossed, silvered, painted and then varnished.

393 Portion with a design commemorating Queen Victoria's Golden Jubilee; stamped on the border *Jubilee—Sanitary Washable Paper-Hangings BV*
1887
Colour print from engraved rollers
67.3 × 55.9 cm
PROVENANCE The stock of F. Scott & Son, 26, High Street, Hawick, Roxburghshire
Given by the Royal Scottish Museum, Edinburgh
E.791–1970 CT 5411 (see col pl, p 182)

See Entwisle, V, pl 21. Another portion, printed in brown, instead of black, is no 394.

394 Another portion of the above design: one roller printing in brown instead of black
1887
Colour print from engraved rollers
108 × 55.9 cm
E.792–1970

See Entwisle, V, pl 21, fig 37.

395 Fragment with a pattern of scrolling formalized plants, in white on a red ground
Circa 1890
Colour print from wood block
20.3 × 54.6 cm
PROVENANCE The gallery of the Theatre Royal, Bath, Avon
Given by Mr Charles Clarke
E.10–1975

The gallery was closed in 1904. This fragment was found above no 373 and below no 452.

396 Fragment showing conventionalized chrysanthemums in pink and yellow, with grey foliage on a light-brown ground
Circa 1890
Machine print
124.5 × 85.8 cm
PROVENANCE Cranford House, Middlesex
Given by the Borough of Heston & Isleworth
E.1250–1937

397

397 'The Sheringham Design'
Circa 1890–95
Machine print
55 × 70 cm (portion)
Given by Miss Mary Peerless
Circ.599–1967 neg GJ.9322

398 Three portions, in different colourways, of a blotch damask design
Circa 1890–1900
Monochrome prints from wood blocks

398

Various sizes
E.2237, 2239, 2241–1913; E.2239–1913 neg GJ.9323

The pattern appears to be based on mid-18th century designs by Anna Maria Garthwaite for Spitalfields damasks.

399 Portion with a pattern of a jar of roses, within a ribbon trellis
Circa 1890–1900
Colour print from wood block on embossed paper
70.2 × 54 cm
E.2234–1913

400 Two portions: one with a pattern of a scrolling plant in silver on a green ground; the other with a design of roses with intertwined stems
Circa 1890–1900
Silk and wool flock; colour print from wood blocks on a micared ground
71.5 × 53.7 cm; 70.5 × 53.5 cm
E.2235, 2236–1913; E.2236 neg GJ.9324

A pencil inscription on the back of E.2236 reads *Blackburn*, possibly the title of the design.

401 Portion with a pattern of tiles, with a design of birds, vines and pomegranates
Circa 1890–1900
Colour machine print
68.6 × 53.3 cm
E.2238–1913

The above 4 items, nos 398–401, were given by Mr Sydney Vacher.

400

402 Nursery paper illustrating 'The Months' from Kate Greenaway's *Almanack*
Produced by David Walker
1893
Colour print from engraved rollers
76.2 × 54.9 cm (portion)
Given by the WM
E.1823–1934 neg B.58 CT 7825 (see col pl, p 183)

403 Waterlilies on a lake overhung by foliage, with a cartouche on the left containing a swag of fruits and flowers, the whole against a latticework background; a colour index in each margin
Produced by David Walker
1895
Colour print from engraved rollers
80 × 54.3 cm (panel)
Given by Mr J. Robertshaw
E.1943–1952 neg Z.2432 CT 8639

See Entwisle, V, pl 36 (wrongly dated *circa* 1860–80).

404

404 Design of poppies, printed in browns and greens, on a cream background
Circa 1895
Colour print from wood blocks
56.5 × 56 cm (portion)
Given by Miss Mary Peerless
E.473–1967 neg GJ.9325

405 Design of birds and vine; inscribed in pencil with notes
Produced by Jeffrey & Co.
Circa 1895
Ink and wash
58.5 × 54 cm
Given by Mrs Margaret Warner
E.5–1945

The pattern of 'Throstle', no 530 (*circa* 1973), is based on this design.

(*opposite*) The Crystal Palace. Probably produced by Heywood, Higginbotham & Smith, Manchester, *circa* 1853–55 (no 271)

403

Paper commemorative of Queen Victoria's Golden Jubilee, 1887 (no 393)

(*opposite*) Nursery paper with designs after Kate Greenaway. Produced by David Walker, 1893 (no 402)

MARCH
APRIL
SEPTEMBER
JULY
AUGUST
JANUARY
NOVEMBER
DECEMBER
MARCH
JUNE
APRIL
SEPTEMBER

Frieze with a landscape. English, *circa* 1905 (no 458)

Nursery paper entitled 'May Day', produced by Jeffrey & Co, *circa* 1905 (no 459)

406 Nursery paper with illustrations of nursery rhymes and stories, the subjects separated by interlaced scrolls and flowers
Circa 1895–1900
Colour print from engraved rollers
56.6 × 54 cm (portion)
Given by Mr J. Robertshaw
E.1946–1952 neg GJ.9318

407 Pattern of peonies and acanthus leaves; stamped on the back with number *36112* etc
Circa 1895–1900
Colour machine print
51.4 × 50.8 cm (portion of frieze)
Given by Miss Mary Peerless
Circ.594–1967 neg GJ.9326

407

408

408 'The Cecil'
Produced by Jeffrey & Co.
1897
Paper embossed in gold and green to simulate leather
108.7 × 57.2 cm
Given by Mr Roger H. M. Warner
E.44–1971 neg GJ.9327 (portion)

406

409 Framed views of the International Exhibition of 1862
Late 19th century
Colour print from wood blocks
91.5 × 53.3 cm (portion)
No 21248 neg 82569

See SE, pl 108; Greysmith, pl 90.

410 Portion with a pattern of orange stems
Produced by Jeffrey & Co.
Last quarter of 19th century
Colour machine print
91.3 × 50.2 cm
E.2367–1932

411 Portion with a pattern of rococo scrolls of leaves and a formalized floral motif
Produced by Jeffrey & Co.
Last quarter of 19th century
Silver and pink flock
88.7 × 51.2 cm
E.2372–1932

The above 2 items, nos 410, 411, were given by Harris & Sons.

409

412

412 Nursery paper with scenes from *The Pilgrim's Progress*, by John Bunyan, within linked cartouches
Last quarter of 19th century
Printed in brown from engraved rollers
88.3 × 56.5 cm (portion)
PROVENANCE The stock of F. Scott & Sons, 26, High Street, Hawick, Roxburghshire
Given by the Royal Scottish Museum, Edinburgh
E.793–1970 neg GJ.9328

413 Nursery paper illustrating episodes from *Robinson Crusoe*, by Daniel Defoe
Last quarter of 19th century
Printed in black and brown from engraved rollers
101.6 × 50.9 cm (portion)
Given by Mr Wyndham Payne
E.714–1952 neg GJ.9329

413

414

414 Pattern based on a brocade, incorporating a pomegranate design
Probably produced by Scott Morton (Tynecastle) Co. Ltd
Last quarter of 19th century
A textile, mounted on board, coloured green, gold and white
75.3 × 54 cm (portion)
PROVENANCE 42, Portland Place, London, W1
Given by Mr P. Lawson
E.291–1977 neg GJ.9330

415 Portion with a baroque floral design
Produced by Jeffrey & Co.
Last quarter of 19th century
Red flock
101.6 × 50.9 cm
Given by Harris & Sons
E.2373–1932

416 Fragment with a pattern of trailing plants with small yellow flowers, on a blue background with white sprigs
Last quarter of 19th century
Machine print
32 × 27.9 cm
PROVENANCE Uppark, West Sussex
E.828–1969

417 Pattern of stylized leaves forming linked circles with rosettes
Last quarter of 19th century
Colour print from wood blocks
25 × 48 cm (fragment)
PROVENANCE Uppark, West Sussex
E.829–1969 neg GJ.9331

The above 2 items, nos 416, 417, were given by Mrs Jean Meade-Fetherstonhaugh.

417

418 Sparrows on branches, in the Japanese style
Last quarter of 19th century
Colour machine print
16.1 × 28.8 cm (fragment)
Given by Mr L. S. Wood
E.481A–1946

419 Portion with a design of vases containing roses and pinks, flanked by sprays of oak, bay and acanthus foliage and linked by festoons of flowers
Second half of 19th century
Colour print from wood blocks
72.4 × 53.4 cm
PROVENANCE Alton Towers, Cheadle, Staffordshire
E.849–1951

Alton Towers was partially demolished in 1951.

420 Portion with a neo-classical design of medallions and formalized husks and leaves
Second half of 19th century
Flock
83.9 × 66 cm
PROVENANCE Alton Towers, Cheadle, Staffordshire
E.850–1951

The above 2 items, nos 419, 420, were given by the Ministry of Local Government and Planning

421

421 Design in imitation of marble, with vertical stripes intended to represent inlays
Second half of 19th century
Colour machine print
99 × 58.5 cm (portion)
Given by Mr Martin Battersby
E.64–1947 neg Z.2443

See Entwisle, V, pl 11, fig 20.

422 Three specimens of wall-coverings, 2 embossed pasteboards simulating leather and 1 printed paper, lacquered and mounted on canvas
Produced by Jeffrey & Co.
Late 19th century
Various sizes
Given by Mrs Margaret Warner
E.7, 9, 11–1945

422

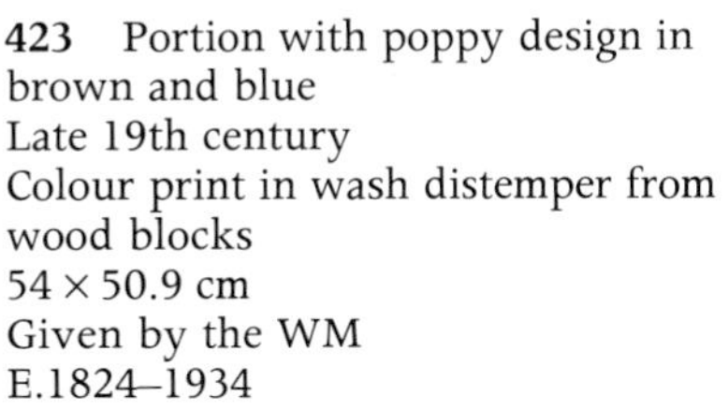

423 Portion with poppy design in brown and blue
Late 19th century
Colour print in wash distemper from wood blocks
54 × 50.9 cm
Given by the WM
E.1824–1934

424 Floral design on a background of scroll work
Late 19th century
Colour machine print
48 × 35 cm (portion)
Given by Mr Charles A. Rowe
E.743–1959 neg GJ.9334

425 Fragment with a trellis pattern containing stylized floral shapes, in magenta and blue-grey
Late 19th century
Machine print
23.3 × 50.6 cm
PROVENANCE Uppark, West Sussex
Given by Mrs Jean Meade-Fetherstonhaugh
E.822–1969

424

426 Fragment with a pattern of small formalized floral shapes in white and grey
Late 19th century
Machine print
70.3 × 36.8 cm
E.823–1969

427 Fragment with a pattern of briar roses and other flowers in white, green and brown
Late 19th century
Machine print
70.3 × 36.8 cm
E.824–1969

428 Portion with a floral pattern in orange, brown and lichen green
Late 19th century
Machine print
70.3 × 36.8 cm
E.825–1969

429 Fragment with a pattern of stylized leaves and flowers in 2 shades of grey
Late 19th century
Colour machine print
35.4 × 55.5 cm
E.826–1969

430 Fragment with a pattern of sprigs of leaves and buds, outlined in magenta on a blue-grey ground
Late 19th century
Machine print
36.6 × 38.6 cm
E.827–1969

431 Fragment with a trellis pattern of leaves and flowers, in brown and blue-grey
Late 19th century
Machine print
39.8 × 28.5 cm
E.830–1969

432 'The Dovedale'
Late 19th century
Print from wood blocks
93.4 × 56.5 cm (portion)
PROVENANCE A house in Surbiton, Surrey
Given by Mr Stuart Durant
E.392–1967 neg GJ.9335

The house is now demolished. Bills found near the paper were dated 1896.

433 Nursery paper showing characters from nursery rhymes and legends
Late 19th century
Colour machine print
57.8 × 57.2 cm (portion)
Given by Miss Mary Peerless
E.472–1967 neg GJ.9336

432

433

434 Portion with a vertical design of sweet peas on a latticework ground
Late 19th century
Print from wood block and colour stencil
69.9 × 54 cm
PROVENANCE St Nicholas' Rectory, Shepperton, Middlesex
Given by the Reverend H. Scholfield
E.555–1956

This paper was taken from between the windows in a front room on the first floor of the Rectory. The wallpapers and borders (nos 55, 93, 111, 155, 181, 215, 282, 332, 434, 440) were superimposed upon each other in this room.

435 Pattern of irises and daisies; numbered in ink on the mount, *Essex No A.30*
Produced by Essex & Co.
Circa 1900
Colour machine print
75.7 × 53.1 cm (portion)
E.818–1974 neg GJ.9337

436 Portion with a pattern of a single rose, within a cartouche of scrolling stems; inscribed in ink on the mount, *Jeffrey B.1*
Produced by Jeffrey & Co.
Circa 1900
Colour machine print
74.7 × 51.2 cm
E.819–1974

437 Pattern of intersecting circles of leaves and berries; lettered in ink on the mount, *Jeffrey B.18*
Produced by Jeffrey & Co.
Circa 1900
Machine print in cream
75 × 53 cm (portion)
E.822–1974

438 Portion of a pattern of lilies and other flowers amid stems with orange berries; inscribed in ink on the mount, *Jeffrey B.19*
Produced by Jeffrey & Co.
Circa 1900
Colour print from wood blocks
76 × 52.7 cm
E.820–1974

The above 4 items, nos 435–438, were given by Courtaulds Ltd.

439 Two portions: one with a landscape pattern; the other with a design of garlands and bunches of flowers
Produced by Allan, Cockshut & Co. from anonymous French designs
Circa 1900
Colour machine prints
95.3 × 56 cm; 93.4 × 56 cm
Given by the WM
E.1826, 1827–1934

441

440 Fragment with a formal design of flowers and barley
Circa 1900
Print from wood block and stencil
5 × 51.5 cm
PROVENANCE St Nicholas' Rectory, Shepperton, Middlesex
Given by the Reverend H. Scholfield
E.554–1956

This paper was taken from above the fireplace in a front room, on the first floor of the Rectory. The wallpapers and borders (nos 55, 93, 111, 155, 181, 215, 282, 332, 434, 440) were superimposed upon each other in this room.

441 High relief pattern of apples, branches and blossom
Circa 1900
Embossed paper, coloured by hand
22.9 × 61 cm (portion)
Given by Mrs P. M. Dowson
Circ.318–1963 neg GJ.9349

This paper was painted by Tom Andrews, of Langport, Somerset.

435

442

Late 19th or Early 20th Century

442 Road bordered by trees in blossom
Late 19th or early 20th century
Colour print from engraved rollers
27 × 53 cm (portion of frieze)
E.475–1967 neg GJ.461

443 Pattern of tiger lilies
Late 19th or early 20th century
Colour print from wood blocks
53.9 × 51.5 cm (portion of frieze)
E.476–1967 neg GJ.9339

The above 2 items, nos 442, 443, were given by Miss Mary Peerless.

443

444 Raised pattern of flowers and fruits, including pomegranates, and a serpent eating from bunches of grapes, intertwining with scrolling foliage
Possibly Japanese
Late 19th or early 20th century
Embossed paper
188.7 × 79.1 cm
Given by Mr John B. Fowler
E.356–1972 neg GJ.9338

444

445 Portion with a chinoiserie design
Late 19th or early 20th century
Colour machine print
57.5 × 50 cm
E.2765–1914

446 Portion of a floral tile pattern
Late 19th or early 20th century
Colour machine print, varnished
49 × 57.3 cm
E.2766–1914

447 Portion with a chinoiserie design in black and grey
Late 19th or early 20th century
Print from wood blocks on white 'satin' ground
47.2 × 50.3 cm
E.2767–1914

448 Portion with a formal design of vertical bands enclosing red and yellow roses, and lace ribbon, on a black ground
Early 20th century
Colour print from wood blocks
53.3 × 47.7 cm
E.2770–1914

The above 4 items, nos 445–448, were given by Mr Henry Butler.

449 Sheet with 10 samples (English and American): one entitled 'Sinclair' and with manufacturer's name, *Shand Kydd*; another with manufacturer's name, *[Jane] way & Carpen[der], New Brunswick Ph. & Chicago*
Late 19th or early 20th century
Colour machine prints
Various sizes (on sheet 86.4 × 63.6 cm)
Given by Courtaulds Ltd
E.823–1974

450 Four portions with various designs of branches and blossoms, large flowers and seed pods, birds and foliage and a formalized damask pattern
Produced by Jeffrey & Co.
Late 19th or early 20th century
Colour machine prints
Various sizes
Given by the WM
E.2780, 2781, 2784, 2785–1914

451 Portion with a pattern of flowers and small auricular scrolls, printed in white on a brown background
Probably English
Late 19th or early 20th century
Machine print
28.6 × 56 cm
PROVENANCE Voigt House, Grand Rapids, Michigan
Given by Mr Samuel J. Dornsife
E.2057–1973

20th Century

452 Fragment with a pattern of chrysanthemums and daffodils
Circa 1900
Colour print from wood block
68.3 × 26 cm

PROVENANCE The gallery of the Theatre Royal, Bath, Avon
Given by Mr Charles Clarke
E.11–1975

The gallery was closed in 1904. This fragment was above nos 373, 395.

453 Pattern of love birds on a prunus branch
1900–1905
Colour print from engraved rollers
26 × 50.8 cm (portion of frieze)
Given by Miss Mary Peerless
Circ.595–1967 neg GJ.9348

454 Frieze entitled 'Tudor'
Produced by Shand Kydd Ltd
Circa 1902
Colour print from wood block and stencil
101 × 180.3 cm
Given by Shand Kydd Ltd
E.1054–1970

See *Decorators' and Painters' Magazine* (1902–1903), vol II, plate on p 28.

455 Portion of a frieze with a stylized design of an orchard
Produced by Arthur Sanderson & Sons Ltd
1903
Colour print from wood blocks
27.6 × 34.3 cm
E.492–1967

This frieze was designed to go with the 'Heysham' filling. *JDA* (1903), plate on p 361; *Decorators' and Painters' Magazine* (1903–1904), vol III, plate on p 308.

456 'The Cupid's Dial'
Produced by Arthur Sanderson & Sons Ltd
1905
Colour machine print
56.4 × 109 cm (portion of frieze)
E.478–1967 neg GE.433

See Greysmith, pl 33 (colour), where it is wrongly dated 1915.

457 Pattern of daisies, harebells and cowslips; the manufacturer's trademark of crossed spears with pennants stamped on the back
1905
Colour machine print
44.5 × 42 cm (portion)
Circ.589–1967 neg GJ.9352

The above 3 items, nos 455–457, were given by Miss Mary Peerless.

453

456

458 Frieze showing a landscape with a river and hills in the background
Circa 1905
Colour machine print
85.7 × 27.4 cm
Given by Mr J. Robertshaw
E.1945–1952 CT 7295 (see col pl, p 184)

459 Nursery paper entitled 'May Day'
Produced by Jeffrey & Co.
Circa 1905
Colour machine print
55.3 × 61 cm (portion)
Circ.587–1967 neg GJ.9353 CT 7296 (see col pl, p 184)

Reproduced in the *Queen*, March 1905, vol CXVII, plate on p 403.

457

460

460 'Shardeloes'; stamped on the back, *Chappell & Payne Art Paper Hangings 11, Queen Street, London, EC*
Produced by Arthur Sanderson & Sons Ltd
Circa 1905
Colour print from wood blocks
106.5 × 56.3 cm (portion of frieze)
E.493–1967 neg GJ.9354

This paper was reproduced in another colourway, which is illustrated in *JDA* (1905), plate to face p 152.

461 Six women dancing in the open air, holding hands in a circle
Circa 1905
Colour print from wood blocks
62.5 × 50.6 cm (portion of frieze)
E.474–1967 neg GJ.9355

The above 3 items, nos 459–461, were given by Miss Mary Peerless.

462 Two portions of 'Manoel'
Produced by Jeffrey & Co.
Circa 1905

461

462

Colour machine print
84.3 × 57.2 cm; 54 × 57.2 cm
Given by Mr Henry Butler
E.2778–1914; E.2769–1914 neg GJ.9356

463 Portion with a design of flowers and foliage, to imitate a furnishing fabric texture
Produced by Allan, Cockshut & Co.
1905–15
Colour machine print
50.2 × 56 cm
Given by the WM
E.1831–1934

464 Portion with a floral design on a white ground, consisting of two sprays of multi-coloured flowers and foliage, each tied with a blue bow
Circa 1906
Machine prints
77.4 × 57.2 cm
Given by Mr Martin Battersby
E.62–1947

465 Portion with a conventional design of blue roses on a darker blue ground
Produced by Lightbown, Aspinall & Co.
Circa 1907
Colour print from 3 engraved rollers
43.5 × 51.1 cm
E.1903–1934

466 Portion of the 'Newbury' frieze
1908
Colour print from 3 wood blocks
57.3 × 95.4 cm
E.1829–1934

The above 2 items, nos 465, 466, were given by the WM

467 Design for 'Sycamore Tapestry'
Produced by Jeffrey & Co.
1908
Body colour
90.2 × 57.2 cm
Given by Mrs Margaret Warner
E.4–1945

A portion of this paper is E.2353–1932.

468 Portion of the 'Ribbon' frieze
Produced by Essex & Co.
Circa 1908
Colour print from 6 wood blocks
28 × 75 cm
Given by the WM
E.1830–1934

469 'Portuguese'
Produced by Charles Knowles & Co.
1909
Colour machine print
94 × 50.8 cm (portion)
E.2356–1932 neg GJ.9357

469

(*opposite left*) Panel entitled 'Romeo', produced by C. & J. Potter, 1910 (no 472) (*right*) 'The Osaka'. English, *circa* 1930–32 (no 516)

·ROMEO·

Design for 'Paddington Bear', a nursery paper. Produced by Shand Kydd Ltd, 1978 (no 536)

470 'Cleves'
Produced by Jeffrey & Co.
1909
Colour machine print (portion)
102.5 × 52.4 cm
E.2357–1932

The above 2 items, nos 469, 470, were given by Harris & Sons.

471 Six portions, in different colourways, of 'Willow Pattern Plate'
Produced by John Perry & Co.
1909
Colour prints from wood blocks
Various sizes
Given by Mr Henry Butler
E.2792–2797–1914

The Patent Office registered number on this pattern is lettered additionally *Also for Fabrics*.

472 Panel of 'Romeo'
Produced by C. & J. Potter (branch, Darwen, Lancashire) for theatres, music halls etc
1910
Colour print from wood blocks
167.7 × 57.2 cm
Given by Mr A. V. Sugden
E.604–1936 CT 7335

473 Panel of 'Cretonne'
Produced by Lightbown, Aspinall & Co.
1910
Colour machine print from 5 engraved rollers
73 × 51 cm
Given by the WM
E.1832–1934

474 Portion with a Moorish pattern; marked with Patent Office registration number *RD No. 583716*
Produced by Arthur Sanderson & Sons
Circa 1910
Colour machine print
67.6 × 55.6 cm
Given by Mr Henry Butler
E.2764–1914

475 Length of a pilaster, showing roses of various types and colours, and jasmine
Circa 1910
Colour print from wood blocks
177.8 × 28.6 cm
Given by the Guildhall Library
E.649–1952

476 Portion with a reproduction of a late 17th-century design
Circa 1910
Print from wood block and red flock
68.6 × 63.6 cm
PROVENANCE The King's Drawing Room, Kensington Palace
Given by Mr H. Clifford Smith, FSA
E.859–1954

This paper was hung when the State Rooms at Kensington Palace were restored by Messrs Bertram, Dean Street, *circa* 1910. The design is the same as that of the wallpaper in the hall of Bowringsleigh, South Devon, surrounding the Jacobean screen. See W. H. Pyne, *The History of the Royal Residences* . . . (1819), vol II, p 74: 'It was on the walls of this drawing room that the new art of paper-hangings in imitation of the old velvet flock, was displayed. . . .'

477 Fragment of metal wall covering, with a raised pattern of chrysanthemums
Probably produced by Sherard Cowper-Coles
Early 20th century
Embossed zinc
58 × 47 cm
Given by Mrs N. McLaren
E.667–1969

See SE, p 247: 'The latest comer in relief decorative materials is steel, which is embossed and nailed generally to the rafters.'
Sherard Cowper-Coles (1866–1936), was founder of the Faraday Society: 'inventor of an electrical process for making metallic wallpaper in continuous lengths, and at a price in keen competition with that of other embossed and stamped materials for wall- and ceiling decoration. This wallpaper he claimed was damp-proof, fire-proof, economical, far more sanitary, artistic and durable than any existing wallpaper and especially suitable for railway carriages, cabins and damp walls' (A. A. McGregor, *Phantom Footsteps*, London, 1959, pp 182, 183).
The firm of Cowper-Coles, Sherard & Co. were metallurgists, working during the early 20th century and established in Westminster and Chelsea. Cowper-Coles was the inventor of 'sherardizing': coating with zinc by heating with zinc dust in the absence of air.

478 'The Pipers'
Early 20th century
Colour machine print
56.6 × 106.5 cm (portion of frieze)
E.477–1967 neg GJ.9341

479 Landscape in the Japanese style entitled 'The Kaimamura'
Early 20th century
Colour print from wood blocks
27.8 × 64 cm (portion of frieze)
E.480–1967 neg GJ.9342

478

479

Early 20th century
Colour print from wood blocks
27.4 × 111 cm (portion)
E.491–1967 neg GJ.9344

486 Repeat pattern of formalized rose-bushes, in the art nouveau style, printed in green and red
Early 20th century
Colour print from engraved rollers
53.4 × 56 cm (portion)
E.489–1967 neg GJ.9345

The above 9 items, nos 478–486, were given by Miss Mary Peerless.

480 Hilly landscape with trees and a stream in the foreground; stamped on the back, *Chappell & Payne Art Paper Hangings 11 Queen Street, London, E.C.*
Early 20th century
Colour machine print
56 × 114 cm (portion of frieze)
E.481–1967 neg GJ.9343

481 Portion in the art nouveau style, with a repeat pattern of formalized trees printed in dark- and light-green on a white background
Early 20th century
Colour print from wood blocks
63 × 57 cm
E.482–1967

482 Portion in the art nouveau style, with a repeat design of formalized flowers in vertical bands, printed in gold and brown
Early 20th century
Colour print from engraved rollers
53.4 × 56 cm
E.487–1967

483 Portion in the art nouveau style, showing a pattern of rose-bushes, printed in 4 shades of pink
Early 20th century

480

Colour print from wood blocks
42.2 × 42.6 cm
E.488–1967

484 Portion in the art nouveau style, showing vertical bands of formalized poppies, printed in mauve, green and blue
Early 20th century
Colour print from wood blocks
40.2 × 44.5 cm
E.490–1967

485 Nursery frieze, showing rows of little girls in Dutch costume

487 Design of rose-bush and birds in the art nouveau style
Produced by Shand Kydd Ltd
Early 20th century
Colour print from wood blocks and stencil, on Japanese grass paper
78 × 138.4 cm (frieze)
E.1043–1970 neg GG.5869

488 Formalized flower design in the art nouveau style
Early 20th century
Colour print from wood block and stencil, on Japanese grass paper
84.5 × 61.6 cm (frieze)
E.1044–1970 neg GJ.9346

485

486

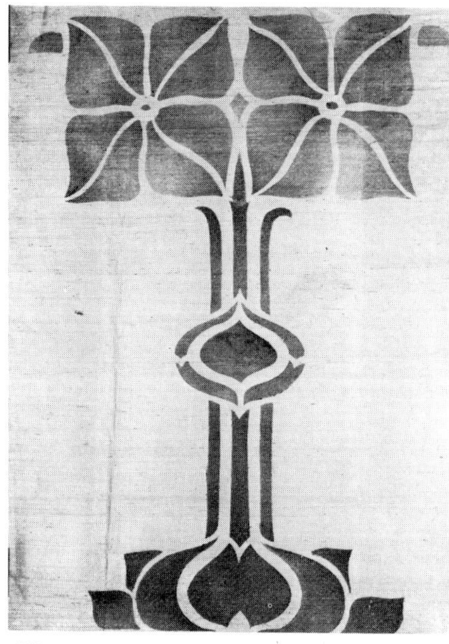
488

491

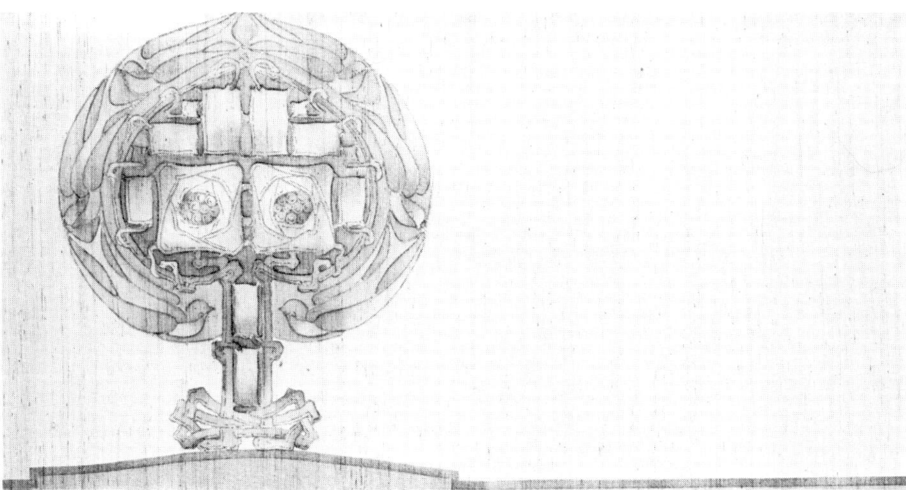
487

489 Frieze with a design of a tree in the art nouveau style
Early 20th century
Colour print from wood block and stencil, on Japanese grass paper
76.2 × 70 cm
E.1046–1970

490 Frieze with panels containing stylized groups of trees
Early 20th century
Colour print from wood blocks and stencil
179.1 × 75.6 cm
E.1048–1970

491 Design of vine-leaves and grapes
Early 20th century
Colour print from wood block and stencil
145 × 76.2 cm (frieze)
E.1049–1970 neg GJ.9347

492 Panel of a wall hanging with a design of poppies against a grating of stems
Early 20th century
Colour print from wood block and stencil, on canvas
130 × 95.9 cm
E.1051–1970

E.1052–1970 shows the same design in other colours.

493 Portion (consisting of 2 pieces joined) entitled 'The Lindyn'; mounted on canvas
Early 20th century
Colour print from wood block and stencil
144.8 × 105.4 cm
E.1053–1970

The above 7 items, nos 487–493, were given by Shand Kydd Ltd

494 Portion of unused plain wallpaper
Sold by Liberty & Co.
Early 20th century
Silk flock
15 × 21 cm
Given by Mrs E. A. Cole
E.1924–1973

495 Portion with a pattern of hollyhocks and other flowers
1910–15
Colour machine print
54 × 114.4 cm
Given by Mrs P. M. Dowson
Circ.319–1963

496 Portion with a formal floral design in crimson on a biscuit ground
Produced by the Lightbown & Aspinall Branch of the WM
1912
Print from engraved rollers
48.5 × 56.4 cm
Given by Mr Henry Butler
E.2771–1914

A sample of this pattern appears in Jeffrey & Co.'s pattern book for 1913 (J.84436): see PATTERN BOOKS, no 694.

497 Portion with a pattern of a landscape with a castle above a river; in the foreground a stone vase of flowers and 2 birds
Produced by the Arthur Sanderson & Sons' branch of the WM
1912
Colour machine print
54.6 × 56.2 cm
PROVENANCE Voigt House, Grand Rapids, Michigan, USA
Given by Mr Samuel J. Dornsife
E.2058–1973

498

498 'Oyama'
Produced by Arthur Sanderson & Sons Ltd
Circa 1913
Colour machine print
55.9 × 58.5 cm (portion)
Circ.600–1967 neg GJ.9358

499

499 Flowering tree, on a black background; with Patent Office registration number *Rd No. for Fabrics 1630*
Produced by Arthur Sanderson & Sons Ltd
Circa 1915
Colour machine print
55.3 × 61 cm
Circ.601–1967 neg GJ.9359

500 'The Daisy Wreath'
Produced by Arthur Sanderson & Sons Ltd
Circa 1920
Colour machine print
49.6 × 53.3 cm (portion)
Circ.596–1967 neg GJ.9360

501 Pattern of baskets of flowers and blue ribbons, on a white ground
Circa 1920
Machine print
45.5 × 45.7 cm (portion)
Circ.597–1967 neg GJ.9361

The above 4 items, nos 498–501, were given by Miss Mary Peerless.

502 Pattern of mauve flowers and green leaves on a black background
Circa 1920
Colour machine print on embossed paper
96.5 × 57.1 cm (portion)
E.41–1971 neg GJ.9362

503 Portion with a pattern of stylized vine-leaves and grapes
Circa 1920

500

Print from wood block in white on a blue ground
71.8 × 57.2 cm
E.47–1971

The above 2 items, nos 502, 503, were given by Mr Roger H. M. Warner

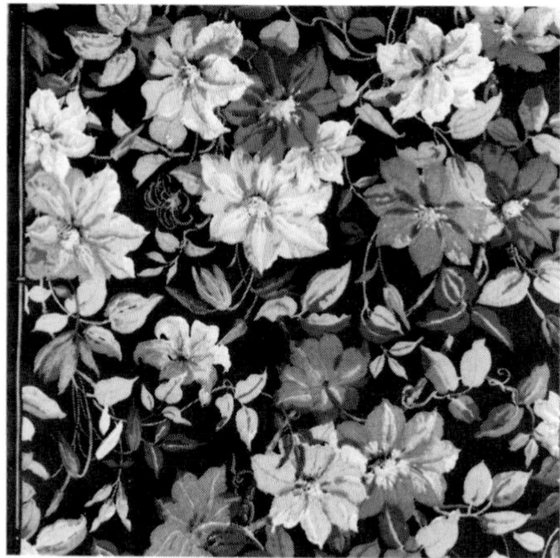

502

504 'Dukesbury'
Produced by Shand Kydd Ltd
Circa 1920
Print from wood block and colour stencil
88.3 × 55.8 cm (portion)
E.1056–1970 neg GJ.9363

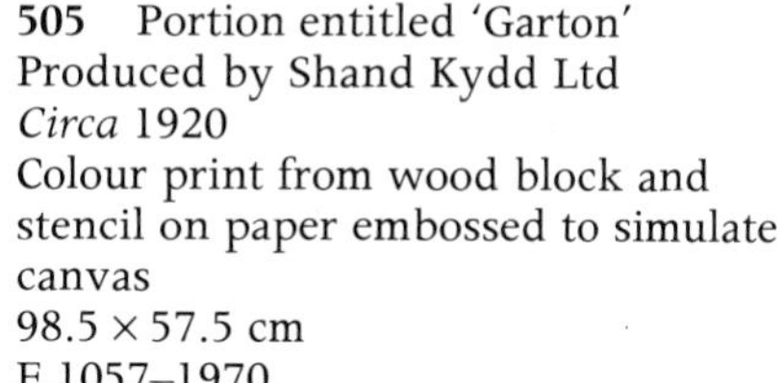

505 Portion entitled 'Garton'
Produced by Shand Kydd Ltd
Circa 1920
Colour print from wood block and stencil on paper embossed to simulate canvas
98.5 × 57.5 cm
E.1057–1970

The above 2 items, nos 504, 505, were given by Shand Kydd Ltd.

504

501

506 Portion with a pattern of roses and other flowers alternating with vertical bands of stripes
Circa 1920–30
Colour machine print
95.3 × 57.2 cm
Given by Mr Roger H. M. Warner
E.48–1971

507 Twenty-six specimens with floral, abstract and 'leather' patterns
Circa 1920
Colour machine prints, some with gauffrage
76.2 × 56 cm (average size)
E.3029–3051–1930

508

508 Six specimens of borders with various floral and abstract patterns
1920–30
Colour prints from wood blocks
Various sizes
E.3101–3106–1930; E.3104–3106–1930 neg GG.5783

509 Twenty-five specimens of various floral and abstract patterns, one with border strip
Circa 1920–30
Colour prints from wood blocks, some with gauffrage
91.5 × 54.7 cm (each)
E.2994–3019–1930; E.2997 neg GG.5786; E.2999 neg GG.5787; E.3007 neg GG.5788; E.3017 neg GJ.9364; E.3018 neg GG.5785; E.3019 neg GG.5784

The above 3 items, nos 507–509, were given by the Arthur Sanderson & Sons' branch of the WM.

509 GG.5786

509 GJ.9364

509 GG.5787

509 GG.5788

509 GG.5785

509 GG.5784

510

510 Pattern of pine branches and cones, hung with Japanese lanterns
Circa 1925
Colour machine print
80 × 58.5 cm (portion)
PROVENANCE 51, High West Street, Dorchester, Dorset
Given by the Dorset Natural History and Archaeological Society
E.1–1975 neg GJ.9366

511 Fragment with a design of roses divided by an undulating dotted band
Circa 1925
Colour print from wood blocks
10 × 28 cm
Given by Mr John B. Fowler
E.2266A–1966

This paper was found above nos 294, 355.

512 A roller for printing a ceiling paper entitled 'Coburn'; lettered with title, name of manufacturer etc
Produced by Shand Kydd Ltd
Circa 1927
Wood, copper strips and felt
152.4 cm (length); 17.8 cm (diameter)
Given by Shand Kydd Ltd
E.1058–1970

513 Portion with a pattern of small stylized flowers
Produced by Arthur Sanderson & Sons Ltd
1928
Colour machine print
58.4 × 55.9 cm
Given by Mr Roger H. M. Warner
E.46–1971

514

514 Geometric pattern of silver, blue and green on white
Produced by Arthur Sanderson & Sons Ltd
Circa 1930
Colour machine print
38 × 46.7 cm (portion)
Given by Miss Mary Peerless
E.494–1967 neg GG.57809

515 Portion of 'Mickey Mouse' border and frieze; after the Disney Studio creations
Produced by Arthur Sanderson & Sons Ltd
Circa 1930
Flock, hand-painted
29.6 × 53 cm (frieze); 23.7 × 53.3 cm (border)

515

Given by Arthur Sanderson & Sons' branch of the WM
E.3100–1930 CT 8586

See *JDA*, vol 50, December 1930, plate on p 392.

516 Nine portions, each with a border strip and cut-out appliqué of flowers, fruit etc
Circa 1930–32
Colour prints from wood blocks, some with gauffrage
103.4 × 56.7 cm (each)
Given by the Arthur Sanderson & Sons' branch of the WM
E.3020–3028–1930

'Daffodils' (E.3020); 'The Sherborne Decoration' (E.3021: reproduced in colour in *Decoration (Beauty and the Home)* (1932), vol 2, p 100; 'The Bay Laurel' (E.3022 neg GG.5790); 'The Ranmore' (E.3023); 'The Midhurst' (E.3024: reproduced in colour, *op. cit.* (1932), vol 2, 24); 'The Cliveden' (E. 3025 neg GG.5791: reproduced in *op. cit.* (1930), vol 1, 30; 'The Virginia Trail' (E.3026 neg GJ.5792); 'The Osaka' (E.3027 CT 7297) (see col pl, p 193).

516 GG.5792

517 Sixteen panels forming a continuous pattern entitled 'The Phoenix Bird'
Circa 1931
Colour print from wood blocks
118.1 × 55.3 cm (pattern area for each panel)
Given by the Arthur Sanderson & Sons' branch of the WM
E.3052–3067–1930

Reproduced in colour in *Decoration (Beauty and the Home)* (1931), vol 1, p 24. The paper was printed from 311 blocks, giving 350 shades.

518 Fourteen marbled papers and 9 marbled cloths
Produced by Douglas Cockerell & Son for book sides and book ends, lampshades and wallpaper
Circa 1932
Various sizes
51.8 × 38.2 cm (in portfolio)
E.519–541–1933

The portfolio, given by Douglas Cockerell, also contains on the inside front cover a printed label, explaining the marbling process, entitled 'A Note on the Craft of Marbling Paper and Cloth'.

519 Portion with a design in the art deco style
Produced by Arthur Sanderson & Sons Ltd
1935
Embossed paper imitating leather; gold on a black background
78.5 × 53 cm
PROVENANCE The Council Chamber in the Town Hall, Chester
Given by the Grosvenor Museum, Chester
E.1616–1977

The work was carried out by Taylor & Son, of Queen Street, Chester, whose estimate, which included wallpaper from Sandersons, was dated June 1935. This paper was recently removed in the course of redecoration.

520 Trellis design incorporating the monogram of George VI and the national emblems; lettered with the name of the manufacturer
Produced for Windsor Castle by John Line & Sons Ltd
1936–40

516 GG.5790

516 GG.5791

520

Colour print from wood blocks
174 × 56.5 cm (length)
Given by Shand Kydd Ltd
E.1069–1970 neg GJ.9367

An adaptation of this design, in a pink colourway, was produced in silkscreen after the Second World War for HM Queen Elizabeth II.

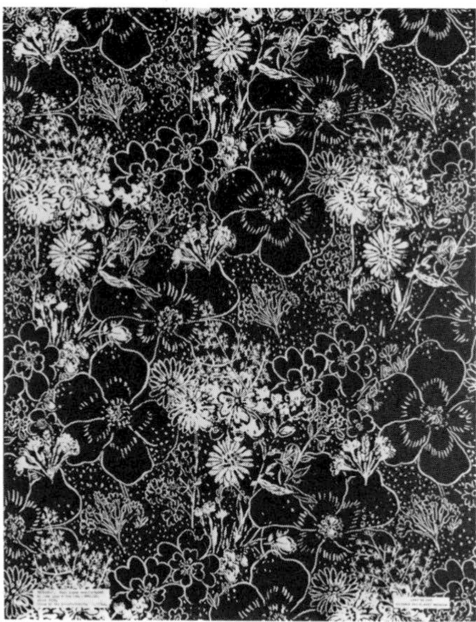

521

521 'Miranda'
Produced by John Line & Sons Ltd
Circa 1950
Silk-screen print
75.2 × 54.6 cm (portion)
Given by John Line & Sons Ltd
E.889–1978 neg GJ.9368

522 Nursery paper showing farmyard scenes; one of the 'Lancastria Line' series
1952
Colour machine print
74.5 × 54.2 cm
Given by Arthur Sanderson & Sons Ltd
E.891–1978 neg GJ.9370

522

523

523 'Stafford'
Produced by John Line & Sons Ltd
1952
Hand-painted blue silk flock, on a watered silk background
75 × 54.5 cm (portion)
Given by John Line & Sons Ltd
E.889–1979 neg GJ.9372

524

524 'Giovanni'
Produced by John Line & Sons Ltd
1952
Flock
45.5 × 48.2 cm (portion)
Given by Shand Kydd Ltd
E.1073–1970 neg GJ.9373

This paper was designed at the request of the Ministry of Works when war damage in St James's Palace was being repaired. This sample shows only one application of flock, but for St James's it was produced with a double layer of flock.

525 Portion with a relief pattern of curvilinear trellis work, on a background simulating hessian
Possibly German
Circa 1960
Colour machine print
56.5 × 43.5 cm
PROVENANCE The Cloisters, Hereford Cathedral
Given by Miss P. E. Morgan
E.120–1972

In 1960 John Line & Sons Ltd produced *Frolic*, a pattern book containing some German imported wallpapers made by the *tiefdruck* method. This deep printing or embossing on flat paper gave the effect of plaster work. This paper was pasted over no 537.

526 Three portions, in different colourways, of a paper entitled 'Besford Court', based on the Tudor pattern from Besford Court, Worcestershire; lettered in the margin with title, manufacturer's name etc and numbered on the back with serial numbers
Produced by Cole & Son (Wallpapers) Ltd
Circa 1963
Colour screen prints
84 × 56.5 cm (average size)
E.1674–1676–1974

The original paper, with a pattern of the arms of England, Tudor roses, etc, dating from 1550–75, on which this wallpaper is based, is no 4. 'Besford Court' was produced for the Shakespeare quatercentenary exhibitions held at the VAM.

527 Portion of a paper entitled 'The Stratford', based on an English wall- or lining paper of the first half of the 17th century; lettered in the margin with title, manufacturer's name etc
Produced by Cole & Son (Wallpapers) Ltd
Circa 1964
Screen print
106.1 × 57 cm
E.1677–1974

This paper is based on a fragment of 'black stitch work' floral paper and was produced for the Shakespeare quatercentenary exhibitions held at the VAM.

The above 2 items, nos 526, 527, were given by Cole & Son (Wallpapers) Ltd.

528 Portion of a paper (2 lengths joined, each with 3-pattern repeats) reproducing a 17th century lining paper, incorporating within its design the arms of the Haberdashers' Company and the initials *GM* (Guillelmus et Maria)
1969
Screen print
114.1 × 108.8 cm (overall size of sheet)
Given by the Haberdashers' Company
E.842–1969

The lining paper, which is a print from a woodcut, is no 26. The small committee room of the Haberdashers' Company's Hall is hung with this reproduction wallpaper, which was made by the Royal College of Art.

529 Four specimens, including different colourways, of 'Decameron', with an illustration of the design; E.1659 lettered in the margin *Design No. 56 By Courtesy Of The Victoria & Albert Museum. Osborne & Little. Printed in England*; E.1659A lettered *Design No: 56 Decameron*; numbered on the backs *56A, C, E* and *F*
Produced by Osborne & Little Ltd
Circa 1973
Colour screen prints and photo offset
E.1659, 1659A–1662–1974; E.1662 neg GJ.9378

The pattern of 'Decameron' is based on an early 20th century design for a printed muslin (E.819–1968) by Albert Edward Hayes (1880–1968), q.v.

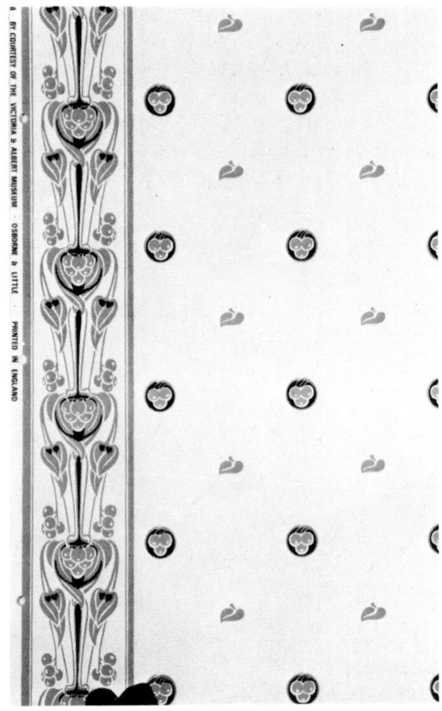

529

530 Four specimens, including different colourways, of 'Throstle', with an illustration of the design
E.1654–1657 numbered on the backs *59A–c*; E.1654A lettered *Design No: 59 Throstle*
Produced by Osborne & Little Ltd
Circa 1973
Colour screen prints and photo offset
60.9 × 38.1 cm (each)
E.1654, 1654A–1657–1974; E.1655 neg GJ.9379

The pattern of 'Throstle' is based on an ink and wash design by an unknown artist for a wallpaper produced by Jeffrey & Co in 1895 (no 405).

531 A roll of the paper described in the entry above, in another colourway
Circa 1973
Colour screen prints and photo offset
931.1 × 80.5 cm
E.1658–1974

532 A roll of the wallpaper described in no 530, in another colourway
Circa 1973
Colour screen prints and photo offset
818.9 × 80.5 cm
E.1659–1974

The above 4 items, nos 529–532, were given by Osborne & Little Ltd

533 'Nowton Court', lettered with title in the margin
A reprint by Cole & Son (Wallpapers)

530

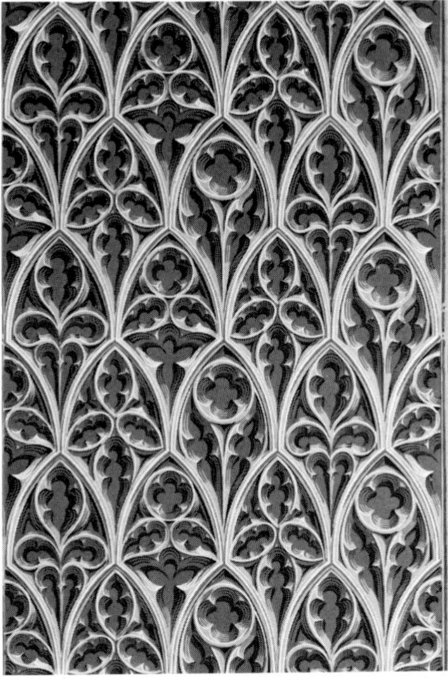

533

Ltd of a flock and block wallpaper
Circa 1975
Colour print from wood blocks
119 × 57.1 cm (portion)
Given by Cole & Son (Wallpapers) Ltd
E.642–1976 neg GJ.472

An order for the original paper, with sample in flock and block, dated 1 December 1840, is in a volume of the Wallpaper Order Books formerly belonging to Cowtan & Sons Ltd (see PATTERN BOOKS, no 692). The reprint was made by Cole & Son from fragments found at Nowton Court, Bury St Edmunds, Suffolk.

534

534 Unused fragment reproducing, in a reduced version, William Morris' design for a wallpaper entitled 'Willow' (1874)
Produced by Osborne & Little Ltd for Liberty & Co.
Circa 1975
Screen print
17.5 × 36 cm
E.180–1978 neg GJ.9380

The paper is produced in another four colourways. A sample of the same pattern in an early 20th century cotton, printed in red, is in the Department of Textiles, no T.209–1953. The exhibition *Liberty's 1875–1975*, for which this paper was produced, was held at the VAM from July to October 1975.

535 Design for a vinyl paper, 'Abelard'
Produced in the Vymura 'Studio One' range by ICI (Ltd) Paints Division
1975–76
Poster colour, acrylic paint and collage on black paper
96 × 46 cm
Given by ICI Ltd (Paints Division)
E.1033–1979

A co-ordinating paper is 'Heloise'. Specimens of both papers are in the pattern-book 'Studio One': see PATTERN BOOKS, no 725.

536 Design for a vinyl nursery paper, 'Paddington Bear'; inscribed with title etc, colour key, measurement and *Job No. 35,330*; E.2730 signed *C. Bailey*, inscribed with measurement etc and mounted on board
Produced by Shand Kydd Ltd
1978
2 sheets of art work
Indian ink, coloured inks and rotagravure
54.7 × 80 cm (size of board, E.2730)
Given by Shand Kydd Ltd
E.2730, 2731–1980 CT 8750 (see col pl, p 194)

The design is based on illustrations by Peggy Fortnum for Michael Bond's series of children's books.

537 Portion of an unprinted green paper
20th century (?)
PROVENANCE The Cloisters, Hereford Cathedral
Given by Miss P. E. Morgan
E.119–1972

This paper was pasted beneath no 525, possibly only serving as a lining paper.

See also 'France': nos 594, 612; 'United States': nos 625–629, 642

FRANCE

18th Century

538 Three wall hangings with designs of flowers, birds etc within rococo scrolls
Mid-18th century
Oil on canvas
242.5 × 118.2 cm; 243.9 × 118.2 cm; 238.7 × 94.2 cm
Given by Mr John B. Fowler
E.449–451–1973

539 Floral design in 2 tones of blue, on a stripe and pin-point background
Fabrique de Martin Bijou à Paris, no 90
Circa 1760
Print from wood block and colour stencil
19.1 × 12.8 cm (fragment)
Given by the WM
E.1555–1934 neg GH.915

See H. Clouzot, 'Le Papier Peint au Début du XVIIIe siècle au L'Enseigne du Papillon', *Renaissance de l'Art française*, April, 1925, vol 8, p 159.

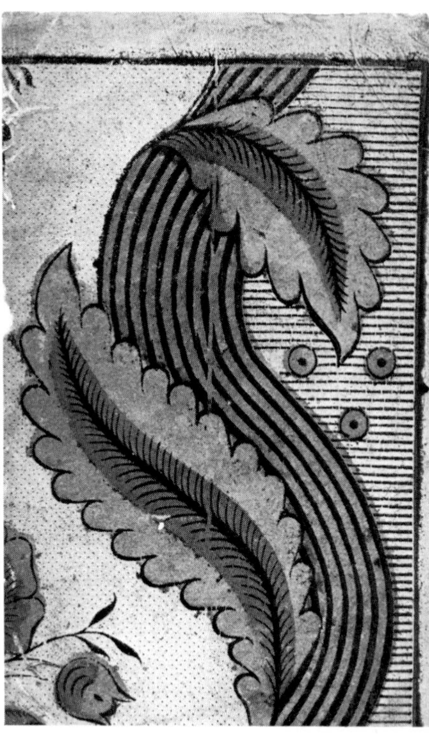

539

540 Two panels: one showing a man and woman beside a stream, fishing; the other, a man and woman fleeing from a burning cottage
Circa 1770
Etchings: each printed from 2 plates, coloured by hand
135 × 50 cm (average size of each)
E.5398, 5399–1919; E.5398 neg 56527; E.5399 CT 7299 (see col pl, p 211)

541 Grisaille *dessus-de-porte*, showing a youth soliciting alms from 2 country women
Circa 1770–80
Print from wood blocks
60.4 × 83.9 cm
PROVENANCE A house in La Haute Ville, Vaison, France, formerly the residence of the Marquis de Taulignan
Given by Mrs Tremayne
E.1237–1930

542 Fragment of an arabesque panel, with a design of medallions, vases, cupids, doves and garlands of flowers; with a separate border of moulding
Produced by Réveillon, Paris
Circa 1770–80
Colour print from wood blocks
86.4 × 67.3 cm (size of sheet); 3.8 cm (size of border)
Given by Mr Martin Battersby
E.57–1947

540

543 Length with a design of 2 panels repeated, of scroll work, birds, vases of flowers, tripods, medallions and a Pan figure; stamped on the back with the cypher of the manufacturer (?) and numbered *3*
Circa 1780
Colour print from wood blocks
398.9 × 53.4 cm
E.738–1912

544 Panel (consisting of 4 sheets joined) with a pattern based on 'L'Eau et le Feu' (produced by Réveillon, Paris)
Circa 1780
Chiaroscuro colour print from wood blocks
165.5 × 54.5 cm
E.835–1980 CT 8744 (see col pl, p 211)

The pattern shows slight variations from the Réveillon paper and may be an early 19th century copy. It was acquired from the archives of Berthaud et Perrin, a Lyons textile firm. Some of Réveillon's most popular designs were copied in textiles.

545 Grisaille *dessus-de-porte* showing a Swiss peasant scene; with a separate border of Greek key pattern
Circa 1780–90
Print from wood blocks
73.8 × 114 cm; 12.4 cm (depth of border)
PROVENANCE A house in La Haute Ville, Vaison, France, formerly the residence of the Marquis de Taulignan
E.46–1937

With no 541, part of a set of scenic designs.

546 Panel with Etruscan vase, flowers, doves and, below the vase, a Greek style frieze of figures; with a separate border of roses and scrolls along the lower and upper edges and the left-hand side
Probably produced by Réveillon, Paris
Late 18th century
Colour print from wood blocks
236.4 × 95.3 cm; 19.1 cm (depth of border)
PROVENANCE A house in La Haute Ville, Vaison, France, formerly the residence of the Marquis de Taulignan
E.1037–1925 neg 56528

E.2263–1929, mounted with this paper, forms part of the same pattern. For another fragment of the border, see no 605.

547 Hunting scene: a dead buck, watched by 2 hounds, alternating with a tripod vase of roses; with a separate border of Greek key pattern in green affixed to 3 edges
Late 18th century
Colour print from wood blocks
185.5 × 110.6 cm (portion); 9.6 cm (border)
PROVENANCE An old house at Avèze, Gard, France
E.2262–1929

548 Pattern of brown with white spots, decorated with cupids and flowers, with a border of reed and acanthus leaf
Late 18th century
Colour print from wood blocks
89 × 49 cm (portion)
PROVENANCE A house in La Haute Ville, Vaison, France, formerly the residence of the Marquis de Taulignan
E.1038A–1925

This paper was beneath no 576.

The above 4 items, nos 545–548, were given by Mrs Tremayne

549 Panel (several fragments joined) of grisaille with a design showing a fisherman and 2 country women on a river bank; with additional designs in colour, cut out and pasted on, to represent a fringed pelmet above and a border below
Late 18th century (?)
Body colour
54.4 × 46 cm
Given by Mr D. N. Japp
E.83–1956 neg GJ.9473

The donor states that this paper was removed from the Château du Poucy, Jégun, Gers, France.

546

549

551 *Dessus-de-porte* showing (?) Chastity extinguishing the flames of Love
Circa 1800
Colour print from wood blocks
71.8 × 101.6 cm
PROVENANCE A house in La Haute Ville, Vaison, France, formerly the residence of the Marquis de Taulignan
E.1238–1930

The paper was discovered beneath no 599 and over no 541.

552 Two portions: one has festooned, fringed drapery, with a border of galloon pattern and a dado with an arcade; the other (illustrated) is in a different colourway and has a different border of leaf and flower pattern
Circa 1800
Colour print from wood blocks
125.2 × 73.1 cm
PROVENANCE A house in La Haute Ville, Vaison, France, formerly the residence of the Marquis de Taulignan
E.1039, 1042–1925; E.1042 neg GJ.9474

553 Fragment with medallions of animals and insects arranged singly and in groups of 4, background pattern of stepped lozenge shapes and border with bunches of grapes
Circa 1800
Colour print from wood blocks
71.2 × 39.4 cm (fragment); 55.2 × 85.1 cm (border)
PROVENANCE A house in La Haute Ville, Vaison, France, formerly the residence of the Marquis de Taulignan
E.1040–1925

19th Century

550 A Greek vase pattern between vertical stripes, on a yellow ground; stamped on the back with the Georgian Excise duty stamp and *Foreign Paper Customs*
Circa 1800
Colour print from wood block and black flock
27 × 41.9 cm (portion)
Given by Mr A. L. Cowtan in memory of his father, Arthur Barnard Cowtan, OBE
E.98–1939 neg GG.5875

This paper is very similar in style and production to the Egyptian paper from Crawley House, no 153 (*circa* 1806).

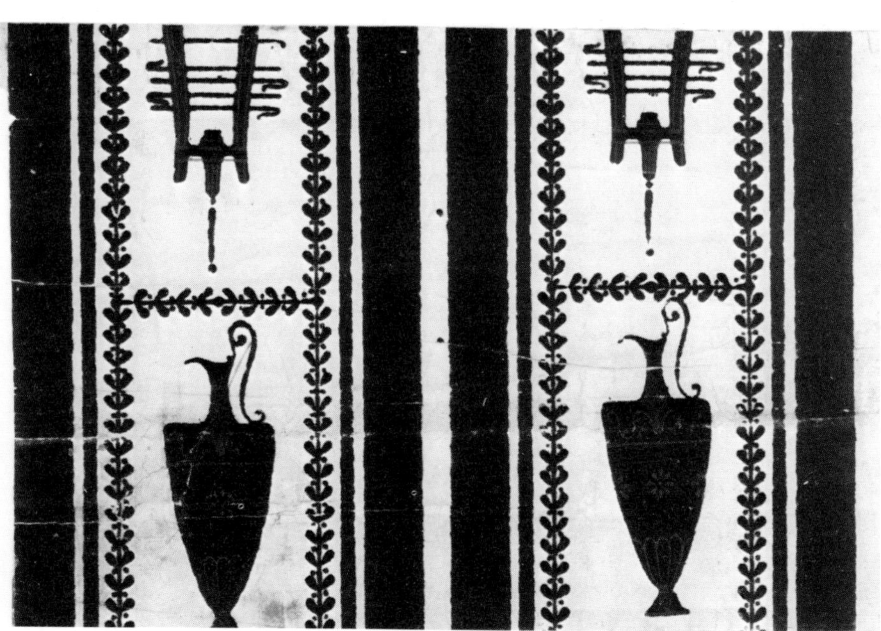

550

552

554 Fragment with a pattern of festoons of hanging silk
Circa 1800
Colour print from wood blocks
47 × 29.2 cm
PROVENANCE A house in La Haute Ville, Vaison, France, formerly the residence of the Marquis de Taulignan
E.1043–1925 neg GJ.9475

This paper was discovered above no 548 and beneath no 576.

555 Fragment with flowers and ribbon, and with a separate border
Circa 1800
Colour print from wood blocks
47.7 × 55.4 cm (overall size); 6.4 cm (depth of border)
PROVENANCE A house in La Haute Ville, Vaison, France, formerly the residence of the Marquis de Taulignan
E.1044–1925

The above 5 items, nos 551–555, were given by Mrs Tremayne

556 Portion with a repeat pattern of leaves forming a circle round six petalled flowers, printed in grey and white on a plain background
Circa 1800
Colour print from wood blocks
34 × 48.5 cm
PROVENANCE The Désert de Retz, near Chambourcy, Seine et Oise, France
Given by Mr John B. Fowler
E.2284–1966

557 *Dessus-de-porte* with trophy consisting of vase, dish, pan-pipes, thyrses, fruit etc in grey and brown on a brown ground
Possibly French
Circa 1810
Colour print from wood blocks
109.8 × 81.3 cm
E.481–1931

558 *Dessus-de-porte* with black lamp, decorated in red, on a purplish ground, surrounded by golden leaves on a brown ground
Circa 1810
Colour print from wood blocks
86.1 × 135.3 cm
E.482–1931 neg GJ.9477

554

558

559 *Dessus-de-porte* with a cupid drinking within a formalized garland, grey on a grey ground
Circa 1810
Colour print from wood blocks
83.2 × 108.7 cm
E.483–1931 neg GJ.9478

560 Panel with green flowers and leaves crossed by diagonal shading, on a bluish-green ground
Possibly produced by Zuber et Cie, Rixheim
Circa 1810–20
Colour print from wood blocks
165.1 × 48.7 cm
E.480–1931

561 Fragment of border: design in black on red and brown ground, with splatterwork in grey, in imitation of marble
Early 19th century
Colour print from wood blocks
24.1 × 21.6 cm (size of sheet)
E.48–1947

562 Seven fragments of wallpaper, corner-pieces and borders: classical mouldings, marbles, ribbons, leaves etc
Early 19th century
Colour prints from wood blocks, and flock
Various sizes
E.49–56–1947

The above 2 items, nos 561, 562, were given by Mr Martin Battersby

563 Diaper pattern, a frieze of drapery and a border of convolvulus climbing up a pole; at the bottom a border of roses
Early 19th century
Colour print from wood blocks
198.1 × 58.4 cm (length)
PROVENANCE A house in La Haute Ville, Vaison, France, formerly the residence of the Marquis de Taulignan
E.3403–1922

This paper had E.3409–1922 as a border. See no 570.

564 Portion with a grisaille pattern of a dancing child holding a rose garland in the centre of each panel
Early 19th century
Colour print from wood blocks
48.2 × 58.4 cm
PROVENANCE A house in La Haute Ville, Vaison, France, formerly the residence of the Marquis de Taulignan
E.3404–1922

This piece forms a dado to no 548.

559

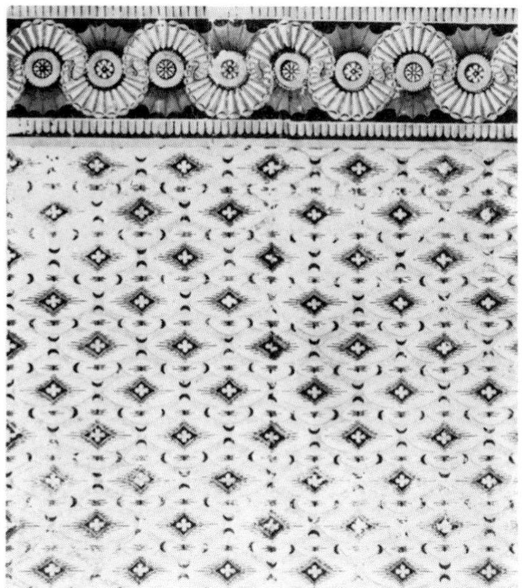

565

565 Design of trellis and quatrefoils in diamonds, and a border of ribbon pattern
Early 19th century
Colour print from wood blocks
55.9 × 49.5 cm (portion)
PROVENANCE A house in La Haute Ville, Vaison, France, formerly the residence of the Marquis de Taulignan
E.3405–1922 neg GJ.9476

Another piece is E.2513–1930

The above 3 items, nos 563–565, were given by Mrs Tremayne

566 Panel imitating a white satin curtain, on a rail against a green wall
Produced by Dufour et Leroy, Paris
Circa 1812
Colour print from wood blocks and flock
227.4 × 57.1 cm (overall size of sheet)
Given by Mr W. L. Wood
E.2906–1938

Reproduced in catalogue (no 120) of exhibition, *Trois Siècles des Papiers Peints*, held at the Musée des Arts Décoratifs, Paris, 1967. See Greysmith, pl 70c.

567 'La Chasse de Compiègne' ('La Chasse aux Courses')
Twenty-five panels with a continuous hunting scene, after Carle Vernet
Produced by Jacquemart et Bénard, 39, Rue de Montreuil, Paris
1814
Colour prints from wood blocks
226.7 × 53.3 cm (each)
Given by Sir William James Ingram, Bart
E.3683–3707–1913; E.3683–3686 CT 8741 (see col pl, p 212)

567 59971

567 49489

567 49490

567 58329

59971; E.3687–3689 neg 49489; E.3690–3692 neg 49490; E.3693–3695 neg 58329; E.3696–3698 neg 59973; E.3699–3701 neg 59974; E.3702–3704 neg 59975; E.3705–3707 neg 59976.

Entwisle, *FS*, p. 64.

568 Portion showing a flowering cactus amid Egyptian remains
Second quarter of 19th century
Colour print from wood blocks
115 × 50 cm
Given by Shand Kydd Ltd
E.1263–1980

569 Three specimens of borders, with mouldings, medallions and formalized leaves; E.99 stamped on the back with the Excise duty stamp and *Foreign Paper Customs 48*; E.100, 101 stamped *34* and *L*
Circa 1820
Colour prints from wood blocks and flock
Various sizes
Given by Mr A. L. Cowtan in memory of his father, Arthur Barnard Cowtan, OBE
E.99–101–1939

570 Portion of a frieze: in an oval formed by a green wreath a cupid driving a 2 horse chariot; and, in an octagonal panel, a torch
Circa 1820
Colour print from wood blocks
54.7 × 45.1 cm
PROVENANCE A house in La Haute Ville, Vaison, France, formerly the residence of the Marquis de Taulignan
E.2502–1930

See Nancy McClelland, *Historic Wall-Papers* (Philadelphia and London, 1924), plate on p 222. This paper formed a border to nos 541, 563. Other portions are nos 575 and E.3409–1922.

Panel based on Réveillon's 'L'Eau et le Feu'. French, *circa* 1780 (no 544)

Pictorial panel. French, *circa* 1770 (no 540)

Panels from 'La Chasse de Compiègne'.
French, 1814 (no 567)

Corner-pieces. French, third quarter of 19th century (no 613)

Panel from 'Les Incas', produced by Dufour et Leroy, Paris, 1826 (no 578)

Panel with birds on a rock, bamboo and flowers. Chinese, late 17th century (no 652)

567 59973

567 59974

571 Three fragments of a frieze: in a panel, a pack ass with sheep (yellow ochre on a grey ground)
Circa 1820
Colour print from wood blocks
59.8 × 64.8 cm
PROVENANCE A house in La Haute Ville, Vaison, France, formerly the residence of the Marquis de Taulignan
E.2504–1930

572 An almost naked child with a garland in an inverted heart-shaped panel (dark grey on light grey ground)
Circa 1820

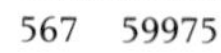

567 59975

567 59976

Colour print from wood blocks
48.6 × 36.2 cm (portion of a frieze)
PROVENANCE A house in La Haute Ville, Vaison, France, formerly the residence of the Marquis de Taulignan
E.2505–1930 neg GJ.9479

573 Panel with a greenish-blue marbled centre, surrounded by a pattern resembling iron work; another design, with a flame-like pattern on a ground strewn with arrowheads
Circa 1820
Colour print from wood blocks
54.6 × 89 cm (panel); 62.2 × 18.4 cm (fragment)

572

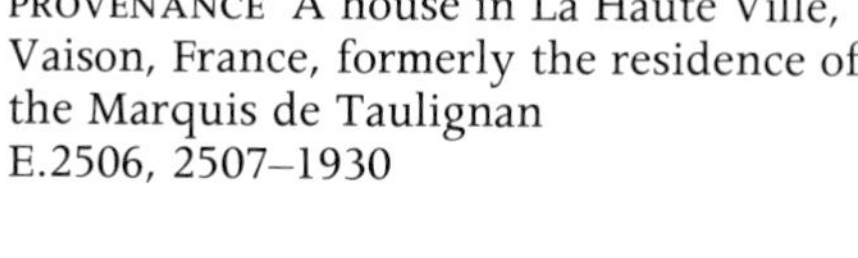

PROVENANCE A house in La Haute Ville, Vaison, France, formerly the residence of the Marquis de Taulignan
E.2506, 2507–1930

574 Two portions with a pattern of vertical stripes of light and dark green: at the top a frieze consisting of a reddish-brown floriated strip; below, sheaves of corn
Circa 1820
Colour print from wood blocks
67.2 × 48 cm; 49 × 49.5 cm
PROVENANCE A house in La Haute Ville, Vaison, France, formerly the residence of the Marquis de Taulignan
E.3407–1922 neg GJ.9480; E.2508–1930

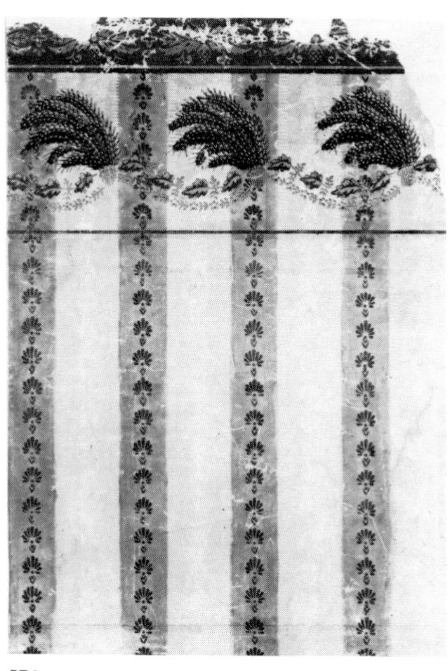

574

575 GJ.9481

575 Two fragments with a pattern of fringed silk hangings decorated with lyre shapes, on a diaper background
Circa 1820
Colour prints from wood block and flock
Various sizes
PROVENANCE A house in La Haute Ville, Vaison, France, formerly the residence of the Marquis de Taulignan
E.2503–1930; E.3408–1922 neg GJ.9481; E.3408A–1922 neg GJ.9482

The above 6 items, 570–575, were given by Mrs Tremayne

576 Portion of frieze with a landscape background and cloisters with cavaliers promenading, together with a border of flowers and arabesques
Circa 1820
Colour print from wood blocks
69.2 × 127 cm
E.1038–1925

This paper was superimposed upon nos 548, 554.

577 Eight lengths from the scenic paper entitled 'Vues d'Italie' or 'La Baie de Naples': views of Tivoli, Amalfi, Vesuvius and the Bay of Naples, some surmounted by a frieze of Pompeian arabesques with putti and running pattern imitating a modillion cornice
Produced by Dufour et Leroy, Paris
Circa 1822
Colour prints in grisaille from wood blocks
Various sizes
PROVENANCE The dining room of the White Hart Hotel (Rashleigh House), St Austell, Cornwall
Given by the St Austell Brewery Co. Ltd
E.1942–1949–1938

Ewart Dudley, 'The Bay of Naples Wallpaper', *Connoisseur* (1936), vol XCVIII, plate on pp 86–88; Entwisle, *FS*, figs 52–54; Clouzot, *TT*, pls XV–XVII; McClelland, p 389.

1. Bridge with houses in background
   106 × 49.5 cm
   E.1942
2. Group of 4 figures listening to a flute player in the gardens of a villa
   83.8 × 91.5 cm
   E.1943
3. View of the Bay of Naples with fisherwomen in foreground
   101 × 52.1 cm
   E.1944
4. Peasants dancing round a bust of Virgil in a landscape with cypress trees; a ship in the bay to the right and Vesuvius in the distance to the left; portion of frieze at top
   246.4 × 119.3 cm
   E.1945
5. Figures on the steps of a quay and ships in the harbour; portion of frieze at top
   241.3 × 99 cm
   E.1946
6. Groups of peasants standing before an obelisk fountain on a quay, against which rides a barque; view of mountains across a bay; portion of frieze at top
   236.3 × 99.1 cm
   E.1947
7. View of ships with workmen, stevedores etc
   138.4 × 99.1 cm
   E.1948 neg 74194
8. Group of fisherfolk standing on the shore of a bay; view of town behind
   61 × 99.2 cm
   E.1949 neg 75689

578 Four lengths from the series of 30 entitled 'Les Incas', illustrating scenes from *Les Incas, ou la Destruction de l'Empire de Perou*, by Jean François Marmontel (1723–99)
Produced by Dufour et Leroy, Paris
1826
Colour prints from wood blocks
271.8 × 55.9 cm (average size)
Given by Mrs Thomas Robbins
E.812–814–1939; E.812 CT 7441 (see col pl, p 213)

See Clouzot, *TT*, pls XXII–XXV (colour); Entwisle, *FS*, pls 25–27.

One of 5 unnumbered lengths in the series, intended for use as required (E.811–1939); no 7, part of 'Celebration de la fête du Soleil au temple de Cusco' (nos 3–9) (E.812); no 15, part of 'Éruption de Volcan' (nos 14–16) (E.813); no 17, part of 'Le Cacique accorde la vie à Gonsalve à la prière de Barthelemy de Las Casas' (nos 17, 18) (E.814)

575 GJ.9482

577 74194

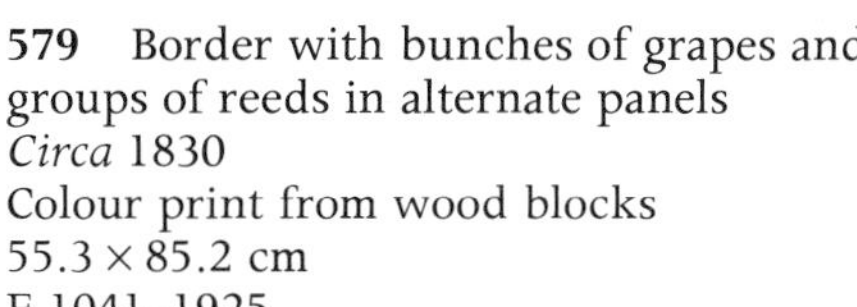

579 Border with bunches of grapes and groups of reeds in alternate panels
Circa 1830
Colour print from wood blocks
55.3 × 85.2 cm
E.1041–1925

580 Vertical pattern of brown and green conventional foliage, with a border strip of brown and cerise
Circa 1830
Print from wood blocks, and flock border
25.8 × 43.3 cm (fragment)
PROVENANCE A house in La Haute Ville, Vaison, France, formerly the residence of the Marquis de Taulignan
Given by Mrs Tremayne
E.2509–1930 neg GJ.9485

581 Portion of a scenic paper entitled 'Don Quixote', showing a tree in full foliage

577 75689

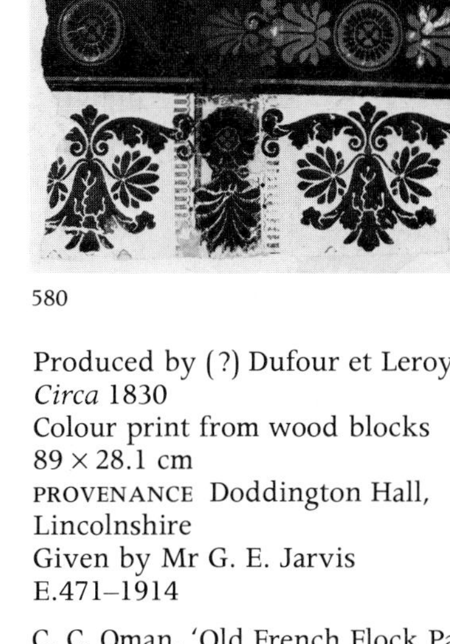

580

Produced by (?) Dufour et Leroy, Paris
Circa 1830
Colour print from wood blocks
89 × 28.1 cm
PROVENANCE Doddington Hall, Lincolnshire
Given by Mr G. E. Jarvis
E.471–1914

C. C. Oman, 'Old French Flock Papers', *Country Life*, vol 63, 625–627, fig 4. See also Olligs, vol II, pp 251, 252, figs 506, 507; McClelland, p 299. For other papers from Doddington Hall, see nos 130, 132–136.

582 Panel with a design of macaws and herons among foliage, on a blue ground; another paper, pasted on the back, with a regular pattern of small red stars
Probably French
Circa 1830
Colour print from wood blocks on embossed paper
233.1 × 99.1 cm
E.1281–1935

583

583 Portion with a pattern of small stars, and 2 borders: one with a pattern of lilies, the other with stylized floral shapes within strap work
Probably French
Circa 1830
Colour prints from wood blocks, on felted paper
Various sizes

PROVENANCE The gothic bathroom, Haseley Court, Oxfordshire
Given by Mr John B. Fowler
E.2281–2283–1966 neg GJ.9486

The star-patterned paper is identical to the above item.

584 Panel with a nymph and lamb among flowers
Circa 1830
Print in grisaille from wood blocks
171.5 × 55.3 cm (average size)
E.2902–1938

585 Panel from a series entitled 'Courses des Chevaux', showing an Italian horse race, with a view of part of the arena
Produced by J. Zuber et Cie, Rixheim
1838
Print in grisaille from wood blocks
152.5 × 50.3 cm
E.2900–1938

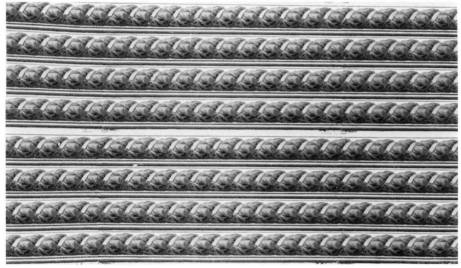

The above 2 items, nos 584, 585, were given by Mr. W. L. Wood

586 Border paper with Pompeian motifs
1840
Colour print from wood blocks
177.9 × 57.2 cm (overall size of sheet)
E.89–1937

587 Border paper with design of fantastic swans, medallions, masks and foliated arabesques
Circa 1840
Colour print from wood blocks
29 × 157.2 cm (overall size of sheet)
E.90–1937

588 Panel with a figure of Diana as a huntress
Circa 1840
Colour print from wood blocks
183 × 57.3 cm
E.85–1937

This panel is one of a series of 5 goddesses: Hebe, Juno, Ceres, Venus and Diana. It is reproduced in N. McClelland, plate on p 177, described as *circa* 1830, printed by Dufour. H. Olligs, vol II, fig 347, shows 2 figures from another series, with the same pedestals, entitled 'Die Erdteile', produced by E. Delicourt, printed later than 1830 and probably copies of designs by Dufour et Leroy. See also no 595.

The above 3 items, nos 586–588, were given by Mr William McEwan through the WM.

589

589 Thirty four sheets: some with the same pattern (in different colourways) of wallpaper borders and angle-pieces, with classical mouldings, ribbons, flowers etc; a single border of birds and flowers; 2 portions of wallpaper, one imitating marble, the other watered silk
Circa 1840–50
Colour prints from wood blocks and flock: E.76A machine print
Various sizes
Given by Sir Gerald Kelly, KCVO, PPRA
E.60–92–1965; E.80 neg GJ.9483

One of the borders (E.76A) appears to be a print from engraved copper cylinders, which were introduced into the manufacture of wallpapers in France *circa* 1838.

590 Twenty-three borders of various patterns
Circa 1840–50
Colour printed from wood blocks, and flock
Various sizes
Given by Mr Owen Little, FRIBA
E.657–679–1922

These borders duplicate some of those in the above item.

591 Panel with a figure of (?) Ferdinand Philippe, Duke of Orléans, in military costume
Possibly French
Circa 1840–50
Print in grisaille from wood blocks
134.6 × 57.2 cm (size of sheet)
Given by Mr William McEwan through the WM
E.81–1937

Two similar figures, perhaps from the same series, 'The Young Queen Victoria' and 'John Milton', are in the Whitworth Art Gallery, Manchester (nos W.133–1967 and W.168–1967). See also no 592.

592 Panel with a figure of an unidentified man, full length, in civilian costume
Possibly French
Circa 1840–50
Print in grisaille from wood blocks
111.1 × 54 cm
E.59–1947

593 Fragment of a frieze, with mouldings and coloured bands of floral and leaf motifs interspersed
Second quarter of 19th century
Colour print from wood blocks
29.8 × 14 cm
E.47–1947

594 Six panels from an unidentified set, including 3 mountain landscapes and 3 seascapes, each surrounded by a cartouche in the Louis XVI style
French or English
Second quarter of 19th century
Centre panels hand-painted in gouache; cartouches, colour prints from wood blocks, 2 with gilding
119.4 × 66 cm (average size)
E.81–86–1947; E.85 neg GJ.9484

For English papers, similarly depicting scenes within cartouches, see nos 375–378.

The above 3 items, nos 592–594, were given by Mr Martin Battersby

595 Panel with an allegorical figure of (?) Winter
Circa 1850

594

595

597

Colour print from wood blocks
196.3 × 70 cm (size of sheet)
Given by Mr William McEwan through the WM
E.86–1937 neg B.59

Possibly one of a series produced by E. Delicourt (see no 588, note).

596 Two portions, intended for use together to show the complete repeat, with a design of bunches of roses, dahlias and hollyhocks and sprays of convolvulus, on a blue ground, with borders simulating moulding
Circa 1850–60
Colour print from wood blocks
269.3 × 49.3 cm (each)
Given by the Curator of the City Museum, Gloucester
E.771, 771A–1955

These unused specimens of wallpaper were discovered at Hardwicke, near Gloucester.

597 Three wall hangings printed in gold on green, blue and crimson respectively; each one stamped with

manufacturer's name and *Exposition Universale, Paris 1855 etc*
Produced by Santesson & Cie, Paris
Circa 1855
Colour prints from wood blocks on silk
75.5 × 44 cm (each)
E.3688–3690–1956; E.3690 neg GJ.9488

598 Fragment with a pattern of bronze oak leaves, on a deep blue ground
Possibly French
Circa 1855
Colour print from wood block
28 × 33 cm
PROVENANCE Berrymead Priory, Acton
Given by Mr J. J. Wade
E.2416–1929

Note by the donor: 'I conjectured that it was at least 80 years old—from the time of Lieut. Heald, husband of the celebrated Lola Montez, who lived at the Priory and did a great deal of decoration there from the year 1851.'

599 Four fragments, mounted on 1 sheet, of borders, including patterns of ironwork, beading etc
Mid-19th century
Colour print from wood block and flock
Various sizes
PROVENANCE A house in La Haute Ville, Vaison, France, formerly the residence of the Marquis de Taulignan
Given by Mrs Tremayne
E.1239–1930

These pieces were superimposed above no 551 and E.1237–1930. One of the fragments is another piece of the border of no 548.

600 Portion with a design of acanthus leaves and scrollwork cartouches, with a pineapple, urns and flowers; stamped on the back with a French duty stamp (partly truncated) and numbered *3498*
Probably French
Mid-19th century
Colour print from wood blocks on varnished paper
113.7 × 70.5 cm
Given by the Geffreye Museum
E.782–1959

601 Fragment with a design of rococo and chinoiserie motifs
Mid-19th century
Colour print from wood blocks
61.5 × 45 cm
PROVENANCE The Désert de Retz, near Chambourcy, Seine et Oise, France
Given by Mr John B. Fowler
E.2285–1966

602 Border with 4 panels, each with a monochrome landscape in the style of Carle Vernet, within a framework of mouldings and pilasters with vase ornaments
French or Italian
Mid-19th century
Colour print from wood blocks
54.3 × 435.6 cm
E.737–1912 neg 51390

See McClelland, plate on p 225, where this example is described as 'Louis XVI wall-paper'.

603 Panels (3 on 1 roll), showing Christ on the Cross, with backgrounds of olive green, carmine and blue-green flock

603

602

Mid-19th century
Colour print from wood blocks and flock
84.5 × 50.8 cm (each panel)
Given by Mr A. L. Cowtan in memory of his father, Arthur Barnard Cowtan, OBE
E.102–1939 neg GG.5883

604 Panel with a baldacchino with floral design framed in arabesque
Mid-19th century
Colour print from wood blocks
158.7 × 57.2 cm (size of sheet)
Given by Mr William McEwan through the WM
E.88–1937

605 Two designs, imitating textile patterns: one with diamond shapes and small red, white and blue flowers, on a brown ground; the other with white roses encircled by a banderole
Mid-19th century
Colour prints from wood blocks
63.6 × 22.9 cm; 49.5 × 20.3 cm (portions)
PROVENANCE A house in La Haute Ville, Vaison, France, formerly the residence of the Marquis de Taulignan
E.2510, 2511–1930

606 Two pieces of ceiling (?) paper with a pattern of linked octagons, enclosing stepped pyramids and rosettes, in imitation of carving or stucco work
Mid-19th century
Colour print from wood blocks
59 × 35 cm; 66 × 46.6 cm
PROVENANCE A house in La Haute Ville, Vaison, France, formerly the residence of the Marquis de Taulignan
E.2512–1930; E.3406–1922 neg GJ.9487

The above 2 items, nos 605, 606, were given by Mrs Tremayne

607 Panel with a foliated design in grisaille on a green ground, based on 18th century designs
Produced by Réveillon; possibly French
Mid-19th century
Print from wood blocks
255.3 × 57.3 cm
E.2903–1938

608 Panel with a foliated design in buff on a blue ground, based on 18th-century designs
Produced by Réveillon; possibly French
Mid-19th century
Flock on silk
195.6 × 53.3 cm
E.2904–1938

A panel with the same design as the above, on a red ground, is E.2905–1938

606

The above 2 designs, nos 607, 608, were given by Mr W. L. Wood

609 Two designs: one with a small diamond-shaped pattern and a narrow frieze with a corrugated band winding amid a row of disks; the other with a variegated floral design on a white ground, imitating watered silk
Circa 1860–70
Colour print from wood blocks
123.8 × 51.1 cm; 63.5 × 64.1 cm (portions)
PROVENANCE A house in La Haute Ville, Vaison, France, formerly the residence of the Marquis de Taulignan
Given by Mrs Tremayne
E.2513–1930; E.1960–1934

610 Panel of scenic paper from an unidentified set: a turreted castle on a cliff, with a man and woman on a cliff

path and sailing vessels in the distance
English or French
Circa 1870
Gouache and watercolour
172.8 × 55.9 cm
Given by Mr Martin Battersby
E.60–1947

This appears to be a hand-painted wallpaper.

611 Portion with a rococo ornamental design with flowers and scenic medallions on a white satin ground
Circa 1880
Colour print from 19 wood blocks
75.3 × 48.3 cm
E.1958–1934

612 Portion with a design of a vase of flowers on a bracket in gold, yellow and grey, on a white ground imitating watered silk
Possibly produced by Turquetil, Malzard et Caillebotte, Paris
Circa 1880
Colour hand print from 3 wood blocks, and gold
73.7 × 48.3 cm
E.1959–1934

The above 2 items, nos 611, 612, were given by the WM

613 Forty-five sheets, some with the same pattern in different colourways, of wallpaper borders and angle-pieces, with mouldings, stripes, formalized flowers, decoration in the Japanese style etc; E.112 stamped on the back
A.P. 2314 Paris
Third quarter of 19th century
Colour prints from wood blocks and flock
Various sizes
Given by Sir Gerald Kelly, KCVO, PPRA
E.93–136–1965; E.113A–1965 CT 8748
(see col pl, p 213)

614 Six corner-pieces with designs of strap work and foliage
Late 19th century
Colour prints from wood blocks
25.4 × 24.1 cm (average size)
Given by Mr Martin Battersby
E.65–70–1947

615 Fourteen designs with various floral patterns
Second half of 19th century
Watercolour and body colour
Various sizes
Given by Mr J. D. Crace
E.1713–1725, 1727–1912

20th Century

616

616 Panel of panoramic paper showing a view with palms and exotic plants
No. 1 from the 'Eldorado' series, produced by Zuber et Cie, Rixheim
Circa 1915
Colour print from wood blocks
172.8 × 57.3 cm
Given by Mr W. L. Wood
E.2901–1938 neg B.67

The 'Eldorado' series was first produced by Zuber *circa* 1848, from designs by George Zipelius (1808–90) and Ehrmann (worked 1830-post-1857), painters and wallpaper designers. Entwisle, *FS*, fig 9; Olligs, vol 2, fig 483 (colour).

See also 'England': no 316.

GERMANY

617

617 Pattern of small hexagons containing leaf and flower motifs
Produced by Erismann & Cie, Breisach
Circa 1955
Colour machine print
267.5 × 53.2 cm (length)
E.979–1978 neg GJ.9493

618 'Toledo'
Produced by Tapetenfabrik H. Strauven, Bonn
Circa 1955
Colour machine print
267.5 × 80 cm (length)
Given by Tapetenfabrik H. Strauven
E.978–1978 neg GJ.9494

619 'Reigen'
Designed by the Werkkunstschule, Krefeld, and produced by Schleu & Hoffmann, Beuel
1956–57
Machine print, black on yellow
75 × 52.5 cm (portion)

618

Given by Schleu & Hoffmann
E.977–1978 neg GJ.9495

H. Olligs, plate on p 318.

620 'Medium'
Designed by the Werkkunstschule, Krefeld, and produced by Schleu & Hoffmann, Beuel
1956–57
Machine print, yellow on black
267.5 × 54 cm (length)
Given by Dr Hoffmann
E.980–1978 neg GJ.9496

H. Olligs, vol 3, plate on p 342.

621 Curvilinear pattern on a background simulating hessian
German or English
Circa 1960
Colour machine print (embossed)
56.5 × 43.5 cm (portion)
Given by Miss P. E. Morgan
E.120–1972

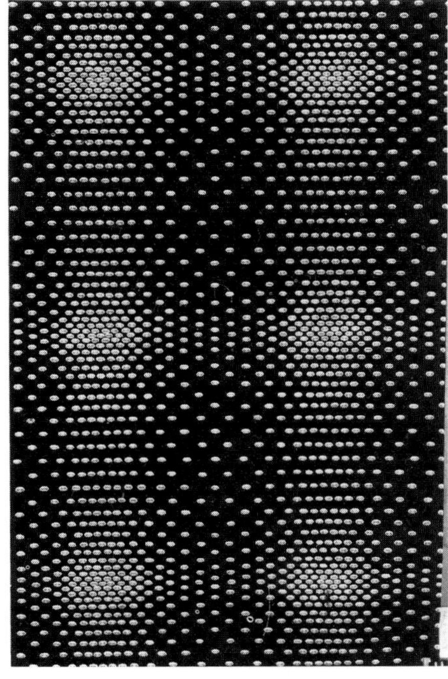

620

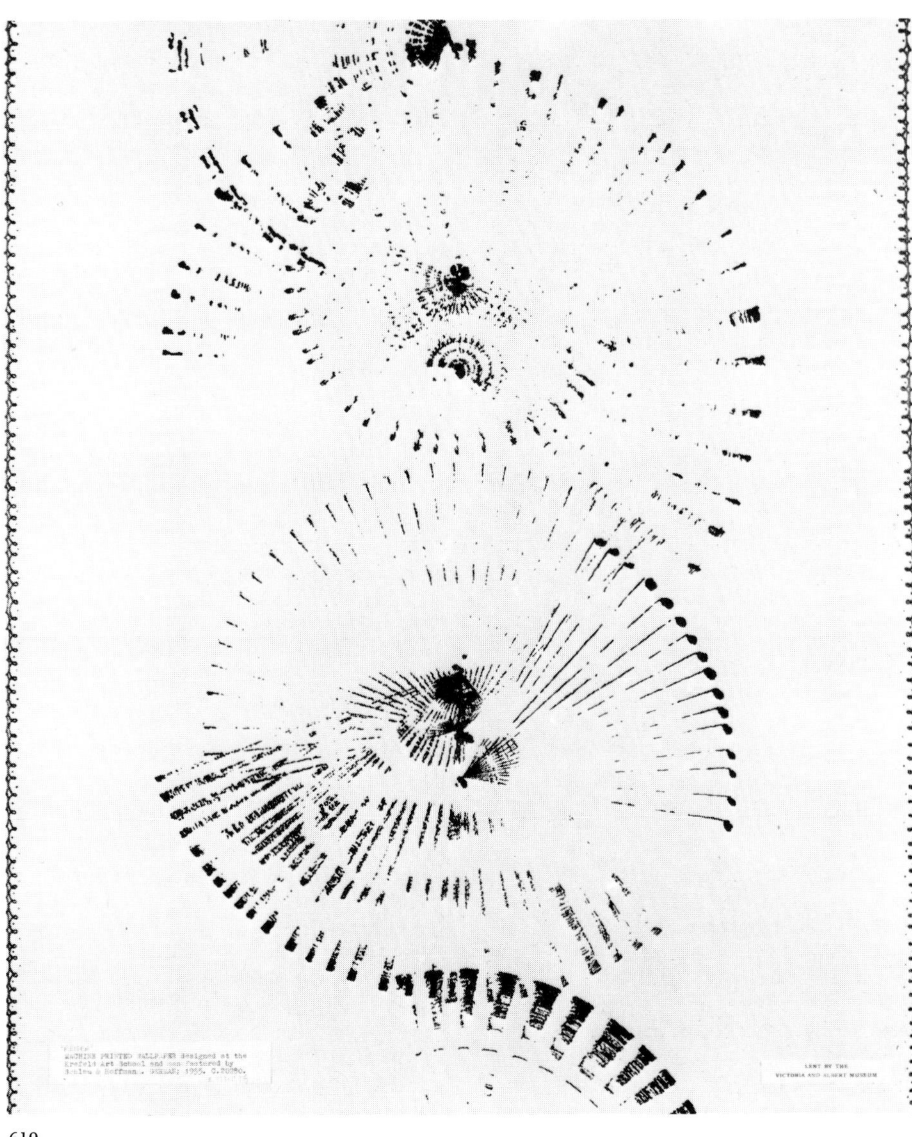

619

In 1960 John Line & Sons Ltd produced *Folio*, a pattern book containing some German imported wallpapers made by the *tiefdruck* method. This 'deep-printing', or embossing on a flat paper, gave the effect of plaster work. This paper was pasted over no 537.

See also 'England': no 525.

ITALY

622 Panel with a design of trees, monkeys and American Indians
Mid-19th century
Colour print from wood blocks
142.2 × 76.3 cm
Given by Miss Winifred Swayne
E.424–1921

THE NETHERLANDS

623 Two rolls of wall hangings with a conventional foliate design, on a white ground with green and red pigments
Possibly French
Circa 1680
Brown flock
262.9 × 97.8 cm (average size of each)
PROVENANCE A house in Folkestone
Given by Mr Ionides
E.3614, 3615–1922

See also 'England': no 33.

NORWAY

624 'Sondagsmorgon'
Washable wallpaper produced by Norma Tapetfabrik, Fredrikstad
1956
Colour machine print
57 × 46.5 cm
Given by Norma Tapetfabrik
E.892–1979 neg GJ.9499

UNITED STATES

625 Corner-piece with roses and small blue flowers, within scrolling acanthus, with a matching border
American or English
Mid-19th century
Colour prints from wood blocks
23.8 × 24.2 cm (size of sheet);
52.5 × 6.4 cm (border)
E.211, 212–1973

626 Border with roses and other flowers, within scrolling acanthus
American or English
Mid-19th century
Colour machine print and flock
58.8 × 18.5 cm
E.213–1973

627 Pattern of vine leaves and stems in chiaroscuro
American or English
Mid-19th century
Colour machine print and flock
71.1 × 25.6 cm (border)
E.214–1973 neg GJ.9448

628 Three borders with scrolling acanthus, strap work and formalized floral motifs etc
American or English
Mid-19th century
Colour prints from wood blocks, flock and gold
Various sizes
E.1671–1673–1974

629 Sheet of uncut borders with a formalized palmette motif
American or English
Third quarter of 19th century
Colour machine print
49.2 × 28.6 cm
E.643–1976

630 Portion with a pattern of scrolling foliage
Produced by Fr. Beck & Co.
Circa 1890
Embossed paper
90 × 57.1 cm
E.1913–1973

631 Portion with a pattern of bunches of flowers and scrolling foliage; lettered *Birge Made in USA*
1895
Embossed paper
41.5 × 56.5 cm
PROVENANCE The parlour of Voigt House, Grand Rapids, Michigan
E.2055–1973

For other papers from Voigt House, see nos 451, 632, 640, 642, 643.

632 Portion with a pattern of circular medallions containing part of a colonnade, with flowers etc between vertical stripes; numbered *1035*
Circa 1895
Embossed paper
55 × 57 cm
PROVENANCE Voigt House, Grand Rapids, Michigan
E.2056–1973

633 Corner-piece showing Cupid in a medallion, within a floral wreath, and edged with a diaper pattern and beading; lettered *Patented in USA Dec. 12*
1899
Colour print from wood blocks
50.3 × 49.8 cm (size of sheet)
E.907–1973

The above 10 items, nos 624–633, were given by Mr Samuel J. Dornsife

624

627

634 Fragment with naturalistic pattern of vine-tree round a column
Produced by M. H. Birge & Sons Co., USA
Late 19th century
Colour print from wood blocks
76.3 × 56 cm (size of sheet)
E.2895–1938

635 Panel of 'satin' paper with motif of basket or roses within a laurel frame
Produced by M. H. Birge & Sons Co., USA
Late 19th century
Colour print from wood blocks
49.5 × 57.2 cm (size of sheet)
E.2896–1938

636 Panel of 'satin' paper, with motif of daisies and knots
Produced by M. H. Birge & Sons Co., USA
Late 19th century
Colour print from wood blocks
49.5 × 48.3 cm (size of sheet)
E.2897–1938

637 Panel with rose wreaths hanging from violet ribbon festoons on a grisaille ground
Produced by M. H. Birge & Sons Co., USA
Late 19th century
Colour print from wood blocks
72.5 × 49.6 cm (size of sheet)
E.2898–1938

The above 4 items, nos 634–637, were given by Mr W. L. Wood

638 Portion with a formal pattern of poppies and other flowers, simulating a leather hanging
American or English
Last quarter of 19th century
Embossed paper, coloured by hand and varnished
68.5 × 56.3 cm
Given by Mr Samuel J. Dornsife
E.644–1976

639

639 Four portions with floral tapestry and other patterns
Produced by M. H. Birge & Sons Co., USA
Late 19th or early 20th century
Colour machine prints
Various sizes
Given by Mr Henry Butler
E.2772–2775–1914; E.2774 neg GJ.9449

640 Portion with a pattern of a vase of flowers, within borders of small trailing flowers and drapery tied in bows with tassels
American or English
1905
Flock
56 × 50.2 cm
PROVENANCE The hall of Voigt House, Grand Rapids, Michigan
Given by Mr Samuel J. Dornsife
E.2054–1973

641 112 portions, including friezes with stags' heads, galleons, panels, imitations of Spanish leatherwork etc
Produced by M. H. Birge & Sons Co., USA
Early 20th century
Colour prints from wood blocks, embossed paper etc
Various sizes
Given by M. H. Birge a Sons Co., USA
E.359–470–1914; E.415 neg GJ.9452; E.423 neg GJ.9450; E.430 neg GJ.9451; E.445 neg GJ.9453; E.450 neg GJ.9454; E.453 neg GJ.9455; E.454 neg GJ.9456; E.460 neg GJ.9457

642 Portion of blue 'oatmeal' paper
American or English
1910–14
Colour machine print
157.5 × 49.5 cm
PROVENANCE Voigt House, Grand Rapids, Michigan
E.2053–1973

643 Portion with a pattern of a landscape with a castle above a river; in the foreground a stone vase of flowers and 2 birds
Produced by the WM (Arthur Sanderson & Sons Ltd)
1912
Colour machine print
54.6 × 56.2 cm

641 GJ.9452

641 GJ.9450

641 GJ.9451

641 GJ.9456

641 GJ.9453

641 GJ.9454

641 GJ.9456

641 GJ.9457

PROVENANCE Voigt House, Grand Rapids, Michigan
E.2058–1973

The above 2 items, nos 642, 643, were given by Mr Samuel J. Dornsife.

644 Nursery paper, 'Montauk', and a matching frieze, showing children skipping, playing with dolls and sledging
Circa 1930
Colour machine print
34.5 × 38.5 cm (portion); 21 × 36 cm (frieze)
Given by Miss Mary Peerless
E.495, 496–1967 neg GJ.9458

644

645 'Les Fleurs Chinoise' (*sic*)
Produced by C. M. Stockwell & Co., California
Circa 1950
Colour screen print
130.5 × 76 cm (portion)
E.981–1978 neg GJ.9459

646 'La Course'
Produced by C. M. Stockwell & Co., California
Circa 1950
Colour screen print
115 × 75.7 cm (portion)
E.982–1978 neg GJ.9460

645

647

647 'Carnet de Bal'
Produced by C. M. Stockwell & Co., California
Circa 1950
Colour screen print
133 × 75.6 cm (portion)
E.983–1978 neg GJ.9461

648 Portion of 'Happy Leaves'
A 'Vera' design, produced by F. Schumacher & Co., New York
1952
Colour screen print
54.5 × 74.8 cm
E.584–1966

649 'Little Bouquet'
Produced by F. Schumacher & Co., New York
1952
Silk screen print
54.5 × 74.7 cm (portion)
E.984–1978 neg GJ.9464

650 'Patchwork Plaid'
Produced by F. Schumacher & Co., New York
Circa 1952
Colour print from wood blocks
74.8 × 54.5 cm (portion)
E.586–1966 neg GJ.9462

651 'Double Entendre'
Produced by F. Schumacher & Co., New York

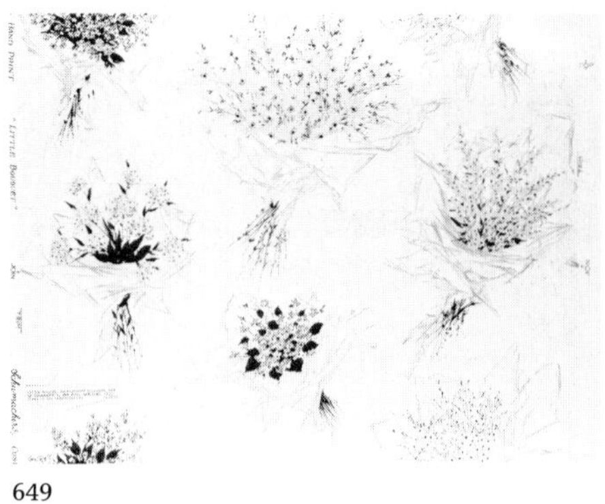

649

Circa 1952
Colour screen print
54.5 × 74.7 cm (portion)
E.585–1966 neg GJ.9463

The above 4 items, nos 648–651, were given by F. Schumacher & Co.

646

650

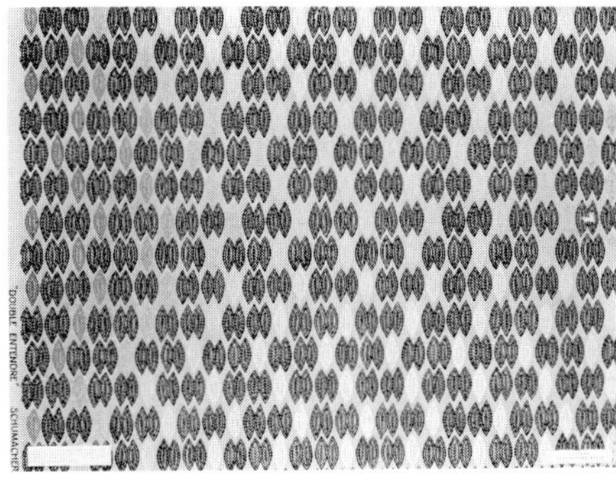

651

CHINA

17th to 18th Centuries

652 Panel showing 2 birds perched on a rock, with bamboo and flowers
Late 17th century
Tempera
38.7 × 45.8 cm
PROVENANCE Found at the back of a framed *petit point* panel in coloured wools and silks (Department of Textiles, VAM, T.111–1922)
E.1211–1922 CT 1181 (see col pl, p 214)

See SE, pl 51.

653 A Chinese garden scene, with 2 figures within a decorative cartouche
Cantonese
Circa 1730–40
Pen and ink, watercolour and body colour
276.2 × 108.6 cm (fragments of a panel)
PROVENANCE The library of Hampden House, Great Missenden, Buckinghamshire
Given by the Earl of Buckinghamshire
E.51–1968 CT 7739 (see col pl, p 231)

The decorative motifs of the cartouche are derived from a design by Watteau, *circa* 1710–20, engraved by Gabriel Huquier and published with 3 similar designs in a set of 4 plates, *circa* 1730. Copies of the set were made by Thomas Kitchen and published under the title *The Diversions of Children*. The Chinese inscription over the gateway in the central scene can be translated as 'The Place of the Valley of Deception (Error or Illusion)'. The fragments have been

654

laid down on a sheet of paper mounted on canvas and some missing parts of the design have been indicated. Another panel made up of fragments is in the Buckinghamshire County Museum, Aylesbury, Buckinghamshire. Some wallpapers at Harrington House, Bourton-on-the-Water, Gloucestershire (see Introduction, p 26), attributed to John Baptist Jackson, have similar motifs after Watteau. These are illustrated in E. Donnell, 'The Van Rensselaer Wall Paper and J. B. Jackson: A Study in Disassociation', *Metropolitan Museum Studies* (New York, 1932), vol IV, pp 95 ff, figs 17–19, and in N. McLelland, pp 147, 148. A set of 20 of these panels, mounted in bamboo frames, was put on sale at Sotheby's on 3 June 1977.

654 Ten panels forming the complete decoration of a room, with plant forms and birds
Second quarter of 18th century
Tempera
Various sizes
Given by HM Commissioners of Woods, Forest, and Land Revenues
E.2083–2092–1914 neg 38419 CT 7740
(see col pl, p 232)

This paper originally hung in Eltham Lodge (now let on lease by the Commissioners of Woods as the Clubhouse of the Eltham Golf Club), from where it was removed by the Commissioners in 1911. A design by William Turner (q.v.), entitled 'The Golden Pheasant', was produced by Jeffrey & Co. in 1912 and was based on the paper described above.

655 Two portions which were apparently adjacent panels in a continuous series depicting scenes in the everyday life of the Chinese
First half of 18th century
Wood engraving and tempera
241.3 × 83.9 cm (average size of each)
Given by Major E. R. Trevor Corbett
E.412, 413–1924 neg 56530

These 2 pieces were on a screen, the back of which was covered with English flock paper of the early 18th century. The colours in tempera were added by hand. At Salthrop House, Swindon, Wiltshire, are a set of 5 pieces identical to these panels. C. C. Oman, 'Old Wall-papers in England', *Old Furniture* (1928), vol 3, plate on p 16.

656 Ten panels pasted together, with a design of trees and plant forms growing out of pots, birds, butterflies, lanterns and birdcages, and with other birds pasted on, against a blue background
Circa 1750
Tempera and watercolour
413.6 × 1,425 cm
PROVENANCE Moor Park, Hertfordshire
Given by Moor Park Ltd
E.533–1937 negs P.770–773

655

657 Nine panels with trees, flowers and birds against a blue background; fragments of rock, and insects on the ground at the base
Mid-18th century
Tempera
318.8 × 88.9 cm (average size of each)
Given by Sir William Ingram, Bart
E.3674–3682–1913; E.3676 neg 45691; E.3677, 3678 neg 45692 CT 7783 (see col pl, p 241)

See C. C. Oman, 'Old Wall-papers in England', *Old Furniture* (1928), vol 3, plate on p 15; SE, pl 54 (detail).

658 Landscape with flowers, rocks and large birds
Mid-18th century
Print from wood block and tempera, applied by hand

Chinese garden scene. Cantonese, *circa* 1730–40 (no 653)

656 P.770

656 P.772

656 P.771

656 P.773

657 45691

25.5 × 151 cm (fragment)
PROVENANCE Haseley Court, Oxfordshire
Given by Mr John B. Fowler
E.2286–1966

659 Plant forms, birds and butterflies on a pink ground
Mid-18th century
Gouache
318.8 × 89 cm (length)
Given by Messrs Green & Abbott
E.3195–1920 neg 50582

660 Bird in a cage hanging from a branch in blossom: to the right of the cage a bird perched on a branch; to the left another bird and a butterfly
Mid-18th century

(*opposite*) Plant forms and birds. Chinese, second quarter of 18th century (no 654)

Tempera
105.4 × 114.3 cm (fragment)
Given by Mrs Finding
E.1667–1920

661 Bamboo, flowers, birds and butterflies on a pink ground
Mid-18th century
Tempera
390.4 × 110.6 cm (length)
Given by Mr A. H. Parkhurst
E.76–1940

662 Two portions with sprays of green foliage with red and yellow flowers on a background of rose-pink; among the foliage brightly coloured birds
Circa 1790
Tempera
266.8 × 111.8 cm; 157.5 × 94 cm
Given by Miss A. Edith Kennedy
E.869, 870–1930

663 Seven panels with buds, butterflies and flowering trees
Late 18th century
Pen, watercolour and body colour
Various sizes

659

PROVENANCE Archdeaconry House, Peterborough
Given by the Right Reverend the Lord Bishop of St Edmundsbury and Ipswich
E.3587–3593–1922; E.3588 neg 57213; E.3592 CT 7744 (see col pl, p 242)

663

664

664 A portion and 2 fragments with a bird and flower design in 2 shades of blue
Late 18th century
Pen and ink and gouache
106 × 89 cm
Given by Mr John B. Fowler
E.2287, 2287A, B–1966 neg GK.3070

665 Floral pattern with birds and butterflies
Second half of 18th century
Tempera
113.8 × 70.8 cm (portion)
Given by Mrs Leonard B. Keyser
E.2712–1929

666

666 Panel depicting an outdoor theatrical performance
Second half of 18th century
Tempera
298.5 × 233.8 cm
Given by Colonel R. C. Cottell, CBE
E.3017–1921 neg K.2249

This panel is almost identical to one of 12 panels at Avebury Manor, Wiltshire, and to paper at Youlston Park, Devon. See SE, pl 55.

667 Three panels with hunting, boating and festival scenes
Second half of 18th century
Gouache
395 × 118.2 cm (overall size of first 2 panels); 243.9 × 118 cm (third panel)
Given by Mr H. B. Darby
E.1181–1183–1921; E.1181 neg 54279; E.1182 neg Y.1280; E.1183 neg Y.1281

See Greysmith, pl 50, for third panel.

667 54279

668 Three portions: the upper part decorated with branches of magnolia and almond, camellia, pomegranate and plum, and with birds and butterflies on a green ground; the lower part depicting the story of tea-making amid scenery with tea houses, pagodas, rock gardens and water
Second half of 18th century
Tempera
398.9 × 119.5 cm; 401.4 × 118.2 cm; 386.2 × 85.1 cm
PROVENANCE Shernfold Park, Sussex
E.2847–2849–1923; E.2847 neg Y.1283; E.2848 neg 55021; E.2849 neg 56531

This paper is said to have been given to a former owner of Shernfold Park by a Chinese ambassador.

669 Two fragments, each showing a part of a wooden building and strips of a separate border pasted along 2 sides
Second half of 18th century
Tempera
27.4 × 14.6 cm; 22.9 × 16.2 cm
Given by Mr Aymer Vallance
E.1472–1933

667 Y.1280

667 Y.1281

670 Two portions showing a design of birds and trees
Second half of 18th century
Tempera
99.8 × 34.7 cm; 156.8 × 36.9 cm
PROVENANCE The drawing room of The Mansion, Ditton Park, Slough, Buckinghamshire, now used as an Admiralty Compass Observatory
Given by Sir Leopold Sackville, KCB, MICE
E.1822, 1823–1930

The Mansion was rebuilt in 1817 on the site of an earlier house destroyed by fire in 1812. It is thought that the Chinese wallpaper was hung by the Duchess of Buccleuch, who was living in the house *circa* 1900. The remainder was sold at Sotheby's on 4 March 1930 by the Lords Commissioners of the Admiralty.

668 Y.1283

672 Two portions from a run of about 170 m: the lower part showing sporting scenes; the upper part decorated with branches of flowering shrubs and birds and butterflies
Second half of 18th century
Gouache
134.7 × 88.3 cm; 134.7 × 91.5 cm
PROVENANCE The Old Brewery House, Watford
Given by Mr Harold Sedgwick
E.252, 253–1924; E.252 neg 78296
CT 7742 (see col pl, p 243); E.253 neg Y.1282

See Greysmith, pl 49 (E.252).

668 55021

668 56531

671 Three panels with flowering shrubs and fruit-trees in pots, and birds and butterflies on a pale-green background
Second half of 18th century
Gouache
315.1 × 116 cm; 196.3 × 98.2 cm; 148.6 × 83.2 cm
Given by Mr W. E. Soltau
E.3881, 3882, 3944–1915; E.3881 neg 45043; E.3944 CT 7741 (see col pl, p 242)

This paper belonged to the donor's family at least as early as 1820.

673 Four lengths with birds and a pot containing a dwarf plant on a stand in the foreground; in the background flowering plants and trees with birds and butterflies
Second half of 18th century
243.9 × 122 cm (each)
E.2851–2854–1913; E.2851 neg 37291; E.2852 neg 58803; E.2853 neg 58804; E.2854 neg 58805

See SE, pl 53 (detail). The layout and device used in this paper are exactly similar to those in the papers at Temple Newsam House, Leeds, and at Houghton Hall, Norfolk.

Late 18th to Early 19th Century

671

672 78296

673 37291

674 Eight panels with bird and plant forms on a white background
Late 18th or early 19th century
Tempera
365.9 × 116.9 cm (each)
E.25–31A–1912; E.25 neg 46913; E.27 neg 46915; E.30 neg Y.1284; E.31 neg 46919; E.31A neg 46913 CT 7743
(see col pl, p 243)

675 Flowers on a blue background
Late 18th or early 19th century
Tempera
32.4 × 49.5 cm (fragment)
29301.20 neg GJ.9467 CT 8704

676 Chinese landscape with a bridge over a river, figures and a house
Late 18th or early 19th century
Print from wood block, coloured by hand
195.7 × 47.4 cm (length)
Given by Mr Roger H. M. Warner
E.21146–1957

677 Pattern of a trellis work of ribbons, containing in the intersections flowers, fruit, insects, ceremonial pots, a mask, a fan, a *sheng* (bamboo flute) etc

673 58803

673 58804

Circa 1800
Body colour
236 × 98 cm (panel)
PROVENANCE Hampden House, Great Missenden, Buckinghamshire
E.948–1978 CT 7745 (see col pl, p 244)

678 Three fragments of borders with bamboo trellis and flowers, surrounding the above
Circa 1800
Body colour
Various sizes
E.948A–C–1978; E.948A neg GJ.9468

The above 2 items, nos 677, 678, were given by the Earl of Buckinghamshire.

679 Panel with sprays of leaves and flowers and 2 butterflies
Early 19th century
Body colour, touched with gold
142.3 × 25.4 cm
Given by Lieutenant-Colonel B. T. Reading
E.409–1932 CT 7744 (see col pl, p 244)

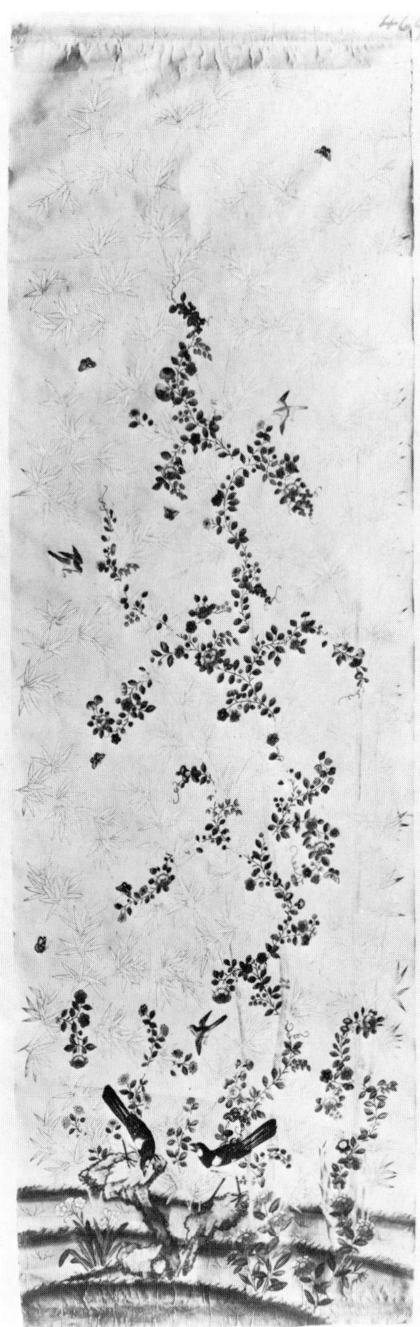

674 46913

JAPAN

19th Century

680 Forty-five specimens (sheets printed on both sides) for use on screens and sliding doors; bound in a volume with silk boards; inscribed in ink inside the front cover *Sir Rutherford Alcock K C B Japanese papers. Vol 1 Wallpaper hanging patterns* and with note on the papers
Mid-19th century

674 46915

Colour prints from wood blocks with gold, silver and embossing
28.7 × 43.2 cm (size of volume)
E.140–184–1955

Sir Rutherford Alcock was appointed the first Consul General in Japan in 1858. He came to England on leave in 1862 and returned to Japan in 1864. In his *Art and Industries in Japan* (1878), p 230, he states, 'I sent to the [Paris International] Exhibition in 1862 a collection of several

675

hundred patterns . . . but I am not aware that they were utilized.' The present specimens possibly formed part of this collection.

681 Five wall- or lining papers with abstract, bird and flower patterns
Circa 1850–60
Colour prints from wood blocks
Various sizes
854, 854A–D–1869

These papers were exhibited at the Paris Exhibition in 1867.

682 Twenty-two wall- or lining papers with abstract and floral patterns
Circa 1850–60
Colour prints from wood blocks
Various sizes
Given by Professor T. C. Archer
79–79u–1866

683 Five portions with birds and plants, fans and a formalized trellis pattern
Circa 1880
Colour prints from wood blocks
Various sizes
Given by Mr A. L. Cowtan, in memory of his father Arthur Barnard Cowtan, OBE
E.93–97–1939

684 Specimen, possibly for use on a screen, with a pattern of floral and geometric designs on an embossed gilt ground
Second half of 19th century
Colour print from wood blocks
32 × 31.7 cm (size of sheet)
Given by Mrs G. C. Arnot
E.577–1947

Late 19th to Early 20th Century

685 Ten leather papers
Circa 1890–1900
Various sizes
Given by Mr Sydney Vacher
E.2245–2254–1913

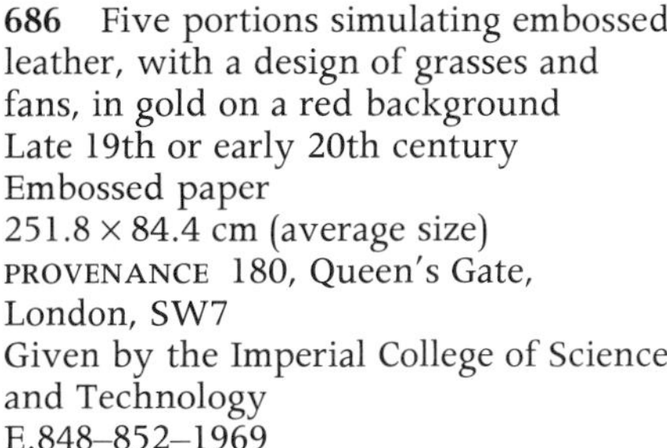

686 Five portions simulating embossed leather, with a design of grasses and fans, in gold on a red background
Late 19th or early 20th century
Embossed paper
251.8 × 84.4 cm (average size)
PROVENANCE 180, Queen's Gate, London, SW7
Given by the Imperial College of Science and Technology
E.848–852–1969

The house, which was built by Norman Shaw, RA, in 1879, has been demolished.

687 Eight portions with various patterns (peacock feathers, pineapples, orchids etc), simulating embossed leather
Late 19th or early 20th century
Embossed paper with gilt backgrounds
Various sizes
PROVENANCE The stock of Thomas Avery, builder, of Ivy House, Tenterden, Kent
Given by Mr Alexander Reynell
E.2247–2254–1913

See no 212.

688 Portion with a raised pattern of lilies and honeysuckle
Probably Japanese
Circa 1900
Embossed paper
90.5 × 50.3 cm
E.911–1965

689 Portion with a raised pattern of formalized leaves and flowers; numbered on the edge *108* and in Japanese characters *Middle of 225*
Circa 1900
Embossed paper
106.6 × 90.8 cm
E.910–1965

The above 2 items, nos 688, 689, were bequeathed by Miss Estella Canziani.

690 Portion simulating embossed leather, with a design of birds and foliage, printed in red and gold
Produced in Japan for Alexander Rottmann & Co., London; the registered trade labels pasted to the back
Early 20th century
Colour print from wood block
67.3 × 46.7 cm
Given by Miss Mary Peerless
E.479–1967

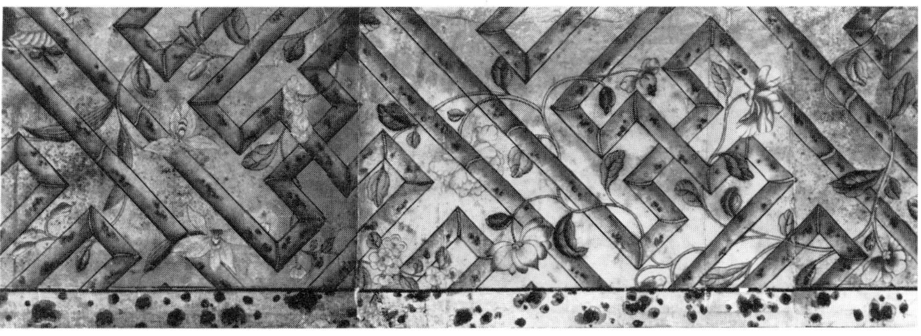

678

(*opposite*) Panels with trees, flowers and birds. Chinese, mid-18th century (no 657)

(*following page, left to right*) Panel with butterflies and flowering trees. Chinese, late 18th century (no 663)
Panel with flowering shrubs and fruit trees in pots. Chinese, second half of 18th century (no 671)
Panel showing a sporting scene. Chinese, second half of 18th century (no 672)
Panel with bird and plant forms. Chinese, late 18th or early 19th century (no 674)

Panel with a trellis of ribbons, with flowers, fruit, insects etc. Chinese, *circa* 1800 (no 677)

Panel with leaves, flowers and butterflies. Chinese, early 19th century (no 679)

Pattern Books

ENGLAND

19th Century

691 Fifty-five specimens from the stock of Cowtan & Sons Ltd; E.71, 74, 88 stamped on the back with Excise duty stamp *First Account Taken*
Circa 1800–90
Colour prints from wood blocks, flock, etc
Various sizes
Given by Mr A. C. Cowtan in memory of his father, Arthur Barnard Cowtan, OBE
E.43–97–1939

Nineteen borders from the first quarter of the 19th century (E.43–61); 4 borders, *circa* 1820 (E.62–65); 14 borders, *circa* 1830 (E.66–79); 10 borders, *circa* 1840 (E.80–89); 1 border, *circa* 1850 (E.90); 2 wallpapers, *circa* 1850 (E.91, 92); 5 wallpapers in the Japanese style, *circa* 1880 (E.93–97).

Cowtan & Sons were the successors of J. Duppa, J. G. Crace etc.

692 Twenty-four order books, containing cuttings of wallpapers and other materials for interior decoration; bound in vellum; some books lettered on the spine *Paper-Orders* and dated consecutively 1824 to 1938
Sold by Cowtan & Sons Ltd, formerly of Oxford Street, London
33 × 25.4 cm (average size of each volume)
Given by Mr A. L. Cowtan in memory of his father, Arthur Barnard Cowtan, OBE
E.1862–1885–1946

692A Three pattern books, containing 932 specimens of papers, borders, corner-pieces etc; inscribed in ink throughout with titles and notes; E. 431 dated in ink at the beginning of each annual section *1837–1844*; E.432, 432A similarly dated *1845–1852*
Probably record books of the firm later known as Jeffrey & Co.
Colour prints from wood blocks, flock etc
57 × 50 cm (approximate size of each vol)
Given by Mrs F. E. Warner
E.431, 432, 432A–1943;
E.432 negs GJ.9381–9424 CT 7298 (see col pl, p 261)

693 Three volumes containing bills (*circa* 1838), pamphlets, press-cuttings, price lists etc (*circa* 1848–1915), together with an account book (for 1869), all relating to wallpapers produced by Jeffrey & Co.
44.5 × 28 cm (each)
Given by Mrs Margaret Warner
E.42A (1–3), 42B–1945

694 Fifty-three specimens of wallpaper borders and corners
Log book of Sanderson & Sons; the blocks were destroyed 1874–80
Circa 1840–70
Colour prints from wood blocks, flock, etc
Various sizes
Given by the WM
E.1764–1816–1934; E.1764–1766 neg GJ.9426; E.1779 neg GJ.9425; E.1788 neg GJ.9249

695 Pattern book with 114 specimens
Produced by Jeffrey & Co.

694 GJ.9426

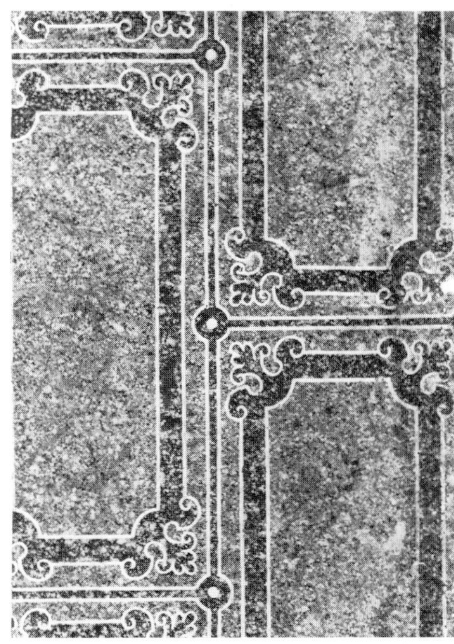
694 GJ.9425

Circa 1850
Flock, stamped gilt and marbled
51.1 × 54 cm (size of volume)
Given by the WM
E.1650–1763–1934

696 Pattern book containing 179 cuttings supplied for the decoration of the Houses of Parliament
1851–59
Colour prints from wood blocks, and flock
57.2 × 39.1 cm (size of volume)
Given by Mr A. L. Cowtan in memory of his father, Arthur Barnard Cowtan, OBE
E.137–1939

692A

692A

692A

692A

692A

692A

692A

692A

692A

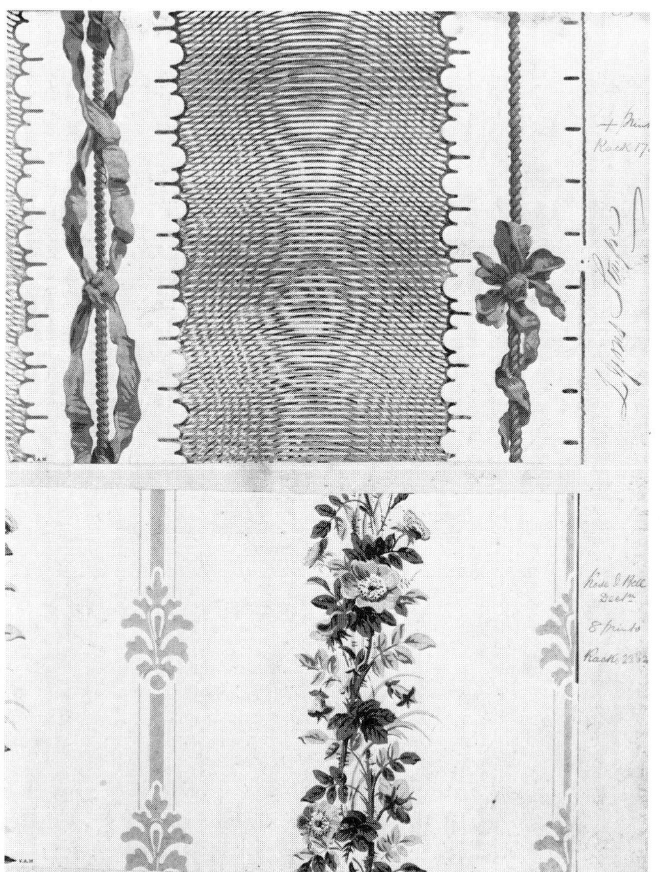

692A

692A

692A

692A

697 Pattern book with 81 specimens; some with Patent Office registration numbers for June, August and November 1853
Produced by Richard Goodlad & Co., Newcastle-upon-Tyne
1853
Colour prints from wood blocks and machine prints
57.2 × 49.2 cm (size of volume)
Given by the WM
E.1569–1649–1934; E.1583 neg GJ.9428; E.1584 neg GJ.9427

698 Pattern book with 80 specimens, including different colourways; each stamped on the back with serial number etc

697 GJ.9428

Produced by John Woollams & Co.
1865–66
Colour prints from wood blocks, flock etc
55.6 × 53.4 cm (size of volume)
Given by John Woollams & Co.
E.1–1897 neg GJ.9429 (p 85)

699 Pattern book with 140 specimens, including different colourways; each stamped on the back with serial number etc
Produced by John Woollams & Co.
1865–66

697 GJ.9427

698

699

Colour prints from wood blocks, marbled papers etc
54.3 × 52.7 cm (size of volume)
Given by John Woollams & Co.
E.2–1897 neg GJ.9430 (p 92)

700 Fourteen decorator's specimen panels of friezes, fillings, dadoes and borders by Bruce James Talbert, Andrew Fingar Brophy, Brightwen Binyon and possibly other artists
Produced by Jeffrey & Co.
Circa 1877–80
Colour prints from wood blocks, flock; some with gold
Various sizes
E.652–665–1953; E.662 CT 7341 (see col pl, p 262); E.665 neg GJ.9753

E.653–655 were exhibited by Jeffrey & Co. at the Paris Exhibition of 1878. E.657 is a panel of staircase paper, with a frieze of dog rose and hips, and a dado of smaller panels of apple branches. The filling of bay-leaves is by A. F. Brophy. This paper was awarded a gold medal at the Paris Exhibition; see catalogue, plate on p 30. Another colourway of the frieze, in flock on a gilt ground, is E.1895–1934.

701 *The New Designs for 1880. Stock Patterns Of Art Colorings And Designs*
Pattern book of wallpaper designs containing 206 specimens, some others torn out; inscribed in ink inside the front cover *The first pattern book issued by John Line & Sons. 1880. Bath. Reading. LHDayes Custodian 213–216 Tottenham Court Rd London W1* etc; each stamped on the back with trademark, serial number etc
Produced by John Line & Sons, 1880
Colour prints from wood blocks, engraved rollers etc
26 × 40.5 (size of volume)
Given by Shand Kydd Ltd
E.1274–1479–1980; E.1340 CT 8751 (see col pl, p 263)

700 GJ.9753

702 *The Westminster Wall Papers*
Pattern book with 169 specimens, including different colourways and photolithographs; most stamped on the back with serial number etc
Produced by Essex & Co.
1897
Colour machine prints
31.2 × 27.4 cm (size of volume)
Given by Mr E. F. Strange
E.6339–1910

'The Magnus', by C. F. A. Voysey; 'The Wykehamist', by C. F. A. Voysey; 'Sparrow Frieze'; 'Shell Border'; 'Crespigny Frieze'; 'Aylsham Frieze'; 'Candidum Frieze'; 'Daisy Chain Frieze'; 'Spray Border'; 'The Burwood'; 'The Woodbine'; 'The Dandelion'; 'The Towton'; 'The Wild Cherry'; 'The Titania'; 'The Godetia Frieze'; 'The Oberon'; 'The Mimosa'; 'The Bullfinch Frieze'; 'The Peasant'; 'The Nubian Frieze'; 'The Perronet'; 'The Trentham Frieze'; 'The Digby'; 'The Sherborne'; 'The Cibber', by C. F. A. Voysey; 'The Egeria'; 'The Anemone Frieze'; 'The Glade', by C. F. A. Voysey; 'The Merion'; 'The Sextus'; 'The Tamsui'; 'The Kintore'; 'The Papaver'; 'The Venici'; 'The Marcus'; 'The Verona Frieze'; 'The Carlton'; 'The Healaugh'; 'The Saladin'; 'The Elaine Frieze'; 'The D'Aumale'; 'The Prior'; 'The Abbot'; 'The Whorl'; 'The Dorothy'; 'The Fuyad'; 'The Bitlis'.

703 *The Westminster Wall Papers*
Pattern book with 163 specimens, including different colourways, borders etc; most stamped on the back with serial numbers etc
Produced by Essex & Co.
1899
Colour machine prints
30.8 × 26.7 cm (size of volume)
Given by Mr E. F. Strange
E.6340–1910

'The Arboreal', by Harrison Townsend (see no 1196); 'The Corea'; 'The Nerissa'; 'The Pindar'; 'The D'Aumale'; 'The Cardinal'; 'The Dandelion'; 'The Halidon'; 'The Melton'; 'The Boscastle'; 'The Astor'; 'The Pergolese'; 'The Genesta'; 'The Zambra'; 'The Katinka'; 'The Flora Frieze'; 'The Bertha'; 'The Trail Frieze'; 'The Empress'; 'The Lorna'; 'The Maisie'; 'The Lancelot Frieze'; 'The Rushill'; 'The Glenfyne Frieze'; 'The Evelyn'; 'The Auroya'; 'The Myra Frieze'; 'The Daisy', by C. F. A. Voysey; 'The Iona'; 'The Hemlock Frieze'; 'The Bimbi'; 'The Malmsley'; 'The Marchway'; 'The Rheims'; 'The Laverstoke'; 'The Leyton'; 'The Comrie'; 'The Wyncote Frieze'; 'The Adaim', by C. F. A. Voysey; 'The Coleherne Frieze', by C. F. A. Voysey; 'The Tokyo', by C. F. A. Voysey; 'The Elaine Frieze', by C. F. A. Voysey; 'The Columba', by C. F. A. Voysey; 'The Welbeck Frieze', by C. F. A. Voysey; 'The Squire's Garden', by C. F. A. Voysey; 'The Bitlis'; 'The Fuyad'; 'The Kintore'; 'The Tulip'.

'The Comrie' is reproduced in *The Magazine of Art* (1892), 168.

20th Century

704 Pattern book of papers, borders and lining papers, containing 223 specimens, including different colourways; some cut; bound in canvas boards, with a cover designed by Reginald L. Knowles, incorporating the manufacturer's trademark; signed within the cover design with initial *K* in a heart, and in letterpress *Plain Tints Self Coloured Stripe & Ceiling Wallpapers From 6d to 10/- per piece 1913*; each specimen with a serial number etc on the back
Produced by Jeffrey & Co.
Colour machine prints
33 × 25.4 cm (size of volume)
E.549–1971
Ex coll. Jeffrey & Co., 64, Essex Road, London, N1; The Library, Morton Sundour Fabrics Ltd, Carlisle. Reginald L. Knowles was a wallpaper designer for Jeffrey & Co. ('The Ilex', 1910).

705 Pattern book of hand-made flock wallpapers, containing 72 specimens, including different colourways; some cut; mounted on a display stand; cloth cover lettered with title etc; each stamped on the back with trademark, serial number etc
Produced by John Line & Sons Ltd
Circa 1921–*circa* 1940
Flock
85.5 × 53 cm (size of volume)
Given by Shand Kydd Ltd
E.2657–2725–1980; E.2667 neg HA.391

The display stand bears the title 'Studies in Harmony', a name which John Line had used for their collections since the 19th century.

705

706 Pattern book containing 277 specimens, including different colourways, of wallpaper, including two borders; bound in red canvas boards, with a leather handle; inscribed in capitals on the spine in white paint *Surface* and dated 1924–25; the majority inscribed on the back with orders; each stamped on the back with a serial number etc
Produced by the WM
Colour machine prints
39.3 × 47 cm (size of volume)
Given by the WM
E.2973–1962 neg GJ.9431

706A Pattern book containing 80 specimens, each duplicated; bound in buckram, with canvas spine; stencilled on the spine *Surface* and dated *1929–30*; each stamped on the back with a serial number

706

Produced by the Holmes Chapel Branch of the WPM
1929–30
Colour machine prints
Size of volume 54.5 × 52 cm
Given by the WPM
E.2974–1962 neg GJ.9432

Pattern no. X 8421, in the 'Egyptian' style, is reproduced in *JDA*, vol XLIX, 1929, 26.

707 Pattern book, incorporating a studio log, compiled by the donors, of obsolete designs, 1936–59; 151 specimens, including different colourways; each with title etc lettered on the front, and the pages of the original pattern book with title, serial number etc in letterpress on the back; some of the patterns interleaved with screen-printed versions, reduced in size; bound in cloth boards, with typescript list of titles, designers and printing methods affixed to the inside of the front cover and to the fly leaf
Produced by John Line & Sons Ltd
1952–53
38 × 50.5 cm (size of volume)
Given by Shand Kydd Ltd
E.2296–2446–1980

'Aegean', by Frank Jaffe (also known as 'Hurry') (E.2296); 'Amala' (not the pattern designed by Donald Melbourne, q.v.) (E.2297); 'Arbour', by Bianca Minns (E.2298); 'Arcadia', by John Minton (E.2299); 'Arcady', by W. W. C. Pitts (E.2300, 2301); 'Ardennes', by William J. Odell (E.2302); 'Argosy', by William J. Odell (E.2303); 'Aria', by William J. Odell (E.2304); 'Atlantis', (E.2305); 'Avondale', by William J. Odell (E.2306); 'Balmyle', by 'Rosal' (E.2307, 2308); 'Bamboo', by William J. Odell (E.2309); 'Belcombe', by Mary Storr (E.2310); 'Belfairs', by Armfield-Passano (E.2311); 'Bermuda', by Mary Storr (E.2312); 'Bird and Tree', by W. W. C. Pitts (E.2313); 'Bolingbroke', by William J. Odell (E.2314); 'Bouquet', (E.2315); 'Bracken', by William J. Odell (E.2316); 'Broads', by Henry Skeen (E.2317, 2318); 'Burleigh', by Mary Storr (E.2319); 'Camelot', by W. W. C. Pitts (E.2320); 'Camilla', by Henry Skeen (E.2321); 'Canton', by H. Close (E.2322); 'Chequers', by Addison (E.2323); 'Cherwell', by William J. Odell (E.2324); 'Chisholm', by Walter Krauer (E.2325); 'Clematis', by William J. Odell (E.2326); 'Cobham', by Henry Skeen (E.2327); 'Colville', by William J. Odell (E.2328); 'Conlowe', by Armfield-Passano (E.2329); 'Corinda' (E.2330, 2331); 'Courcy', by William J. Odell (E.2332); 'Crossley', by Henry Skeen (E.2333); 'Daphne' (E.2334); 'Derswell', by Henry Skeen (E.2335); 'Dominoes', by Willy Hermann (E.2336); 'Dudley', by Edgar Cattermole (E.2337); 'Early Bird', by Sylvia Priestley (E.2338); 'Emily', by Mary Storr (E.2339); 'Fairy Dell', by W. W. C. Pitts (E.2340); 'Fantasy', by Olga Lehmann (E.2341); 'Insulin 8.25', by Robert Sevant (E.2342); 'Boric Acid 8.34', by William J. Odell (E.2346); 'Insulin 8.27', by William J. Odell (E.2344); 'Afwillite 8.45', by William J. Odell (E.2345); 'Flora' (E.2346); 'Florida', by William J. Odell (E.2347); 'Fontaine', by William J. Odell (E.2348, 2349); 'Forest Glade', by W. W. C. Pitts (E.2350); 'Granada', by William J. Odell (E.2351); 'Greta', by William J. Odell (E.2352); 'Gretchen', by Beatrice V. Leyson (E.2353); 'Gustave', by Walter Krauer (E.2354); 'Harlequin', by Henry Skeen (E.2355); 'Haslam', by A. Raisin (E.2356); 'Hassan', by G. Fisher-Jones (E.2357); 'Hatherley', by William J. Odell (E.2358, 2359); 'Heaton', by Henry Skeen (E.2360); 'Hector' (E.2361); 'Hiawatha', by Daphne Barder (E.2362); 'Huntingdon', by William J. Odell (E.2363); 'Isabella', by Jacqueline Groag (E.2364); 'Jacqueline', by William J. Odell (E.2365); 'Jennifer', (?Linx Co., Paris) (E.2366); 'Julian', by Henry Skeen (E.2367); 'Katrina', by Virginia James (E.2368); 'Kiddies' Town', by Jacqueline Groag (E.2369); 'Leaf and Berry', by G. Fisher-Jones (E.2370); 'Lomond', by Henry Skeen (E.2371); 'London Square', by Miriam Wornum (E.2372); 'Lysander', by William J. Odell (E.2373); 'Maidenhair', by Robert Scott (E.2374); 'Marina', by Sylvia Priestley (E.2375); 'Marston', by Henry Skeen (E.2376); 'Maxwell', by Henry Skeen (E.2377); 'Medina', by William J. Odell (E.2378); 'Melford', by William J. Odell (E.2379); 'Melville', by Daphne Barder (E.2380); 'Millicent', by 'Rosal' (E.2381, 2382); 'Mirabel', by G. Kingbourne (E.2383); 'Miranda', by Jacqueline Groag (E.2384, 2385); 'Morelle', by ? E. Calvetti (E.2386); 'Mostyne', by Willy Hermann (E.2387); 'Murania', by William J. Odell (E.2388); 'Neville', by William J. Odell (E.2389); 'Ninette', by William J. Odell (E.2390); 'Odette', by Artur Litt (E.2391); 'Orville', by William J. Odell (E.2392); 'Paeony', by Henry Skeen (E.2393); 'Penrose', by 'Lees' (E.2394); 'Perugia', by Graham Rice (E.2395); 'Priscilla', by 'Rosal' (E.2396, 2397); 'Provence', by Lucienne Day (E.2398); 'Quartic Trellis', by Eric Ayers (E.2399); 'Quiltie', by Arnold Lever (E.2400); 'Ribbon', arranged from a drawing by M. McGregor (E.2401); 'Riga', by Barbara Hirsch (E.2402); 'Romaine', by 'Rosal' (E.2403, 2404); 'Rowan', by G. Kingbourne (E.2405); 'Roxburgh', by Helène Gallet (E.2406); 'Saigon', by Henry Skeen (E.2407, 2408); 'Salon', by Willy Hermann (E.2409); 'Saville', by William J. Odell (E.2410); 'Seahorses', by Bruce Hollingsworth (E.2411); 'Sefton', by Henry Skeen (E.2412); 'Shalimar', by William J. Odell (E.2413); 'Shell', by Henry Skeen (E.2414); 'Shelley', by William J. Odell (E.2415); 'Shenstone', by Mary Storr (E.2416); 'Sherwood', by G. Fisher-Jones (E.2417); 'Sprig', by P. Pompa (E.2418); 'Summer Flowers', by Daphne Barder (E.2419); 'Tamrico', by William J. Odell (E.2420); 'Tartan', by Mary Storr (E.2421); 'Thalia', by Esmé Grace (E.2422); 'Titania', by W. W. C. Pitts (E.2423); 'Trellis', by William J. Odell (E.2424); 'Troy', by John Minton (E.2425); 'Turnberry', by Anne Loosely (E.2426); 'Turnberry Thistle', by Anne Loosely (E.2427); 'Tuscany', by John Minton (E.2428); 'Val Rosa', by Joyce E. Morgan (E.2429); 'Vanessa', by Henry Skeen (E.2430); 'Vanessa Trellis', by Henry Skeen (E.2431); 'Vermont', by William J. Odell (E.2432); 'Victoria', by Mary Storr (E.2433); 'Vienna', by Daphne Barder (E.2434); 'Walbrook', by N. Hart (E.2435); 'Waldron' (E.2436); 'Vivienne', by William J. Odell (E.2437); 'Western Isles', by William J. Odell (E.2438); 'Wheatley', by Mary Storr (E.2439); 'Windsor Castle', by William J. Odell (E.2440); 'Wisley', by Henry Skeen (E.2441); 'Woodlands', by W. W. C. Pitts (E.2442); 'Wycliffe', by M. Glover (E.2443); 'Yolande', by H. Hofbauer (E.2444); 'Zambesi', by Walter Krauer (E.2445); 'Zephyr', by Henry Skeen (E.2446).

708 *British Wallpaper Base. Papier Peint Vierge Anglais*
Pattern book containing 47 specimens produced by Arthur Sanderson & Sons Ltd and Crown Wallpaper 1950–62; letterpress introduction, etc, in English and in French; full bound in leather, with title, manufacturer's name, etc, on the front cover; notes on the type of paper and weight per square metre on sheets interleaved between each specimen
Produced by M. R. Berra (London) Ltd, 1962
Rotagravure, silk screen, flock, embossed paper
25 × 38.6 cm (size of volume)
Given by Mr M. R. Berra
E.1211–1258–1978

The specimens of rotagravure printing include imitation wood grain, a wove wood fence, and various types of stone walling.

709 *Wallpaper for the Small Home*
Twelve sheets of samples of wallpapers, together with 2 sheets of illustrations of

709 GJ.9433

709 GJ.9434

709 GJ.9436

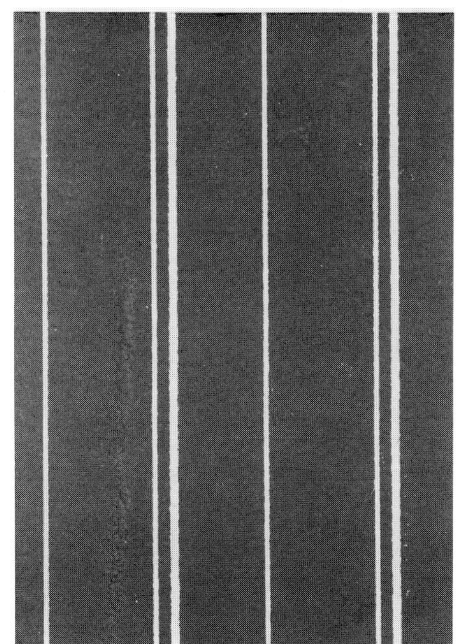

709 GJ.9335

709 GJ.10021

709 GJ.9437

709 GJ.9439

709 GJ.9438

709 GJ.9440

709 GJ.9441

the various designs decorating a room; each inscribed in letterpress on the mounts with the manufacturer's name, description etc and *Design Folios Book K Plate 1 to 12*
Folio issued by the Council of Industrial Design
Circa 1950 (including 2 reprints)
Colour prints from wood blocks, machine, and screen prints
44.5 × 37 cm (each)
Given by an anonymous donor
E.1221–1234–1974

1 Pattern of leaves and flowers in green on white
Produced by Arthur Sanderson & Sons Ltd
Hand block-printed
E.1221 neg GJ.9433
2 Diaper cinquefoil pattern on a background simulating watered silk
Produced by Shand Kydd Ltd
Embossed and roller-printed
E.1222 neg GJ.9434
3 Narrow- and broad-stripe pattern in green
Produced by John Line & Sons Ltd
Trough-printed stripes
E.1223 neg GJ.9435
4 Abstract shapes in white on yellow
Designed by Graham Sutherland
Produced by Cole & Son (Wallpapers) Ltd
Hand block-printed
E.1224 neg GJ.10021
See Entwisle, L. H., pl 107.
5 Pattern of white leaves and trailing stems on a background of undulating vertical stripes
Produced by the WM
Roller-printed
E.1225 neg GJ.9436
6 Pattern of a formalized leaf motif in pink, half-dropped on a background of grey stripes
Produced by Arthur Sanderson & Sons Ltd
Hand block-printed on a trough-printed stripe
E.1226 neg GJ.9437
7 Pattern of a formalized floral motif, alternating with small cinquefoils, in white on a red background
Reprint of a hand block-printed paper of *circa* 1810
Produced by Cole & Son

(Wallpapers) Ltd
E.1227

8 Pattern of birds, flowers and leaves within coiling stems
Produced by the WM
Embossed and roller-printed
E.1228 neg GJ.9438

9 Pattern of a small flower-and-leaf motif in gold, half-dropped on a background embossed to simulate linen weave
Produced by Arthur Sanderson & Sons Ltd
Embossed and roller-printed
E.1229 neg GJ.9439

10 Pattern of bunches of violets within a trellis of ribbons, on a dotted background
Reprint of a roller-printed paper of *circa* 1860–70
Produced by the WM
E.1230

11 Pattern of flowers and grasses in yellow on a blue background
Produced by John Line & Sons Ltd
Screen print
E.1231 neg GJ.9440

12 Pattern of star shapes on a background of dots
Produced by John Line & Sons Ltd
Hand block-printed
E.1232 neg GJ.9441

710 *'1951' Wallpapers Limited Editions*
Pattern book containing 52 specimens, including different colourways; each with designer's name, name of pattern, serial number etc in letterpress on the back; with price-list and preface by Derek Patmore
Produced by John Line & Sons Ltd
1951
Colour prints from wood blocks and screen prints
49.5 × 53 cm (size of volume)
Given by Shand Kydd Ltd
E.1480–1531–1980

The first British screen-printed set. The pattern book is discussed in *Design*, no 36, 1951, pp 10–12, where a number of the patterns are reproduced: namely, 'Isabella', 'Orpheus', 'Provence', 'Early Bird', 'Troy', 'Tuscany' and 'Murania'.

'Isabella', by Jacqueline Groag (E.1480); 'Troy' and 'Tuscany', by John Minton (E.1481–1487); 'Stanstead' (E.1488, 1529–1531); 'Estelle' (E.1489, 1491); 'Early Bird', by Sylvia Priestley (E.1490, 1492); 'Carlyon' (E.1493, 1495, 1498, 1500, 1504); 'Mexico', by Armfield-Passano (E.1494, 1496); 'Belfairs', by Armfield-Passano (E.1497); 'Arcadia', by John Minton (E.1499, 1503, 1505); 'Crossley' (E.1506, 1508); 'Conlowe', by Armfield-Passano (E.1507, 1509); 'Quiltie', by Arnold Lever (E.1510–1512); 'Amala', by Donald Melbourne (E.1513); 'Wyndham' (E.1514); 'Orpheus', by Arnold Lever (E.1515); 'Arbour', by Bianca Minns (E.1516, 1517); 'Sea Horses', by Bruce Hollingsworth (E.1518, 1519); 'Langdon' (E.1521); 'Auratum', by Henry Skeen (E.1520, 1522); 'Murania', by William J. Odell (E.1523, 1524); 'Frivolité', by Mary Storr (E.1525); 'Fantasy', by Olga Lehmann (E.1526–1528).

711 *Beauty in Wallpaper*
Pattern book containing 33 specimens, including different colourways; each with title, serial number etc in letterpress on the back; bound in paper boards, with letterpress introduction
Produced by John Line & Sons Ltd
1952–53
Colour prints from wood blocks, most embossed
16.9 × 22.3 cm (size of volume)
Given by Mr L. R. King
E.839–871–1977

The sheets are interleaved with an artist's impressions of contemporary interiors, each with a commentary on the use of the wallpaper. Each scheme consists of a combination of two different patterned papers.

'The Grosvenor Decoration' (E.839, 840); 'The Lansdowne Decoration' (E.841, 842); 'The Alison Decoration' (E.843–846); 'The Cadogan Decoration' (E.847–851); 'The Lonsdale Decoration' (E.852, 853); 'The Chester Decoration' (E.854, 855); 'The Leamington Decoration' (E.856, 857); 'The Wild Rose Decoration' (E.858–861); 'The Sherwood Decoration' (E.862–865); 'The Mayfair Decoration' (E.866, 867); 'The Adrian Decoration' (E.868–871).

712 *Coronation Decoration*
Pattern book of hand-printed wallpapers containing 27 specimens, including different colourways, commemorating the coronation of Queen Elizabeth II; each with serial number etc on the back; in a paper folder, with letterpress description
Produced by Arthur Sanderson & Sons Ltd
1953
Colour prints from wood blocks, some embossed and one flock
20.3 × 25.4 cm (size of folder)
Given by Mr L. R. King
E.872–898–1977; E.885 neg GJ.9442; E.886 neg GJ.9443; E.887 neg GJ.9444

712 GJ.9442

712 GJ.9443

712 GJ.9444

713 *The Significance of Line*
Pattern book containing 128 specimens, including different colourways; each with title, serial number etc in letterpress on the back; 3 sheets inserted with screen prints of the patterns reduced to one-eighth of the size; bound in cloth-covered boards and lettered on the spine *Traditional Collection*
Produced by John Line & Sons Ltd
Circa 1955
Flock, and screen prints
42.4 × 52.2 cm (size of volume)
Given by Shand Kydd Ltd
E.2529–2656–1980

Miniature patterns: 'Double Venetian', 'Dauphin', 'Lombardy' and 'Ravenna', by G. Fisher-Jones; 'Palermo' and 'Bologna', by Clement Cooke; 'Andalusia' and 'Atherstone' (E.2529),

713 'Kaiwan'

by L. Wildgoose; 'Saigon' and 'Avignon', by Henry Skeen; 'Nizami', by George Kingbourne; 'Pastoral', by George Dufond; 'Lorenzo', 'Orleans', 'June' and 'Mansfield' (E.2530), by William J. Odell.

Standard-sized patterns: 'Athene' (E.2531); 'Russell' (E.2532); 'Kaiwan' (E.2533 neg HA.399, 2534); 'Pompadour' (E.2535–2537); 'Etienne' (E.2538–2540); 'Yunnan' (E.2541–2543); 'Garland' (E.2544, 2545); 'Clarence' (E.2546, 2547); 'Belvedere' (E.2548–2550); 'Bologna', by Clement Cooke (E.2551, 2552); 'Lorraine' (E.2553–2555); 'Orleans', by William J. Odell (E.2556, 2557); 'Ceylon Chintz' (E.2558); 'Mathilde' (E.2559, 2560); 'Steyne' (E.2561, 2563, 2642, 2643); 'Beauchamp' (E.2562, 2564–2566); 'Bathurst' (E.2567, 2568); 'Clarendon' (E.2569, 2570); 'Antoinette' (E.2571–2573); 'Rosetta' (E.2574, 2575); 'Clarissa' (E.2576, 2577); 'Linton' (E.2578, 2579); 'Marcus' (E.2580, 2581); 'Milan' (E.2582); 'Apsley' (E.2583–2585); 'Burford' (E.2586); 'Josephine' (E.2587, 2588); 'Villiers' (E.2589, 2590); 'Bow' (E.2591, 2593); 'Charlotte' (E.2592, 2594); 'Priscilla' (E.2595–2597); 'Creighton' (E.2598, 2599); 'Jennifer' (E.2600, 2601); 'Mentone' (E.2602); 'Claremont' (E.2603–2605); 'Radnor' (E.2606, 2607); 'Dauphin' (E.2608, 2609); 'Padua' (E.2610); 'Camilla' (E.2611–2613); 'Shansi' (E.2614–2616); 'Armand' (E.2617, 2618); 'Palmette' (E.2619–2621); 'Teheran' (E.2622, 2623); 'Messina' (E.2624–2626); 'Shelburne' (E.2627, 2628); 'Kenilworth' (E.2629, 2630); 'Arlington' (E.2631, 2632); 'Hubert' (E.2633, 2634); 'Hector' (E.2635–2637); 'Berkeley' (E.2638); 'Star' (E.2639–2641); 'Vernay' (E.2644–2646); 'Denstone' (E.2647); 'Buckingham' (E.2648, 2649); 'Wyndham' (E.2650–2653); 'Osterley' (E.2654, 2655); 'Garrick' (E.2656).

714 *Epoch*
Pattern book of vinyl papers, containing 151 specimens, including different colourways; each with title, serial number etc in letterpress on the back; some sheets interleaved with photographs of the patterns and notes concerning them; bound in plastic-covered boards
Produced by John Line & Sons Ltd
1964
Screen prints
51.5 × 50.6 cm (size of volume)
Given by Shand Kydd Ltd
E.2045–2145–1980

'Shiraz' (E.2045, 2047); 'Lucretio' (E.2046, 2090); 'Arlington' (E.2049, 2110, 2115, 2193–2195); 'Globe' (E.2050); 'Garrick' (E.2051, 2052, 2058, 2086, 2190–2192); 'Stanmer' (E.2053, 2144); 'Wykeham' (E.2054, 2077); 'Verrio' (E.2055, 2085, 2111); 'Sarah' (E.2056, 2063, 2114); 'Kedleston' (E.2057, 2105); 'Bayonne' (E.2059, 2060); 'Solvay' (E.2061, 2070, 2080); 'Istanbul' (E.2062, 2091); 'Berkeley' (E.2064, 2126, 2172, 2184–2186); 'Apsley' (E.2065, 2066, 2117); 'Rudloff' (E.2067, 2078); 'Aversa' (E.2068, 2069); 'Bordeaux' (E.2071, 2072); 'Samarkand' (E.2073, 2074, 2076); 'Steyne' (E.2075, 2145, 2158, 2181–2183); 'Achmin' (E.2079, 2104, 2116); 'Chantilly' (E.2081, 2084); 'Denise' (E.2082, 2083); 'Prologue' (E.2087, 2088); 'Samos' (E.2089); 'Verdona' (E.2092–2096); 'Rosalys' (E.2097–2099); 'Lucienne' (E.2100, 2101, 2107); 'Hickleton' (E.2102, 2103); 'Samisen' (E.2106, 2119); 'Plumage' (E.2108, 2109); 'Mantua' (E.2112, 2113, 2121, 2123); 'Wynn' (E.2118, 2120, 2142, 2146); 'Buckingham' (E.2122, 2139, 2151, 2187–2189); 'Rendezvous' (E.2124); 'Selwyn' (E.2125, 2127); 'Syon' (E.2128, 2129); 'Arbutus' (E.2130, 2131, 2152–2154); 'Marnier' (E.2132–2136); 'Beaufoy' (E.2137, 2161); 'Montcalm' (E.2138, 2140, 2141); 'Belvedere' (E.2143, 2165, 2166); 'Hidcote' (E.2147, 2148); 'Vincennes' (E.2149, 2150); 'Trades' (or 'Arts and Crafts') by Brian Moore (E.2155); 'Kaiwan' (E.2156, 2157); 'Mentone' (E.2159, 2160); 'Sassanid' (E.2162–2164); 'Victoria' (E.2167–2169); 'Nicolas' (E.2170, 2171); 'Dauphin' (E.2173, 2174); 'Malaga' (E.2175, 2176); 'Delphic' (E.2177–2180)

715 *Focus*
Pattern book containing 187 specimens, including different colourways; each with designer's name, name of pattern, serial number etc in letterpress on the back; a few sheets interleaved with photographs of the papers in contemporary settings; bound in boards, with a design by John Griffiths on the front cover
Produced by Shand Kydd Ltd
1964–65
Colour prints from wood blocks, rotagravure and ink emboss
40 × 50.5 cm (size of volume)
Given by Shand Kydd Ltd
E.1532–1718–1980

Some of the papers are washable; the remainder are described as 'spongeable'. The volume is divided into sections: 'Lounge & Dining Room'; 'Hall, Landings & Attic'; 'Bedroom & Nursery'; 'Bathroom & Kitchen', and 'Ceilings, Specials & Stripes'. See under Charles Raymond (no 1127) for his design for 'Sweet Pea'. 'Shiro', 'Festival' and 'Fontaine' were exhibited at the Whitworth Art Gallery, Manchester, 1972. 'Festival', by Donald Melbourne, was printed from rubber rollers on a Heidemann ink embossing machine and is probably the first flexographic paper printed in this country (reproduced in F. Lewis, *Best Designs versus Best Seller*, 1965, fig 66).

'Silk' (E.1532, 1534, 1563, 1564, 1573, 1574, 1599, 1601, 1623, 1625, 1627, 1630, 1700–1707); 'Korin', by Peter Sumner (E.1533, 1535, 1537, 1643); 'Osmond' (E.1536, 1613, 1667–1669); 'Tamana', by James Heath (E.1538, 1540, 1542, 1664–1666); 'Bamboo', by Donald Melbourne (E.1539, 1541, 1543); 'Rosa', by Michael Dauban (E.1544–1546); 'Powys', by John Harbour (E.1547, 1549, 1551, 1621, 1708–1710); 'Gaverne', by John Harbour (E.1548, 1550, 1552); 'Belinda', by Gordon Davies (E.1554, 1556, 1558); 'Sudbury' (E.1555, 1557, 1717, 1718); 'Alwyn', by Donald Melbourne (E.1559–1561); 'Shiro', by Tessa Hagity (E.1562, 1563, 1565, 1644); 'Gisburn', by Fay Hillier (E.1566–1568); 'Melvyn' (E.1569); 'Mistra', by José Bonnet (E.1570–1572); 'Orvieto', by Gordon Davies (E.1574, 1576); 'Kaduna', by Willy Hermann (E.1577); 'Halsbury', by Peter Sumner (E.1578); 'Selbury' (E.1579, 1713); 'Festival', by Donald Melbourne (E.1580 CT8747 (see col pl, p 264, 1582, 1648); 'Kansvik', by James Heath (E.1583, 1584, 1619, 1652); 'Lindell' (E.1585, 1587, 1711, 1712); 'Kent', by John Harbour (E.1586, 1588); 'Axford', by Evelyn Pauker (E.1589–1591); 'Carna', by Donald Melbourne (E.1592, 1597); 'Barra', by Donald Melbourne (E.1593–1596, 1598); 'Fontaine', by Charles Raymond (E.1600, 1602, 1642); 'Ballina', by Joyce Storey (E.1603–1606); 'Vernon', by John Harbour (E.1607, 1609, 1611); 'Wild Rose', by John Harbour (E.1608, 1610, 1612); 'Deronda', by Joyce Storey (E.1614, 1616, 1618); 'Dunning' (E.1615, 1617, 1640, 1714–1716); 'Dolls', by Donald Melbourne (E.1620, 1622); 'Sweet Pea', by Charles Raymond (E.1624, 1626); 'Clematis', by Donald Melbourne (E.1628, 1629, 1631); 'Marietta', by Mondial Designs (E.1632, 1633); 'Verity', by John Harbour (E.1634, 1637); 'Valerie', by John Harbour (E.1635, 1636, 1638); 'Posy', by José Bonnet (E.1639, 1641); 'Hayling', by Harry Cadney (E.1645–1647); 'Herbal' (E.1649–1651); 'Rondel', by John Harbour (E.1653, 1654); 'Corsham', by Donald Melbourne (E.1655–1657); 'Mellor', by Rudi Colme (E.1658–1660); 'Vernon', by John Harbour (E.1661–1663)

716 *Folio*
Pattern book of vinyl papers containing 100 specimens, including different colourways; each with designer's name, name of pattern, serial number etc in letterpress on the back; some of the sheets interleaved with screen prints of the patterns reduced to one-eighth of the size; bound in boards
Produced by Shand Kydd Ltd
1964–65
Colour screen prints
46.5 × 51 cm (size of volume)
Given by Shand Kydd Ltd
E.2196–2295–1980

'Folio', a John Line brand name, was taken over by Shand Kydd when the 2 companies merged in 1958. Shand Kydd produced 3 'Folio' collections. 'Portals' and 'Perseus' were exhibited at the Whitworth Art Gallery, Manchester, 1972.

'Carola', by Carola and Daniel Olsen (E.2196–2199); 'Adamantine', by Elizabeth Gould (E.2200–2202); 'Bezique', by Harry Cadney (E.2203–2205, E.2203 neg HA.342); 'Biscari', by Harry Cadney (E.2206–2208); 'Cymbria', by Fritz Wurthmuller (E.2209–2211); 'Aubrey', by William J. Odell (E.2212–2214); 'Tabard', by James Heath (E.2215–2217); 'Carousel', by Donald Melbourne (E.2218–2221); 'Portals', by Robert Dodd (E.2222–2225); 'Tarascan', by Carola and Daniel Olsen (E.2226–2228); 'Kinna', by Bessie Wells (E.2229–2231); 'Pandora', by John Harbour (E.2232–2235); 'Bardolph', by Fritz Wurthmuller (E.2236–2238); 'Palm Frond', by Veronica Midgley (E.2239–2242); 'Kalevada', by Cliff Holden (E.2243, 2244); 'Latium', by John Wright (E.2245–2248); 'Auriga', by Carola and Daniel Olsen (E.2249–2251); 'Venado', by William J. Odell (E.2252–2255); 'Nineveh', by Harry Cadney (E.2256–2259); 'Gala', by Joyce Storey (E.2260–2262); 'Berain' (E.2263, 2264);

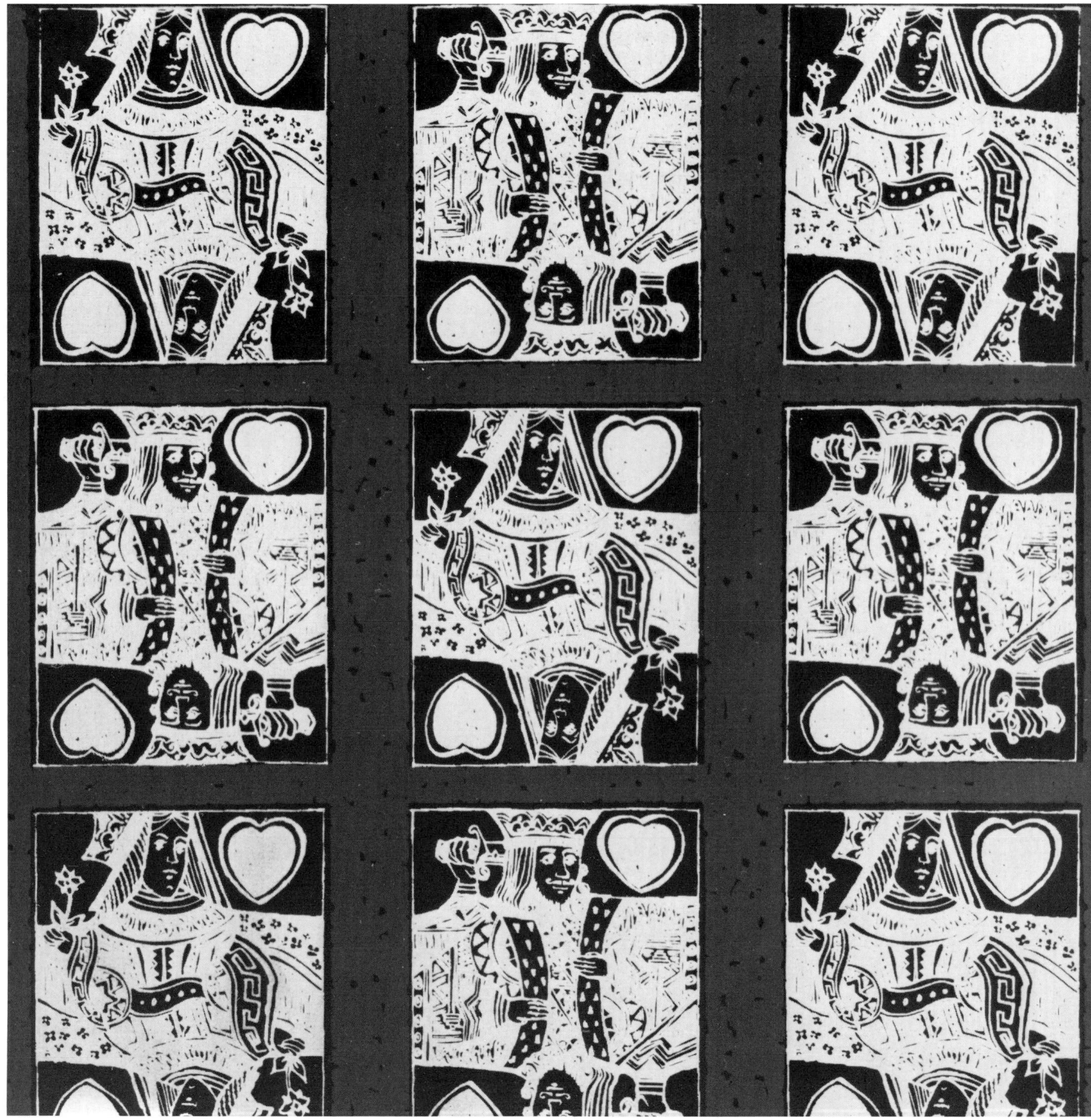

716 'Bezique'

'Thicket', by John Harbour (E.2265–2267); 'Aztec', by Carola and Daniel Olsen (E.2268–2271); 'Osten' (E.2272, 2273); 'Terrazzo', by Harry Cadney (E.2274–2277); 'Zoltan', by Karin Warming (E.2278–2280); 'Vervolde', by Fritz Wurthmuller (E.2281–2283); 'Diabolo', by Carol Williams (E.2284–2286); 'Telston', by Malcolm Jones (E.2287–2289); 'Conrad' (E.2290); 'Perseus', by Jean G. Hopes (E.2291–2293); 'Garnier', by James Heath (E.2294, 2295)

717 *Folio (Shand Kydd Folio Vinyl Protected Handprints)*
A selection of 17 miniature designs from the complete Shand Kydd Book of 33 designs in 90 colourways; each with designer's name, title, serial number etc in letterpress on the back; bound in paper covers
1964–65
Screen prints
19.5 × 24.5 cm (size of volume)
Given by Shand Kydd Ltd
E.2867–2883–1980

'Latium', by John Wright (E.2867); 'Aubrey', by William J. Odell (E.2868); 'Carola', by Carola and Daniel Olsen (E.2869); 'Aztec', by Carola and Daniel Olsen (E.2870); 'Biscari', by Harry Cadney (E.2871); 'Portals', by Robert Dodd (E.2872, 2873); 'Carousel', by Donald Melbourne (E.2874); 'Adamantine', by Elizabeth Gould (E.2875); 'Tarascan', by Carola and Daniel Olsen (E.2876); 'Bezique', by Harry Cadney (E.2877); 'Thicket', by John Harbour (E.2878); 'Palm Frond', by

Veronica Midgley (E.2879); 'Gala', by Joyce Storey (E.2880); 'Venado', by William J. Odell (E.2881); 'Terrazzo', by Harry Cadney (E.2882); 'Pandora', by John Harbour (E.2883)

718 'Wood Mosaic'

718 *Focus*
Pattern book containing 151 specimens, including different colourways, each with designer's name, name of pattern, serial number etc in letterpress on the back; a few sheets interleaved with photographs of the papers in contemporary settings
Produced by Shand Kydd Ltd
1966–67
Colour prints from wood blocks, rotagravure and emboss
40 × 50.5 cm (size of volume)
Given by Shand Kydd Ltd
E.1719–1869–1980

Some of the papers are washable; the remainder are described as 'spongeable'. The volume is divided into sections: 'Dining-room & Lounge'; 'Hall, Landings & Attic'; 'Bedroom & Nursery'; 'Bathroom & Kitchen' and 'Ceilings, Specials & Stripes'. See under Donald Melbourne for his designs for 'Areca' and 'Amala' (nos 1055, 1056).

'Oswald' (E.1719, 1736, 1788, 1790, 1792, 1808, 1841–1846); 'Kaleidoscope', by Donald Melbourne (E.1720, 1722, 1822); 'Salvador' (E.1721, 1745, 1768, 1849–1851); 'Pandang' (E.1723, 1726, 1831–1834); 'Bonnington', by John Harbour (E.1724, 1725, 1727); 'Naughton', by William J. Odell (E.1728–1730); 'Patna', by Henry Skeen (E.1731–1733); 'Silk' (E.1734, 1738, 1750, 1853–1855); 'Selina' (or 'Celina'), by Peter Sumner (E.1735, 1737, 1739, 1820); 'Dorado' (E.1740, 1795, 1796, 1803, 1810, 1859–1861); 'Cannetti', by Eric Thompson (E.1741, 1744, 1746, 1821); 'Garvald', by John Harbour (E.1742, 1743, 1762, 1772–1774); 'Andorra', by John Harbour (E.1747–1749); 'Areca' (or 'Arica'), by Donald Melbourne (E.1751, 1753, 1755); 'Wood Mosaic', by Deryck Healey (E.1752, 1818, 1828 neg HA. 396, 1852); 'Screen' (E.1754, 1758, 1770, 1778, 1837–1840); 'Blain', by Deryck Healey (E.1756, 1757); 'Amala', by Donald Melbourne (E.1759, 1761, 1816); 'Maze', by Mea Angerer (E.1763, 1765); 'Donovan', by Donald Melbourne (E.1764, 1856–1858); 'Stefan' (E.1766, 1786, 1862–1864; 'Lychees', by Peter Sumner (E.1767, 1769, 1771); 'Tamana', by James Heath (E.1768, 1775, 1866, 1867); 'Canvas' (E.1777, 1847, 1848); 'Osaka', by William J. Odell (E.1776, 1779); 'Blendon', by Donald Melbourne (E.1780–1782); 'Alcombe', by Deryck Healey (E.1783–1785); 'Roxana', by F. Luckett (E.1787, 1789, 1791); 'Dalkeith', by Frank Designs (E.1793, 1794, 1797); 'Dallas' (E.1798, 1865); 'Pauline', by Patricia Smart (E.1799, 1802, 1804); 'Granthorpe' (E.1800, 1801, 1813, 1835, 1836); 'Eveleigh', by John Harbour (E.1805–1807); 'Flora', by Peter Sumner (E.1809, 1811); 'Charleston', by Evelyn Pauker (E.1812, 1814, 1815); 'Cullerne', by Peter Sumner (E.1817, 1819); 'Gourds', by Joyce Storey (E.1823, 1824); 'Alicante', by Leon Joiner (E.1825, 1826); 'Fontaine', by Charles Raymond (E.1827); 'Popham' (E.1829, 1830); 'Dovedale', by Rudi Colme (E.1868, 1869).

719

719 *Palladio 8*
Pattern book of wallpaper containing 105 specimens, including different colourways; each with title, artist's name, serial number etc in letterpress on the back; bound in plastic-covered boards
Produced by Sanderson-Rigg Ltd, Bridlington
1968
Silk screen prints
50.8 × 50.8 cm (size of volume)
Given by the WM
E.5084–5188–1968

'Contre', 'Parti', by Pat Albeck (E.5106–5111); 'Tournament', by Deirdre Baker (E.5177, 5178); 'Hecuba', 'Zohak', by David Bartle (E.5096–5098, 5112–5114); 'Athena', 'Calyx', 'Charlotte', by Ann Berwick (E.5151–5153, 5171–5173, 5183, 5184); 'Crescendo', 'Primavera', 'Ziggurat', by Margaret Cannon (E.5091 neg GH.3294, 5092, 5115–5117, 5179, 5180); 'Ceramica', 'Ida', 'Impact', by Judith Cash (E.5125, 5126, 5134 CT 8592, 5135,

5148); 'Dorado', 'Octavia', 'Portico', by Inge Cordsen (E.5084–5086, 5145, 5146, 5154–5157); 'Celtic', by Ann Cotton (E.5136, 5137); 'Bokhara', 'Chantilly', 'Clementine', by Robert Dodd (E.5118–5120, 5121, 5122, 5131–5133); 'Sedge', by Evelyn Erlbeck (E.5093–5095); 'Jardin', by Tony Fraser (E.5163–5165); 'Quentin', by John Halton (E.5149, 5150); 'Gambit', 'Roulette', by Deryck Healey (E.5166–5168, 5174–5176); 'Compendium', by Rosemary Newsom (E.5089, 5090); 'Zircon', by Althea McNish (E.5186); 'Berkley', 'Tarascon', by Edward Pond (E.5101–5103, 5123, 5124, 5138–5144); 'Zandra', by Zandra Rhodes (E.5088); 'Sable', by Humphrey Spender (E.5169, 5170); 'Telemachus', by Edward Squires (E.5127–5130); 'Boulevard', 'Fontana', by Jeremy Talbot (E.5099, 5100, 5158–5162); 'Metropole', by Sandra Watts (E.5181, 5182); 'Pomona', by Erica Willis (E.5104, 5105); 'Carnavel', 'Totem' (studio designs) (E.5185, 5187, 5188)

721 'Apollo'

720 *Focus*
Pattern book containing 167 specimens, including different colourways; each with designer's name, name of pattern, serial number etc in letterpress on the back; a few sheets interleaved with photographs of the papers in contemporary settings
Produced by Shand Kydd Ltd
1968–69
Colour prints from wood blocks, rotagravure and emboss
40 × 50.3 cm (size of volume)
Given by Shand Kydd Ltd
E.1870–2036–1980

Some of the papers are washable. The volume is divided into sections: 'Hall, Landings & Attic'; 'Bathroom & Kitchen'; 'Lounge & Dining-room'.

'Vesiga', by Peter Sumner (E.1870, 1880, 1881, 1883, 1885, 1946, 2001–2003); 'Odessa', by John Harbour (E.1871, 1873); 'Matsu' (E.1872, 1926, 1944, 1956); 'Keswick' (E.1874, 1887, 1912, 1913, 1948, 1973, 2014); 'Marbella', by John Harbour (E.1875, 1877, 1879); 'Verne' (E.1876, 2030); 'Seaton' (E.1878, 1896, 1904, 1906, 1935, 1996, 1997, 2009, 2010); 'Izmir', by Patricia Smart (E.1882); 'Rondo', by Donald Melbourne (E.1884, 1886, 1888, 1979); 'Merlyn' (E.1889, 1891, 1937, 2011–2013); 'Pandava' by Leon Joiner (E.1890, 1892, 1894); 'Alomo' (E.1893, 1915, 1991); 'Nivram', by John Harbour (E.1895, 1897, 2004, 2005); 'Novak', by Russell Greenslade (E.1898, 1900, 1987); 'Kumara' (E.1899, 1908, 1929, 1931, 1942, 1950, 1952, 1953, 1975, 2017–2024); 'Alhambra', by Charles Raymond (E.1901, 1994, 2015, 2016); 'Monstera', by José Bonnet (E.1902); 'Pharaoh', by Lawrence Corre (E.1903, 1905, 1907); 'Platter', by Michael Griffin (E.1909, 1911, 1914); 'Andover' (E.1910, 2025); 'Tyrrel', by John Harbour (E.1916, 1918); 'Linstrand' (E.1917, 1922, 1924, 2031–2033); 'Marvin', by Henry Skeen (E.1919–1921); 'Begonia', by Peter Sumner (E.1923, 1925); 'Arbury', by John Harbour (E.1927, 1928, 1930); 'Olsen', by Carola and Daniel Olsen (E.1932, 1934, 1936); 'Kintai', by Peter Sumner (E.1938, 1939); 'Jaspe' (E.1940, 1958, 1962, 2026–2029); 'Harlequin', by Harry Cadney (E.1941, 1943, 1945, 1993); 'Valentine', by Donald Melbourne (E.1947, 1949); 'Ships', by Harry Cadney (E.1951, 1954); 'Patsy', by Patricia Smart (E.1955, 1957, 1959); 'Floribunda', by F. Luckett (E.1960, 1961, 1963, 1984); 'Petra', by Dorothy Evans (E.1964, 1965, 1990); 'Gaylin', by Joyce Storey (E.1966, 1967, 1986); 'Vindora', by John Harbour (E.1968–1970); 'Alexandra', by Donald Melbourne (E.1971, 1972); 'Lollipops', by Dorothy Evans (E.1974, 1976, 1985); 'Mabel', by Sally Markes (E.1977, 1978); 'Capano', by Rudi Colme (E.1980, 1995); 'Evesham', by F. Luckett (E.1981); 'Sevilla', by Leon Joiner (E.1982, 1983); 'Torino', by F. Luckett (E.1988, 1989); 'Holidays', by Faith Jacques (E.1992); 'Woodform', by Rudi Colme (E.1998, 2034, 2035); 'Domingo', by Rudi Colme (E.1999); 'Arcia', by John Harbour (E.2000); 'Valletta', by Donald Melbourne (E.2006–2008); 'Barkwood', by Rudi Colme (E.2036)

(*opposite*) Page from a pattern book. English, *circa* 1837–44 (no 692A)

22
Tintern Abbey
6 Prints
Rack 30
Rack 345
3 Prints
Club Trellis
2 Prints
Rack
373
Swans Oak
V.A.M.
V.A.M.

Sample from the pattern book of John Line & Sons, 1880 (no 701)

(*opposite*) Decorator's specimen panel of combined frieze, filling and dado. Produced by Jeffrey & Co., *circa* 1877–80 (no 700)

'Festival', by Donald Melbourne, 1964–65 (no 715)

721 *Palladio 9*
Pattern book containing 103 specimens, including different colourways; each with artist's name, serial number, etc in letterpress on the back; the sheets interleaved with photographs of contemporary interiors; bound in plastic-covered boards
Produced by Arthur Sanderson & Sons Ltd, Perivale
1971
Screen prints
50 × 50 cm (size of volume)
Given by Arthur Sanderson & Sons Ltd
E.159–261–1977

Palladio 9 was the first of the 'Palladio' series to be sold abroad.

'Gandalf', by David Bartle (E.168–171); 'Annabelle', 'Calyx', 'Charlotte', by Ann Berwick (E.200–203, 255–259); 'Deco', by Judith Cash (E.225–228); 'Angela', 'Constance', by Robert Dodd (E.239–241, 244–247); 'Chantilly', 'Exotique', by Evelyn Erlbeck (E.186–189, 197–199); 'Monte Carlo', 'Parisienne', 'Neon', by Tony Fraser (E.162–164, 210–212, 231–233); 'Broadway East', 'Broadway West', 'Leonora', 'Mata-Hari', by John Garnett (E.219–224, 176–182; E.177 neg GJ.9445); 'Venessa', by Natalie Gibson (E.183–185); 'Ophelia', 'Cranston', by Clare Hartley Jones (E.204–209); 'Solaria', 'Sikhara', by Peter Jones (E.172–175, 229, 230); 'Bellaphron', by Brian Knight (E.236–238); 'Brynkir', by Patricia Pollard (E.190–193); 'Minotaur', 'Zeppelin', 'Berkley', by Edward Pond (E.165–167, 242, 243, 251–254); 'Fontana', by Jeremy Talbot (E.260, 261); 'Stereo one', 'Stereo two', by Shelagh Wakely (E.214–218); 'Kashan', by Sandra Watts (E.248–250); 'Main Street', 'Apollo', 'Zero', by John Wilkinson (E.159–161, 194–196, 234, 235; E.194 neg GJ.9446)

722 *Cole's Wallpapers*
Pattern book containing 120 specimens, including different colourways, some with borders attached; each with serial number on the back; full bound in cloth-covered boards, with title etc on the front
Produced by Cole & Son (Wallpapers) Ltd
1971
Colour machine prints and wood block prints, some on embossed paper
32.7 × 50.8 cm (size of volume)
Given by Cole & Son (Wallpapers) Ltd
E.102–220, 220A–1979

The collection includes striped and embossed papers in imitation of woven materials, and several *jaspés*. Some of the borders are reproductions in other colourways of 18th- and 19th-century borders in the Museum's collection.

721 'Mata-Hari'

723 *Pavilion*
Pattern book of vinyl papers designed by David Bartle, Anne Berwick, Alan Dunn, John Garnett, John Harbour ('Wandyke'), Alan Johnston, Susan Phillips and Anne Redhead, containing 82 specimens, including different colourways; each with name of pattern, serial number etc on the back; interleaved throughout with photographs of sportsmen and women against a background of the patterns; bound in plastic-covered boards
Produced by Arthur Sanderson & Sons Ltd
1973–74
In volume 50 × 50 cm
Given by Shand Kydd Ltd
E.2447–2528–1980

'Dolphins' (E.2447, 2448); 'Rosana' (E.2449, 2451, 2453); 'Tarquin' (E.2454, 2455, 2457); 'Grotto' (E.2450, 2472, 2522); 'Hilcote' (E.2458, 2460); 'Vanilla' (E.2452, 2486, 2515); 'Panatella' (E.2456, 2527); 'Bilberry' (E.2459, 2523); 'Caterpillar' (E.2461); 'Kaftan' (E.2462-2464); 'Wandyke' (E.2465, 2467, 2470, 2471); 'Astra' (E.2466, 2521); 'Wild Lilac' (E.2468, 2478, 2517); 'Raspberry' (E.2469, 2526); 'Kasim' (E.2473, 2474); 'Baldock' (E.2475–2477); 'Pergola' (E.2479–2481); 'Black' (E.2482, 2513, 2528); 'Tagus' (E.2483, 2484); 'Kenzan' (E.2485, 2487, 2488); 'Corvette' (E.2489); 'Faubourg' (E.2490–2492); 'Leybourne' (E.2493, 2494 neg HA.398); 'White' (E.2495, 2509, 2514); 'Kyoto' (E.2496–2498); 'Tineton' (E.2499–2501); 'Peterkin' (E.2502, 2503); 'Portcullis' (E.2504); 'Ophelia' (E.2505, 2506); 'Myriad' (E.2507, 2508); 'Sultan' (E.2510–2512); 'Mistletoe' (E.2516); 'Aztec' (E.2518); 'Corvette' (E.2519); 'Caterpillar' (E.2520); 'Rawhide' (E.2524).

723

724 *Swedish Vinyl Collection*
Pattern book containing 109 specimens, including different colourways; several of the papers shown in photographs of contemporary interiors interleaved throughout the volume; full bound in plastic-covered boards, with title etc on the front
Produced by Cole & Sons (Wallpapers) Ltd
1975–76
Colour machine prints on embossed or textured paper
36.6 × 50.5 cm (size of volume)
Given by Cole & Son (Wallpapers) Ltd
E.263–371–1979

725 *Studio One*
Pattern book of vinyl papers containing 92 specimens, including different colourways; each with title, artist's name, serial number etc printed on the back; the volume interleaved with photographs of contemporary interiors; bound in cloth covered boards, with carrying handle and clip fastener
Produced in the Vymura range by ICI (Ltd) Paints Division
1976
Screen prints
60.5 × 50 cm (size of volume)
Given by ICI (Ltd) Paints Division
E.1034–1124–1979

For the design for 'Abelard', see ANONYMOUS WALLPAPERS AND WALLPAPER DESIGNS, no 535; for the designs for 'Plaza' and 'Piazza', see under Faulkner, Sue (nos 961, 960).

'Plaza', 'Piazza', by Sue Faulkner (E.1034–1037); 'Rondo', 'Roulette', by Robert Dodd (E.1038–1041); 'Apex', 'Zenith', by Hadyn Williams (E.1042–1045); 'Admiral', by Sue Faulkner (E.1046–1048); 'Fiji' (E.1049–1052); 'Treillage', 'Cane', 'Bower' (E.1053–1056); 'Concourse', 'Precinct', by Sue Faulkner (E.1057–1064); 'Nereid', 'Aurora' (E.1065–1070); 'Jardinière', 'Fleur' (E.1071–1076); 'Cane' (E.1077, 1078); 'Khayyam', 'Kashan', 'Kazak', by Phillipa Jones-Richards (E.1079–1084); 'Beatrice', 'Nancy', by Tessa Smith (E.1085–1090); 'Cassandra' (E.1091–1094); 'Tansy' (E.1095–1098); 'Lalique' (E.1099–1101); 'Kelpie' (E.1102, 1103); 'Shibui', 'Satsuma', 'Saki', by Sue Faulkner (E.1104–1112); 'Abelard', 'Heloise' (E.1113–1118); 'Belle', by Sue Faulkner (E.1119–1121); 'Songthrush' (E.1122–1124)

726 *Designers Guild Wallpaper Collection No 1*
Pattern book containing 88 specimens, including different colourways; each with title, serial number etc in letterpress on a label affixed to the back; bound in boards, with the 'Blockflower' pattern
Produced by The Designers Guild, London
1977
Colour machine prints
44 × 37 cm (size of volume)
Given by The Designers Guild
E.1092–1180–1977

These designs are also produced in fabrics.

'Peaweed' (E.1092–1110); 'Turkish Delight' (E.1111–1114); 'Blockflower' (E.1115–1120); 'Phulwari' (E.1121–1124); 'Gagan' (E.1125–1128); 'Chrispin' (E.1129–1132); 'Amrapali' (E.1133–1136); 'Pretty Ropey', by Sheila Reeves (E.1137–1140; E.1137 neg

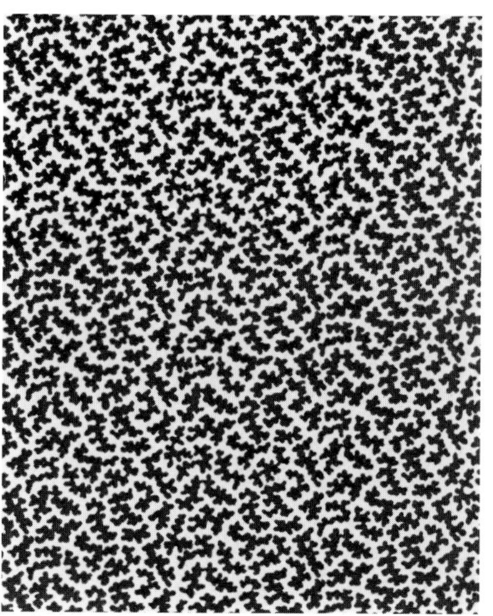

726 'Gibweed'

GJ.9447); 'Tasket' (E.1141–1148); 'Gibweed' (E.1149–1157; E.1149 neg GJ.451); 'Jaal' (E.1158–1162); 'Pebbledash', by Kaffee Fassett and Tricia Guild (E.1163–1169); 'Fossils' (E.1170–1176); 'Rosebud' (E.1177–1180)

FRANCE

727 Pattern book containing 166 specimens, including different colourways, among them a floral and trellis pattern and a Chinese vase pattern; each stamped on the back with a serial number; bound in green cloth; stamped on the cover *Collection PD London Stock 1927*
Produced by Paul Dumas, Paris
1927
Colour machine prints
47 × 61.5 cm (size of volume)
Given by Miss Mary Peerless
E.499–1967 negs GJ.9489, GJ.9490 (serial nos 10713, 10702)

728 *Collection Leroy De Paris 1974–75*
Pattern book containing 113 specimens, including different colourways; each stamped on the back with serial number etc; some papers shown in photographs of contemporary interiors interleaved in the volume; full bound in plastic-covered boards, with title etc on the front
Produced by Papiers Peints I. Leroy, Ponthierry, Seine-et-Marne, France, for Cole & Son (Wallpapers) Ltd
Colour machine prints, most on embossed or textured paper; some pre-pasted and strippable
40 × 51 cm (size of volume)
Given by Cole & Son (Wallpapers) Ltd
E.512–624–1979

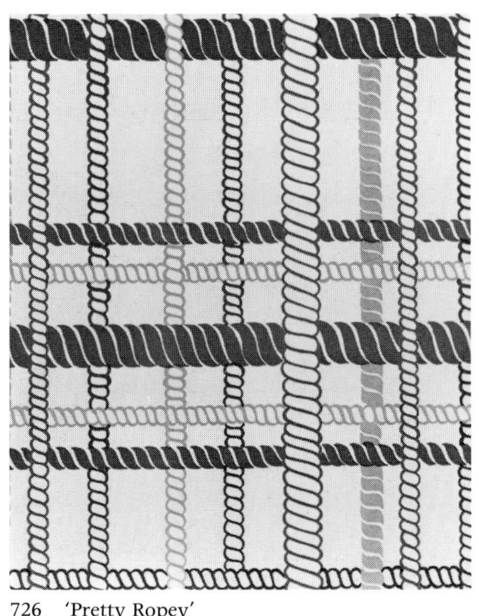
726 'Pretty Ropey'

727 GJ.9490

727

729 *Europa IV*
Pattern book containing 140 specimens, including different colourways, some cut out; each stamped on the back with serial number etc and *Made in France* [and] *Italy*; the papers shown in photographs of contemporary interiors interleaved throughout the volume; full bound in cloth-covered boards, with title etc on the front
Produced by Cole & Son (Wallpapers) Ltd; containing papers made in France and Italy
1974–75

Colour machine prints; photogravure, embossed or lightly textured
36.7 × 51.2 cm
Given by Cole & Son (Wallpapers) Ltd
E.372–511–1979

Some of the papers are tile or marble patterns in vinyl.

730 *Collection Zuber*
Pattern book containing 67 specimens, including different colourways; each with title, serial number etc on the back; with 6 samples of matching fabrics printed in England, and with a few photographs of the papers in contemporary interiors interleaved; full bound in plastic-covered boards with title etc on the front
Produced by Zuber & Cie, Rixheim, Haut-Rhin, Mulhouse, France, for Cole & Son (Wallpapers) Ltd
1977
Colour prints from engraved rollers, rotagravure etc
43 × 51 cm (size of volume)
Given by Cole & Son (Wallpapers) Ltd
E.740–806–1979

The contents include two Toile de Jouy designs and their matching fabrics.

'Robinson' (E.740–742); 'Feuillantine' (E.743); 'Clematis' (E.744); 'Belle de Nuit' (E.745–748); 'Belle de Jour' (E.749–752); 'Marie-Galante' (E.753–756); 'Bali' (E.757–760); 'Gavotte' (E.761–764); 'Perrette' (E.765, 766); 'Les Lavandières' (E.767–769); 'Pontoise' (E.770–773); 'Le Paon' (E.774–776); 'Samarcande' (E.777, 778); 'Bahamas' (E.779–781); 'Indienne' (E.782, 783); 'Rameaux' (E.784–786); 'Cloe' (E.787–789); 'Lutin' (E.790–792); 'Amarante' (E.793–796); 'Lisette' (E.797–799); 'Trophées de Jardin' (E.800); 'Les Lilas' (E.801); 'Chevrefeuille' (E.802); 'Chinoiserie' (E.803); 'Panama' (E.804–806)

731 *Europa VI*
Pattern book of wallpapers containing 146 specimens, including different colourways, of French, German, Italian and Swedish patterns; each with serial number etc stamped on the back; some designs interleaved with photographs of the wallpapers in contemporary settings; bound in cloth-covered boards, with a sheet of colour samples of Cole's vinyl matt emulsion paints
Produced by Cole & Son (Wallpapers) Ltd
1978–79
Flock, rotagravure and emboss
43.7 × 51 cm (size of volume)
Given by Cole & Son (Wallpapers) Ltd
E.1078–1125–1980

732 *Collection Zuber French Wallpapers & Fabrics*
Pattern book containing 115 specimens, including different colourways; each with title, serial number etc in letterpress on the back; several papers shown in photographs interleaved throughout the volume; full bound in cloth-covered boards, with title etc on the front
Produced by Zuber & Cie, Rixheim, Haut-Rhin, Mulhouse, France, for Cole & Son (Wallpapers) Ltd
1979
Colour prints from engraved rollers, rotagravure etc; a few on embossed paper
41.2 × 45.8 cm (size of volume)
Given by Cole & Son (Wallpapers) Ltd
E.625–739–1979

There is a letterpress price list in a transparent envelope at the front of the volume. There are 36 samples of matching fabrics. All but 6 of the fabrics were made in France; these are marked accordingly

'Perse' (E.625, 626); 'Estelle' (E.627, 628); 'Tabriz' (E.629–632); 'Lhassa' (E.633–638); 'Srinagar' (E.639); 'Le Paon' (E.640–643); 'Pundjab' (E.644, 645); 'Samarcande' (E.646–651); 'Menuet' (E.652); 'Chalon' (E.653–655); 'Fontainebleau' (E.656–658); 'Annabelle' (E.659–661); 'Pontevedra' (E.662–665); 'L'Abreuvoir' (E.666); 'La Violetta' (E.667, 668); 'L'Urne' (E.669, 670); 'Losanges' (E.671–674); 'Philippe' (E.675–678); 'Igrec' (E.679–682); 'Fleurette' (E.683–686); 'Diamants Fleuris' (E.687–689); 'Jaipur' (E.690–692); 'Beton' (E.693–695); 'Châle Indien' (E.696–699); 'Chinoiserie' (E.700); 'Les Faisans' (E.701–705); 'Les Lavandières' (E.706–709); 'Pontoise' (E.710–713); 'Louis XVI à Cherbourg' (E.714); 'Don Quichotte' (E.715, 716); 'Eugénie' (E.717); 'Trophées de Jardin' (E.718); 'Beaugency' (E.719, 720); 'Rose et Fougère' (E.721); 'Rose et Lilas' (E.722); 'Les Lilas' (E.723, 724); 'Les Chevrefeuilles' (E.725); 'Bahamas' (E.726); 'Colibris' (E.727); 'La Bequée' (E.728, 729); 'Les Dauphines' (E.730–734); 'Mogador' (E.735–737); 'Moustier' (E.738, 739).

GERMANY

See 'France': no 731

ITALY

See 'France': nos 729, 731

SWEDEN

733 *Duro Gammal-Svenska Tapeter . . .*
Pattern book of wallpapers containing 123 specimens, including different colourways, reproducing old wallpaper designs; each stamped on the back with manufacturer's name, serial number and measurements; the papers shown in photographs of contemporary interiors, interleaved throughout the volume; bound in boards with plastic spine
Produced by Duro, Gävle, Sweden
1976
Colour machine prints
30 × 22 cm (size of volume)
Given by Duro
E.439–561–1977; E.523 neg GJ.9502

The volume is prefaced with a list of titles.

734 *Duro, NK*
Pattern book of wallpapers containing 93 specimens, including different colourways, of various formal patterns, and some nursery papers; each stamped on the back with manufacturer's name and serial number; the papers by named designers shown in photographs of contemporary settings interleaved in the volume; bound in paper, with a plastic spine
Produced by Duro, Gävle, Sweden
1976
Colour machine prints
30 × 22 cm (size of volume)
Given by Duro
E.562–654–1977; E.620 neg GJ.10026

'Gästgivars', after a design by Jonas Wallström (1798–1862) from the hotel in Vallsta (E.610); 'Beata', by Inez Svensson (E.613–615); 'Jordgubbe', by Gunnel Ginsburg (E.623); 'Tornhem', by Monica Widlund (E.632); 'Förgätmigej', by Lotta Hagerman (E.637); 'Djurriket', by Clees Kock (E.654).

735 *Duro 17*
Pattern book of wallpapers containing 133 specimens, including different colourways, of various floral and formal patterns; each stamped on the back with manufacturer's name and serial number; nearly all the papers shown in photographs of contemporary interiors interleaved throughout the volume
Produced by Duro, Gävle, Sweden
1976
Colour machine prints
30 × 22 cm (size of volume)
Given by Duro
E.655–787–1977

These are acrylic papers.

733

734 'Beata'

735 'Löjtnantshjärtan'

'Jefta', by Rolf Engströmer (E.658–662); 'Apel', by Mona Johansson (E.663–665); 'Fjärilar', by Gun Rosen (E.666–672); 'Fleur', by Louise Carling (E.674); 'Möln', by Gunila Axen (E.677–679); 'Django', by Elisabeth Carlström (E.680–682); 'Äng', by Kjell Bohlin (E.683–685); 'Fjällviol', by Tage Möller (E.686, 687); 'Penseer', by Viel Carlsson (E.688–690); 'Körsbärsblom', by Tage Möller (E.691); 'Härsan Tvärsan', by Marie Dolck (E.692–696); 'Prästkragar', by Viel Carlsson (E.697, 698); 'Skogen', by Lotta Hagerman (E.699–703); 'Löv', by Mildred Samuelsson (E.704–707); 'Skogsvision', by Lilo Hörstadius (E.708–714); 'Par om Par', by Kerstin Nilsson (E.715–717); 'Par', by Kerstin Nilsson (E.718–720); 'Blom-String', by Anna-Lena Emden (E.721–726); 'Lina', by Elisabeth Carlström (E.727–729); 'Nyponkvist' by Elisabeth Carlström (E.730–732); 'Bark', by Birgit Ullhammer (E.733); 'Löjtnantshjärtan', by Gunnel Ginsburg (E.734 neg GJ.9503); 'Kröson', by Ulla Klevert (E.735–738); 'Lingonblom', by Lotta Hagerman (E.739–742); 'Karolina', by Birgitta Lamm (E.743–753); 'Körsbär', by Ulla Aström (E.754–756); 'Lin', by Tage Möller (E.757–760); 'Tula', by Anne-Lie Lantz (E.761–767); 'Pomona', by Gun Rosen (E.768–772); 'Flygande Blad', by Inez Svensson (E.773–775); 'Rally', by Inez Svensson (E.776–778); 'Varflora', by Tage Möller (E.779, 780); 'Storstänk', by Anna-Johanna Angström (E.781–787).

736 *Land*
Pattern book of wallpapers containing 53 specimens, including different colourways, reproducing earlier designs; each stamped on the back with manufacturer's name, serial number and measurement; the papers shown in photographs of contemporary interiors interleaved throughout the volume; bound in boards, with plastic spine
Produced by Duro, Gävle, Sweden
1977
Colour machine prints
34.2 × 24.5 cm (in volume)
Given by Duro
E.1488–1534–1977; E.1528 neg GJ.9504

The volume is prefaced with a foreword on the collection, which was a result of a nation-wide appeal for specimens of old Swedish wallpaper.

'Spolargarden' (E.1482, 1483); 'Lilla Dockekulla' (E.1484–1487); 'Signeshög' (E.1488–1492); 'Västansjö' (E.1493–1496); 'Johannelund' (E.1497–1502); 'Sjömarken' (E.1503–1507); 'Fjärsman' (E.1508–1510); 'Sanna' (E.1511–1515); 'Furuskallen' (E.1516–1520); 'Västra Amtervik' (E.1521–1522); 'Ekenäs' (E.1523–1527); 'Värmslandes Säby' (E.1528–1534, E.1528 neg GJ.9504).

737 *Swedish Linen and Jute Wallcoverings*
Pattern book containing 42 specimens, including different colourways; each stamped on the back with name of pattern and shade number; full bound in plastic-covered boards, with title etc on the front
Produced by Tasso Skandinaviska Jute, AB, Oskarström, near Holmstad, Sweden, for Cole & Son (Wallpapers) Ltd
1979
Linen, jute, flax, glass-fibre; most paper-backed
27.8 × 37.9 cm (size of volume)
Given by Cole & Son (Wallpapers) Ltd
E.221–262–1979

'Aquarell' (E.221–226); 'Fresco' (E.227–229); 'Kapri' (E.230–233); 'Relief 218' (E.234–239); 'Relief 244' (E.240–243); 'Tassolin 336' (E.244–256); 'Natural' (E.257–262).

See also 'England': no 731.

736 'Varmslandes Säby'

Designers

Addison. See PATTERN BOOKS, no 707.

Albeck, Pat (Mrs Peter Rice). See PATTERN BOOKS, no 719(2).

Aldridge, John Arthur Malcolm, A.R.A., b. 1905

Painter in oils, book-illustrator and wallpaper designer. Assistant at the Slade School 1949–70. Examples of his work are in the Tate Gallery, the Contemporary Arts Society, the Arts Council.

738 'Lace'
Produced by Cole & Sons (Wallpapers) Ltd, as part of their 'Bardfield' series
Circa 1938
Line block printed by hand in distemper colours
81.2 × 57.8 cm (portion)
E.1631–1939 neg GE.462

F. J. Harris, 'Wallpaper: Its Design and Use in the Modern Interior', *Architectural Review* (1939), vol 86, 253–58.

739 'Moss', with another colourway in light-blue ground
Produced by Cole & Sons (Wallpapers) Ltd, as part of their 'Bardfield' series
Circa 1939
Colour print from line blocks
81.2 × 55.9 cm (portion)
E.1632, 1633–1939; E.1633 neg GG.5778

These papers were hand-printed in distemper colours from blocks designed and cut by Aldridge.

738

739

Andersen, Aagaard, working *circa* 1955

740 'Mille Points'
Produced by Rodia Tapetfabriken, Copenhagen
Circa 1955
Colour machine print
57.3 × 47 cm
Given by Rodia Tapetfabriken
E.893–1979 neg GJ.9472

Angerer, Mea. See PATTERN BOOKS, no 718.

Angström, Anna-Johanna. See PATTERN BOOKS, no 735.

Angus, Peggy (Mrs Richards), b. 1904

Abandoned her earlier career as a leading design consultant to the tile industry and set up a workshop for hand-printed wallpapers, tiles and stones. She specializes in Celtic design, and produces individual patterns for clients. She had studied at the RCA for four years.

740

741 'Velvet'
Produced by Arthur Sanderson & Sons Ltd
1959
Colour screen print
60.5 × 55.8 cm
Given by Arthur Sanderson & Sons Ltd
E.822–1978 neg GJ.9505

This design won a prize in the international competition organized by the manufacturers in 1960.

742 'Corn Stooks'
Designed for Philippa Trefall
Circa 1970
Lino cut
21 × 17.2 cm; 84.4 × 51.5 cm (size of sheet)
E.823–1978

743 'Beasties'
Designed for Alex Kasanthis
Circa 1970
Lino cut
28 × 26.8 cm; 56 × 54.5 cm (size of sheet)
E.824–1978

744 'Persian Pear'
Designed for Keith Grant
Circa 1970
Lino cut
29.5 × 26.5 cm; 65 × 53 cm (size of sheet)
E.825–1978

745 'Grapes'
Designed for Diana Hall
Circa 1970
Lino cut
26.5 × 26 cm; 86 × 53 cm (size of sheet)
E.826–1978

'Church and Dove', by Edward Bawden. Printed and published by the Curwen Press Ltd, *circa* 1925 (no 756)

Formal pattern by Maria Brooks, produced by Corbière, Son & Brindle, 1868 (no 777)

'Les Monuments de Paris', after designs by Jean Broc. French, 1814 (no 776)

741

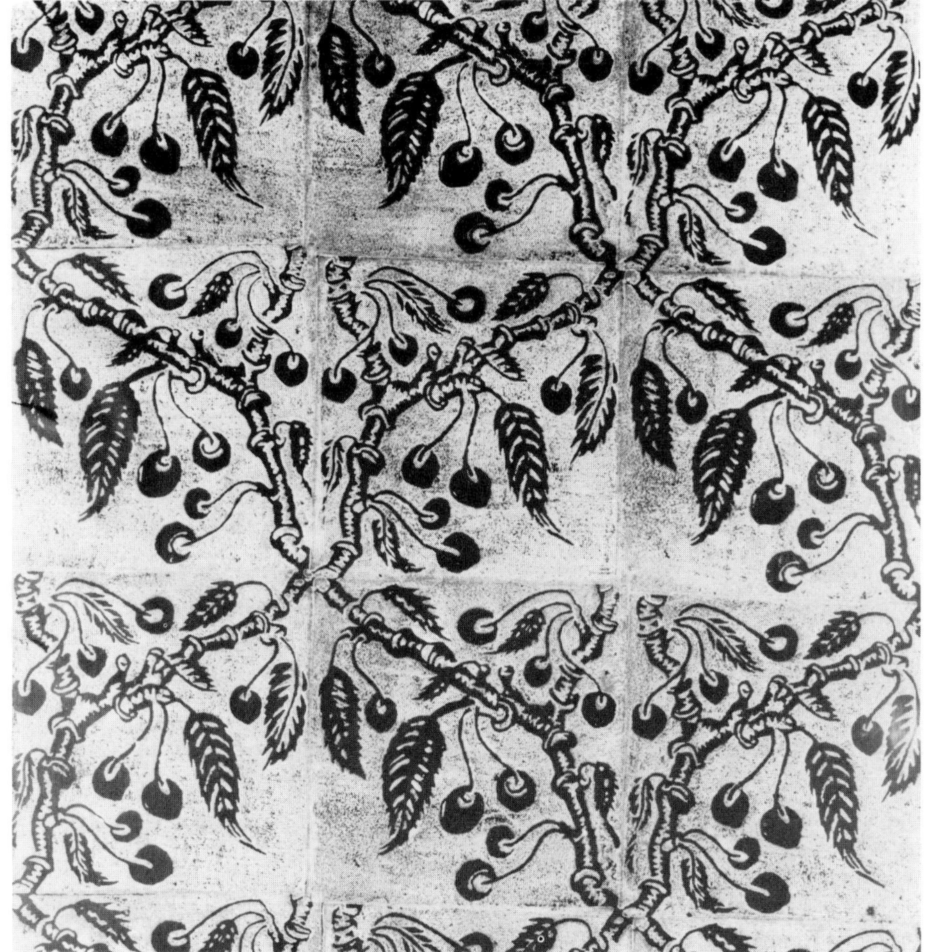
747

746 'Circle and Square'
Designed for Kenneth Rowntree
Circa 1970
Lino cut
13.3 × 13.3 cm; 52.7 × 52.7 cm (size of sheet)
E.827–1978

747 'Cherries'
Designed for Jasmin Rose-Innes
Circa 1970
Lino cut
15.3 × 15 cm; 63 × 46 cm (size of sheet)
E.828–1978 neg GJ.9506

748 'Willow and Bird'
Designed for Max Fry
Circa 1970
26 × 26 cm; 56 × 56 cm (size of sheet)
E.829–1978

749 'Welsh Dragons'
Designed for Ian Langland
Circa 1970
Lino cut
32.5 × 28 cm; 98.5 × 56 cm (size of sheet)
E.830–1978 neg GJ.9507

750 Portion with a pattern composed of Celtic knot, birds and beasts
Circa 1970
Three lino cuts
17.7 × 17.8 cm (each); 53.3 × 53.3 cm (size of sheet)
E.831–1978

The above 9 items, nos 742–750, were given by the London Borough of Camden Libraries and Arts Department

---

Armfield, Diana M. (Mrs Bernard Dunstan), M.S.I.A, N.E.A.C., R.W.A., b. 1920, and John Passano, working early 1950's

Diana Armfield is a painter and textile and wallpaper designer, and a partner in Armfield-Passano. She was taught at the Central School and at the Byam Shaw School of Art. She has exhibited at the Royal Academy, the Royal West of England Academy and the New English Art Club. Examples of her work are in the collection of the RWA. See also PATTERN BOOKS, nos 707(2), 710(3).

751 'Conlowe'
Produced by John Line & Sons Ltd
1951
Screen print
75 × 54.5 cm
E.878–1978 neg GJ.9508

749

752

752 'Mexico'
Produced by John Line & Sons Ltd
1951
Screen Print
74 × 54.5 cm
E.879–1978 neg GJ.9509

'The new papers: a preview', *Interiors*, Vol 112, pt 1, August 1952, pl on p 102.

The above 2 specimens, nos 751, 752, were given by John Line and Sons Ltd

---

Aström, Ulla. See PATTERN BOOKS, no 735.

Attwell, Mabel Lucie (Mrs Harold Earnshaw), 1879–1964

Illustrator and writer of children's stories, she studied painting and life drawing at the Regent Street Art School and at Heatherley's. She has illustrated children's classics, including *The Water Babies* and *Alice in Wonderland*.

753 Frieze with scenes from nursery tales, including 'Bo-Peep', 'Mother Goose' and others
Produced by C. & G. Potter
1913
Colour print from engraved rollers
26.7 × 179.8 cm
Given by the WM
E.1834–1934 neg GE.426

See SE, pl 214; Greysmith, pl 131.

751

753

754

Axen, Gunila. See PATTERN BOOKS, no 735.

Ayers, Eric. See PATTERN BOOKS, no 707.

Baker, A. J., working *circa* 1912–28

Designer for C. & J. G. Potter from *circa* 1912 to *circa* 1928.

754 'Delphinium and Trellis'
Produced by C. & J. Potter
1914
Colour machine print
93.4 × 54.6 cm
Given by the WM
E.1835–1934 neg GJ.9510

See SE, pl 164 (colour).

Baker, Deirdre. See PATTERN BOOKS, no 719.

Balin, Paul, d. 1898

Bought the firm of Genoux et Bader in 1863, and specialized in the production of quality papers. In 1867 he won a medal for his designs and began to work for A. Saegers. His work was widely copied and he began to institute proceedings against numerous manufacturers, including Zuber. He committed suicide in 1898. His reproductions of ancient materials, silks, velvets, brocades and leather work are unrivalled.

755 Fifty-seven specimens of wallpapers and wall coverings
The designs (except for 1333, 1335) are taken from textiles
Produced by Paul Balin, Paris
Second half of 19th century
81.3 × 58.4 cm (each)
Given by Monsieur Paul Balin
(VAM Cat. No. 202) 1329–1352A–L–1874
(some missing items written off)

The specimens were exhibited at the Vienna Exhibition of 1873.

Lace pattern on a lilac ground
From a mid-16th century embroidery formerly in the possession of Paul Balin
Embossed paper and muslin
1329

Lace pattern on a primrose ground
From an 18th-century textile formerly in the possession of Paul Balin
Embossed paper and muslin
1330

See also 1342, based on the same textile.

Lace pattern on a lilac ground
From an 18th century embroidery formerly in the possession of S. Decloux
Embossed paper and muslin
1331

See also 1341, based on the same embroidery.

Lace pattern on a pink ground (border and paper)
From a 19th-century embroidered muslin
Embossed paper and muslin
1332

Gold diaper on a black ground and gold arabesques on a gold background
From the background of a 15th-century picture formerly in the possession of Paul Balin
1333, 1334; 1334 neg GJ.9511

755 GJ.9511

Scrolls and conventional flowers on a black ground
From an early 16th-century Portuguese leather hanging formerly in the possession of Paul Balin
Flock on satin
1335

Four borders mounted on a satin ground: a 16th-century velvet border formerly in the possession of Paul Balin; a fragment of 13th-century material in the VAM; a material of the period of Louis XIII in the Industrial Museum at Lyons (see also 1350d, based on the same textile); a velvet border of the period of Louis XIII formerly in the possession of Paul Balin
Flock on embossed satin
1336 neg GE.421

See Greysmith, pl 119.

Border with dark-red conventional pattern on a yellow ground mounted on paper
From a 13th-century material formerly in the possession of Paul Balin
Machine print on embossed paper
1338

Border with scroll foliage and flowers on a black ground, mounted on paper
From an embroidery of the period of Louis XIII, formerly in the possession of Paul Balin
Machine print on embossed paper
1339

Blue design on a yellow satin ground
From a material of the end of the 16th century, formerly in the possession of Paul Balin
Flock on satin
1340

755 GE.421

Flowers in colours and gold on a blue ground
From a Persian material, formerly in the possession of Paul Balin
Machine print on embossed paper
1340a

Gold flower and scroll ornament on a red ground
From an 18th-century embroidery, formerly in the possession of S. Decloux
Embossed paper
1341

See also 1331, based on the same embroidery.

From an embroidery of the period of Henri II, formerly in the possession of Paul Balin
Embossed, coloured and gilt
1341a

Flowers with gold outline on a red ground
From an 18th-century textile, formerly in the possession of Paul Balin
Embossed satin
1342

See also 1330, based on the same textile.

Gold flowers on a blue satin ground
From a material of the period of Henri II, formerly in the possession of P. Récapé.
Embossed satin
1342a

Formalized floral pattern
From a mid-15th century Chinese material, formerly in the possession of Paul Balin
Machine print on embossed paper
1343

Flower-and-fruit pattern in colours on a blue ground
Machine print on embossed paper
1343a

Fruit pattern on a drab ground
From a material of the period of Louis XV, in the Japanese style, formerly in the possession of Paul Balin
Machine print on embossed paper
1343b

Gold pattern on a crimson satin ground
From a material of the period of Louis XIV, formerly in the possession of Paul Balin
Embossed satin
1344

Damask pattern on a red satin ground
From a 15th-century material, formerly in the possession of V. Poterlet
Flock on satin
1344a

Crimson damask pattern of flowers and eagles
From a 15th-century material
Flock on satin
1344b

Damask pattern on a red satin ground
From a mediaeval material, formerly in the possession of Paul Balin
Flock on satin
1344c

Two borders mounted on a satin ground
From materials in the Industrial Museum at Lyons, formerly in the possession of V. Poterlet
Embossed satin
1345

Border with pattern in white and gold mounted on a flock ground
From the bed hangings of Marshal d'Effiat in the Cluny Museum, Paris
Embossed paper
1345a

Border mounted on paper
From an appliqué-work embroidery, in the Renaissance style, formerly in the possession of Paul Balin
Embossed paper
1345b

Pattern on green satin
From a material of the period of Louis XIII, in the Cluny Museum, Paris
Flock on satin
1346

Pattern of flowers in vases on green satin
From a material of the period of Louis XVI, formerly in the possession of Paul Balin
Flock on satin
1346a

Damask pattern on yellow satin
From a material of the period of Louis XIV, formerly in the possession of Paul Balin
Embossed satin
1347

Leaf pattern on green satin
From a 15th-century material, formerly in the possession of Paul Balin
Embossed satin
1347a

Border with conventional lions and other ornament on a gold-and-green ground, mounted on paper
From a 16th-century Chinese material, formerly in the possession of V. Poterlet
Machine print on embossed paper
1349

Flower pattern in purple and gold on a gilt ground
From a 16th-century material, formerly in the possession of V. Poterlet
Flock on embossed paper
1350

See also 1350b, based on the same textile.

Flower pattern on a chocolate satin ground
From a 16th-century embroidery, formerly in the possession of Paul Balin
Flock on embossed satin
1350a

Flower pattern on a green satin ground
From a 16th-century material, formerly in the possession of V. Poterlet
Flock on embossed satin
1350b

See also 1350, based on the same textile.

Flower pattern on a green satin ground
From a velvet of the period of Louis XIII, in the Industrial Museum at Lyons
Flock on embossed satin
1350c

Flower pattern on a green satin ground
From a velvet of the period of Louis XIII, in the Industrial Museum at Lyons
Flock on embossed satin
1350d

See also 1336 (3), based on the same textile.

Flower pattern on a red ground
From a velvet of the period of Louis XIII, in the Cluny Museum, Paris
Flock on embossed paper
1350e

Flower pattern in light- and dark-pink, on a red ground
From a velvet of the period of Louis XIV, formerly in the possession of Paul Balin
Flock on embossed paper
1350f

Red flower pattern on a yellow satin ground
From an 18th-century velvet, formerly in the possession of Paul Balin
Flock on embossed satin
1350g

Flower pattern with griffins, in colours
From a 12th-century material, formerly in the possession of A. Martin
Machine print on embossed paper
1351

Birds and animals on a yellow satin ground
From a mid-13th century Venetian material, formerly in the possession of V. Poterlet
Flock on satin
1351a

Gold and yellow, with griffins, on a maroon ground
From a 13th-century material, formerly in the possession of Paul Balin
Machine print on embossed paper
1351b

Conventional flowers, with fruit and birds, in dark-red and gold on a red satin ground
From an early 16th-century material, formerly in the possession of Paul Balin
Flock on embossed satin
1351e

See also 1351f, based on the same textile.

Conventional flowers, with fruit and birds, in gold and black on a crimson ground
From a material of the beginning of the 16th century, formerly in the possession of Paul Balin
Machine print on embossed paper
1351f

See also 1351e, based on the same textile.

Gold lions etc on a grey ground
From a material of the period of Henri III, formerly in the possession of Paul Balin
Machine print on embossed paper
1351g

Flower pattern in colours on a gold ground
From a material of the period of Henri II, formerly in the possession of A. Martin
Machine print on embossed paper
1352

Coloured flowers on a metallic ground
From an old French material
Machine print on embossed paper
1352a

Flower pattern on a pink ground
From a material of the period of Louis XIII, formerly in the possession of Paul Balin
Machine print on embossed paper
1352b

Flower-and-leaf pattern, with vases
From a material of the period of Louis XIII, formerly in the possession of Paul Balin
Machine print on embossed paper
1352c

Damask pattern in colours and gold on a green ground
From a material of the period of Louis XIII, formerly in the possession of Paul Balin
Machine print on embossed paper
1352d

Flowers in colours and silver on a green ground
From a material of the period of Louis XIII, formerly in the possession of Paul Balin
Machine print on embossed paper
1352e

Pattern in gold and colours on a green ground
From a material of the period of Louis XIII, formerly in the possession of Paul Balin
Machine print on embossed paper
1352f

Flowers in colours and gold on a green ground
From a material of the period of Louis XIII, formerly in the possession of Paul Balin
Machine print on embossed paper
1352g

Gold-and-silver pattern on a green ground
From an embroidery of the period of Louis XIV, in the Cluny Museum, Paris
Machine print on embossed paper
1352h

Coloured flowers on a drab ground
From a material of the period of Louis XV, formerly in the possession of Paul Balin
Machine print on embossed paper
1352i

Flower pattern in colours on a gold ground
From a material of the period of Louis XV, formerly in the possession of Paul Balin
Machine print on embossed paper
1352j

Floral trellis pattern, with ribbon, ties and sprigs, on a chocolate ground
Machine print on embossed paper
1352k

Vases of flowers and birds in silver on a blue watered-silk ground
From a material of the period of Louis XVI, formerly in the possession of Paul Balin
Machine print on embossed paper
1352l

Barder, Daphne. See PATTERN BOOKS, no 707(4).

Bartle, David. See PATTERN BOOKS, nos 719(2), 721, 723.

Bawden, Edward, C.B.E., R.A., R.D.I., b. 1903

Landscape artist in watercolour, book-illustrator and mural painter, he studied at the Royal College of Art under Paul Nash. He was a War Artist and saw active service. He has taught at the Goldsmith's College and the R.C.A. from 1930. His murals include decorations for Morley College.

756 Portion of 'Church and Dove'
Printed and published by the Curwen Press Ltd
Circa 1925
Colour lithograph

758

56.4 × 54.5 cm
Given by Modern Textiles
E.1398–1979 CT 7794 (see col pl, p 273)

Reproduced in D. P. Bliss, *Edward Bawden* (Godalming, 1979) p 78.

757 Portion of 'Mermaid'
Printed and published by the Curwen Press Ltd
Circa 1930
Colour lithograph
73 × 56.5 cm (size of sheet)
E.543–1931

Another portion is E.3874–1934

758 'Conservatory'; signed within the design *EB* (monogram)
Printed and published by the Curwen Press Ltd
Circa 1930
Colour lithograph
71.1 × 55.7 cm (portion)
E.544–1931 neg GG.5480

759 'Desert and Camels'
Printed and published by the Curwen Press Ltd
Circa 1930
Colour lithograph
70.8 × 53.7 cm (portion)
E.545–1931 neg GG.5780

759

760 Portion of 'Leaf'
Printed and published by the Curwen Press Ltd
Circa 1930
Colour lithograph
58.1 × 57.2 cm
E.546–1931 CT 8590

761 Four portions of 'Salver', 'Node', 'Façade' and 'Ashlar'
Printed and published by the Curwen Press Ltd
Circa 1930
Colour lithographs
86.4 × 54.5 cm (each)
Given by the Curwen Press Ltd
E.1388–1391–1933; E.1388 neg GG.5781

'Salver' and 'Node' are reproduced in *Design for Today* (1933), vol 1, p 65.

762 Portion of 'Waves and Fish'
Printed and published by the Curwen Press Ltd
Circa 1930
Colour lithograph
71.2 × 55.7 cm
E.3874–1934

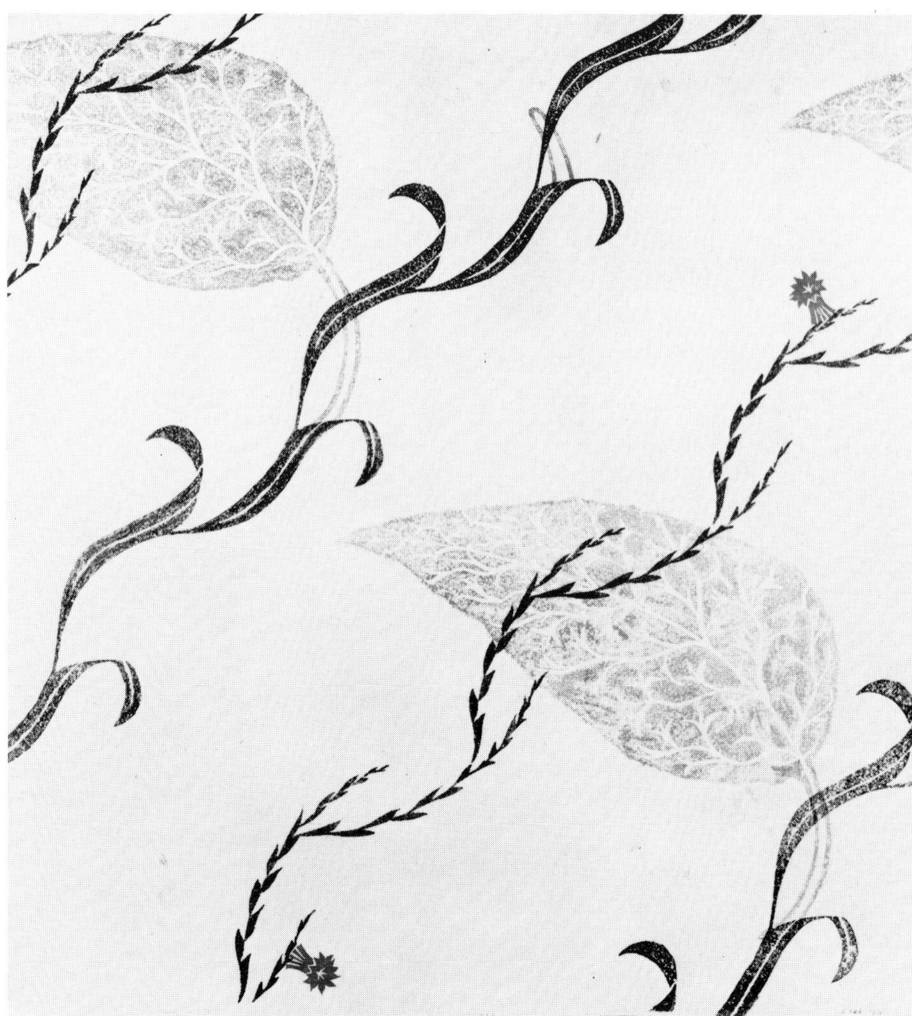
760

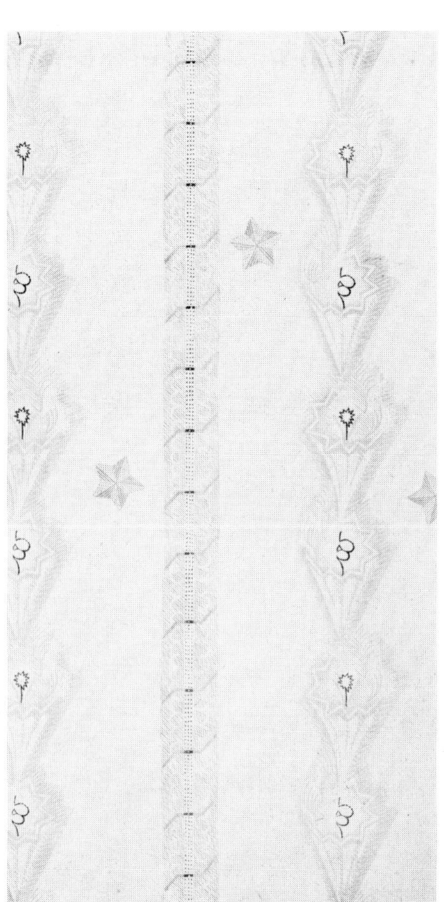
761

763 Portion of 'Trees and Cows'
Printed and published by the Curwen Press Ltd
Circa 1930
Colour lithograph
54.6 × 56 cm
E.3875–1934

764 Portion of 'Napkins and Fruit'
Printed and published by the Curwen Press Ltd
Circa 1930
Colour lithograph
54.6 × 56 cm
E.3876–1934

The above 3 items, nos 762–764, were given by Modern Textiles.

765 Portion of 'Knole Park'
Hand-printed in distemper by Cole & Son from blocks designed and cut by the artist, as part of their 'Bardfield' range
Circa 1931
Colour print from lino blocks
82 × 56 cm
E.960–1978

766 'Grid and Cross'
Hand-printed in distemper by Cole & Son from lino blocks designed and cut by the artist, as part of their 'Bardfield' range
Circa 1938
Colour print from lino blocks
81.3 × 56 cm (portion)
E.1636–1939 neg GG.5782

See *Architectural Review* (1939), vol 86, plate on page 53; Entwisle (1970), pl 67.

767 Portion of 'Grass and Swan' (cream ground) and of 'Grass and Swan' (grey ground)
Hand-printed in distemper by Cole & Son from blocks designed and cut by the artist, as part of their 'Bardfield' range
Circa 1938

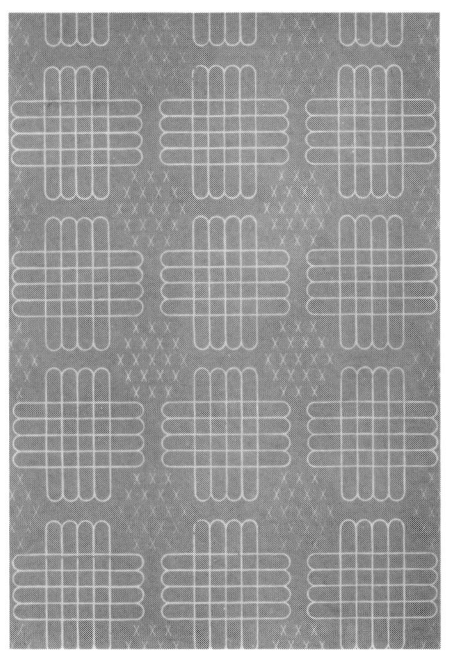

766

Colour print from lino blocks
81.3 × 56 cm
E.1634, 1635–1939

768 Portion of 'Rose'
Hand-printed in distemper by Cole & Son from lino blocks designed and cut by the artist, as part of their 'Bardfield' range
Circa 1938
Colour print from lino blocks
81.3 × 56 cm
E.1637–1939

769 'Quatrefoil'
Produced by Cole & Son (Wallpapers) Ltd
Circa 1950
Colour print from wood blocks
99.5 × 55 cm
E.890–1979 neg GJ.9512

See Entwisle, *LH*, pl 113; *Architectural Review* (1952), vol 112, p 224, fig 14 (this is reproduced in a red colourway).

Beham, Hans Sebald. See no 803.

Belcher, John, R.A., F.R.I.B.A., 1841–1913

Architect, musician and author of works on architecture and music. President of the R.I.B.A. from 1904 to 1906. His work includes the Institute of Chartered Accountants, Moorgate, London, and the Royal Society of Medicine, Marylebone. He exhibited at the R.A. from 1882 to 1910.

770 'Haarlem'
Produced by Hayward & Son Ltd
1885
Colour print from wood blocks
142.3 × 53.3 cm (portion)
Given by the WM
E.1836–1934 neg GJ.9513

See SE, pl 127.

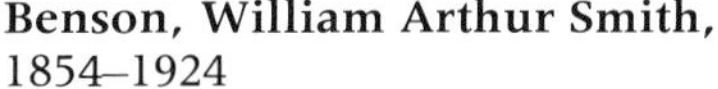

Benson, William Arthur Smith, 1854–1924

Benson was trained as an architect under Basil Champneys from 1877 to 1880, but he became a craftsman in metal work, and was associated with William Morris in schemes where metal work and lighting were included. After Morris' death he became chairman of Morris & Co. He was an original member of the Artworkers' Guild. See also under Dearle, J. H., and Benson, W. A. S., no 946.

771 'Garden Craft'
Printed by Jeffrey & Co. for Morris & Co.
1908
Colour print from wood blocks
57.2 × 86.5 cm (portion)
Circ.250–1964 neg GJ.9514

770

Berwick, Ann. See PATTERN BOOKS, nos 719(3), 721(3), 723.

Binyon, Brightwen, F.S.A., A.R.I.B.A., worked *circa* 1875-post 1895

Architect. Of Ipswich. He exhibited at the Royal Academy from 1887 to 1895. See also PATTERN BOOKS, no 700.

769

771

772 Dado of poppies, corn and swallows
Produced by Jeffrey & Co.
1875
Colour print from wood blocks
53.3 × 45.8 cm (portion)
E.1850–1934 neg GG.5867

See SE, pl 184. The dado was originally introduced by Jeffrey & Co., in flock, with this design by Binyon.

773 Portion of a frieze of swallows and dragonflies
Produced by Jeffrey & Co.
1875
Colour print from wood blocks
27.3 × 45.8 cm
E.1881–1934

The above 2 items, nos 772, 773, were given by the WM

772

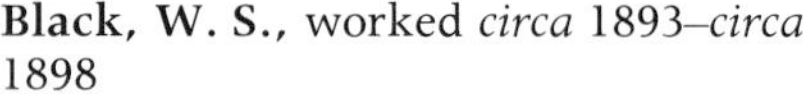

Black, W. S., worked *circa* 1893–*circa* 1898

Possibly William S. Black of Edinburgh, who exhibited at Manchester City Art Gallery, and at the Royal Scottish Academy, from 1881 to 1897, and designed for lithographs.

774 Designs for a paper and frieze, entitled 'The Seasons'; with stamps lettered *James Barrett Print Cutter* and numbered in ink respectively *3970* and *3969*
Produced by Jeffrey & Co.
1893
Indian ink and pencil, touched with white
114.4 × 76.2 cm; 53.3 × 124.5 cm
Given by Mrs Margaret Warner
E.12–1945 neg GJ.10025; E.13–1945 neg GJ.10022

774 GJ.10022

774 GJ.10025

Building News, 3 February 1893, plate on pp 172, 173. Exhibited at the World's Fair, Chicago, 1893. The paper was printed in monochrome; the example discussed in *Building News* was red.

Blondel, Méry-Joseph. See Lafitte, Louis.

Bodley, George Frederick, 1827–1907

Architect and designer, the first pupil of George Gilbert Scott, he helped in setting up Watts & Co. as a depot for the sale of textiles, furniture, wallpaper and other decorative goods. He was the first architect to commission Morris & Co. to execute decorative work, in 1862.

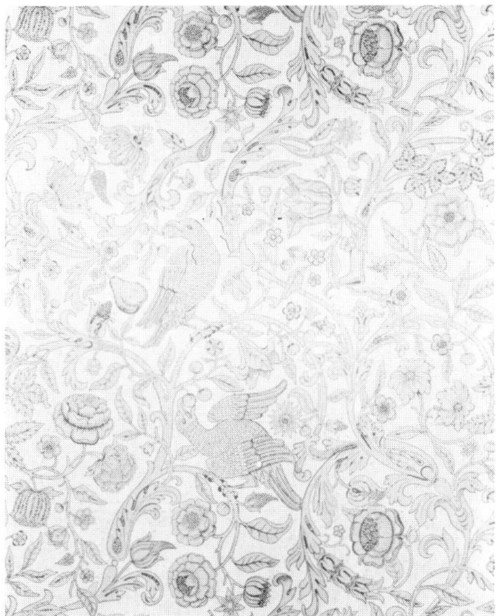

775

775 'The Bird'
Made for Watts & Co., probably by Cole & Sons
1874
Colour print from wood blocks
93.5 × 63.5 cm (portion)
E.951–1978 neg GJ.9515

Bohlin, Kjell. See PATTERN BOOKS, no 735.

Bonnet, José. See PATTERN BOOKS, nos 715(2), 720.

Broc, Jean, 1780–1850, after

Painter. Pupil of David.

776 *Les Monuments de Paris.* Thirty lengths forming a continuous panorama of the chief monuments of Paris, arranged along one of the banks of the Seine
Produced by Dufour et Leroy
1814
Colour prints from wood blocks
240 × 49.5 cm (each)
E.848–871–1924; negs H.1455–1459, B.121

The horses on the top of the Arc du Carrousel are those removed by Napoleon from St Mark's, Venice, and returned there in 1815. The statue of the Emperor has already been removed from the chariot, which shows that the paper was made after the entry of the Allies into Paris on 30 March 1814. The guards in front of the arch have changed the Imperial cockade for the white one of the Royalists. The paper was produced and sold by Joseph Dufour. His account books show that the original price of the paper was 50 francs, and that it was published in 1814. C. C. Oman, 'Old French Flock Papers', *Country Life* (1928), vol 63, p 626; Greysmith, pl 69; Clouzot, *TT*, pls 6–8 (colour).

Brooks, Maria, worked *circa* 1868–*circa* 1890

A student of the National Arts Schools in 1868, she also made designs for muslins, which were exhibited at the

776 B.121

776 H.1459

Royal Albert Hall in 1873. As a portrait painter she exhibited at the Royal Academy and at the Royal Society of British Artists from 1873 to 1890.

777 Four portions, in different colourways, with formal patterns
Produced by Corbière Son & Brindle
1868
Colour prints from wood blocks
40.6 × 57.3 cm (each)
Given by Corbière Son & Brindle
1111B, 1112B, 1113B, 1114B–1868;
1112B CT 7443 (see col pl, p 274)

These designs were made while the artist was a student at the National Art Training Schools.

Brophy, Andrew Fingar, 1846–1912

Born at Limerick, he began as a teacher of mechanical drawing. In 1882 he was appointed Master of the City of London

776 H.1458

776 H.1456

776 H.1455

Guilds Technical Institute, and was examiner in the National Science and Art competitions at South Kensington. He was also an architect. See also PATTERN BOOKS, no 700.

778 'Adam'
Produced by Arthur Sanderson & Sons Ltd
1903
Colour print from wood blocks
81.6 × 55.8 cm
Given by the WM
E.2148–1929 CT 7444 (see col pl, p 291)
See SE, pl 149.

Burges, William, A.R.A., 1827–81

Trained as an architect under Blore and Sir Matthew Digby Wyatt, he restored, rebuilt and furnished Castel Coch and Cardiff Castle, 1865–75. His own house, 9, Melbury Road, Kensington, was designed by him 'as a model residence of the 15th century' (1875–81).

779

780

776 H.1457

779 Frieze with squirrels and leaves, within a border of trefoils
Produced by Jeffrey & Co.
1872
Colour machine print
36.3 × 41 cm
Given by the WM
E.1862–1934 neg GJ.9516

See *Building News*, 11 October 1872, plate on p 11.

780 Fragment with a design of birds and interlaced ornament
Produced by Jeffrey & Co.
1872
Wood block and flock on embossed paper
34.3 × 27.3 cm
Given by Mr R. Ede England
E.97–1955 neg GJ.9517 CT 8495

A specimen of the frieze is E.1862–1934. See *Building News*, 11 October 1872, p 287; Entwisle, *V*, pl 24, fig 42. Another example of this paper, in a different colour, lent by the Royal Institute of British Architects, was shown in the Exhibition of Victorian and Edwardian Decorative Arts, held at the VAM in 1952 (Catalogue no. J.10b).

Burges, William, A.R.A., possibly by

781 Frieze of arcades containing in the centre an illustration of Aesop's fable, 'The Fox and the Crane', and, on either side, a rose and a pomegranate in a vase
Circa 1870
Print from wood block; black on terracotta
26.5 × 47.4 cm
Given by the WM
E.1874–1934 CT 4207 (see col pl, p 292)

Butler, Henry, R.B.A., worked *circa* 1917–*circa* 1927

Textile designer. Member of the Design & Industries Association. Also drew designs for interiors (reproduced in *Studio Year Book of Decorative Art*, 1927) and for inlay (*op. cit.*, 1919).

782 Portion of 'The Hawes', from a design based on textiles in the Victoria & Albert Museum
1919
Colour machine print
104.1 × 53.4 cm
E.30–1923

783 Nine sheets with designs based on textiles in the Victoria & Albert Museum
Circa 1919
Colour machine prints
Various sizes
E.35–43–1923

E.40–42 bear the Patent Office registration marks for the year 1919.

784 Portion with a chinoiserie pattern, from a design based on textiles in the Victoria & Albert Museum
1919–24
Colour machine print
106.7 × 53.4 cm
E.29–1923

785 Hunting scene in a forest, from a design based on textiles in the Victoria & Albert Museum
Circa 1920
Colour machine print
78.7 × 53.3 cm
Given by Arthur Sanderson & Sons Ltd
E.28–1923

786 Brick work pattern with 7 landscapes
Circa 1921
Lithograph
120.6 × 52.8 cm
E.31–1923

787 Portion with a design based on textiles in the Victoria & Albert Museum
Circa 1921

789

Flock
105.4 × 53.4 cm
E.33–1923

788 Portion with a pattern based on textiles in the Victoria & Albert Museum
Circa 1921–22
Colour machine print, embossed
86.4 × 54 cm
E.34–1923

789 Rural and hunting scenes, based on textiles in the Victoria & Albert Museum
Circa 1921–22
Colour machine print
108 × 55.2 cm (portion)
E.32–1923 neg GJ.473

Butterfield, Lindsay Phillip, 1869–1948

He entered the National Art Training Schools competition, 1889–90, with designs for surface decoration. He was a designer of textiles and wallpaper, who confessed that C. F. A. Voysey was his main inspiration. Author of *Floral Forms in Historical Design, mainly from objects in the Victoria and Albert Museum*, 1922, London. He lived at Bedford Park, London.

790 Four designs: 'Alpinus', produced by Essex & Co., 1900; 'Hawkweed', produced by Essex & Co., 1902; a stylized floral pattern within undulating bands, produced by Arthur Sanderson & Sons Ltd, 1905; a frieze with a pattern of apple blossoms; each signed *Lindsay Butterfield*
Watercolour
Various sizes
Given by the artist
E.3056–3059–1934; E.3056 neg GJ.9518; E.3057 CT 7795 (see col pl, p 301); E.3058 neg GJ.9519; E.3059 neg GJ.9520

791 Portion with a pattern of irises and daisies; numbered in ink on the mount *Essex No. A.30*
Produced by Essex & Co.

790 GJ.9519

790 GJ.9518

Circa 1900
Colour machine print
75.7 × 53.1 cm
E.818–1974

792 Portion with a pattern of a single rose within a cartouche of scrolling stems; inscribed in ink on the mount *Jeffrey B.1.*
Produced by Jeffrey & Co.
Circa 1900
Colour machine print
74.7 × 51.2 cm
E.819–1974

(*opposite*) 'Adam', by Andrew F. Brophy, produced by Arthur Sanderson & Sons Ltd, 1903 (no 778)

790 GJ.9520

'The Fox and the Crane', possibly by William Burges, *circa* 1870 (no 781)

793 Portion with a pattern of lilies and other flowers amid stems with orange berries; inscribed in ink on the mount *Jeffrey B.19*.
Produced by Jeffrey & Co.
Circa 1900
Colour print from wood blocks
76 × 52.7 cm
E.820–1974

794 Portion with a pattern of stripes composed of leaves and berries, with a single sprig half-drop between the stripes; inscribed in ink on the mount *Jeffrey B.16*.
Produced by Jeffrey & Co.
Circa 1900
Colour print from a wood block
74.6 × 53 cm
E.821–1974

795 Portion with a pattern of intersecting circles of leaves and berries; lettered in ink on the mount *Jeffrey B.18*.
Produced by Jeffrey & Co.
Circa 1900
Colour machine print
75.3 × 53 cm
E.822–1974

796 'Lilburn'; signed in ink on the mount *LP Butterfield*, inscribed with title and numbered *93119*
Colour machine print
62.2 × 49.4 cm (portion)
E.812–1974 neg GJ.9521

797 Portion with a pattern of swirling leaves and yellow roses; signed in ink on the mount *LP Butterfield* and numbered *29771*
Colour machine print, part squared in pencil
66.4 × 46.7 cm
E.813–1974

798 'The Woodham'; signed in ink on the mount *LP Butterfield*, inscribed with title and numbered *63537*
Machine print in red
75.6 × 47.6 cm (portion)
E.814–1974 neg GJ.9522

The above 8 items, nos 791–798, were given by Courtaulds Ltd.

Butterfield, Lindsay Phillip, probably by

799 Portion with a pattern of acanthus leaves and poppies in shades of blue
Circa 1895
Colour machine print
55.2 × 55.8 cm
Given by Miss Mary Peerless
Circ.598–1967

796

798

800 Two portions of 'The Courtland' and 'The Hanover'
Produced by Essex & Co.
Colour machine prints
196.9 × 56.5 cm; 78.2 × 56.5 cm
Bequeathed by Miss Estella Canziani
E.913, 914–1965

'The Hanover' is described in *JDA* (1902), p 21.

Butterfield, Lindsay Phillip, possibly by

801 Portion with a swirling pattern of daisies and other flowers; numbered in ink on the mount *Jeffrey B.22.*

Produced by Jeffrey & Co.
Late 19th century
Colour machine print
75.7 × 53.4 cm
E.815–1974

Cadney, Harry. See PATTERN BOOKS, nos 715, 716(4), 717(3), 720(2).

Calvetti. See PATTERN BOOKS, no 707.

Cannon, Margaret. See PATTERN BOOKS, no 719(3).

Carling, Louise. See PATTERN BOOKS, no 735.

Carlsson, Viel. See PATTERN BOOKS, no 735.

Carlström, Elisabeth. See PATTERN BOOKS, no 735.

Carpenter, Alfred C., worked *circa* 1899–1900

He was awarded a silver medal while studying at Birkbeck College for the best design for tapestry entered in the National Art Competition of 1895. He also designed embossed paper for Lincrusta Walton.

802 'The Thibet'
Produced by Jeffrey & Co.
1913
Colour print from wood blocks
102.5 × 56.6 cm (portion)
Given by Jeffrey & Co.
E.1777–1914 neg GJ.9523

See *The Studio Year Book of Decorative Art* (1913), plate on p 89.

Cash, Judith. See PATTERN BOOKS, nos 719(3), 721.

802

Cattermole, Edgar. See PATTERN BOOKS, no 707.

'Celtis-Meister', working *circa* 1530

Frankish artist of the school of Dürer, known by the above name.

803 Reproduction of a woodcut wallpaper, reconstructed from fragments, showing a satyr playing a wind instrument, a nymph and a child among grape vines; with description etc in German in the margin
Published by Kurt Weber, Dreye bei Bremen
Circa 1530
Silk screen, black on cream
123 × 87 cm (size of sheet)

Given by the Deutsches Tapetenmuseum, Kassel
E.1218–1979 neg GJ.9491

The design, described as for a tapestry, has also been attributed to Hans Sebald Beham.

Cerio, Letizia, b. 1908

Argentinian painter, illustrator and craftswoman, born in Buenos Aires. She studied for 3 years at the Art Students League in New York, where she lives. She has also designed tapestry.

804 'Capri'
Produced by Rasch & Co., Bramsche, Germany
Circa 1955
Machine print, brown on cream
267.5 × 53 cm
Given by Dr Emil Rasch
E.989–1978 neg GJ.9524

See *Gebrauchsgraphik* (1958), vol 29, no 1, pl 4.

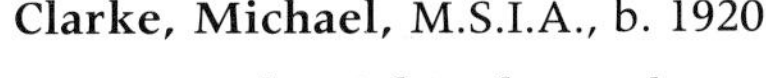

Clarke, Michael, M.S.I.A., b. 1920

Artist in indian ink and gouache, typographer, wood-engraver and advertising agent.

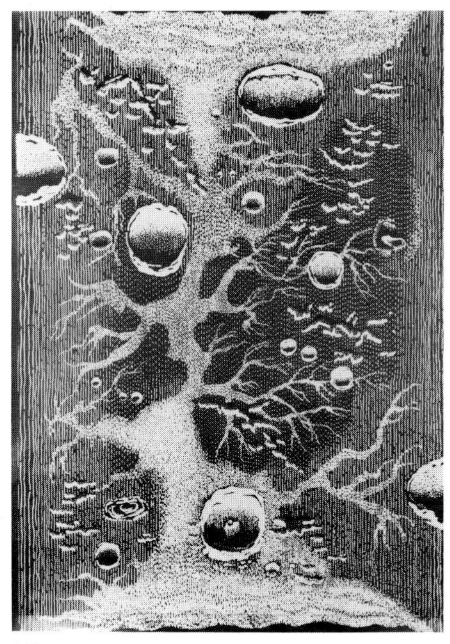

805

803

804

805 'Lunar'
Produced by Cole & Son (Wallpapers) Ltd
1964
Colour screen print
72.5 × 57 cm (portion)
Given by Cole & Son (Wallpapers) Ltd
E.952–1978 neg GJ.9525

Close, H. See PATTERN BOOKS, no 707.

Cockerell, Mrs S., working *circa* 1922

806 'Deer' frieze
Produced by Jeffrey & Co.
Circa 1922
Colour machine print
51 × 85.6 cm (portion)
Given by Harris & Sons
E.2368–1932 neg GJ.9365

See W. G. Paulson Townsend, fig 166.

Cockshut, J. Cheetham, worked *circa* 1905–*circa* 1922

Nephew of John and James Cockshut, directors of the firm of Allan, Cockshut & Co.

807 Portion of a nursery paper with a design adapted by J. C. Cockshut from Randolph Caldecott's *Nursery Books*
Produced by Allan, Cockshut & Co.
Circa 1900
Colour machine print
73.6 × 52.2 cm
Given by the WM
E.1825–1934

Another piece is E.715–1952 CT 8487

806

Coleman, William Stephen, 1829–1904, attributed to

Designer, illustrator, landscape, genre and figure painter, he exhibited at the Dudley Gallery, London, *circa* 1865–79. In 1869 he took up pottery decoration, and in 1871 Minton's Art Pottery Studio in Kensington Gore, London, was established under his direction.

808 Two portions of a frieze, showing different sections of the same design, embodying a nude girl holding a pomegranate and surrounded by sprays of apple blossom
Circa 1885
Colour prints from wood blocks
26.7 × 45.7 cm (each)
Given by the WM
E.1870–1934 neg GG.5865; E.1871–1934 neg GG.5866

807

808 GG.5866

808 GG.5865

Colme, Rudi. See PATTERN BOOKS, nos 715, 718, 720(3).

Cooke, Clement. See PATTERN BOOKS, no 713.

Cordsen, Inge. See PATTERN BOOKS, no 719(3).

Corre, Lawrence. See PATTERN BOOKS, no 720.

Cotton, Ann. See PATTERN BOOKS, no 719.

Crane, Walter, R.W.S., 1845–1915

A designer of mural decoration, plaster and gesso relief work, stained glass, metal work, tiles and pottery, wallpapers and textiles. A prolific illustrator of children's books. First President of the Arts & Crafts Exhibition Society, from 1888 to 1890 and from 1895 to 1915, member of the Council of Art, from 1898 to 1899. Author of books on design and, like Morris, a socialist.

809 Nursery paper, 'The Queen of Hearts'; with a floral border affixed
Produced by Jeffrey & Co.
1875
Colour machine prints
63.3 × 60.1 cm (overall size of fragment); 6.4 cm (depth of border)
E.42–1971 neg GJ.9526

This paper was joined to nos 367 and 810. It was the artist's first wallpaper design. SE, pl 180.

810 Nursery paper, 'Nursery Rhymes' (Humpty Dumpty etc); with floral border affixed
Produced by Jeffrey & Co.
1876
Colour machine prints
64.8 × 58.4 cm (overall size of portion); 6.4 cm (depth of border)
E.42A–1971 neg GJ.9527

This paper was joined to nos 367 and 809, backed with pages from *The Graphic* (1879). I. Spencer, *Walter Crane* (1975), London, plate on p 105.

The above 2 items, nos 809, 810, were given by Mr Roger H. M. Warner

811 Two portions, in different colourways, of no 812
Produced by Jeffrey & Co.
1876
Colour prints from wood blocks
86.4 × 53.3 cm; 105.5 × 52.2 cm
Given by Mr Emslie John Horniman and Harris & Sons respectively
E.4028–1915; E.2322–1932

Both portions are printed without the legend *Si douce est La Margarete*. This paper, with the 'Alcestis' frieze and 'Dove' dado, were exhibited at the Philadelphia Exhibition of 1876. *Easter Art Annual* (1898), plate on p 22. See SE, pl 129 (colour).

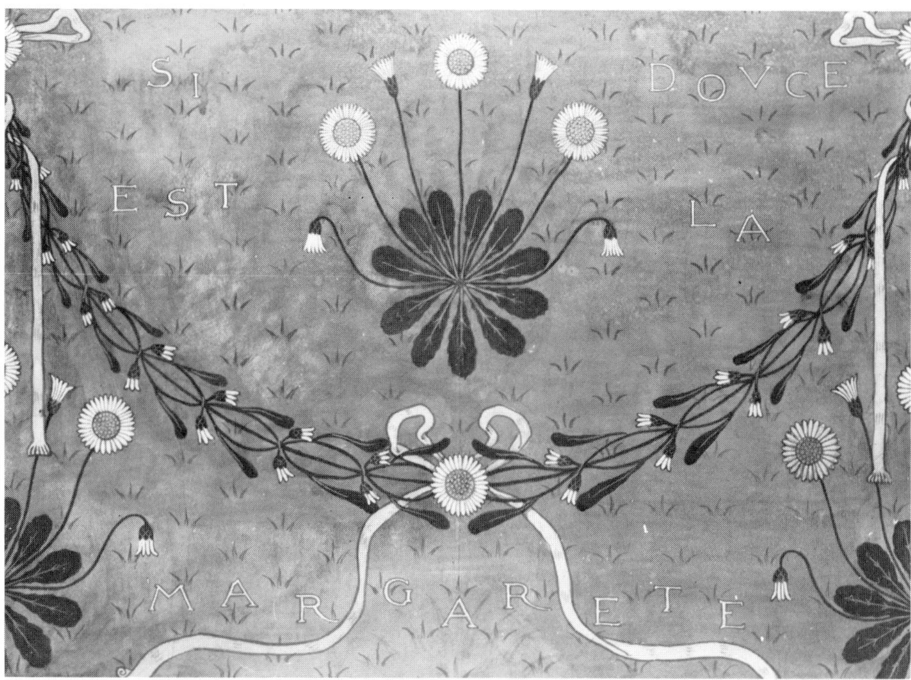

812

810

812 'La Margarete'; signed in ink *Walter Crane* and inscribed in pencil with notes
Produced by Jeffrey & Co.
1876
Body colour
38.1 × 53.3 cm
Given by Mrs Margaret Warner
E.18–1945 neg GJ.9528

'La Margarete'—wallpaper, frieze (no 813) and dado—were exhibited at the Philadelphia Exhibition of 1876.

813 Four portions of a frieze entitled 'Alcestis'
Produced by Jeffrey & Co.
1876
Colour prints from wood blocks
Various sizes
Given by Mr Emslie John Horniman and the WM respectively
E.4034–1915 CT 7796 (see col pl, p 302); E.1843–1845–1934

809

A detail of the block for this frieze is reproduced in *Art Journal*, November 1901, plate on p 333.

814 'La Margarete' with 'Alcestis' frieze
Produced by Jeffrey & Co.
1876
Colour print from wood blocks
170.8 × 49.5 cm (panel)
Given by the WM
E.1837–1934

An inscription on a piece of paper pasted on the back gives the price of the wallpaper as 8d a yard and of the frieze as $4\frac{1}{2}$d a yard.

817

815 Portion of ceiling paper showing a dove and olive branch, intended for use with no 812
Produced by Jeffrey & Co.
1876
Colour prints from wood blocks
71.1 × 52.7 cm
E.5115–1919

See Greysmith, pl 112.

816 Portion of a dado showing lilies and doves, intended for use with no 812
Produced by Jeffrey & Co.
1876
Colour print from wood blocks
68.6 × 50.2 cm
Given by Mr Emslie John Horniman
E.4027–1915

817 Frieze showing doves and marguerites, intended, as an alternative to the 'Alcestis' frieze (no 813), for use with no 812
Produced by Jeffrey & Co.
1876
Colour print from wood blocks
27.1 × 51 cm (portion)
Given by the WM
E.1886–1934 neg GJ.9529

818 Design for the above
Body colour
26.7 × 53.4 cm
Given by Mrs Margaret Warner
E.19–1945

819 Design for no 815; signed with the artist's monogram
1876
Body colour
52.7 × 52.7 cm
Given by the Guildhall Library
E.642–1952

820 Portion of the 'Iris and Kingfisher' wallpaper
Produced by Jeffrey & Co.
1877
Colour print from wood blocks
43.8 × 53.3 cm
Given by Mr Emslie John Horniman
E.4035–1915

See catalogue of the International Exhibition, Paris, 1878, plate on p 30.

821 Design for the above
Watercolour and body colour
53.3 × 53.3 cm
Given by Mrs Margaret Warner
E.15–1945

822 Portion showing only the irises of the 'Iris and Kingfisher' design (no 820)
Produced by Jeffrey & Co.
1877
Colour print from wood blocks
95.3 × 53.3 cm
E.5166–1919

823 Design for the above; signed with the artist's emblem
Body colour
38.1 × 26.7 cm
Given by Mrs Margaret Warner
E.16–1945

824 Two portions of a dado entitled 'Swan, Rush and Iris', intended for use with the 'Iris and Kingfisher' wallpaper (no 820)
Produced by Jeffrey & Co.
1877
Colour prints from wood blocks
53.8 × 104.1 cm (each)
E.5124, 5125–1919

825 Design for the above; signed with the artist's emblem
1875
Body colour
53.3 × 53.3 cm
Given by Mrs Margaret Warner
E.17–1945

Exhibited *Art Nouveau in Britain*, Arts Council, 1965, no 27.

826 Two portions, in different colourways, of a frieze showing irises, to be used either alone or jointly with a frieze of boats and irises intended to accompany the 'Iris and Kingfisher'

wallpaper (no 820)
Produced by Jeffrey & Co.
1877
Colour print from wood blocks
38.2 × 52.1 cm; 38.8 × 53.3 cm
E.1854, 1866–1934; E.1866 neg GJ.9530

827 Frieze showing boats and irises, intended for use with the 'Iris and Kingfisher' wallpaper (no 820)
Produced by Jeffrey & Co.
1877
Colour print from wood blocks
38.8 × 55.8 cm (portion)
E.1867–1934 neg GJ.9531

Exhibited at the International Exhibition, Paris, 1878.

828 Portion of a dado showing rushes and irises, intended for use either alone or jointly with the 'Swan, Rush and Iris' dado (no 824) intended to accompany the 'Iris and Kingfisher' wallpaper (no 820)
Produced by Jeffrey & Co.
1877

826

Colour print from wood blocks
53.3 × 49.6 cm
E.1849–1934

The above 3 items, nos 826–828, were given by the WM.

829 Two portions, in different colourways, of no 830
Produced by Jeffrey & Co.
1878
Colour prints from wood blocks
84.4 × 53.3 cm (each)
Given by Mr Emslie John Horniman
E.4047, 4048–1915

830 Design for 'Peacocks and Amorini', showing scheme for 2 different treatments: (1) for flat printing; (2) for embossed leather paper
1878
Watercolour
106.7 × 53.1 cm
E.595–1925 neg 56524

'In the arabesque, the ever-ascending stem and interlacing branches may figure the constant growth of an ideal life, like a tree bearing flowers and living fruit. Amorini suspend its festal garlands and light the flame of its thoughts, or play with the masks of grief and gladness, overhung by the bow and quiver of Love, and crowned with his roses. Pride and splendour as of the peacock lodge in its boughs, and the craft of the serpent is ruled over by the benign wings of the dove, while the

827

830

corn is ever in the sickle, and the cornucopia is full of fruit.' (Description of the design by the artist, in *Building News* (1879), XXXVI, p 198.) This, with the frieze (no 832) and dado (no 834), was exhibited at the International Exhibition, Paris, 1878, where it received the Gold Medal Award. For a wallpaper made after this design, see no 831.

831 Specimen of 'Peacocks and Amorini', made from the above design
Produced by Jeffrey & Co.
1878
Embossed leather, lacquered in gold
134 × 57.5 cm
E.596–1925

This was exhibited with others made by the same manufacturer at the International Exhibition, Paris, 1878, where it gained a gold medal. See *Building News* (1879), XXXVI, pl on p 198.

The above 2 items, nos 830, 831, were given by Mr Metford Warner.

832 Portion of a frieze showing a peacock with outspread tail, intended for use with no 830
Produced by Jeffrey & Co.
1878
Colour print from wood blocks
53.3 × 49 cm
Given by Mr Emslie John Horniman
E.4032–1915

Another length, given by Mrs Margaret Warner, is E.14–1945.

833 Frieze showing peacocks and winged figures with sickles, intended for use with no 830
Produced by Jeffrey & Co.
1878
Body colour and gold
53.3 × 54.1 cm (design for frieze)
Given by Mrs Margaret Warner
E.23–1945 neg GJ.9532

834 Portion of a dado showing a fish in a roundel within a classical panel, intended for use with no 830
Produced by Jeffrey & Co.
1878
Colour print from wood blocks
69.2 × 49 cm
E.4031–1915

835 Two portions, in different colourways, of a frieze, 'Almond Blossom and Swallow', for use with the filling 'Almond Blossom and Wallflower' (no 836)
Produced by Jeffrey & Co.
1878

836

Colour prints from wood blocks
54 × 71.7 cm; 54 × 59.7 cm
E.4037, 4038–1915

Building News (1879), XXXVI, plate between pp 326, 339. Exhibited at the International Exhibition, Paris, 1878, together with the filling, where it was awarded a gold medal.

The above 2 items, nos 834, 835, were given by Mr Emslie John Horniman.

836 'Almond Blossom and Wallflower'
Produced by Jeffrey & Co.
1878
Body colour
37.8 × 53.3 cm (design)
Given by the Guildhall Library
E.641–1952 neg GJ.10024

833

Design for 'Hawkweed', by Lindsay P. Butterfield, produced by Essex & Co., 1902 (no 790)

'Alcestis' frieze, by Walter Crane, produced by Jeffrey & Co., 1876 (no 813)

'Trio' pilaster, by Walter Crane, produced by Jeffrey & Co., 1893 (no 863)

Day

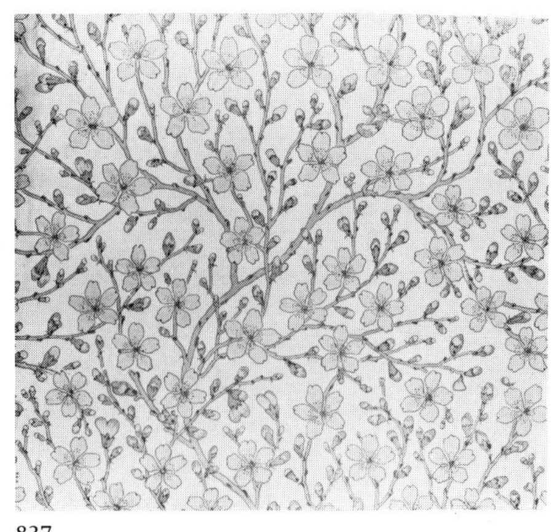
837

837 Almond blossom adapted from the frieze, 'Almond Blossom and Swallow' (no 835)
Produced by Jeffrey & Co.
Circa 1878
Colour print from wood blocks
53.3 × 47 cm (portion)
E.4021–1915 neg GJ.9533

838 Portion of 'Billow'
Produced by Jeffrey & Co.
1879
Colour print from wood blocks
53.3 × 45.7 cm
E.4024–1915

This paper was produced in another version, showing fish.

839 Portion of a dado for use with the 'Billow' wallpaper (see above), showing shells and starfish
Produced by Jeffrey & Co.
1879
Colour print from wood blocks
73.7 × 54 cm
E.4029–1915

840 Portion of a frieze, 'Mermaid', for use with the 'Billow' wallpaper (see no 838)
Produced by Jeffrey & Co.
1879
Colour print from wood blocks
59.3 × 89 cm
E.4042–1915

The above 4 items, nos 837–840, were given by Mr Emslie John Horniman.

841 Nursery paper, 'Sleeping Beauty'
Produced by Jeffrey & Co.
1879
Colour machine print
85 × 53.5 cm (portion)
E.4036–1915 neg 21962

(*opposite*) Design for 'The Magnolia', by Lewis F. Day, 1891 (no 924)

Exhibited at the International Health Exhibition, London, 1884 (*British Architect* (1884), vol XXI, plate between pp 254, 255); *V & A Picture Book*, pl 20; Entwisle, *V*, pl 26, fig 46. Two more portions are Circ.566 CT 8585, 566a–1915. A roll of the paper is E.60–1968.

842 Three portions, in different colourways, of a staircase wallpaper, 'Awakening Day'
Produced by Jeffrey & Co.
1880
Colour prints from wood blocks
79.3 × 53.3 cm (each)
E.5158–5160–1919; E.5158 neg GJ.9534

843 Frieze, 'Girls Skipping'
Produced by Jeffrey & Co.
1880
Colour print from wood blocks
50.8 × 74.3 cm (portion)
Given by Mr Emslie John Horniman
E.4030–1915 neg GJ.9535

This paper was exhibited at the International Health Exhibition, London, 1884.

842

844 'Briar Rose'
Produced by Jeffrey & Co.
1880
Colour print from wood blocks
50.3 × 50.8 cm (portion)
E.5090–1919 neg GJ.9536

Another portion, 86.3 × 56.6 cm, is E.2783–1914.

841

843

845 Portion of a frieze for use with 'Briar Rose' (see no 844)
Produced by Jeffrey & Co.
1881
Colour print from wood blocks
38.7 × 56.5 cm
Given by the WM
E.1869–1934

846 Dado, 'Rose and Cupid', for use with 'Briar Rose' (no 844)
Produced by Jeffrey & Co.
1881
Colour print from wood blocks
61 × 53.3 cm (portion of dado)
E.5089–1919 neg GJ.9537

847 Three portions, in different colourways, of 'Woodnotes'
Produced by Jeffrey & Co.
1886
Colour prints from wood blocks; E.4022–1915 flock
Various sizes
Given by Jeffrey & Co. and Mr Emslie John Horniman respectively
E.1766–1914; E.4022, 4039–1915

SE, pl 30 (colour). Exhibited in Manchester, Royal Jubilee Exhibition, 1887.

848 Design for no 851; signed with monogram, dated *WC Oct:86* and inscribed in ink *Oct. 1886*
Watercolour and body colour
101 × 66.7 cm
Given by Mrs Margaret Warner
E.20–1945

This design was reproduced in embossed leather and pasteboard simulating leather (no 852).

849 Nursery paper, 'The House that Jack Built'
Produced by Jeffrey & Co.
1886
Colour machine print

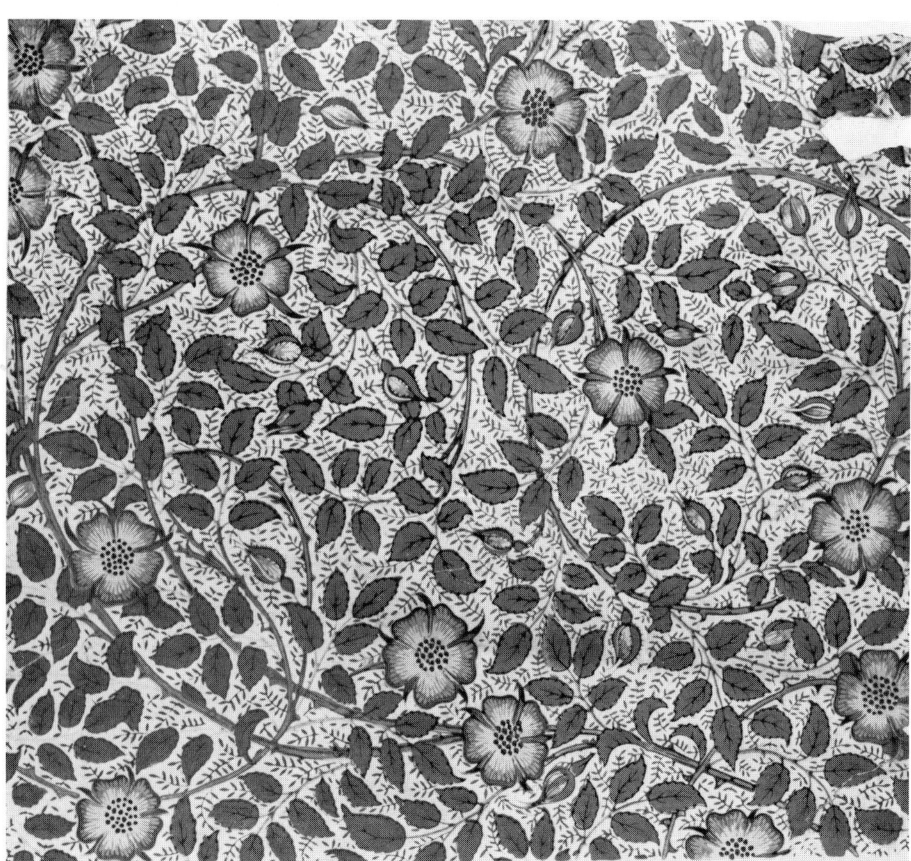
844

846

108 × 54.6 cm (portion)
Given by Miss E. Spiller, O.B.E.
E.2292–1931 neg GE.424

P. G. Konody, *Walter Crane* (1902), plate on p 116; Greysmith, pl 109.

850 Portion of a frieze, 'Deer and Rabbits', for use with the 'Woodnotes' wallpaper (no 847)
Produced by Jeffrey & Co.
1887
Colour print from wood blocks
50.8 × 70.6 cm
Given by Mr Emslie John Horniman
E.4040–1915

851 Two portions of 'The Golden Age'
Produced by Jeffrey & Co.
1887
Colour prints from wood blocks
116.9 × 54 cm; 85.1 × 49.2 cm
Given by Jeffrey & Co. and Harris & Sons respectively
E.1760–1914; E.2319–1932

Exhibited at the Royal Jubilee Exhibition, Manchester, 1887.

852 Two portions of wall coverings entitled 'The Golden Age'
Produced by Jeffrey & Co.
1887
E.21 embossed pasteboard simulating leather, with coloured lacquer; E.22 embossed leather with brown-and-gold lacquer
89 × 50.8 cm; 79.4 × 59.1 cm
Given by Mrs Margaret Warner
E.21, 22–1945

853 Portion of 'Peacock Garden'
Produced by Jeffrey & Co.
1889

Colour print from wood blocks
132.1 × 53.3 cm
Given by Jeffrey & Co.
E.1762–1914

SE, pl 31 (colour). Sold with the 'White Peacock' frieze.

854 Three portions, in different colourways, of 'Corona Vitae'
Produced by Jeffrey & Co.
1890
Colour prints from wood blocks
Various sizes
Given by Mr Emslie John Horniman and Messrs Harris & Sons respectively
E.4045, 4046–1915; E.2315–1932;
E.4045–1915 neg GE.425

Exhibited at the Fine Art Society, London, 1891, illustrated in catalogue; Greysmith, pl 110.

855 Portion of a frieze for use with 'Corona Vitae' (see above)
Produced by Jeffrey & Co.
1890
Colour print from wood blocks
61 × 83.8 cm
E.4041–1915

849

854

856 Specimen of ceiling paper, 'Four Winds', for use with 'Corona Vitae' (no 854)
Produced by Jeffrey & Co.
1890
Colour print from wood blocks
53.3 × 84.5 cm
E.4049–1915

The above 2 items, nos 855, 856, were given by Mr Emslie John Horniman

857 Design for the above; inscribed in pencil with notes
1890
Watercolour and body colour
71.8 × 71.8 cm
Given by Mrs Margaret Warner
E.24–1945 neg GJ.9538

858 Portion of nursery paper, 'Fairy Garden'
Produced by Jeffrey & Co.
1890
Colour machine print
70.4 × 53.3 cm
E.4043–1915

859 Two portions, in different colourways, of 'Cockatoo'
Produced by Jeffrey & Co.
1891
Colour prints from wood blocks
71.1 × 49.7 cm; 62.8 × 50.2 cm
E.4017, 4018–1915

Exhibited at the International Exhibition, Paris, 1900.

857

860 Two portions, in different colourways, of a frieze, 'Iris and Pomegranate', for use with the 'Cockatoo' wallpaper (see above)
Produced by Jeffrey & Co.
1891
Colour prints from wood blocks
45.7 × 50.8 cm (each)
E.4025, 4026–1915

The above 3 items, 858–860, were given by Mr Emslie John Horniman

861 Design for a pilaster showing pomegranates, peacocks, squirrels, a serpent, lizards etc, possibly intended to go with the 'Cockatoo' wallpaper (see no 859); signed with the artist's emblem and dated *1891*
Body colour
217.2 × 31.7 cm
E.5034–1919

862 Two portions, in different colourways, of a wallpaper, 'Plumes', for use with the 'Trio' pilaster decoration
Produced by Jeffrey & Co.
1893
Colour prints from wood blocks
71.7 × 52.1 cm; 73.1 × 52.1 cm
Given by Mr Emslie John Horniman
E.4019, 4020–1915

863 Portion of a pilaster showing a winged figure with a violin etc, being part of the 'Trio' decoration
Produced by Jeffrey & Co.
1893
Colour print from wood blocks
104.1 × 30.5 cm
E.5167–1919

This decoration was exhibited with the 'Plumes' paper (see no 862) and 'Singing Bird' frieze (no 864) at the Chicago Exhibition of 1893. Another portion is E.38–1971 CT 8745 (see col pl, p 303)

864 Portion of a frieze, 'Singing Bird', for use with the 'Trio' pilaster decoration
Produced by Jeffrey & Co.
1893
Colour print from wood blocks
57.1 × 53.3 cm
E.4044–1915

865 Two portions, in different colourways, of 'Seed and Flower'
Produced by Jeffrey & Co.
1893
Colour prints from wood blocks
46.3 × 53.3 cm; 43.2 × 53.3 cm
E.4023, 4033–1915

The Studio, December 1894, plate on p 77.

867

The above 2 items, nos 864, 865, were given by Mr Emslie John Horniman

866 Two portions of 'Teazle'
Produced by Jeffrey & Co.
1894
Colour print from wood blocks
89.5 × 51.4 cm; 75 × 54 cm
Given by Harris & Sons and the WM respectively
E.1839–1934; E.2323–1932

867 Four portions, in different colourways, of 'Lily and Rose'
Produced by Jeffrey & Co.
1894
Colour prints from wood blocks
92.7 × 53.3 cm (first three); 59.6 × 53.3 cm (last portion)
E.2318–1932 given by Harris & Sons
E.5143, 5144–1919; E.2318–1932;
E.5164–1919; E.2318–1932 neg GJ.9539

868 Portion of a frieze for use with the 'Lily and Rose' wallpaper (see above)
Produced by Jeffrey & Co.
1894
Colour print from wood blocks
30.5 × 61 cm
E.5165–1919

869 Two portions, in different colourways, of 'Artichoke'
Produced by Jeffrey & Co.
1895
Colour prints from wood blocks
75 × 53.3 cm (each)
E.5131, 5132–1919; E.5132 neg GJ.9540

870 Three portions, in different colourways, of 'Fig and Peacock'
Produced by Jeffrey & Co.
Circa 1895
Colour prints from wood blocks
101.6 × 51.7 cm; 88.2 × 52.1 cm; 77.5 × 50.8 cm
Given by Jeffrey & Co., Harris & Sons and Arthur Sanderson & Sons Ltd respectively
E.1765–1914; E.2325–1932; E.266–1949; E.1765–1914 neg K.2934

Exhibited in *Arts & Crafts*, London, 1896. See *Artist* (1896), XVIII, plate on p 9. Another portion, on embossed paper, is E.39–1972

871 Six portions, in different colourways, of 'Meadow Flowers'
Produced by Jeffrey & Co.
1896

869

870

Colour prints from wood blocks
96.5 × 55.2 cm (average size)
E.5083–5088–1919

872 Three portions, in different colourways, of a frieze, 'May Tree', for use with the 'Meadow Flowers' wallpaper (see above)
Produced by Jeffrey & Co.
1896
Colour prints from wood blocks
53.3 × 81.2 cm (average size)
E.5112–5114–1919; E.5112 CT 4210 (see col pl, p 321)

873 Eight portions, in different colourways, of 'National', and another portion
Produced by Jeffrey & Co.
1897
Colour prints from wood blocks, 2 with flock additions
83.8 × 50.8 cm (average size); 142.3 × 105.4 cm
E.5116–5123–1919; E.2331–1920; E.5118–1919 neg GJ.9541

873

874 Nine portions, in 8 colourways, of 'Day Lily'
Produced by Jeffrey & Co.
1897
Colour prints from wood blocks
Various sizes
E.2316–1932 given by Harris & Sons
E.5145–5151–1919; E.2316, 2317–1932

Reproduced in *St James' Budget*, 15 April 1898. Exhibited *Art Nouveau in Britain*, Arts Council, 1965, no 28.

875 Three portions, in different colourways, of 'Cockatoo and Pomegranate'; the third portion dated in pencil *1898*
Produced by Jeffrey & Co.
1899
Colour prints from wood blocks
123.8 × 54 cm; 88.9 × 51.5 cm; 23.5 × 50.8 cm
Given by Jeffrey & Co., Harris & Sons and Arthur Sanderson & Sons Ltd respectively
E.1761–1914; E.2320–1932; E.265–1949

876 'Rose Bush'
Produced by Jeffrey & Co.
1900
Colour print from wood blocks
91.5 × 54.6 cm (portion)
Given by Mr Sydney Vacher
E.2229–1913 neg K.2933

Exhibited at the International Exhibition, Paris, 1900.

877 Portion of a frieze, 'Lion and Dove', for use with 'Rose Bush' (see above)
Produced by Jeffrey & Co.
1900

876

Colour print from wood blocks
111.7 × 68.5 cm
Given by Jeffrey & Co.
E.1759–1914

Exhibited International Exhibition, Paris, 1900.

878 Portion of 'Lily'
Produced by Jeffrey & Co.
1900
Colour print from wood blocks
73.6 × 52 cm
Given by Harris & Sons
E.2326–1932

879 Portion of 'Olive Stripe'; inscribed in ink on the mount *Jeffrey B.16*.
Produced by Jeffrey & Co.
1900
Colour print from wood block
74.6 × 53 cm
Given by Courtaulds Ltd
E.821–1974

'New Designs for Wallpaper', *AJ* (1902), plate on p 286.

880 Two portions of 'Francesca'
Produced by Jeffrey & Co.
1902
Colour print from 6 wood blocks
68.6 × 51.4 cm; 89.5 × 51.5 cm
Given by the WM
E.1838–1934; E.2358–1932; E.1838–1934
neg GJ.9542

884

881 Portion of 'Dawn'
Produced by Jeffrey & Co.
1902
Colour print from wood blocks
90.2 × 51.4 cm
Given by Harris & Sons
E.2314–1932

882 Five portions, in different colourways, of 'Orange Tree'
Produced by Jeffrey & Co.
1902
Colour prints from wood blocks
94 × 52 cm (each)
E.2307–1932 given by Harris & Sons
E.5139–5142–1919; E.2307–1932

SE, pl 153 (colour).

883 Two portions of a frieze, 'Fruit', for use with the 'Orange Tree' wallpaper (no 882)
Produced by Jeffrey & Co.
1903
Colour prints from wood blocks
53.3 × 105 cm; 53.3 × 104.2 cm
E.2308–1932 given by Harris & Sons
E.5126–1919; E.2308–1932

884 Design for a frieze, 'Mistress Mary'; dated *1903*
Watercolour
54 × 76.8 cm
E.2329–1920 neg GJ.9543

885 Portion of a wallpaper and frieze, 'Mistress Mary', made from the above design
Produced by Lightbown, Aspinall & Co.
1903
Machine-printed from 6 engraved rollers
243 × 106.4 cm
E.2330–1920

A. S. Jennings, *Wallpaper Decoration* (1907), plate facing p 60 (colour).

886 Portion of a frieze, 'Mistress Mary'
Produced by Lightbown, Aspinall & Co.
1903
Machine-printed from engraved rollers
53.3 × 64.7 cm
E.5161–1919

A. S. Jennings, *Wallpaper Decoration* (1907), plate facing p 60 (colour). See also no 884.

880

887

887 Seven portions, in 6 colourways, of 'The Formal Garden'
Produced by Jeffrey & Co.
1904
Colour prints from wood blocks
83.8 × 57.2 cm (average size)
E.1840–1934 given by the WM
E.5100–5105–1919; E.1840–1934 neg GJ.9544

I. Spencer, *Walter Crane* (1975), plate on p 117 (colour); Greysmith, pl 25 (colour).

888 Ten portions, in 9 colourways, of 'Dulce Domum'
Produced by Jeffrey & Co.
1904
Colour prints from wood blocks
85.1 × 54 cm (average size)
E.1764–1914 given by Jeffrey & Co.
E.1764–1914; E.5091–5099–1919

Exhibited at St Louis in 1904, no 204 (catalogue, plate on p 257); *Decorators' & Painters' Magazine* (1903–1904), vol III, plate on p 340.

889 Six portions, in different colourways, of 'Myrtle Wreath'
Produced by Jeffrey & Co.
1904
Colour prints from wood blocks
83.8 × 57.2 cm
E.5106–5111–1919

Decorators' & Painters' Magazine (1903–1904), vol III, plate on p 339.

890 Design for a wallpaper showing medallions of flowers on a green ground, and with pilaster and frieze of lilies; signed and dated *Walter Crane May 04*
Watercolour
137.2 × 91.3 cm
E.5037–1919

891 Thirty-eight portions, in different colourways, of a frieze, border and corner sections, 'Oak'
Produced by Jeffrey & Co.
1904
Colour prints from wood blocks
Various sizes
E.5045–5082–1919

892 Four portions, in 2 colourways, of 'Macaw'
Produced by Jeffrey & Co.
1908
Colour prints from wood blocks
Various sizes
E.1763–1914 given by Jeffrey & Co.;
E.2321–1932 given by Harris & Sons;
E.267–1949 given by Arthur Sanderson & Sons Ltd
E.1763–1914; E.4163–1919;
E.2321–1932; E.267–1949; E.2321–1932 neg GJ.463

SE, pl 159; *The Studio Year Book of Decorative Art* (1915), plate on p 172.

892

895

893 Two portions, in different colourways, of 'Rosamund'
Produced by Jeffrey & Co.
1908
Colour prints from wood blocks
103 × 52.1 cm (each)
Given by Harris & Sons
E.2312, 2313–1932

894 Portion of a frieze for use with the 'Rosamund' wallpaper (see above)
Produced by Jeffrey & Co.
1908
Colour print from wood blocks
53.3 × 51.5 cm
E.1847–1934

895 'Saxon'
Produced by Jeffrey & Co.
1909
Colour print from wood blocks
73.7 × 52.1 cm (portion)
Given by Harris & Sons
E.2324–1932 neg GJ.9545

Reproduced in *The Studio Year Book of Decorative Art* (1909).

896 Three portions, in different colourways, of a wallpaper showing a design of crowns and bay, probably intended as an alternative for use with the 'Classic' pilaster and frieze (nos 897, 900)
Produced by Jeffrey & Co.
1910
Colour prints from wood blocks
89 × 54.5 cm (average size)
E.2311–1932 given by Harris & Sons
E.5137, 5138–1919; E.2311–1932

897 Design for the 'Classic' pilaster (no 899); signed with the artist's emblem
1910

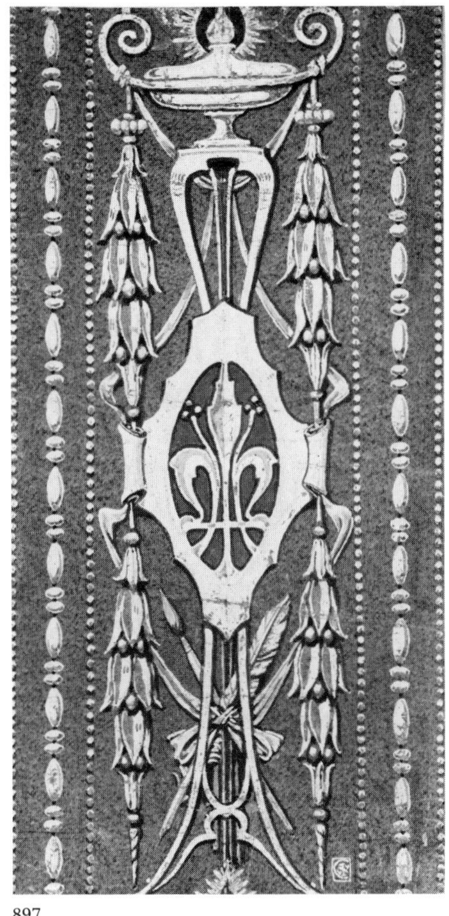
897

Tempera
53.3 × 26.7 cm
E.5039–1919 neg GJ.9546

898 Two designs for pilasters, probably alternatives to the above design
1910
Tempera
91.5 × 26.6 cm; 54.6 × 26.6 cm
E.5041, 5042–1919

899 Two portions, in different colourways, of the 'Classic' pilaster (no 897)
Produced by Jeffrey & Co.
1910
Colour prints from wood blocks
76.2 × 26.7 cm (each)
E.5135, 5136–1919

900 Design for a frieze for use with the 'Classic' pilaster (no 897); signed with the artist's emblem and dated *1910*
Tempera
109.2 × 45.7 cm
E.5043–1919

901 Two portions, in different colourways, of 'Scallop Diaper' (no 902), for use with the 'Classic' pilaster (no 897)
Produced by Jeffrey & Co.
1910
Colour prints from wood blocks
86.3 × 55.9 cm (each)
E.5127, 5128–1919

902 Design for 'Scallop Diaper' (see above), for use with the 'Classic' wallpaper; signed with the artist's emblem
Tempera
55.2 × 55.5 cm
E.5040–1919

903 Design for no 896; signed with the artist's emblem and dated *1910*
1910
Tempera
58.2 × 55.6 cm
E.5038–1919

904 Two portions, in different colourways, of a frieze for which no 900 is the design
Produced by Jeffrey & Co.
1911
Colour prints from wood blocks
45.2 × 83.8 cm (each)
E.5133, 5134–1919; E.5133 neg GJ.9547

904

905 Design for 'Laurel'; signed with the artist's emblem
1911
Watercolour
96.5 × 59.6 cm
E.5044–1919

906 Five portions, in different colourways, of 'Laurel' (see above)
Produced by Jeffrey & Co.
1911
Colour prints from wood blocks
88.8 × 53.3 cm (each)
E.5153–5157–1919

The Studio Year Book of Decorative Art (1911), plate on p 98.

909

907 Three portions, in different colourways, of 'Vineyard' (see no 908)
Produced by Jeffrey & Co.
1912
Colour prints from wood blocks
Various sizes
Given by Jeffrey & Co. and the WM respectively
E.1767, 1768–1914; E.1841–1934

908 Two sheets of the original design for 'Vineyard'
1912
Pencil and coloured chalks
53.3 × 53.3 cm (each)
E.5035, 5036–1919

Undated and unidentified wallpapers

909 A ceiling paper: a central roundel, made up from a repeat of a semicircular design, with a formal decoration and 4 draped female figures, on a blue ground, within a rim of Greek key pattern
Circa 1880–90?
Colour machine print
80.5 cm (diameter)
Given by Mr Martin Battersby
E.61–1947; E.629–1972 neg GJ.9548

910 Portion showing a design of pine-needles and cones
Colour print from wood blocks
93.3 × 53.3 cm
E.5162–1919

911 Two portions, in different colourways, showing a sun decoration
Colour prints from wood blocks
81.3 × 53.3 cm (each)
E.5129, 5130–1919

912 Portion of a frieze showing poppies, lizard and cockatoo; another portion in flock
Colour print from wood blocks
47.7 × 104.6 cm; 46.4 × 56.7 cm
E.5152–1919; E.1894–1934

Reproductions

913 Eight sheets of advertisement reproductions of wallpapers by Crane; E.4050 also showing papers by Stephen Webb
Process half-tone engraving
Various sizes
Given by Mr Emslie John Horniman
E.4050–4057–1915

'Trio' pilaster, 'Plumes' filling, 'Singing Bird' frieze (E.4050); 'Venetia', 'Boy and Dolphin' frieze by Stephen Webb (E.4050); 'Trio' pilaster, 'Plumes' filling, 'Singing Bird' frieze (E.4051); 'Four Winds' ceiling paper (E.4052); 'The Cockatoo' (E.4053); 'The Peacock Garden' decoration (E.4054); 'Corona Vitae' paper and frieze (E.4055); 'The Golden Age' (E.4056); 'Woodnotes' (E.4057).

Cutler, Thomas William, F.R.I.B.A., worked *circa* 1873 to *circa* 1908

Architect and author of *A Grammar of Japanese Ornament* (1880) and *Cottages and Country Buildings* (1896). He exhibited at the Royal Academy between 1873 and 1901.

914 Pattern of sparrows in flight
Late 19th century
Colour prints from wood blocks
38.1 × 54.6 cm (portion)
Given by Mr Sydney Vacher
E.2231–1913 neg GJ.9549

914

Dahlström, Preben, working 1956

915 'Ljus i Flaske' ('Light in Bottles')
Produced by Dahls Tapetfabrik, Copenhagen
1956
Colour print from wood blocks
57.5 × 54.6 cm (portion)
Given by Dahls Tapetfabrik
E.568–1966 neg GJ.471

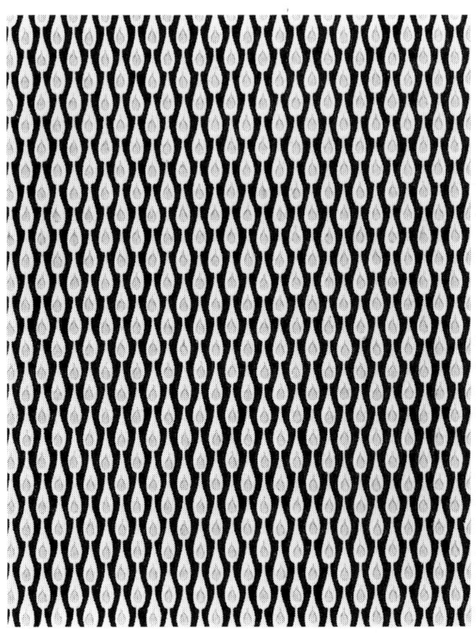

915

Dauban, Michel. See PATTERN BOOKS, no 715.

Davies, Gordon. See PATTERN BOOKS, no 715(2).

Day, Lewis Foreman, 1845–1910

Designer, lecturer and author of numerous books on ornament and design. In 1870 he joined the firm of Clayton & Bell as a designer of stained glass, but in the same year set up his own business designing textiles, wallpapers, stained glass, embroidery, carpets, tiles etc. In 1881 he was made director of Turnbull & Stockdale. A founder-member of the Artworkers' Guild, he became Master in 1884. Among other official appointments, he was made a member of the committee to report on the arrangement of collections in the VAM in 1909.

916 GJ.9552

916 GJ.9553

916 Three portions of paper, and 1 ceiling paper
Produced by Jeffrey & Co. for W. B. Simpson
1874
Colour prints from wood blocks
106.5 × 52.5 cm (average size)
Given by Mrs G. F. Rawnsley
E.607–610–1954; E.608 neg GJ.9552; E.609 neg GJ.9553

These 4 papers were exhibited in the *Exhibition of Victorian and Edwardian Decorative Arts*, VAM, 1952.

'Pomegranate' (E.607); 'Trellis Dado' (E.608); 'Apple Blossom' (Entwisle, *V*, pl 24, fig 43) (E.609); ceiling paper (unidentified) (E.610).

917 Design for 'The Medici', for Jeffrey & Co.; signed and dated in ink *Lewis F. Day 1885*
Watercolour
91.5 × 63.5 cm
E.1071–1911

918 Design for 'The Brocade'; signed and dated in ink *Lewis F. Day 1885* and *L. F. Day*, inscribed in ink with title and with colour notes
Watercolour and body colour
58.4 × 76.8 cm
Given by Mrs Margaret Warner
E.25–1945 neg GE.428

919 Four designs of formalized floral shapes; E.990 signed *Lewis F. Day* and dated *1886*
Watercolour and pencil
Various sizes
E.987, 990, 992, 994–1911

920 One hundred and twelve papers, dadoes, friezes and borders, including different colourways; in a volume with cover designed by the artist and lettered *Low-price Wallpapers for Staircase Decoration designed by Lewis F. Da[y] manufactured by Jeffrey & Co. 64, Essex Road Islington London N*; the backs of the sheets lettered with titles, manufacturers' serial numbers and prices
Produced by Jeffrey & Co.
Circa 1887-*circa* 1900
Machine prints
Various sizes; 57.7 × 41.3 cm (size of volume)
Given by Turnbull & Stockdale Ltd
E.23086–23195, 23086A, 23090A–1957

'Acacia' and border (E.23086, 23086A); 'Athenian' (E.23087, 23088); 'Arab Vine' (E.23089); 'Arabesque' and frieze (E.23090, 23090A); 'Athens' (E.23091, 23092); 'Brace' (E.23093, 23094); 'Brick' dado (E.23095, 23096); 'Cactus' (E.23097–23099); 'Cedric' (E.23100, 23101); 'Chaplet' (E.23102); 'Chevron' (E.23103); 'Conway' (E.23104, 23105); 'Damask' (E.23106, 23107); 'Dual' (E.23108); 'Elvas' (exhibited Manchester Royal Jubilee Exhibition, 1887) (E.23109, 23110); 'Etruscan' (E.23111, 23112); 'Festoon' frieze (E.23185); 'Flick' border (E.23189–23192); 'Greek' (E.23113, 23114); 'Henri II' (E.23115, 23116); 'Holbein' and border (E.23117, 23118); 'Indian' (E.23119); 'Interchange' frieze (E.23183–23186); 'Interlace' dado (E.23120, 23121); 'Istria' (E.23122, 23123); 'Kaiser' (E.23124); 'Lettice' dado (E.23125); 'Mandarin' (E.23126); 'Mason' (E.23127, 23128); 'Mecca' and frieze (E.23129, 23132); 'Memphis' and frieze (E.23131); 'Mercury' (E.23134–23136); 'Milan' (E.23137); 'Minerva' border and frieze (E.23138–23140, 23195); 'Orbit' frieze and dado (E.23141, 23142); 'Panel' frieze (E.23182); 'Peony' (E.23143); 'Photo' and frieze (E.23144–23146, 23147, 23148); 'Piccolomini' (reproduced in *Magazine of Art*, 1893; exhibited Chicago, 1893) (E.23149); 'Quarry' dado (E.23150); 'Renaissance' (E.23151); 'Sandringham' (E.23152, 23153); 'Seed' (E.23154, 23155); 'Shell' (E.23156, 23157); 'Sienna' (E.23158, 23159); 'Smyrna' (E.23160); 'Sprig and Scroll' (E.23161, 23162); 'Strasburg' border (E.23187, 23188); 'Tigris' (E.23163, 23164); 'Tooling' and frieze (E.23165, 23166); 'Tread' (E.23167, 23168); 'Trefoil' (E.23169, 23170); 'Trellis' dado (E.23171–23173); 'Troas' (E.23174); 'Trocadero' (E.23175); 'Veneer' border and dado (E.23176–23178); 'Wave' dado (E.23179); 'Wreath' (E.23180, 23181)

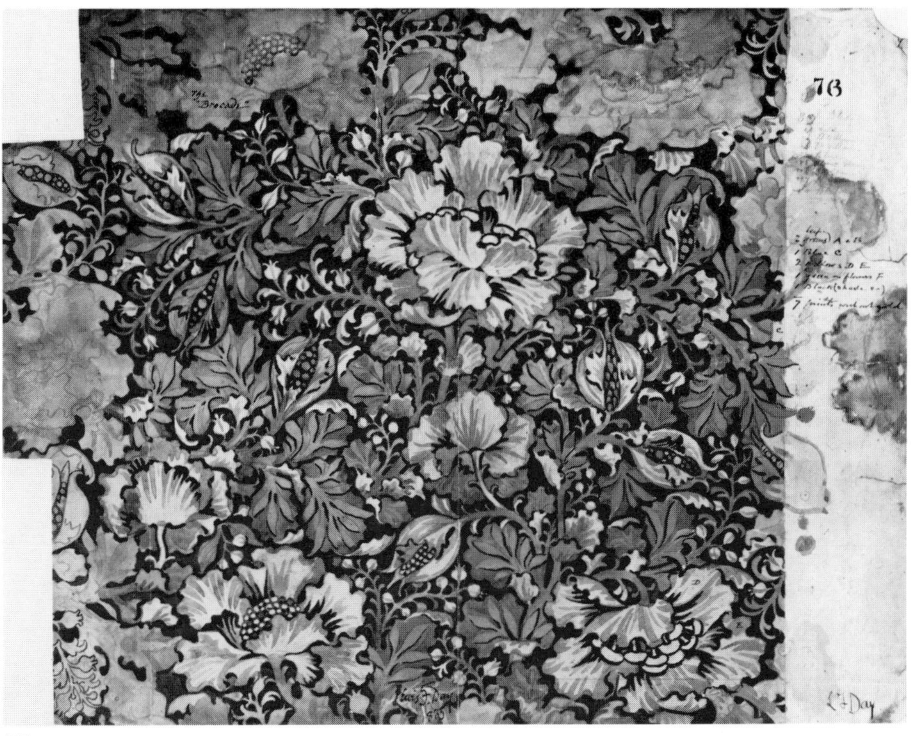

918

921 Design for 'The Turk's Cap', for Jeffrey & Co.
1890
Watercolour
64.7 × 38.6 cm
E.1063–1911

922 Design for 'The Poppy Head', for Jeffrey & Co.
1890
Watercolour
73.6 × 59.1 cm
E.1070–1911

923 Design for 'The Horns', for Jeffrey & Co.
1891
Watercolour
83.1 × 60.3 cm
E.1068–1911

This design differs from that of no 941, also entitled 'The Horns' and probably by Day.

924 Design for 'The Magnolia', for Jeffrey & Co; dated *1891*
Watercolour
85.1 × 63.5 cm
E.1064–1911 CT 7797 (see col pl, p 304)

925 Design for 'The Artichoke'; signed and dated *Lewis F. Day 1887*; inscribed in ink with title and with colour notes
1892
Watercolour
69.2 × 68 cm
E.26–1945

926 Design for a frieze, 'Poppy Head'; signed and dated *Lewis F. Day 1891*; inscribed with title and in pencil with colour notes
1892
53.3 × 86.4 cm
E.27–1945

The above 2 items, nos 925, 926, were given by Mrs Margaret Warner

927 Design for 'Cactus'; signed and dated *Lewis F. Day 1891*; inscribed with title and in pencil with working notes, with a stamp lettered *James Barrett Print Cutter* and numbered in ink *3476*
1892
Watercolour
74.2 × 59.6 cm
Given by the Guildhall Library
E.639–1952

The House, March 1897, plate on p 43. Exhibited *Art Nouveau in Britain*, Arts Council, 1965, no 30.

928

928 'Como'
Produced by Jeffrey & Co.
1894
Colour print from wood blocks
69.2 × 51.7 cm (portion)
Given by the WM
E.2149–1929 neg GG. 5864

929 Design showing conventional lilies and foliage; signed and dated *Lewis F. Day 1894*; inscribed in pencil with working notes, with a stamp lettered *James Barrett Print Cutter* and numbered in ink *4640*
Watercolour on toned paper
72.3 × 60.3 cm
Given by the Guildhall Library
E.638–1952

930 Design for a gilt, embossed 'leather' paper, 'The Abercorn', for Jeffrey & Co.
1896
Watercolour
110.4 × 64.8 cm
E.1067–1911

SE, pl 225.

931 Design 'to go with' the 'Paris' frieze, for Jeffrey & Co.; signed and dated in ink *Lewis F. Day 1896*
Watercolour
86.3 × 61.6 cm
E.1069–1911

932 Two friezes, on 1 sheet, of daisies, on a blue ground
Late 19th century
Colour prints from wood blocks
53.3 × 73.5 cm (overall size); 26.8 × 73.5 cm (each)
Given by Mr Roger H. M. Warner
E.40–1971 neg GJ.9551

932

933 Design showing a damask pattern of conventionalized foliage; signed and dated *Lewis F. Day 1899*, inscribed with working notes and numbered *1183*
1900
Body colour on brown paper
116.9 × 85.7 cm
Given by the Guildhall Library
E.640–1952

934 Design for a staircase paper, with undulating bands of foliage; signed and dated in ink *Lewis F. Day 1902*, inscribed with notes and numbered *422*
Watercolour and pencil
81.9 × 54.7 cm
E.1065–1911

935 Design for 'Neo-Grec'; signed and dated in ink *Lewis F. Day 1902*, with pencil note and numbered *431*
Circa 1904
Pencil and watercolour
66.4 × 46.7 cm
E.1066–1911

The paper reproduced from this design is illustrated in *Art Journal* (1904), plate on p 60 (colour). The artist also designed a ceiling paper of the same title, which is illustrated in the *Magazine of Art* (April 1892), p 192.

936 Three portions, in different colourways, of 'The Jacobite'
Produced by Jeffrey & Co.
Circa 1904
Colour prints from wood blocks
Various sizes
Given by Harris & Sons
E.2332–2334–1932

SE, pl 139; *AJ* (1905), plate facing p 284 (colour).

937

937 Pattern based on a Renaissance velvet
Produced by Jeffrey & Co.
Colour print from wood blocks
96.3 × 51.4 cm (portion)
E.2330–1932 neg GJ.9550

938 Portion with a pattern of a formalized palm-tree motif
Produced by Jeffrey & Co.
Colour print from wood blocks, on embossed paper
90.5 × 50.5 cm
E.2331–1932

939 Three portions, in different colourways, with a pattern of formalized (?) camelias
Produced by Jeffrey & Co.
Colour prints from wood blocks
102 × 57.5 cm (each)
E.2327–2329–1932

940 Portion with a flower and seed pod motif
Produced by Jeffrey & Co.
Colour print from wood blocks
89 × 52 cm
E.2335–1932

The above 5 items, nos 936–940, were given by Harris & Sons

Day, Lewis Foreman, probably by

941 'The Horns'
Produced by Jeffrey & Co.
1897
Leather, embossed, coloured and gilded
69 × 54 cm (portion)
Given by Mrs Margaret Warner
E.6–1945 neg GJ.9554

See also no 923.

941

Day, Lucienne, A.R.C.A., F.S.I.A., b. 1917

Textile and wallpaper designer, wife of furniture designer Robin Day, she studied at the Royal College of Art and later taught at Beckenham Art School. In 1946 she gave up teaching to go into private practice. See also PATTERN BOOKS, no 707.

942

942 'Provence'; lettered on the selvedge with facsimile signature *Lucienne Day*
Produced by John Line & Sons Ltd in their series 'Limited Editions 1951'
Hand screen print
74.4 × 54.2 cm (portion)
Given by John Line & Sons Ltd
E.569–1966 neg GJ.449 CT 8591

Designers in Britain (1951), vol 3, plate on p 243; *Design* (1951), vol 3, plate on p 11 (colour); *Gebrauchsgraphik* (1959), vol 30, plate on p 54; N. Carrington, *Design and Decoration in the Home* (1952), pl 111 (colour).

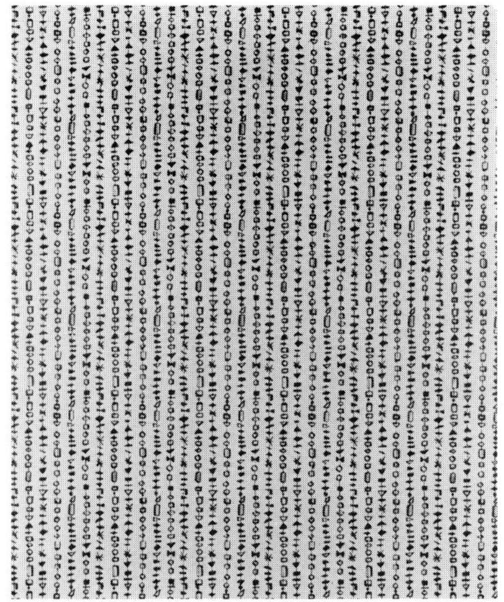
943

943 Pattern of vertical strings of geometrical shapes, in brown on white
Produced by the Crown Branch of the WM
1954
Machine print, on a lightly embossed ground
66.7 × 55.5 cm (portion)
Given by the WM
E.953–1978 neg GJ.9555

See Entwisle, *LH*, pls 114, 118 (colour).

944

944 'Prisma'
Produced by Rasch & Co, Bramsche, Germany
Circa 1955
Colour machine print
77.5 × 56.2 cm (portion)
Given by Dr Emil Rasch
E.954–1978 neg GJ.9556

Dearle, John Henry, 1860–1932

Designer of textiles, tapestry and stained glass, he joined Morris & Co. in 1878. After Morris' death in 1896 he took over the designing of textiles and wallpapers and backgrounds for many of the tapestries, and became art director of the firm. His designs included 'Iris', *circa* 1887, and 'Thistle', a machine-printed paper: see Morris, William, nos 1066, 1068.

945

945 Portion of 'The Oak Tree'
Printed by Jeffrey & Co. for Morris & Co.
1896
Colour machine print
74.5 × 53 cm
Given by Mr E. A. Morrison
Circ. 88–1968 neg GJ.9557

Other portions in different colourways are E.729–732–1915 (no 1066).

Dearle, John Henry, and **William Arthur Smith Benson,** 1854–1924

See also no 771.

946 'Sweet Pea'
Produced by Jeffrey & Co. for Morris & Co.
1908
Colour print from wood blocks
57.3 × 76.3 cm (portion)
Circ. 251–1964 neg GJ.9558

Another portion in a different colourway is Circ. 252–1964.

946

Delefant, Luise, working *circa* 1955, possibly by

947

947 Length with a pattern of birds among branches of blossom
Produced by Erismann & Cie, Breisach, Germany
Circa 1955
Colour machine print
267.5 × 54.2 cm (length)
E.961–1978 neg GJ.9562

Dennington, W., working 1900

948 Portion of a frieze, 'Peacock'; inscribed on the back in blue chalk *The Peacock No. 7703 5/6 per yard*
Produced by Shand Kydd Ltd
1900
Stencil
72.3 × 101.6 cm
Given by Shand Kydd Ltd
E.1535–1954 CT 7294 (see col pl, p 321)

See SE, pl 190.

Denst, Jack R., working 1968

President of Denst Designs Inc.

949 'I wish to fly'; signed within the design *Jack Denst*
Produced by Jack Denst Designs Inc., Chicago, U.S.A.
Circa 1968
Colour screen print
75.8 × 45.6 cm (portion)
E.781–1968 neg GJ.9559

950 'Oh promised land—oh, sweet freedom'; signed *J.R.D.*
Produced by Jack Denst Designs Inc., Chicago, U.S.A.
Circa 1968
Colour screen print
150.5 × 65.5 cm (portion)
E.782–1968

949

Denst & Soderlund Studio

953 'The Broken Ladder', printed in blue on a white ground
Produced by Denst & Soderlund, Chicago, U.S.A.
1952
Colour screen print
74 × 54 cm (portion)
Given by Denst & Soderlund
E.583–1966 neg GJ.9561

This paper, in another colourway, is reproduced in 'Wallpapers, A–W', *Interiors*, August 1952, vol 112, p 99.

951 'A Dialogue of Color'
Produced by Jack Denst Designs Inc., Chicago, U.S.A.
Circa 1968
Screen print in white on silver 'mirror' paper
76 × 46 cm (portion)
E.783–1968

952 'A gentle pleasure roaming in Indiana'
Reduced version of a design produced by Jack Denst Designs Inc., Chicago, U.S.A.
Circa 1968
Colour screen print
27 × 46.7 cm
E.784–1968 neg GJ.9560

The above 4 items, nos 949–952, were given by Jack Denst Designs Inc.

952

Desfossé, Jules, d. 1889

In 1851 he acquired the firm of Mader and issued a series of large papers in a new style: 'Le Rêve de Bonheur' (1852), 'Le Jardin d'Hiver' (1854) and 'Le Jardin d'Armide' (1854). In 1863 he became associated with his brother-in-law, Hippolyte Karth. After the Second World War Desfossé et Karth became the property of the Société Isidore Leroy.

954 Panel entitled 'Le Souper à la Maison d'Or', or 'Les Prodiges'
After the painting, dated 1855, by Thomas Couture (1815–79)
Produced by the firm of Jules Desfossé
1862
Colour machine print
186.6 × 259.1 cm (overall size)
E.147–1946 neg H.1453

See Entwisle, *FS*, pl 66; Clouzot, pl 25 (colour); Greysmith, pl 91.

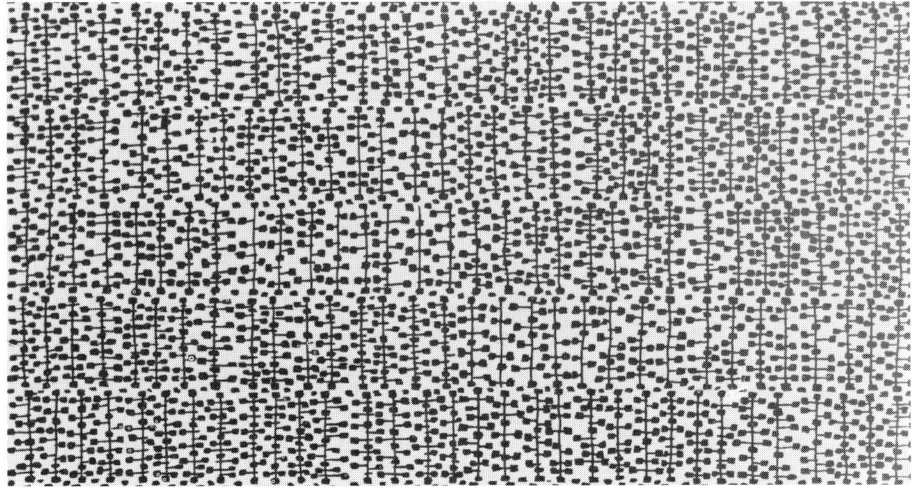

953

(*above*) The 'May Tree' frieze, by Walter Crane, produced by Jeffrey & Co., 1896 (no 872)

(*below*) The 'Peacock' frieze, by W. Dennington, produced by Shand Kydd Ltd, 1900 (no 948)

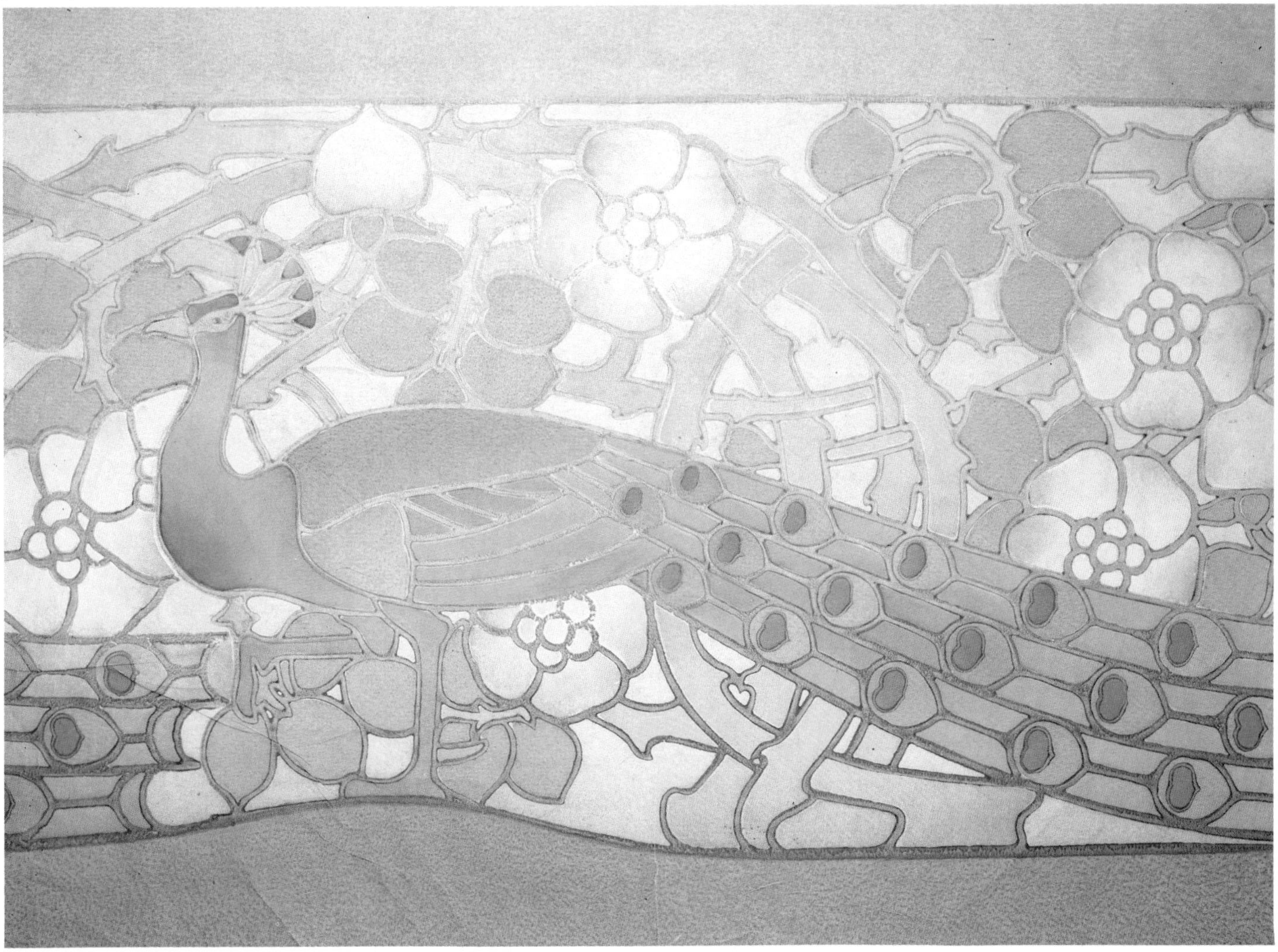

Design for 'Cranbourne', by Robert Dodd, produced by Shand Kydd Ltd, *circa* 1977 (no 955)

(*opposite*) 'Coq et Perroquet', panel by Jean-Baptiste Fay, produced by Réveillon, Paris, *circa* 1785–88 (no 962)

Design for a wallpaper or textile by Henri Gaudier-Brzeska, *circa* 1911 (no 966)

954

956 GJ.9563

Dodd, Robert W., des R.C.A., M.S.I.A., b. 1934

Textile and wallpaper designer. See also PATTERN BOOKS, nos 716, 717, 719(3), 721(2), 725(2).

955 Design for 'Cranbourne'; inscribed and dated on the mount *Robert Dodds* [*sic*] *1977*, and with title, colour key and measurements
Produced by Shand Kydd Ltd
Circa 1977
Poster colours
63.2 × 51.4 cm
Given by Shand Kydd Ltd
E.2726–1980 CT 8742 (see col pl, p 322)

Dolck, Marie. See PATTERN BOOKS, no 735.

Doran, Joseph M., working early 20th century

Designer of wallpapers and of printed and woven fabrics, also a worker in metal and enamel. His work was shown at the Royal Academy Exhibition of British Art in Industry, 1935.

956 GJ.9564

956 Ten original designs for wallpapers, cretonnes etc (not produced): 'Jasmine', 'Flanders', 'Dolly Varden', 'Bletchingley', 'Nevis', 'Greensted', 'The Bunch of Flowers', 'Angus 09', 'The Tunbridge' (frieze and filling), 'Ypres'
Early 20th century
Watercolour and pencil
Various sizes
Given by the artist
E.3841–3850–1915; E.3844 neg GJ.9563; E.3846 neg GJ.9564

Doran, Joseph M., attributed to

957 Design for a wallpaper showing pomegranates, grapes and lemons; inscribed in pencil with colour notes
Produced by Jeffrey & Co.
Circa 1910
Body colour
75 × 57 cm
Given by Mrs Margaret Warner
E.2–1945

Dresser, Christopher, 1834–1904

Designer and author of *The Art of Decorative Design* (1862), he began as a lecturer in botany. He visited Japan in 1876 as official representative of the British Government. He was art adviser to the Linthorpe Pottery, 1879–82, and art editor of the *Furniture Gazette*. He established a studio at Sutton in 1882, and at 'Elm Bank', Barnes, in 1889. From 1891 to 1896 he designed pottery for William Ault.

958 Portion of a frieze with a design of sweet peas with open seed pods, intertwined with scroll borders
Probably produced by Woollams
Circa 1880
Colour print from wood blocks
55 × 76 cm
Given by Mr T. F. Cardwell
E.950–1978 neg GJ.9598

Dufond, George. See PATTERN BOOKS, no 713.

Dunn, Alan. See PATTERN BOOKS, no 723.

Dunstan, Mrs Bernard. See Armfield, Diana M.

Ehrmann. See ANONYMOUS WALLPAPERS AND WALLPAPER DESIGNS, no 616 (note).

Emden, Anna-Lena. See PATTERN BOOKS, no 735.

Engströmer, Rolf. See PATTERN BOOKS, no 735.

Erbeck, Evelyn. See PATTERN BOOKS, nos 719, 721(2).

Evans, Dorothy. See PATTERN BOOKS, nos 720(2).

Farleigh, John William Frederick, C.B.E., R.B.A., R.E., 1900–1965

Painter in oils and watercolour, and wood engraver, he was educated at the Central School of Arts and Crafts and was for a time head of the book production department there. He exhibited with the London Group. Author of *Graven Image*.

959 GJ.9565

959 Pattern book with 36 specimens, including different colourways, and notes by the artist about each design; each lettered on the selvedge with title etc; full bound in grey buckram, with coiled wire spine and *Line* on the front cover
Produced by John Line & Sons Ltd
1956
Screen prints
54 × 54 cm (size of volume)
Given by Shand Kydd Ltd
E.1074–1109–1970

958

Discussed in *Design* (1956), vol 8, p 21, where 'Ceres' and 'Arbour' are reproduced in colour. This pattern book was the first to contain designs by one artist only.

'Downlands' (E.1074–1076); 'Ormulu' (E.1077–1080); 'Arbour' (E.1081–1083); 'Flower Burst' (E.1084–1086; E.1085 neg GJ.9565); 'Willow Herb' (E.1087–1089); 'Woodland' (E.1090–1092; E.1090 neg GJ.9566); 'Pirouette' (E.1093–1095); 'Bouquet' (E.1096–1098; E.1096 CT 7445 (see col pl); 'Pot Pourri' (E.1099–1101); 'Ceres' (E.1102–1105; E.1102 neg GJ.9567); 'Vignette' (E.1106–1109)

959 GJ.9566

Fassett, Kaffe. See PATTERN BOOKS, no 726.

Faulkner, Kate, working 1877–*circa* 1880

Artist and designer, sister of Charles Faulkner, one of the original partners in the Morris firm, she worked for the firm painting tiles and executing gesso work. She designed 'Loop Trail' (1877), 'Mallow' (1879) and 'Carnation' (*circa* 1880). See no 1066.

Faulkner, Sue, b. 1942

See also PATTERN BOOKS, no 725(9).

960 Design for a vinyl paper, 'Piazza'; numbered in pencil *101* and on the back, in ballpoint pen, *RS.101 PS 165*; stamped *000164*
Produced in the Vymura 'Studio One' range by ICI (Ltd) Paints Division
1975–76
Poster colour
60.5 × 53 cm
E.1031–1979

'Piazza' and 'Plaza' were designed to hang individually or together, vertically or horizontally, in any direction. M. Timmers, *The Way We Live Now . . .*, catalogue issued by the VAM, 1979, p 31; *Design*, 1976, p 38, no 328, illus. of 'Piazza', 'Plaza', 'Rondo', 'Concourse', 'Precinct', 'Treillage' and 'Cane'.

961 Design for a vinyl paper, 'Plaza'; numbered in pencil *100* and on the back, in ballpoint pen, *RS 100 PN 164*; stamped *000165*
Produced in the Vymura 'Studio One' range by ICI (Ltd) Paints Division
1975–76
Poster colour and pencil
61 × 53 cm
E.1032–1979

The above 2 items, 960, 961, were given by ICI (Ltd) Paints Division

---

Fay, Jean-Baptiste, working *circa* 1780 to *circa* 1790

Designer of engraved ornament and arabesques.

962 Six panels and fragments with designs of a cock, a parrot, swans, vases, floral festoons etc
Printed at Réveillon's works in the Rue de l'Arbre Sec, Paris
Circa 1785–88
Colour prints from wood blocks
Various sizes
PROVENANCE A house at Longford, Newport, Salop
Given by Colonel Ralph Leeke
E.15–20–1916; E.17 CT 7446 (see col pl, p 323); E.18, 19 neg D.265

The complete rolls are illustrated in P. Gusman, *Panneaux Decoratifs et Tentures Murales du XVIIIe siècle* (1913), pls 9–11. A complete set of these papers, consisting of ten panels, exists at the house of General Lafayette at Chavagnac, Haute-Loire (see M. L. le Verrier, 'Old Wall-paper of France', *Antiques* (1928), vol 13, p 128, where they are wrongly attributed and described as hand-painted). The paper was bought from Elliot in 1793. E.16 is reproduced in Clouzot, plate on p 49 ('Coq et Perroquet'). See also Entwisle, *FS*, pl 35; Olligs, I, plate on p 248.

959 GJ.9567

962

Fischer-Jones, G. See PATTERN BOOKS, nos 707(3), 713(4)

Fletcher, F. W. H., working *circa* 1880

Possibly related to Edwin Fletcher of Royston, near Barnsley, the designer and manufacturer.

963 Frieze with a pattern of peonies; inscribed in ink on the back *No. 1 Lacquer. Blocked all over then painted with Crimson Lake, Raw Sienna & Prussian Blue. Duplicate of Pattn. sent to George, New York 19/1/81*
Produced by Jeffrey & Co.
1880

963

Embossed pasteboard imitating leather, lacquered by hand
65.4 × 57.8 cm
Given by Mrs Margaret Warner
E.10–1945 neg GJ.9568

The British Architect, 29 December 1882, plate between pp 618, 619.

Forrer, Karl Gustav, b. 1852, after

Designer, born at Winterthur, who worked in Paris from 1879. He was professor of Design at the School of Industrial Arts, Leipzig.

964

964 Woodland scene
Produced by Allan, Cockshut & Co.
1906
Colour machine print
101.7 × 50.5 cm (portion)
Given by the WM
E.1897–1934 neg GJ.9569

SE, pl 158 (colour).

Frank Designs. See PATTERN BOOKS, no 718.

Fraser, Tony, working 1970s

See also PATTERN BOOKS, nos 719, 721(4).

965 Design for 'Alicia'; signed *Tony Fraser*; inscribed with title etc. and *Job No 38497*
Produced by Shand Kydd Ltd
Circa 1975
Artwork
Pen and ink and coloured inks, mounted on board
39.5 × 29 cm (size of sheet)
Given by Shand Kydd Ltd
E.2733–1980 neg HA.390

Gallet, Helène. See PATTERN BOOKS, no 707.

Garnett, John. See PATTERN BOOKS, nos 721(4), 723.

Gaudier-Brzeska, Henri, 1891–1915

Sculptor. He made a few designs for materials and carpets, also for wallpaper and book jackets.

966 Design for a wallpaper or textile, with a half-drop pattern of cockatoos
Circa 1911
Coloured inks
50.5 × 38 cm
E.13–1980 neg GK.724 CT 7908 (see col pl, p 324)

Gear, William, b. 1915

Scottish abstract painter and lithographer. Designed textiles for Edinburgh Weavers.

967

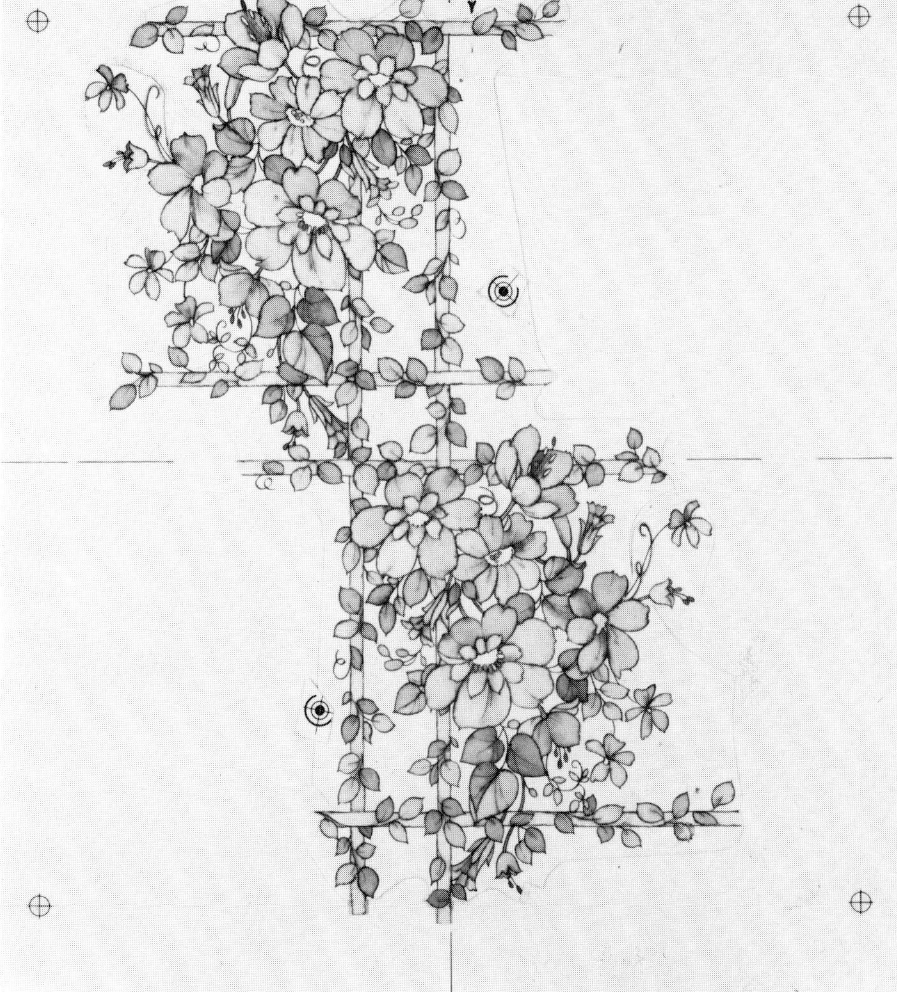
965

967 Two portions, in different colourways, of 'Palette'
Produced by the WM as one of their 'Modus' series
1960
Screen prints
49.5 × 55.5 cm (each)
Given by the WM
E.955, 955A–1978; E.955 neg GJ.9570

Entwisle, *LH*, pl 127; *Design* (1961), 145, plate (inside cover).

Gibson, Natalie. See PATTERN BOOKS, no 721.

Ginsburg, Gunnel. See PATTERN BOOKS, nos 734, 735.

Glover, M. See PATTERN BOOKS, no 707.

Godwin, Edward William, F.S.A., 1833–86

Architect and designer, born in Bristol, he began to design wallpapers in 1866, and from 1868 onwards furniture, wallpapers, carpets and textiles. His association with Ellen Terry led him to design costumes and sets for theatre productions. Among his buildings are Dromore Castle for the Earl of Limerick and The White House, Chelsea, for Whistler. He published *Dress in Relation to Health and Climate* in 1885.

968 Design for 'Sparrow and Bamboo'
Produced by Jeffrey & Co.
1872
Pencil on tracing paper
35.6 × 43.8 cm
E.514–1963 neg GJ.9571

W. Watt, *Art Furniture from Designs by E. W. Godwin . . .* (1877), pl 20; *Building News*, 11 October 1872. Two versions were made of this paper.

968

969 Design showing bamboo leaves and formalized Japanese flowers; inscribed and dated on the back by the artist *Wall Decoration, November 1872*
Produced by Jeffrey & Co.
Watercolour on tracing paper
52.5 × 52.5 cm
E.515–1963 neg GG.5868

Illustrations of the wallpaper produced from this design, used alternatively as a length and as a frieze, are shown in W. Watt, *Art Furniture from Designs by E. W. Godwin* . . . London, 1877, pl 20.

970 Design for a paper (or tiles): a frieze with the 'Japanese Sparrow' design and a formalized flower pattern with a geometrical border below; inscribed by the artist in ink and watercolour with notes
Circa 1872
Watercolour and body colour over preliminary pencil
30.5 × 38 cm (size of sheet)
E.512–1963

971 Formalized design showing the head and wings of a peacock, within a roundel, for part of the 'Peacock' dado; signed *E. W. G.* and inscribed by the artist with a colour note
Produced by Jeffrey & Co.
1873
Pencil and watercolour on tracing paper
29.5 cm (diameter)
E.513–1963 neg GJ.9572

Illustrations of the 'Peacock' dado, used alternatively as a frieze and as a dado, are shown in W. Watt, *Art Furniture from Designs by E. W. Godwin* . . . London, 1877, pl 20; *Building News*, 8 May 1874, illus.; SE, pl 123; *Magazine of Art* (1878–79), vol I, plate on p 90.

The above 4 items, nos 968–971, were given by Mr Edward Godwin, son of the artist

---

Goes, Hugo. See ANONYMOUS WALLPAPERS AND WALLPAPER DESIGNS, no 1.

Gould, Elizabeth. See PATTERN BOOKS, nos 716, 717.

Grace, Esmé. See PATTERN BOOKS, no 707.

969

971

Gråsten, Viola, b. 1910

Finnish textile designer and draughtswoman, she studied at the Ateneum in Helsinki. In 1937 she went to France, and in 1946 to Copenhagen. She worked for N.K.'s textile concern in Stockholm, and was a member of the Röhsska Museum staff.

972 'G.-Sträng'
Produced by AB Durotapet, Sweden
1953
Machine print
74.5 × 54.5 cm
Given by AB Durotapet
E.976–1978 neg GJ.9501

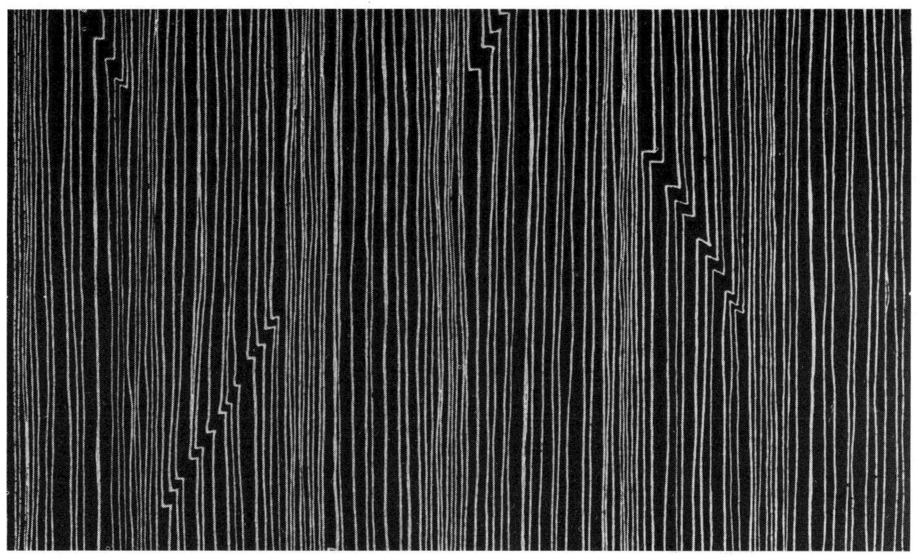

972

Greenslade, Russell. See PATTERN BOOKS, no 720.

Griffiths, Albert, worked *circa* 1914–post 1920

Designer of wallpapers and textiles.

973 Portion with a rhododendron pattern, from a design finished by Griffiths
Produced by Jeffrey & Co.
Circa 1910–14
Colour print from wood block
87.2 × 51.7 cm
E.3688–1915

974 'The Mikado'
Produced by Jeffrey & Co.
1914
Colour print from wood blocks
133.4 × 66 cm (length)
E.1775–1914 neg GJ.9573

Studio Year Book of Decorative Art (1915), plate on p 172.

The above 2 items, nos 973, 974, were given by Jeffrey & Co.

Griffiths, Elizabeth, working 1950s

Designer of 'The Red Dog Biscuit' (1953), which became a best-seller.

975 'Colophon'
Produced by the Lightbown, Aspinall Branch of the WM as one of their

974

'Palladio' range
Circa 1957
Screen print, black on red
72 × 55.5 cm (portion)
E.962–1978 neg GJ.9574

Griset, Ernest Henry, 1844–1907

See ANONYMOUS WALLPAPERS AND WALLPAPER DESIGNS, no 334.

Groag, Jacqueline, F.S.I.A., b. 1903

Textile and wallpaper designer. See also PATTERN BOOKS, nos 707(3), 710.

976 'Isabella'; lettered with manufacturer's name etc and *Rd. no. 864900*
Produced by John Line & Sons Ltd, in their series 'Limited Editions 1951'
Colour print from wood blocks
72.5 × 54.5 cm
E.880–1978 neg GJ.9575

Designers in Britain (1951), vol 3, plate on p 242; *Design* (December 1951), vol 3, p 10; N. Carrington, *Design and Decoration in the Home* (1952), pl 137.

977 Portion of a nursery paper, 'Kiddies Town'
Produced by John Line & Sons Ltd
1951
Colour machine print
72.7 × 54.5 cm
Given by John Line & Sons Ltd
E.881–1978 neg GJ.9576

Designers in Britain (1951), vol 3, pl on p 242.

976

978 Design for 'April'; signed and dated *jacqueline 1976*
Produced by Sandudd Vantaa, Finland
Collage and poster-colour over dye-line print
50.2 × 49.7 cm
E.944–1978

Exhibited in *The Way We Live Now: Designs for Interiors 1950 to the Present Day*, Department of Prints and Drawings, VAM, 7 November 1978 to 4 March 1979.

Guild, Tricia. See PATTERN BOOKS, no 726.

Gwatkin, Arthur L., worked *circa* 1890–*circa* 1903

Originally trained at Hayward & Son Ltd, he became designer for Wyllie & Lochhead. He exhibited designs for friezes at the Royal Academy from 1890 to 1899.

975

977

Panel with an heroic landscape, by John Baptist Jackson, after Marco Ricci, 1744 (no 1018)

Page from an album of designs by John Baptist Jackson, mid-18th century (no 1020)

981

980 Portion of 'Flaming Tulip'
Produced by Wyllie & Lochhead Ltd
Circa 1901
Colour print from engraved rollers
88 × 56 cm
Given by Miss Mary Peerless
E.467–1967 neg GK.4564 CT 8566

Decorators' & Painters' Magazine (1901–1902), I, plate on p 433, described as 'Sanitary, Engraved on Ingrain', No.04141. This hall wallpaper is a 'sanitary' paper.

981 'The Thunberg'
Produced by Hayward & Son Ltd
1904–1905
Colour print from wood blocks
89.5 × 57.2 cm (portion)
Given by the WM
E.1899–1934 neg GG.5878

Decorators' & Painters' Magazine (1904–1905), IV, plate on p 24.

Hagerman, Lotta. See PATTERN BOOKS, nos 734, 735(2).

Hagity, Tessa. See PATTERN BOOKS, no 715.

979 'The Poppy'
Produced by Hayward & Son Ltd
Circa 1890–1900
Colour print from wood blocks
82 × 56 cm (portion)
Given by the WM
E.1898–1934 neg GJ.9577

979

(*opposite*) 'Eltham', probably by William Shand Kydd, *circa* 1905 (no 1037)

980

Haité, George Charles, R.I., R.B.A., 1855–1924

Son of the Paisley textile designer, George Haité, he was a painter of landscapes in oil and watercolour, and a designer of wallpapers, carpets, leaded glass and metal work. He came to London in 1873, and from 1883 exhibited at the Royal Academy. He became President of the Langham Sketching Club and President of the Society of Designers. The Anaglypta Co. made several of his designs for ceilings, dadoes, fillings and friezes, and he also worked for Jeffrey & Co., William Woollams & Co., Sanderson & Sons, Wyllie & Lochhead and David Walker.

982 Volume of designs for textiles, stained glass, ceiling papers and wallpapers etc
Circa 1876–*circa* 1883
Pencil, pen and ink, gouache etc
37.5 × 24.8 cm (size of volume)
E.23237 (1–1068)–1957

Among the identified designs for wallpaper are the following: (1) a preliminary sketch for a design for flock, reproduced in the *Builder* (28 January 1882), vol 42, plate on p 107 (E.23237 (851)); (2) a design for a paper produced by W. Woollams & Co., reproduced in Gleeson White, *Practical Designing* (London, 1894), fig 2 in Haite's chapter on wallpapers (E.23237 (853)); (3) seven designs for textiles and wallpaper for Bruce Talbert, furniture designer (q.v.) (E.23237 (241, 320–322, 325, 395, 430)).

983

983 Design for a paper with a formalized fern-and-flower pattern in blue and gold; signed and dated *Geo C. Haité 1879* and inscribed in pencil with measurement and *Carry out for Scott Cuthbertson & Co, 3 June 1879*
Watercolour and pencil
35.5 × 38.2 cm (size of sheet)
E.23239–1957 neg GJ.9578

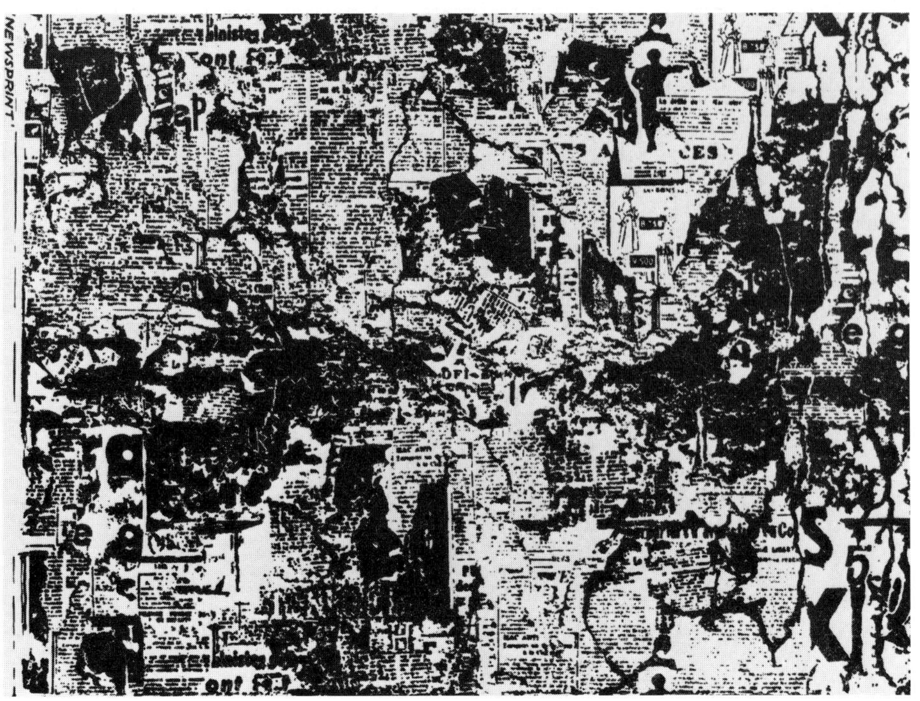

985

The above 2 items, nos 982, 983, were given by Miss Elsie Haité, daughter of the artist.

Haité, George Charles, R.I., R.B.A., possibly by

984 Portion with a design incorporating a lion's head and vertical oak stems
Produced by Jeffrey & Co.
Last quarter of 19th century
Colour machine print on embossed paper
90.2 × 52 cm
Given by Harris & Sons
E.2355–1932

An article by Aymer Vallance, 'New Designs for Wallpapers', *AJ* (1902), p 287, mentions 'Mr. Haité's characteristic designs of heraldic lions and oak leaves, obviously conceived as appropriate souvenirs of the Coronation'.

Halton, John. See PATTERN BOOKS, no 719.

Hammer Prints

Designers of textiles and wallpaper. Now part of the Hull Traders Ltd.

985 'Newsprint'
Produced by Cole & Son (Wallpapers) Ltd
1963
Screen print in black
70 × 57 cm (portion)
Given by Cole & Son (Wallpapers) Ltd
E.965–1928 neg GJ.9579

986 'Portobello'
Produced by the WM
1964
Machine print, in white on red
139.5 × 57 cm (portion)
Given by the WM
E.964–1978 neg GJ.9580

986

991

Harbour, John. See PATTERN BOOKS, nos 715(8), 716(2), 717(3), 718(4), 720(7), 723.

Hart, N. See PATTERN BOOKS, no 707.

Haward, Sidney, worked *circa* 1882–*circa* 1940

He was an assistant to his father and brother, who were cabinet-makers and furnishers in Darlington. He went to London in 1882 and entered the studio of Arthur Silver, becoming Silver's chief assistant. In 1892 he set up his own studio and continued to design wallpaper. He lived at Bedford Park, London.

987 Portion of 'Burmese Poppy'
Produced by Jeffrey & Co.
1896
Colour print from wood blocks
92.9 × 56 cm
Given by Miss Mary Peerless
E.471–1967

Builder's Reporter, 3 June 1896.

988 Portion of 'Cineraria'
Motif designed by Albert Warner and finished by Sidney Haward
Produced by Jeffrey & Co.
Early 20th century
Colour print from wood blocks
160 × 56.5 cm
Given by Jeffrey & Co.
E.3687–1915

989 Two portions, in different colourways, of 'Nankin'
Produced by Jeffrey & Co.
Early 20th century
Colour print from wood blocks
59.6 × 89 cm
Given by the WM
E.1946, 1947–1934

Paulson Townsend, fig 125 (colour).

990 Portion of 'Elizabeth's Garden'
Produced by John Line & Sons
Early 20th century
Colour print from wood blocks
84.9 × 53 cm
Given by Mr Henry Butler
E.2786–1914

Studio Year Book of Decorative Art (1915), plate on p 174.

991 Two portions of 'Sackville'
Produced by Jeffrey & Co.
1912
Colour print from wood blocks
122 × 56.7 cm; 115.4 × 57 cm
Given by Mr Henry Butler and Jeffrey & Co. respectively
E.2789–1914; E.1776–1914 neg GJ.9582

992 Birds and flowers in blues and browns on a mottled ground
Produced by Jeffrey & Co.
Circa 1912
Colour print from wood blocks
84.7 × 50.8 cm
E.1900–1934 neg GJ.9581

992

993

993 Portion of 'Chinese Flowers and Birds'
Produced by C. & J. G. Potter
Circa 1914
Machine print
76.2 × 51.4 cm
E.1901–1934 neg GG.5863

SE, pl 166 (colour).

The above 2 items, nos 992, 993, were given by the WM

994 Portion of 'Stafford'
Produced by Jeffrey & Co.
Circa 1915
Colour machine print
72.3 × 53.3 cm
Given by Mr Henry Butler
E.2763–1914

995 Roll with a pattern of exotic birds on branches of blossom
Produced by Jeffrey & Co.
Circa 1919
Colour machine print
655.3 × 57.2 cm
Given by Mr Roger H. M. Warner
E.37–1971

The Studio Year Book of Decorative Art (1919), top plate on p 105.

Hayes, Albert Edward, 1880–1968

Of Walthamstow, Essex, a designer of textiles and wallpaper. He exhibited at the R.I. in 1924. See also ANONYMOUS WALLPAPERS AND WALLPAPER DESIGNS, no 529 (note).

996

996 Design with a repeat pattern of formalized leaves and blossom, within square borders of leaves
Early 20th century
Body colour
52.5 × 52.5 cm
E.813–1968 neg GJ.9583

997 Design with a repeat pattern of formalized nasturtiums
Early 20th century
Body colour
48.7 × 48.6 cm
E.814–1968 neg GJ.9584 CT 7447 (see col pl)

The above 2 items, nos 996, 997, were given by Mrs Majorie Wilson, daughter of the artist

---

Healey, Deryck, working early 1960s

Fellow of the School of Advanced Studies, Manchester College of Art, then head of the London design studio of the WM (1964). See also PATTERN BOOKS, nos 718(3), 719(2).

998

998 'Florian'
Produced by the WM
1963
Colour screen print
75 × 54.2 cm (portion)
Given by the WM
Circ.18–1964 neg GJ.9585

999 Two portions, in different colourways, of 'Lamina'
Produced by the Lightbown, Aspinall Branch of the WM in their 'Palladio' range
1964
Colour screen prints
104 × 55.7 cm; 81 × 55.7 cm
Circ.128A, B–1965; Circ.128B
neg GJ.9586

This paper received a Design Centre Award in 1964. *Design*, June 1964, vol 186, p 50 (colour).

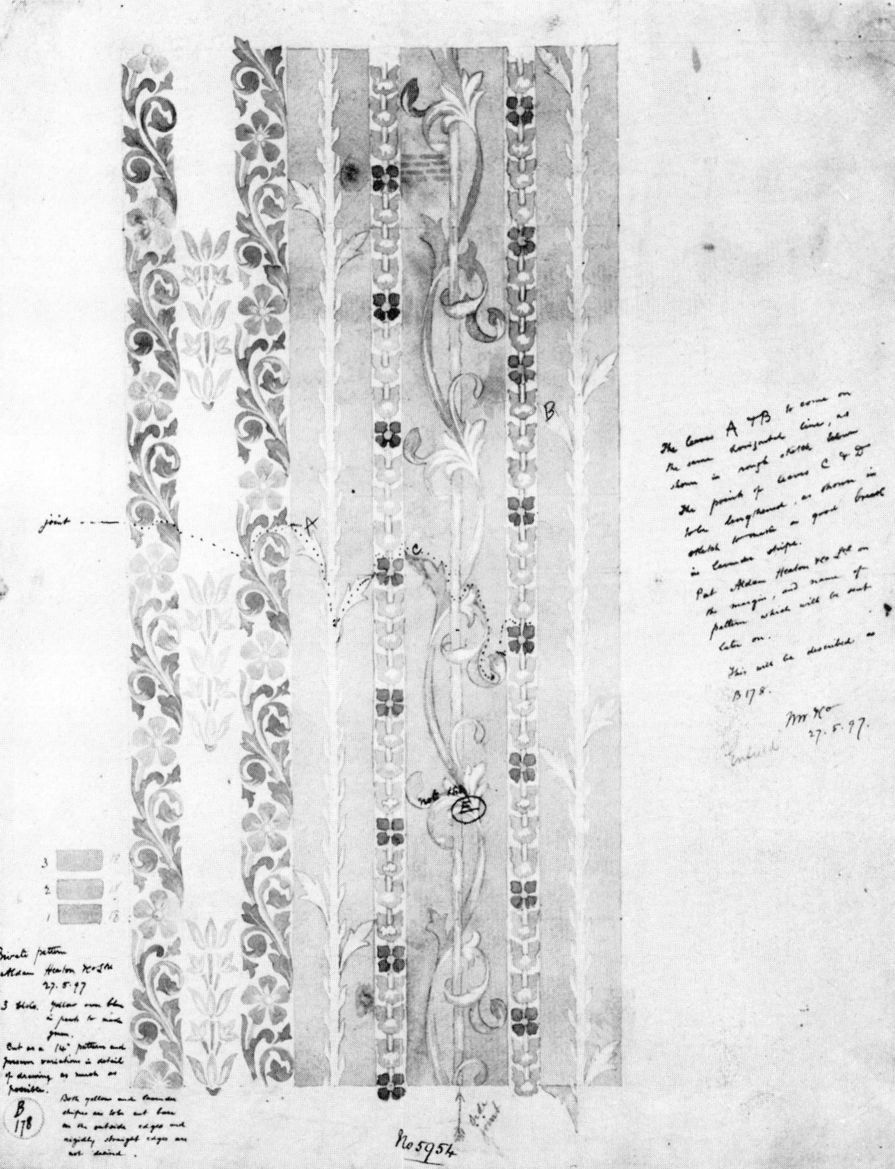

1001

999

Heath, James. See PATTERN BOOKS, nos 715(2), 716(2), 718.

Heaton, John Aldam, 1830–98

He came to London from Yorkshire in 1876 and began business as a decorator, producing gesso panels, stained glass, beaten copper and brass, and inlay. He also designed carpets, wallpaper and damasks. He was involved in the initiation of the School of Art Needlework at South Kensington. He exhibited 3 friezes at the Royal Academy in 1888.

1000 Design for a paper with a formalized pattern of undulating leaves and flowers; signed and dated *J. A. Heaton 18/11/80*, inscribed with notes and *Private Pattern B WW* [*William Woollams*] *& Co* and numbered *5653*
Pencil and body colour, squared
65.5 × 64.9 cm
E.2694–1929

A. Heaton, *Designs and Decorations* (1893), pl 72, etc.

1001 Design entitled 'Enfield'; inscribed in ink with working notes etc and *WW* [*William Woollams*] *& Co. Private Pattern Aldam Heaton & Co Ltd*, numbered *5954* and blind stamped with the Heaton Co.'s stamp

Circa 1897
Pencil and watercolour
61.7 × 49.5 cm
E.2696–1929 neg GJ.9588

1002 Design with a pattern of formalized leaf shapes in cusps; inscribed *Heaton Private Pattern D* etc and numbered *5738*
Watercolour, squared
44.8 × 30.1 cm
E.2695–1929 neg GJ.9587

1002

1003 Design for a ceiling paper: flowers and leaves within panels
Watercolour and pencil
53 × 53.2 cm
E.2697–1929 neg GJ.9589

1004 Design entitled 'Romana'; inscribed with notes and *WW* [*William Woollams*] *& Co* and numbered *6407*
Pencil and body colour
61 × 70.6 cm
E.2698–1929

1005 Design entitled 'Miniato'; inscribed with title and notes and numbered *6308*
Pencil, watercolour and Chinese white, squared
66.4 × 69.8 cm
E.2699–1929

1006 Design with a pattern of large flowers and foliage
Pencil and watercolour

1003

80.5 × 53.8 cm
E.2700–1929

The above 7 items, nos 1000–1006, were given by Heaton Tabb & Co. Ltd.

Hermann, Willy. See PATTERN BOOKS, nos 707(3), 715.

Hildebrand, Margit (Margret), working from 1950s

Of Hamburg. Apart from the example given below, she designed other wallpapers for Rasch & Co. in 1966.

1007 'Konifere'
Produced by Rasch & Co., Bramsche, Germany
Circa 1955
Machine print, black on cream
267.5 × 55 cm (length)
Given by Dr Emil Rasch
E.965–1978 neg GJ.9590

1007

Hillerbrand, Josef, b. 1892

Glass painter, and designer of furniture and textiles.

1009

1008 Varnished wallpaper with formalized flower and grass shapes
Produced by Erismann et Cie, Germany
1955
Colour machine print
72 × 52.5 cm (portion)
Given by Erismann et Cie
E.895–1979 neg GJ.9591

Hillier, Fay. See PATTERN BOOKS, no 715.

Hirsch, Barbara. See PATTERN BOOKS, no 707.

1008

Hodgetts, T. C., working late 19th century

He seems to be known only from the design listed below, which was found in the VAM in 1908. Possibly he was a student at the South Kensington Art Schools.

1009 Design of purple hellebore; signed in pencil *T. C. Hodgetts*
Tempera
30.6 × 22.9 cm
D.1752–1908 neg GJ.9592

Hofbauer, H. See PATTERN BOOKS, no 707.

Holden, Cliff, b. 1919

He studied art at the Borough Polytechnic, where he worked with David Bomberg, and was the first president of the Borough Group. He was a partner with Lisa Grönwall and Maj Nilsson in Marstrand Designers, Sweden. See also PATTERN BOOKS, no 716.

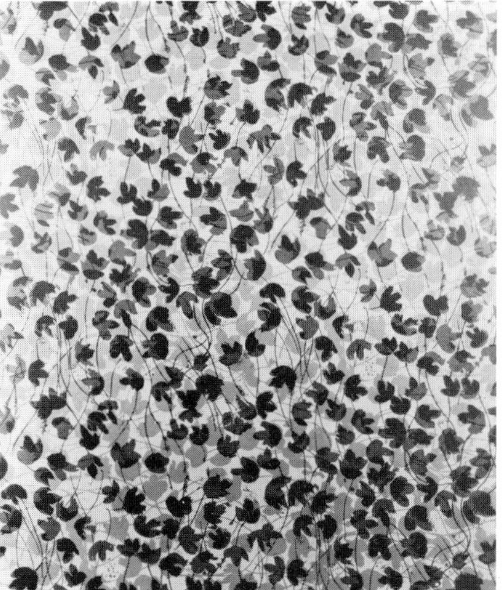

1010

1010 'Trifoliate'
Produced by the Lightbown, Aspinall Branch of the WM, in their 'Palladio 5' range
1962
Colour screen print
74.5 × 54.5 cm (portion)
Given by the WM
Circ.596–1963 neg GJ.9593

Design Centre Award, 1962. *Design* (June 1962), vol 162, plate on p 60. The pattern was produced in 3 colourways: green, lilac and grey.

Hopes, Jean G. See PATTERN BOOKS, no 716.

Horne, Herbert Percy, 1864–1916

He went into partnership with A. H. Mackmurdo, and worked with the firm of Mackmurdo & Horne from *circa* 1882 to 1890. He edited the magazine *Hobby Horse*, which first appeared in 1884, from 1886 to 1893.

1011 'The Bay Leaf', with frieze
Produced by Jeffrey & Co.
Circa 1882
Colour print from wood blocks
110 × 72 cm (portion)
E.966–1978 neg GJ.9594 CT 8589

The paper was designed by Horne for the Century Guild. The design for the filling is E.1166–1920 (see no 1012). The frieze is reproduced in *AJ* (1892), p 44. Exhibited at the Inventions Exhibition, London, 1885; *Arts and Crafts*, London, 1888.

1013 GJ.9597

1011

1013 GJ.9596

1012 Three designs showing stylized floral motifs; inscribed *CG* (monogram of the Century Guild)
Tempera
Various sizes
E.1166–1168–1920; E.1166 neg GJ.9595

1013 Eighteen designs showing stylized floral motifs; E.1473 dated in pencil on the back *Jan.1885*; E.1474–1481 dated variously on the mounts from *Jan. 1886* to *August 1886*
Watercolour and pencil
Various sizes
Given by Mr Aymer Vallance
E.1473–1490–1933; E.1479, 1480 neg GJ.9596; E.1481, 1484 neg GJ.9597

Hollingsworth, Bruce. See PATTERN BOOKS, nos 707, 710.

Hörstadius, Lilo. See PATTERN BOOKS, no 735.

Hughes, Edward H., A.R.C.A., M.S.I.A., working 1950s

Of the firm of designers Clarke, Clements & Hughes, and agent for Roger & Robert Nicholson Ltd.

1014 'Adelphi' and 'Basuto'
Produced by the WM
Circa 1955
Colour screen prints
97 × 55.7 cm; 74.5 × 52.5 cm (portions)
Given by the WM
E.1399–1979; E.967–1978 neg GJ.9599

'Basuto' is reproduced (colour) in *Design* (December 1955), p 22, no 84.

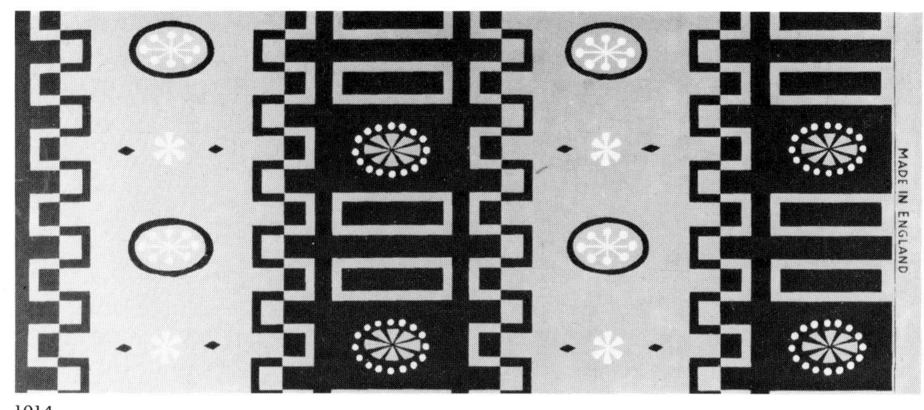

1014

Huntington, James, 1826–78

The eldest brother of W. B. & C. P. Huntington, founders of the firm of Huntington Frères, which represented English firms in Paris. Originally a designer of Paisley shawls and silks, he started a business of designing, engraving and print-cutting (known as pattern drawing) in Holloway, London, in 1848. He joined Potters of Darwen in 1864, together with his principal staff, and in 1875 became managing partner.

1015 Two borders with formalized flower motifs, from a log book of Sanderson & Sons
Produced by Jeffrey & Co.
1862
Colour prints from wood blocks
26.4 × 43.1 cm; 16.1 × 43.1 cm
Given by the WM
E.1800–1934 neg GJ.9600; E.1802–1934 neg GJ.9601

These borders form part of a pilaster decoration exhibited by Jeffrey & Co. at the Great Exhibition, London, 1862. SE, pl 106 (colour).

1015 GJ.9601

Huntington, James, probably by

1016 Specimen of the 'Huntington Rosette', from a log book of Sanderson & Sons
Circa 1860
Colour print from wood blocks
Given by the WM
E.1773–1934

Ireland, ——, working third quarter of 19th century

This designer appears to be unknown except for the example listed below. A pencil inscription on the back of the mount records that the paper was designed by Ireland and *published by Woollams Marylebone Lane.*

1017 Pattern of arabesques
Third quarter of 19th century
Colour print from wood blocks
53 × 58 cm (portion)
Given by Mr W. D. Dawkins
E.522–1914 neg GJ.9602

1015 GJ.9600

1017

Jackson, John Baptist, 1700 or 1701–1777

Little is known of Jackson's early life in England; he is said to have been a pupil of the wood-engraver, Elisha Kirkhall. He arrived in Paris in 1725, and received advice from the wood-engravers, Vincent Le Sueur and Jean M. Papillon, also employment from the latter. In 1731 he settled in Venice, where he designed a cylinder press. He returned to England in 1745 and worked for a calico firm for some years. In 1752 he set up as a wallpaper printer in chiaroscuro at Battersea, and in 1754 published *An Essay On the Invention of Engraving and Printing in Chiaroscuro.* In spite of his original style and methods, Jackson failed in competition with the London manufacturers, and by 1755 he was out of business as a producer of wallpaper. His subsequent career is obscure, though in 1761 he was at Salisbury making a drawing of the cathedral for a bookseller, Edward Eaton. The wood-engraver Thomas Bewick recalled meeting Jackson in Newcastle, implying that he lived there for a time, and that he died in an asylum 'at some place on the border near Teviot, or on Tweedside.' See Introduction, pp 22–7; also J. Kainen, *John Baptist Jackson: 18th-Century Master of the Color Woodcut*, Smithsonian Institution Bulletin No.222, Washington, D.C., 1962.

1018 Panel with an heroic landscape with fisherman, cows and horsemen
After Marco Ricci
1744
Chiaroscuro wood engraving
42.6 × 59.6 cm
E.2696–1920 CT 7798 (see col pl, p 333)

E. Donnell, 'The Van Rensselaer Wall Paper and J. B. Jackson', *Metropolitan Museum Studies* (1932), vol 4, pt 1, p 77; J. Kainen (see under biography, above), nos 40, 43 and pls 40, 43.

1019 Panel with an heroic landscape, with watering place, riders and obelisk
After Marco Ricci
1744
Chiaroscuro wood engraving
42.6 × 59.6 cm
E.2695–1920 neg 55910

See note below above item.

1020 Album containing drawings of flowers, foliage, details of ornament, proofs etc, used by the artist as working material for his wallpaper designs: 52 sheets, together with an engraved title-

1019

page by Jackson, an engraving by Bonneau, and 3 anonymous engravings of plant forms; several signed *J:B:J.*, inscribed with notes and dated from 1740 to 1753; the title-page dated 1738
Pen and ink, pencil and watercolour
49.5 × 31.7 cm (size of volume)
E.4486–4542–1920; E.4486 neg R.506; E.4487 neg R.504 CT 7448 (see col pl, p 333)

According to Kainen (see under biography, above) the collection is the work of Jackson's studio, rather than his own work. The title-page was designed for *Gajo Suetenio tranquillo, le vite de'dodici Cesari* (1738), Piacentini, Venice (Kainen, plate facing p 35).

Jacques, Faith. See PATTERN BOOKS, no 720.

Jaffe, Frank. See PATTERN BOOKS, no 707.

1020 R.506

1020 R.504

James, Virginia. See PATTERN BOOKS, no 707.

Johansson, Mona. See PATTERN BOOKS, no 735.

Johnston, Alan. See PATTERN BOOKS, no 723.

Joiner, Leon. See PATTERN BOOKS, nos 718, 720(2).

Jones, Clare Hartley. See PATTERN BOOKS, no 721(2).

Jones, Malcolm. See PATTERN BOOKS, no 716.

Jones, Owen, 1809–74

Designer, writer and architect, he was educated at the Academy Schools. He toured the Middle East and Spain in 1833 and 1834. He published *Plans, Sections and Details of the Alhambra* in 1842. He was appointed Superintendant of the Works of the Great Exhibition in 1851, and in 1852 joint Director of Decoration of the Crystal Palace. When this building was removed to Sydenham he designed the Egyptian, Greek, Roman and Alhambra Courts. In 1856 he published (with Sir Matthew Digby Wyatt) *Grammar of Ornament*. He advocated formality of design in wallpapers and textiles, which influenced his contemporaries.

1021 Portion with a conventionalized foliate pattern
Produced by Townsend, Parker & Co.
1850
Green flock
73.8 × 53.4 cm
PROVENANCE The stock of W. B. Simpson, 456, W. Strand
E.164–1934

1022 Ten pattern books
Some produced by John Trumble, some by Jeffrey & Co. and some by Townsend, Parker & Co.
Circa 1852–74
Colour prints from wood blocks, flock
Various sizes
8335.1–91
8336.1–132
8337.1–184
8338.1–109 (8338.65, Townsend, Parker & Townsend, 1852)
8339.1–178
8340.1–94
8341.1158 (8341.50, J. Townsend & Co., 1858)
8342.1–181
8343.1–162
8344.1–56 (8344.33, Jeffrey & Co., 1860)
Given by Miss Catherine Jones, daughter of the artist
8344.27 neg L.1943; 8344.43 neg L.1944; 8342.56 neg Y.1385; 8342.77 neg Y.1386; 8338.65 neg Y.1387; 8336.71 neg GJ.9603; 8336.106 neg GJ.9604; 8342.78 neg GJ.9605; 8344.27 neg GJ.9606; 8343.44 neg GJ.9607; 8342.41 neg GJ.9608; D.762–1897 neg GD.2232 CT 7449 (see col pl); D.809–1897 neg GD.2256; D.810–1897 neg GD.2257; D.756–1897 neg GD.2287.

Designs for many of the patterns are D.732–736–1897. 8342.87 is reproduced in *Building News*, 8 June 1858; 8344.43 is reproduced in *Building News*, 8 May

1022 L.1943

1022 L.1944

1022 Y.1385

1022 Y.1386

1022 GJ.9607

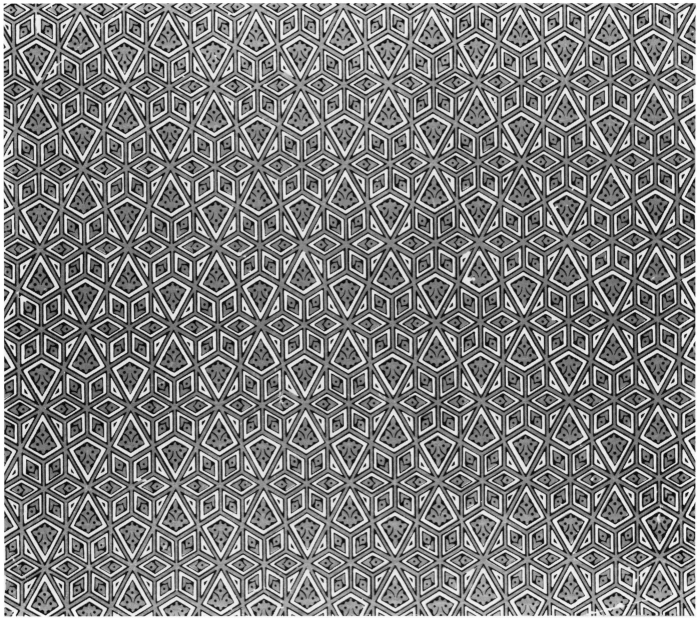

1874; 8344.27, Entwisle, *V*, pl 23, fig 41; 8344.43, Entwisle, V, pl 23, fig 40; Greysmith, pl 97.

1023 Portion of a border with acorns and leaves arranged in triangles
Produced by Jeffrey & Co.
Circa 1872
Colour print from wood blocks
14 × 41.3 cm
Given by the WM
E.1888–1934

Building News (1872), vol XXIII, p 289 (E).

Jones, Peter. See PATTERN BOOKS, no 721(2).

1022 GJ.9606

1022 GJ.9605

1022 GD.2257

1022 GD.2287

1022 GJ.9608

1022 GD.2256

1022 GJ.9603

Jones, Robert, worked first quarter of 19th century

Designer of furniture, mural painter and decorator, who collaborated with Frederick Crace in the work on the interior of the Royal Pavilion, Brighton.

1024 Two portions, each consisting of 2 sheets joined, with designs of dragons and exotic flowers; on paper watermarked *1820* and stamped on the back with the Excise duty stamps and *First Account Taken 208*
Probably produced by Crace & Sons
Prints from wood blocks in yellow and white
50.8 × 60.3 cm
PROVENANCE The Royal Pavilion, Brighton
Given by the Brighton Corporation
E.9847, 9848–1958; E.9848 neg GJ.9609

These wallpapers and those listed under nos 1025–1027 were intended for rooms on the upper floor of the Pavilion, which include the Duke of York's and the Duke of Clarence's bedrooms and the lobbies of them, all on the east side, the King's old bedroom on the south-east and the west bedrooms. See also ANONYMOUS WALLPAPERS AND WALLPAPER DESIGNS, no 185. Another portion in a red colourway is Circ.4–1959 neg GJ.9610.

1022 GJ.9604

Jones, Robert, possibly by

1025 Six portions of borders with bamboo designs; E.9839, 9842, 9843 stamped on the back with the Excise duty stamps
Probably produced by Crace & Sons
1820
Colour prints from wood blocks
Various sizes
PROVENANCE The Royal Pavilion, Brighton
Given by the Brighton Corporation
E.9839–9844–1958; E.9839 neg GJ.9611; E.9840 neg GJ.230; E.9842 neg GJ.9612

These wallpapers and E.9845–9850–1958 were intended for rooms on the upper floor of the Pavilion, which include the Duke of York's and the Duke of Clarence's bedrooms and the lobbies to them, all on the east side, the King's old bedroom on the south-east and the west bedrooms. Another piece of the bamboo trellis design (E.9840) is Circ.2–1959, and another piece of the vertical bamboo design (E.9841) is Circ.3–1959, which is stamped on the back with the *First Account Taken* duty stamp and number *220*.

Design showing monoplanes and clouds, by Raymond McGrath, *circa* 1933 (no 1047)

1024 Circ. 4–1959

1024 GJ.9609

1026 Portion, consisting of 2 sheets joined, of border with a bamboo design; stamped on the back with Excise duty stamp and *First Account Taken 208*.
Probably produced by Crace & Sons
1820
Colour print from wood blocks
69.2 × 57.4 cm
PROVENANCE The Royal Pavilion, Brighton
Given by the Brighton Corporation
E.9846–1958 neg GJ.9613

1027 Two portions, 1 consisting of 2 sheets joined, of dado with a chinoiserie fretwork design
E.9850 stamped on the back with the Excise duty stamp and *First Account Taken 208*
Probably produced by Crace & Sons
1820
Colour print from wood blocks
34.2 × 60; 59 × 62.2 cm
PROVENANCE The Royal Pavilion, Brighton
Given by the Brighton Corporation
E.9849, 9850–1958; E.9849 neg GJ.9614
CT 8492

E.9850 is a dado for the paper with a dragon design (no 1024).

(*opposite*) Swirling leaf design, by Arthur H. Mackmurdo, produced by Jeffrey & Co., *circa* 1884 (no 1050)

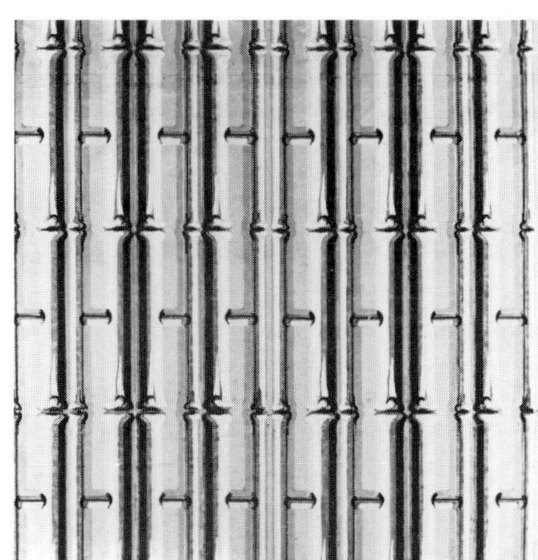
1025 GJ.9611

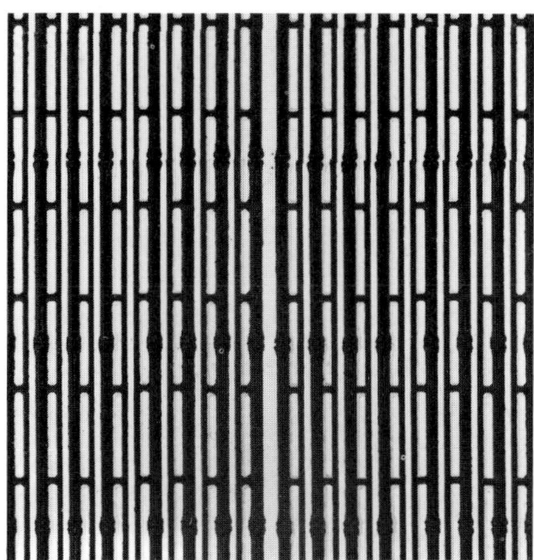
1025 GJ.9612

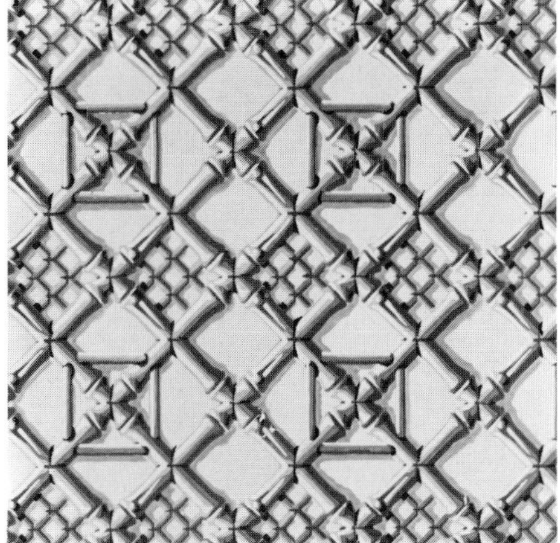
1025 GJ.230

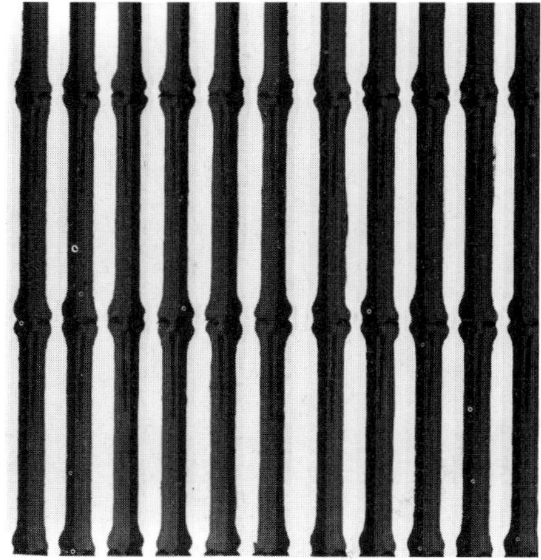
1025 GJ.9613

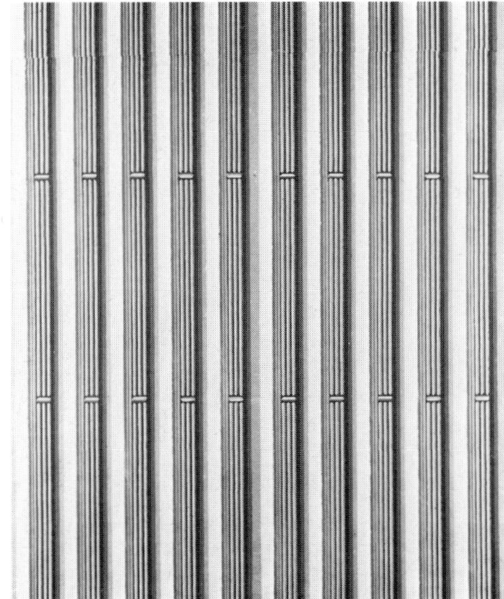
1026

1028

Jones-Richards, Philippa. See PATTERN BOOKS, no 725(3).

Karlby, Bent, b. 1912

Danish designer who exhibited hand-printed textiles, produced for Dahls Tapetfabrik, Copenhagen, at the exhibition 'Deense Schilderkunst', held at The Hague Gemeentemuseum in 1948.

1028 'Haelderne'
Produced by Dahls Tapetfabrik, Copenhagen
1951
Colour print from wood blocks
57.5 × 46.5 cm (portion)
Given by Dahls Tapetfabrik
E.897–1979 neg GJ.9469

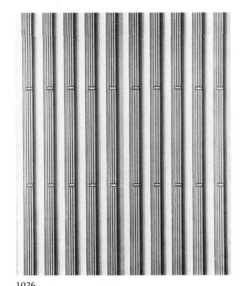

1029 'Flora Danika'
Produced by Dahls Tapetfabrik, Copenhagen
1951
Colour print from wood blocks
56.8 × 47 cm (portion)
Given by Arthur Sanderson & Sons Ltd
E.570–1966 neg GJ.9470

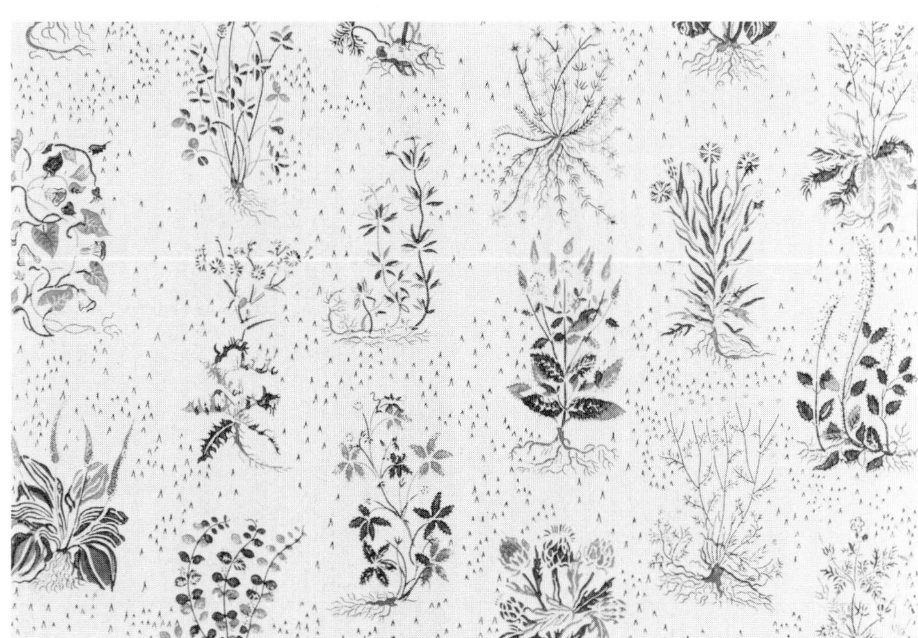
1029

1030 'Expansion'
Produced by Dahls Tapetfabrik, Copenhagen
1956
Colour machine print
57.5 × 47 cm
Given by Dahls Tapetfabrik
E.896–1979 neg GJ.9471

Kingbourne, G. See PATTERN BOOKS, nos 707(2), 713.

Kingman, ——, ? working second half of 19th century

Probably the same as George Kingman (worked second half of 19th century), a volume of whose designs for carpets is E.544–1956. Kingman attended the R.C.A. Schools.

1031 Five portions with stylized flower-and-leaf motifs within trellises, and heptagonal and triangular shapes
Produced by Corbière Son and Brindle
Circa 1868
Colour prints from wood blocks
Various sizes
Given by Corbière Son and Brindle
E.1105B, 1106B, 1115B, 1116B, 1117B–1868; E.1105B neg GJ.9615

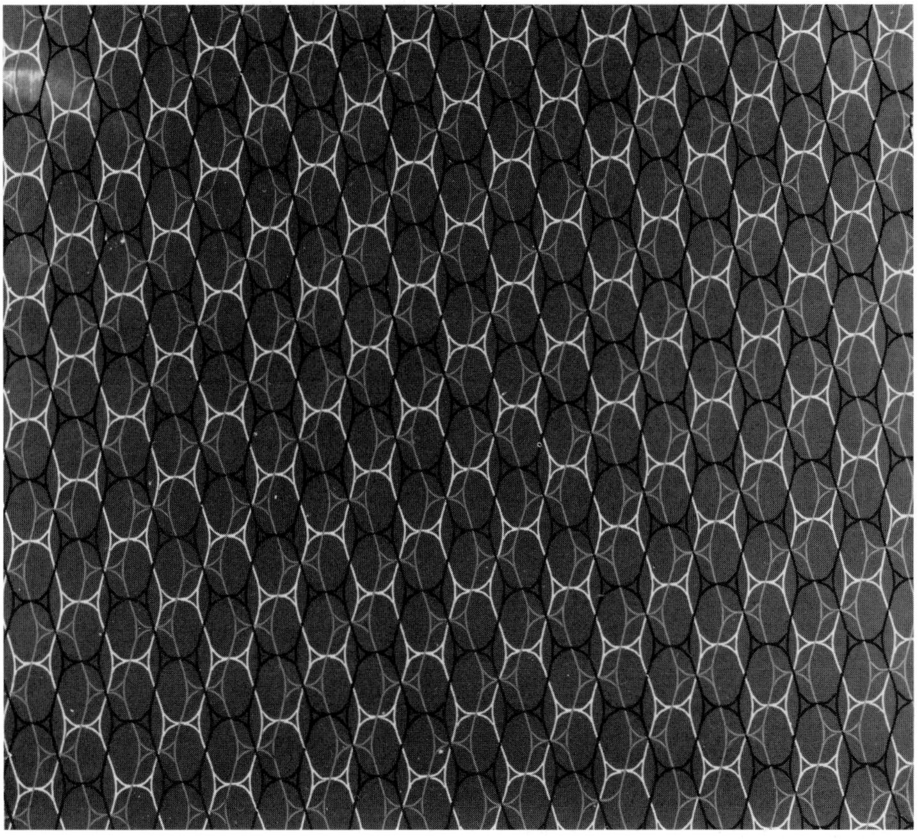

1030

1032 'Neue Form'
Produced by Marburger Tapetenfabrik
J. B. Schaefer
1956–57
Machine print, white on grey
E.894–1979 neg GJ.10384

Olligs, plate on p 334.

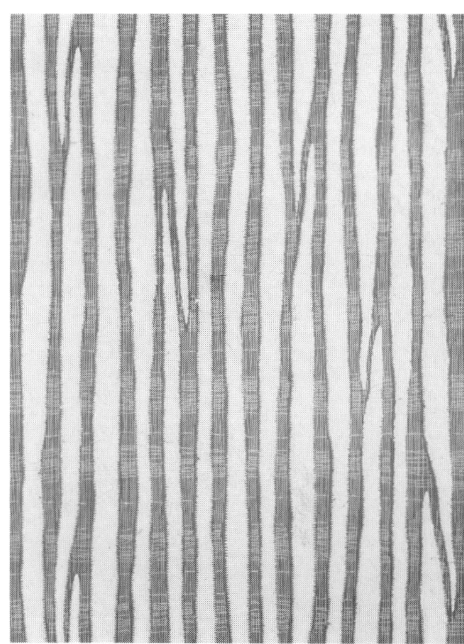

1032

Klevert, Ulla. See PATTERN BOOKS, no 735.

Knight, Brian. See PATTERN BOOKS, no 721.

Knowles, Reginald L. See PATTERN BOOKS, no 704 (note).

Kock, Claes. See PATTERN BOOKS, no 734.

Krauer, Walter. See PATTERN BOOKS, no 707(2).

Kupferoth, Elsbeth, b. 1920

German designer of textiles and wallpapers. Worked in Maria May's (q.v.) fashion house. Living in Munich.

1031

Kydd, William Shand, 1864–1936

He joined Hayward & Son in about 1881. In 1890 he set up business on his own in a house in the Marylebone Road. Here he designed and cut stencils and blocks to print decorative friezes of bold design, and these were bought by Liberty's, Warings, Maples and other firms. In 1896, to cope with the expansion of work, Shand Kydd moved to a factory in Seaton Steet. In 1906 fresh premises were needed and the firm was moved to Highgate Road, Kentish Town, where machine production was introduced, and by 1930, 95 per cent of production was done by machinery. Until recent years the firm, which was incorporated into the WM, was situated at Christchurch, Hampshire. Shand Kydd Ltd was closed down in 1980.

1033 Six portions of papers and friezes
Produced by Shand Kydd Ltd
1895–1905
Stencil
Various sizes
E.1524–1528, 1534–1954; E.1524 neg GJ.9616 CT 8485; E.1527 neg GJ.9617; E.1528 neg GJ.9618

E.1524 ('Ravenna'), E.1525 ('The Arum') and E.1528 ('The Atmy') were exhibited in *Victorian and Edwardian Decorative Arts*, VAM, 1952 (SE, pl 195). Three other samples of 'Ravenna' in different colourways are E.1040–1042–1970. E.1526 ('Lytham') is an embossed paper; E.1527 ('Roma') is a frieze printed on Japanese grass-paper. 'Atmy' and 'Ravenna' were first produced in 1896.

1034 'Sherland': frieze with a design of rose bushes in the art nouveau style
Produced by Shand Kydd Ltd
1905
Colour print from wood blocks and stencil, on canvas
91.5 × 195.7 cm
E.1055–1970

Exhibited in *Exhibition of Historical & British Wallpapers*, Suffolk Galleries, London, May 1945, no 133. A portion of this design, printed on paper, is E.1534–1954 neg GJ.9619.

1035 'Carlton' frieze; inscribed in pencil on the back with title etc and numbered *6491*
Produced by Shand Kydd Ltd
1905
Colour print from wood block and stencil, on Japanese grass-paper
37.5 × 56.5 cm (portion)
E.1045–1970 neg GJ.9620

1033 GJ.9616

1033 GJ.9618

1033 GJ.9617

1034 E.1534–1954

1037 GJ.9621

1035

1036 Two portions, joined, of 'Orwell'; mounted on linen; inscribed in pencil on the back with title etc and numbered *5*
Produced by Shand Kydd Ltd
Colour print from wood block and stencil
129.4 × 104.8 cm
E.1047–1970

The above 4 items, nos 1033–1036, were given by Shand Kydd Ltd

---

Kydd, William Shand, probably by

1037 Five specimens of papers and friezes
Produced by Shand Kydd Ltd
Circa 1905
Stencil
Various sizes
Given by Shand Kydd Ltd
E.1529–1533–1954

Frieze of formalized roses and vine (E.1529); 'Gayton' (E.1530 neg GJ.9621); 'Eltham' (E.1531 CT 7450; see col pl, p 334); 'Allendale' (E.1532 neg GJ.9622); 'Regent' (E.1533)

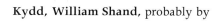

Kydd, William Shand, attributed to

1038 Portion of 'Romney'
Produced by Shand Kydd Ltd
1911
Colour machine print
64.8 × 55.9 cm
E.2777–1914

1039 Portion of 'Framley'
Produced by Shand Kydd Ltd
Circa 1911
Colour machine print
E.2776–1914

The above 2 items, nos 1038, 1039, were given by Mr Henry Butler

---

Lafitte, Louis, 1770–1828, and Méry-Joseph Blondel, 1781–1853

Lafitte was a history painter and designer; Blondel, a history painter.

1037 GJ.9622

1040

1040 'Psyché au Bain': 4 panels from the scenic paper illustrating the story of Cupid and Psyche (from La Fontaine's *Les Amours de Psyché*, 1669); lettered *Psyche au Bain. en 4 les* and numbered 5–8
First produced in 26 lengths by Dufour et Cie
1816
Print in grisaille from wood blocks
152.5 × 57.2 cm (each)
E.695–698–1937 neg 78276

Seven scenes from the series are in the Whitworth Art Gallery, Manchester, W.174, 175–1967. Clouzot, II, pls X–XIV.

Lamm, Birgitta. See PATTERN BOOKS, no 735.

Lantz, Anne-Lie. See PATTERN BOOKS, no 735.

'Lees'. See PATTERN BOOKS, no 707.

Lehmann, Olga. See PATTERN BOOKS, nos 707, 710.

Leschke, Paul, working early 1900s

1041 'Sanitary' damask, with a conventional floral design in brown on a red ground
Produced by Lightbown, Aspinall & Co.
1903
Colour print from 3 engraved rollers
43.1 × 50.3 cm (portion)
Given by the WM
E.1902–1934 neg GJ.9350

The second engraved 'sanitary' damask produced by the firm. See SE, pl 172.

Lever, Arnold, working early 1950s

See also PATTERN BOOKS, nos 707, 710(2).

1042 'Orpheus'
Produced by John Line & Sons Ltd for their series 'Limited Editions 1951'
Screen print

1041

1042

74.7 × 54.5 cm (portion)
Given by John Line & Sons Ltd
E.882–1978 neg GJ.9371

See *Design* (1951), vol III, no 36, plate on p 10.

Levy, Audrey, working 1950s

Textile, wallpaper and interior designer, she attended Nottingham College of Arts and Crafts, then studied textile design at the Royal College of Art. In 1951 she left and worked for 3 years as a consultant designing dress prints for wholesale dress firms. She has also designed pottery for T. G. Green & Co Ltd.

1043 'Tracery'
Produced by the WM as one of their 'Palladio' range of 'Crown' wallpapers
1956
Colour screen print
101.5 × 55.7 cm (portion)
Given by the WM
E.968–1978 neg GJ.9623

Design (October 1956), vol VIII, p 20, pl 10.

1043

1044 Roll of 'Phantom Rose'
Produced by the WM as one of their 'Palladio 2' range
1957
Screen print, black on white
671 × 55.5 cm
Circ.296–1963 neg GJ.9624

Design Centre Award, 1958. *Design* (June 1958), vol X, no 114, plate on p 24 (colour).

1044

Leyson, Beatrice V. See PATTERN BOOKS, no 707.

Linx Co. See PATTERN BOOKS, no 707.

Litt, Artur. See PATTERN BOOKS, no 707.

Little, Antony, b. 1942

Partner and designer of the firm of Osborne & Little Ltd, founded *circa* 1968, Council of Industrial Design award winners. See also ANONYMOUS WALLPAPERS AND WALLPAPER DESIGNS, nos 529–532.

1045 Four designs for wallpaper
Produced by Osborne & Little Ltd
1968–75
Gouache, poster colour
Various sizes
Given by Osborne & Little Ltd
E.855–858–1978

1045 GJ.9625

Branches with berries and blossom in the Japanese style, 1971 (E.855 neg GJ.9625); 'Koh-i-Noor', 1968 (E.856 neg GJ.9626), reproduced in *Design* (1970), p 48, no 3; trellis and climbing plant, 1975 (E.857 neg GH.1555); 'Jonas Cord', 1968 (E.858 neg GJ.9627), reproduced in *Design* (1970), p 48.

Loosely, Anne. See PATTERN BOOKS, no 707(2).

Luckett, F. See PATTERN BOOKS, nos 718, 720(3).

1045 GH.1555

MacDougall, W. B., ?d. 1936

Possibly William Brown MacDougall (d. 1936), a landscape and figure painter, etcher, wood engraver and illustrator.

1046 Formalized pattern of peacocks in a garden
Produced by Jeffrey & Co.
Circa 1902
Colour machine print
56 × 55 cm (portion)
Given by Miss Mary Peerless
E.469–1967 neg GJ.9351

See *AJ* (1902), plate on p 285.

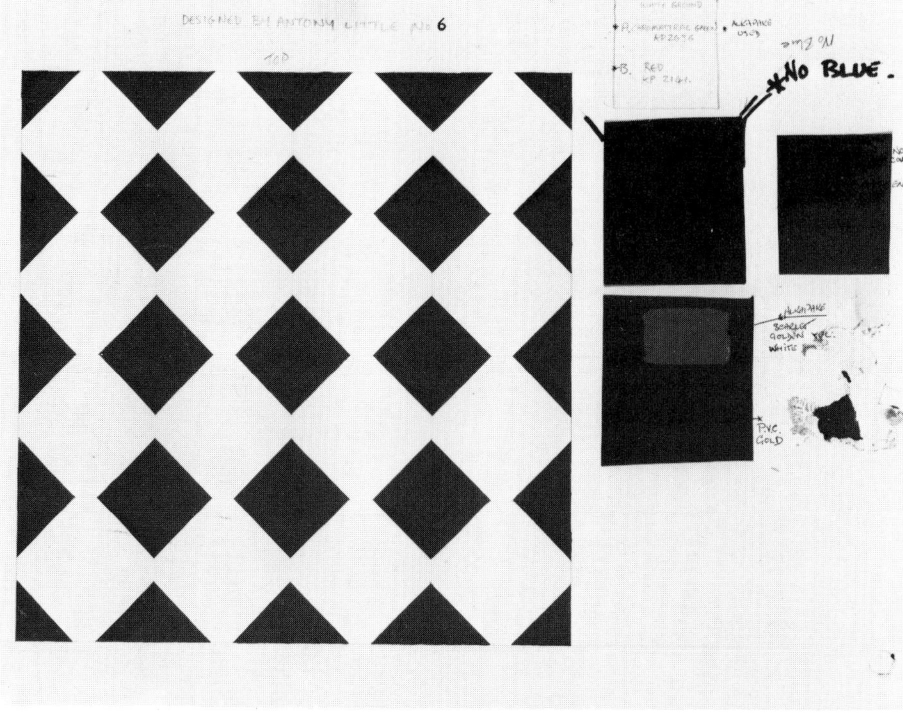

1045 'Koh-i-Noor'

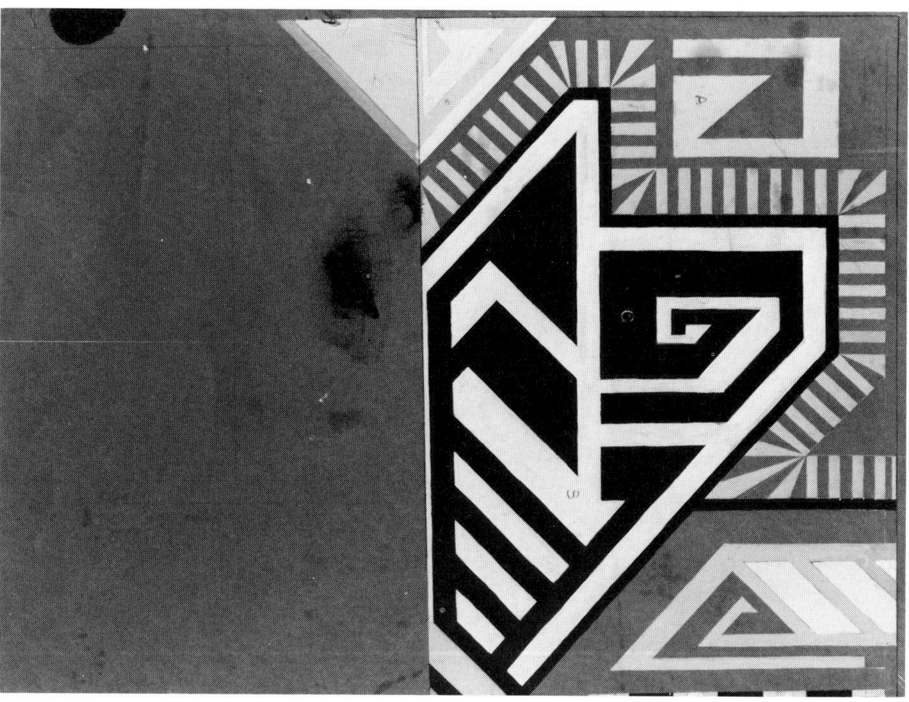

1045 'Jonas Cord'

McGrath, Raymond, 1903–77

Architect and designer.

1047 Design showing monoplanes and clouds
Circa 1933
Gouache
32 × 41.5 cm
Circ.568–1974 neg GK.4717 CT 8583 (see col pl, p 351)

This design might have been intended for the projected house for a woman aviator, 'Rudderbar', which was not built.

(*opposite*) 'Maxwell', by Sidney G. Mawson, produced by Jeffrey & Co., *circa* 1907 (no 1052)

Wallpaper by Albert Moore, 1875
(no 1061)

(*opposite*) 'Trellis', by William Morris,
1862 (no 1065, vol 1)

'Blackthorn', by William Morris, 1892
(no 1065, vol 2)

1046

1049 Design, possibly for a wallpaper, of formalized leaves; lettered within the design with the monogram of the Century Guild *CG*
Circa 1882
Tempera
54 × 75.9 cm
E.1165–1920 neg GJ.9628

See no 1048 (note): no 64

1050 Vertical swirling leaf design
Produced by Jeffrey & Co. for the Century Guild
Circa 1884
Colour print from wood blocks
74.5 × 53.7 cm (portion)
E.888–1979 neg FD.51 CT 8746 (see col pl, p 352)

Greysmith, pl 118.

See no 1048 (note): no 65.

McNish, Althea. See PATTERN BOOKS, no 719.

Markes, Sally. See PATTERN BOOKS, no 720.

Martin, Joe, working early 1950s

American designer.

Mackmurdo, Arthur Heygate, 1851–1942

Architect, designer and currency reformer, he attended Ruskin's lectures and travelled to Italy with him *circa* 1874. He established the Century Guild in 1882 and its magazine *Hobby Horse* in 1884. He abandoned architecture after *circa* 1904 and devoted himself to the study of economics and social and currency reforms.

1048 Design of birds and plants for a wall decoration; lettered within the design with the monogram of the Century Guild *CG*
Circa 1882
Tempera
47.3 × 127.7 cm
E.1164–1920

Arts Council exhibition, *Art Nouveau in Britain*, 1965, catalogue illustration (63).

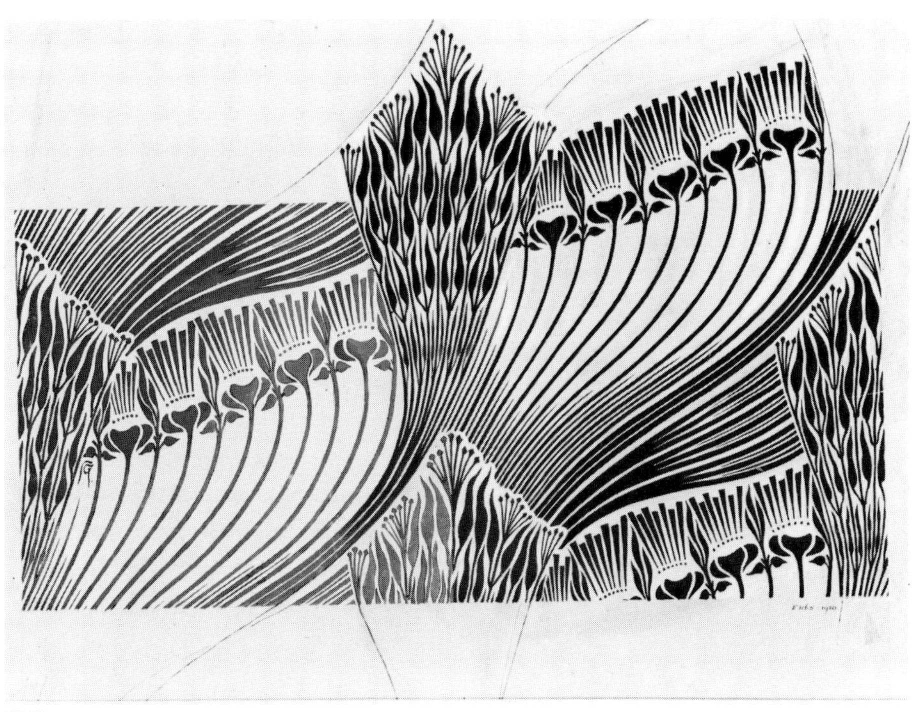

1049

1051

1051 'Coffee and Tea'
Produced by Harben Papers, New York
1953
Colour screen print
53.4 × 74.7 cm (portion)
Given by Herndon Papers Inc.
E.571–1966 neg GJ.9466

Mawson, Sidney G., working from *circa* 1882, d. 1941

Landscape painter and lecturer in textile design at the Slade School. Designer of textiles and wallpaper.

1052 'Maxwell'
Produced by Jeffrey & Co.
Circa 1907
Colour machine print
53.3 × 110.4 cm (portion)
E.1779–1914 neg GJ.9629 CT 7333 (see col pl, p 361)

Cabinet Maker & Complete House Furnisher (April 1907), plate on p 69.

1054

1053

1053 'Locksley' (or 'Rose and Trellis')
Produced by Jeffrey & Co.
Circa 1907
Colour print from wood blocks
88.3 × 51.4 cm (portion)
Given by the WM
E.1904–1934 neg GJ.9630

Studio Year Book of Decorative Art (1907), plate on p 127.

May, Maria, b. 1900

Born in Berlin where she lives now, she studied at the Staatliche Kunstschule there. She has designed wall paintings, mosaics, textiles and posters.

1054 'Christliche Seefahrt'
Produced by Rasch & Co., Bramsche, Germany
Circa 1955
Machine print, white on red
267.5 × 53.9 cm (length)
Given by Dr Emil Rasch
E.969–1978 neg GJ.10023

Melbourne, Donald, b. 1921

Design director of Shand Kydd Ltd, for whom he worked since leaving school. See also PATTERN BOOKS, nos 710, 715(8), 716, 717, 718(4), 720(4).

1055 Design for 'Areca', for the pattern book, *Focus 2*; inscribed with title, colour notes etc; a label with a description of the job affixed
Produced by Shand Kydd Ltd
Artwork and 2 samples of the wallpaper
1966–67
Coloured inks and rotagravure
72.5 × 54.7 cm (size of sheet);
42 × 53.9 cm (each wallpaper)
Given by the artist
E.2037–2039–1980

1056 Design for 'Amala', for the pattern book *Focus 2*; inscribed with title, colour key, measurements etc; a label with a description of the job affixed
Produced by Shand Kydd Ltd
1966–67
Artwork and 2 samples of the wallpaper
Coloured inks, some pencil on card and rotagravure
82 × 56.5 cm (size of sheet)
Given by the artist
E.2040–2042–1980

1057

Méry, Alfred Emile, 1824–96, and possibly other artists

Méry, a French designer, was a painter of interiors, animals, still life and genre.

1057 Fifteen designs for wallpapers with formalized floral patterns; E.1726 inscribed on the back *Méry*
Second half of 19th century
Watercolour and body colour
Various sizes
Given by Mr J. D. Crace
E.1713–1727–1912; E.1719, 1722, 1723, 1725, 1727 neg GJ.9631

Midgley, Veronica. See PATTERN BOOKS, nos 716, 717.

Minns, Bianca. See PATTERN BOOKS, nos 707, 710.

Minton, (Francis) John, M.S.I.A., 1917–57

Painter, illustrator, mural and poster artist, and designer of textiles and stage sets. See also PATTERN BOOKS, nos 707(3), 710(2).

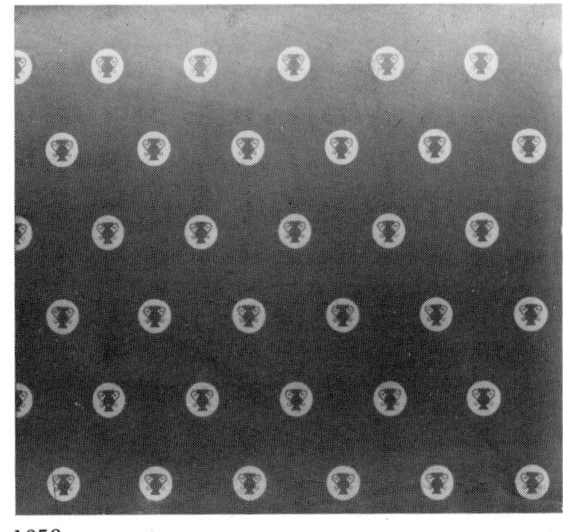

1058

1058 Two portions of 'Tuscany' and 'Troy', matching it
Produced by John Line & Sons Ltd in their series 'Limited Editions'
1951
Colour screen prints
73.3 × 54.6 cm; 48 × 56.2 cm
E.572, 572A–1966; E.572 neg GG.5874; E.572A neg GJ.9632

Design (December 1951), vol 3, no 36, plate on p 11 (colour); N. Carrington, *Design and Decoration in the Home* (1952), plate III (colour).

1058

1059 'Arcadia'; lettered with manufacturer's name etc
Produced by John Line & Sons Ltd
1951
Colour screen print
74.5 × 54.5 cm (portion)
E.883–1978 neg GJ.9633

Not to be confused with a wallpaper with the same title designed by Cliff Holden for the 'Palladio 6' series, produced by Arthur Sanderson & Sons Ltd, 1963 (*Design* (1963), no 170, pl 15).

The above 2 items, nos 1058, 1059, were given by John Line & Sons Ltd.

1060 Ten designs for wallpapers with various classical and floral motifs, for Shand Kydd Ltd
Circa 1956
Poster colours, and some pencil; E.1273 a photostat
Various sizes
Given by Shand Kydd Ltd
E.1264–1273–1980

These designs were not used by the manufacturer.

Möller, Tage. See PATTERN BOOKS, no 735(4).

Mondial Designs. See PATTERN BOOKS, no 715.

Moore, Albert Joseph, A.R.W.S., 1841–93

Painter of classical and emblematical subjects who entered the Royal Academy Schools in 1857, and went to Rome in 1859. He was elected A.R.W.S. in 1884. Jeffrey & Co. produced 2 wallpapers designed by him, 'The Yewberry' and 'The Bulb'.

1059

1061 Flowers and foliage in red, green and yellow, and biscuit, on a cream ground
Produced by Jeffrey & Co.
1875
Colour print from wood blocks
26 × 37.2 cm (portion)
Given by the WM
E.1905–1934 neg GJ.9634 CT 7334 (see col pl, p 362)

Moore, Brian, working 1960s

See also PATTERN BOOKS, no 714.

1062 Design for foam vinyl wallpaper, 'Arts and Crafts'; inscribed with title, colour key, measurements etc
Produced by Shand Kydd Ltd
Post 1964
Indian ink on board and poster colours on tracing paper
71 × 54.7 cm (size of sheet)
E.2727–1980

1063 Two samples, on one mount, of 'Arts and Crafts', showing different colourways; inscribed on the mount with title etc
Embossed foam vinyl
52 × 32 cm (size of sheet)
E.2728, 2729–1980; E.2728 neg HA.400

The above 2 items, nos 1062, 1063, were given by Shand Kydd Ltd

---

Morgan, Joyce E. See PATTERN BOOKS, no 707.

Morley, Mrs L. H., ? working 1897–1907

1063

1064

Possibly Mrs Ida Morley, the landscape painter, who exhibited between 1897 and 1907.

1064 Baroque flowers on vertical scrolling stems, on a black background
Produced by John Line & Sons Ltd
1907
Colour machine print
136.5 × 53 cm (portion)
Given by Mr H. Butler
E.2768–1914 neg GJ.9635

Morris, Mary (May), 1862–1938

Designer and embroideress, daughter of William Morris, by whom she was trained. She designed textiles and wallpapers for Morris & Co., and took over the embroidery section of the firm in 1885. In 1910 she lectured in England and in the U.S.A. on embroidery, jewellery, costume and pattern designing. She was one of the founders of the Women's Guild of Arts, 1907, and for some time its chairman. She designed 'Honeysuckle' (1883, see no 1065); 'Horn Poppy' (1885, see no 1066) and 'Arcadia' (*circa* 1886, see no 1065).

Morris, William, 1834–96

Designer, craftsman, poet and socialist. He founded the firm of Morris, Marshall & Faulkner in 1861. His first wallpaper to be issued ('Daisy', 1864) was printed by Jeffrey & Co., who continued to print the Morris designs until 1930, when they closed down. The work was carried on by Arthur Sanderson & Sons Ltd, who bought the blocks when Morris & Co. went into voluntary liquidation in 1940. See Aymer Vallance, *The Art of William Morris. A Record* (1897); Peter Floud, 'The Wallpaper Designs of William Morris', *The Penrose Annual* (1960), vol 54, also 'Dating Morris Patterns', *Archaelogical Review* (1959), vol 126; Fiona Clark, *William Morris Wallpapers and Chintzes* (New York, 1973). These publications are cited below as AV, PFF, PFAR and FC respectively. See also no 771.

1065 Two pattern books, containing patterns (25 and 27, on 168 sheets, including different colourways); each inscribed on the back in ink with title, number and price
1862–96
68.5 × 53.3 cm (size of each volume)
Given by Morris & Co.
E.441–608–1919

These are the original patterns as kept together by William Morris. The numbers after the names of the patterns are taken from Morris & Co.'s log books.

Volume 1 (1862–81)
'Daisy', 1862, produced 1864 (E.441–444; E.3718–1927). The second paper Morris designed, but the first to be issued. AV, pl 4 (colour); SE, pl 110 (colour); FC, no 1.

1065 'Acanthus', R.01

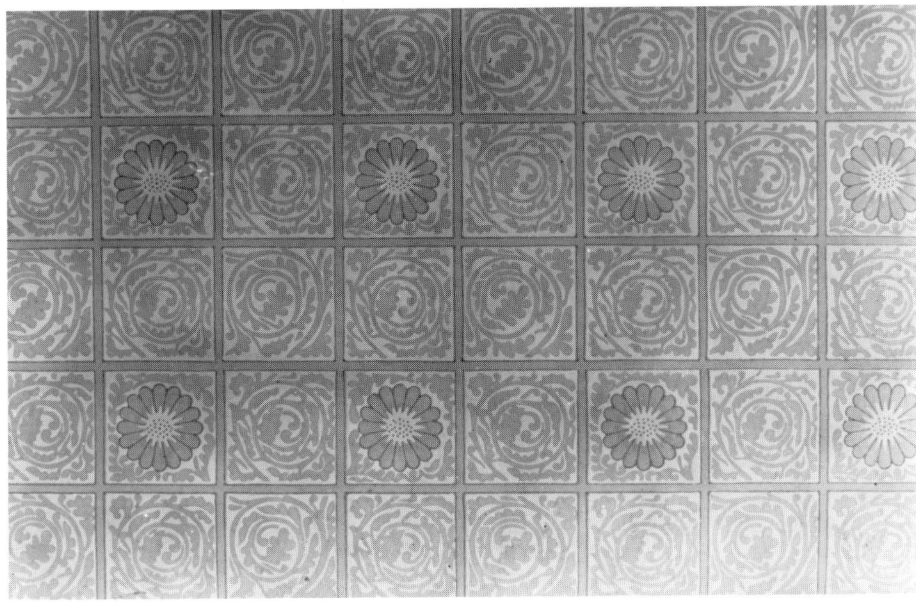
1065 'Diaper'

1065 'Scroll'

1065 'Branch'

'Fruit' (or 'Pomegranate'), 1862, produced 1864 (E.445–449). The second paper to be issued. SE, pl 11 (colour); FC, no 2. Another portion is Circ.248–1964.

'Trellis', November 1862, produced 1864 (E.450–453 CT 4206 (see col pl, p 363). The first paper Morris designed, but the third to be issued. The birds were designed by Phillip Webb. AV, pl 4 (colour); SE, pl 109 (colour); FC, no 3. Another portion is Circ.247–1964.

'Diaper', *circa* 1870 (E.454–462 neg S.1630). FC, no 6.

'Scroll', *circa* 1872 (E.463–465; E.3698–1927). FC, no 9. Other portions are E.3470–1913; Circ.279–1959 neg GJ.9637.

'Branch', *circa* 1872 (E.467). Underlay of 'Scroll'. FC, no 10. Another portion is Circ.274–1959 neg GJ.9638.

'Larkspur', 1874 (E.468–474; E.476 neg M.8). Also produced in monochrome, and as a chintz and a woven silk. PFP, pl 6 (colour); FC, no 11. E.778–1915 (see no 1066) neg L.1958.

'Jasmine', 1872 (E.475–477 neg M.86). PFP, pl 1 (colour); FC, no 12. Another portion is Circ.23–1954.

'Marigold', 1875 (E.478–483). AV, pl 6 (colour); FC, no 16. Another portion is Circ.275–1959.

'Lily', 1873 (E.484 neg Q.1715). FC, no 13. Another portion is Circ.276–1959.

'Vine', 1873 (E.485, 486). AV, pl 7 (colour); FC, no 14. E.485–1914 neg GE.2074.

'Powdered', 1874 (E.487 neg M.10). PFP, pl 5; FC, no 15. Another portion is Circ.277–1959.

'Willow', 1874 (E.488–493). PFAR, pl 16; FC, no 17. Another portion is Circ.285–1959 neg S.1629.

'Acanthus', 1875 (E.494–496). AV, pl 8 (colour); SE, pl 112 (colour); FC, no 18. The pencil and watercolour design for this paper is Circ.297–1955 neg R.01. Other portions are Circ.24–1954; Circ.281–1959 CT 8743 (see col pl, p 389; Circ.24–1954 neg M. 1791.

'Pimpernel', 1876 (E.497–499; E.497 neg 56526). Greysmith, pl 22 (colour); FC, no 19. Other portions are Circ.280–1959; Circ.249–1964.

'Wreath', 1876 (E.500, 501; E.500 neg M.11). PFP, pl 8; FC, no 51.

'Rose', 1877 (E.502, 503; E.503 neg M.12). FC, no 21.

'Chrysanthemum', 1877 (E.504, 505; E.2173–1889). PFP, pl 9; Greysmith, pl 100; FC, no 22. Other portions are E.350–1972; E.802–1915 (see no 1066) neg L.1959.

'Apple', 1877 (E.506–508; E.506 neg M.13). AV, pl 9 (colour); FC, no 23.

'Bower', 1877 (E.509 neg Q.1720). FC, no 24. For a sample of this pattern see

1065 'Larkspur'

1065 'Vine'

1065 'Acanthus'

1065 'Jasmine'

1065 'Powdered'

1065 'Pimpernel'

1065 'Lily'

1065 'Willow'

1065 'Wreath'

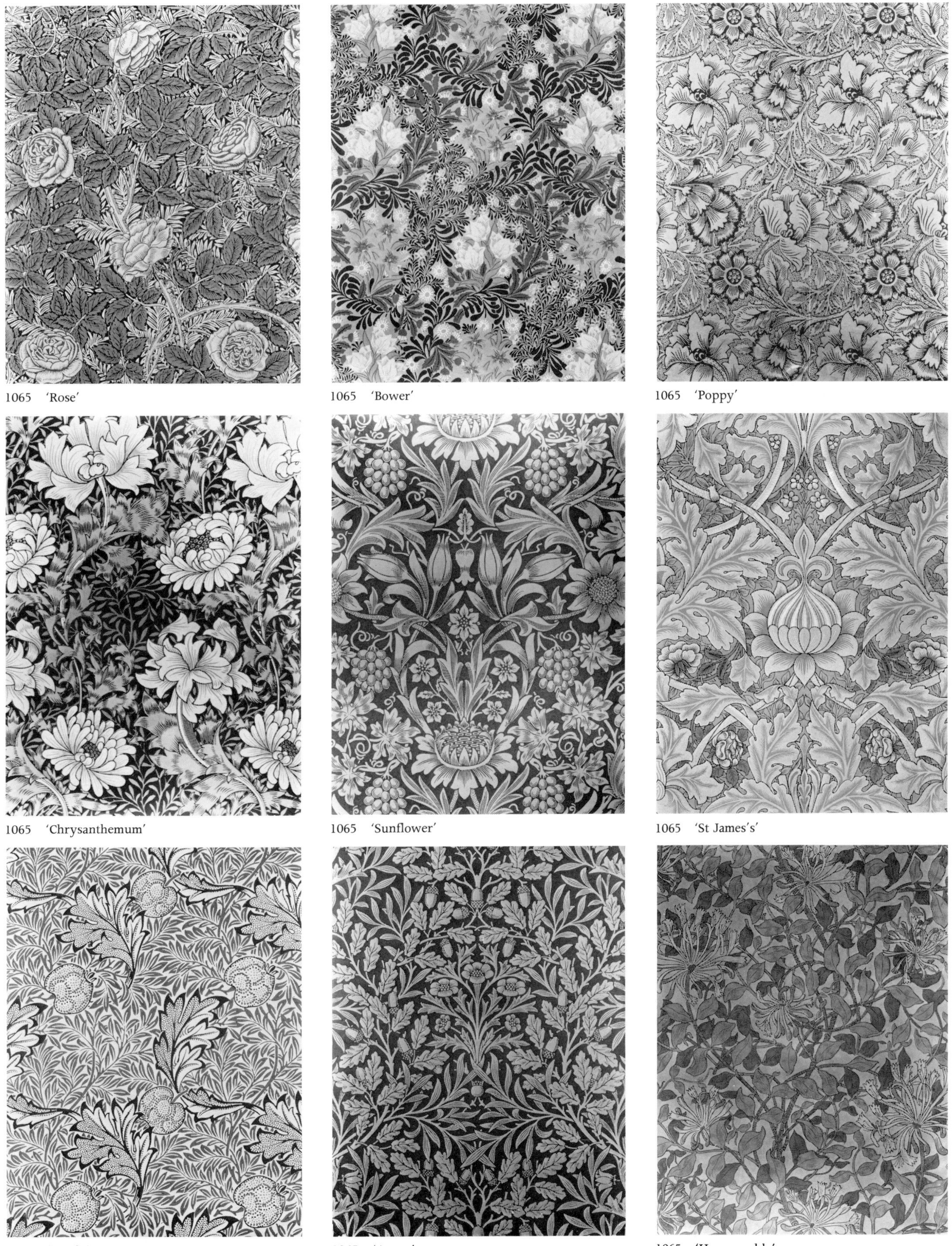

1065 'Rose'

1065 'Bower'

1065 'Poppy'

1065 'Chrysanthemum'

1065 'Sunflower'

1065 'St James's'

1065 'Apple'

1065 'Acorn'

1065 'Honeysuckle'

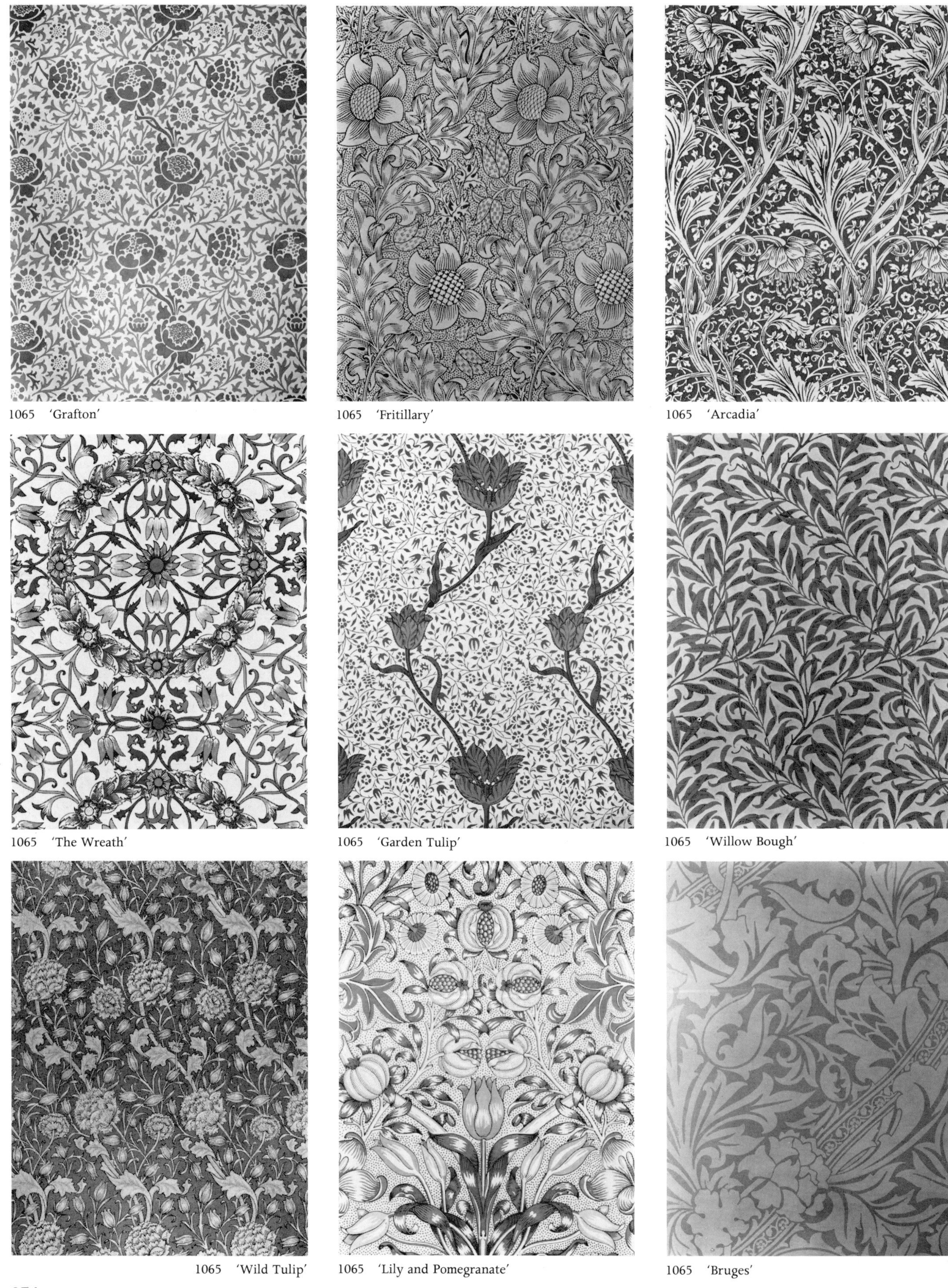

1065 'Grafton'

1065 'Fritillary'

1065 'Arcadia'

1065 'The Wreath'

1065 'Garden Tulip'

1065 'Willow Bough'

1065 'Wild Tulip'

1065 'Lily and Pomegranate'

1065 'Bruges'

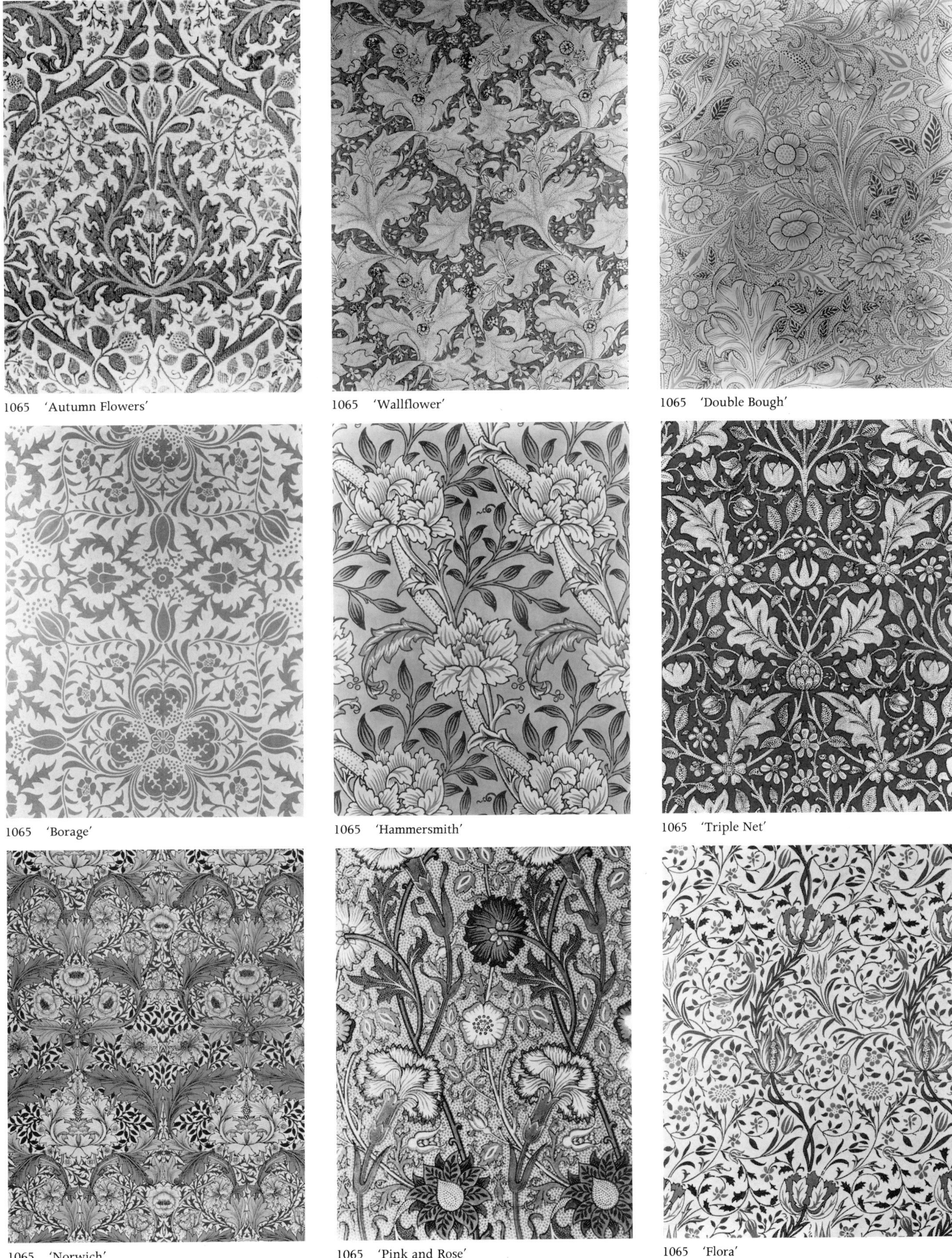

1065 'Autumn Flowers'

1065 'Wallflower'

1065 'Double Bough'

1065 'Borage'

1065 'Hammersmith'

1065 'Triple Net'

1065 'Norwich'

1065 'Pink and Rose'

1065 'Flora'

Architectural Review (1931), vol 69, p 151.

'Ceiling', November 1877 (E.510, 511). FC, no 50.

'Sunflower', 1879 (E.512–517). PFAR, pl 21; FC, no 25. E.817–1915 (see no 1066) neg L.1960.

'Acorn', 1879 (E.518–520; E.520 neg M.14). PFAR, pl 21; FC, no 26. A preliminary design for this paper is E.38–1940. Another portion is Circ.282–1959.

'Poppy', 1881 (E.521–527 neg GJ.9639). FC, no 27.

'St James's', 1881 (E.528, 529). Designed for the Throne Room and the Wellington Room in St James's Palace. The decorative scheme for the palace was begun in 1866 and was Morris & Co.'s first secular commission. AV, pl 11 (colour); SE, pl 113 (colour); FC, no 28. Another portion of this paper is Circ.25–1954 neg M.1792.

Volume 2 (1882–96)

'Bird and Anemone', 1882 (E.530, 531; E.530 neg R.671). Also used for a chintz (AV, pl 15 (colour)). FC, p 58, no 16.

'Honeysuckle', 1883 (E.532 neg S.1632). By Mary (May) Morris. A different design with this title is for a chintz (AV, pl 16 (colour)).

'Grafton', 1883 (E.533, 534; E.533 neg P.1520). PFP, pl 12; FC, no 31. A preliminary design for this paper is E.955–1954.

'The Wreath', or 'New Ceiling' (with colours), 1883 (E.535). *Magazine of Art* (April 1892), p 193. FC, no 52 (called in error 'Borage', q.v., below). Another portion is Circ.288–1959 neg GJ.9640.

'Wild Tulip', 1884 (E.536–541 neg Q.1714). PFP, pl 13; FC, no 32.

'Fritillary', 1885 (E.542–548; E.542 neg P.1521). PFP, pl 14; FC, no 33.

'Garden Tulip', 1885 (E.549–552 neg GJ.9641).

'Lily and Pomegranate', 1886 (E.553, 554; neg GJ.9642; E.2225–1913). FC, no 34.

'Arcadia', *circa* 1886 (E.555, 556; neg GJ.9643). By Mary (May) Morris.

'Willow Bough', 1887 (E.557–559). SE, pl 114 (colour); FC, no 35. The design for this paper is Circ.297–1955. Another portion is Circ.281–1959 neg S.1635.

'Bruges', 1888 (E.560–566; neg P.1522). AV, pl 13 (colour); FC, no 36.

'Autumn Flowers', 1888 (E.567, 568; neg S.1637). FC, no 37.

'Borage', 1888–89 (E.569 neg GJ.9644). A ceiling paper. The paper illustrated in FC, no 52, is 'The Wreath' or 'New Ceiling', q.v., above.

'Norwich', 1889 (E.570–574;

1065 'Bachelor's Button'

1065 'Spring Thicket'

1065 'Compton'

1065 'Net Ceiling'

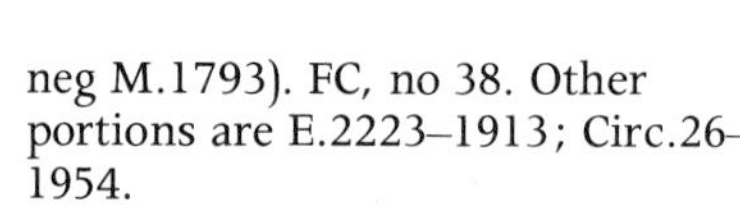

neg M.1793). FC, no 38. Other portions are E.2223–1913; Circ.26–1954.

'Wallflower', 1890 (E.575–578; neg P.1525). PFP, pl 15; FC, no 39.

'Hammersmith', 1890 (E.579 neg S.1638). Entwisle, *V*, pl 9, fig 34; FC, no 40.

'Pink and Rose', *circa* 1890 (E.580–584; neg GJ.9645). PFAR, pl 30; FC, no 41.

'Double Bough', 1890 (E.585–591; neg S.1640). PFP, pl 16. Other portions are E.2221–1913.

'Triple Net', 1891 (E.592 neg GJ.9646). PFP, pl 17; FC, no 42.

'Flora', 1891 (E.593 neg GJ.9647). FC, no 43.

'St James's Ceiling', 1881 (E.594, 595). AV, pl 10 (colour); FC, no 29.

'Bachelor's Button', 1892 (E.596–601; neg P.1523). PFP, pl 18; FC, no 44. Another portion is Circ.44–1954.

'Blackthorn', 1892 (E.602). PFP, pl 18; FC, no 45. Other portions are Circ.22A–1953; E.2232–1913 neg S.1642 CT 755 (see col pl, p 364)

'Lechlade', 1893 (E.603, 604). FC, no 46.

'Spring Thicket', 1894 (E.605 neg P.1524). FC, no 47.

'Compton', 1896 (E.606, 607; neg GJ.9648). Morris' last design, commissioned by Laurence Hodson for his house, 'Compton', outside Wolverhampton, and executed both as a wallpaper and as a printed textile. PFP, pl 20 (colour); Greysmith, pl 23 (colour); FC, no 47.

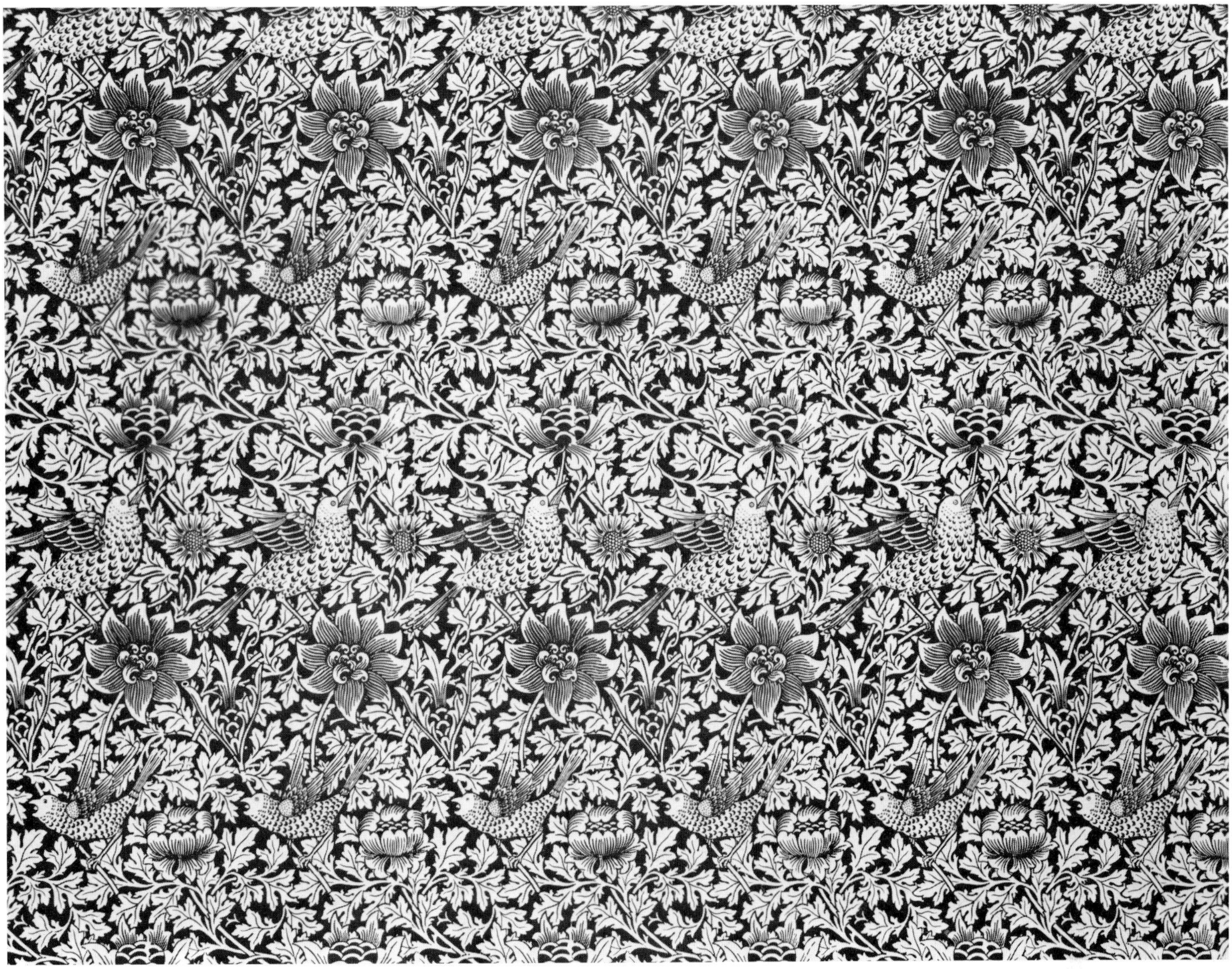

1065 'Bird and Anemone'

Another portion is Circ.290–1959 neg GJ.9648.

'Net Ceiling', or 'The Net', 1895 (E.608 neg GJ.9649). A ceiling paper. FC, no 53.

1066 Two pattern books, containing patterns (117 and 109, on 226 sheets, including different colourways); each sheet inscribed in ink on the back with title, number and price
Published by Morris & Co. and printed by Jeffrey & Co.
Colour prints from wood blocks, and machine prints
84.7 × 66.7 cm (size of each volume)
Given by Mr Allan F. Vigers
E.633–858–1915

With the exception of those listed below, the papers in these volumes are duplicates of those in no 1065.

'Iris', *circa* 1887, by J. H. Dearle (E.642, 643, 699, 703 neg S.1636); 'Merton', by

1066 'Iris'

'Horn Poppy', by Mary (May) Morris, 21 September 1885 (E.707, 845–852; E.707 neg GJ.9651); 'Single Stem', by J. H. Dearle, *circa* 1905 (E.712 neg S.1644); 'Woodland Weeds', by J. H. Dearle, *circa* 1905 (E.712 neg S.1643), another portion, Circ.252–1954; 'Granville', by J. H. Dearle (E.724, 725 neg GJ.9652); 'Celandine', by J. H. Dearle (E.728 neg GJ.9653); 'Oak Tree', machine print, by J. H. Dearle (see no 945) (E.729–732); 'Anemone', machine print (E.734–738); 'Tom Tit', machine print, by J. H. Dearle (E.739–742 neg GJ.9654); 'Thistle', machine print, by J. H. Dearle (E.743–747 neg GJ.9655); 'Indian', *circa* 1871 (FC, no 5) (E.748, 757–759 neg GJ.9656); 'Venetian', *circa* 1871 (FC, no 4) (E.749, 754–756, 783–785, 834 neg GJ.9657); 'Queen Anne', *circa* 1870 (FC, no 7) (E.762–764, 784 neg GJ.9658); 'Loop Trail', by Kate Faulkner, 12 May 1877 (E.803–805, 843 neg S.1631); 'Mallow', by Kate Faulkner, 1879 (E.811–813, 826, 829, 834, 844; E.811 neg GJ.9659); 'Carnation', machine print, by Kate Faulkner, *circa* 1880 (E.818 neg GJ.9660), another portion, Circ.46–1954; 'Christchurch', 1882 (PFP, pl 11; Greysmith, pl 101; FC, no 30) (E.833 neg P.1526).

1066 'Woodland Weeds'

1066 'Merton'

1066 'Horn Poppy'

1066 'Queen Anne'

1066 'Granville'

1066 'Celandine'

1066 'Tom Tit'

1066 'Thistle'

1066 'Single Stem'

1066 'Venetian'

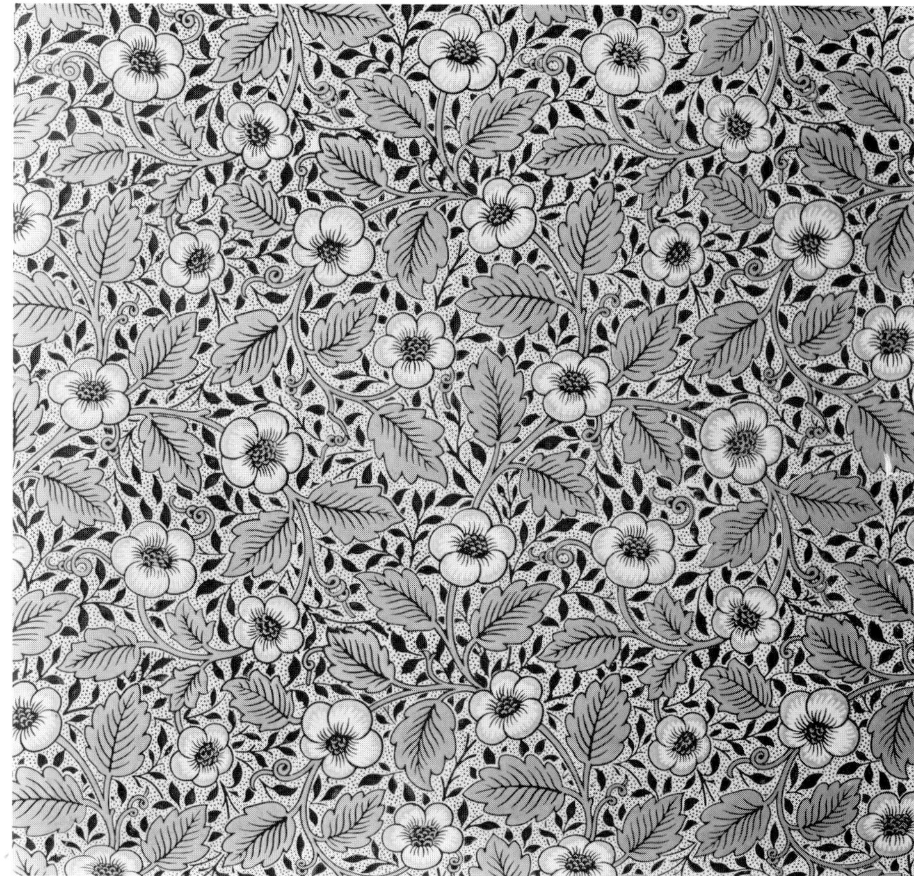

1066 'Christchurch'

1066 'Indian'

1066 'Mallow'

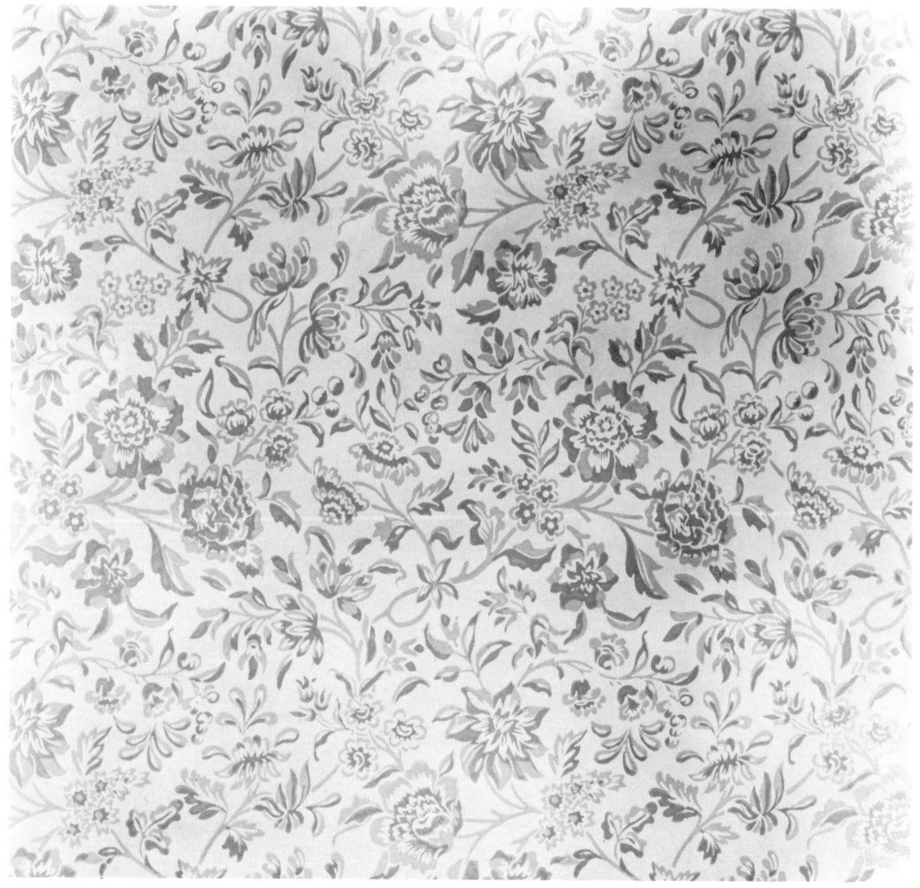

1066 'Loop Trail'

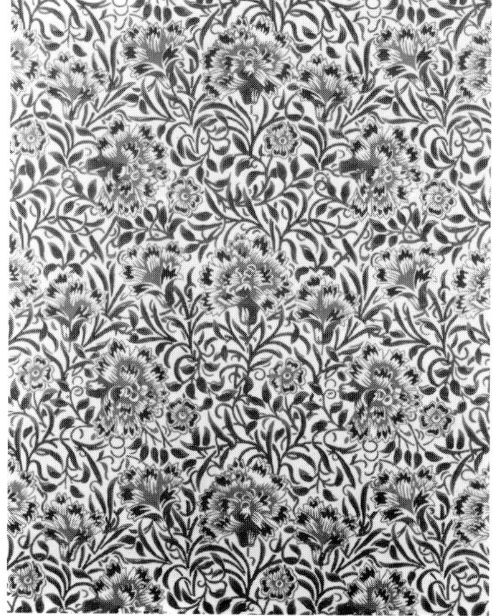

1066 'Carnation'

1067 Pattern book containing 23 patterns; each inscribed on the back in ink with title, number etc
Published by Morris, Marshall, Faulkner & Co., 26, Queen Square, Bloomsbury
1865–75
Colour prints from wood blocks
54.6 × 77.5 cm (average size)
Bequeathed by J. R. Holliday
E.3698–3704, 3706–3718, 3720–3722–1927

Originally in a volume, this set was split up, and E.3705, 3719–1927 are missing. One of these papers ('Spray') was not designed by Morris, but was produced by the firm and was based on an earlier paper removed from a house, 'Palace Ann', near Brandon, County Cork, and given to Morris by Charles C. Townsend, architect, in 1866. (Information found on the backs of photographs of the house by Miss Caroline C. Townsend, daughter of the architect.)

'Scroll', *circa* 1871 (E.3698); 'Branch', *circa* 1871 (E.3699); 'Trellis', 1864 (E.3700–3703); 'Diaper', *circa* 1868–70 (E.3704); 'Indian', *circa* 1868–70 (E.3706–3709); 'Fruit', 1862, produced 1864 (E.3710–3712; E.3710 neg GJ.9636); 'Spray', *circa* 1871 (E.3713, 3714; E.2807 neg GJ.9661); 'Venetian', *circa* 1868–70 (E.3715–3717); 'Daisy', 1864 (E.3718, 3720); 'Queen Anne', *circa* 1868–70 (E.3721, 3722).

1067 'Fruit'

1068 Seventeen portions, including different colourways, of papers published by Morris & Co.
Colour prints from wood blocks and machine prints
Various sizes
Given by Mr Sydney Vacher
E.2209–2211, 2213–2225, 2232–1913

Most of these papers are duplicates of those listed in no 1065.

'Thistle', machine print, by J. H. Dearle (E.2209); 'Fruit', 1862, produced 1864 (E.2210); 'Fritillary', 1885 (E.2211), another portion (Circ.283–1957); 'Celandine', by J. H. Dearle (E.2213); 'Autumn Flowers', 1888 (E.2214, 2215); 'Compton', 1896 (Morris's last design, executed both as a wallpaper and as a printed textile: PFP, pl 20) (E.2216), another portion (Circ.290–1959); 'Apple', 1877 (PFP, pl 10) (E.2217); 'Larkspur', 1874 (PFP, pl 6, colour) (E.2218); 'Bachelor's Button', 1892 (PFP, pl 18) (E.2219), another portion (Circ.44–1954); 'Iris', by J. H. Dearle, *circa* 1887 (E.2220); 'Double Bough', 1890 (PFP, pl 16) (E.2221); 'Daisy', 1862, produced 1864 (E.2222); 'Norwich', 1889 (E.2223); 'Lily and Pomegranate', 1886 (E.2224, 2225); 'Blackthorn', 1892 (PFP, pl 19, colour; Greysmith, pl 21, colour) (E.2232), another portion (Circ.22A–1953).

1069 Pattern book of wallpapers containing 132 specimens, including different colourways; most stamped on the back with title and serial number; some inscribed in ink; mounted on a display stand; cloth cover
Produced by Morris & Co., 449, Oxford Street, London
1880–1917
Colour prints from wood blocks, some machine prints
Various sizes
Given by Shand Kydd Ltd
E.2734–2866–1980

'Tree Frieze' (E.2734); 'Net Ceiling', 1895 (E.2735, 2736, 2866); 'Ceiling', 1883 (E.2737); 'Tulip Frieze' (E.2738); 'Daisy', 1862, produced 1864 (E.2739–2742); 'Fruit', 1862, produced 1864 (E.2743–2746, 2840); 'Trellis', November 1862 (E.2747–2750, 2795, 2811); 'Jasmine', 1872 (E.2751–2753); 'Lily', 1873 (E.2754, 2766); 'Double Bough', 1890 (E.2755, 2841–2847); 'Seaweed', 1901, by J. H. Dearle (E.2756); 'Planet', by J. H. Dearle (E.2757); 'Christchurch', 1882 (E.2758); 'Powdered', 1874 (E.2759–2761); 'Bower', 1877 (E.2762); 'Flora', 1891 (E.2763, 2764); 'Celandine', by J. H. Dearle (E.2765); 'Blossom', by Kate Faulkner (E.2767); 'Orchard', by J. H.

1067 'Spray'

Dearle (E.2768–2770); 'Larkspur', 1874 (E.2771); 'Autumn Flowers', 1888 (E.2772–2776); 'Bruges', 1888 (E.2777); 'Clover', by J. H. Dearle (E.2778, 2779); 'Daffodil', by J. H. Dearle (E.2780, 2792); 'Blackthorn' (E.2781); 'Chrysanthemum', 1877 (E.2782, 2783); 'Myrtle' (E.2784); 'Iris', *circa* 1887, by J. H. Dearle (E.2785–2787); 'Honeysuckle', by Mary (May) Morris (E.2788–2791); 'Blackberry', 1903, by J. H. Dearle (E.2793, 2794, 2839); 'Foliage', 1899, by J. H. Dearle (E.2796, 2797); 'Woodland Weeds', *circa* 1905, by J. H. Dearle (E.2798); 'Hammersmith' (E.2799); 'Vine', 1873 (E.2800, 2801, 2865); 'Garden Tulip', 1885 (E.2802–2804); 'Garden', by J. H. Dearle (E.2805); 'Rose' (E.2806, 2807); 'Scroll [& Flower]', *circa* 1871 (E.2808–2810); 'Meadow Sweet', by J. H. Dearle (E.2812–2814); 'Golden Lily', by J. H. Dearle (E.2815–2817); 'Compton', 1896 (E.2818–2819); 'Wild Tulip', 1884 (E.2820–2824); 'Single Stem', by J. H. Dearle (E.2825–2827); 'Lechlade' (E.2828, 2829); 'Artichoke', by J. H. Dearle (E.2830, 2831); 'Spring Thicket', 1894, by J. H. Dearle (E.2832–2834); 'Granville', by J. H. Dearle (E.2835, 2836); 'Persian', by J. H. Dearle (E.2837, 2838); 'Pink and Rose', *circa* 1890 (E.2848); 'Norwich', 1889 (E.2849–2851); 'Lily and Pomegranate', 1886 (E.2852, 2853); 'Pimpernel', 1876 (E.2854–2856); 'Acanthus', 1875 (E.2857–2860); 'St James's', 1881 (E.2861, 2862); 'Sunflower', 1879 (E.2863, 2864).

1070 Fragment of 'Chrysanthemum'
1877
Colour print from wood blocks
45.7 × 34.3 cm
PROVENANCE 'Greenfields', near Manchester
Given by Mrs J. M. Weekes
E.350–1972

For other portions of this paper in different colourways, see no 1065. Another Morris paper, 'Triple Net' (1891), was taken from the same house.

1071 Preliminary drawing for 'Acorn'
Circa 1879
Watercolour
102.5 × 66.7 cm
E.38–1940

Only part of the drawing appears to be by Morris; the repeat is evidently the work of assistants. For specimens of the wallpaper, designed by Morris in 1879, see no 1065.

1072 Preliminary drawing for 'Grafton'
1883
Pencil and watercolour
42.5 × 34.9 cm
E.955–1954

The above 2 items, nos 1071, 1072, were bequeathed by Miss Mary (May) Morris, daughter of the artist.

1073 Design of crowns, thistles and initials *VRI*, for Balmoral Castle, 1887
Reprint from the original blocks, by Arthur Sanderson & Sons Ltd
Print from wood block
109 × 76.7 cm (portion)
Given by Mr E. A. Entwisle
Circ.16–1961 neg GJ.9662

The original design (Entwisle, *LH*, pl 92) is inscribed *Design for flock wallpaper Morris & Company* and bears a pencilled note: *Their Majesties prefer this design with the diamonds as big again . . . the design to be in flock (not coloured).*

1074 'Myrtle'
1899
Colour print from wood blocks
136 × 100.3 cm (portion)
Given by the WM (Sanderson's branch)
Circ.27–1954 neg M.1794

FC, no 49. The design is one made by

1073

Morris for needlework, probably *circa* 1875, and was produced by the firm after his death.

1075 Two portions of 'Marigold' and 'Scroll'
Removed from the Sheepshanks and Jones Galleries in the Victoria and Albert Museum
Colour prints from wood blocks
71.1 × 114.4 cm; 71.1 × 91.3 cm
E.3469, 3469A, 3470–1913

'Marigold', 1875 (AV, pl VI, colour; SE, pl 112, colour) (E.3469, 3469A); 'Scroll', 1871, produced 1872 (E.3470).

1076 Wallpapers by Morris & Co., reprinted by Arthur Sanderson & Son Ltd, *circa* 1955
Various sizes
E.1401–1432–1979

'Planet', by J. H. Dearle (E.1401 neg GJ.9663); 'Orchard', by J. H. Dearle (E.1402 neg GJ.9664); 'Michaelmas Daisy', by J. H. Dearle (E.1403 neg GJ.9665); 'Leicester' (E.1404 neg GJ.9666); 'Sweet Briar', by J. H. Dearle (E.1405 neg GJ.9667); 'Artichoke', by J. H. Dearle (E.1406 neg GJ.9668 CT 7336 see col pl, p 390); 'Golden Lily', by J. H. Dearle (E.1407 neg GJ.9669); 'Lily Border' (E.1408 neg GJ.9670); 'Orange Border' (E.1409 neg GJ.9671); 'Verdure', by Kathleen Kersey (Mrs Allington) (E.1410 neg GJ.9672); 'Persian', by J. H. Dearle (E.1411 neg GJ.9673); 'Clover', by J. H. Dearle (E.1412 neg GJ.9674); 'Arbutus', 1903, by Kathleen Kersey (Mrs Allington) (E.1413 neg GJ.9675); 'Bramble', by Kate Faulkner (E.1414 neg GJ.9676); 'Blackberry', by J. H. Dearle (E.1415 neg GJ.9677); 'Hyacinth', by J. H. Dearle (E.1416 neg GJ.9678); 'Brentwood', by J. H. Dearle (E.1417 neg GJ.9679); 'Seaweed', by J. H. Dearle (E.1418 neg GJ.9680); 'Daffodil', by J. H. Dearle (E.1419 neg GJ.9681); 'Harebell', 1911, by J. H. Dearle (E.1420 neg GJ.9682); 'Foliage', by J. H. Dearle (E.1421 neg GJ.9683); 'Tulip' frieze (E.1422 neg GJ.9684); 'Little Tree' frieze (E.1423 neg GJ.9685); 'Garden', by J. H. Dearle (E.1424 neg GJ.9686); 'Brocade' (E.1425 neg GJ.9687); 'Bird and Pomegranate' (E.1426 neg GJ.9688); 'Blossom', by Kate Faulkner (E.1427 neg GJ.9689); 'Sprig' (E.1428 neg GJ.9690); 'Meadow Sweet', by J. H. Dearle (E.1429 neg GJ.9691); 'Rambler', by J. H. Dearle (E.1430 neg GJ.9692); 'Flowering Scroll', by J. H. Dearle (E.1431 neg GJ.9693); 'Thistle' (not the same design as J. H. Dearle's; see no 1066) (E.1432 neg GJ.9694).

1074

1076 'Lily Border'

1076 'Orchard'

1076 'Planet'

1076 'Leicester'

1076 'Orange Border'

1076 'Golden Lily'

1076 'Sweet Briar'

1076 'Michaelmas Daisy'

1076 'Verdure'

1076 'Arbutus'

1076 'Garden'

1076 'Persian'

1076 'Bramble'

1076 'Hyacinth'

1076 'Clover'

1076 'Blackberry'

1076 'Brentwood'

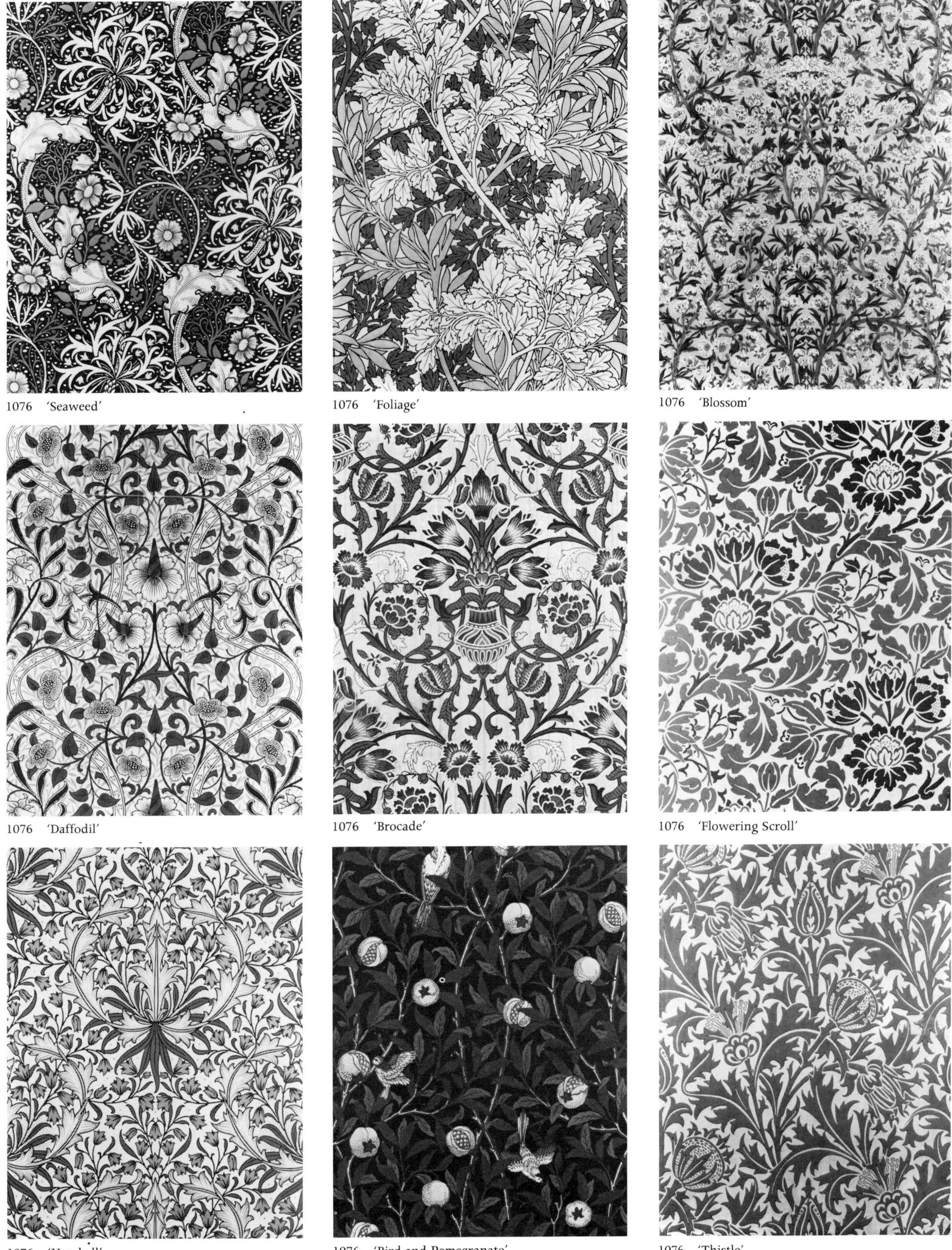

1076 'Seaweed'

1076 'Foliage'

1076 'Blossom'

1076 'Daffodil'

1076 'Brocade'

1076 'Flowering Scroll'

1076 'Harebell'

1076 'Bird and Pomegranate'

1076 'Thistle'

1076 'Sprig'

1076 'Tulip'

1076 'Meadow Sweet'

Morton, William Scott, *circa* 1840–1903

Founder in 1870 of the firm of Scott Morton (Tynecastle), producers of 'art furniture', who later specialized in raised wall coverings, which became known as 'Tynecastle' canvas. Later 'leather' papers, 'vellums' and other types of embossed wall coverings were produced.

1077 Raised pattern of formalized leaves and flowers
Produced by the Scott Morton (Tynecastle) Company
Circa 1900
Embossed canvas, gilded and mounted on paper
200.6 × 62 cm (portion)
Bequeathed by Miss Estella Canziani
E.912–1965 neg GJ.9695

This paper is reproduced on p 20 (design no 1029) of the firm's trade pattern book (VAM Library). The design was still in use when the pattern book was issued by the new Scott Morton Tynecastle Co. Ltd, *circa* 1920.

Mott, Henry H., worked second half of 19th century

Member of the firm of H. Scott Richmond & Co., for whom he made a range of designs. The firm's blocks were taken over by John Perry & Co. in the late 1890s.

(*opposite*) 'Acanthus', by William Morris, 1875 (no 1065, vol 1)

1076 'Rambler', GJ.9692

1076 'Little Tree', GJ.9685

1078

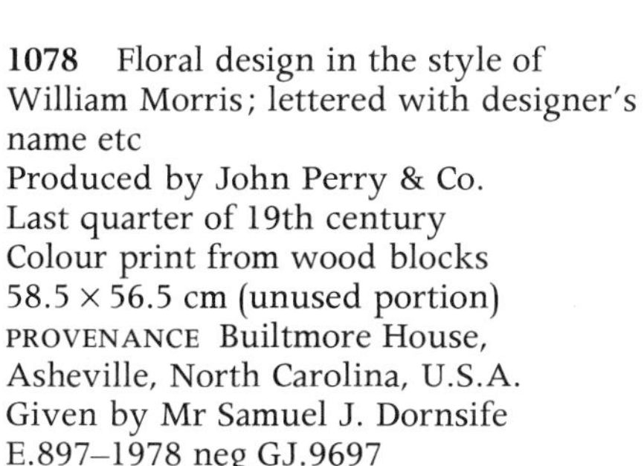

1078 Floral design in the style of William Morris; lettered with designer's name etc
Produced by John Perry & Co.
Last quarter of 19th century
Colour print from wood blocks
58.5 × 56.5 cm (unused portion)
PROVENANCE Builtmore House, Asheville, North Carolina, U.S.A.
Given by Mr Samuel J. Dornsife
E.897–1978 neg GJ.9697

Mould, Phyllis A., working *circa* 1930

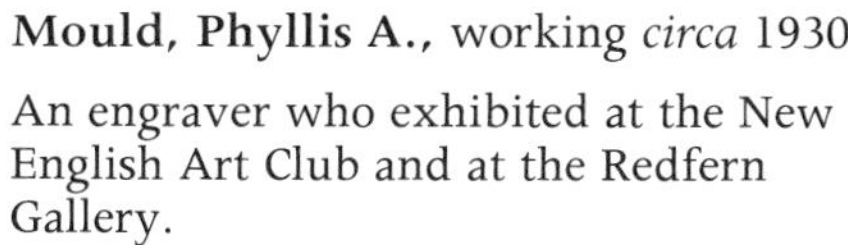

An engraver who exhibited at the New English Art Club and at the Redfern Gallery.

(*opposite*) 'Artichoke', by J. H. Dearle, produced by Morris & Co., reprinted by Sanderson & Sons Ltd, *circa* 1955 (no 1076)

1077

1079

1079 Portion of 'Steamboats'
Printed and published by the Curwen Press
Circa 1930
Colour lithograph
61.6 × 58.4 cm (size of sheet)
E.548–1931 neg GJ.9696

Another sample is E.4045–1934 (BGM).

Napper, Harry, d. 1930

Watercolour artist and designer of wallpapers, carpets and other textiles, he managed the Silver Studio for a while after Arthur Silver's death in 1896. English interpreter of the art nouveau style.

1080 Two portions of 'Kingsbury'
Produced by Alexander Rottmann & Co.
Circa 1900
Colour machine print
57.5 × 62.5 cm; 51.7 × 62 cm
E.464–1967; Circ.586–1967 neg GJ.9698

Moderne Stil (1900), vol II, pl 43, fig 2. The frieze to accompany this paper is reproduced in *Artist* (1900), vol XXVIII, plate on p 160.

1081 Portion of 'Whitchurch'
Produced by Alexander Rottmann & Co.
Circa 1900
Colour machine print
61.7 × 61.7 cm
Circ.585–1967

The above 2 items, nos 1080, 1081, were given by Miss Mary Peerless.

1082 Formalized tulips and vetch in vertical lines; inscribed in ink on the mount *Napper No.C.6.*
Circa 1900
Colour machine print
76.2 × 48.2 cm (portion)
E.643–1974 neg GJ.9699

1083 'The Springfield'; inscribed in ink on the mount *Napper No.C.5.*
Produced by Alexander Rottmann & Co.
Circa 1902
Colour machine print
75.7 × 48.1 cm (portion)
E.642–1974 neg GJ.9702

ASJ, plate on p 51; *JDA*, vol 22, p 55; *Decorators' and Painters' Magazine* (1902–1903), vol I, plate on p 423.

1080

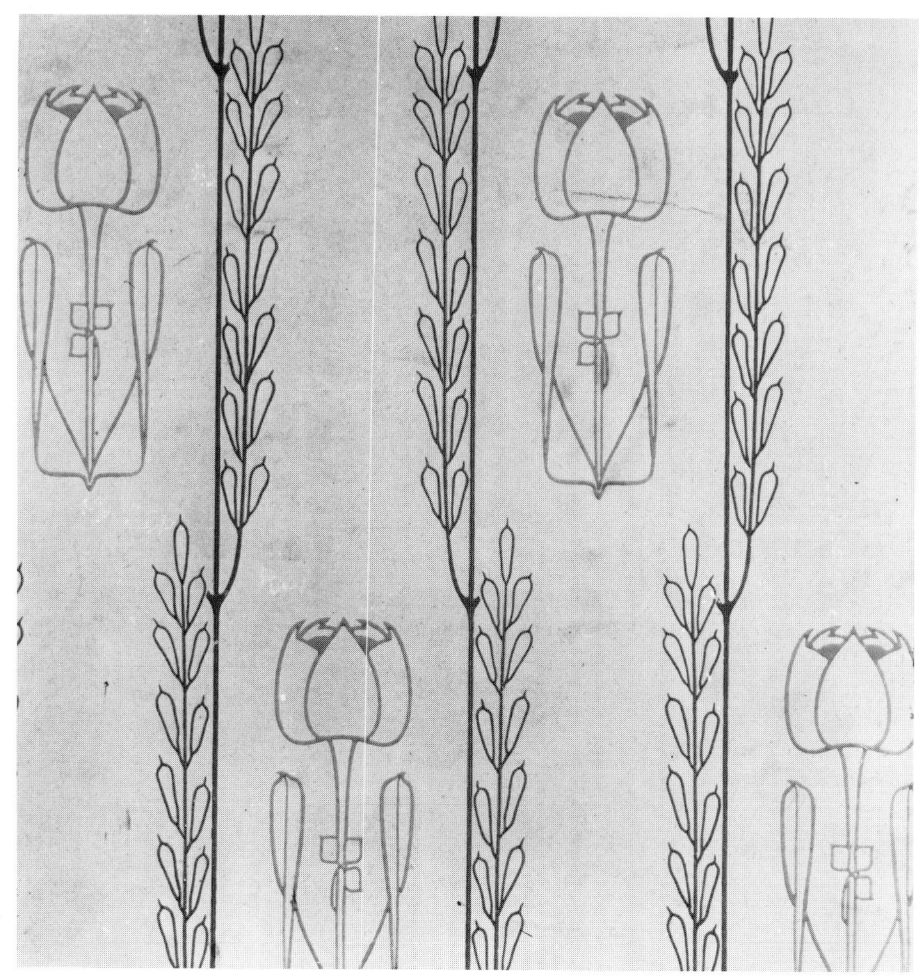

1082

1083

1084 'The Braunton'; inscribed in ink on the mount *Napper No.C.1.*
Produced by Alexander Rottmann & Co.
Circa 1902
Colour machine print
75.8 × 48.2 cm (portion)
E.641–1974 neg GJ.9700 CT 8486

ASJ, plate on p 48; *JDA*, vol 22, p 55.

The above 3 items, nos 1082–1084, were given by Courtaulds Ltd.

1085 Portion of 'Stanmore'
Produced by Alexander Rottmann & Co.
Circa 1903
Colour machine print
54.3 × 62.2 cm
Given by Miss Mary Peerless
E.465–1967

ASJ (1), plate on p 44. The frieze to accompany this paper is reproduced in *Artist* (1900), vol XXVIII, plate on p 162.

1084

1087 'Sanitary' paper in the art nouveau style, with a repeat design of formalized roses, printed in brown and green on white, with a matching border
Early 20th century
Colour print from engraved rollers
51.5 × 56 cm; 28.2 × 52 cm (portions)
E.483, 484–1967; E.484 neg GJ.462

1088 Portion of 'sanitary' paper in the art nouveau style, with a pattern of formalized roses, within a rectangular border of stems, printed in shades of brown and green, and 2 identical matching borders, uncut
Early 20th century
Colour print from engraved rollers
51.6 × 56 cm; 12.6 × 57.8 cm (each border)
E.485, 486–1967

The above 2 items, nos 1087, 1088, were given by Miss Mary Peerless

1089 'The Rowan'; inscribed in ink on the mount with title and *Knapper* [*sic*]
Machine print in black on a red paper
75.3 × 45.8 cm (portion)
Given by Courtaulds Ltd
E.644–1974 neg GJ.9701

Napper, Harry, possibly by

1090 Portion of 'Pinner'
Produced by Alexander Rottmann & Co.
Circa 1900

1087

Colour machine print
61 × 62 cm
Given by Miss Mary Peerless
E.463–1967

Moderne Stil (1900), vol II, pl 43, fig 1.

Neatby, William James, 1860–1910

Painter and designer of mural decorations, he was chief designer for John Line & Sons between 1907 and 1910. He exhibited a series of wall paintings illustrating Browning and Burns at the Franco–British Exhibition in Vienna, 1908. Other works included a painted dome in the Masonic Temple of the New Gaiety Restaurant, panels for the Imperial Hotel, London, and decorations in tile work for Harrods' Food Halls.

1091 'Lancaster Frieze'
Produced by Jeffrey & Co.
1904
Colour print from 8 wood blocks
54 × 107 cm (portion)
E.1906–1934 neg GJ.9703

1092 'Orchard'
Produced by Jeffrey & Co.
Circa 1904

1089

1091

1092

1093

Colour print from 5 wood blocks
73.3 × 50.2 cm (portion)
E.1911–1934 neg GG.5862

AJ (1905), plate 284 (colour); Greysmith, pl 134.

1093 'Lancelot', alternatively known as the 'Oak Tree Shield'
Produced by Jeffrey & Co.
Circa 1905
Colour print from wood blocks
88 × 51.2 cm (portion)
E.1910–1934 neg GJ.9704

1094 Portion of a dado for the 'Hanover' decoration (no 1095)
Produced by Jeffrey & Co.
1907
Colour print from wood blocks
85.4 × 51.5 cm (portion)
E.1907–1934

'Hanover' is reproduced in ASJ (2), plate on p 58. See also *Decorators' and Painters' Magazine* (1906–7), vol VI, plate on p 353.

1095 'Hanover' decoration
Produced by Jeffrey & Co.
1907
Colour print from wood blocks
71.1 × 51.4 cm (portion)
E.1909–1934 neg GJ.9705

1096 Portion of the 'Curzon' decoration, with stuck-on border
Produced by Jeffrey & Co.
1911
Colour print from 10 wood blocks
50.8 × 83.2 cm
E.1908–1934

The above 6 items, nos 1091–1096, were given by the WM.

Newsom, Rosemary. See PATTERN BOOKS, no 719.

Nicholson, Robert, working from 1950s

Of Robert and Roger Nicholson Ltd.

1097 Small globes within vertical bars, in white on grey
Produced by the Crown Branch of the WM
1954
Colour machine print, on a lightly embossed ground
78.5 × 55.5 cm (portion)
E.986–1978 neg GJ.9706

Entwisle, *LH*, pl 118 (in another colourway).

1098 'Columns'
Produced by the WM as one of their 'Palladio 1' range
1955
Colour screen print
74.8 × 52.9 cm (portion)
E.574–1966 neg GJ.9707

Design (1955), vol 7, no 84, plate on p 22 (colour).

1099 Portion of 'Avenue'
Produced by the WM as one of their 'Palladio 1' range
1955
Colour screen print
74.8 × 52.8 cm
E.575–1966 neg GK.3071 CT 7799 (see col pl, p 407)

Design (1955), vol 7, no 84, plate on p 18. 'Palladio I' was the product of the WM's first screen-printing plant.

1095

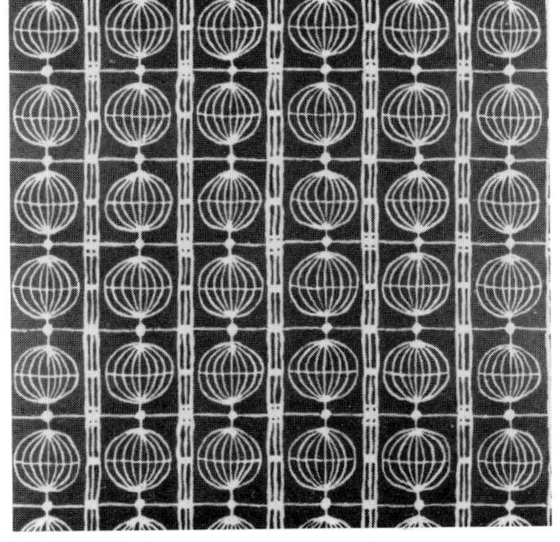

1097

1098

1100

1101

1100 'Colonnade'
Produced by the WM as one of their 'Palladio 1' range
1956
Colour screen print
74.8 × 52.9 cm (portion)
E.573–1966 neg GJ.450

Design (1956), vol 8, no 89, p 62, fig 72.

1101 'Sicilian Lion'
Produced by the WM as one of their 'Palladio 2' range
Circa 1957
Colour screen print
96 × 55.6 cm (portion)
E.970–1978 neg GJ.9708

Design (1957), vol 99, plate on p 34.

The above 5 items, nos 1097–1101, were given by the WM.

1102

Nicholson, Roger, working from 1950s

Of Robert and Roger Nicholson Ltd. Formerly Professor at the School of Textile Design, Royal College of Art.

1102 Pattern of vertical strips of small leaf and star shapes in white between broadly spaced bands of red stars and lines
Produced by the Crown Branch of the WM
1954
Colour machine print
78 × 55.5 cm (portion)
Given by the WM
E.987–1978 neg GJ.9374

Nilsson, Kerstin. See PATTERN BOOKS, no 735.

Odell, William J., working from early 1950s

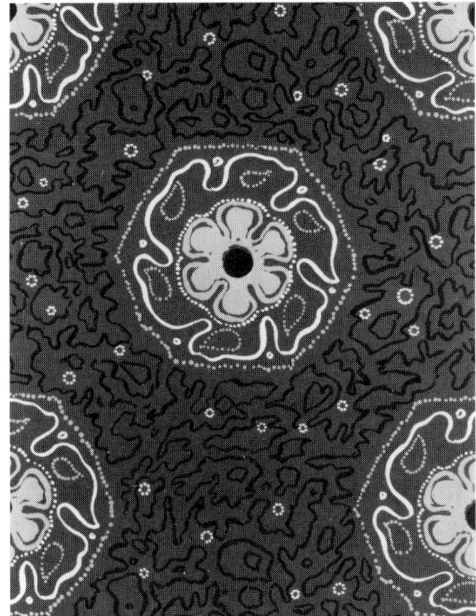
1104

Staff designer, and later head designer, with John Line & Sons Ltd. See also PATTERN BOOKS, nos 707(37), 710, 713(4), 716(2), 717(2), 718(2).

1103 'Murania'; lettered with manufacturer's and designer's names etc
Produced by John Line & Sons Ltd for their series 'Limited Editions 1951'
Screen print
73.5 × 54.5 cm (portion)
E.971–1978 neg GJ.9709

Design (1951), vol III, plate on p 12 (colour).

1104 Design based on the crystalline structures of insulin, pattern group 8.27; lettered with manufacturer's name etc
Produced by John Line & Sons Ltd for the Festival of Britain
1951
Screen print
75 × 54.5 cm
E.884–1978 neg GJ.9710

Design (1951), vol III, plate on p 17. See also no 1140.

1105 Design based on the crystalline structures of afwillite, pattern group 8.45; lettered with manufacturer's name etc
Produced by John Line & Sons Ltd for the Festival of Britain
1951
Screen print
75 × 54.5 cm (portion)
E.885–1978 neg GJ.9711 CT 7337 (see col pl)

1103

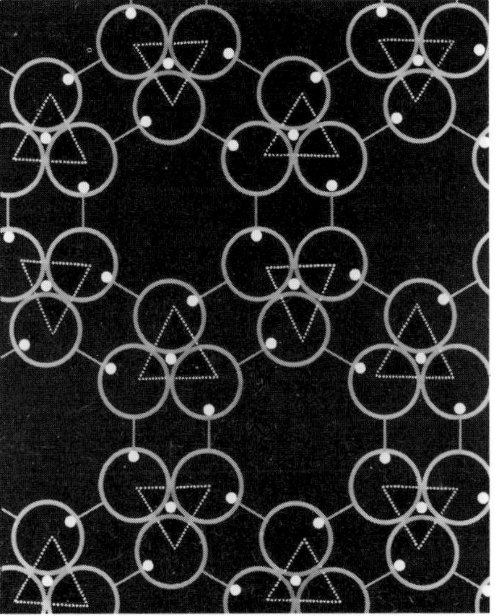
1106

1106 Portion of a design based on the crystalline structures of boric acid, pattern group 8.34; lettered *1951 Festival of Britain* etc
Produced by John Line & Sons Ltd for the Festival of Britain
1951
Screen print
75 × 54.5 cm
E.886–1978 neg GJ.9712

Design (1951), vol III, plate on p 21 (colour). See also no 1140.

1107 'Mantova'; lettered with manufacturer's name etc
Produced by John Line & Sons Ltd
1958

1107

Pink flock
67.3 × 55.4 cm (portion)
Given by Shand Kydd Ltd
E.1110–1970 neg GJ.9713

Olsen, Carola and Daniel. See PATTERN BOOKS, nos 716(4), 717(3), 720.

Orr, ? J., working until *circa* 1940

Possibly the painter Jack Orr (worked until *circa* 1940).

1108

1109

1110

1108 'The Prestwick'; inscribed in pencil on the mount *J [?] Orr Glasgow* and with title
Colour print from wood blocks
54.3 × 47.5 cm (portion)
Given by Courtaulds Ltd
E.616–1974 neg GJ.9714

Owen, Will, R. Cam.A., 1869–1957

A poster designer and illustrator who studied at the Lambeth School of Art. Born in Malta. He published *Old London Town* etc.

1109 Portions of nursery friezes: 'Bo-Peep' and 'Simple Simon'
Produced by Lightbown, Aspinall & Co.
1910
Machine prints from 6 engraved rollers
26.7 × 243.8 cm (size of sheet)
E.1912–1934 neg GJ.9715

SE, pl 213.

Passano, John. See Armfield, Diana M.

Pattison, Edgar L., 1872-post 1935

Painter, etcher and designer, he studied at the Lambeth School of Art, and exhibited at the Royal Academy and elsewhere from 1906 until 1935.

1110 'Cotter'
Produced by Jeffrey & Co.
1913
Colour machine print
85 × 53.8 cm (portion)
Given by Mr Henry Butler
E.2782–1914 neg GJ.9716

Reproduced in *Lady's Pictorial* (1913).

1111 'Torrington'
Produced by Jeffrey & Co.
1914
Colour machine print
120.7 × 57.3 cm (length)
Given by Jeffrey & Co.
E.3686–1915 neg GJ.9717

Pauker, Evelyn. See PATTERN BOOKS, nos 715, 718.

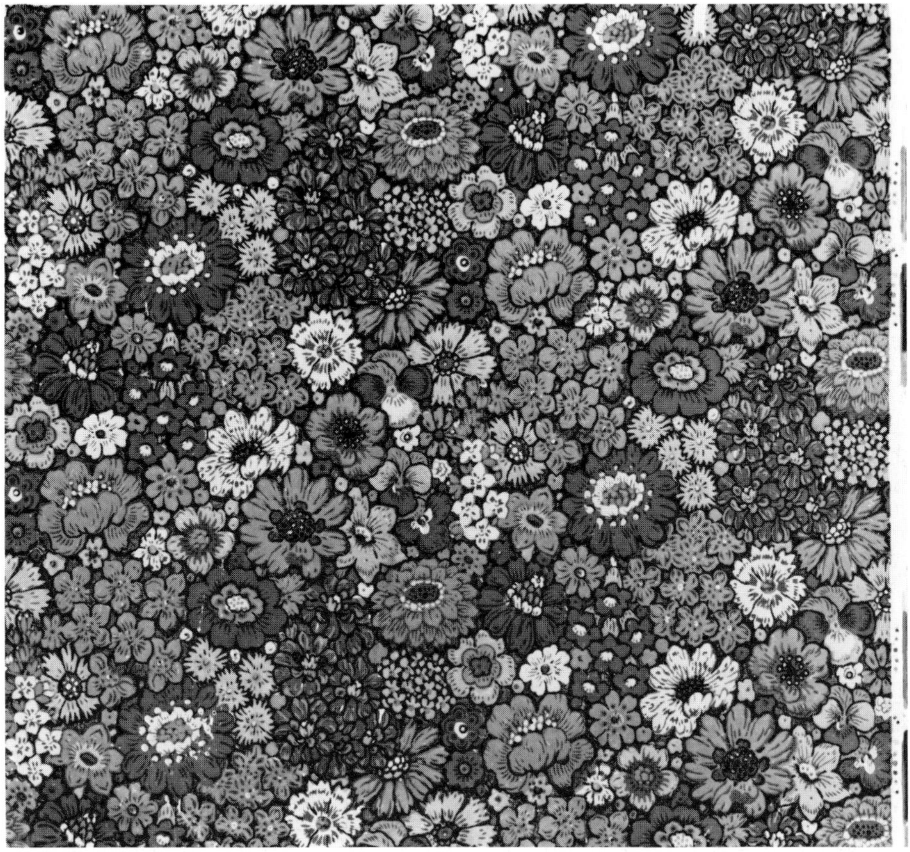
1111

Phillips, Susan. See PATTERN BOOKS, no 723.

Pienkowski, Jan, working 1960s–1970s

Designer of cards, stickers etc.

1112 Four reduced versions of wallpaper friezes
Circa 1970
Colour off-set
5.7 × 48.2 cm (each)
Given by Gallery Five Ltd
E.1584–1587–1974

Children's frieze: 'ABC' (E.1584 neg GJ.9249); children's frieze: 'Colours' (E.1585); children's frieze: 'Shapes' (E.1586); children's frieze: '123' (E.1587)

Pitts, W. W. C. See PATTERN BOOKS, no 707(7).

Platter, Michael. See PATTERN BOOKS, no 720.

Pollard, Patricia. See PATTERN BOOKS, no 721.

Pompa, P. See PATTERN BOOKS, no 707.

Pond, Edward Charles, Des R.C.A., F.S.I.A. See PATTERN BOOKS, no 719(2).

Priestley, Sylvia Nancy, M.S.I.A., working early 1950s

Textile and wallpaper designer, daughter of J. B. Priestley, she studied at the Slade School of Art and at the Central School of Arts and Crafts. Worked for Jacqmar Ltd, Warner & Sons and Helios Ltd. See also PATTERN BOOKS, nos 707(2), 710.

1113 'Early Bird'
Produced by John Line & Sons Ltd in their series 'Limited Editions 1951'
1951
Colour screen print
75 × 54.5 cm (portion)
E.887–1978 neg GJ.9718

Design (1951), vol III, plate on p 11 (colour); N. Carrington, *Design and Decoration in the Home* (1952), pl 111 (colour).

1113

Pugin, Augustus Welby Northmore, 1812–52

Trained by his father Augustus Charles Pugin, he designed goldsmith's work and furniture at an early age. He delighted in mediaeval art and put all his energies into the promotion of the gothic style. He was in charge of the decorative furnishing of the Houses of Parliament. He wrote several books on gothic architecture, and exhibited at the Royal Academy, 1849–52.

1114 Length with a design incorporating a crown, and thistles and formalized flowers
Later printing (1969), in 2 shades of green on a gold background, from the original blocks used in the decoration of the Red Drawing Room of Scarisbrick Hall, Lancashire
1847
Colour print from wood blocks
108.6 × 57 cm
E.332–1970 neg GJ.9719

The original paper, printed in red and gold, was used in the Red Drawing Room, Scarisbrick Hall, which was rebuilt by A. W. N. Pugin and Edward Pugin, 1837–70. Design, D.769–1908.

1115 Printing block for a diaper-pattern wallpaper for the Houses of Parliament
Produced by Samuel Scott for J. G. Crace
Circa 1848
Wood
31 × 56 cm
E.146–1976

1116

1116 'Crace Diaper', printed from the above
Colour print from wood block, in blue on a white background
57 × 58 cm
E.147–1976 neg GJ.9721

Samples of this paper, in the same and different colourways, also in flock, are in a pattern book of wallpapers supplied for the decoration of the Houses of Parliament between 1851 and 1859. See PATTERN BOOKS, no 696.

1117 Length with a design of an heraldic leopard and 2 Tudor roses within roundels against a background of conventionalized foliage and pineapples
Later printing, from the original blocks, of a paper made by Samuel Scott for J. G. Crace and used in the decoration of the Houses of Parliament
Circa 1848–50
Print from wood block and gold flock
154.8 × 55.2 cm
E.1705–1953

This example was shown in the *Exhibition of Victorian and Edwardian Decorative Arts*, VAM, 1952 (catalogue, No.C.38). SE, fig 83 (designs, D.969, 739, 755–1908).

1118 Tudor roses and fleur-de-lis, surmounted by crowns, within vertical ogival borders
Later printing (*circa* 1953) of a paper made by Samuel Scott for J. G. Crace and used in the decoration of the Houses of Parliament
Circa 1848–50
Print from wood block in white, on a bronze-gold ground
70.5 × 54.8 cm (portion)
E.887–1979 neg GJ.9720

The original (SE, pl 86) was printed in green flock on a gold ground.

The above 5 items, nos 1114–1118, were given by Cole & Son Wallpapers Ltd.

1114

1118

1119 Thirty-four specimens, including different colourways, made for J. G. Crace, for several decorative schemes; after designs in the gothic manner by Pugin, with heraldic motifs
Mid-19th century
Colour prints from wood blocks and flock
81.3 × 52 cm
Given by Mr A. L. Cowtan in memory of his father, Arthur Barnard Cowtan, O.B.E.
E.103–136–1939

For Lord Gough, Lough Cutra Castle: 3 pieces (E.118, 119, 136); for the Manchester Assize Courts: 4 pieces (E.120–123); for Tennyson D'Eyncourt, Esq, Bayons Manor (E.124); for the Marquis of Breadalbane, Taymouth Castle: ceiling paper (E.125); for Henry Sharples, Oswaldcroft: 2 pieces (E.126, 127; design, D.889–1908); for Lady Macdonald Lockhart, Lee Castle: 2 pieces (E.128, 129), another portion, E.153–1976, design, D.1160–1908; for S. J. Cooper, 6 pieces (E.130–135); fleur-de-lis design (E.103); for Magdalen College, Oxford: 4 pieces (E.104–107); for Captain Washington Hibbert: 2 pieces (E.108, 109), another portion, E.154–1976 neg GG.5860; for the Duke of Devonshire, Lismore Castle: 4 pieces (E.110–113, preliminary design, D.838–1908); for Viscount Campden (later Earl of Gainsborough): 4 pieces (E.114–117).

Greysmith, pl 96 (E.130–135, Cooper).

1120 Unused portion of wallpaper with a design of a crown, fleur-de-lis and pomegranate, within ogival bands, for the Committee Rooms and throughout the buildings of the Houses of Parliament

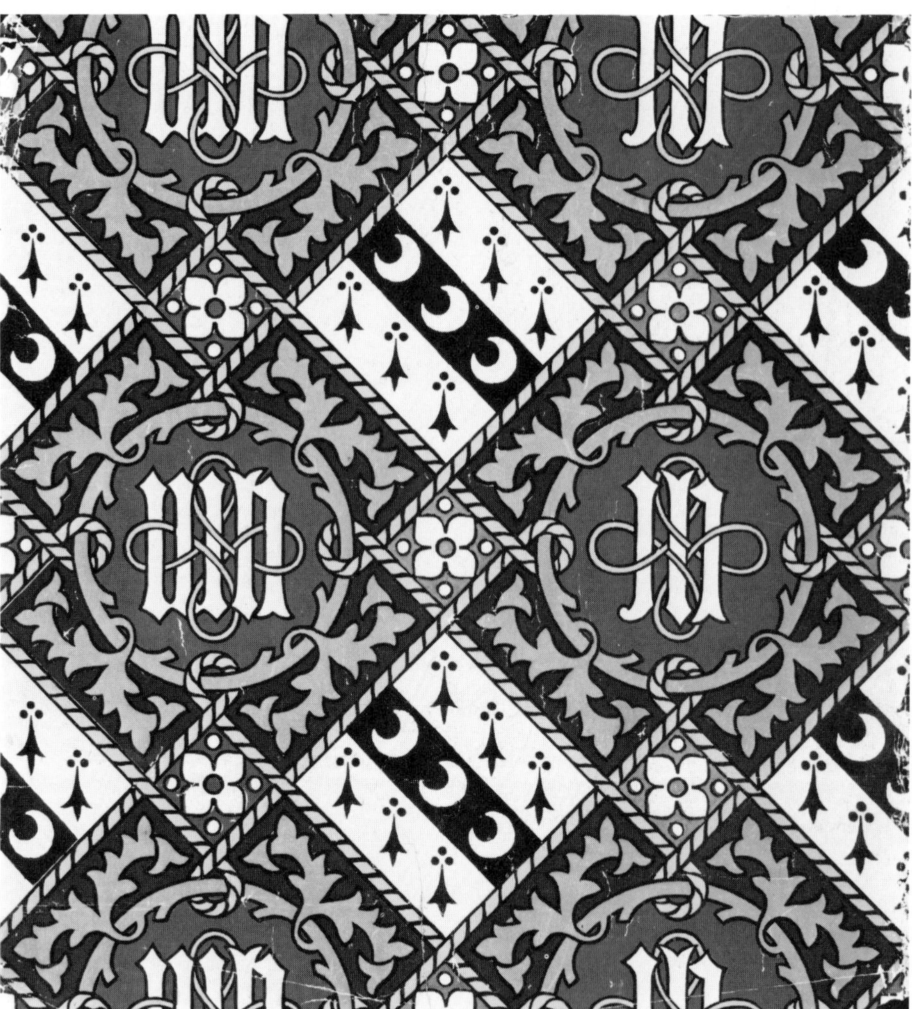

1119

Produced by Samuel Scott for J. G. Crace
Colour print from wood block and flock
103 × 58.5 cm
E.148–1976

Pugin's design for this paper, showing a different colourway, is D.825–1908.

1121 Unused portion of a wallpaper with a pattern of the Tudor rose and portcullis, and the initials *VR*, for the Houses of Parliament
Produced by Samuel Scott for J. G. Crace
Colour print from wood blocks
63 × 57 cm
E.150–1976 CT 8494

Pugin's body-colour design for this paper is D.719–1908.

1122 Fragment with a formalized leaf-and-fruit pattern, on a background of basket-weave pattern, for the Royal Gallery of the Houses of Parliament
Produced by Samuel Scott for J. G. Crace
Colour print from wood block and flock
84 × 57 cm
E.155–1976

Pugin's watercolour design for this paper, signed and dated 1850, is D.791–1908. In the pattern book of wallpapers (no 696) supplied for the redecoration of the Houses of Parliament examples of this paper are noted as 'Exhibition Pattern', perhaps indicating that it was shown in the Mediaeval Court at the Great Exhibition.

The above 2 items, nos 1121, 1122, were given by Cole & Son (Wallpapers) Ltd.

1123 Formalized thistle-and-leaf pattern, for the Houses of Parliament
Produced by Samuel Scott for J. G. Crace
Flock
86.5 × 52 cm (portion)
Given by the Department of the Environment
E.151–1976 neg GJ.9722

Pugin's watercolour design for this paper is D.827–1908.

1124 Unused portion of wallpaper with a half-drop pattern of a star, within a trefoil border, on a background simulating oak grain

1125

Colour print from wood blocks
145 × 53.5 cm
E.149–1976

Pugin's pencil design for the star pattern is D.995–1908, but the paper is probably a late design by Crace based on Pugin's motif.

1125 Reprint of wallpaper with a pattern of the national emblems within a trellis, used at the Houses of Parliament, and said to have been designed for the Great Exhibition, 1851
Produced by Arthur Sanderson & Sons Ltd
Circa 1951
Print from wood block
31.5 × 55.8 cm
E.1400–1979 neg GJ.9723

1126 Unused portion with a formalized crown-and-flower pattern, for the Houses of Parliament
Produced by Samuel Scott for J. G. Crace
From a modern copy of the original block
Produced by Cole & Son (Wallpapers) Ltd for the Refreshment Room of the House of Lords
1974
Colour print from wood block and flock
65.5 × 57.3 cm
Given by Cole & Son (Wallpapers) Ltd
E.152–1976

1123

Pugin's watercolour design for this paper, in a different colourway, is D.778–1908.

Raisin, A. See PATTERN BOOKS, no 707.

Raymond, Charles, working 1960s

See also PATTERN BOOKS, nos 715(2), 718, 720.

1127 Two sheets with a design for 'Sweet Pea', for the pattern book *Focus 1*; E.2043 signed and dated in pencil *Charles Raymond 1964./65* and inscribed with note and measurement; E.2044 inscribed with notes and numbered on the back of the mount *A41*
Produced by Shand Kydd Ltd
1964–65
Art work, and a 'test print' of part of the design
Watercolour, some pencil, mounted on card, and rotagravure
60.5 × 49.9 cm (art work)
Given by Shand Kydd Ltd
E.2043, 2044–1980

Reason, Ann, working 1950s

1128

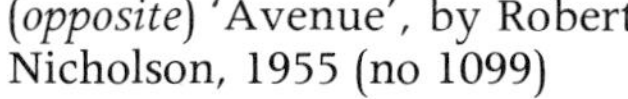

(*opposite*) 'Avenue', by Robert Nicholson, 1955 (no 1099)

1129

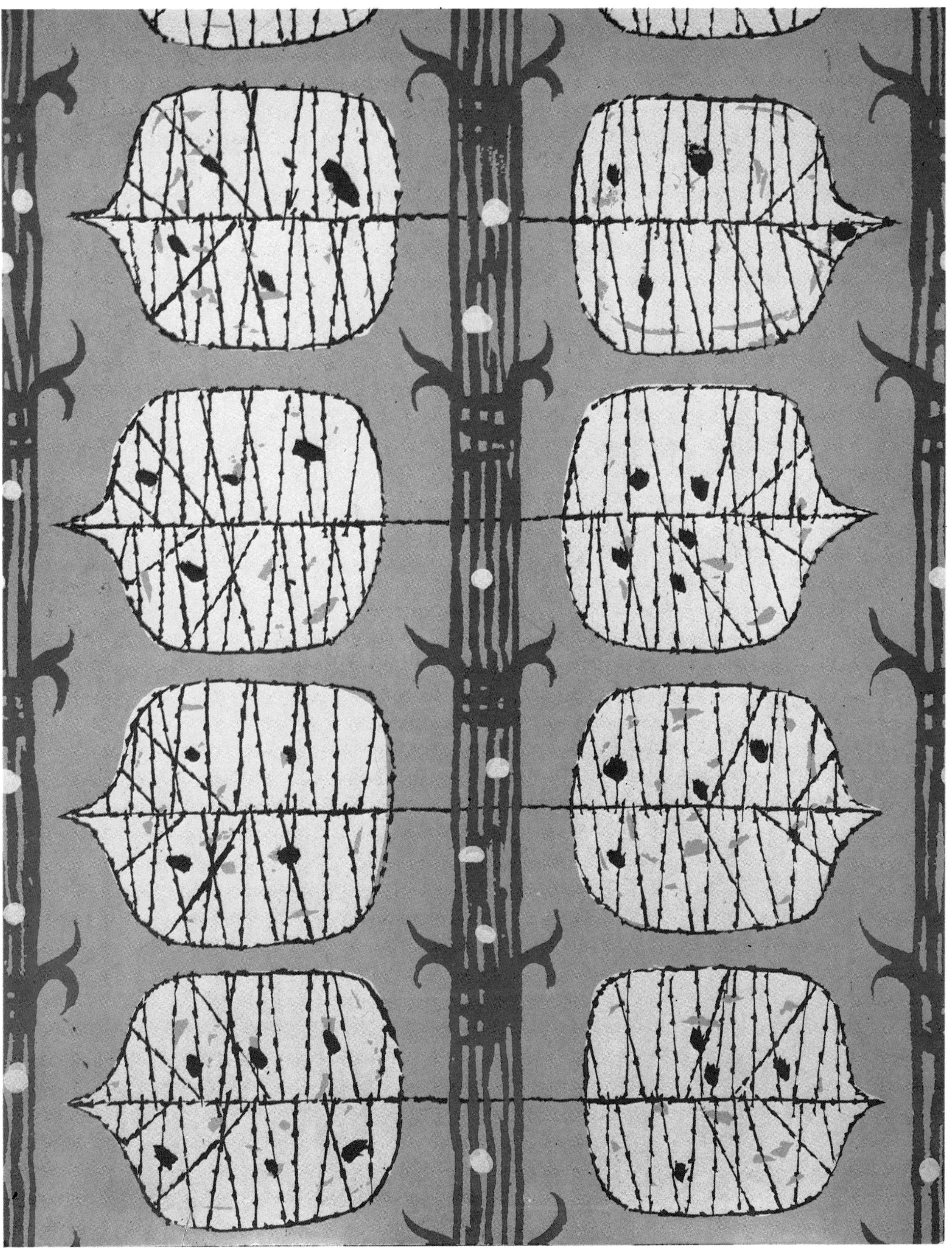

Frieze of flying birds, dado and filling by T. W. Sharp, produced by Jeffrey & Co., *circa* 1882 (no 1141)

1128 'Bouquet'
Produced by the WM as one of their 'Palladio' range
Circa 1957
Screen print
73.5 × 52.9 cm (portion)
Given by the WM
E.576–1966 neg GJ.9375

Redhead, Anne. See PATTERN BOOKS, no 723.

Reeves, Sheila. See PATTERN BOOKS, no 726.

Rhodes, Jennie, working 1970s

1129 Design for 'Sugar and Spice'; inscribed on the mount with title, colour key, note and measurement; with the designer's stamp on the back
Produced by Shand Kydd Ltd
Circa 1976
Pen and ink and watercolour, heightened with chinese white
58.3 × 31 cm
Given by Shand Kydd Ltd
E.2732–1980 neg HA.401

Rhodes, Zandra. See PATTERN BOOKS, no 719.

Rice, Graham. See PATTERN BOOKS, no 707.

Rice, Mrs Peter. See Albeck, Pat.

Richards, Mrs Peggy. See Angus, Peggy.

1130

Rigby, John Scarratt, worked *circa* 1887–*circa* 1940

1130 Design of an exotic bird and flowers; signed *J. Scarratt Rigby,* inscribed for block-printing and with colour notes etc and numbered *1477.*
Circa 1930
Indian ink and watercolour, squared
132 × 75.5 cm
E.1064–1970 neg GJ.9724

1131 Design based on a Chinese painted paper, with a pattern of trees and exotic birds and flowers; signed *J. Scarratt Rigby,* inscribed with measurements, colour notes etc and numbered *200–201.*
Circa 1930
Watercolour and some body colour, squared
133 × 60 cm
E.1065–1970

The above 2 items, nos 1130, 1131, were given by Shand Kydd Ltd.

Risley, Christine, working 1950s

1132 'Joanna', a nursery paper
Produced by the WM as one of their 'Palladio' range
Circa 1957
Screen print, black on yellow
66.5 × 55.2 cm (portion)
E.893–1978 neg GJ.9376

'Rosal'. See PATTERN BOOKS, no 707(4).

'Rose, A. F.'. See Vigers, Allan Francis

Rose, Ben, working early 1950s

American designer.

1133 'Interlace'
Circa 1952
Colour screen print
267.5 × 69 cm (length)
E.985–1978 neg GJ.9465

'The New Papers: a Preview', *Interiors* (August 1952), vol 112, plate on pp 98, 99 (another colourway).

Rosen, Gun. See PATTERN BOOKS, no 735(2).

Samuelsson, Mildred. See PATTERN BOOKS, no 735.

Sanderson-Rigg Studio. See PATTERN BOOKS, no 719.

Sattler, Frau Katharina, working 1840–48

German designer. Wife of Wilhelm Sattler of Schweinfurt-am-Main.

1132

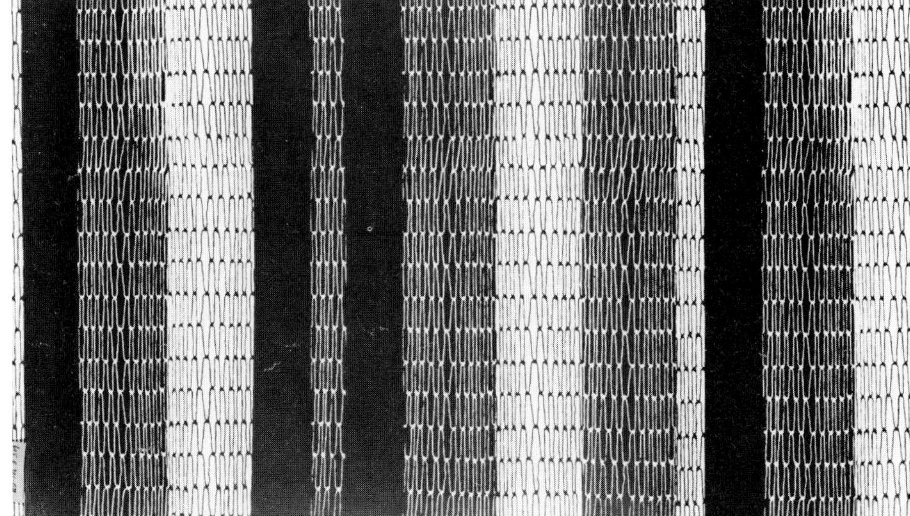

1133

1135

1136

1134 'Die Moritat': one of a pair of supraportes in brown and white on a buff ground
After drawings by Frau Sattler and produced by Wilhelm Sattler of Schweinfurt-am-Main
Circa 1840–48
Colour print from wood blocks
93.5 × 103.5 cm
E.484–1931 BGM

The scene is of a boy holding up a banner with pictures to 2 little girls. Reproduced in Olligs, vol 2, fig 284; Entwisle, *FS*, pl 13.

1135 Supraporte, one of a pair (see above) in brown and white on a buff ground
After drawings by Frau Sattler and produced by Wilhelm Sattler of Schweinfurt-am-Main
Reproduction from the original by Kurt Weber, Dreye bei Bremen
Circa 1840–48
Silk-screen
87.5 × 101 cm (size of sheet)
Given by Deutsches Tapetenmuseum, Kassel
E.1217–1979 neg GJ.9492

A disguised political theme is contained in the picture, which shows a boy with a banner (Ludwig I of Bavaria), a girl (Lola Montez) holding a doll (the Queen of Bavaria), and a kneeling boy (Lola Montez's father). Olligs, vol 2, fig 285.

Schinkel, Herman, d. 1568?

See ANONYMOUS WALLPAPERS AND WALLPAPER DESIGNS, no 33.

Scott, George Gilbert, II, 1839–97

Architect, son of Sir Gilbert Scott.

1136 Two portions, in different colourways, of 'Genoese'
First produced by Watts & Co. Ltd
1877
Colour prints from wood blocks
114.5 × 57.3 cm (each)
Given by Watts & Co. Ltd
E.990, 991–1978 neg GJ.9725

The design for this paper is in the R.I.B.A. collection. Exhibited in *Sir Gilbert Scott (1811–1878) Architect of the Gothic Revival*, VAM, 31 May to 10 September 1978.

Scott, Robert. See PATTERN BOOKS, no 707.

Sedding, John Dando, 1838–91

Architect and designer, who worked in G. E. Street's office originally. In 1874 he set up as a designer of embroidery, wallpapers and church metal work. In 1880 he was appointed Diocesan Architect of Bath and Wells.

1137 Portion of 'The Tapestry'
Produced by Jeffrey & Co.
Circa 1882
Colour machine print
91.4 × 50.1 cm
Given by Harris & Sons
E.2366–1932

1138 Portion with a scrolling foliate pattern
Circa 1885
Print from a wood block in white on brown paper
72 × 53.2 cm
E.2228–1913 neg GJ.9726

1139 Portion of 'Jacobean'
Produced by Jeffrey & Co.
1886
Colour print from wood blocks
92.8 × 54 cm
E.2233–1913

The above 2 items, nos 1138, 1139, were given by Mr Sydney Vacher

1138

Sevant, Robert, working *circa* 1950
See also PATTERN BOOKS, no 707.

1140 Design based on the crystalline structures of insulin (pattern group 8.25); lettered with manufacturer's name etc
Produced by John Line & Sons Ltd for the Festival of Britain in 1951
Colour screen print
74 × 56.5 cm (portion)
E.888–1978 neg GJ.464 CT 8084

See *Design* (1951), vol III, no 36, plate on p 17; N. Carrington, *Design and Decoration in the Home* (1952), pl 138. See also no 1104.

1140

Sharp, T. W., working early 1880s

Possibly the 'T. F. Sharp' referred to in SE.

1141 Frieze of flying birds, a dado of oak leaves and a shell, and a filling (the 'Albion')
Produced by Jeffrey & Co.
Circa 1882
Colour prints from wood blocks
53.8 × 47.6 cm
Given by the WM
E.1852–1934 neg GJ.9727; E.1858–1934 neg GJ.9728 CT 7338 (see col pl, p 408)

Exhibited at the Manchester Exhibition, 1882. *British Architect* (1882), vol XVIII, plate between pp 618, 619.

Shuffrey, L. A. See ANONYMOUS WALLPAPERS AND WALLPAPER DESIGNS, nos 382–387.

Shuttleworth, Peter, working late 1950s

1142 'Toccata'
Produced by the Lightbown & Aspinall branch of the WM as one of their 'Palladio' range
Circa 1952
Colour screen print
73 × 56 cm (portion)
E.958–1978 neg GJ.9377

1142

1141

Silver, Arthur, 1852–96

Founder of the Silver Studio (q.v.) at Brook Green, Hammersmith, London, in 1880. Designer of wallpapers, textiles and gesso panels.

1143 Portion of 'The Flowers of the Field'; stamped with the Patent Office registration number *146905* and with Japanese characters
Produced by Alexander Rottmann & Co.
1891
Embossed paper simulating leather, hand-painted
99 × 93.5 cm
Given by Miss Mary Peerless
Circ. 224–1966

Repr. *JDA* (December 1891), Vol xi, p 191.

Silver, Arthur, probably by

1144 'The Robin Hood'
Probably produced by the Silver Studio, London
Late 19th century
Colour print from wood blocks
56.2 × 59 cm (portion of frieze)
Given by Miss Mary Peerless
E.498–1967 neg GJ.9729

Silver, Rex, 1879–1965

Eldest son of Arthur Silver. Designer of textiles, wallpapers and art nouveau silver. He produced the ranges of 'Cymric' and 'Tudric' pewter ware sold by Liberty & Co.

1145 Trees and fields; stamped on the back with a trademark
Produced by John Line & Sons Ltd

Circa 1905
Stencil
26.4 × 43.1 cm (frieze)
Given by Miss Mary Peerless
Circ. 590–1967 neg GJ.9730 CT 8588

Silver Studio, probably by

See under Silver, Arthur.

1146 Galleons in full sail
Circa 1900–1905
Colour print from engraved rollers
55.9 × 63.5 cm (frieze)
Circ. 593–1967 neg GJ.9733

1147 Trees against a sunset sky; stamped on the back *Chappell & Payne, Art Paper Hangings, 11, Queen's St*
1902
Colour machine print
27.3 × 60.3 cm (frieze)
Circ. 592–1967 neg GJ.9732

1148 Tulips and trees
Stencil
53.4 × 36.8 cm (frieze)
Circ. 591–1967 neg GJ.9731

Greysmith, pl 117.

1144

1145

1148

1146

1149

The above 3 items, nos 1146–1148, were given by Miss Mary Peerless.

Skeen, Henry, working mid-20th century

Studio designer for John Line & Sons Ltd. See also PATTERN BOOKS, nos 707(19), 710, 713(2), 718, 720.

1149 'Verona'
Produced by John Line & Sons Ltd
1950
Flock on a background of glazed paper imitating watered silk
47 × 48.3 cm (portion)
E.1070–1970 neg GJ.9734

For the blocks from which this paper was printed, see no 1149.

1147

1150 Two printing blocks for the above; lettered in copper strips with title, manufacturer's name etc
Produced by John Line & Sons Ltd
Wood
66 × 55.8 cm; 66 × 57.1 cm
E.1071, 1072–1970

The above 2 items, nos 1149, 1150, were given by Shand Kydd Ltd

1151 Portion of 'Crossley'
Produced by John Line & Sons Ltd
1952
Colour machine print
74.4 × 54.5 cm
Given by John Line & Sons Ltd
E.892–1978

Slocombe, F. A., ? 1847–*circa* 1920

Possibly Frederick Albert Slocombe, R.E. (1847–*circa* 1920), a painter and etcher of landscape and genre.

1152

1152 Sixteen portions, including different colourways, of papers with formalized floral motifs
Produced by Corbière Son & Brindle
Circa 1868
Colour prints from wood blocks
Various sizes
Given by Corbière Son & Brindle
1107B–1110B, 1118B–1128B–1868; 1123B neg GJ.9735

Smart, Patricia. See PATTERN BOOKS, nos 718, 720(2).

1153

Smith, Tessa. See PATTERN BOOKS, no 725(2).

Smith, W. J., working early 20th century

1153 'Koto'
Produced by Shand Kydd Ltd
1910
Colour print from wood block and stencil
120.7 × 105 cm (frieze and appliqué filling)
Given by Shand Kydd Ltd
E.1050–1970 neg GJ.9736

Spence, Thomas Ralph, b. 1885

Architect, painter and designer of wrought iron work. He also designed 'The Parthenon Frieze' for Essex & Co. in 1902.

1154 'Syon'
Produced by Essex & Co.
Circa 1906
Colour print from wood block
59 × 57 cm (portion)

1154

Given by Miss Mary Peerless
E.468–1967 neg GJ.9737

Studio Year Book of Decorative Art (1906), plate on p 130.

Spender, (J.) Humphrey, A.R.I.B.A., F.S.I.A., b. 1910

Lithographer, textile and wallpaper designer, and designer of graphics. See also PATTERN BOOKS, no 719.

(*opposite*) 'Trains', by Saul Steinberg, *circa* 1950 (no 1159)

275
SECOND CLASS

'Fig and Vine', by George H. M. Sumner, produced by Jeffrey & Co., *circa* 1900 (no 1173)

(*opposite*) 'The Seraph', by Sydney Vacher, produced by Jeffrey & Co., 1897 (no 1203)

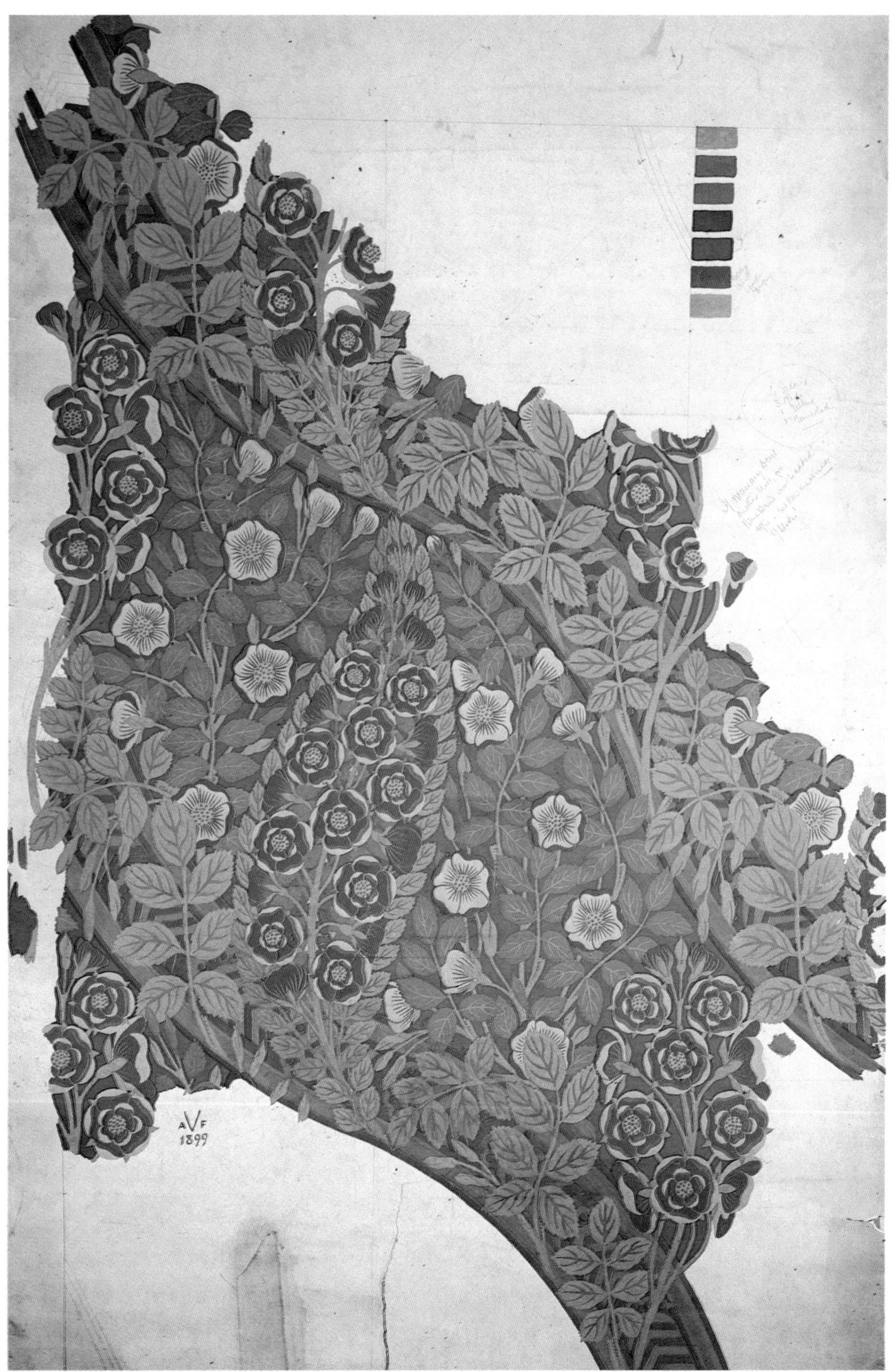
AVF
1899

(*opposite*) Design for 'Japanese Rose', by Allen F. Vigers, produced by Jeffrey & Co., 1901 (no 1214)

1155

1155 Pattern of linked hexagons, in gold and green
Produced by Arthur Sanderson & Sons Ltd
1964
Screen print
54 × 55.7 cm (portion)
E.956–1978 neg GJ.9738

Designers in Britain (1964), vol 6, p 183 (top left).

Spiers, Charlotte Horne, worked from *circa* 1873, d. 1914

A landscape painter in oils and watercolour, she exhibited at the Royal Academy, the Royal Society of British Artists and the New Watercolour Society. She was a relative, probably a sister, of the architect, Richard Phené Spiers.

1156 GJ.9740

1156 Thirty-seven designs for friezes and dadoes, with naturalistic and semi-naturalistic floral patterns
Watercolour
Various sizes
Given by Mr Walter L. Spiers, A.R.I.B.A.
E.22–58–1917; E.23 neg GJ.9739; E.39 neg GJ.9740

1156 GJ.9739

Squires, Edward. See PATTERN BOOKS, no 719.

Stahl, Louis, working early 20th century

He was appointed chief designer for Percy Heffer & Co. *circa* 1914, and was at one time on the staff of Arthur Sanderson & Sons Ltd. He specialized in design in the oriental style.

1157 'Peacock'
Produced by Arthur Sanderson & Sons Ltd for the Franco-British Exhibition, Vienna, 1908
1908
Colour machine print
193.1 × 52.1 cm (length)
Given by Mr Henry Butler
E.2762–1914 neg GJ.9741

SE, pl 155 (colour).

1157

1158

1160

Steinberg, Saul, b. 1914

A Russian-born cartoonist, he began by studying architecture at Milan University in 1932. From 1941 he was on the staff of the *New Yorker* and he became a United States citizen in 1943.

1158 'Views in Paris'; signed and dated in facsimile *Steinberg 46*
Produced by Piazza Prints Inc., New York
1946
Screen print in black
54.6 × 74.8 cm
E.577–1966 neg GJ.452

1159 'Trains'
Produced by Piazza Prints Inc., New York
Colour screen print
97 × 63.5 cm (portion)
E.959–1978 neg GJ.9742 CT 7339 (see col pl, p 417)

1160 'Horses'
Produced by Piazza Prints Inc., New York
Circa 1950
Colour screen print
57 × 75.7 cm (portion)
E.957–1978 neg GJ.9743

The above 3 items, nos 1158–1160, were given by Piazza Prints Inc.

Stéphany, H., working 1920s

Designer of wallpapers in the art deco style of the 1920s, mainly for Desfossé et Karth, he exhibited wallpapers and textiles at the Exhibition in Paris in 1925.

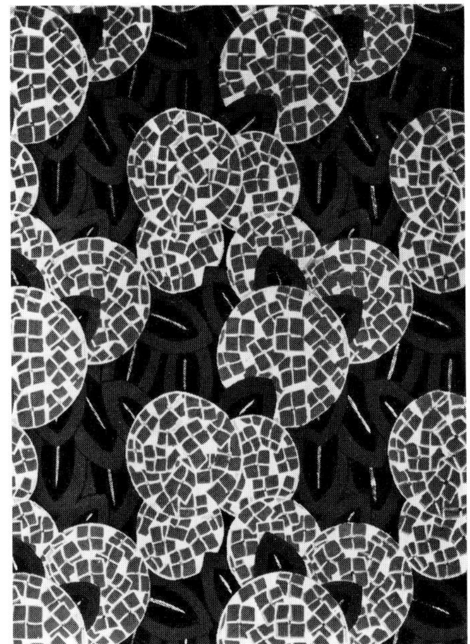
1161

1161 Abstract pattern based on leaves and blossoms, printed in silver and 3 shades of blue
Produced by the Societé Français des Papiers Peints
Circa 1925
Colour machine print
38.4 × 49.8 cm (portion)
Given by Miss Mary Peerless
E.497–1967 neg GJ.9744

H. Clouzot, *Tentures Murales et Papiers Modernes* (Paris, 1928), pl 1 (colour). The illustration reproduced in this work shows the entire design.

Storey, Joyce. See PATTERN BOOKS, nos 715(2), 716, 717, 718, 720.

Storr, Mary. See PATTERN BOOKS, nos 707(8), 710.

Sumner, George Heywood Maunoir, 1863–1940

Designer, archaeologist, painter and etcher, he exhibited at the Royal Academy from 1880 to 1883. He joined the Art Workers' Guild and was associated with A. H. Mackmurdo and the Century Guild in 1884. One of the founders of the Fitzroy School Picture Society, 1893, and Master of the Artworkers' Guild in 1894. He specialized in *sgraffito* work, with which he decorated several churches. He also designed stained glass.

1163 GE.422

1163 GE.423

1162 Design, on 3 sheets joined, for 'The Vine', together with 2 variant arrangements on 4 additional sheets
Produced by Jeffrey & Co.
1893
Body colour on brown paper
Various sizes
Given by the Guildhall Library
E.632–634, 633A, B–1952

1163 'The Vine'
Produced by Jeffrey & Co.
1893
Colour machine print
167.6 × 51.4 cm (portion)
Given by Mr Sydney Vacher
E.2336–1932 negs GE.422, 423

Exhibited in Chicago, 1893; *Art Nouveau in Britain*, Arts Council, 1965, no 89.

1164 Design for the 'Tulip' frieze; inscribed in pencil with working notes, with a stamp lettered *James Barrett* and numbered in ink *3550*
Produced by Jeffrey & Co.
Circa 1893
Body colour
47 × 106.1 cm
Given by Mrs Margaret Warner
E.36–1945

The frieze printed from this design was exhibited at the Glasgow Exhibition, 1901, on the walls of a pavilion designed by W. A. S. Benson. The 'Tulip' frieze is mentioned in *Building News*, 3 February 1893, p 161.

1165 Portion of 'Fig and Olive', a staircase paper
Produced by Jeffrey & Co.
1895
Colour print from wood blocks
E.2342–1932

Builder (1895), plate on p 349. Exhibited *Art Nouveau in Britain*, Arts Council, 1965, no 88.

1166

1166 'The Oak and the Ash and the Bonnie Ivy Tree'
Produced by Jeffrey & Co.
1896
Colour print from wood blocks
E.1770–1914 neg GJ.9745

Journal of Gas and Sanitary Engineering (1899), plate on p 97. Another portion is E.2340–1932.

The above 2 items, nos 1165, 1166, were given by Harris & Sons

1167 'The Crown Imperial'
Circa 1898
Colour print from wood blocks
62 × 55.9 cm (portion)
Given by Mr Roger H. M. Warner
E.36–1971 neg GJ.9746

1167

1168

1168 'Camelia'; inscribed in ink on the mount with the artist's name and numbered *45001*
Produced by Jeffrey & Co.
Circa 1898
Colour print from wood blocks
73.6 × 53.1 cm (portion)
Given by Courtaulds Ltd
E.576–1974 neg GJ.9748

The design for this paper, dated 1898, is E.635–1970. It shows another colourway.

1169 Design for 'Rhododendron'; inscribed in pencil with colour notes
Produced by Jeffrey & Co.
1899
Watercolour and body colour
70.5 × 77.5 cm
E.647–1952 neg GJ.9747

1169

Portions of this wallpaper in different colourways are E.2338, 2339–1932 and E.575–1974 neg GJ.9747. *AJ* (1899), plate on p 91.

1170 Design for 'Knapweed'; inscribed in pencil with colour notes and numbered *91*
Produced by Jeffrey & Co.
1899
Black chalk, watercolour and body colour
102 × 83.9 cm
E.645–1952

A portion of this wallpaper is E.2341–1932 neg L.1942. *Magazine of Art* (March 1900), plate on p 230; Entwisle, *V*, plate 27, fig 49.

1170

1171 Design for 'The Woodlanders'; inscribed in pencil with working notes
Produced by Jeffrey & Co.
Circa 1899
Body colour
53.4 × 106 cm
E.643–1952

A portion of this wallpaper is E.2360–1932 (*Magazine of Art*, December 1899).

1172 Design for 'Arbutus'; inscribed in pencil with working notes
Produced by Jeffrey & Co.
Circa 1899
Watercolour and body colour
87.6 × 106.7 cm
E.646–1952

A portion of this wallpaper is E.2337–1932.

The above 4 items, nos 1169–1172, were given by the Guildhall Library

1173 'Fig and Vine'
Produced by Jeffrey & Co.
Circa 1900
Colour print from wood blocks
71.1 × 50.8 cm (portion)
Given by Mr Sydney Vacher
E.2226–1913 neg L. 1941 CT 7340 (see col pl, p 418)

1174 Design for a staircase paper showing conventionalized flowers and foliage; signed and dated in pencil *Heywood Sumner Jany, 1900* and inscribed with working notes
Produced by Jeffrey & Co.
1902
Watercolour and body colour
91.5 × 91.5 cm
E.637–1952

Reproduced in the *Builder*, 3 May 1902.

1175

1175 Design for 'Brockhurst'; signed and dated in pencil *Heywood Sumner Aug. 1902*; inscribed by the artist *"The Sumerley"* and with working notes
Produced by Jeffrey & Co.
1903
Body colour
86.3 × 81.2 cm
E.636–1952 neg GJ.9749

A portion of this wallpaper is E.1771–1914. *Magazine of Art* (March 1904), plate on p 225.

The above 2 items, nos 1174, 1175, were given by the Guildhall Library

1176 Portion entitled 'Bindweed'
Produced by Jeffrey & Co.
1904
Colour print from wood blocks
85.3 × 51.2 cm
Given by the WM
E.1918–1934

1177 Portion of 'The Apple Tree' (or 'Springtime')
Produced by Jeffrey & Co.
1905
Colour print from wood blocks
71.1 × 50.8 cm
E.2310–1932

The Studio Year Book of Decorative Art (1906), plate on p 129. Other portions are E.2309–1932 and E.1769–1914.

1178 Portion with a pattern of leaves and berries
Produced by Jeffrey & Co.
Early 20th century
Colour machine print
85 × 52.1 cm
E.2343–1932

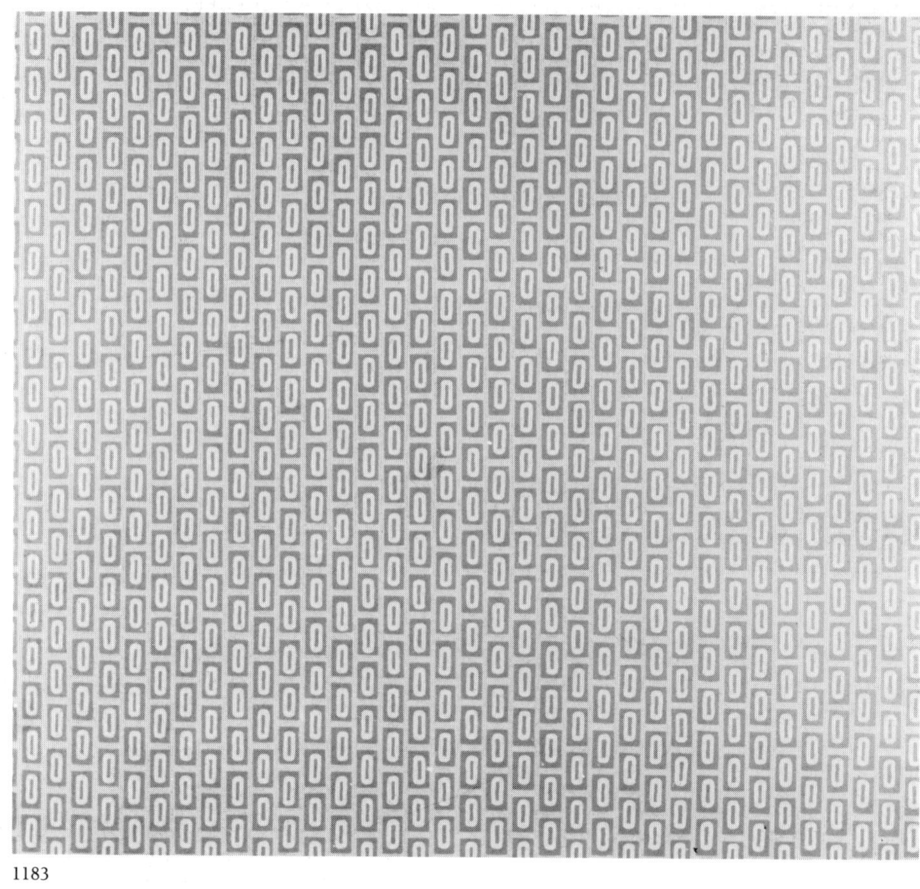

1183

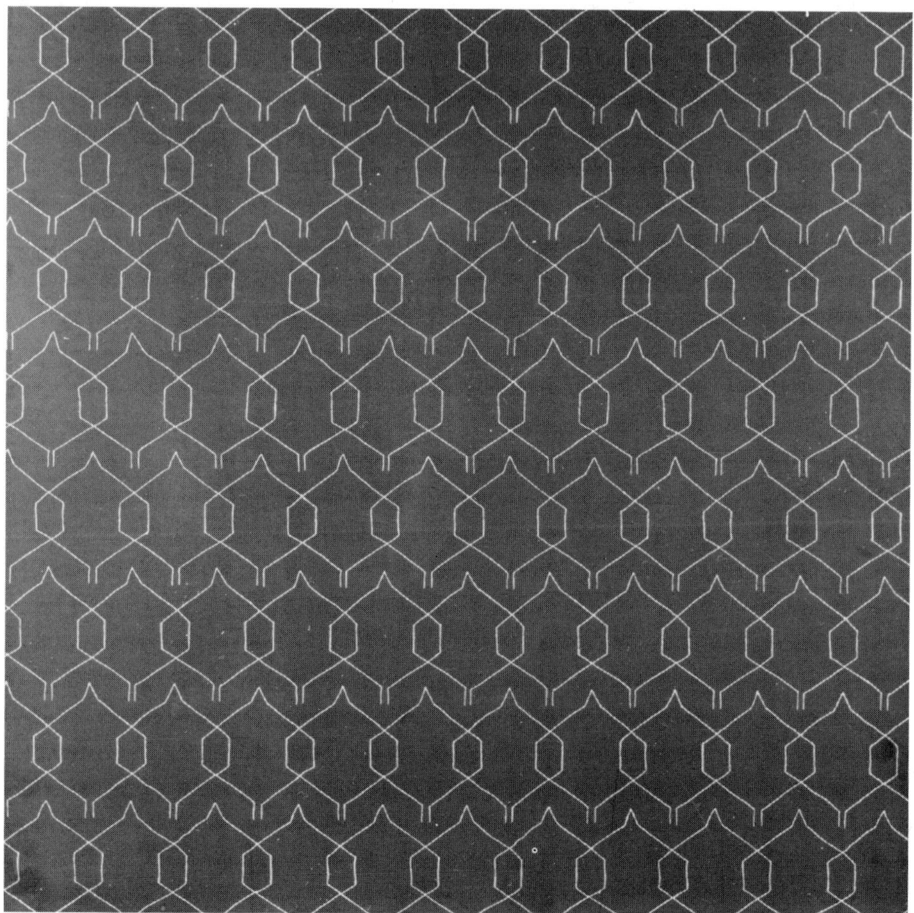

1182

1179 Portion of 'The Evergreen'
Produced by Jeffrey & Co.
1911
Colour print from wood blocks
85 × 50.8 cm
E.1913–1934

1180 Portion of 'Rambler Rose', with border
Produced by Jeffrey & Co.
1913
Colour print from wood blocks
86.4 × 51.4 cm
E.1914–1934

The above 2 items, nos 1179, 1180, were given by the WM

1181 Design showing a flowering plant with intertwining ribbons; inscribed in pencil with working notes
Black chalk, watercolour and body colour
106.7 × 106.7 cm
Given by the Guildhall Library
E.648–1952

Sumner, Peter. See PATTERN BOOKS, nos 715(2), 718(4), 720(3).

1184

Sundberg, Folke, working 1950s

Swedish furniture and wallpaper designer.

1182 'Alle'
Produced by Engblads Tapetfabrik, Göteborg, Sweden
1953
Screen print
74.9 × 54.3 cm
Given by Engblads Tapetfabrik
E.578–1966 neg GJ.9500

1183 Pattern of light oblong forms on a mustard-coloured ground
Produced by Vallo Tapetfabrik, Vallo, near Tonsberg, Norway
1956
Colour machine print
74.6 × 54.2 cm
E.579–1966 neg GJ.9497

1184 Lattice pattern in grey on a blue ground
Produced by Vallo Tapetfabrik, Vallo, near Tonsberg, Norway
1956
Colour machine print
74.9 × 54.2 cm
E.580–1966 neg GJ.9498

The above 2 items, nos 1183, 1184, were given by Vallo Tapetfabrik

---

Sutherland, Graham. See PATTERN BOOKS, no 709.

1185

Svensson, (Gudrup) Inez (Linnea). See PATTERN BOOKS, nos 734, 735(2).

Tajiri, Shinkichi, b. 1923

American sculptor, painter and designer, born in Los Angeles of Japanese extraction. He studied at the Art Institute of Chicago, and in Paris under Zadkine and Fernand Léger.

1185 'Louisiana'
Produced by Rasch & Co., Bramsche, Germany
Circa 1955
Colour machine print
268 × 53 cm (length)
E.972–1978 neg GJ.9750

Gebrauchsgraphik (1958), vol 29, no 1, pl 6.

1186 'Raris'
Produced by Rasch & Co., Bramsche, Germany
Circa 1955
Machine print, lightly embossed
267.5 × 56.5 cm (length)
E.973–1978 neg GJ.9751

The above 2 items, nos 1185, 1186, were given by Dr Emil Rasch

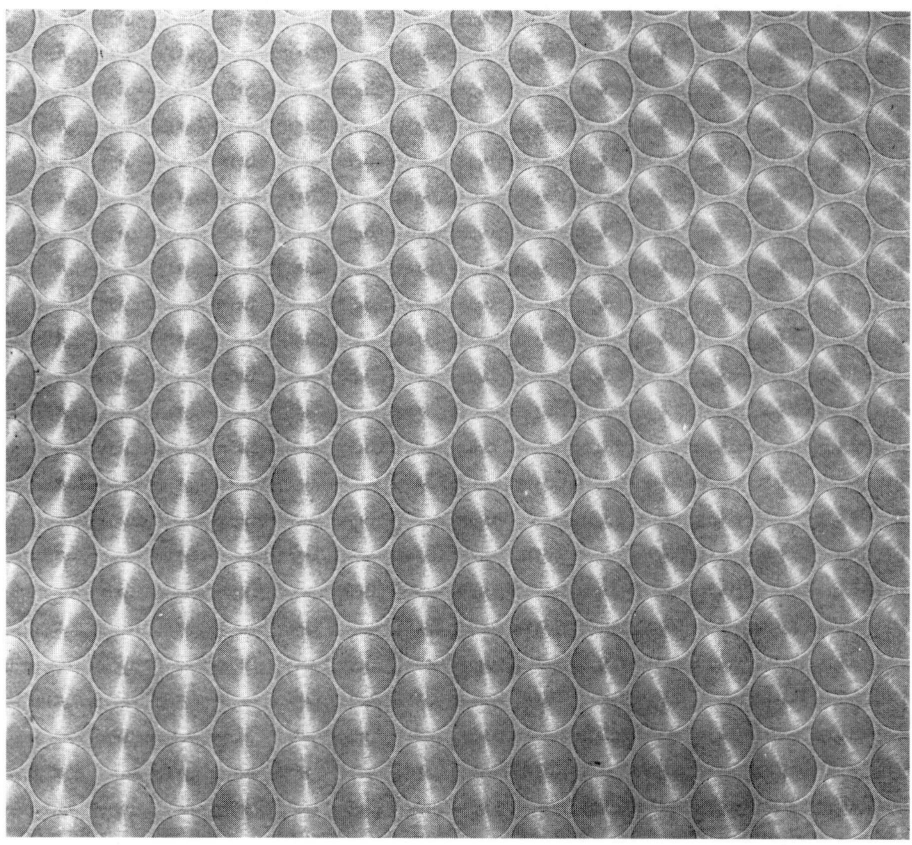

1186

1189 Panel with a frieze of apples and butterflies, a filling of bay leaf and a dado of trellis and fan shapes
Produced by Jeffrey & Co.
1877
Colour prints from wood blocks; the dado, flock
152.4 × 52.7 cm
E.1842–1934

The filling is the same as that exhibited at the International Exhibition, Paris, 1878 (see no 1192).

1190 Another portion of the frieze of the above
E.1855–1934 neg GJ.9754

1191 Branches of pomegranates
Produced by Jeffrey & Co.
1878
Colour print from wood blocks
26.7 × 45.7 cm (frieze)
E.1880–1934 neg GJ.9755

The design for this paper is no 9077.13.

Talbert, Bruce James, 1838–81

A designer and writer, he trained as an architect and was apprenticed in Glasgow from 1856 until 1862. In the latter year he began as a furniture designer for Doveston, Bird and Hull of Manchester. In 1865 he moved to London, where he became known as the leading furniture designer of his time, winning many international awards. He published *Gothic Forms Applied to Furniture* (1867). See also PATTERN BOOKS, no 700.

1187 Trailing leaves, on a background with Greek key pattern
Circa 1875
Paper embossed to simulate leather, on a gilt background
51.7 × 51.2 cm (portion)
E.526–1914 neg GJ.9752

1188 Two portions, 1 a colour variant, with branches of flowers and butterflies
Produced by Jeffrey & Co.
Circa 1875
Colour prints from wood blocks
E.1875, 1876–1934

Greysmith, pl 24.

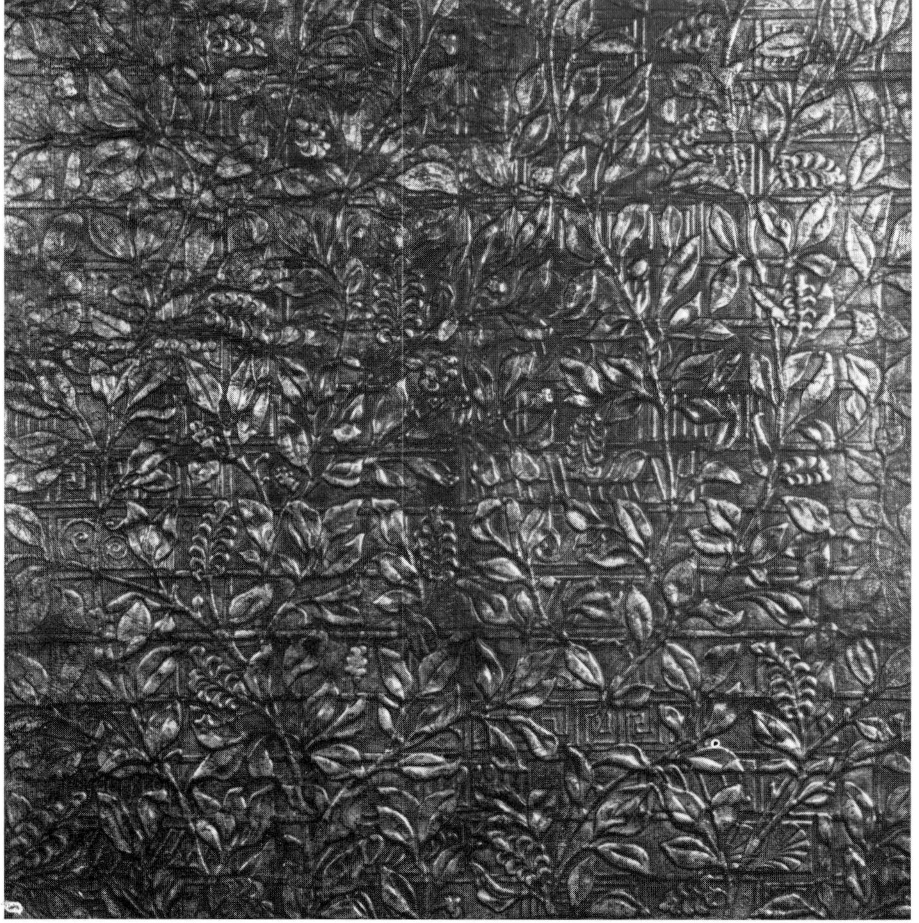

1187

1192 'Clematis'
Produced by Jeffrey & Co.
Colour print from wood blocks
25.4 × 45.7 cm (portion of frieze)
E.1882–1934 neg GJ.9756

International Exhibition, Paris, 1878 (catalogue, plate on p 30). The frieze, filling and dado are E.1853–1934 and E.665–1953 (for both, see no 1189).

The above 5 items, nos 1188–1192, were given by the WM

1193 Pattern of sunflowers and dahlias
Produced by Jeffrey & Co.
Embossed pasteboard imitating leather, coloured by hand
37.5 × 55.9 cm (portion)
E.8–1945 neg GJ.9757

This paper was adapted from a similar paper designed by the artist which was exhibited at the International Exhibition, Paris, 1878 (see no 1194).

1194 Design for 'The Sunflower'
Produced by Jeffrey & Co.
1878
Watercolour and body colour
38.7 × 53.4 cm
E.37–1945 neg K.845

This design originally bore a signature and address on the mount: *B. J. Talbert, 5, Euston Sq. N.W.* The paper printed from this design was exhibited at the International Exhibition, Paris, 1878, where it was awarded a gold medal. See above item. Reproduced in *Building*

1190

1191

1192

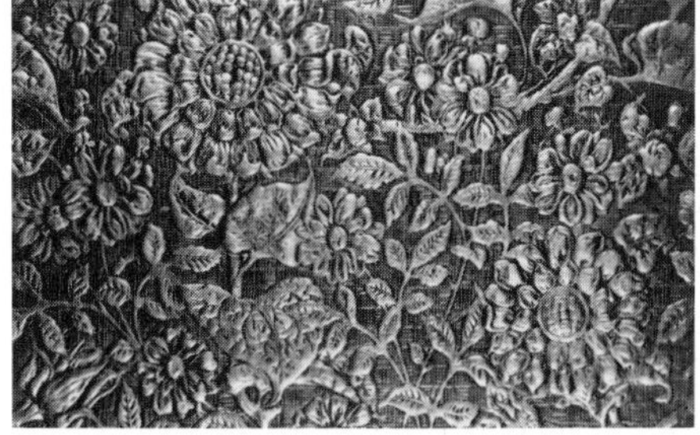

1193

News, 21 February 1879; Greysmith, pl 106. The frieze for the wallpaper is E.1879–1934 (reproduced in *Building News*, loc. cit.); Entwisle, *V*, pl 25, figs 44, 45.

The above 2 items, nos 1193, 1194, were given by Mrs Margaret Warner

1195 Frieze or dado of vertical stems of flowers and foliage, within borders of mouldings
Colour machine print
51.5 × 53.3 cm
Given by the WM
E.1846–1934

1194

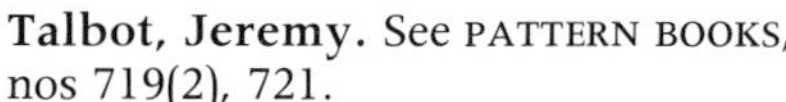

Talbot, Jeremy. See PATTERN BOOKS, nos 719(2), 721.

Taylor, E. Ingram. See Warner, Albert.

Townsend, Charles Harrison, F.R.I.B.A., 1852–1928

Architect of the Horniman Museum, London (1902). Master of the Art-workers' Guild, also a designer of textiles and wallpaper. See also PATTERN BOOKS, no 703.

1196 'The Arboreal Decoration'
Produced by Essex & Co.
1897
Colour machine print
148 × 50.8 cm (panel)
Given by the WM
E.1828–1934 neg GJ.9758

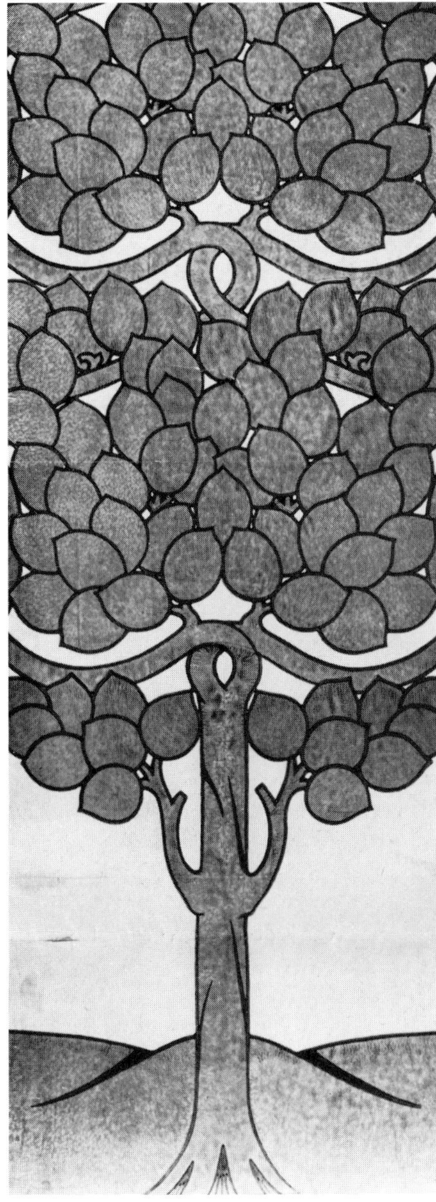

1196

This paper was designed for the drawing room of a house called 'Cliff Towers', built by Townsend near Salcombe, Devon. *Studio* (1898), vol 13, plate on p 244.

Townsend, William George Paulson, 1868–1941

Author of *Embroidery, or the craft of the Needle* (1899), *Plant and Floral Studies for designers, art students and craftsmen* (1901), *Modern Decorative Art in England . . .* (1922).

1197 Seven designs for textiles or wallpapers, with floral, pictorial and chinoiserie patterns

1197 GJ.9759

Early 20th century
Pencil, watercolour and body colour
Various sizes
Given by Mr G. Paulson Townsend, son of the artist
E.794–800–1959; E.798 neg GJ.9759; E.797 neg GJ.9760

Turner, William, ? 1867–1936

His designs were also produced by Lightbown, Aspinall & Co. He was possibly William Lakin Turner (1867–1936), a landscape artist. See also under Warner, Albert.

1198 Three portions, in different colourways, of 'Rubens'
Produced by Jeffrey & Co.
1904
Colour machine prints
Various sizes
E.1773–1914; E.2362, 2363–1932

1199 Portion of 'Sycamore'
Produced by Jeffrey & Co.
1908
Colour machine print
28.7 × 50.6 cm
Given by Harris & Sons
E.2353–1932

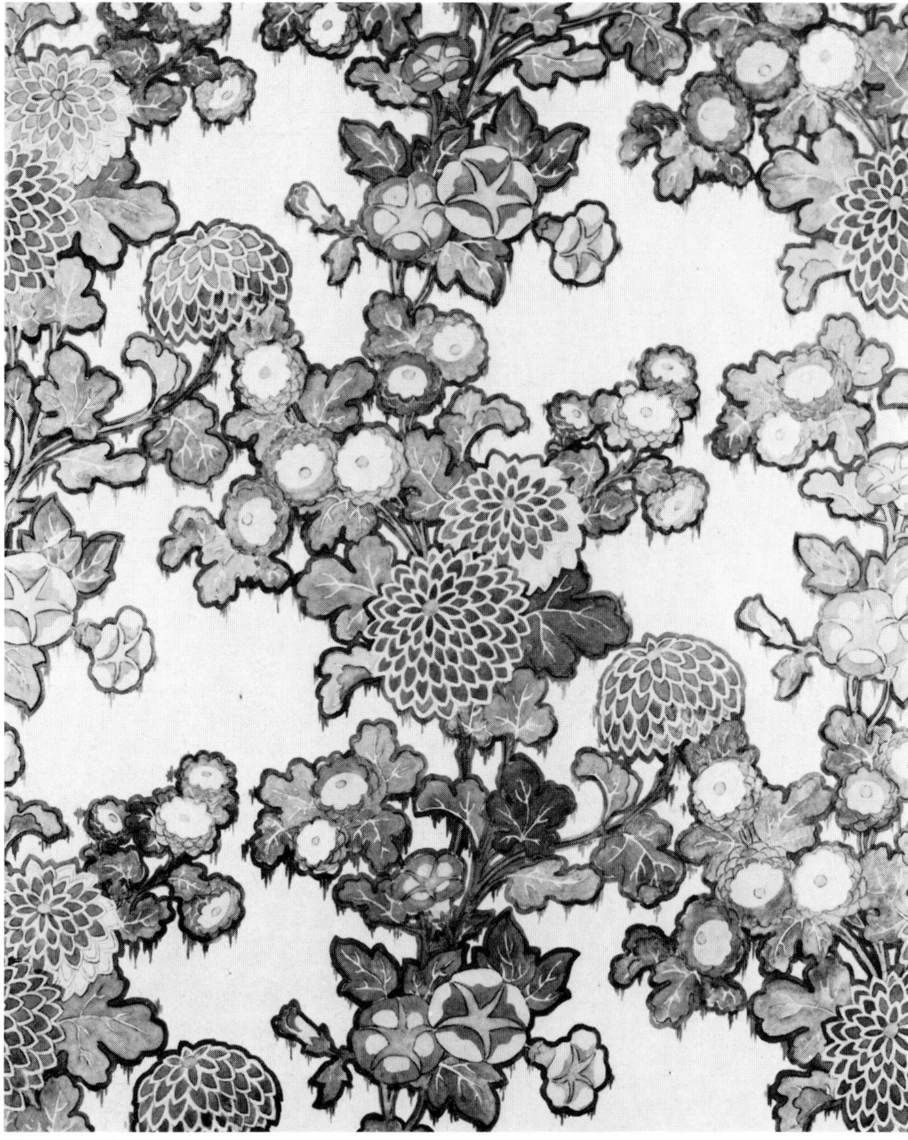

1197 GJ.9760

1202 E.3–1945

Paulson Townsend, fig 126 (colour). The design for this paper is E.3–1945 neg GJ.9761. The Chinese paper on which this design is based is E.3679–1913 (see ANONYMOUS WALLPAPERS AND WALLPAPER DESIGNS, no 657). The annotations in French on the back of the design suggest that it may also have been used by a French firm as a colour guide in making replicas of the paper.

Paulson Townsend, fig 137. The design for this paper is E.4–1945.

1200 Three portions, in different colourways, of 'The Chinese Tree'
Produced by Jeffrey & Co.
1909
Colour machine prints
120.6 × 66 cm (each)
E.1772, 2787–1914; E.1188–1916

The design is based on some Chinese papers from Eltham Lodge (see ANONYMOUS WALLPAPERS AND WALLPAPER DESIGNS, no 654. Yet another colourway, dated 1907, is in the collection of G.P. & J. Baker Ltd. The artist produced many designs for this firm.

1201 Two portions, in different colourways, of 'The Golden Pheasant'
Produced by Jeffrey & Co.
1912
Colour machine prints
121.3 × 63.5 cm (each)
E.1774–1914; E.1186–1916

The Studio Year Book of Decorative Art (1915), plate on p 171. Not to be confused with another design of this title (produced by Charles Knowles & Co., *circa* 1907), based on a Chinese paper; see ANONYMOUS WALLPAPERS AND WALLPAPER DESIGNS, no 654.

1202 Three portions, in different colourways, of 'Chinese Magpie'
Produced by Jeffrey & Co.
1915
Colour machine prints
Various sizes
E.278–1914; E.3683, 3685–1915

Ullhammar, Birgit Eivor. See PATTERN BOOKS, no 735.

Vacher, Sydney, 1854–1935

Architect and etcher. He exhibited at the Royal Academy from 1882 until 1893.

1203 Three portions, including different colourways, of a ceiling paper entitled 'The Seraph'
Produced by Jeffrey & Co.
1897
Colour machine prints
71 × 52.3 cm (each)
E.2199–2201–1913; E.2199 neg GJ.9762
CT 7342 (see col pl, p 419)

House (1897), plate on p 204.

1204 Three portions, in different colourways, of a ceiling paper, with a pattern of briar roses enclosed in circles of branches
Colour machine prints
63.3 × 50.8 cm (average size)
E.2197, 2202, 2207–1913

1206

1205 Two portions of a (?) ceiling paper with a scrolling 'ironwork' pattern
Colour machine prints; E.2205, beige flock
70.9 × 53 cm (each)
E.2198, 2205–1913

1206 Design of birds, dogs, acorns and cherubs holding branches
Colour machine print on a mica ground
43.2 × 56.7 cm (portion)
E.2208–1913 neg GJ.9763

1207 Three portions, in different colourways, with a crown-and-thistle strap-work design, 2 on a mica ground
Colour machine prints
95.9 × 53.4 cm
E.2195, 2203, 2204–1913

1208 Two portions, in different colourways, of a large flower-and-leaf pattern
Colour machine prints
71.2 × 53.4 cm (each)
E.2239, 2241–1913

1209 Portion with a formalized flower-and-leaf design
Colour machine print
69.2 × 53.7 cm (each)
E.2196–1913

1210 Portion with a design of roses in a vase within scrolling leaves and garlands of small flowers
Colour machine print, on embossed ground simulating watered silk
71.9 × 50.8 cm
E.2242–1913

1211 Portion with a strap work and formalized floral pattern
Colour machine print
72.4 × 53.3 cm
E.2206–1913

The above 9 items, nos 1203–1211, were given by the artist

Vigers, Allan Francis, 1858–1921

Wallpaper designer and book-illuminator.

1212 Design for a paper with a pattern of white roses and pinks for Jeffrey & Co.; signed and dated *AFV 1898*

1213

Watercolour and pencil
91.5 × 52.1 cm
Circ. 306–1960

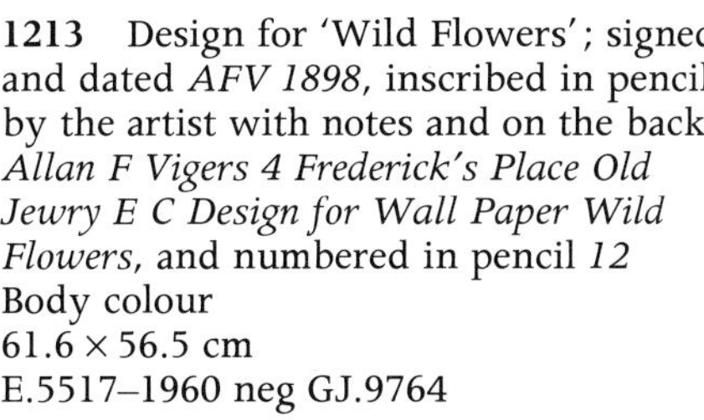
1213 Design for 'Wild Flowers'; signed and dated *AFV 1898*, inscribed in pencil by the artist with notes and on the back *Allan F Vigers 4 Frederick's Place Old Jewry E C Design for Wall Paper Wild Flowers*, and numbered in pencil *12*
Body colour
61.6 × 56.5 cm
E.5517–1960 neg GJ.9764

The above 2 items, nos 1212, 1213, were given by Miss Mary A. R. Vigers, daughter of the artist

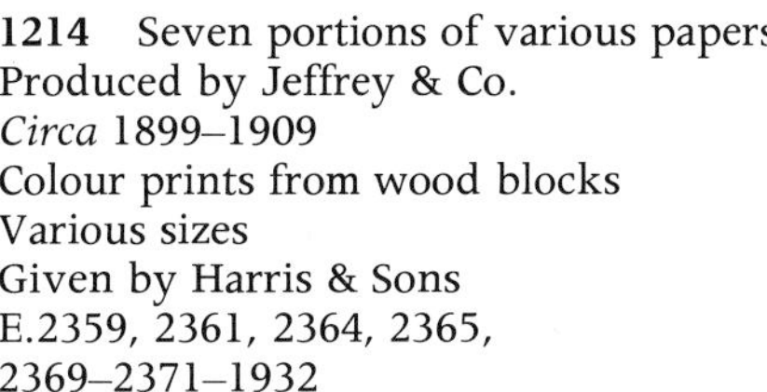
1214 Seven portions of various papers
Produced by Jeffrey & Co.
Circa 1899–1909
Colour prints from wood blocks
Various sizes
Given by Harris & Sons
E.2359, 2361, 2364, 2365, 2369–2371–1932

1214 Circ.308–1960

1214 L.1939

'Pansy', 1899 (*AJ*, plate on p 378) (E.2370), another colourway (E.604–1974); 'Mallow', 1900 (E.2371), another portion (Circ. 308–1960 neg GJ.9765); 'Columbine', 1901 (*Der Moderne Stil* (1901), vol 3, pl 33 (CT 7344; see col pl, p 437); Entwisle (1970), pl 65; Greysmith, pl 116 (E.2369 neg L.1939); 'Japanese Rose', 1901 (*Builder*, 1902, vol 82) (E.2359); 'Lavender', 1905 (E.2365); 'The Arrowhead' (or 'The Bray'), 1901 (*Der Moderne Stil* (1901), vol 3, pl 33; *AJ* (1902), plate on p 286) (E.2364 neg L.1940); 'Chancellor', 1909 (*The Studio Year Book of Decorative Art* (1909), plate on p 75 (E.2361)

'Japanese Rose' (E.2359) is described in *Builder* (1902), vol 82, as being by 'A. F. Rose', in error for A. F. Vigers. The design for 'Japanese Rose' is E.5511–1960 neg GJ.9766 CT 7343 (see col pl, p 420), dated 1899. The design for 'Columbine' (E.2369) is E.2230–1913, and the design for 'Mallow' (E.2371) is Circ. 307–1960, dated 1898.

1215 Design for 'Campanula'; signed and dated *A F V 1900*, inscribed by the artist with colour notes etc, with the stamp *James Barrett Print Cutter*, inscribed in ink *10 Blocks* and numbered *7202*
Produced by Jeffrey & Co.
Body colour over preliminary pencil
134.6 × 80 cm
E.5512–1960

The Studio Year Book of Decorative Art (1906), plate on p 128.

1216 Design for a paper or printed textile, with flowering horse chestnut, wisteria etc; signed and dated *A F V 1901* and inscribed by the artist with notes
Pencil and body colour
80 × 63.5 cm
E.5514–1960

The above 2 items, nos 1215, 1216, were given by Miss Mary A. R. Vigers, daughter of the artist

1217 Six portions of various papers
Produced by Jeffrey & Co.
Circa 1901–1904
Colour prints from wood blocks
Various sizes
Given by the WM
E.1915–1917, 1919–1921–1934

'Aragon', 1901 (*Der Moderne Stil* (1901), vol 3, pl 33) (E.1921); 'Chevrons', 1901 (E.1919); 'Climber', 1901 (E.1916); 'Shrewsbury', 1904 (E.1917)

The design for 'Climber' (E.1916–1934) is E.5520–1960.

Vigers, Frederick, worked *circa* 1884–post 1910

Designer of wallpapers, hangings, tapestries, embroideries and furniture. He was awarded the Grand-Prix at the Franco-British Exhibition, Vienna, 1908, for wallpaper shown by Jeffrey & Co.

1218 Portion of 'Chinese Chippendale'
Produced by Jeffrey & Co.
1910
Colour print from wood blocks
87.6 × 53.3 cm
E.2779–1914 neg GJ.10383

Cabinet Maker (1910), vol 44, plate on p 432; *The Studio Year Book of Decorative Art* (1910), plate on p 104.

1219 Two portions, in different colourways, of 'Pagoda'
Produced by Jeffrey & Co.
1910

1218

1223

Colour machine prints
Given by Mr Henry Butler
E.2790, 2791–1914

The Studio Year Book of Decorative Art (1910), plate on p 104.

1220 Portion with a pattern of climbing roses and large foliage
Produced by Jeffrey & Co.
Circa 1911
Colour print from wood blocks
84.3 × 50 cm
Given by Harris & Sons
E.1920–1934

The Studio Year Book of Decorative Art (1911), plate on p 97.

1221 Portion of 'Blenheim'
Produced by Jeffrey & Co.
Circa 1915
Colour print from wood blocks
79.7 × 51 cm
E.1922–1934

The Studio Year Book of Decorative Art (1915), plate on p 173.

Voysey, Charles Francis Annesley, F.R.I.B.A., 1857–1941

Architect and designer, articled to J. P. Seddon in 1874. He set up practice in 1882. Designed his first wallpapers and textiles under the influence of A. H. Mackmurdo, and joined the Art-workers' Guild in 1884. He also designed furniture, and wrote on economic theories related to the decorative arts. He designed for Jeffrey & Co., Turnbull & Stockdale, Essex & Co., Woollams, Wyllie & Lochhead, Anaglypta & Co., Charles Knowles, Lightbown, Aspinall & Co., John Line, Lincrusta Walton, Arthur Sanderson & Sons and Scott Cuthbertson.
See also PATTERN BOOKS, nos 702(4), 703(8).

1222 Twenty-one portions
Produced by Essex & Co.
Circa 1889–1903
Colour prints from wood blocks
Various sizes
Given by Morton Sundour Fabrics Ltd
E.1883–1903–1953; Circ. 261–1953

'The Saladin', *circa* 1897 (*The House* (1897), vol 1, p 112, fig 10) (Circ. 261); 'The Glade', 1897 (E.1883); 'The Merle', *circa* 1901 (Greysmith, pl 121) (E.1884); 'The Nure', *circa* 1889 (E.1885); 'The Xipon', 1899 (E.1886); 'Briar', 1901 (E.1887), another colourway (E.313–1974); 'The Gidus', 1901 (E.1888); 'The Ilmore', *circa* 1897 (E.1889); 'The Maestro', *circa* 1899 (E.1890 neg GJ.9769); 'The Teynham', *circa* 1903 (E.1891); 'The Morgiana', *circa* 1901 (E.1892); 'The Cestrefeld', 1895 (E.1893); 'The Tierney', *circa* 1897 (E.1894); 'The Savaric', *circa* 1897 (E.1895); 'The Wykehamist', 1897 (E.1896); 'The Columba', *circa* 1898 (*Artist* (1899), vol 25, plate on p 46) (E.1897); 'The Gordon', *circa* 1897 (E.1898 CT 7345 (see col pl, p 438)); 'The Iolanthe', *circa* 1897 (E.1899); 'The Adaim', *circa* 1897 (E.1900); 'The Collina', 1901 (E.1901); 'The Owl', 1897 (E.1902); 'The Standard Rose', *circa* 1901 (E.1903)

Most of these pieces were shown in the exhibition, *Victorian and Edwardian Decorative Arts*, VAM, 1952.

1223 Design for wallpaper and a textile, showing birds perched among formalized plants; inscribed in pencil with colour notes and *Sold to Essex & to Newman without bird. April 1891*
Pencil, black chalk and watercolour
61 × 54 cm
E.267–1913 neg Q.829

The firm of 'Newman' is that of Newman, Smith & Newman, cotton-printers.

1224 'Tokio'
Produced by Essex & Co.
1893
Colour machine print
73.1 × 51.5 cm (portion)
Given by the WM
E.1923–1934 neg K.2935

SE, pl 145, *JDA* (April 1893), p 113. Another piece is Circ. 267–1953. Exhibited *Art Nouveau in Britain*, Arts Council, 1965, no 96.

1224

1225 Design for 'Isis'; signed in ink *C. F. A. Voysey: Architect*, inscribed *11, Melina Place Grove End Road S.John's Wood. N.W*; also inscribed with notes in pen and pencil and *8gns*
Produced by Jeffrey & Co.
Circa 1893
Watercolour and body colour
66 × 100.3 cm
Given by Mrs Margaret Warner
E.39–1945 neg GK.4565 CT 8567

JDA (April 1895), plate on p 83. Also mentioned in *Building News*, 3 February 1893, p 175. 'Isis', the design for the frieze, is E.40–1945. Greysmith, pl 27 (colour).

1226 'The Oswin'
Produced by Essex & Co.
Circa 1895
Colour machine print
70.5 × 48.2 cm (portion)
Circ. 264–1953 neg GJ.9768

1227 'The Aylmer'
Produced by Essex & Co.
Circa 1896
Colour machine print
71.8 × 47 cm (portion)
Circ. 266–1953 neg GJ.9770
Exhibited *Art Nouveau in Britain*, Arts Council, 1965, no 95.

The above 2 items, nos 1226, 1227, were given by Morton Sundour Fabrics Ltd

(*opposite*) Design for 'Columbine', by Allen F. Vigers, *circa* 1901 (no 1214)

1227

1225

Design for a wallpaper by C. F. A. Voysey, *circa* 1900 (no 1239)

(*opposite*) 'The Gordon', by C. F. A. Voysey, produced by Essex & Co., *circa* 1897 (no 1222)

(*opposite*) 'The Norse', by Horace Warner, produced by Jeffrey & Co., 1920 (no 1283)

1228 'The Squire's Garden'
Produced by Essex & Co.
Circa 1896
Colour machine print, varnished
83.2 × 55.9 cm (portion)
Given by the WM
E.1924–1934 neg Q.1073

Greysmith, pl 122; SE, pl 146; Entwisle (1970), pl 63. Another piece in a different colourway is E.306–1974

1229 Design for 'The Owl'
Produced as a paper by Essex & Co., 1897; as a hanging in woollen cloth tissue by Alexander Morton & Co., 1898
Pencil and watercolour
50.8 × 40.1 cm
E.263–1913

A specimen of the textile was shown in the exhibition, *Victorian and Edwardian Decorative Arts*, VAM, 1952, catalogue no S.22. Portions of the paper are E.305–1974 and E.1902–1953. *Artist* (1899), vol XXV, plate on p 42; *AJ* (1899), p 91.

1230 'The Owl'; numbered in ink on the mount *Essex No. A.36*
Produced by Essex & Co.
1897
Colour machine print
62.3 × 44 cm (portion of frieze)
Given by Courtaulds Ltd
E.305–1974 neg R.206

The design for a hanging in woollen cloth, showing the same pattern, which was produced by Alexander Morton & Co. in 1898, is no 1229. The frieze is reproduced in *AJ* (1899), p 91. Another portion of the frieze is E.1902–1953.

1230

1231 Design showing crown, rose, thistle, shamrock and acanthus; signed in ink *C. F. A. Voysey. Architect. 23, York Place W.*
Possibly intended for the Diamond Jubilee year, 1897
Pencil and watercolour
58.5 × 53.3 cm
E.261–1913

1232 'The Lerena'
Produced by Essex & Co.
Circa 1897
Colour machine print
75 × 47 cm (portion)
Circ. 265–1953

Catalogue of the exhibition, *C. F. A. Voysey . . .*, held at the Art Gallery and Museum, Brighton, 1978, pl D.33.

1228

1233 'The Galahad'
Produced by Essex & Co.
Circa 1899
Colour machine print
69.2 × 53.3 cm (portion)
Circ. 263–1953 neg GJ.9772

The above 2 items, nos 1232, 1233, were given by Morton Sundour Fabrics Ltd

1234 Portion of a frieze with a pattern of birds in a tree with red berries; numbered *Essex A.5.*
Produced by Essex & Co.
Late 19th century
Colour machine print
76.5 × 50.5 cm
Given by Courtaulds Ltd
E.316–1974

1235 Two portions: one with a pattern of tulip-shaped flowers, the other with a pattern of birds among oak branches; E.319–1974 numbered *Essex No. A.17.*
Produced by Essex & Co.
Late 19th century
Colour machine prints
61 × 53.5 cm; 75.6 × 53.5 cm
Given by Miss Mary Peerless and Courtaulds Ltd respectively
Circ. 588–1967; E.319–1974 Circ. 588–1967 neg GJ.9773

1236 Design for 'Hemlock'; signed in ink *C. F. A. Voysey Architect*; inscribed *11 Melina Place Grove End Rd. S.John's Wood NW*; also inscribed with title, instructions for printing and *7 gns*; with a stamp lettered *James Barrett Print Cutter* and numbered in ink *4279*
Produced by Jeffrey & Co.
1900
Pencil and watercolour
45 × 40 cm
Given by Mrs Margaret Warner
E.38–1945

1237 Portion of 'The Wild Olive'
Produced by Essex & Co.
Circa 1900
Colour machine print
76 × 47.5 cm
Circ. 259–1953

1238 Portion of 'The Libra'
Produced by Essex & Co.
1901
Colour machine print
68 × 52.7 cm
Circ. 260–1953

JDA, January 1902, p 18.

The above 2 items, nos 1237, 1238, were given by Morton Sundour Fabrics Ltd

1233

1239 Design showing flowers, birds and foliage; signed in ink *C.F.A. Voysey. Architect*; inscribed with notes and *45, Tierney Road Streatham Hill. S.W.*; with a stamp lettered *James Barrett Print Cutter* and numbered in ink *3416*
Produced by Jeffrey & Co.
Circa 1900
Ink and watercolour
61 × 53.3 cm
Given by Mrs Margaret Warner
E.41–1945 CT 7800 (see col pl, p 439)

1240 Two portions, in different colourways, of 'The Shallop'; each signed and dated on the mount *C.F.A. Voysey 1901* and inscribed *The Shallop Design*; numbered *84629* and *84632*
Produced by Essex & Co.
Given by Courtaulds Ltd
E.307, 308–1974; E.307 neg R.211

Der Moderne Stil (1903), vol 5, pl 43, fig 4; P. C. Floud, 'The Wallpaper designs of C. F. A. Voysey', *Penrose Annual* (1958), vol 52, pl 16.

1241 'The Grategus'
Produced by Essex & Co.
1901
Colour machine print
68.6 × 53.3 cm (portion)
Given by Morton Sundour Fabrics Ltd
Circ. 268–1953 neg GJ.9774

1242 'Briar'; signed and dated in ink on the mount *C.F.A. Voysey 1901*, inscribed with title and numbered *64024*

1235

1241

1240

1242

Produced by Essex & Co.
Colour machine print
67.9 × 53.2 cm (portion)
E.313–1974 neg R.213

Another portion of this paper, printed in a different colourway, is E.1887–1953. SE, pl 147; *Decorators' and Painters' Magazine* (1902–1903), vol 1, plate on p 375. For the same paper, with the pattern reduced to half-size, see no 1253.

1243 'Cibber'; signed and dated in ink on the mount *C. F. A. Voysey 1901*, inscribed with title, numbered *6* and inscribed with pencil notes
Machine print in yellow

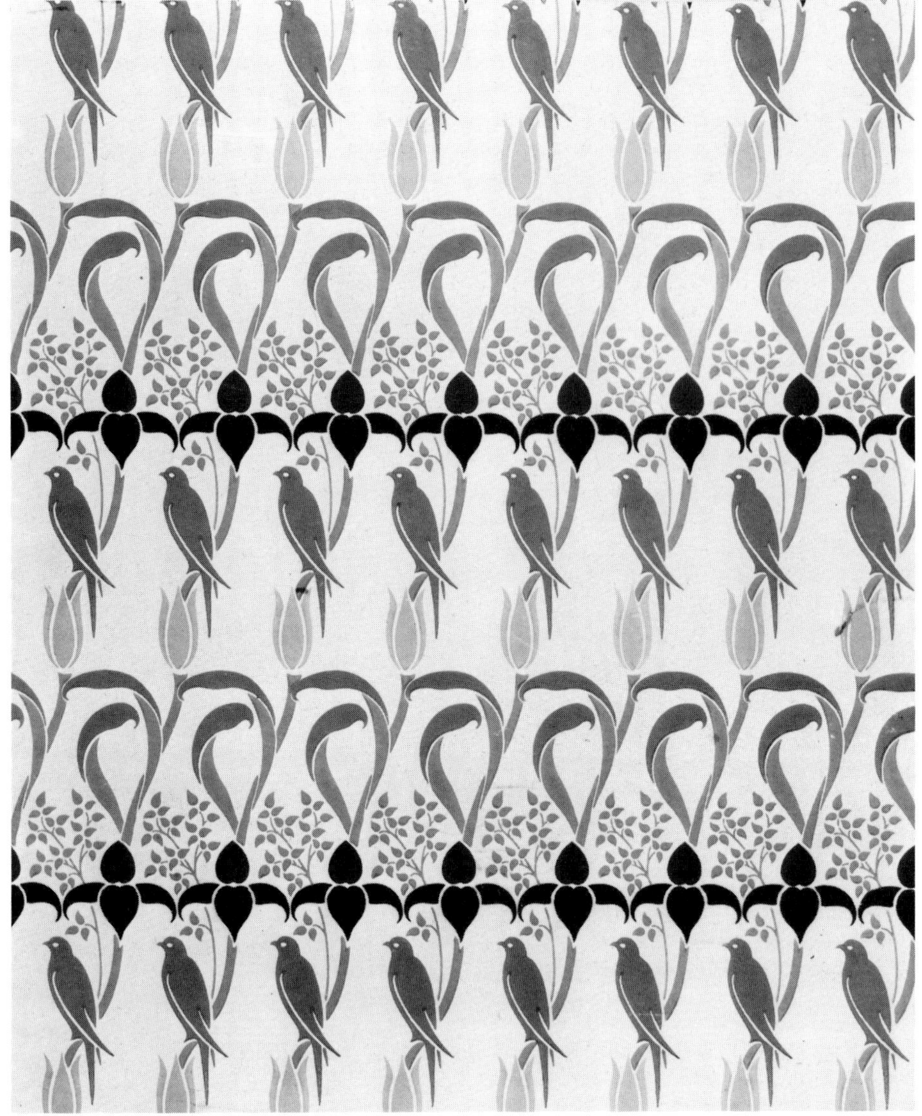

1244

67.7 × 52.8 cm (portion)
E.310–1974

This pattern, printed in blue, red, pink, green and yellow, on a different paper, appears in Essex & Co.'s pattern book for the year 1897 (See PATTERN BOOKS, no 702).

1244 'Minto'; signed and dated in ink on the mount *C. F. A. Voysey 1901*, inscribed *The Minto Design* and numbered *63927*
Produced by Essex & Co.
Colour machine print
67.6 × 54 cm (portion)
E.311–1974 neg R.204

P. C. Floud, 'The Wallpaper Designs of C. F. A. Voysey', *Penrose Annual* (1958), vol 52, pl 15 (there dated *circa* 1898); *Decorators' and Painters' Magazine* (1902–1903), vol 1, plate on p 373.

The above 3 items, nos 1242–1244, were given by Courtaulds Ltd

1245 Design for 'Heraldic'
Produced by Essex & Co.
1902
Pencil and watercolour
66.6 × 53.3 cm
E.264–1913

Decorators' and Painters' Magazine (1902–1903), vol 1, plate on p 373.

1246 'The Furrow'; signed and dated on the mount in ink *C. F. A. Voysey 1901*, inscribed *The Furrow Design* and numbered *64332*
Produced by Essex & Co.
1902–1903
Colour machine print
68 × 53.3 cm (portion)
E.312–1974 neg R.212

A design for this paper showing a different colourway is E.182–1974. *Der Modern Stil* (1903), vol 5, pl 87, fig 3; *Decorators' and Painters' Magazine* (1902–1903), vol 1, plate on p 375.

1247 Two portions, in different colourways, with a pattern of birds, branches and berries, hearts and crowns; numbered in ink on the mounts *Essex No. A.4* and *Essex No. A.29*
Produced by Essex & Co.
Circa 1903
Colour machine prints
75.8 × 53.5 cm (each)
E.317, 318–1974

Voysey worked for Essex & Co., producing wallpaper designs, between 1890 and 1900. *Der Moderne Stil* (1903), vol 5, pl 43, fig 7.

The above 6 items, nos 1243–1247, were given by Courtaulds Ltd

1248 Design (incomplete) for paper or textile, showing a formalized plant; inscribed in pencil *For 1907*
Pencil and watercolour
72.5 × 53.5 cm (size of sheet)
E.266–1913

This design is related to no 1249.

1249 Design for 'Fool's Parsley'; signed and dated in ink *C. F. A. Voysey Architect. 23 York Place W September 1907* and inscribed *S. & Sons*
Produced by Sanderson & Sons
1907
Pencil, watercolour and Indian ink
63.5 × 53.3 cm
E.265–1913

1250 Design with a pattern of birds in a tree; signed and dated in ink on the back *C. F. A. Voysey Archt. Invt. et delt February 1919*; inscribed *73 St. James's Street, S.W.1.*
Process engraving, coloured by hand
38.6 × 40 cm (size of sheet)
E.240–1974

The original design for this wallpaper is E.239–1974.

1251 Design, on 3 sheets joined, for 'Huntsmen'; signed and dated on the back *C. F. A. Voysey. Architect invt. et delt. 73 St. James's St S.W.1 August 1919*
Process engraving, coloured by hand
50.5 × 31.5 cm (overall size)
E.321–1974

Another design for this is in the R.I.B.A. collection (M. Richards, 'The Wallpapers of C. F. A. Voysey', *Journal of the R.I.B.A.* (August 1965), vol LXXII, plate on p 40). Paulson Townsend, fig 169.

1252 Design for 'Fidelis'; signed and dated in ink on the back *C. F. A. Voysey Archt. 73 St. James's St. S.W.1 Decr. 1919*

Process engraving, coloured by hand
36.3 × 32.9 cm
E.322–1974

Paulson Townsend, fig 143.

The above 3 items, nos 1250–1252, were given by Courtaulds Ltd

1253 Portion of 'Briar'
Produced by Lightbown, Aspinall & Co.
1924
Colour machine print
73.4 × 52.2 cm
E.1927–1934

This design was produced at twice this size by Essex & Co. in 1901. See no 1242; SE, pl 147.

1254 Portion of 'Buttercup and Daisy'
Produced by Lightbown, Aspinall & Co.
1924
Colour machine print
74.8 × 51.1 cm
E.1928–1934

This design was originally produced at twice this size by Essex & Co., *circa* 1898. SE, pl 148.

1255 Portion of 'Birds, Squirrel, Acorn and Oakleaf'
Produced by Lightbown, Aspinall & Co.
1924
Machine-printed in oil, one colour
70.8 × 56.2 cm
E.1925–1934

1256 Portion of 'The Daisy'
Produced by Lightbown, Aspinall & Co.
1924
Colour machine print
73.6 × 51.1 cm
E.1926–1934

This design was originally produced at twice this size by Essex & Co., *circa* 1898.

The above 4 items, nos 1253–1256, were given by the WM

1257 Design for 'Birds and Berries'; signed *C. F. A. Voysey. Architect 45, Tierney Road, Streatham Hill S. W.*, with inscribed measurements etc and numbered *80*
Watercolour and pencil
57 × 43.2 cm (size of sheet)
E.145–1974

Reproduced in 'An Interview with Mr. C. F. A. Voysey', *Studio* (1893), vol 1, plate on p 234. The artist was at Tierney Road *circa* 1893 or earlier.

1246

1258 Design (incomplete) used for a frieze and for a wall hanging entitled 'The Minstrel'; numbered *56*
The paper, produced by Essex & Co.; the textile, by Alexander Morton & Co.
Watercolour and pencil
54 × 26.9 cm
E.148–1974

The design is possibly a copy. The whole frieze is reproduced in 'An Interview with Mr. C. F. A. Voysey' (see under above item) and in *JDA* (1900), vol 20, on p 366. The wall hanging is reproduced in J. L. Caw, 'The Mortons of Darvel', *AJ*, 1900, plate on p 9.

1260

1259 'The Anselm'; inscribed in ink on the mount *C. F. A. Voysey* and with title (wrongly spelt)
Colour machine print, part squared in pencil
74 × 47.2 cm
E.304–1974

Reproduced in *JDA*, April 1895, plate on p 84.

The above 3 items, nos 1257–1259, were given by Courtaulds Ltd

1260 'The Fairyland'
Produced by Essex & Co.
Colour machine print
76 × 53.3 cm (portion)
Given by Morton Sundour Fabrics Ltd
Circ. 262–1953 neg GJ.9771

1261 Portion of 'Feudal'; numbered in ink on the mount *Essex No. A.14*
Produced by Essex & Co.
Colour machine print
76 × 53.4 cm
Given by Courtaulds Ltd
E.309–1974

1262 Design for the frieze to go with the wallpaper 'Feudal' (above)
Pencil and watercolour
33.3 × 65.4 cm
E.269–1913

Der Moderne Stil (1903), vol 5, pl 43, fig 3.

1263 Design showing birds, leaves and waterlilies
Produced by Jeffrey & Co.
Ink wash
61 × 53.3 cm
Given by Mrs Margaret Warner
E.42–1945

1264 Portion with a pattern of birds on fruit-bearing branches; numbered *Essex No. A.16*
Produced by Essex & Co.
Colour machine print
75.9 × 53.1 cm
E.315–1974

Der Moderne Stil (1903), vol 5, plate 43, fig 1.

1270

1265 Design for a wallpaper, with a pattern of an owl in a tree, mobbed by small birds; signed in ink on the back *C. F. A. Voysey Architect Invt. et delt 73 St. James's Street, S.W.1.* and inscribed with measurement
Process engraving and Indian ink
74 × 60.7 cm (size of sheet)
Given by Courtaulds Ltd
E.323–1974

The artist lived at St James's Street from 1917. Another copy of this design is Circ.42–1928.

1266 Design for wallpaper or textile showing birds and poppies; signed in ink *C. F. A. Voysey. Archit*; inscribed with notes for printing and in pencil on the back *Never published*
Pencil and watercolour
57.2 × 42 cm
E.260–1913

1267 Design showing formalized birds and mistletoe; signed in ink *C. F. A. V* and inscribed with notes
Pencil and watercolour
66.6 × 53.3 cm
E.262–1913

1268 Portion of 'The Lisston'; signed in ink on the mount *C. F. A. Voysey*, inscribed in ink with title, numbered *1377* and inscribed in pencil *4 shuttle broc. Use three weaves for leaves*
Colour machine print
70 × 41.6 cm
E.314–1974

This design was also intended for a textile.

1269 Design entitled 'The Ornamental Tree'; signed *C. F. A. Voysey. Archt. 23 York Place. W.* and inscribed in pencil *Essex & Pilkington for tile. Never published*
Pencil and watercolour
57.8 × 53.3 cm
E.270–1913

This design was used by Pilkington Bros Ltd as a tile decoration. A set of tiles made after this design is in the Nordenfjeldske Kunstindustrimuseum, Trondheim, Norway. The reference to Essex & Co. in the inscription indicates that the design was also originally intended for use as a wallpaper.

Voysey, Charles Francis Annesley, probably by

1270 'The Syracuse'
Produced by Essex & Co.
1902–1903
Colour print from wood block
58.5 × 55.7 cm (portion)
Given by Miss Mary Peerless
E.470–1967 neg GJ.9775

Decorators' and Painters' Magazine (1902), vol II, plate on p 290.

Wagner, ——, worked *circa* 1845–*circa* 1864

1273 'Flying Heart'

Painter and wallpaper designer who was noted for his skill in painting flowers and for his large-scale compositions with romantic subjects in cartouches. He designed mainly for Desfossé et Karth.

1271 Floral decoration with putto and cartouche, framed in arabesque
Circa 1850
Colour print from wood blocks
177.8 × 57 cm (size of sheet)
Given by Mr William McEwan, through the WM
E.87–1937

1272 Panel in the neo-Greek style; on a pink ground, a vase containing flowers on a tall tripod, the whole surrounded by a thin gold border
Produced by Desfossé et Karth, Paris 1863–64
Colour print from wood blocks
130.2 × 52.8 cm
E.3474–1932

Two panels with this design, one on either side of a large central panel, printed on a grey-green ground, were No 111 in the exhibition *Trois Siècles des Papiers Peints*, Musée des Arts Décoratifs, Paris, 22 June to 15 October 1967.

Wakely, Shelagh. See PATTERN BOOKS, no 721(2).

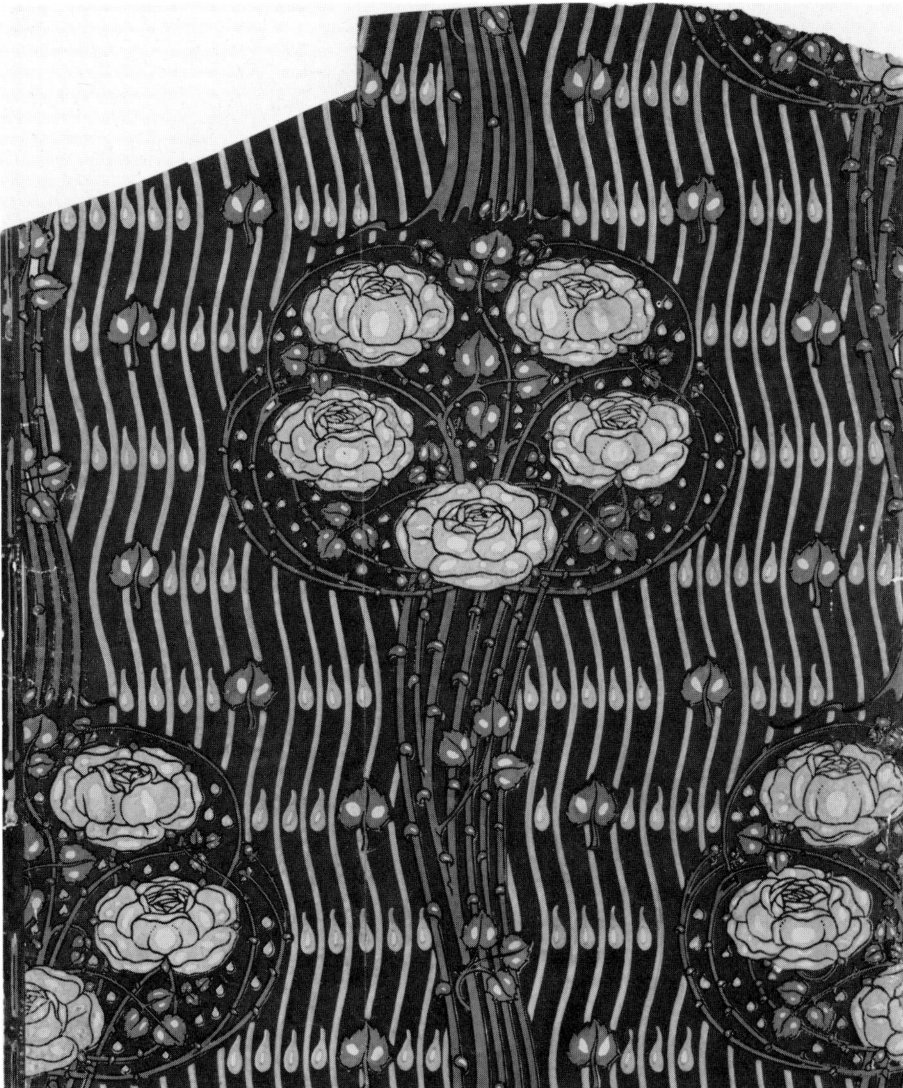

1273 'The Rambler Rose'

Walton, George, 1867–1933

Architect and designer, who set up as a decorator and designer under the title of George Walton & Co., Ecclesiastical and Home Decorators, Glasgow, 1888. He first exhibited with the Arts and Crafts Society, 1890, and moved to London in 1897. He designed shop fronts, interiors and furniture for Kodak's in London, Glasgow and abroad. Among the houses designed and decorated by him are 'The Leys', Elstree, and 'The White House', Shiplake. He also produced textile designs for Morton Sundour Fabrics from 1926 until 1930.

1273 Nine portions, including different colourways
Produced by Jeffrey & Co.
Colour prints from wood blocks
Various sizes
Given by Harris & Sons
E.2344–2352–1932

'Flying Heart', 1905 (E.2347, E.2348 neg GK.4712 CT 8587); 'Privet', 1905 (E.2351, 2352); 'The Rambler Rose', 1905 (E.2344–2346; E.2345 neg GG.5877); 'Stag within an Oak Wreath' (E.2349, 2350).

'The Rambler' and 'Privet' are illustrated in *AJ* (1905), plate on p 284 (colour).

Wardle, George Young, working from *circa* 1860, d. 1910

Wardle made drawings for Morris, Marshall & Co., from 1865 to 1866.

1274 Design for a paper and border with leaves and berries
Circa 1860
Watercolour on tracing paper
22.9 × 23.2 cm
Given by Mr Aymer Vallance
E.1469–1933 neg GJ.9776

1274

1277

Warming, Karin. See PATTERN BOOKS, no 716.

Warner, Albert, working early 1900s

Son of Metford Warner (owner of the firm of Jeffrey & Co.) and a partner in the firm. See also no 988.

1275 Border of formalized roses and tulips connected by straight stems of leaves with a filling
Produced by Jeffrey & Co.
1903
Colour machine prints
83.9 × 50.8 cm (overall size)
E.1932–1934

The filling was also used for the 'Standard Rose' decoration, reproduced in *Cabinet Maker & Complete House Furnisher* (April 1904), plate on p 321.

1276 Portion of 'Aspen'
Produced by Jeffrey & Co.
1903
Colour print from wood blocks
73.6 × 50.8 cm
E.1929–1934

1277 'Chequers'
Produced by Jeffrey & Co.
1903
Colour print from wood blocks
66.4 × 49.5 cm (portion)
E.1930–1934 neg GJ.9777

Decorators' and Painters' Magazine (1903–1904), vol III, plate on p 336.

1278 Portion with a design of harebells, tansies and clover
Produced by Jeffrey & Co.
Circa 1905
Colour machine print
83.9 × 49.8 cm
E.1931–1934

The above 4 items, nos 1275–1278, were given by the WM

Warner, Albert, and Ingram Taylor

1279 Frieze of formalized rose-bushes, forming part of the 'Stamford' decoration
Produced by Jeffrey & Co.
Circa 1903

Colour print from wood block and stencil
232.2 × 56.8 cm
Given by Mr Roger H. M. Warner
E.35–1971 neg GJ.9778

Der Moderne Stil (1903), vol 5, pl 69. Ingram Taylor designed the 'Falcon' wallpaper for Jeffrey & Co., 1897.

Warner, Albert, and William Turner

1280 Portion of the 'Bermudas'
Produced by Jeffrey & Co.
1914
Colour print from wood block
Given by Jeffrey & Co.
E.1778–1914

Decorators' and Painters' Magazine (1914), plate on p 351.

Warner, Horace, 1871–1939

A son of Metford Warner. owner of Jeffrey & Co. When the firm was taken over by the WM in the early 1920s he worked for a time as a designer at their Perivale factory; subsequently he worked freelance. See also ANONYMOUS WALLPAPERS AND WALLPAPER DESIGNS, no 1.

1281 Two portions, in different colourways, of 'The Mill Stream'
Produced by Jeffrey & Co.
1904
Colour print from wood blocks
40 × 49.8 cm
E.1933, 1934–1934 neg GJ.9779

1282 Portion of 'The Rock Peony'
Produced by Jeffrey & Co.
Colour print from wood blocks
86.3 × 59 cm
E.1935–1934

1283 Portion of 'The Norse'
Produced by Jeffrey & Co.
1920
Colour print from wood blocks
62.2 × 51.5 cm
E.1936–1934 CT 7346 (see col pl, p 440)

1284 Portion with a floral design taken from a specimen of Elizabethan needlework
Produced by Jeffrey & Co.
Colour print from wood blocks
85.1 × 50 cm
E.1937–1934

1281

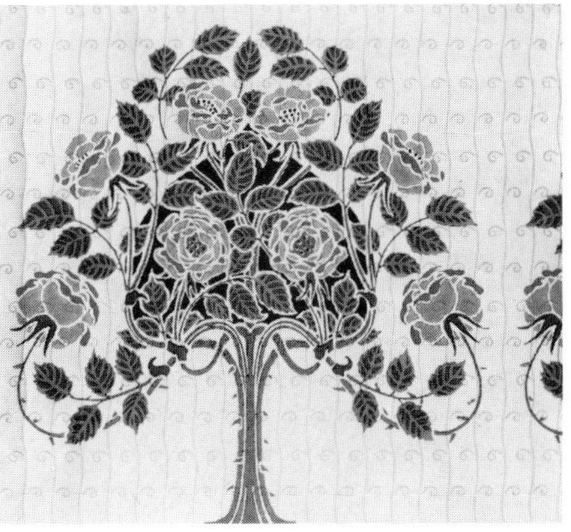

1279

1285 Portion of 'The Sunflower'
Produced by Jeffrey & Co.
Colour print from wood blocks
86.3 × 51.5 cm
E.1938–1934

1286 Portion of 'Borneo'
Produced by Jeffrey & Co.
Colour print from wood blocks
85.7 × 50.1 cm
E.1939–1934

The above 6 items, nos 1281–1286, were given by the WM

1291

Warner, Metford, 1843–1930

Became junior partner of Jeffrey & Co. in 1866 and sole proprietor in 1871. William Morris entrusted him with the printing of his wallpaper designs. Warner encouraged many artists to design for the wallpaper industry, among them William Burges, E. W. Godwin, Walter Crane and C. L. Eastlake. He gained admittance for wallpaper into the *Fine Arts Exhibition* at the Albert Hall for the first time in 1873, and did much to further the high standards of the industry.

1287 Portion with a design of larch twigs, butterflies, birds etc; the birds by Harrison Weir
Produced by Jeffrey & Co.
1878
Colour print from wood blocks
68.5 × 50.8 cm
Given by the WM
E.1940–1934

For a study for the birds by Weir, see no 1294.

1288 Portion of 'The Periwinkle'
Produced by Jeffrey & Co.
1908
Colour print from wood blocks
67.6 × 51.5 cm
E.1941–1934

1289 Portion of 'The Burford'
Produced by Jeffrey & Co.
1912
Colour print from wood blocks
76.8 × 51.4 cm
E.1942–1934

1290 Three portions, in different colourways, of 'Juno'
Produced by Jeffrey & Co.
1920
Colour prints from wood blocks
Various sizes
E.1943–1945–1934

1291 Two portions, in different colourways, with a design of flowers in a vase on a stand
Produced by Jeffrey & Co.
Colour prints from wood blocks
88.5 × 60 cm
Given by the WM
E.1946, 1947–1934; E.1946–1934
neg GJ.9780

Watts, Sandra. See PATTERN BOOKS, nos 719, 721.

Webb, Stephen, 1849–1933

Professor of Sculpture at the Royal College of Art. He designed several wallpapers for Jeffrey & Co. See also no 913.

1292 Portion of a frieze, 'Boy and Dolphin'
Produced by Jeffrey & Co.
1894
Paper embossed in gold to simulate leather
213.4 × 57.1 cm
Given by Mr Roger H. M. Warner
E.43–1971 neg GJ.9781

Studio (1894), vol 2, plate on p 191.

Weir, Harrison William, 1824–1906

Animal painter, illustrator and author who learned colour printing under George Baxter. He drew for the *Illustrated London News, The Graphic*

1292

and other magazines. He wrote *Alphabet of Birds* (1858) and exhibited at the Royal Academy and elsewhere between 1843 and 1880.

1293 Portion of 'The Daisy'
Produced by Jeffrey & Co.
1871
Colour print from wood blocks
49.8 × 47.3 cm
E.1948–1934

SE, pl 122.

1294 Study of blue-tits and apple blossom, intended as the basis of a design for wallpaper to be produced by Jeffrey & Co.; inscribed on the back *Painted by Harrison Weir for Metford Warner for a Paper Hanging Design, 1874, in which these birds were to be introduced*
Pencil, watercolour and body colour
29.5 × 36.9 cm (size of sheet)
Given by the Guildhall Library
E.644–1952

For the wallpaper produced by Metford Warner, see no 1287.

1295 Portion of 'The Berthault Frieze'
Produced by Essex & Co.
1906
Colour machine print
49.5 × 76.2 cm
Given by the WM
E.1833–1934

1296

1296 'The Dimsdale'
Produced by Jeffrey & Co.
Circa 1907
Colour print from wood blocks
88.5 × 50.3 cm (portion)
Given by Harris & Sons
E.2354–1932 neg GJ.9782

ASJ (2), fig 47.

Wells, Bessie. See PATTERN BOOKS, no 716.

Whistler, Rex (John), 1905–44

After studying at the Slade School, he worked as a painter of murals (including those in the Tate Gallery restaurant) and portraits, and also as a book-illustrator and stage designer. He was killed in action during the Second World War.

1297 Portion in the chinoiserie style, with a picture frame as its central motif, painted to house Picasso's 'L'Enfant au Pigeon'; signed and dated *Rex Whistler 1932*
Oil on canvas
182.9 × 155 cm
PROVENANCE Above the chimneypiece of a bedroom in 12, North Audley Street, London
Given by an anonymous donor
P.13–1977 neg GG.1701

The artist has provided this missing section of a chinoiserie wallpaper, bought by Mr Samuel Courtauld at Bath. A similar work was executed by the artist on the walls of a room at 39, Preston Park Avenue, Brighton, a month before he was killed. A strip of the original 19th century chinoiserie wallpaper is P.13A–1977.

1297

Widlund, Monica. See PATTERN BOOKS, no 734.

Wildgoose, L. See PATTERN BOOKS, no 713(2).

Wilkinson, John. See PATTERN BOOKS, no 721(3).

Willcock (Wilcock), Arthur, working early 20th century

He designed for Allan, Cockshut & Co., Lightbown, Aspinall & Co. and John Line & Sons Ltd.

1298 Thirty-three floral and neo-classical designs
1910–13
Watercolour and pencil
Various sizes
Given by the artist
E.3925–3957–1923; E.3940 neg GJ.10011; E.3935 neg GJ.10012

E.3937, 3938 are inscribed with a note stating that they were produced for Zuber et Fils, Rixheim, Alsace. E.3940, a frieze, is inscribed with the words 'sold to Stather, probably in 1904'. E.3926–1923, 'Trojan Bird'.

Willement, Thomas, F.S.A., 1786–1871

Heraldic writer and artist in stained glass.

1299 Formalized flowers, fruit and leaves
Circa 1832
Print from wood block and red flock
61 × 68.6 cm (portion)
PROVENANCE Alton Towers, Cheadle, Staffordshire
Given by the Ministry of Local Government and Planning
E.848–1951

Alton Towers was partially demolished in 1951. This paper has the same pattern as no 1301, which is printed in green and gold.

1300 Floral arabesques
Circa 1832
Flock on embossed gold paper
36.2 × 57.7 cm
PROVENANCE Charlecote Park, Warwickshire
E.23196–1957 neg GJ.10014

This paper is from the dining room in the 19th-century wing of Charlecote. It is illustrated and referred to by Christopher Hussey in *Country Life* (May 1952), pp 1330, 1331.

1301 Formalized flowers, fruits and leaves
Circa 1832
Print from wood block and flock
37.7 × 53.3 cm (portion)
PROVENANCE Charlecote Park, Warwickshire
E.23199–1957 neg GJ.10016

This paper is from a bedroom in the 19th-century wing of Charlecote. The decoration of the 19th-century wing is referred to by Christopher Hussey, *Country Life* (May 1952) pp 1330 *et seq*. For another portion in red flock, see no 1299

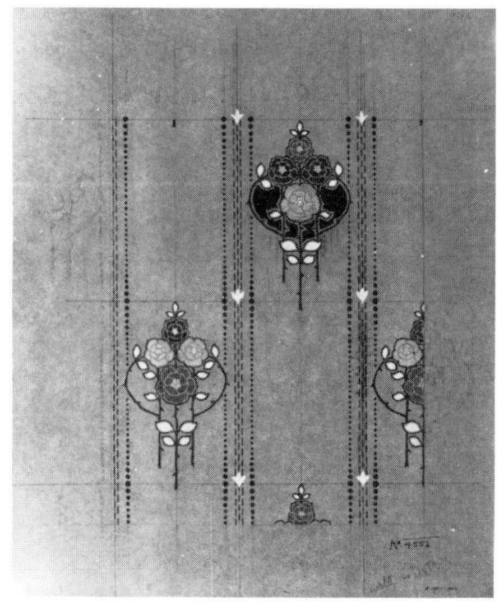

1298 GJ.10011

1298 GJ.10012

1303

1302 Strap-work design; stamped on the back with the William IV Excise duty stamp and *Paper 222 Stained*; with frame mark *137B 179 62 1258*
1832
Print from wood block
45.7 × 54 cm (portion)
PROVENANCE Charlecote Park, Warwickshire
E.23200–1957 neg GE.431

This paper is from a bedroom in the 19th-century wing of Charlecote. The decoration of the 19th-century wing is referred to by Christopher Hussey, *Country Life* (May 1952), pp 1330 *et seq*.

1303 Formalized fleur-de-lis design
1832
Flock
35 × 53.3 cm (portion)
PROVENANCE Charlecote Park, Warwickshire
E.23201–1957 neg GJ.10017

This paper is from a bedroom in the 19th-century wing of Charlecote. See above item (note).

1300

1301

1302

1304

1304 Two portions with a strap-work design, 1 on embossed gold paper
1837
Flock
51.4 × 58.4 cm; 56.5 × 57.7 cm
PROVENANCE Charlecote Park, Warwickshire
E.23197, 23198–1957; E.23198
neg GJ.10015

The specimen on embossed paper is from the library in the 19th-century wing of Charlecote. It is illustrated and referred to by Christopher Hussey, *Country Life* (May 1952), p 1329. An order for this pattern in a green colourway is in the Cowtan order book for 1837 (see PATTERN BOOKS, no 692).

The above 5 items, nos 1300–1304, were given by the Hon. Mrs Brian Fairfax-Lucy.

Williams, Carol. See PATTERN BOOKS, no 716.

Williams, Hadyn. See PATTERN BOOKS, no 725.

Willis, Erica. See PATTERN BOOKS, no 719.

Wilson, Henry, 1864–1934

Architect and sculptor, metal worker and silversmith, he set up a workshop *circa* 1895, and from 1901 taught at the R.C.A. He was Master of the Artworkers' Guild in 1917, and President of the Arts and Crafts Exhibition Society from 1915 to 1922.

1305

1305 'The Tree'
Produced by Jeffrey & Co.
1893
Colour print from a wood block
90.5 × 56 cm (portion)
Given by Miss Mary Peerless
E.466–1967 neg K.1418

Exhibited at the *Arts and Crafts Exhibition*, New Gallery, Regent's Street, London, October 1893. The whole design of which this forms a section is reproduced in the *Studio* (1894), vol 2, plate on p 22. The block from which the paper was printed is reproduced in *AJ* (1901), plate on p 332.

Wolfe, Arthur Theobald, 1870–1944

Of P. A. Staynes & A. T. Wolfe, designers and supervisors to Norman & Stacey, furnishers, of Tottenham Court Road, London.

1306 Design for a wallpaper or a textile, showing a repeat pattern of formalized peonies; inscribed in ink on the back *55 Rossetti Mansions Cheyne Walk SW* (crossed through) and *The Heights Queens Rd Loughton Essex*, numbered *1271* and stamped *A. T. Wolfe Designer*

1306

Produced by P. A. Staynes & A. T. Wolfe
Circa 1900–1905
Watercolour
76 × 56 cm
E.300–1966 neg GJ.10018

1307 Design for a wallpaper or a textile: 'Cluster Leaves' or 'Laburnum'; inscribed in pencil on the back *Cluster Leaves and Laburnam*, with addresses as below; stamped *A. T. Wolfe Designer* and numbered *1200*; inscribed in ink *55 Rossetti Mansions Cheyne Walk SW* (crossed through) and *The Heights, Queens Road, Loughton, Essex*
Produced by P. A. Staynes & A. T. Wolfe
1900–1905
Watercolour and gouache
74.1 × 52.5 cm
E.301–1966

1308 Design for a wallpaper or a textile, showing a repeat pattern of formalized honeysuckle; numbered in ink on the back *1261* and stamped *A. T. Wolfe Designer*
Produced by P. A. Staynes & A. T. Wolfe
Circa 1900–1905
Watercolour and gouache
65 × 55.7 cm
E.302–1966

The above 3 items, nos 1306–1308, were given by Mrs D. M. Scott, daughter of the artist

---

Wornum, Miriam, working early 1950s

See also PATTERN BOOKS, no 707.

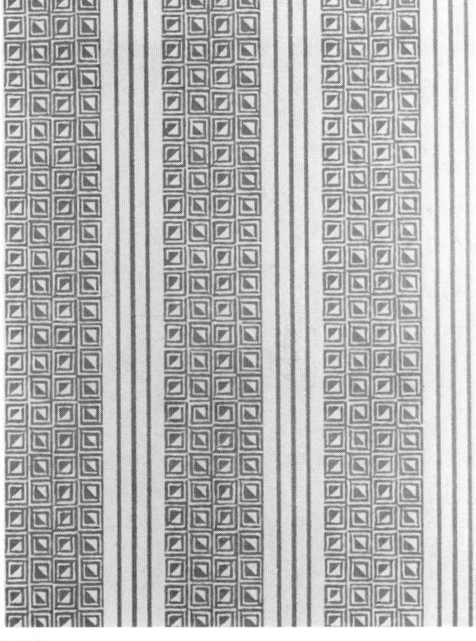

1309

1309 'London Square'
Produced by John Line & Sons Ltd
1951
Colour print from wood blocks
73.7 × 54.7 cm (portion)
Given by John Line & Sons
E.890–1978 neg GJ.9369

Wright, Frank Lloyd, 1867–1959

American architect. Became leader of a group of mid-Western architects known as the 'Prairie School'. Designed the carpets and upholstery of an office in the Kaufmann Department Store in Pittsburg and other interior work.

1310 'Design 103', one of the 'Taliesin Line' range
Produced by F. Schumacher & Co., New York
1956
Colour screen print
110.3 × 76 cm (portion)
E.974–1978 neg GJ.10019

Also produced by Schumacher as a textile.

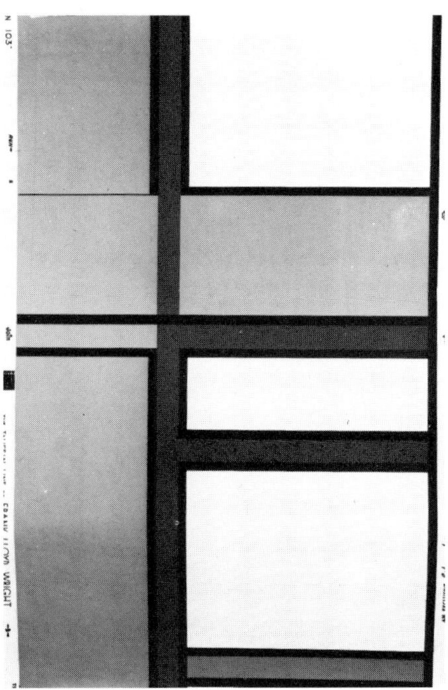

1310

Wurthmuller, Fritz. See PATTERN BOOKS, no 716(3).

Zipelius, Georges. See ANONYMOUS WALLPAPERS AND WALLPAPER DESIGNS, no 616.

1311

1311 'Malacca Texture' (Design 704), one of the 'Taliesin Line' range
Produced by F. Schumacher & Co., New York
1956
Colour screen print
95.5 × 76 cm (portion)
E.975–1978 neg GJ.10020

1312 Portion of Design 705, one of the 'Taliesin Line' range
Produced by F. Schumacher & Co., New York
1956
Colour screen print
74.7 × 54.6 cm
E.581–1966

Also produced by Schumacher as a textile, 1960.

1313 Design 706, one of the 'Taliesin Line' range
Produced by F. Schumacher & Co., New York
1956
Colour screen print
75 × 54.6 cm (portion)
E.582–1966 neg GG.5873

Reproduced in *Design* (April 1960), vol 12, p 43, fig 7. This design was also produced by Schumacher as a furnishing fabric.

The above 3 items, nos 1311–1313, were given by F. Schumacher & Co.

Wright, John. See PATTERN BOOKS, nos 716, 717.

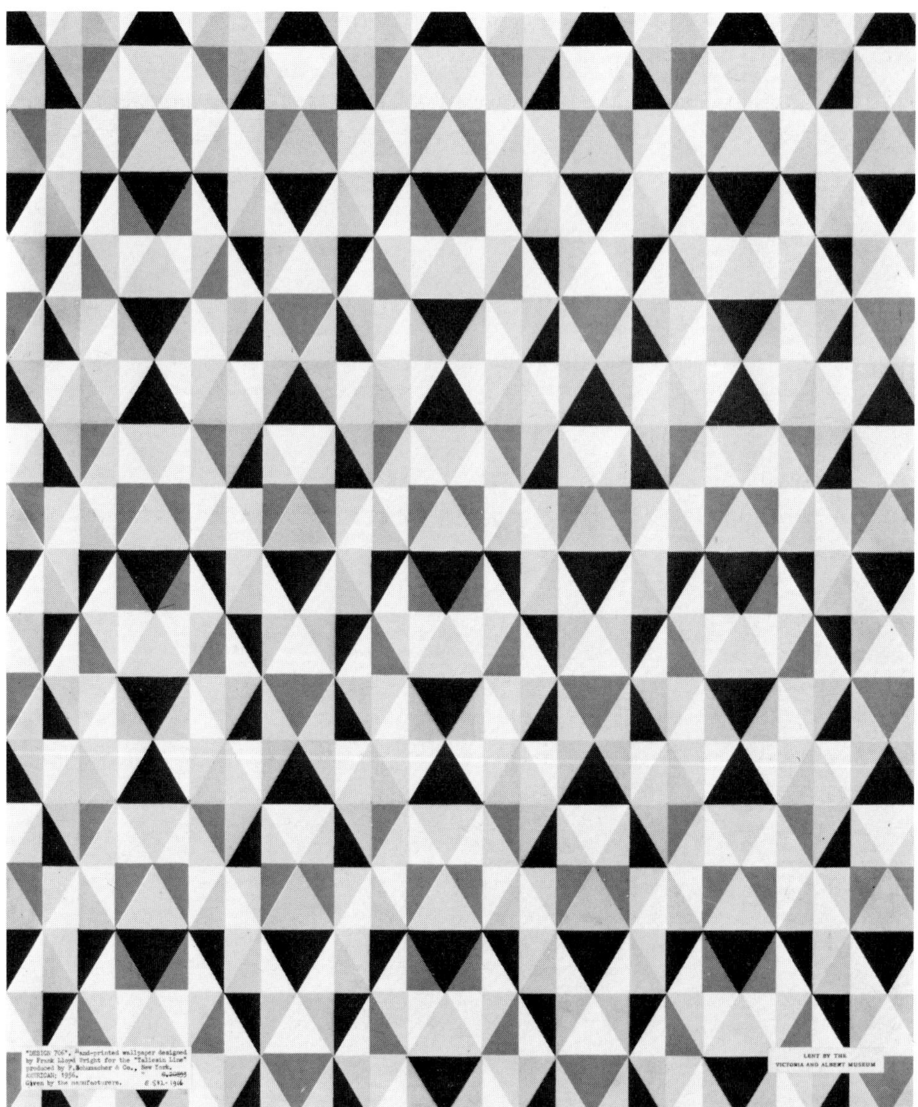

1313

Bibliography

By E. A. Entwisle

Of the publications listed below the following should be singled out as being of primary importance to the student of the history of wallpaper: Nancy V. McClelland, *Historic Wallpapers from their Inception to the Introduction of Machinery* (1924); A. V. Sugden and J. L. Edmondson, *A History of English Wallpaper. 1509–1914* (1926); C. C. Oman, *Catalogue of Wallpaper* (the first edition, which appeared in 1929, of the present work); Henri Clouzot and Charles Follot, *Histoire du Papier Peint en France* (1935); E. A. Entwisle, *A Literary History of Wallpaper* (1960), with its valuable index; Brenda Greysmith, *Wallpaper* (1976), also with a valuable index; H. Olligs, ed., *Tapeten—ihre Geschichte bis zur Gegenwart* (3 vols, 1969–70). Volume II of the last-mentioned work contains a long list of references as well as useful contributions by Josef Leis (former Director of the German Museum of Wallpaper, Cassel) and F. Machmar.

PUBLICATIONS AND OTHER SOURCES UNTIL 1900

1692 First English Patent for Paperhangings granted to William Bayly in October

1699 John Houghton, F.R.S., ed., *A Collection of Letters for the Improvement of Husbandry and Trade* (periodical, London, 1692–1703)

1723 Jacques Savary des Bruslons, *Dictionnaire Universel de Commerce* (Geneva). Reference to flock hangings. New ed. 1742.

1747–95 P. Toynbee, 'Strawberry Hill Accounts. A record of expenditure in building, furnishing etc . . . kept by Mr H. W. from 1747–1795'. Reprinted from the original MSS, 1927.

1751–57 Denis Diderot and Jean Le Rond d'Alembert, *Encyclopédie ou Dictionnaire Raisonné des Sciences etc* (Paris)

Malachy Postlethwayt, *Universal Dictionary of Trade and Commerce*, trans. from Bruslons (see under 1723)

1754 John Baptist Jackson, *Essay on the Invention of Engraving and Printing in Chiaro Oscuro* (London). See the account of Jackson's printing methods: Edna K. Donnell, 'Enquiry into the Origin of Printing in Europe', *Metropolitan Museum Studies* (New York, 1932); see also Jacob Kainen, *John Baptist Jackson, Eighteenth Century Master of the Color Woodcut* (Smithsonian Institution, Washington, 1962)

1756 *Journal Oeconomique*, February, p. 92

1758 R. Dossie, *Handmaid to the Arts* (2 vols, London), vol II, under 'Paperhangings'

1763 Thomas Mortimer, *Universal Director*. Lists ten prominent London wallpaper makers. See also under 1810

1764 Orders of the Board of Excise, 17 July. Reference to taxation. See also Longfield, Ada K., 'History of the Dublin Wallpaper Industry in the 18th Century', under 'Articles', below.

1766 Jean Baptiste Michel Papillon, *Traité Historique et Pratique de la Gravure en Bois* (Paris)

1774 'Manufacture of Paperhangings', *Practical Magazine* (America)

1778–83 *Encyclopaedia Britannica* (2nd ed.), under 'Wallpaper', section III

1795 R. Ackermann, *Repository of Arts and Manufacturers* (London); reprinted 1809, 1819, 1829

1797 Johann Beckmann, trans. William Johnston, *History of Inventions and Discoveries*; further eds 1814, 1817, 1846

Jean Zuber, *Reminiscences et Souvenirs de Jean Zuber père* (Mulhouse). See also under 1897

1810 Thomas Mortimer, *A General Dictionary of Commerce, Trade and Manufactures* (London); 2nd ed. 1819

1819 Abraham Rees, *The Cyclopaedia; or Universal Dictionary of Arts, Sciences, and Literature*

1820 Louis Sebastien Le Normand, *Manuel du Fabricants d'Etoffes Imprimées, et Papiers Peints* (Paris); new ed. 1830

1821 John Wilkes, ed., *Encyclopaedia Londiniensis* (1810–29)

1839 W. A. Chatto, illustrated by John Jackson, *Treatise on Wood Engraving. Historical and Practical*

John Gregory Crace, 'The History of Paperhangings'. Paper read to the Royal Institute of British Architects, 14–18 February; published in the society's journal.

Patent 8302. Printing Calicoes and other Fabrics. Granted to Harold Potter. See Sugden, A. V., and E. A. Entwisle, *Potters of Darwen*, under 'Books', below.

Circa 1840 Fleury-Chavant, *Le Dessinateur des Papiers Peints* (Paris)

1844 Mawer Cowtan, lecture read to the Decorative Arts Society, 9 October; published in the proceedings of the society

1849–51 *Journal of Design and Manufacture* (6 vols, London). Contains samples of wallpaper, textiles etc.

1851 Year of the Great Exhibition. See catalogue and jurors' reports.

Matthew Digby Wyatt, *The Industrial Arts of the Nineteenth Century* (2 vols, London)

Year Book of Facts in Science and Art (published by David Boque), section on paper-staining

Jean Zuber Fils, 'The Manufacture of Paperhangings'. Paper read before Mulhouse Société Industrielle, 27 August

1854 James Arrowsmith, *Paperhangers' and Upholsterers' Guide . . .* (London))

Charles Tomlinson, ed., *Cyclopaedia of Useful Arts . . . and Manufactures . . .*, vol 2, 374–6

1855 Jules Désfossé, comment on Exposition Universelle, Paris, of this year

1857 'Origin of the machine for making endless paper', *Journal of the Society of Arts* (27 February), vol 5, 237

1858–59 F. B. Thompson, ed., *The Universal Decorator* (3 vols, London)

1860 Andrew Ure, *Ure's Dictionary of Arts, Manufactures, and Mines* (5th ed., London)

1861 John Stewart, 'French and English Paper-staining', *Art Journal* (pts I–III, January, February, April), vol 7, pp 6, 55, 105

1862 W. F. Exner, *Geschichte des Papiers* (Vienna)

Children's Employment Commission. Government report.
International Exhibition, London, catalogue
1863 J. B. Waring, *Masterpieces of Industrial Art and Sculpture at the International Exhibition, 1862* (London)
1867 Prosper Poitevin, *Les Papiers Peints en l'Exposition Universelle de 1867*
1868 Charles L. Eastlake, F.R.I.B.A., *Hints on Household Taste in Furniture, Upholstery . . .* (London)
1869 W. F. Exner, *Die Tapeten und Buntpapierindustrie* (Weimar)
1871–94 Marius Vachon, *Les Arts et les Industries du Papier en France* (Paris)
1872 *The House Furnisher* . . . (London, 1 July), 77. Contains list of contemporary wallpaper manufacturers
Building News (11 October), vol XXIII, 291
1875 Guillaume Louis Figuier, *Les Merveilles de l'industrie* . . . (4 vols, illustrated, Paris, 1873–77), vol 2, chapter on paper-staining
G. H. Morton, 'History of Paperhangings'. Paper read before the Liverpool Architectural and Archaeological Society, 10 February
1876 Richard Redgrave, compiled from the writings of, *Manual of Design* (South Kensington Museum Art Handbooks, no 6); reprinted 1887
1880 Exposition Universelle, Paris, 1878, jurors' reports, groupe III, class 22 (Paris)
1881 *Journal of Decorative Art* (Manchester and New York). First published this year; contains frequent references to wallpaper over many years.
William Morris, 'Some Hints on Pattern Designing'. Lecture in the series 'The Lesser Arts of Life', given at the Working Men's College, London
1882 Alexandre A.P. C. Blanc, *Grammaire des Arts Décoratifs* . . . (Paris)
V. Portalet and P. Rioux de Maillou, 'Le Papier Peint' (Union Centrale des Arts Décoratifs . . ., Paris)
Theodor Seeman, *Die Tapete, ihre ästhetische Bedeutung* . . . vol XCII of A. Hartleben, ed., 'Chemisch-Technische Bibliothek' (Vienna)
1883 P. Rioux de Maillou, *Les Arts du Bois . . . et du Papier* (Union Centrale des Arts Décoratifs . . ., Paris)
G. T. Robinson, 'Household Decoration—Wallpapers', *Art Journal*, new series, no VIII, 353–6
1884 William Morris and J. H. Middleton, *Encyclopaedia Britannica* (9th ed.), under 'Wallpaper'
1885 G. C. Haité, 'Wallpapers and their Manufacture'. Lecture given at the Society for the Encouragement of the Fine Arts, 12 February
1887 F. Follot, *Causerie sur le Papier Peint* (Paris)
La Grande Encyclopédie (Paris), under 'Papiers Peints'
1888 Tapeten Zeitung (Darmstadt). First published this year.
1889 Friedrich Fischbach, *Beitrag zur Geschichte der Tapeten Industrie* (Darmstadt)
M. Pierre Larousse, *Grande Dictionnaire Universel du XIXe Siecle*
1891 W. R. Bradshaw, *Wallpaper, its History, Manufacture and Decorative Importance* (New York)
1893 J. S. Corder, *Christchurch or Withepole House* (Ipswich))
G. C. Haité, 'Wallpaper Design', in G. White, *Practical Designing* (London), 283
T. R. Spence, 'Wallpapers and Stencilling'. Paper read before the Royal Society of Arts, 12 February

1894 'A Designer of Paperhangings', *Studio* (December), vol 4, 76–82. Interview with Walter Crane

1895 Frédèric Aumonier, 'Wallpapers, their Manufacture and Design'. Paper read before the Society of Architects.

Charles Booth, *Life and Labour of the People in London* (London), vol 2, section on paper-staining

Lewis F. Day, 'The Art and Craft of Paperstaining', *Good Words* (April), 244

1896 Metford Warner, 'History of Paperhangings'. Paper read before the Art Workers' Guild.

1897 G. C. Haité, 'Designs of the Victorian Reign', *Architectural Review* (vol 2, June–November), 81–89

Jean Zuber et Cie, *La Fabrique de Papiers Peints de Jean Zuber à Rixheim, 1797–1897*

1898 L. P. Butterfield, 'Discovery and Restoration of two Old Wallpapers', *Artist*, vol 23, 102, 103

1900–1901 F. Follot, *Rapport du Comité de Classe 68 à 18 Exposition Universelle et Internationale, Paris*

BOOKS

Ackerman, Phyllis, *Wallpaper, its History, Design and Use* (New York, 1923)

Appuhn, Horst, *Riesenholzschnitte und Papiertapeten der Renaissance* (Unterschneidheim, 1976)

Auguste, Pierre, *Les Papiers Peints . . .* (Paris, 1978)

Carlhian, André, *Panoramic Wallpapers* (Paris, 1936)

Clark, Fiona, *William Morris: Wallpapers and Chintzes* (London and New York, 1974)

Clouzot, Henri, *Papiers Peints et tentures modernes* (Paris, 1928)

Le Papier Peint en France du xviie au xixe siècle (Paris, 1931)

Les chefs d'oeuvres du Papiers Peints. Tableaux-tentures de Dufour et Leroy (Paris, 1931)

Clouzot, Henri, and Charles Follot, *Histoire du Papier Peint en France* (Paris, 1935)

Cooper Union Museum, New York, illustrated catalogue, *Chronicle* (April 1938), vol I, no 4

Cordonnier-Détrie, Paul, and Jacques Gaugain, *Cartier Dominotier en la ville de Mons au 18me siècle* (Le Mans, 1928)

Council of Industrial Design, *Folio K: Wallpaper for the Small Home*, designs prepared by Stella Carlisle (1950)

Dunn, Edward J., *The History of Wallpaper as a Decoration* (New Jersey, 1919)

Entwisle, E. A., *The Book of Wallpaper* (2nd ed, Bath, 1970)

British Fabrics. A Century of British Fabrics, 1850–1950 [Wallpapers] (Leigh-on-Sea, 1955)

A Literary History of Wallpaper (London, 1960)

Wallpapers of the Victorian Era (Leigh-on-Sea, 1964)

French Scenic Wallpapers (Leigh-on-Sea, 1972)

Fagu, Gabriel, and J. Braudey, *Le Papier Peint* (Paris, 1957)

Farr, Michael, *Design in British Industry. A Mid-century Survey . . .* (Cambridge, 1956)

Frangiamore, Catherine L., *Wallpapers in Historic Preservation* (Washington, 1978)

Greysmith, Brenda, *Wallpaper* (London, 1976)

Gusman, P., *Panneaux Décoratifs et tentures murales du xviie siècle . . .* (Paris, 1913)

Hascall, F. K., *Harry Wearne. A Short Account of his Life and Work* (New York, 1933)

Hurst, A. E., *Painting & Decorating* (London, 1949), chap. 3

Jeans, Herbert, *The Periods of Interior Decoration* (London and New York, 1921), last chap., on wallpaper, by Metford Warner

Jennings, A. S., *Wallpapers and Wall Coverings* (London, 1903)

Jourdain, Margaret, *English Interior Decoration 1700–1830* (London, 1950); see also under Lenygon, Francis

Katzenbach, Lois and William, *The Practical Book of American Wallpaper* (Philadelphia, 1951)

Koch, Alexander, *Deckorationstoffe, Tapeten und Teppiche* (Stuttgart, 1951)

Labarre, E. J., *Dictionary and Encyclopaedia of Paper and Papermaking . . .* (Amsterdam, 1952)

Leis, Josef, *Bildtapeten aus alter und neuer Zeit* (Hamburg, 1961)

Lenygon, Francis [M. Jourdain], *Decoration in England, 1660–1770* (London, 1914)

Lichten, Frances M., *Decorative Art of Victoria's Era* (New York, 1950)

Machmar, F., *Führer durch das Deutsches Tapetenmuseum . . .* (1950), catalogue of the Wallpaper Museum, Cassel

McClelland, Nancy V., *Historic Wallpapers from their Inception to the Introduction of Machinery* (Philadelphia and London, 1924)

The Practical Book of Decorative Wall Treatments . . . (Philadelphia and London, 1926)

Olligs, H., *Tapeten. Ihre Geschichte bis zur Gegenwart* (Brunswick, 1969–70)

Oman, C. C., *Catalogue of Wallpaper* (Victoria and Albert Museum, London, 1929)

Pazaurek, Gustav E., *Die Tapete. Beiträge zu ihrer Geschichte und ästhetische Wertung* (Stuttgart, 1922)

Pevsner, Nikolaus, *An Enquiry into Industrial Art in England* (Cambridge, 1937)

Rasch, Emil, *Lage der Tapetenindustrie* (Bramsche, 1937)

Die Zukunft der Tapete (brochure, 1954)

Rullmann, Franz, *Die Tapete . . .* (Stuttgart, 1939)

Sanborn, Kate, *Old Time Wallpapers* (Greenwich, Connecticut, 1905)

Selling, Carl Gösta A., *Hur Gammal ar Stoftapetan* (Stockholm, 1927)

Sugden, A. V., and J. L. Edmondson, *A History of English Wallpaper. 1509–1914* (London, 1926)

Sugden, A. V., and E. A. Entwisle, *The Crace Papers: Two Lectures on the history of paperhangings delivered by John Gregory Crace to the Royal Institute of British Architects on 4th and 18th February 1839 with foreword and comments by A. V. Sugden and E. A. Entwisle* (Birmingham, 1939)

Potters of Darwen . . . A Century of Wallpaper Printing by Machinery (Manchester, 1939)

Tipping, H. Avray, *English Homes* (10 vols, London, 1912–37)

Townsend, W. G. P., *Modern Decorative Art in England* (London, 1922), pt I

Tunander, Ingemar, *Tapeter* (Stockholm, 1955)

Ward, G. Whiteley, *Wallpaper* (London, 1922)

Wilson, John, *Decoration and Furnishing . . .* (London, 1960), chap. 4, 80–92

Yarwood, Doreen, *The English Home* (London, 1956)

ARTICLES

Aars, Harold, 'New Norwegian Wallpapers', *Foreningen Brukskunst Arbok* (1920)

Ackerman, Phyllis, 'Wallpapers in Early American Homes', *Arts and Decoration* (June 1922), vol 17, 100, 101, 138, 140

Archer, Michael, 'Gothic Wallpapers . . .', *Apollo* (August 1963), vol 78, 109–16

Blake, J. E., 'Designing Wallpapers', *Design* (December 1955), vol 84, 18–23
'Wallpapers', *Design* (March 1957), no 99, 33–5
Bouteille, L., 'Les Vieux Décors en Papier Peint', *L'Art Décoratif* (September 1912), vol 28, 175–80
Brackett, Oliver, 'English Wallpapers of the 18th Century', *Connoisseur* (October 1918), vol 52, 83–8
Clouzot, Henri, 'Tradition du Papier Peint en France', *Gazette des Beaux Arts* (4 période, 1912), vol VII, 131–43
Le Papier Peint à l'Epoque Impériale Napoléonienne', *Gazette des Beaux Arts* (4 période, 1914), vol XII, 42–52
'Le Papier Peint au Début du XVIIIe siècle au l'Enseigne du Papillon', *Renaissance de l'Art Français* (April 1925), VIII, 149–60
'L'Atelier du Cartier Dominotier', *La Renaissance de L'Art Français* (February 1927), X, 83–90
Crick, Clare, 'Wallpapers by Dufour et Cie', *Connoisseur* (December 1976), vol 193, 310–16
Cuffe, Lionel [John Betjeman], 'William Morris', *Architectural Review* (May 1931), vol 69, 151
Donnell, Edna B., 'The Van Rensselaer Painted Wallpaper', *Bulletin of Metropolitan Museum of Art* (New York, December 1931), vol 26 (supplement), 10–16
Entwisle, E. A., 'Painted Chinese Wallpapers', *Connoisseur* (June 1934), vol 93, 367–74
'Early Black and White Papers', *Connoisseur* (January 1936), vol 97, 16–17
'Bromwich of Ludgate Hill', *Journal of Decorative Art* (November 1941)
'Eighteenth-century Paperstainers' and Decorators' Bills', *Connoisseur* (September 1943), vol 112, 38–41
'A Pioneer of Wallpaper—Walmsley Preston', *Journal of Decorative Art* (January 1945), 45
'Historians of Wallpaper', *Connoisseur* (March 1945), vol 115, 23–9
'The Blew Paper Warehouse in Aldermanbury', *Connoisseur* (May 1950), vol 125, 94–8
'18th-century London Paperstainers, Thomas Bromwich at the Golden Lyon', *Connoisseur* (American ed., November 1952), vol 130, 106–10
'Early Wallpapers', *Country Life* (16 July 1953), vol 114, 212–13
'The German Wallpaper Museum at Kassel', *Decorator* (6 August 1953)
'The Eckhardt Brothers of Chelsea', *Connoisseur* (American ed., March 1959), vol 143, 74–7
Review of the exhibition of wallpaper, *Trois siècles des Papiers Peints*, Musée des Arts Décoratifs, Paris, 1967, *Connoisseur* (January 1968), vol 167, 17–21
'Wallpaper Ladies', *Lady* (3 July 1969)
'Collecting Wallpaper', *Antique Dealer and Collector's Guide* (September 1970), 79–80
'Panoramas on the Wall. French Scenic Wallpapers', *Country Life* (7 June 1973), vol 153, 1654–7
'Adding the Finishing Touches. Wallpaper Borders', *Country Life* (17 April 1975), vol 157, 1006–7
Illustrated article, signed 'E.A.E', in *Encyclopaedia Britannica* (1957), under 'Wallpaper', 309–11
Flick, Pauline, 'Nursery Wallpapers in Victorian Times', *Country Life* (December 1969), vol 146, 1519–21
Floud, Peter C., article in *Decorator* (January 1953)
'Wallpaper Designs of C. F. A. Voysey', *Penrose Annual* (1958), vol 52, 10–14

'Dating Morris Patterns', *Architectural Review* (July 1959), vol 126, 14–20

'The Wallpaper Designs of William Morris', *Penrose Annual* (1960), vol 54, 41–5

Francesco, Grete De, 'Birds and Beasts in Wallpaper Patterns', *Ciba Review* (Basel, November 1937), no 3, 93

'The History of Mural Hangings', *Ciba Review* (Basel, November 1937), no 3, 70

'Wallpapers', *Ciba Review* (Basel, November 1937), no 3, 75

Frangiamore, Catherine L., 'Wallpapers used in 19th-century America', *Antiques* (1972), vol 102, 1042–53

Gianni, E., 'Le Tappezzerie di Carta', *Revista di Ingegneria* (1952), no 6

Gooden, Wyndham, 'Palladio Wallpapers. Problems for a Pace-setter', *Design* (October 1957), no 118, 39–41

Gusman, Pierre, 'J. B. Papillon et ses papiers de tenture (1698–1776)', *Byblis* (1924), III, 18–23

Hamilton, Jean, 'Early English Wallpapers', *Connoisseur* (July 1977), vol 195, 201–6

'Dating Wallpapers', *Antique Collecting* (1979), vol 13, no 8, 18–23

Harris, F. J., 'Wallpaper', *Architectural Review* (Supplement, December 1939), vol 86, 253–8

Heal, Ambrose, 'Paper Stainers of the 17th and 18th Centuries', *Country Life* (22 July 1949), vol 106, 258–60

Hellmann, B. H., 'The Story of Wallpaper', *American Wallpaper Magazine* (1953)

Hunter, George Leland, *Decorative Textiles . . .*, (Philadelphia and London, 1918)

'Early American Wallpapers', *Good Furniture* (July 1922), vol 19, 27–36

Ionides, Basil, 'Wallpaper in a 16th-century House', *Architectural Review* (December 1924), vol 56, 195–6

Jayne, H. H. F., 'The Captain Cook Wallpaper', *Pennsylvania Museum Bulletin* (1921), vol 17, no 69, 6–10

Jenkinson, Hilary, 'English Wallpapers of the Sixteenth and Seventeenth Centuries', *Antiquaries Journal* (1925), V, no 3, 237–53

Jourdain, Margaret, 'Some Early Printed Papers', *Connoisseur* (March 1922), vol 62, 156–9

'Old English Wall-papers and Wall Hangings', pt I (English Wallpapers), *Country Life* (29 March 1924), vol 55, 499–501

'Old English Wall-papers and Wall Hangings', pt II (Chinese), *Country Life* (24 May 1924), vol 55, 835–7

Laver, James, 'Wallpapers', *Lady* (March 1945)

Longfield, Ada K. (Mrs Ada Leask), 'History of the Dublin Wallpaper Industry in the 18th Century', *Journal of the Royal Society of Antiquaries of Ireland* (December 1947), vol LXXVII, pt 2, 101–120

'French Scenic Wallpapers', *Country Life* (15 March 1956), vol 119, 490–93

'Old Wallpapers in Ireland: 5. More English, Chinese and French Examples', *Journal of the Royal Society of Antiquaries of Ireland* (1957), vol 87, 141–6

'Some Later Excise Marks on English Wallpapers', *Papermaker* (1966), vol 35

McClelland, Nancy V., 'The Dominotiers, Inventors of Wallpaper', *Arts and Decoration* (November 1923), vol 20, 28–9

'Wallpaper', article in *Encyclopaedia Britannica* (14th ed., London and New York, 1929)

Menzies, A. C., 'The Decoration of the Nursery', *Decorators' and Painters' Magazine* (1903), no 39, vol IV, 74–7

Mills, D. Dewar, 'Wallpapers', *Architectural Review* (October 1952), vol 112, 218–26

Neuberger, M. C., 'Modern Wallpaper Manufacture', *Ciba Review* (Basel, November 1937), no 3, 102

Oman, C. C., 'Old Wallpapers in England: 1. The Black and White Papers', *Old Furniture* (1927), vol 1, 272–6
'Old Wallpapers in England: 2. Early Coloured Papers', *Old Furniture* (1927), vol 2, 168–71
'Old Wallpapers in England: 3. Chinese Papers', *Old Furniture* (1928), vol 3, 15–22
'Old Wallpapers in England: 4. Later Coloured Papers and Print Rooms', *Old Furniture* (1928), vol 4, 217–22
'Old French Flock Papers', *Country Life* (28 April 1928), vol 63, 625–7
'Wallpapers of Early England: 1495–1770', *Fine Arts* (New York, March 1932), vol 18, 25–8
'Wallpapers made in England—1760–1800', *Fine Arts* (New York, December 1932), vol 19, 15–17
'English Chinoiserie Wallpapers', *Country Life* (11 February 1933), vol 73, 150–51
Percival, MacIver, 'Old Wallpapers', *Connoisseur* (February 1917), vol 47, 79–85
'Jackson of Battersea and his Wallpapers', *Connoisseur* (January 1922), 25–35
'English Wallpapers of the Chippendale Period', *Journal of Decorative Art* (July 1925), 231–4
'Wallpaper of the Sheraton Period', *Journal of Decorative Art* (September 1925), 297–300
'Old Flock Wallpapers', *Journal of Decorative Art* (October 1925), 340–43
'In the Indian Taste', *Antique Collector* (August 1932), vol 3, 287
Rasch, Emil, 'Die Deutsche Tapete seit 1900', *Architektur und Wohnform* (November 1960), 306–10
Reilly, Paul, 'German Enterprise in Wallpaper Design', *Design* (July 1953), vol 55, 16–19
Roches, Fernand, 'Vieux Papiers Peints', *L'Art Décoratif* (February 1912), vol 27, 117–23
Sayle, C., 'Cambridge Fragments', *Library* (1911), 3rd series, vol II, 340
Sheffield, Noel D., 'Wallpapers', *Journal of the Society of Architects* (April 1913), new series, vol 6, 206–18
Smith, J. H., 'History of Wallpapers in England', *Ciba Review* (Basel, November 1937), no 3, 96
Stewart-Greene, W., 'Chinese Wallpapers', *Architects' Journal* (6 September 1922), vol 56, 303–7
Storey, Helen A., 'Foreign Wallpapers in American Decoration', *Antiquarian* (1930), vol XV, 68–100
Stratton, Deborah, 'People who study Old Wallpaper', *Art and Antiques Weekly* (November 1969), no 14, 11, 14
Sutherland, W. G., 'Modern Wallpaper Design', *Country Life* (Supplement, 21 July 1917), 12–14
Temple, Grace L., 'Hunting Old Time Wallpapers', *American Magazine of Art* (September 1920)
Vizetelly, Frank H., 'Wallpapers, their Origin and History', *New Age Magazine* (November 1910), 389
Wellman, Rita, 'Wallpapers of the 18th Century', *International Studio* (New York, October 1930), vol 97, 36–43
Yorke, F. R. S., 'Modern Wallcoverings', *Architectural Review* (February 1932), vol 71, 71–80
'German Wallpaper Museum at Kassel, The', *Architectural Review* (October 1935), vol 78, 140–41
'Historic Wallpapers', in symposium, *Preservation of New England Antiquities* (Boston, April 1973)

Oxford Companion to the Decorative Arts, ed. Harold Osborne (Oxford, 1973), article on wallpaper
'Papier Peint à travers les Ages, Le', *L'Architecture* (April 1922)
'Story of Wallpaper, The', *Hobbies. The Magazine for Collectors* (Chicago, 1954), 59
Tapeten Zeitung, articles on the English wallpaper industry (Darmstadt, March 1955)

EXHIBITION CATALOGUES

American Museum of Decorative Art and Design, An, exhibition at the Victoria and Albert Museum, June–August 1973, catalogue by Catherine L. Frangiamore
British Sources of Art Nouveau, Whitworth Art Gallery, Manchester, 1969 (an exhibition of 19th and 20th century British textiles and wallpapers)
Exhibition in Holland reviewing the development of the wallpaper industry, 1937, catalogue by F. Machmar
Exhibition of Domestic Interior Paintings and Wallpaper, Department of Engraving, Illustration and Design, Victoria and Albert Museum, Christmas 1916
Exhibition of Victorian and Edwardian Arts, Victoria and Albert Museum, November 1952, catalogue with introduction by Peter C. Floud
Exhibition of Wallpaper, Albright Art Gallery, Buffalo Fine Arts Academy, New York, December 1937–January 1938
Exposition des Papiers et Toiles Imprimées, Musée Galliera, Paris, 1909
Exposition des Toiles Imprimées et Papiers Peints, Musée Galliera, Paris, 1928
Historical and Modern Wallpapers, Suffolk Galleries, London, May 1945
Internationale Tapetenaustellung 1960, Munich, October 1960
Papier peint et la conquête de l'air, Le, Musée Galliera, Paris, November 1933 (Réveillon commemorative exhibition)
Papiers peints au musée Galliera, Les, Musée Galliera, Paris, December 1953
Trois Siècles des Papiers Peints, Musée des Arts Décoratifs, Paris, 1967, catalogue with article by Jean Seguin

LECTURES AND PAPERS

Beckett, J. J., lecture on paper-hanging delivered in the Lecture Hall, Lancaster, 1 February 1907
Cowtan, M. Cowtan, 'Reminiscences and Changes in Taste in Home Decoration', paper read before the Incorporated Institute of British Decorators, 6 March 1914
Dowling, H. G., 'Wallpaper, its History, Production and Possibilities', lecture delivered to the Royal Society of Arts, 25 March 1925
Entwisle, E. A., lecture on wallpaper delivered to the International Design Congress, London, 1956 (Council of Industrial Design)
Laver, James, lecture on wallpaper delivered at the National Gallery, London, May 1945
Masters, C. O., 'Wallpapers and their History', lecture, *Decorator* (22 January 1916), vol XIV
Pevsner, Nikolaus, 'Design in Relation to Industry through the Ages', lecture delivered to the Royal Society of Arts, 24 November 1948
Rasch, Emil, lecture on wallpaper delivered to the International Design Congress, London, 1956 (Council of Industrial Design)

Sugden, A. V., 'The Crace Papers', paper read before the Institute of British Decorators, December 1924; see also Sugden, A. V., and E. A. Entwisle, *The Crace Papers . . .*, under 'Books' above

Warner, Metford, 'The Progress of Design in Paperhangings', paper read before the Institute of British Decorators, 10 January 1910

General Index

Figures in roman type refer to catalogue numbers. Figures in italic type refer to page numbers; from 271 onwards these refer to the biographies of the designers.

Index of Titles and Pictorial Subjects

All entries refer to titles except those followed by (S), *which indicates a pictorial subject. Figures in roman type refer to catalogue numbers. Figures in italic type refer to page numbers; from 271 onwards these refer to the biographies of the designers.*